S0-BSI-095

# ELEMENTS

OF

# CIVIL GOVERNMENT

A TEXT-BOOK FOR USE IN PUBLIC SCHOOLS
HIGH SCHOOLS AND NORMAL SCHOOLS

AND

A MANUAL OF REFERENCE FOR TEACHERS

BY

## ALEX. L. PETERMAN

LATE PRINCIPAL AND PROFESSOR OF CIVIL GOVERNMENT IN THE NORMAL
SCHOOL OF THE KENTUCKY STATE COLLEGE, AND MEMBER
OF THE KENTUCKY STATE SENATE

NEW YORK ·:· CINCINNATI ·:· CHICAGO
AMERICAN BOOK COMPANY

Copyright, 1891, 1903, by

AMERICAN BOOK COMPANY

E-P 40

# DEDICATION.

---

To the thousands of devoted Teachers in every part of the land, who are training the boys and girls of to-day to a true conception of American citizenship, and to a deeper love for our whole country, this little book is dedicated by a Brother in the work.

# PREFACE.

THIS text-book begins "at home." The starting-point is the family, the first form of government with which the child comes in contact. As his acquaintance with rightful authority increases, the school, the civil district, the township, the county, the State, and the United States are taken up in their order.

The book is especially intended for use in the public schools. The plan is the simplest yet devised, and is, therefore, well adapted to public school purposes. It has been used by the author for many years, in public schools, normal schools, and teachers' institutes. It carefully and logically follows the much praised and much neglected synthetic method. All students of the science of teaching agree that beginners in the study of government should commence with the known, and gradually proceed to the unknown. Yet it is believed this is the first text-book that closely follows this method of treating the subject.

The constant aim has been to present the subject in a simple and attractive way, in accordance with sound principles of teaching—that children may grow into such a knowledge of their government that the welfare of the country may "come home to the business and bosoms" of the people.

The recent increase of interest among the people

upon the subject of government is a hopeful sign. It will lead to a better knowledge of our political institutions, and hence give us better citizens. Good citizenship is impossible unless the people understand the government under which they live.

It is certainly strange that every State in the Union maintains a system of public schools for the purpose of training citizens, and that the course of study in so many States omits civil government, the science of citizenship.

The author's special thanks are due Hon. Joseph Desha Pickett, Ph.D., Superintendent of Public Instruction of Kentucky, for the suggestion which led to the preparation of the work and for excellent thoughts upon the plan. The author also desires to confess his obligation to President James K. Patterson, Ph.D., and Professor R. N. Roark, A.M., of the Kentucky State College, Lexington, for valuable suggestions as to the method of treatment and the scope of the book.

The author has derived much assistance from the many admirable works upon the same subject, now before the country. But he has not hesitated to adopt a treatment different from theirs when it has been deemed advisable. He submits his work to a discriminating public, with the hope that he has not labored in vain in a field in which so many have wrought.

ALEX. L. PETERMAN.

# A FEW WORDS TO TEACHERS.

**1. Purpose of the Study.**—Every school should teach, and every child should study, the principles of our government, in order:

1. That by knowing his country better he may learn to love it more. The first duty of the school is to teach its pupils to love " God, home, and native land."

2. That the child may learn that there is such a thing as just authority; that obedience to it is right and manly; that we must learn to govern by first learning to obey.

3. That he may know his rights as a citizen, and, "knowing, dare maintain;" that he may also know his *duties* as a citizen, and, knowing, may perform them intelligently and honestly.

4. That he may understand the sacredness of the right of suffrage, and aid in securing honest elections and honest discharge of official duties.

5. That he may better understand the history of his country, for the history of the United States is largely the history of our political institutions.

**2. Oral Instruction.**—There is no child in your school too young to learn something of geography, of history, and of civil government.

These three subjects are so closely related that it is easier and better to teach them together. **All**

(7)

pupils not prepared for the text-book should, at least on alternate days, be instructed by the teacher in a series of familiar talks, beginning with " The Family," and proceeding slowly to " The School," " The Civil District or Township," " The County," " The State," and " The United States." In this system of oral instruction, which is the best possible preparation for the formal study of civil government, the plan and outlines of this book may be used by the teacher with both profit and pleasure.

**3. Proper Age for Study of the Text-book.**—The plan and the style of this book are so simple that the subject will be readily understood by pupils reading in the " Fourth Reader." Even in our ungraded country schools the average pupil of twelve years is well prepared to begin the study of the text-book in civil government. It is a serious mistake to postpone this much neglected subject until a later age. Let it be introduced early, that the child's knowledge of his government may " grow with his growth, and strengthen with his strength."

**4. Two Parts.**—It will be observed that the book is divided into two parts : the former treating the subject concretely, the latter treating it abstractly.

Beginners should deal with things, not theories; hence, the abstract treatment of civil government is deferred until the pupil's mind is able to grasp it.

For the same reason, definitions in the first part of the book are few and simple, the design of the author being *to illustrate* rather than *to define ;* to lead the child *to see*, rather than to burden his mind with fine-spun statements that serve only to confuse. In an elaborate work for advanced students the method of treatment would, of course, be quite different.

**5. Topical Method.**—The subject of each paragraph is printed in bold-faced type, thus specially adapting the book to the topical method of recitation. This feature also serves as a guide to the pupil in the preparation of his lesson.

**6. Suggestive Questions.**—In deference to the best professional thought, the author has omitted all questions upon the text, knowing that every *live* teacher prefers to frame his own questions. The space usually allotted to questions upon the text is devoted to suggestive questions, intended to lead the pupil to think and to investigate for himself.

The author sincerely hopes that the teacher will not permit the pupil to memorize the language of the book, but encourage him to express the thought in his own words.

# CONTENTS.

## CHAPTER I.

### THE FAMILY.

## CHAPTER II.

### THE SCHOOL AND SCHOOL DISTRICT.

## CHAPTER III.

### THE CIVIL DISTRICT.

## CHAPTER IV.

### THE TOWNSHIP, OR TOWN.

( II )

## CHAPTER V.

### THE COUNTY.

PAGE

## CHAPTER VI.

### MUNICIPAL CORPORATIONS—VILLAGES, BOROUGHS, AND CITIES.

## CHAPTER VII.

### THE STATE.

## CHAPTER VIII.

### THE STATE—(*Continued*).

# CHAPTER IX.

## THE STATE—(*Continued*).

# CHAPTER X.

## THE STATE—(*Continued*).

# CHAPTER XI.

## THE UNITED STATES.

# CHAPTER XII.

## THE UNITED STATES—(*Continued*).

# CHAPTER XIII.

## THE UNITED STATES—(*Continued*).

## CHAPTER XIV.

### THE UNITED STATES—(*Continued*).

## CHAPTER XV.

### GOVERNMENT.

## CHAPTER XVI.

### JUSTICE.

## CHAPTER XVII.

### LAW AND LIBERTY.

## CHAPTER XVIII.

### SUFFRAGE AND ELECTIONS.

## CHAPTER XIX.

### THE AUSTRALIAN BALLOT SYSTEM.

## CHAPTER XX.

### PARTIES AND PARTY MACHINERY.

## CHAPTER XXI.

### LEGISLATION.

## CHAPTER XXII.

### REVENUE AND TAXATION.

# ELEMENTS

OF

# CIVIL GOVERNMENT.

## PART I.

## CHAPTER I.

### THE FAMILY.

**Introductory.**\* — People living in the United States owe respect and obedience to not less than four different governments; that is, to four forms of organized authority. They have duties as citizens of a township or civil district, as citizens of a county, as citizens of some one of the States, and as citizens of the United States. All persons are, or have been, members of a family; some also live under a village or city government; and most children are subject

---

\* To the Teacher.—Do not assign to the average class more than two or three pages of the text as a lesson. Make haste slowly. When each chapter is completed let it be reviewed at once, while the pupil's interest is fresh.

See that the "Suggestive Questions" at the end of the chapter are not neglected. If necessary, devote special lessons to their consideration. Assign the "questions" to the members of the class, to be answered on the following day, giving not more than two "questions" to any pupil.

Pet. C. Go.—2

to the government of some school. Many people in this country live under six governments—namely, the family, the township or civil district, the village or city, the county, the State, and the United States; while children who live in villages or cities, and attend school, are subject to seven different governments. These organizations are so closely related that the duties of the people as citizens of one do not conflict with their duties as citizens of the others. The better citizen a person is of one of these governments the better citizen he is of all governments under which he lives.

**Definition.**—Each of us is a member of some family. We were born into the family circle, and our parents first taught us to obey. By insisting upon obedience, parents govern their children, and thus keep them from evil and from danger. The family, then, is a form of government, established for the good of the children themselves, and the first government that each of us must obey.

**Purposes.**—The family exists for the rearing and training of children, and for the happiness and prosperity of parents. All children need the comforts and restraints of home life. They are growing up to be citizens and rulers of the country, and should learn to rule by first learning to obey. The lessons of home prepare them for life and for citizenship.

### MEMBERS.

The members of the family are the father, the mother, and the children, and the family government exists for all, especially for the children, that they may be protected, guided, and taught to become useful men and women. The welfare of each and of all depends upon the family government, upon the care of the parents and the obedience of the children.

**Rights.**—The members have certain rights; that is, certain just claims upon the family. Each has a right to all the care and protection that the family can give: a right to be kindly treated; a right to be spoken to in a polite manner; a right to food, clothing, shelter, and an opportunity to acquire an education; a right to the advice and warning of the older members; a right to the respect of all.

**Duties.**—As each of the members has his rights, each also has his duties; for where a right exists, a duty always exists with it. It is the duty of each to treat the others kindly; to teach them what is right and what is wrong; to aid them in their work; to comfort them in their sorrows; and to rejoice with them in their gladness. It is the duty of the children to love their parents; to obey them in all things; to respect older persons; and to abstain from bad habits and bad language.

### OFFICERS.

The officers of the family government are the father and the mother. They were made officers when they were married, so that the rulers of the family are also members of the family. The office of a parent is a holy office, and requires wisdom for the proper discharge of its duties.

**Powers.**—The parents have power to make rules,

to decide when these have been broken, and to insist that they shall be obeyed. They make the law of the family, enforce the law, and explain the law. They have supreme control over their children in all the usual affairs of life, until the children arrive at the legal age—twenty-one years.

**Duties, Responsibility.**—Parents should be firm and just in their rulings; they should study the welfare of their children, and use every effort to train them to lives of usefulness and honor. It is the duty of parents to provide their children with food, clothing, shelter, and the means of acquiring an education. There is no other responsibility so great as the responsibility of fathers and mothers. They are responsible for themselves, and the law makes them partly responsible for the conduct of their children. Therefore, one of the highest duties of a parent to his children is to exact obedience in all right things, in order that the children may be trained to true manhood and womanhood.

### SUGGESTIVE QUESTIONS.

1. Name some of the restraints of home life.
2. Why does the welfare of all depend upon the family government?
3. Why do rights and duties always exist together?
4. Name some bad habits.
5. Why should children abstain from bad habits?
6. What is true manhood?
7. Are disobedient children apt to make good citizens?
8. Should a father permit his bad habits to be adopted by his children?

# CHAPTER II.

## THE SCHOOL.

**Introductory.**—When children reach the age of six or seven years, they enter the public school and become subject to its rules. We are born under government, and we are educated under it. We are under it at home, in school, and in after life. Law and order are everywhere necessary to the peace, safety, liberty, and happiness of the people. True liberty and true enlightenment can not exist unless regulated by law.

**Definition and Purposes.**—A school district or sub-district is a certain portion of the town or county laid off and set apart for the purpose of establishing and maintaining a public school. It exists for educational reasons only, and is the unit of educational work. The public schools are supported by funds raised partly by the State, and partly by the county or the township. They are frequently called common schools or free schools. It is the duty of the State to provide all children with the means of acquiring a plain English education, and the State discharges this duty by dividing the county into districts of such size that a school-house and a public school are within reach of every child.

**Formation.**—The limits of the school district are usually fixed by the chief school officer of the county, by the town, by the school board, or by the peo-

ple living in the neighborhood. In most of the
States districts vary greatly in size and shape; but
in some of the States they have a regular form, each
being about two miles square.

**Functions.**—The functions, or work, of the school
are solely educational. The State supports a system
of public schools in order that the masses of the
people may be educated. The country needs good
citizens: to be good citizens the people must be
intelligent, and to be intelligent they must attend
school.

### MEMBERS.

The members of the school district are the people living in it. All are interested, one way or another, in the success of the school. In most States
the legal voters elect the school board, or trustees,
and in some States levy the district school taxes.
Those who are neither voters nor within the school
age are interested in the intelligence and good name
of the community, and are therefore interested in
the public school.

**Children.**—The children within the school age are
the members of the school, and they are the most
important members of the school district. It is for
their good that the school exists. The State has
provided schools in order that its children may be
educated, and thus become useful men and women
and good citizens.

**Rights.**—Children, as members of the school, have
important rights and duties. It is the right, one of
the highest rights, of every child to attend the full

session of the public school. Whoever prevents him from exercising this right commits an offense against the child and against the State. The State taxes its citizens to maintain a system of schools for the benefit of every child, and so every child has a right to all the State has provided for him.

**Duties.**—As it is the right, it is also the duty of all children to attend the full session of the public school, or of some other equally as good. They should be regular and punctual in their attendance; they should yield prompt and cheerful obedience to the school government, and try to avail themselves of all advantages that the school can give. As it is the duty of the State to offer a plain English education to every child, so it is the duty of all children to make the most of all means the State has provided for their education.

**Parents, their Rights and Duties.**—All parents have the right to send their children to the public school, and it is also their duty to patronize the public school, or some other equally as good. Fathers and mothers who deprive their children of the opportunities of acquiring an education do them lasting injury. Parents should use every effort to give their children at least the best education that can be obtained in the public schools.

## GOVERNMENT.

The school has rules to govern it, that the pupil may be guided, directed, and protected in the pursuit of knowledge. Schools can not work without order, and there can be no order without government.   The members of the school desire that good order be maintained, for they know their success depends upon it; so that school government, like all other good government, exists by the consent and for the good of the governed.

**Officers.**—The school, like all other governments, has its officers.   These are the school board, or trustees, and the teacher.   They are responsible for the government and good conduct of the school.   There are, in most governments, three kinds of officers, corresponding to the three departments of government—the legislative, the judicial, and the executive. The legislative department of the government makes the laws, the judicial department explains them, and the executive department executes them.   School officers are mostly executive; that is, their chief duties are to enforce the laws made by the legislature for the government of the public schools.   As they also make rules for the school, their duties are partly legislative.

**Appointment, Term of Office.**—The district officers are usually elected by the legal voters of the school district; but in some States they are appointed by the county superintendent, or county school commissioner as he is often called.   In most States the term of office is three years, but in some it is two years, and in others it is only one year.   Directors receive no pay for their services.

**Duties.**—In most States it is the duty of the district officers to raise money by levying taxes for the erection of school-buildings, and to superintend their construction; to purchase furniture and apparatus; to care for the school property; to employ teachers and fix their salaries; to visit the school and direct its work; to take the school census; and to make reports to the higher school officers. In some States, as in Indiana, most of these duties belong to the office of township trustee.

**The Teacher.**—The teacher is usually employed by the directors or trustees, but in some States he is employed by the township trustee or by the county superintendent. He must first pass an examination before an examiner, or board of examiners, and obtain therefrom a certificate or license entitling him to teach in the public schools.

**Powers.**—The teacher has the same power and right to govern the school that the parent has to govern the family. The law puts the teacher in the parent's place and expects him to perform the parent's office, subject to the action of the directors or trustees. It clothes him with all power necessary to govern the school, and then holds him responsible for its conduct, the directors having the right to dismiss him at any time for a failure to perform his duty.

**Duties.**—The teacher is one of our most important officers. The State has confided to him the trust of teaching, of showing boys and girls how to be useful men and women, of training them for citizenship. This is a great work to do. The State has clothed him with ample power for the purpose, and it is his duty to serve the State faithfully and well. The teacher should govern kindly and firmly. Every pupil in school, of whatever age or size, owes him cheerful and ready obedience. It is his duty, the duty for which he is paid, to insist upon this obedience; to govern the school; to teach the pupils to obey while they are children, in order that they may rule well when they become rulers; that is, when they become citizens.

## SUGGESTIVE QUESTIONS.

1. Why are law and order necessary to the peace and happiness of the people?

2. Why are public schools sometimes called free schools or common schools?

3. About how many square miles are there in a school district in this county?

4. What is the official title, and what the name, of the chief school officer of this county?

5. Why does the State want its people educated?

6. Why should children be regular and punctual in their attendance?

7. What can parents do to aid their children to acquire an education?

8. What number of directors do you think would be best for the school district? Why?

9. Should directors receive compensation? How much?

10. Why should the teacher pass an examination?

11. Should he be examined every year?

12. Why does the law place the teacher in the parent's place?

13. Why are citizens said to be rulers?

## QUESTION FOR DEBATE.

*Resolved*, That it is right for a man without children to pay school taxes.

# CHAPTER III.

## THE CIVIL DISTRICT.

**Introductory.**—In our study, thus far, we have had to do with special forms of government as exercised in the family and in the school. These are, in a sense, peculiar to themselves. The rights of government as administered in the family, and the rights of the members of a family, as well as their duties to each other, are natural rights and duties; they do not depend upon society for their force. In fact, they are stronger and more binding in proportion as the bands of society are relaxed.

In the primitive state, before there was organized civil society, family government was supreme; and, likewise, if a family should remove from within the limits of civil society and be entirely isolated, family government would again resume its power and binding force.

School government, while partaking of the nature of civil government, is still more closely allied to family government. In the natural state, and in the isolated household, the education of the child devolves upon the parents, and the parent delegates a part of his natural rights and duties to the teacher when he commits the education of his child to the common school. The teacher is said to stand *in loco parentis* (in the place of the parent), and from this direction, mainly, are his rights of government derived.

The school, therefore, stands in an intermediate position between family government and civil government proper, partaking of some features of each, and forming a sort of stepping-stone for the child from the natural restraints of home to the more complex demands of civil society. The school district, also, while partaking of the nature of a civil institution, is in many respects to be regarded as a co-operative organization of the families of the neighborhood for the education of their children, and its government as a co-operative family government.

### THE CIVIL UNIT DEFINED.

In nearly every part of the United States there is a unit of civil society in which the people exercise many of the powers of government at first hand. This civil unit is variously named in the different States, and its first organization may have been for some minor purpose; but it has grown to be an important sphere of government in many States, and throughout the entire country it is the primary school of the citizen and the voter.

There are many different names by which this civil unit is known.

In the State of Mississippi it is called the *Beat*, and this name is no doubt derived from the original purpose of the organization, as the jurisdiction of a watchman or constable.

In Delaware it is called the *Hundred*, which is the old English subdivision of a county, supposed to contain one hundred families, or one hundred men able to bear arms in the public service.

In the New England States, in New York, and in Wisconsin it is called the *Town*, from the old Anglo-Saxon civil unit, which antedates the settlement of England by its Saxon invaders, and is probably older than the Christian era.

In Arkansas, Indiana, Iowa, Kansas, Michigan, Minnesota, Missouri, Montana, New Jersey, the Carolinas, Ohio, Pennsylvania, and parts of Illinois, Nebraska, and the Dakotas, it is called the *Township*, only a variation of name from the "town," and having the same origin.

In California it is called the *Judicial Township*, and in parts of the Dakotas it is called the *School Township*.

In Alabama, Colorado, Florida, Idaho, Oregon, Utah, Washington, and parts of Illinois and Nebraska, it is called the *Election Precinct*, from the fact that it was the subdivision made for the convenience of voters.

In Georgia it is called the *Militia District*, from the fact that each subdivision furnished a certain proportionate number of men for the militia service of the State.

In Kentucky, Virginia, and West Virginia, it is called the *Magisterial District*, from the fact that it was constituted as the limit of the jurisdiction of a local magistrate.

In Louisiana it is called the *Police Jury Ward*, perhaps for the reason that from each one of these subdivisions a warden was elected to administer the parish government.

In Maryland and Wyoming it is called the *Election*

*District*, from the fact that it was the subdivision made for the convenience of voters.

In Tennessee it is called the *Civil District*—probably, next to " town " or " township," the most fitting name for the smallest subdivision of civil government.

In Texas it is called the *Justice's Precinct*, as being the limit of a justice's jurisdiction.

In some of the New England States, also, districts which have not the entire town organization are provisionally called *Plantations* or *Grants*, being subject to the administration, in some local affairs, of other towns.

But under whatever name the civil unit may exist, it is the primary seat of government. In many cases the original reason for the name has disappeared, while the character of the government has greatly changed, and been modified and developed from the first crude forms.

**Three General Classes.**—As a result, there are at present but three general classes into which we need subdivide the civil unit in the various States: these are the *Civil District*, which would include the "Beat," "Hundred," "Election Precinct," "Militia District," and numerous other classes, embracing about one half the States of the Union; the *Town*, which has its fullest development in the New England States; and the *Township*, which in some States has nearly the full development of a New England town, while in other States it has a looser organization, approximating the civil district of the Southern and Southwestern States.

## THE CIVIL DISTRICT, PROPER.

We shall treat of the various forms of the civil unit which we have classed under the general name of civil district before we speak of the town and the township, because they are simpler and much less developed, and therefore naturally constitute the simplest form of the civil unit.

**Number, Size.**—In number and size, civil districts vary widely in different States and in different counties of the same State. There are rarely less than five or more than twelve districts to the county.

**Purposes.**—The division of the county into districts, each with its own court of law, brings justice to the people's doors. It secures officers to every part of the county, thus affording better means for the punishment of crimes. It provides a speedy trial for minor offences and minor suits. It aids the higher courts by relieving them of a multitude of small cases. As each district has one or more polling-places, it secures convenience to the electors in casting their votes.

**Government.**—The functions of the civil district are judicial and executive, and lie within a narrow range. Its government possesses no legislative or corporate power whatever; it can not make a single law, however unimportant. Within a narrow jurisdiction or sphere, it applies the law to particular cases, and this is the chief purpose for its existence. Whenever the civil unit possesses more powers than are herein set forth, it is more properly described under the township in the next chapter, no matter what name it may go by locally.

## CITIZENS.

The citizens of the civil district are the people residing within it. It exists for their benefit, that they may be secure in life, liberty, and property. In a certain sense they constitute the district, since its government concerns them directly, and others only remotely.

**Rights.**—All citizens have a right to the full and equal protection of the laws. Each has a right to be secure in his person and property; to demand that the peace be preserved; to do all things according to his own will, provided he does not trespass upon the rights of others. No one in the family, in the school, in the civil district, in the county, in the State, or in the nation, has the right to do or say any thing which interferes with the life, liberty, property, or happiness of another. Any act which interferes with the rights of others is an offence against the common good and against the law. It is chiefly for the prevention and punishment of these unlawful acts that the civil district exists, with its court and its officers.

All legal voters of the district have the right to participate in its government by exercising a free choice in the selection of its officers, except in States where these officers are appointed. They have the right to cast their votes without fear or favor. This is one of the most important and sacred rights that freemen possess. Free government can not exist without it. The law guarantees it, and all the power

of the State may be employed to maintain it. Therefore, whoever prevents a voter from exercising the
right of suffrage does it at his own peril.

**Duties.**—As the citizens of the civil district have
rights, they also have corresponding duties. As they
may demand protection and the preservation of the
peace, so it is their duty to obey the law and assist
the officers in its enforcement, in order that the same
protection may be extended to the whole people.
Each should abstain from acts that injure others, and
render cheerful aid to all in securing their rights
through the law.

All qualified voters have the right, and it is also
their duty, to vote. The voters elect the officers of
the district, and are therefore its rulers. When they
fail to vote, they fail to rule—fail in their duty to the
people and to themselves. The duty to vote implies
the duty to vote right, to vote for good men and for
good measures. Therefore, men should study their
duty as voters, that they may elect honest, capable,
faithful officers, and support the parties and principles that will best promote the good of the country.
Every man should study his political duty with the
best light that he can obtain, decide what is right,
and then vote his sentiments honestly and fearlessly.
If the district has good government, the voters deserve the credit; if it has bad government, the voters
deserve the blame.

## OFFICERS.

The officers of the district are the justices of the
peace and the constable. In some States there is only

one justice to each district, in other States there are two, and in others there are three.

**Justice of the Peace.**—The office of justice of the peace is one of dignity and importance. Justices can render great service to society by the proper discharge of their duties. They may have much to do with enforcing the law, and therefore the best men should be elected to this office.

**Election, Term of Office.**—Justices of the peace are usually elected by the qualified voters of the district. In some States the governor appoints them. The term of office is two, three, four, or even seven years, varying in different States.

**Duties.**—The duties of justices of the peace are principally judicial, and their jurisdiction extends throughout the county. Upon the sworn statement of the person making complaint, they issue warrants for the arrest of offenders. With the aid of juries, they hold court for the trial of minor offences—such as the breach of the peace—punishable by fine or brief imprisonment. They sometimes try those charged with higher crimes, and acquit; or, if the proof is sufficient, remand the accused to trial by a higher court. This is called an *examining trial.* They try civil suits where the amount involved does not exceed a fixed amount—fifty dollars in some States, and one hundred dollars in others—and prevent crime by requiring reckless persons to give security to keep the peace. Justices sometimes preside, instead of the coroner, at inquests, and in some States they have important duties as officers of the county.

**Constable, Election, Term of Office.**—There is usually one constable—in some States more—in each civil district. Constables, like the justices, are elected in most States; but in some they are appointed. The term of office is usually the same as that of the justice in the same State.

**Duties.**—The constable is termed a ministerial officer because it is his duty to minister to, or wait upon, the justice's court. He serves warrants, writs, and other processes of the justice, and sometimes those of higher courts. He preserves the public peace, makes arrests for its violation, and in some States collects the taxes apportioned to his civil district.

### SUGGESTIVE QUESTIONS.

1. In what respect does civil government differ from family or school government?

2. Why does the government of the civil district concern its people directly and others remotely?

3. What is meant by the civil unit? By what names is it known in the various States?

4. What are the three general classes under which the civil unit may be considered?

5. Why can not free government exist without the right to vote?

6. Why should the people try to secure their rights through the law?

7. What is the purpose of the subdivision of a county into districts?

8. Define in general terms the rights and duties of the citizens of civil districts.

9. By what other names are justices of the peace sometimes called?

10. Why is the jurisdiction of a justice's court limited?

11. Who are the justices of this civil distri
12. When elected, and what is their term ffice?
13. Who is constable of this district?

## QUESTION FOR DEBAT

*Resolved*, That the government of the civ istrict should have a legislative department.

# CHAPTER IV.

## THE TOWNSHIP OR TOWN.

**Introductory.**—We have learned that in the Southern States the civil unit under various names may be described under the common name of the civil district; that in the New England States it is called the town, and in many of the Western States it is known as the township. As the powers and functions of the town and the township are the same in kind, differing only in extent, and as the two names are so often used, the one for the other, we shall consider both under the head of the township.

As a rule, the township possesses more extensive governmental functions in the Eastern than in the Western States, and in the West it possesses functions much more extensive than those of the civil district in the South. Many of the most important powers that belong to the county in the Southern States belong to the township in the Eastern and the Western States.

**Formation.**—In the Eastern States the townships were formed in the first settlement of the country, and afterward a number of townships were combined to form the county. In the Western States the townships were surveyed, and their boundaries marked, by agents of the general government, before the Territories became States of the Union. As a natural result, the townships of the Eastern States are irreg-

( 37 )

ular in shape and size, while those of the Western
States have a regular form, each being about six
miles square.   In the Western States the township
is usually composed of thirty-six sections, each section being one mile square, and containing six hundred and forty acres of land.

**Purposes.**—It is an old and true maxim that
government should be brought as near the people as
possible.   This the township system does.   In our
country all power resides in the people, and the
township provides a convenient means of ascertaining their wishes and of executing their will.   The
farther away the government, the less will be the
people's power;   the nearer the government, the
greater will be the people's power.   The township
system enables each community to attend to its own
local affairs—a work which no other agency can do so
well—to remove readily and speedily its local public
grievances, and to obtain readily and speedily its
local public needs.

### CITIZENS.

The citizens of the township are the people living
in it, whether native or foreigners who have become
citizens.   It exists for their benefit, to afford them
a means of securing their rights and of redressing
their wrongs.   It is these persons that the law has
in view when setting forth the privileges and immunities of citizenship.

**Rights.**—All citizens of the township are entitled
to enjoy the rights of "life, liberty, property, and
the pursuit of happiness."   The township govern-

ment exists for the purpose of securing these rights to the people. All have equal claims to the fullest protection of the law. They may use their own property as they choose, and do whatever pleases them, so long as they do not interfere with the rights of others. Whenever one's act, speech, or property interferes with the rights of others, he falls under the censure of the law and becomes subject to its penalty.

All male inhabitants born in the United States, and foreigners who have become citizens, who have resided within the State, county, and township the time required by law, are entitled to vote at all township, county, state, and national elections. Several States require the payment of poll-tax as a qualification to vote; others permit the subjects of foreign countries to vote; and in a few States, women are permitted to vote in municipal elections. Lunatics, idiots, paupers, and persons convicted of certain high crimes are disfranchised; that is, are not permitted to vote. The right of suffrage is one of great power and value, being the basis of all free government, and is jealously guarded by the laws of the land.

**Duties.**—The people have extensive rights and they have equally extensive duties. Each citizen has rights that others must respect. It is the duty of each to observe and regard the rights of all other persons; and when he does not, the law interferes by its officers and deprives him of his own rights by fine or imprisonment, and in some instances by a still more severe penalty. It is the duty of the people to love and serve the country; to be good citizens; to labor for the public good; to obey the law, and to assist the officers in its enforcement.

It is the duty of the qualified voters to give the township good government by electing good officers. A vote cast for a bad man or a bad measure is an attack upon the rights of every person in the community. The power of suffrage is held for the public good; but it is used for the public injury when incompetent or unfaithful men are elected to office. Good government and the happiness and prosperity of the country depend upon an honest and intelligent vote.

### GOVERNMENT.

The township government possesses legislative, judicial, and executive functions. It has a legislative department to make local laws, a judicial department to apply the laws to particular cases, and an executive department to enforce these and other laws. The three functions are of nearly equal prominence in the Eastern States, but in the West the executive function is more prominent than the legislative and the judicial.

**Corporate Power.**—Each township is a corporation; that is, in any business affair it may act as a single person. In its corporate capacity it can sue and be sued; borrow money; buy, rent, and sell property for public purposes. When it is said that the township possesses these powers, it is meant that the people of the township, acting as a single political body, possess them.

**Officers.**—The officers of the township are more numerous, and their functions are more extensive than those of the civil district. Many officers are the same in name, and others have the same duties as those of the county in the Southern States.

**Legislative Department ; the People.**—In the Eastern States the legislative department of the township government has more extensive functions than in the West. In the New England States most local affairs belong to the township government, and the county is of minor importance. In these and a few other States the people make their own local laws instead of delegating this power to representatives. The electors of the township meet annually at a fixed place, upon a day appointed by law, discuss questions of public concern, elect the township officers, levy township taxes, make appropriations of money for public purposes, fix the salaries and hear the reports of officers, and decide upon a course of action for the coming year. Thus the people themselves, or more strictly speaking, the qualified voters, are the government. In some States special town meetings may be called for special purposes. The town meeting places local public affairs under the direct control of the people, and thus gives them a personal interest in the government, and makes them feel a personal responsibility for its acts. Another benefit of the system is that it trains the people to deal with political matters, and so prepares them to act intelligently in all the affairs of the State and the nation.

In the Western States the county government **is**

more important, and township legislation is confined to a narrow range. In power and importance the township of most Western States is intermediate between the town of the East and the civil district of the South.

**Selectmen or Trustees.**—The legislative power of the township is vested in the trustees, town council, or selectmen, as they are variously termed. The number of trustees or selectmen is not the same in all parts of the Union, being fixed at three in most States of the West, and varying in New England with the wishes of the electors. The trustees, councilmen, or selectmen are elected by the qualified voters of the township for a term of one, two, or three years, varying in different States. They are the legal guardians of the public interests of the township, and make laws or *ordinances*, sometimes called *by-laws*, expressly pertaining to the local wants of the community, and to a limited extent may levy taxes.

In some States, especially those of the East, the principal duties of the trustees or selectmen are executive. They divide the township into road districts; open roads on petition; select jurors; build and repair bridges and town halls, where the expenditure is small; act as judges of elections; purchase and care for cemeteries; have charge of the poor not in the county charge; and act for the township in its corporate capacity. If any thing goes wrong in the public affairs of the town, complaint is made to these officers.

**Executive Department.**—Most of the public affairs of the township, as well as of all other governments, pertain to the executive department. Its duties are far more extensive, and its officers are more numerous, than those of the other departments. The executive officers of the township are the clerk, the treasurer, the school directors, the assessor, the supervisors, and the constables. In most States all these officers are elected by the qualified voters; but in some the clerk, the treasurer, and the constables are elected by the town council.

**Clerk.**—The clerk of the township is clerk of the trustees, council, or selectmen, and in some States of the school board. He attends the meetings of the trustees, and makes a careful record of the proceedings. He keeps the poll-lists and other legal papers of the township, administers oaths, and notifies officers of their election. In the New England States, and some others, he keeps a record of the marriages, births, and deaths, calls the town meeting to order, reads the warrant under which it is held, presides until a moderator is chosen, and then acts as clerk of the meeting.

**Treasurer.**—Taxes collected from the people for local purposes are paid to the treasurer. He receives all fines, forfeitures, and license-fees paid to the township. He is the keeper of the township funds, giving bond for the faithful performance of his duties, and pays out money upon the written order of the trustees, attested by the clerk. In some States, as in New York, there is no separate township treasurer, the above and other duties being performed by the supervisor, who is the chief officer of the township.

**School Directors.**—The school directors have

charge of the public schools of the township. The number of directors varies widely, being usually three, five, or more. In a few States, as in Ohio, the clerks of the district trustees constitute the township school directors, or township board of education. The directors levy taxes for school purposes, visit and inspect the public schools, adopt text-books, regulate the order of studies and length of the term, fix salaries, purchase furniture and apparatus, and make reports to the higher school officers. In some States they examine teachers and grant certificates to teach. In many States a part of these duties falls to the county superintendent.

**Assessor.**—The assessor makes a list of the names of all persons subject to taxation, estimates the value of their real and personal property, assesses a tax thereon, and in some States delivers this list to the auditor, and in others to the collector of taxes. In most States there is also a poll-tax of from one to three dollars, sometimes more, laid upon all male inhabitants more than twenty-one years of age. In some States there are two or more assessors to the township, and in others real estate is valued only once in ten years.

**Commissioners,** or surveyors of highways, have charge of the construction and repair of highways, summon those subject to labor on the road, and direct their work.

**Supervisor.**—In some States the chief executive duties of the town fall upon the supervisor, but his principal duties are rather as a member of the county board of supervisors.

**Constables.**—Constables are ministerial and police officers. There are usually two or three in each township. They wait upon the justice's court, and are subject to his orders. They preserve the public peace, serve warrants and other processes, and in some States act as collectors of taxes.

**Collector, etc.**—In some States the township has a collector and three or more auditors. They are usually elected by the trustees, or council, but in a few of the States they are elected by the town meeting. The collector collects the township taxes, giving bond for the faithful performance of his duties. In order to secure honesty and efficiency in public office, and to exhibit the financial condition of the township, the auditors annually examine the books of the treasurer and the collector, and publish a report showing the receipts and expenditures of public money.

In a few States the township has a field-driver and a pound-keeper, whose respective duties are to take stray animals to the pound, an enclosure kept for the purpose, and to retain them with good care until the owner is notified and pays all expenses; two or more fence-viewers, who decide disputes about fences; surveyors of lumber, who measure and mark lumber offered for sale; and sealers, who test and certify weights and measures used in trade. These officers are usually appointed by the selectmen.

**Judicial Department; Justices.**—The judicial power is vested in the justices who are elected by the qualified voters of the town. There are usually two or three justices, but in some States there is only one in each township. The term of office is one, two, three, four, or more years, varying in different States. Justices preside in the justice's court to hear and determine suits at law. "This is the humblest court in the land, the court of greatest antiquity, and the court upon which all other courts are founded." * The justice's court tries petty offences and civil suits for small amounts. In some States the justices preside at the town meetings, and in others they perform the duties of coroner in the township.

## SUGGESTIVE QUESTIONS.

1. Has this State the township system ? If so, give the name and number of your township.

2. How does the township system provide a convenient means of ascertaining and of executing the people's will ?

3. Why is the people's power greater when the government is near ?

4. Why can the community manage its own affairs better than any other agency can manage them ?

5. How do people secure their rights ?

6. What is meant by falling under the censure of the law ?

7. What is a naturalized person ?

8. Is it right for subjects of foreign governments to vote ? Why ?

9. Is it right for women to vote in municipal elections ?

10. Why is suffrage the basis of all free government ?

11. What is a more severe penalty than imprisonment ?

12. How can people serve the country ?

13. What is a good citizen ?

14. Why is a bad vote an attack on the rights of the people ?

15. What other laws than those made by the legislative

---

* Thorpe's *Civil Government.*

department of the township does the executive department enforce?

16. How do you like the New England town meeting? Why?

17. Name some duties that belong to the executive department.

18. What is a poll-list?

19. What are the duties of judges of election?

20. Of what use is a record of marriages, births, and deaths?

21. What is meant by license-fees?

22. What persons are subject to taxation?

23. What is a poll-tax, and is it right? Why?

24. Who are subject to road duty in this State?

25. Give the names of the officers of this township.

## QUESTION FOR DEBATE.

*Resolved*, That the town meeting is the best system of local government yet devised.

# CHAPTER V.

## THE COUNTY.

**Introductory.**—The county is a political division of the State, and is composed of civil districts or of townships. It bears the name of county in all parts of the country except in Louisiana, where a similar organization is known as a parish. In New England the county has less power than the town; in the Western States it has more than the township; and in the Southern States it has far more than the civil district, being there the unit of political influence.

**Purposes.**—The county organization brings justice near the people, enables them to attend to local affairs too extensive for a smaller community, and affords a medium by which they may transact business with the State. It serves as a convenient basis of apportioning members of the legislature among the people. It maintains local officers, such as sheriff and prosecuting attorney, whose duties would be too narrow if confined to a township. It secures a competent and higher tribunal than the justice's court for the trial of suits at law. This was the original purpose, and is still the controlling reason for the division of the States into counties.

**Formation, Area.**—Counties are formed, their rights are conferred, and their duties imposed, by act of the State legislature. In most States counties vary greatly in shape and size, but in some of the

Western States they have a regular form. The average area of counties in the United States is eight hundred and thirty square miles; the average area of those east of the Mississippi River is only three hundred and eighty square miles.

**County Seat.**—The county government resides at the county seat, county town, or shire town, as it is variously called. The court-house, the jail, the public offices, and sometimes other county buildings are located at the county seat. Here are kept the records of the courts; also, usually copies of the deeds, wills, mortgages, and other important papers of the people.

## COUNTY GOVERNMENT.

The county, like the United States, the State, and the township, has a republican form of government; that is, it is governed by representatives elected by the people. In nearly all States the county government has three departments, legislative, executive, and judicial: but the functions of making, of executing, and of explaining the laws, are not always kept separate and distinct. In a few States the county does not have a judicial department.

**Officers.**—County officers and township officers have duties similar in kind, but the former have charge of the larger interests. The usual officers of the county are the commissioners or supervisors, the county attorney or prosecuting attorney. the county superintendent of schools or school commissioner, the sheriff, the treasurer, the auditor, the county clerk or common pleas clerk, the surveyor, the coroner, and the county judge and surrogate, or probate judge. In the counties of many States one or more of these officers are lacking, and others have different names from those here given. In the Western and the Southern States county officers are elected by the direct vote of the people ; in most of the New England States some of them are chosen in other ways. The terms of county officers vary in different parts of the Union, being usually two, three, or four years ; but in some States certain officers are elected for a longer term.

**Legislative Department: County Commissioners, or Board of Supervisors.**—In most States the public interests of the county are intrusted to a board of officers, three or five in number, called county commissioners. In some States the board consists of one or more supervisors from each township, and is called the board of supervisors. In a few States the board consists of all the justices of the county, with the county judge as presiding officer.

The county commissioners, or board of supervisors, have charge of the county property, such as the court-house, the jail, and the county infirmary; make orders and raise funds for the erection of county buildings, and for the construction and improvement of highways and bridges; provide polling-places; make appropriations of money for public purposes; and act as the chief agents of the county in its corporate capacity. In some States they fix the salaries of county officers; in others they have power to form new townships and to change the township boundaries. In several States the functions of the board are almost wholly executive.

**Executive Department: County Attorneys, or Prosecuting Attorneys.**—The county attorney, or prosecuting attorney, is the county's counsellor at law, and when requested gives legal advice to all the county officers. It is his duty to prosecute the accused in the trial of crimes and offences, in the justice's court, the county court, and in some States in the circuit court or district court; to represent the county in all civil suits to which it is a party; and to act for it in all cases in which its legal interests are involved.

**County Superintendent of Schools.** — In some States there is no county superintendent of schools. In most States there is such an officer elected by the township school directors or by the people of the county, or appointed by the State superintendent of public instruction. In a few States the county is divided into two or more districts, each having a commissioner of schools.

The county superintendent, or school commissioner, is the chief school officer of the county. He administers the public school system, condemns unfit school-houses and orders others built, examines teachers and grants certificates, holds teachers' institutes, visits and directs the schools, instructs teachers in their duties, interests the people in education, and reports the condition of the schools to the State superintendent of public instruction. He is one of the most important officers of the county, a capable administration of his duties being of the greatest benefit to the whole people.

**Sheriff.**—" The sheriff is the guardian of the peace

of the county and the executive officer of its courts."*
He preserves the peace, arrests persons charged with
crime, serves writs and other processes in both civil
and criminal cases, makes proclamation of all elections, summons jurors, and ministers to the courts
of his county. In States having no county jailer,
the sheriff has charge of the prisons and prisoners,
and is responsible for their safe-keeping. When persons refuse to pay their taxes, he seizes and sells
enough property to pay the sum assessed; and in
some States he is the collector of all State and
county revenue.

**County Treasurer.**—The duties of the treasurer
are indicated by the title of his office. He receives
all county taxes, licenses, and other money paid into
the county treasury. In most States he is custodian
of the county's financial records, and of the tax-collector's books, and in others he collects all the taxes
assessed in the county. He gives bond for the faithful performance of his duties, and pays out funds
upon the warrant of the county commissioners. In
most States having no county treasurer, the sheriff
is keeper of the public money.

**Auditor.**—The auditor is the guardian of the
county's financial interests. He examines the books
and papers of officers who receive or disburse county
funds; keeps a record of receipts and expenditures;
draws all warrants for the payment of public money;
and publishes a report of the county's financial transactions. In some States he receives the assessor's

---

* Thorpe's *Civil Government.*

returns, apportions taxes among the people, and prepares the tax-collector's duplicate list. In States having no county auditor, these duties are performed by other officers.

**County Clerk, or Common Pleas Clerk.**—The county clerk, or common pleas clerk, is the recording officer of the county court, or probate court, and in some States of the circuit court. He issues writs, preserves papers, and records judgments. In many States he issues licenses, preserves election returns, and records wills, deeds, mortgages, and other important papers.

**Recorder, or Register.**—In many States the county has a recorder, or register, instead of the county clerk, and in some States it has both. The recorder, or register, makes a record in books kept for that purpose, of wills, deeds, mortgages, village plats, and powers of attorney. Some of these instruments must be recorded in order to make them valid in law. In some States having no recorder, these duties are performed by the township clerk, and in others by the county clerk.

**Surveyor.**—The county surveyor, or engineer, surveys tracts of land to locate lines, determine areas, and to settle conflicting claims. In some States his services are frequently needed in the transfer of real estate. In most States he makes plots of surveys, issues maps of the county, and has charge of the construction of roads and bridges.

**Coroner.**—The coroner investigates the death of persons who have died by violence, or in prison, or from causes unknown. He receives notice of the

death ; a jury is summoned; witnesses testify; and
the jury renders a verdict in writing, stating the cause
and the manner of the death.　This inquiry is known
as the *coroner's inquest*.　In some States when the office
of sheriff is vacant, the coroner performs the duties.

**Other Officers.**—In some States there are superintendents of the poor, or infirmary directors, who
have charge of the county infirmary in which the
dependent poor are maintained ; in others the township overseers of the poor support these unfortu-
nates with funds furnished for that purpose by the
county.　In some States there is a collector who collects all the taxes of the county ; a county jailer who
holds prisoners in custody and has charge of the
county buildings, under the commissioners' directions ; and also a circuit clerk, or district clerk, who
is the recording officer of the circuit court, or district court as it is often called.

**Judicial Department : County Judge or Pro-
bate Judge.**—The judicial power of the county is
vested in the county judge, or probate judge, who in
many States is its most prominent and important
officer.　He has jurisdiction of wills and estates, appoints administrators and guardians, and settles their
accounts.　In many states he grants licenses; presides over the legislative body of the county ; makes
orders opening roads and appointing overseers of
the public highway ; appoints officers of elections ;
holds examining trials ; sits in the county court to
try minor offences and civil suits for small amounts ;
and in a few States acts as county superintendent of
schools.

In some States there is a probate judge, or judge of the orphan's court, in addition to the county judge.

## SUGGESTIVE QUESTIONS.

1. What is meant by unit of political influence?
2. What affairs are too extensive for a smaller community than the county?
3. Why is the county seat so called?
4. State the terms and the names of the officers of this county.
5. Why do the officers of the county need legal advice?
6. What is meant by the sheriff administering to the courts?
7. What are licenses?
8. Of what use is the treasurer's bond?
9. What is the collector's duplicate list?
10. What is a writ?
11. What is the plot of a survey?
12. What is a will? an administrator?
13. What is an examining trial?
14. Do you think the county judge or probate judge should act as superintendent of schools? Why?

## QUESTION FOR DEBATE.

*Resolved*, That a poll-tax is unjust.

# CHAPTER VI.

## MUNICIPAL CORPORATIONS.

**Villages, Boroughs, and Cities.**—The county usually has within its limits villages or cities, organized under separate and distinct governments. When the people become so thickly settled that the township and county government do not meet their local public wants, the community is incorporated as a village. Villages are often called towns, and incorporated as such, especially in the Southern States; but the word taken in this sense must not be confounded with the same word, denoting a political division of the county in New England, New York, and Wisconsin.

### THE VILLAGE, OR BOROUGH.

**Incorporation.**—In most States, villages, boroughs, and towns are incorporated under general laws made by the State legislature. A majority of the legal voters living within the proposed limits must first vote in favor of the proposition to incorporate. In some States, villages are incorporated by special act of the legislature.

**Government Purposes.**—The purposes of the village or borough government are few in number, and lie within a narrow limit. It is a corporate body, having the usual corporate powers. Under the village organization, local public works, such as streets, sidewalks, and bridges, are maintained more readily and in better condition than under the government of the township and county. The presence of the village officers tends to preserve the peace and make crime less frequent.

**Officers.**—The usual officers of the village or borough are the trustees or councilmen, whose duties are mostly legislative; the marshal, and sometimes a president or mayor: a collector and a treasurer, whose duties are executive; and the recorder, or police judge, or justices of the peace, whose duties are judicial. The officers are usually elected by the legal voters, and serve for a term of one or two years. In many villages the president and the collector are elected by the trustees, the former from among their own number.

**Duties.**—The trustees or council pass laws, called *ordinances*, relating to streets, fast driving, lamps, water-works, the police system, public parks, public health, and the public buildings. They appoint minor officers, such as clerk, regular and special policemen, keeper of the cemetery, and fire-wardens; prescribe the duties, and fix the compensation of these officers.

The president or mayor is the chief executive officer, and is charged with seeing that the laws are enforced. In villages having no president or mayor, this duty devolves upon the trustees. The marshal is a ministerial officer, with the same duties and often the same jurisdiction as the constable, and is sometimes known by that name. He preserves the peace, makes arrests, serves processes, and waits upon the recorder's court. The collector collects the village taxes. The treasurer receives all village funds, and pays out money upon the order of the trustees.

The recorder or police judge tries minor offences, such as breach of the peace, and holds examining trials of higher crimes. His jurisdiction is usually equal to that of justices of the peace in the same State. In some States the village has two justices of the peace instead of the recorder, these being also officers of the county.

## THE CITY.

When the village, borough, or town becomes so large that its government does not meet the people's local public needs, it is incorporated as a city. Where the country is sparsely settled the peace is seldom broken, private interests do not conflict, the people's public needs are small, and therefore the functions of government are few and light. As the population grows dense, the public peace is oftener disturbed, crime increases, disputes about property arise, the public needs become numerous and important, and the officers of the law must interfere to preserve order and protect the people. The fewer the people to the square mile, the fewer and lighter are the functions of government; the more people to the square mile, the more and stronger must be the functions of government.

**Incorporation.**—Cities and villages or boroughs differ principally in size and in the scope of their corporate authority. A city is larger in area and population, and the powers and privileges of its government are more extensive. In some States cities may be incorporated under general laws, but they are usually incorporated by special acts of the State legislature. The act or deed of incorporation is called the city charter. The charter names the city, fixes its limits, erects it as a distinct political corporation, sets forth its powers and privileges, names its officers, prescribes their duties, and authorizes the city to act as an independent government. The legislature may amend the charter at any time, and the acts and laws of the city must not conflict with the constitution of the State or of the United States.

**Wards.**—The city is usually divided into wards for convenience in executing the laws, and especially in electing representatives in the city government. Wards vary greatly in area and population, and their number depends in a measure upon the size of the city. Each usually elects a member of the board of education, and one or more members of each branch of the city council. Each ward is subdivided into precincts for convenience in establishing polling-places.

**City Institutions.**—Cities maintain a number of institutions, peculiar to themselves, for the public welfare. The frequency of destructive fires causes the formation of a fire department. A police force must be organized to protect life and property. A system of sewerage is necessary to the public health. There must be gas-works or electric-light works, that the streets may be lighted, and water-works to supply water for public and private use. In many cities

gas-works and water-works are operated by private
parties or by private corporations.

**Finances.**—Each city has an independent financial
system, which requires skillful management. The
city borrows money, issuing interest-bearing bonds in
payment, and engages in extensive public improvements. The large outlays for paving the streets,
constructing water-works, laying out parks, erecting
public buildings, and for maintaining police systems
and fire departments, cause cities to incur debts often
amounting to many millions of dollars. As the result
of the greater expense of its government, and as its
people also pay State and county taxes, the rate of
taxation in a city is far greater than in rural districts
and villages.

**Citizens: Rights and Duties.**—The qualifications,
the rights, and the duties of citizens of the city are
the same as those of citizens of the township and the
county. The qualifications of voters are also usually
the same. The duties of voters are the same in all
elections, whether in the school district, the civil
district, the city, the county, the State, or the United
States; namely, to vote for the best men and the
best measures. Under whatever division of government the people are living, they always have the
same interest in the maintenance of order, in the
enforcement of the laws, in the triumph of right
principles, and in the election of good men to office.

**Government.**—A city often has a more complex
government than that of the State in which the city
is situated. The massing of so many people, representing so many interests, requires a government

with strong legislative, executive, and judicial functions. One of the great questions of our time is how
to secure economy and efficiency in city government;
and, as our cities are growing with great rapidity, the
problem is daily becoming more difficult to solve.

**Officers.**—The legislative power is vested in the
city council, usually composed of the board of aldermen and of the common council. The executive
authority is vested in the mayor, the city attorney
or solicitor, the city clerk, the assessor, the collector,
the treasurer, the city engineer or surveyor, the board
of public works, the street commissioner, the school
board or board of education, and the superintendent
of schools. The judicial power is vested in the city
court, police court, or recorder's court, as it is
variously termed; in a number of justices' courts;
and in the higher courts, which are also courts of the
county in which the city is located. The officers of
the city are usually elected by the legal voters, but
in some cities the collector, the city engineer, the
street commissioner, and a number of subordinate
officers are appointed by the mayor or city council.
The superintendent of schools is elected by the
school board.

**Duties.**—In many small cities, and in several of
the larger, such as New York, Chicago, Brooklyn,
and San Francisco, the council consists only of the
board of aldermen. When the council is composed
of two branches, a law can not be made by one of
them alone; it must be passed by both; and if
vetoed by the mayor, it must be passed again, and
in most cities by a two thirds vote, or it is void. The

council makes laws, or ordinances, regulating the police force; fixing the rate of city taxation; ordering the issue of bonds and the construction of public works; and making appropriations for public purposes.

The mayor is the chief executive of the city. It is his duty to see that the laws are enforced. He appoints a number of subordinate officers, and in most cities may veto the acts of the city council. The duties of the city attorney, the city clerk, the assessor, the collector, the treasurer, the school board, and the superintendent of schools are similar to those of township and county officers of the same name. The city engineer has charge of the construction of sewers and the improvement of parks. The street commissioner attends to the construction and repair of the streets, crossings, and sidewalks. There are a number of officers appointed by the mayor or the council, such as chief of police, chief of the fire department, and the city physician, who have duties connected with their special departments.

The city judge, police judge, or recorder, has duties similar to those of the same officer in an incorporated village. Cities also have higher courts, variously named, whose judges have duties and jurisdiction equivalent to those of county officers of the same grade. Because offenses against the law are more frequent, officers are more numerous in cities than in the rural districts.

### SUGGESTIVE QUESTIONS.

1. What is meant by incorporating a village ?
2. What is a breach of the peace ?

3. What are polling-places?

4. To what State officer does the mayor of a city or town correspond?

5. Why are offenses against the laws more frequent in the cities than in the rural districts?

6. What is the largest city of this State? Is its council composed of one body or of two?

## QUESTION FOR DEBATE.

*Resolved*, That the legislative department of a city government should consist of only one deliberative body.

# CHAPTER VII.

## THE STATE.

**Introductory.**—After the county, the government nearest us is that of the State. The political divisions which we have considered are subject to the State, holding their powers as grants from its government. The State can make and unmake them, and we owe them obedience because the State has commanded it. As we sometimes express it, the sovereignty or supreme sway of these local divisions resides in the State.

**Definition.**—A *State* is a community of free citizens living within a territory with fixed limits, governed by laws based upon a constitution of their own adoption, and possessing all governmental powers not granted to the United States. Each State is a republic and maintains a republican form of government, which is guaranteed by the United States. The State is supreme within its own sphere, but its authority must not conflict with that of the national government. A State is sometimes called a commonwealth because it binds the whole people together for their common weal or common good.

**Formation of Original States.**—The thirteen original colonies were principally settled by people from Europe. The colonial rights were set forth and boundaries fixed by charters granted by the crown of England. In the Declaration of Independence these

( 64 )

colonies declared themselves "free and independent States." After the treaty of peace which acknowledged their independence, they framed and adopted the national constitution, and thereby became the United States of America.

**Admission of New States.**—New States are admitted into the Union by special acts of the Congress of the United States. An organized Territory having the necessary population sends a memorial to Congress asking to be admitted as a State. Congress then passes a law called an "enabling act," authorizing the people of the Territory to form a State constitution. When the people have framed and adopted a State constitution not in conflict with the Constitution of the United States, Congress passes another act admitting the new State into the Union "upon an equal footing with the original States in all respects whatever." Sometimes the enabling act provides for admission on proclamation of the President of the United States. Several of the Territories adopted State constitutions and were admitted as States without enabling acts.

**Purposes.**—The State keeps power near the people, and thus makes them more secure in their liberty. "The powers not granted to the United States, nor prohibited to the States, are reserved to the States respectively or to the people." If the whole country were a single republic without State divisions, power would be withdrawn from the people and become centralized in the national government.

Our political system leaves the various functions of government to the smallest political communities that can perform them efficiently. The county has charge of all public interests that can be managed by it as well as by the State. Many public affairs, such as popular education,* private corporations, and the organization of the smaller political divisions, can be better managed by the State than by the National Government, and are therefore properly left to the State's direction.

Parts of the country widely separated differ in climate and soil, giving rise to different industries and occupations, which require different laws, made and administered by different States. The State serves as a convenient basis for the apportionment of members of both houses of Congress, and State institutions preserve and develop the local individuality and self-reliance of the people.

**Functions.**—The functions of the State are very extensive, including the greater part of those acts of government which preserve society by affording security to life, liberty, property, and the pursuit of happiness.

The State government touches the citizens at most points; that is, all those laws that concern the body of the people in their ordinary daily life are made and enforced by the State, or by the smaller political divisions of the State, acting under the State's direc-

---

* Popular education must command the sympathy and respect of the people in each locality in order to remain "popular." While the State, therefore, enforces a general system of public schools, it leaves all the details of local management with the people most closely related to the particular school. The people esteem that which they create and control.

tions. Officers discharge their duties, arrests are made, courts are held, offenders are punished, justice is meted out, and taxes are collected, by the authority of the State.

The National Government has similar functions to perform in every part of the country, but they are far less frequent than those of the State.

**Institutions.**—The State maintains a number of charitable and other institutions for the public welfare. It makes appropriations of land or money for the support of asylums, prisons, reformatories, scientific institutions, schools, colleges, and universities. The support of these institutions, the payment of salaries, the administration of justice, and the conduct of other public interests, involve large annual expenditures, often amounting to several millions of dollars.

## CITIZENS.

The citizens of a State are the people who live in it, whether natives of the United States, or foreigners who have been adopted. Persons who are citizens of the United States are thereby citizens of the State in which they reside. They have all the rights that freemen can possess, and enjoy a larger freedom than do the people of any other country.

The legal voters, often called electors, are the male citizens who have resided in the State, the county, and the township, or voting precinct, the time required by law to entitle them to vote. The length of residence required in the State varies, being two years in some, six months in others, and one year in most States. Several States permit citizens of foreign countries to vote, and a few permit women to vote.

**Rights.**—Every citizen has the right to be secure in his person; to be free from attack and annoyance; to go when and where he may choose; to keep, enjoy, and dispose of his property; and to provide in his own way for the welfare of himself and of those dependent upon him.

The rights of the people are set forth at length and with great precision in a portion of the State constitution called the Bill of Rights. These rights must be exercised under the restrictions of the law, and with due regard for the same rights held by others.

The legal voters have the right to vote in all local, State, and national elections. They are voters in national elections by virtue of being voters in State elections. The right to vote implies the right to be voted for, and the right to hold office; but for many officers the State requires a longer residence and other qualifications than those prescribed for voters.

**Duties.**—For every right, the people have a corresponding duty; and for every privilege they enjoy, there is a trust for them to discharge. The large personal freedom possessed by the American citizens imposes equally as large public responsibilities. It is the duty of every citizen to obey the law, to aid in securing justice, to respect authority, to love his country, and to labor for the public good. No one can be a useful member of society unless he respects the laws and institutions of the land. The people themselves have established this government, both

State and national; it exists for them, and therefore they owe it honor and obedience.

It is the duty of every voter to study the interests of the country, and to vote for men and measures that, in his opinion, will best "promote the general welfare." In this country, government is intrusted to the whole people, and they can govern only by expressing their will in elections. Therefore the majority must rule. The majority will sometimes make mistakes, but these will be corrected after a time.

In order that good government may ensue, good men must take part in elections. The privilege of suffrage is conferred upon an implied contract that it will be used for the public good. He who fails to vote when he can, fails to perform his part of the contract, fails to fulfill his promise, and fails to respect the government that protects him.

## CONSTITUTION.

The constitution is often called the supreme law of the State. In other words, it is the supreme act of the people, for the purpose of organizing themselves as a body politic, of formulating their government, and of fixing the limits of its power. It is a contract between the whole society as a political body, and each of its members. Each binds himself to the whole body, and the whole body binds itself to each, in order that all may be governed by the same laws for the common good. The constitution of each State is a written instrument, modeled after the Constitution of the United States, with which it must not conflict.

The constitutions of England and most other countries of Europe are unwritten. They consist of the common usages and maxims that have become fixed by long experience. In those countries, when a new political custom grows into common practice it thereby becomes a part of the national constitution.

**Formation and Adoption.**—As the whole people can not assemble in one place to frame and adopt a constitution, they elect delegates to a constitutional convention. The convention usually meets at the capital, deliberates, frames articles for a proposed constitution, and in nearly all cases submits them to the people. The people make known their will in a general election, and if a majority vote in favor of adopting the proposed constitution, it becomes the constitution of the State. If the proposed constitution is rejected, another convention must be called to propose other articles to be voted upon by the people.

**Purposes.**—The purposes of the constitution are to guard the rights of the people, to protect the liberties of the minority, to grant authority to the government, to separate the functions of the three departments, to prescribe the limits of each, and to fix in the public policy those maxims of political wisdom that have been sanctioned by time.

The special tendency in recent amendments of State constitutions has been to limit the power of the legislature. Constitutions, like other political institutions, are largely matters of growth, and from time to time must be revised to meet the changing wants of society. For this purpose the constitution of almost every State contains a provision, called the *open clause*, which authorizes the legislature, under certain restrictions, to propose amendments to the constitution to be adopted or rejected by a vote of the people.

**Value.**—The people of any State may, at their pleasure, frame and adopt a new constitution, which must be in harmony with the Constitution of the United States. The right to make their own constitution is one of the highest and most important rights that freemen can possess. It is in this and in the right of suffrage that their freedom principally consists.

The constitution protects the people by prescribing the limits of official authority. The legislature can not legally pass a law which the constitution of the State forbids, and when such a law is passed it is declared unconstitutional by the State courts. A provision of a State constitution becomes void when declared by the supreme court of the United States to be in conflict with the national Constitution.

**Contents.**—The constitutions of the several States are based upon the Constitution of the United States as a model, and are therefore much alike in their general provisions. Each contains :

A preamble setting forth the purposes of the constitution ;

A lengthy declaration called the bill of rights.

Provisions for distributing the powers of government into three departments ; and

Articles relating to suffrage, debt, taxation, corporations, public schools, militia, amendments, and other public affairs.

## BILL OF RIGHTS.

The bill of rights usually declares various rights of the citizen which may be classified under the heads of republican principles, personal security, private property, freedom of conscience, freedom of speech and of the press, freedom of assembly, and freedom from military tyranny.

**Republican Principles.**—Under this head the bill declares :

That all power is inherent in the people ;

That governments exist for their good, and by their consent ;

That all freemen are equal ;

That no title of nobility shall be conferred ;

That exclusive privileges shall not be granted except in consideration of public services ;

That all elections shall be free and equal.

**Personal Security.**—In the interests of the personal security of the citizen it is provided :

That the people shall be secure in their persons, houses, papers, and possessions, from unreasonable seizures and searches ;

That warrants to seize and to search persons and things must describe them by oath or affirmation ;

That there shall be no imprisonment for debt, except in cases of fraud.

**Private Property.**—To secure the rights of private property, the bill declares :

That private property shall not be taken for public use without just compensation ; .

And, in some States, that long leases of agricultural lands shall not be made.

**Freedom of Conscience.**—To induce the entire freedom of conscience of the citizen it is declared:

That there shall be perfect religious freedom, but not covering immoral practices;

That there shall be no State church;

That no religious test shall be required for performing any public function;

That the rights of conscience are free from human control.

**Freedom of Speech and of the Press.**—To maintain the rightful freedom of the press, the bill guarantees:

That printing-presses may be used by all;

That every citizen may freely speak, write, and print upon any subject—being responsible for the abuse of the right.

**Freedom of Assembly.**—The right of assembly is secured by the provision:

That the people may peaceably assemble for the public good, to discuss questions of public interest; and

That they may petition the government for redress of grievances.

**Freedom from Military Tyranny.**—To guard against abuses by the military, it is declared:

That the military shall be in strict subordination to the civil power;

That no standing army shall be maintained in time of peace;

That in time of peace no soldier shall be quartered in any house without the owner's consent;

That the right of people to bear arms shall not be questioned. This does not authorize the carrying of concealed weapons.

**Forbidden Laws.**—To insure the people against improper legislation, the bill of rights provides:

That no *ex post facto* law or law impairing the validity of contracts, shall be made;

That no bill of attainder shall be passed;

That no power of suspending laws shall be exercised except by the legislature.

**Rights of the Accused.**—Among the worst abuses of tyranny in all ages have been the corruption of the courts and the denial of the rights of common justice. To guard against these it is expressly provided:

That the writ of *habeas corpus* shall not be suspended except when, in cases of rebellion or invasion, the public safety may require it;

That, except in capital cases, persons charged with crime may give bail;

That no excessive bail shall be required;

That all courts shall be open;

That the accused shall have a speedy trial in the district in which the offense was committed;

That the ancient mode of trial by jury shall be maintained; but civil suits, by consent of the parties, may be tried without a jury;

That all persons injured in lands, goods, person, or reputation shall have remedy by course of law;

That the accused shall be informed of the nature of the charges against him;

That he shall be confronted by the witnesses against him ;

That he shall be heard in his own defense, and may have the benefit of counsel ;

That he shall not be required to testify against himself ;

That he shall not be deprived of life, liberty, or property except by due process of law ;

That no cruel or unusual punishment shall be inflicted ;

That no one shall be twice placed in jeopardy for the same offense.

No citizen of the United States would deny the justice of these declarations. They are so reasonable it seems strange that they should ever have been questioned. " But in enumerating them we are treading on sacred ground. Their establishment cost our ancestors hundreds of years of struggle against arbitrary power, in which they gave their blood and treasure."*

It was to secure and maintain a part of these rights that the American colonies went to war with Great Britain, and made good their Declaration of Independence by an appeal to arms.

Most of these rights are preserved in the Constitution of the United States, to prevent encroachments upon the liberties of the people by the General Government. They are repeated in the State constitution in order that they may not be invaded by the State Government. There is also a provision in the

* McCleary's *Studies in Civics.*

constitution of the State which declares that "the enumeration of certain rights shall not be construed to deny or disparage others retained by the people."

## SUGGESTIVE QUESTIONS.

1. Why are the smaller political communities subject to the State ?

2. Give the names of the thirteen original States.

3. What is meant by States having different industries and occupations ?

4. How do State institutions develop the self-reliance of the people ?

5. Name some acts of government which you have seen the State perform.

6. What are charitable institutions ?

7. How is justice administered ?

8. Wherein are the people of this country freer than other people ?

9. How long must a person live in this State to entitle him to vote ?

10. What is meant by being secure in person ?

11. Read the bill of rights in the constitution of your State.

12. What is a body politic ?

13. Why can not the whole people assemble to form a State constitution ?

14. What is meant by taking private property for public use ?

15. How may the right to speak and print be abused ?

16. What is meant by the military being subordinate to the civil power ?

17. Are all cases tried by jury ?

## QUESTION FOR DEBATE.

*Resolved,* That there should be an educational qualification for suffrage.

# CHAPTER VIII.

## THE STATE—(*Continued*).

**Government Departments.**—The State government is based upon the State constitution. It has a legislative department charged with the making of the laws, an executive department to enforce the laws, and a judicial department to explain and apply the laws. Each of the departments is independent of the others, being supreme within its own sphere.

The American people believe that the functions of making, of enforcing, and of explaining the laws, should forever be separate and distinct. Experience has shown that it is dangerous to the liberties of the people to permit either of the three departments of government to trespass upon the functions of the others. Therefore, the limits of each department are well defined, and its power closely guarded, by the constitution and laws of the State.

### LEGISLATIVE DEPARTMENT.

The legislative or law-making power of the State is vested in the legislature, sometimes called the general assembly, and in some States known as the general court, or legislative assembly. The legislature is composed of two bodies, or houses, called respectively the Senate and the House of Representatives. In New York the latter body is known as the Assembly, in New Jersey it is called the General Assembly

( 77 )

and in some States the House of Delegates. A bill must be passed by both branches of the legislature in order to become a law. The proceedings of the legislature should be made public, and therefore the sessions are open, and the constitution requires each house to keep and publish a daily record, called the *Journal.*

**Qualifications.**—The State constitution prescribes the age, the length of residence, and other legal qualifications for membership in each branch of the legislature. The constitutions of most States fix a longer term of office and require a more mature age for senators than for representatives. In addition to these legal qualifications a legislator should be a man of unswerving honesty, of broad information, of close thought, well versed in the principles of government, acquainted with the needs of the country, and faithful to the interests of the whole people.

**Privileges.**—Each branch of the legislature consists of members elected by the people. Senators and representatives are responsible for their official acts to the people, and to the people alone. Except for treason, felony, and breach of the peace, members of the legislature are privileged from arrest while attending the sessions of their respective houses, and while going thereto and returning therefrom. For any speech or debate in either house, a member thereof can not be questioned in any other place.

Each house adopts rules for its own government. Each house also elects its own officers, except that in most States the people elect a lieutenant-governor, who is also president of the Senate. These various privileges are granted in the State constitution in order that the actions of the legislature may be free from all outside influences.

**Power.**—The constitution of the State defines the limits of the power vested in the legislative department. The legislature may enact any law not forbidden by the Constitution of the State or of the United States. Every act passed is binding upon the people unless it is declared by the courts to be unconstitutional. An act of the legislature, when declared to be unconstitutional, thereby becomes void; that is, it ceases to have any legal force.

**Sessions.**—The legislature meets at the State capitol. In a few States the legislature holds annual sessions, but in far the greater number it meets biennially; that is, once every two years. In many States the constitution limits the session to a certain number of days, but in a few of these States the legislature may extend its session by a special vote of two-thirds of each house. A majority constitutes a quorum for business, but a smaller number may meet and adjourn from day to day in order that the organization may not be lost.

**Functions.**—The legislature enacts laws upon a great variety of subjects. It fixes the rate of State taxation, it provides for the collection and distribution of State revenue, creates offices and fixes salaries, provides for a system of popular education, and makes laws relating to public works, the administration of justice, the conduct of elections, the management of railways and other corporations, the maintenance of charitable and other institutions, the construction and repair of public roads, the organization of the militia, the conduct of prisons and reformatories, and a number of other public interests.

**Forbidden Powers.**—The Constitution of the United States forbids any State to exercise certain powers:

(1) No State can enter into any treaty, alliance, confederation, contract, or agreement with any other State, or with a foreign power; issue commissions to vessels authorizing them to capture and destroy the merchant ships of other nations; coin money; issue paper money; make any thing but gold and silver coin a legal tender for the payment of debts; pass any bill inflicting the penalty of death without a regular trial, or any law fixing a penalty for acts done before its adoption, or any law affecting the provisions of contracts made before its passage; or grant any title of nobility.

(2) No State can, without the consent of Congress, lay a tax or duty on imports or exports, except what is necessary in executing its inspection laws. The net proceeds of all duties laid by any State for this purpose must be paid into the treasury of the United States; and all such laws are subject to the revision and control of Congress. Without the consent of Congress, no State can tax ships, keep troops or ships of war in time of peace, or engage in war unless invaded or in imminent danger.

(3) "No State shall make or enforce any law which shall abridge the privileges or immunities of citi-

zens of the United States; nor shall any State deprive any person of life, liberty, or property without due process of law, nor deny to any person within its jurisdiction the equal protection of the laws."

(4) "[No] State shall assume or pay any debt or obligation incurred in aid of insurrection or rebellion against the United States, or any claim for loss or emancipation of any slave."

**The Senate.**—The Senate is a less numerous body than the House of Representatives. The presiding officer is addressed as "Mr. President" or "Mr. Speaker," the title varying in different States. There is also a chief clerk, with assistants, who keeps the records; a sergeant-at-arms, who preserves order on the floor; a doorkeeper, who has charge of the senate chamber and its entrances, and a number of subordinate officers.

The Senate has two functions not belonging to the House of Representatives: 1. When the governor nominates persons for appointment as officers of the State, unless the Senate advises and consents to the nominations, the appointments are void; 2. When the House of Representatives presents articles of impeachment against an officer of the State, the Senate sits as a court to try the charges.

**House of Representatives.**—The House of Representatives is often called the popular branch of the legislature. It is sometimes designated as the "House." The title of the presiding officer is "Mr. Speaker." The other officers usually have the same titles and duties as those of the Senate.

In most States bills raising revenue, and in some
States bills making appropriations, must originate
in the House of Representatives. This body also
has the sole power of impeachment. Usually when
charges affecting the official conduct of an officer
of the State are brought before the legislature, the
House of Representatives appoints a committee to
investigate the charges and report. If the report
warrants further action, the House adopts charges
of official misconduct, or of high crimes and misdemeanors in office. This proceeding is called an
*impeachment.*

The Senate sits as a court of impeachment, hears
the evidence, listens to the argument by the managers and the counsel for the accused, and then condemns or acquits. The judgment in cases of impeachment is removal from office and disqualification
to hold any office of honor, trust, or profit under the
State.

### SUGGESTIVE QUESTIONS.

1. Why is the State legislature composed of two houses ?
2. Why should the proceedings of the legislature be
public ?
3. Why should senators and representatives be free from
arrest while discharging their public duties ?
4. How often does the legislature of this State meet ?
5. What is the limit of its session ?
6. Can its session be extended ?
7. What is a reformatory ?
8. What are the age and number of years of residence
required of a State senator in this State ? Who is the senator
from this district ?
9. What is a bill for raising revenue ?

10. What are the age and number of years of residence required of a representative in this State? Who is the representative from this district?

## QUESTION FOR DEBATE.

*Resolved*, That a State legislature should not have more than forty senators and one hundred representatives.

# CHAPTER IX.

## THE STATE—*(Continued)*.

WHEN the laws are enacted it becomes necessary that some one be charged with seeing that they are duly executed and obeyed. The people's representatives in the legislative department make the laws. The people's servants in the executive department execute the laws.

### EXECUTIVE DEPARTMENT.

The chief executive officers of the State are the governor, the lieutenant-governor, the secretary of state, the auditor or comptroller, the treasurer, the attorney-general, and the superintendent of public instruction, who, in most States, are elected by the people. Besides these, an adjutant-general, a commissioner of agriculture, a commissioner of insurance, railway commissioners, a register of the land office or land commissioner, and in some States other subordinate officers, are usually appointed by the governor, and confirmed by the Senate.

The higher State offices are provided for in the constitution, while the subordinate offices are created by act of the legislature. Several States have no lieutenant-governor; in some the secretary of state and the superintendent of public instruction are appointed by the governor, and in others some of the subordinate officers are elected by the people. The titles of many of these officers vary in different States.

The terms of the State officers elected by the people are usually alike in the same State, but in some States the terms of the auditor and the treasurer are less, and in others more, than those of the other officers.

**Governor : Term, Qualifications.**—The supreme executive authority is vested in the governor, who is therefore sometimes called the chief executive of the State. His position is one of great dignity and influence.

The term of office is one, two, three, or four years, varying in different States, and in some the constitution prohibits any person from serving two terms in succession.

The legal qualifications of the office of governor vary in different States. He must be a citizen of the United States ; must have resided in the State at least a fixed term of years ; must not be under a certain age, usually thirty or thirty-five years ; and in some States must own property of a given value.

**Powers, Duties.**—The governor is commander-in-chief of the military forces of the State, and represents it in its dealings with other States. He may call on all other executive officers for written information concerning their respective duties. He is presumed to be well informed upon the affairs of the people, and is therefore required to give the legislature information as to the condition of the State, and to recommend the passage of such laws as he deems proper and expedient.

The governor may call special meetings of the legislature to consider questions of great and immediate public concern.   At the opening of each session he addresses a regular message to the legislature, and from time to time submits special messages upon various subjects.

All acts of the legislature are presented for his approval and signature.   If he approves and signs them, they become laws ; if he retains them for ten days without signing them, they become laws without his signature ; if he refuses to approve them, he returns them within the ten days to the house in which they originated, with a statement of his objections.

This action is called a *veto*, and the vetoed measure, in order to become a law, must pass both houses again, and in some States must secure a two thirds vote of each house.

The governor may grant reprieves and pardons, except in cases of impeachment, and in some States, of treason.   In some States this power is limited by a board of pardons, which must recommend a pardon before it can be granted by the governor ; and in others the consent of one branch of the legislature must be obtained.

Treason against the States consists in an open or overt act of " levying war against them, or in adhering to their enemies, giving them aid and comfort."

*To reprieve* is to delay or postpone for a time the execution of the sentence of death upon a criminal.

*To pardon* is to annul a sentence by forgiving the offense against the law, and by releasing the offender.

The governor may also *commute* the sentence of an offender by exchanging the penalty for one less severe.

**Lieutenant-Governor.**—The term and qualifications of the lieutenant-governor are the same as those of the governor. The lieutenant-governor is also president or speaker of the Senate, but votes only in case of a tie. In States having no lieutenant-governor, the Senate elects its presiding officer.

In case of the death or resignation of the governor, the lieutenant-governor becomes governor of the State. In States having no lieutenant-governor, special laws provide for filling vacancies in the office of governor.

When the chief executive is absent from the State, or disabled, the lieutenant-governor performs the duties of the office.

**Secretary of State.**—The secretary of state is the keeper of all State papers, and usually of the great seal of the State. In some States he is *ex officio* auditor. He keeps a record of the proceedings and acts of the legislature and of the executive department of the State government.

He certifies to the correctness of State documents and commissions, indexes the laws, and attends to their printing and distribution, except in States having a superintendent of printing. He receives and preserves the returns of elections, and in some States has charge of the State buildings at the capital.

**Auditor, or Comptroller.**—The auditor is the financial agent of the State, and in some States acts as register of the land office, and in others as commissioner of insurance. He is also the State's bookkeeper, and attends to the collection of its revenue. He examines and adjusts claims and accounts against the State, and orders the payment of such as he approves. He receives moneys paid to the State, deposits them with the treasurer, and takes receipt therefor. No funds can be paid out of the State treasury except upon the auditor's warrant. He makes an annual or biennial report, showing the financial condition of the State. In some States having no auditor, these various duties fall to other officers, chiefly to the secretary of state.

**Treasurer.**—The treasurer is custodian of the funds of the State. He receives the State's revenues from the auditor, and pays them out only upon the auditor's warrant, keeping an accurate account of all sums paid. The treasurer and the auditor (and also the secretary of state when he handles State funds) give heavy bonds for the faithful performance of their duties.

**Attorney-General.**—The attorney-general is a lawyer who acts as attorney for the State in law cases to which the State is a party. His duties pertain chiefly to the higher courts of the State. He is the legal adviser of the State officers, and, when requested by them, gives opinions upon points of law.

He prosecutes persons who are indebted to the State, and assists in bringing to justice those charged with crime. He represents the State in its legal business in the supreme court at Washington, and in the other courts of the United States.

**Superintendent of Public Instruction.** — The superintendent of public instruction has charge of the public school system, and thus superintends one of the largest interests of the State. He has the general management of State teachers' institutes, and in most States he has an official connection with the State university and the State normal schools, either as a member of the faculty or as president or secretary of the board of trustees.

He is an officer of, and usually president of, the State board of education, a body generally consisting of from three to seven members, and in most States composed, in part, of other high officers of the State. The State board of education decides questions of school law, and performs other important duties varying in different States.

The superintendent of public instruction makes an annual or biennial report to the legislature, showing the condition of the public schools and suggesting amendments to the system. In many States the superintendent is appointed by the governor; in others he is elected by the State board of education, and, as president or secretary of that board, is *ex officio* superintendent of public instruction.

**Other Officers.** — The *adjutant-general* is the active officer of the State militia.

The *commissioner of agriculture*, sometimes called the secretary of the board of agriculture, looks after the agricultural interests of the State.

The *commissioner of insurance* has the general oversight of the insurance companies doing business in the State.

The *railway commissioners* assess the value of railway property, and to a limited extent regulate charges on railway lines.

The *register of the land office*, or *land commissioner*, keeps in his office the patents or title-deeds of land issued by the State in its early settlement, and furnishes copies of land patents and warrants to those who desire them. In a few States this officer is elected by the people.

The *State librarian* has charge of the State library, and in some States is superintendent of the State buildings at the capital.

In a few States there are other executive officers, among whom may be named:

A *surveyor-general*, who surveys the public lands, and keeps in his office maps of counties and townships;

A *State engineer*, who superintends the construction and repair of canals and levees;

A *commissioner of statistics*, who collects statistics relating to public interests;

A *commissioner of immigration*, who attends to the interests of immigrants;

A *labor commissioner*, who looks after the interests of the laboring classes;

A *bank inspector*, or *superintendent of banking*, who inspects State banks for the protection of the public; and

A *State examiner*, who investigates the conduct of State institutions, and inspects the State offices, in order to secure honesty and efficiency in public affairs.

In some States two or more of these offices are combined, and in others their duties are performed by the higher officers of the State.

## SUGGESTIVE QUESTIONS.

1. What is the term of office and what the name of the governor of this State?
2. What are the age and the length of residence required of him?
3. How many terms can he serve in succession?
4. Has this State a lieutenant-governor?
5. If so, name his qualifications.
6. What is the great seal of the State?
7. What is the necessity of an auditor?
8. Why should the superintendent of public instruction make a report?

## QUESTION FOR DEBATE.

*Resolved*, That the governor should hold the power of veto.

# CHAPTER X.

## THE STATE—(*Continued*).

### JUDICIAL DEPARTMENT.

**Purposes.**—The judicial department of the State government exists for the sole purpose of administering justice ; that is, for the purpose of interpreting the laws and of applying them to particular cases. The legislature makes the laws, but it can not execute them. The governor recommends the passage of certain laws, and holds the veto power ; but he has no law-making power, nor can he try the most trivial suit.

So the judiciary has no voice in making or in executing the laws, its sole function being to decide their meaning and to apply them in securing justice. The legislative and executive departments may assist, but it is the peculiar province of the judiciary to protect society and to maintain the rights of the people.

**Supreme Court.**—The higher courts of the State are of two classes—those whose jurisdiction includes the entire State, and those whose jurisdiction is confined to particular districts.

The Supreme Court, called in some States the Court of Appeals, is the highest court of the State. The number of the judges of the supreme court varies in the different States, there being a chief justice and from two to eight associate justices in each State.

In some States the justices are elected by the people; in others they are elected by the legislature; and in some they are appointed by the governor, and confirmed by the Senate.

The term of office is lengthy, not less than four years in any State, except Vermont, where it is two years; six, seven, eight, nine, ten, twelve, fourteen, or fifteen years in most States; twenty-one years in Pennsylvania; during good behavior in Massachusetts; until the judges are seventy years of age in New Hampshire; and practically for life in Rhode Island.

The jurisdiction of the supreme court, or court of appeals, extends over the entire State. It holds sessions at the State capital, and in some States at other prominent places, and is chiefly engaged in the trial of cases in which appeals have been taken from the decisions of the lower courts.

Its decision is final, but in cases in which it is alleged that the State law is in conflict with the constitution or laws of the United States, appeals may be taken to the United States Supreme Court at Washington.

**District, or Circuit Court.**—The people most commonly resort to the district court, circuit court, or superior court, as it is variously called in different States, to secure justice. In it are tried the great body of important civil and criminal cases, and also appeals from the lower courts.

The jurisdiction of the district court is limited to a district created by the State constitution or by act of the State legislature. In some cases the district consists of a single county; usually it includes two or more counties, the court being held successively in each county of the district.

In each district there is usually one district judge, who is elected by the people, appointed by the governor, or elected by the legislature.

The term of office in most States is four, six, or eight years.

In some of the districts of certain States there are criminal courts having jurisdiction in criminal cases, and chancery courts or courts of common pleas having jurisdiction in certain civil cases.

In some States there is a high court of chancery having State jurisdiction, and in others there is a superior court which has State jurisdiction, and whose rank is between the supreme court and the district courts.

## TERRITORIES.

**Organization.**—Congress organizes the public domain into Territories, fixes their boundaries, and establishes their governments. The act of organization is passed as soon as the population is dense enough to require governmental authority.

**Executive Department.**—The governor and the secretary are appointed by the President of the United States, with the consent of the United States Senate, and serve for four years, unless removed. The governor appoints a treasurer, an auditor or comptroller, a superintendent of public instruction, a librarian, and in some cases several other territorial officers.

**Legislative Department.**—The legislature consists of a council, usually of twelve members, and a house of representatives of twenty-four members elected by the people of the Territory. The council is the upper house of the legislature, and is sometimes called the Senate. Although the governor and the legislative assembly rule the Territory, all laws passed by them must be submitted to Congress, and, if disapproved, they become null and void.

**Judicial Department.**—The judiciary consists of a supreme court and inferior courts. The chief justice and two or more associate justices of the supreme court are appointed for four years by the President, with the consent of the Senate. The inferior courts are established by the territorial legislature.

**Representation in Congress.**—Each Territory elects a delegate to the Congress of the United States. Territorial delegates serve upon committees, and have the right to debate, but not to vote. Their real duties are as agents of their respective Territories.

**Laws.**—Territories are governed by the laws of Congress, by the common law, and by the laws passed by the territorial legislatures. The governor may pardon offenses against territorial laws, and may grant reprieves for offenses against the laws of Congress, until the cases can be acted upon by the President.

**Local Affairs.**—The local interests of a Territory are similar to those of a State. Taxation, schools, public works, and the administration of justice are supported by the people. The people of the Territories have no voice in the election of President, and none in the government of the United States except through their delegates in Congress.

**Purposes.**—The chief purposes of the territorial government are to give the people the protection of the law, and to prepare the Territory for admission into the Union as a State. A State is a member of the Union, with all the rights and privileges of self-government; a Territory is *under* the Union, subject at all times, and in all things, to regulation by the government of the United States.

All the States, except the original thirteen (including Maine, Vermont, Kentucky, and West Virginia) and California and Texas, have had territorial governments. A Territory is not entirely self-governing; it may be called a State in infancy, requiring the special care of the United States to prepare it for statehood and for admission into the Union " upon an equal footing with the original States in all respects."

**Arizona, New Mexico, Oklahoma,** and **Hawaii** illustrate the territorial form of government described above. The following are exceptions to the rule:

**Alaska.**—By an act establishing a civil government for Alaska, Congress created a district government, providing for a governor and a district court, but not for any legislature. Congress itself makes laws for Alaska.

**Indian Territory.**—This is another exception to the general rule of territorial government. In 1832 it was set apart as the home of the Indian tribes. Each tribe is supreme on its own reservation in the regulation of its domestic concerns. There is therefore no organized territorial government.

**The District of Columbia** is neither a State nor a Territory. It resembles a Territory in being directly governed by Congress in such manner as that body may choose, but it differs from a Territory since it can never become a State.

It is not represented in the government of the United States, and its inhabitants have no voice in local matters. Its affairs are administered by three commissioners, appointed by the President, with the consent of the Senate, and they are subject to the laws of Congress.

**Porto Rico** and the **Philippines** have each a legislature and are governed much like a Territory; but their people are not citizens of the United States. They are practically colonies.

### SUGGESTIVE QUESTIONS.

1. Is it better that judges be elected, or that they be appointed? Why?

2. Why should a judge's term of office be lengthy?

3. Who is chief justice of this State?

4. Who is the judge of the circuit or district court of this district?

5. At what dates does this court hold sessions in this county?

6. How many organized Territories now in the United States? Give their names.

7. When did this State cease to be a Territory?

8. Why should delegates from the Territories not have the privilege of voting in Congress?

### QUESTION FOR DEBATE.

*Resolved*, That the judges of the higher courts should be appointed by the governor, and hold their positions during life and good behavior.

# CHAPTER XI.

## THE UNITED STATES.

**Introductory.**—Each division of government which we have considered exists for only a part of the whole people. The government of one State has no authority over the people of other States; but the government of the United States, often called the national government or federal government, is for the good of the entire country, and its authority is over the whole people.

All these divisions of government—the family, the school, the township or civil district, the county, the State, and the United States—are dependent upon one another.

If family government were destroyed, society would be ruined and other governments would be worthless.

If there were no schools, the people would be so ignorant that free government would be impossible.

If the township or civil district were neglected, local government would be inefficient.

If the States were blotted out, the national government would assume all power, and the freedom of the people would be greatly abridged, and perhaps finally lost.

If the national government were dismembered, the States would be weak, helpless, at war with one another, and at the mercy of foreign nations.

The distribution of power among the several political organizations prevents any of them from assuming too much authority, and thus tends to preserve the liberties of the people.

**Formation.**—The national government is based upon the Constitution of the United States. It was formed by the union of the several States under the Constitution, and its powers are set forth in that instrument. The thirteen original States ratified the Constitution of the United States between December 7, 1787, and May 29, 1790, and thus organized the national government. It thus became, and has continued to be, the government of the whole people, " by the people and for the people."

## FORM OF GOVERNMENT.

The national government, like the government of each State, is a republic; that is, the authority is exercised by the representatives of the people. As all power resides in the people, our government is called a democracy. As the people elect officers or representatives to act for them in the performance of public duties, it is called a representative democracy.

Our system of government is different from those of all other nations, because part of the political power is vested in the State, and part in the nation; that is, in the United States.

The national Constitution enumerates the powers which may be exercised by the national government, and reserves all other powers " to the States respectively, or to the people." Because of this dual or double character of our system of government, John Quincy Adams called it " a complicated machine."

**Purposes.**—The purposes of the national government are clearly and forcibly set forth in the " preamble," or opening clause, of the Constitution of the United States ;

1. " To form a more perfect *union ;* "
2. " To establish *justice ;* "
3. " To insure domestic *tranquillity ;* "
4. " To provide for the common *defense ;* "
5. " To promote the general *welfare ;* "
6. " To secure the blessings of *liberty* to ourselves and our posterity."

Before the Revolutionary war, the American colonies were subject to Great Britain. By the Declaration of Independence these colonies became " free and independent States." During the period between the Declaration of Independence and the adoption of the national Constitution, the union between the States was weak and unsatisfactory.

Instead of there being " domestic tranquillity," the States were engaged in constant quarrels. There was no power to provide for the " common defense " of the people against foreign enemies ; each State must protect itself as best it could. No provision could be made for the " general welfare " by the passage and enforcement of broad measures for the whole country. Under the Articles of Confederation, as was said at that time, the States might "declare everything, but do nothing." The adoption of the national Constitution and the formation of the national government made the inhabitants of the States one people, and have since brought the United States to be "the first of the nations of the earth."

**Functions.**—The functions of the national government are numerous and important. In adopting the national Constitution, the States delegated or ceded to the United States those powers which are necessary to the strength and greatness of a nation.

The national government administers those public affairs which concern the whole people, such as the regulation of commerce, the granting of patents, and the coinage of money ; and also those which pertain to the United States as a nation dealing with other nations, such as declaring war and making treaties of peace.

The subjects upon which the national Congress may enact laws, and consequently the subjects included in the functions of the national government, are enumerated in Section 8, Article I. of the Constitution.

### CITIZENS.

The people who reside in the United States are either citizens or aliens. The national Constitution declares that " All persons born or naturalized in the United States, and subject to the jurisdiction thereof, are citizens of the United States and of the State wherein they reside." Women and children are citizens, though not entitled to vote.

A citizen is a member of the body politic, bound to allegiance, and entitled to protection at home and abroad. He can renounce his allegiance—that is, lay down his citizenship—by becoming the subject of some other country. Wherever he goes, until he renounces his allegiance, he is a citizen of the United States, and is shielded from insult by the might and majesty of the whole nation. Citizenship is therefore valuable for its protection abroad, as well as for its rights and privileges at home.

**Naturalization.**—Naturalized citizens are persons of foreign birth who have become citizens by naturalization, after a continuous residence of at least five years in the United States. A foreigner is *naturalized* by appearing in court, declaring his intention to become a citizen of the United States, and his purpose to renounce all allegiance to foreign governments. After two years more, he must appear in open court, renounce upon oath all foreign allegiance, and swear to support the Constitution of the United States. If he bears any title of nobility, he must renounce it. Naturalized citizens have all the rights and privileges that belong to native-born citizens, except that no naturalized person can become President or Vice President of the United States.

**Rights.**—The Constitution of the United States does not contain a formal bill of rights, as do most of the State constitutions, but it names the following as among the rights of citizens :

(1) " The citizens of each State shall be entitled to all privileges and immunities of citizens of the several States " ;

That is, a citizen who removes into another State shall enjoy all the rights and privileges that belong to its citizens.

(2) " A person charged in any State with treason, felony, or other crime, who shall flee from justice, and be found in another State, shall, on demand of the executive authority of the State from which he fled,

be delivered up, to be removed to the State having jurisdiction of the crime." A demand for the delivery of a fugitive criminal is called a *requisition*.

(3) "No person held to service or labor in one State under the laws thereof, escaping into another, shall, in consequence of any law or regulation therein, be discharged from such service or labor; but shall be delivered up on claim of the party to whom such service or labor may be due."

This provision refers to the capture and return of fugitive slaves, and is rendered void by the abolition of slavery.

(4) "A well-regulated militia being necessary to the security of a free State, the right of the people to keep and bear arms shall not be infringed."

This clause does not authorize the carrying of concealed weapons.

(5) "No soldier shall, in time of peace, be quartered in any house without the consent of the owner, nor in time of war but in a manner to be prescribed by law."

(6) "The right of the people to be secure in their persons, houses, papers, and effects, against unreasonable searches and seizures, shall not be violated; and no warrants shall issue but upon probable cause, supported by oath or affirmation, and particularly describing the place to be searched and the persons or things to be seized."

(7) *a.* "No person shall be held to answer for a capital or otherwise infamous crime, unless on a presentment or indictment of a grand jury, except in cases arising in the land or naval forces, or in the

militia when in actual service, in time of war or public danger ;

*b.* Nor shall any person be subject for the same offense to be twice put in jeopardy of life or limb, nor shall be compelled, in any criminal case, to be a witness against himself ;

*c.* Nor be deprived of life, liberty, or property without due process of law ;

*d.* Nor shall private property be taken for public use without just compensation."

The first part of this clause secures a civil trial to every private citizen. The land and naval forces, and the militia when in actual service, are under military law, usually called martial law.

(8) " In all criminal prosecutions the accused shall enjoy the right

*a.* " To a speedy and public trial by an impartial jury of the State and district wherein the crime shall have been committed, which district shall have been previously ascertained by law ;

*b.* " To be informed of the nature and cause of the accusation ;

*c.* " To be confronted with the witnesses against him ;

*d.* " To have compulsory process for obtaining witnesses in his favor ;

*e.* " And to have the assistance of counsel for his defense."

(9) " In suits at law where the value in controversy shall exceed twenty dollars, the right of trial by jury shall be preserved, and no fact tried by a jury shall be otherwise re-examined in any court of the

United States than according to the rules of the common law."

(10) " Excessive bail shall not be required, nor excessive fines imposed, nor cruel and unusual punishment inflicted."

(11) " Neither slavery nor involuntary servitude, except as a punishment for crime whereof the party shall have been duly convicted, shall exist within the United States or any place subject to their jurisdiction."

(12) " The right of citizens of the United States to vote shall not be denied or abridged by the United States, or by any State, on account of race, color, or previous condition of servitude."

(13) " The enumeration in the Constitution of certain rights shall not be construed to deny or disparage others retained by the people."

### ALIENS.

Aliens are subjects of foreign governments. They are not citizens of this country, and, in general, have no right to take part in its political affairs. Throughout the Union aliens have full social and moral rights; in some States their property rights are restricted; and in a few States they have certain political rights.

### NATURE OF THE CONSTITUTION.

The Constitution of the United States is the supreme law of the whole land. It is a written instrument, and is often called the fundamental law.

Neither the laws of any State nor the laws of the

United States must conflict with the Constitution.
It is the basis of our system of government, the
model upon which all State constitutions are framed,
and the foundation of our greatness as a people. It
defines the limits of the national government, and
enumerates the powers of each of its departments.
It declares what public interests are within the scope
of the national government, reserves certain powers
to the States, and provides that neither State nor
nation shall enact certain specified laws.

**Formation.**—The national Constitution was framed
by a convention of delegates from twelve of the thirteen original States, Rhode Island alone being un-
represented. The convention was called for the
purpose of revising the Articles of Confederation
under which the States were at the time united.

The convention met at Philadelphia, on Monday,
May 14, 1787, and organized on the 25th day of the
same month by electing as its president George
Washington, one of the delegates from Virginia.
The Articles of Confederation were readily seen to be
inadequate to the purposes of a national government,
and the convention proceeded to draught a " Constitution for the United States of America."

The convention completed its labors, submitted
the Constitution to the several States for their ratification, and adjourned on the 17th of September, 1787.
All the States ratified the Constitution, the last being
Rhode Island, whose convention, called for the purpose, passed the ordinance of ratification, May 29,
1790.

**Necessity.**—The necessity for a written national

constitution is readily seen. The preamble states the purposes of the Constitution, which are also the purposes of the national government. The Constitution defines the limits of State and of national power, and thus prevents conflicts of authority which would otherwise arise between the State and the United States. Through the Constitution, the people, who are the sources of all just authority, grant to the government certain powers, and reserve all other powers to themselves. The Constitution prescribes the functions of each department of the government, and thus preserves the liberties of the people by preventing either Congress, the executive department, or the judiciary from exercising powers not granted to it.

**Amendment.**—The Constitution prescribes two methods by which it may be amended:

1. By a two thirds vote of both houses Congress may propose to the several States amendments to the Constitution.
2. Upon the application of two thirds of the States, Congress shall call a convention of delegates from the several States for proposing amendments.

An amendment proposed by either method, " when ratified by the legislatures of three fourths of the States, or by conventions in three fourths thereof, shall be valid to all intents and purposes as a part of this Constitution."

Nineteen amendments have been proposed by Congress, and fifteen of these have been ratified by three fourths of the State legislatures, and have become parts of the Constitution. The other four proposed amendments were rejected. Congress has never called a convention to propose amendments, and no State has ever called a convention to consider those amendments proposed by Congress.

**Departments.**—The functions of each branch of government are carefully marked in the Constitution, and the people and their representatives jealously guard the rights of each department. They believe that the duties of the law-making power, those of the law-enforcing power, and those of the law-explaining power can not be too clearly separated. If the same officers could make the law, enforce the law, and explain the law, there would be no limit to their authority, and therefore no security to the people.

The framers of the Constitution were wise men; they had seen the abuse of power by Great Britain while the colonies were under her sway, and they determined to guard the liberties of the people by forever separating the legislative, the executive, and the judicial functions. Their example has been followed in the constitutions of all the States.

The President has no right to interfere with the decisions of the courts, and, except by his veto, can not interfere with the action of Congress.

Congress can not question the decisions of courts, nor can it interfere with the legal actions of the President, except that the Senate may refuse to confirm his appointments to office.

Even the Supreme Court of the United States can not call in question the official acts of the President, so long as he conforms to the law; nor has it any power over the acts of Congress, except merely to decide upon the constitutionality of the laws when they are properly brought before it.

While, therefore, Congress and the President have some remote influence upon the actions of each other, neither has the slightest right to invade the functions of the Supreme Court, or of any other court, even the humblest in the land.

## SUGGESTIVE QUESTIONS.

1. Why do foreigners become naturalized?
2. What is a title of nobility?
3. What officer of a State makes requisition for the delivery of a criminal held by another State?
4. When was slavery abolished in the United States?
5. What is the purpose of a militia force?
6. What is a capital crime?
7. Why is the accused entitled to a speedy and public trial?
8. Why is the Constitution called the fundamental law?
9. Read in the history of the United States the account of the formation of the Constitution.
10. How many States were needed to ratify the Constitution in order that it might go into effect?
11. Read the fifteen amendments to the Constitution.
12. Can you name any proposed amendments that have been recently advocated?

## QUESTION FOR DEBATE.

*Resolved*, That a written constitution is best for a free country.

# CHAPTER XII.

## THE UNITED STATES—(*Continued*).

### LEGISLATIVE DEPARTMENT.

**Congress.**—The legislative authority of the national government is vested in the Congress of the United States, consisting of a senate and a house of representatives. The senators represent the States, and the representatives represent the people. Congress holds annual sessions at the city of Washington, the seat of the national government. A measure must pass both houses, and be approved by the President, in order to become a law; or if vetoed, it fails, unless it again passes both houses by a two thirds vote.

Senators and representatives receive an annual salary of five thousand dollars each; and are allowed mileage, or traveling expenses, of twenty cents for each mile in going to and returning from the session of Congress.

**Privileges of the Houses.**—There are certain constitutional privileges guaranteed to Congress in order that its action in legislation may be free from undue influence from other departments of the government.

"The times, places, and manner of holding elections for senators and representatives shall be prescribed in each State by the legislature thereof; but the Congress may, at any time, by law, make or alter such regulations, except as to the places of choosing senators."

" Each house shall be the judge of the elections, returns, and qualifications of its own members;" that is, each House declares who are entitled to membership therein.

" Each house may determine the rules of its proceedings, punish its members for disorderly conduct, and with the concurrence of two thirds expel a member."

Each house keeps and publishes a journal of its proceedings, " excepting such parts as may, in their judgment, require secrecy; and the yeas and nays of the members of either house, on any question, shall, at the desire of one fifth of those present, be entered on the journal."

" Neither house, during the session of Congress, shall, without the consent of the other, adjourn for more than three days, nor to any other place than that in which the two houses shall be sitting."

**Privileges and Disabilities of Members.**—The Constitution of the United States sets forth the following privileges and disabilities relating to membership in both the Senate and the House of Representatives :

(1) " The senators and representatives shall receive a compensation for their services, to be ascertained by law, and paid out of the treasury of the United States.

" They shall in all cases except treason, felony, and breach of the peace be privileged from arrest during their attendance at the session of their respective houses, and in going to and returning from the same; and for any speech or debate in either house they shall not be questioned in any other place."

(2) "No senator or representative shall, during the time for which he was elected, be appointed to any civil office under the authority of the United States which shall have been created, or the emoluments whereof shall have been increased, during such time; and no person holding any office under the United States shall be a member of either house during his continuance of office."

The purpose of the first part of this clause is to prevent members of Congress from voting to create offices, or to affix high salaries to offices, with the hope of being appointed to fill them.

(3) "The senators and representatives before mentioned, and the members of the several State legislatures, and all executive and judicial officers both of the United States and of the several States, shall be bound by oath or affirmation to support this Constitution; but no religious test shall ever be required as a qualification to any office or public trust under the United States."

(4) "No person shall be a senator or representative in Congress, or elector of President and Vice President, or hold any office, civil or military, under the United States, or under any State, who, having previously taken an oath as a member of Congress, or as an officer of the United States, or as a member of any State legislature, or as an executive or judicial officer of any State, to support the Constitution of the

United States, shall have engaged in insurrection or rebellion against the same, or given aid and comfort to the enemies thereof. But Congress may, by a vote of two thirds of each House, remove such disability."

The purpose of the clause was to exclude from office all those who had sworn, as officers of the State or the nation, to support the Constitution of the United States, and who afterward engaged in war against the Union. An act of Congress enabling them to hold office was called a removal of their disabilities. This clause of the Constitution is practically void as regards all past offenses, as the disabilities of nearly all to whom it applied have been removed by Congress.

**Powers of Congress.**—Congress has power:

(1) To *levy and collect taxes*, duties on imported goods, and revenues from articles of manufacture, "to pay the debts and provide for the common defense and general welfare of the United States."

(2) "To *borrow money* on the credit of the United States."

The usual method of borrowing money is to issue government bonds, which are promises to pay the sums specified in them at a given time, with interest at a given rate. The bonds are sold, usually at their face value, and the proceeds applied to public purposes. United States bonds can not be taxed by a State.

(3) "To *regulate commerce* with foreign nations, and among the several States, and with the Indian tribes."

(4) "To establish a uniform rule of *naturalization*, and uniform laws on the subject of bankruptcies, throughout the United States."

(5) "To *coin money;* regulate the value thereof, and of foreign coin; and fix the standard of weights and measures."

(6) "To provide for the *punishment of counterfeiting* the securities and current coin of the United States."

(7) "To establish *post-offices* and post-roads."

(8) "To promote the progress of *science and useful arts*, by securing for limited times, to authors and inventors, the exclusive right to their respective writings and discoveries;"

That is, to grant *copyrights* to authors, and to issue *patents* to inventors.

(9) "To constitute *tribunals* inferior to the supreme court."

(10) "To define and punish *piracies and felonies* committed on the high seas, and offenses against the law of nations."

*Piracy* is robbery committed at sea.

(11) "To *declare war;* grant letters of marque and reprisal, and make rules concerning captures on land and water."

*Letters of marque* are commissions issued to private parties, authorizing them to cross the frontiers of another nation, and to seize the persons and property of its subjects.

*Reprisal* is the forcible taking of the property or persons of the subjects of another nation, in return for injuries done to the government granting the letters. Vessels carrying letters of marque and reprisal are called *privateers*.

(12) " To raise and support *armies*."

(13) " To provide and maintain a *navy*."

(14) " To make rules for the government and regu-lation of the land and naval forces."

(15) " To provide for calling forth the *militia* to execute the laws of the Union, suppress insurrection and repel invasions."

(16) " To provide for organizing, arming, and dis-ciplining the militia, and for governing such part of them as may be employed in the service of the United States."

(17) " To exercise exclusive legislation " over the *District of Columbia*, " and to exercise like authority over all places purchased by the consent of the legis-lature of the State in which the same shall be, for the erection of forts, magazines, arsenals, dockyards, and other needful buildings."

(18) " To make all laws which shall be neces-sary and proper for carrying into execution the foregoing powers and all other powers vested by this Constitution in the government of the United States, or in any department or officer thereof."

(19) " Congress may determine the time of choos-ing the *electors* " for President and Vice President of the United States, " and the day on which they shall give their votes, which day shall be the same through-out the United States."

(20) " Congress may, by law, provide for the case of removal, death, resignation, or inability of both

the President and Vice President, declaring what officer shall then act as President."

(21) " The Congress may, by law, vest the appointment of such *inferior officers* as they think proper, in the President alone, in the courts of law, or in the heads of departments."

(22) " The Congress shall have power to declare the punishment of *treason*."

(23) " Full *faith and credit* shall be given in each State, to the public acts, records, and judicial proceedings of every other State. And the Congress may, by general laws, prescribe the manner in which such acts, records, and proceedings shall be proved, and the effect thereof."

(24) "*New States* may be admitted by the Congress into this Union, but no new State shall be formed or erected within the jurisdiction of any other State, nor any State be formed by the junction of two or more States, or parts of States, without the consent of the legislatures of the States concerned, as well as of the Congress."

(25) " The Congress shall have power to dispose of, and to make all needful rules and regulations respecting the *territory* or other property belonging to the United States; and nothing in this Constitution shall be so construed as to prejudice any claims of the United States or of any particular State."

(26) Congress has " power to enforce, by appropriate legislation," all provisions of the Constitution.

Under the authority " to provide for the general welfare of the United States," Congress exercises powers which are implied—that is, understood—but which are not expressly named in the Constitution. The grants of public lands to railway and canal companies, the annual appropriations for the improvement of rivers and harbors, and numerous similar laws are based upon implied powers.

**Forbidden Powers.**—The following powers are expressly denied to the national government:

(1) "The privilege of the writ of *habeas corpus* shall not be suspended unless when, in cases of rebellion or invasion, the public safety may require it."

*Habeas corpus* means "Thou mayst have the body." A person in prison, claiming to be unlawfully detained, or the friend of such a person, applies to the judge of a court for a writ of *habeas corpus*. The judge issues the writ, which directs the officer to bring the body of the prisoner into court at a certain time and place, in order that the legality of the imprisonment may be tested.

The case against the prisoner is not tried under the writ of *habeas corpus*, but the judge inquires whether any crime is charged, or whether there is a legal cause for the arrest. If the imprisonment is illegal, the judge orders the prisoner released; if the prisoner is lawfully held, the judge remands him to prison. This writ secures the freedom of every person unless detained upon legal charges. Therefore, there is no power in this wide country that can arrest and imprison even the humblest citizen except upon legal grounds. The writ of *habeas corpus* is the most famous writ known to the law, the strongest safeguard of the personal liberty of the citizens, and is regarded with almost a sacred reverence by the people.

(2) " No bill of attainder or *ex post facto* law shall be passed " by Congress.

A *bill of attainder* is an act of a legislative body inflicting the penalty of death without a regular trial. An *ex post facto* law is a law which fixes a penalty for acts done before the law was passed, or which increases the penalty of a crime after it is committed. Laws for punishing crime more severely can take effect only after their passage; they can not affect a crime committed before they were passed.

(3) " No tax or duty shall be laid on articles exported from any State. No preference shall be given, by any regulation of commerce or revenue, to the ports of one State over those of another; nor shall vessels bound to or from one State be obliged to enter, clear, or pay duties in another."

(4) " No money shall be drawn from the treasury but in consequence of appropriations made by law, and a regular statement and account of the receipts and expenditures of all public money shall be published from time to time."

(5) " No title of nobility shall be granted by the United States, and no person holding any office of profit or trust under them shall, without the consent of Congress, accept of any present, emolument, office, or title of any kind whatever, from any king, prince, or foreign State."

(6) " Congress shall make no law respecting establishment of religion, or prohibiting the free exercise thereof; or abridging the freedom of speech or of the press; or the right of the people peaceably to

assemble, and to petition the government for a redress of grievances."

(7) " The validity of the public debt of the United States, authorized by law, including debts incurred for payment of pensions and bounties for services in suppressing insurrection or rebellion shall not be questioned. But neither the United States nor any State shall assume or pay any debt or obligation incurred in aid of insurrection or rebellion against the United States, or any claim for the loss or emancipation of any slave; but all such debts, obligations, and claims shall be held illegal and void."

The Constitution of the United States forbids the national government from exercising certain other powers, relating principally to slavery; but such denials are rendered useless by the freedom of the slaves.

## THE UNITED STATES SENATE.

The Senate is composed of two senators from each State, elected by the legislature; and therefore each State has an equal representation, without regard to its area or the number of its people.

The term of office of a United States senator is six years, and one third of the Senate is elected every two years.

A senator must be thirty years old, must have been for nine years a citizen of the United States, and must be an inhabitant of the State for which he shall be chosen.

A vacancy which occurs in any State's representation in the United States Senate, when the legislature is not in session, is filled by appointment by the governor of the State, until the legislature meets again and fills the vacancy by election.

The Vice President of the United States is *ex officio* president of the Senate, but has no vote except when the Senate is equally divided upon a question. The Senate elects its other officers, including a president *pro tempore*, or temporary president, who presides when the Vice President is absent.

The Senate is a continuous body; that is, it is always organized, and when it meets it may proceed at once to business.

When the House of Representatives impeaches an officer of the United States, the impeachment is tried before the Senate sitting as a court.

The Senate has the sole power to try impeachments, and it requires two thirds of the senators present to convict. Judgment in cases of impeachment shall not extend further than to removal from office, and disqualification to hold and enjoy any office of honor, trust, or profit under the United States; but the party convicted shall, nevertheless, be liable and subject to indictment, trial, judgment, and punishment according to law.

All treaties made by the President of the United States with foreign countries must be laid before the Senate for ratification. If two thirds of the Senate vote for the treaty, it is ratified; otherwise, it is rejected.

*Treaties* are compacts or contracts between two or more nations made with a view to the public welfare of each, and are usually formed by agents or commissioners appointed by the respective governments of the countries concerned.

## HOUSE OF REPRESENTATIVES.

The House of Representatives, often called the lower House of Congress, is a much larger body than the Senate. The last apportionment of representatives, made in 1901, gave the House three hundred and eighty-six members, and this went into effect with the Fifty-eighth Congress, beginning on the 4th of March, 1903.

A census of the people is made every ten years, and upon this as a basis Congress fixes the number of representatives for the entire country, and the number to which each State shall be entitled for the next ten years thereafter. Each legislature divides the State into as many Congress districts as the State is entitled to representatives, and each district elects a representative by direct vote of the people.

The term of office is two years, and the terms of all representatives begin and end at the same time.

A representative must be twenty-five years old, must have been a citizen of the United States seven years, and must be an inhabitant of the State in which he is elected.

A vacancy in a State's representation in the lower house of Congress is filled by special election called by the governor for that purpose.

" All bills for raising revenue "—that is, all bills providing for taxation—" must originate in the House of Representatives; but the Senate may propose or concur with amendments, as in other bills." Taxation is called the strongest function of government, and therefore the Constitution provides that the first step must be taken by the House of Representatives, because its members are elected by the direct vote of the people, and are supposed to represent the people's views.

The Constitution provides that "the House of Representatives shall have the sole power of impeachment;" that is, the House of Representatives must formulate and present the charges to the Senate, and prosecute the accused at its bar. An impeachment by the House of Representatives corresponds to an indictment by a grand jury; specific charges must be made before a trial can be held in any court.

**The Speaker.**—The speaker is elected by the representatives. He is a member of the House, and is nominated for the speakership by a convention, or *caucus*, of the representatives who are of his political party. In rank he is the third, and in influence the second officer of the government. He presides over the House, preserves decorum, decides points of order, and directs the business of legislation. He is the organ of the House, and because he speaks and declares its will is called the *Speaker*. He appoints about sixty standing committees, and thus largely shapes legislation. As almost all laws are matured by the committees, and are passed as the result of their work, the political influence of the speaker is second only to that of the President.

The speaker receives three thousand dollars annually in addition to his salary as a representative.

The clerk of the preceding House presides during

the election of the speaker. Immediately after his election, the speaker is sworn into office by the representative of the longest service in the House. He then assumes the direction of business, and administers the oath to the members as they present themselves by States. The House of Representatives is reorganized every two years at the opening of the first session of each Congress.

**Other Officers.**—The other officers of the House are the clerk, the sergeant-at-arms, the doorkeeper, the postmaster, and the chaplain. They are not members of the House. The sergeant-at-arms and the doorkeeper appoint numerous subordinates.

The sergeant-at-arms is the ministerial and police officer of the House. He preserves order, under the direction of the speaker, and executes all processes issued by the House or its committees. The symbol of authority of the House is the mace, consisting of a bundle of ebony rods surmounted by a globe, upon which is a silver eagle with outstretched wings. In scenes of disturbance, when the sergeant-at-arms bears the mace through the hall of the House at the speaker's command, the members immediately become quiet and order is restored.

The doorkeeper has charge of the hall of the House and its entrances. The postmaster receives and distributes the mail matter of the members. The chaplain opens the daily sessions of the House with prayer.

### SUGGESTIVE QUESTIONS.

1. Why do not the people of the United States make their laws in person, instead of delegating this power to Congress ?

2. Is it right that the President should hold the veto power?

3. Why is each House "judge of the elections, returns, and qualifications of its own members"?

4. Why are the yeas and nays entered on the Journal?

5. Why are senators and representatives privileged from arrest during the session, except for certain specified offenses?

6. Is it right to grant copyrights and patents?

7. What is counterfeiting?

8. Should United States senators be elected by the legislature or by the people?

9. How many senators in Congress now?

10. Who are the two United States senators from this State?

11. What is an impeachment?

12. How many representatives in Congress from this State?

13. Give the name of the representative from this district.

14. Who at present is speaker of the national House of Representatives?

15. Of what State is he a representative?

16. Name six of the most important committees of the House of Representatives.

## QUESTION FOR DEBATE.

*Resolved*, That the members of the President's cabinet should be members of the House of Representatives.

# CHAPTER XIII.

## THE UNITED STATES—(*Continued*).

### EXECUTIVE DEPARTMENT.

**President: Qualifications.**—The executive power of the national government is vested in the President of the United States.

The President and the Vice President must be natural born citizens of this country, must have attained the age of thirty-five years, and must have resided fourteen years in the United States.

In case of the President's death, resignation, or removal from office, his duties devolve upon the Vice President; and if a vacancy occurs in the office, the Vice President becomes President of the United States. At other times the only duty of the Vice President is to preside over the Senate.

The President receives a salary of fifty thousand dollars per year; the annual salary of the Vice President is eight thousand dollars.

**Election.**—The President holds his office for a term of four years, and, together with the Vice President chosen for the same term, is elected in the following manner: Each of the political parties meets in the several States in State conventions during the earlier part of the regular year for the election of a President, and appoints delegates to the national convention of the party. Each party meets in national convention later on in the year, and nominates the candidates whom it will support for President and Vice President, and puts forth a declaration of principles called a "platform."

On Tuesday after the first Monday in November the people of the several States meet at their usual polling-places, and elect as many electors of President and Vice President as the State has senators and representatives in Congress. For this purpose candidates for electors have previously been nominated by the several parties naming candidates for President and Vice President.

The election returns are forwarded to the State capital, where they are compared, and the result declared by the election board of the State. The governor and secretary of state issue certificates to the persons chosen as electors of President and Vice President.

On the second Monday in January the electors of each State meet at the State capital and cast their votes for the candidates of their party for President and Vice President. They make, sign, certify, and seal three separate lists of their votes for President and Vice President; transmit two lists to the president of the United States Senate—one by mail and the other by special messenger—and file the remaining list with the judge of the United States district court of the district in which the electors meet.

On the second Wednesday in February the United States Senate and House of Representatives meet in joint session. The president of the Senate opens the certificates of votes from all the States, and the votes are then counted. The person having the highest number of votes for President is declared elected President, if his votes are a majority of all the electors elected in the whole Union.

If no person receives a majority of all the electoral votes, then the House of Representatives elects the President from the three candidates receiving the highest numbers of votes. A quorum for the purpose is a representative or representatives from two thirds of the States. Each State has one vote, cast as a majority of its representatives present directs; and a majority of all the States is necessary to elect.

The person receiving the highest number of votes for Vice President is elected Vice President, if his votes are a majority of the whole number of electors chosen.

If his votes are not a majority of all the electors, then the Senate proceeds to elect the Vice President from the two candidates receiving the highest number of votes for Vice President. A quorum for the purpose consists of two thirds of the senators from all the States. Each senator has one vote, and a majority of the whole number is necessary to elect.

The people do not vote directly for President and Vice President, but for electors by whom the President and the Vice President are chosen. The electors of all the States are called collectively the *electoral college*.

The electors *may* vote for some other person than the candidate nominated by their respective parties; but no elector has ever chosen to exercise this privilege. They consider themselves in honor pledged and instructed to cast their votes for the candidate of their own political faith.

The vote of the people for electors is called the *popular vote*, and the vote of the electors for President is called the *electoral vote*. As has several times happened in our history, a candidate may be elected President or Vice President and yet be in a minority of the popular vote.

**Inauguration.**—On the 4th of March following the election the President and the Vice President assume the duties of their respective offices amid imposing ceremonies.

The Vice President is first sworn into office in the presence of the United States Senate. The following oath of office is then administered to the President-elect by the Chief Justice of the United States Supreme Court: "I do solemnly swear (or affirm) that I will faithfully execute the office of President of the United States; and will, to the best of my ability, preserve, protect, and defend the Constitution of the United States."

In the presence of a vast concourse of citizens the President delivers an address, outlining the public policy to be pursued during his term of office. There is usually a display of civil and military organizations representing all sections of the country. The political differences of the people are in great part forgotten in the enthusiasm attending the inauguration of the President.

**Official Residence.**—The presidential mansion in the city of Washington is called the White House. It was erected and is maintained by the national government at public expense. Here the President resides with his family, and receives private citizens, members of Congress, officers of other departments of the government, and foreign ministers and dignitaries.

At his public receptions, held at stated times, he may be called upon by the humblest person in the land. This shows the spirit of equality which prevails even in the highest station under our system of government. Our institutions are based upon the principle embodied in the Declaration of Independence, " That all men are created equal."

**Dignity and Responsibility.**—The office of President of the United States is the highest in the gift of the people. " He represents the unity, power, and purpose of the nation." He is the first citizen of the United States, holding the position of highest dignity, influence, and responsibility in the whole country. He directs the machinery of the government, and is therefore held responsible by the people for the conduct of public affairs, and largely for the condition of the country.

His term of office is called an administration. He and his official advisers have the appointment of more than one hundred and fifteen thousand officers of the national government.

**Messages.**—At the opening of each regular session of Congress the President sends to both houses his annual message, in which he reviews the public events of the previous year, gives " information of the state of the Union," and recommends the passage of such laws as he deems " necessary and expedient." From

time to time he gives information upon special subjects, and recommends the passage of measures of
pressing importance. The heads of departments
make yearly reports to the President, which he lays
before Congress and the country in his message.

**Duties and Powers.**—The duties of the President
are so extensive, the burdens of his office so heavy,
and his power so great, that the people believe that
no man, however wise and eminent, should hold the
office for more than two terms. Washington set
the example of voluntary retirement at the end of
the second term, and it seems to be an unwritten law
that no President shall serve more than eight years
in succession. The duties of the office, so various
and so burdensome, are summed up in the provision
of the Constitution : "He shall take care that the
laws be faithfully executed."

The President approves or vetoes all bills and joint-
resolutions passed by Congress, except those relating
to questions of adjournment. All measures vetoed
must, within ten days after they are received, be returned to the house in which they originated. The
power to veto acts of Congress is called the legislative power of the President.

He is *commander-in-chief* of the army and the navy
of the United States, and of the militia of the several
States when engaged in the national service. He
does not command in person, but places the forces
under the orders of officers of his choice.

He may require information in writing from the
heads of departments upon subjects relating to their
respective offices. As he appoints these officers,

and may remove them at his pleasure, the people hold him responsible for their official conduct. He is held responsible for the official actions of all officers of the executive department of the government.

He may grant *reprieves and pardons* for offenses against the United States, except in cases of impeachment. Frequent appeals are made to his pardoning power.

He may make *treaties* with foreign countries, but before a treaty can have any effect it must be submitted by him to the Senate, and must be ratified by a vote of two thirds of the senators present. With the consent of the Senate, he appoints ministers to foreign courts, consuls to foreign countries, judges of the United States Supreme Court, and other officers of the national government. He fills vacancies in office which occur during recesses of the Senate, by granting commissions which expire at the close of the next session of the Senate.

He may, in cases of extreme necessity, call *special sessions* of Congress, or of either house. If the Senate and the House of Representatives fail to agree upon a time to which they shall adjourn, the President may adjourn them to such time as he may think proper. Such a necessity has never arisen, and therefore this power has never been exercised.

The President may receive or refuse to receive ministers and other agents of foreign governments. *To receive* a minister is to recognize the nation which he represents. He may also dismiss foreign ministers who do not prove acceptable to our government.

He commissions all officers of the United States.

The power to make appointments of office is called his *patronage*. A civil service commission, consisting of three commissioners, has been established by act of Congress, to secure efficiency in the public service, and to prevent the appointment of men to office as a reward for party work. Before applicants for certain offices can be appointed they must pass an examination prescribed by the civil service commission.

## CABINET.

The President's cabinet is a council of nine official advisers, appointed by him and confirmed by the Senate. They are often called heads of departments. The members of the cabinet are the secretary of state, secretary of the treasury, secretary of war, secretary of the navy, postmaster-general, secretary of the interior, attorney-general, secretary of agriculture, and secretary of commerce and labor.

They may be removed by the President at pleasure, and are directly responsible to him for the conduct of their respective departments. The President holds frequent meetings of the cabinet for the purpose of conferring upon official business; but he may, if he choose, disregard their advice and act upon his own judgment.

In case of the death, resignation, removal, or disability of both President and Vice President, the presidential office would be filled by the members of the cabinet, in this order: The secretary of state, the secretary of the treasury, the secretary of war, the attorney-general, the postmaster-general, the secretary of the navy, the secretary of the interior.

Each of the cabinet officers receives a salary of eight thousand dollars per year.

**Department of State.**—The secretary of state is the head of the department of state, formerly called the department of foreign affairs. His office is the highest rank in the cabinet, and is next in importance to that of the President. He preserves the original draughts of all treaties, laws, public documents, and correspondence with foreign countries. He keeps the great seal of the United States, and fixes it to all commissions signed by the President. He furnishes copies of records and papers kept in his office, impressed with the seal of his department, and authenticates all proclamations and messages of the President.

He has charge of the negotiation of treaties and other foreign affairs, conducts correspondence with foreign ministers, issues instructions for the guidance of our ministers and other agents to foreign countries, and from time to time reports to Congress the relations of the United States with other governments. He is the organ of communication between the President and the governors of the States.

He issues traveling papers, called *passports,* to citizens wishing to travel in foreign countries. When foreign criminals take refuge in this country, he issues warrants for their delivery according to the terms of existing treaties. He presents to the President all foreign ministers, and is the only officer authorized to represent him in correspondence with foreign governments.

The secretary of state has three assistants, called

respectively, first assistant secretary of state, second assistant secretary of state, and third assistant secretary of state.

The department of state conducts the foreign affairs of the government chiefly through the diplomatic service and the consular service.

**The Diplomatic Service.**—The officers of the diplomatic service are called *ministers*, and represent the United States in a political capacity. They negotiate treaties under the direction of the secretary of state, and maintain friendly relations between the United States and the countries to which they are accredited. They are forbidden to engage in any commercial transaction, or to exercise any control over the commercial interests of the United States.

By the laws of nations, foreign ministers in all countries enjoy many rights and privileges not accorded to other foreign persons. They are assisted by interpreters, who explain speeches made in foreign tongues; and by secretaries of legation, who keep the records, and attend to the minor duties of the ministers.

The diplomatic service consists of ambassadors extraordinary and plenipotentiary, of envoys extraordinary and ministers plenipotentiary, and of ministers resident. These officials rank in the order named, but the duties are the same; the chief difference being in the rank and influence of the countries to which they are accredited.

The ambassadors and ministers of the higher rank receive salaries ranging from seven thousand five hundred dollars to seventeen thousand five hundred dollars each, the latter sum being paid to those accredited to Great Britain, Germany, France, Russia, and Mexico.

Ministers resident, most of whom are also consuls general, receive from four thousand dollars to seven thousand dollars each. Ministers sent to foreign countries upon special service, such as the negotiation of special treaties, are sometimes called *commissioners*.

**Consular Service**.—The consular service includes about thirty consuls general, some of whom are ministers resident, and more than three hundred consuls.

The chief duties of consuls are to enforce the commercial laws, and to protect the rights of American citizens. Consuls reside at the principal cities of the consular districts to which they are accredited. The interests of American shipping and American seamen are specially intrusted to their care. They keep the papers of American vessels while in port ; they record the tonnage, the kind and value of the cargo, and the number and condition of the sailors. They hear the complaints of seamen, cause the arrest of mutinous sailors, send them home for trial, and care for mariners in destitute condition. They take possession of the property of American citizens dying abroad, and forward the proceeds to the lawful heirs.

They collect valuable information relating to the commerce and manufactures of foreign countries, which is distributed among our people by the department of commerce and labor.

In Turkey and China, American citizens who are charged with crime are tried by the American consul. Most consuls receive salaries ranging from one thousand dollars to six thousand dollars each, but some are paid by the fees received in the discharge of their duties.

**Treasury Department.**—The secretary of the treasury is the head of the treasury department. He manages the entire financial system of the national government. He suggests to Congress plans for raising revenue and maintaining the credit of the United States, and makes detailed reports on all the operations of his department.

He superintends the collection of revenue; the coinage of money; the operation of national banks; the conduct of custom-houses, where taxes on imported foreign goods are collected. The schedule or table showing the duties levied on foreign goods is called the *tariff;* this is fixed by act of Congress. The management of the marine hospitals, established for disabled sailors, and the operation of the life-saving service, maintained along the seacoast for the rescue of persons from drowning, are also under the charge of the secretary of the treasury. His greatest responsibility is the management of the national debt, which still amounts to many hundred millions of dollars.

**Bureaus.**—The secretary of the treasury is assisted by three assistant secretaries of the treasury, a comptroller, six auditors, a treasurer, a register of the treasury, and numerous other responsible officers in charge of the bank currency, internal revenue, the mint, the erection of public buildings, and other important bureaus and divisions of the treasury department.

The *comptroller* directs the work of the six auditors, and superintends the recovery of debts due the United States.

The *auditor for the treasury department* settles — that is, examines and passes on — all accounts in the collection of customs duties and internal revenue, the national debt, and other accounts immediately connected with the operations of the treasury department.

The *auditor for the war department* settles the army accounts.

The *auditor for the interior department* settles pension accounts, accounts with the Indians, and all other accounts arising in the department of the interior.

The *auditor for the navy department* settles the accounts of the navy.

The *auditor for the state and other departments* has charge of the accounts of the secretary of state, the attorney-general, the secretary of agriculture, and the secretary of commerce and labor, and of all the officials under their direction; the accounts of the United States courts; and those of various institutions which are not under the control of any department.

The *auditor for the post-office department* examines and passes on the accounts of the postal service.

The *treasurer* is custodian of the funds of the United States. All funds and securities are kept in vaults made for the purpose, or deposited in reliable banks for safe keeping.

The *register of the treasury* has charge of the account-books of United States bonds and paper money. They show the exact financial condition of the United States at all times. The register's name is upon all bonds and notes issued by the government.

The *comptroller of the currency* has charge of the national banking system. A *bank* is a place for the safe keeping of money. A bank holding its charter —that is, its power to do business—from a State government is called a State bank. A bank chartered by the national government is called a *national bank*.

By the laws of the United States, any five or more persons with sufficient capital may organize a national bank under the directions of the comptroller of the currency. A national bank may issue its notes—that is, its promises to pay—as currency, to an amount not exceeding the amount of United States bonds deposited by the bank with the national government. There are about four thousand national banks in the United States.

The *commissioner of internal revenue* supervises the collection of internal revenue. Internal revenue is derived from taxes laid upon tobacco and spirituous and malt liquors.

The *director of the mint* has charge of the coinage of money, and reports to Congress upon the yield of precious metals. There are mints at Philadelphia, Carson, San Francisco, Denver, and New Orleans, and assay offices also at other places.

The Constitution vests the power to coin money in the national government alone.

The *director of the bureau of engraving and printing* supervises the execution of designs and the engraving and printing of revenue and postage stamps, national bank notes, and the notes, bonds, and other financial paper of the United States.

The *supervising architect* selects plans for the erection of custom-houses, court-houses, post-offices, mints, and other public buildings of the United States.

The *surgeon-general of the public health and marine hospital service* has charge of the marine hospitals, and helps to enforce the laws which aim to prevent the introduction of contagious diseases into the country.

The *solicitor of the treasury* is the chief lawyer for the department. He has charge of prosecutions for violations of the customs laws, and other crimes against the financial interests of the United States. Like similar lawyers for other departments, he is included in the department of justice, under the attorney-general.

**War Department.**—The secretary of war is the head of the war department. He has charge of the land forces, under the direction of the President. He supervises the expenditure of money voted by Congress for the improvement of rivers and harbors, and for the United States Military Academy at West Point, as well as for the support and operations of the army. In the management of his department he is aided by an assistant secretary of war.

**Bureaus.**— The war department has numerous offices and bureaus, each of which is in charge of a responsible officer.

The *adjutant-general* issues the military orders of the President, conducts the army correspondence, issues commissions, and keeps the army records.

The *quartermaster-general* provides quarters, storage, and transportation for the army, and has charge of barracks and national cemeteries.

The *commissary-general* provides food for the troops.

The *paymaster-general* supervises the payment of the army and the military academy.

The *surgeon-general* superintends the army hospitals, and the distribution of medical stores for the army.

The *inspector-general* attends to inspection of the arms and equipments of the soldiers.

The *chief of engineers* supervises the construction of forts, the improvement of rivers and harbors, and the surveys relating to them.

The *chief of ordnance* furnishes guns and ammunition to the army and to forts, and has charge of armories and arsenals.

The *judge-advocate-general*, who is chief of the bureau of military justice, prosecutes crimes committed in the army, and reviews all sentences passed by military courts and military commissions.

**Military Academy.** — The military academy at West Point is maintained by the national government, for the education and training of officers for the army. Each member of Congress appoints one cadet to the academy, and the President appoints one from the District of Columbia and forty from the United States at large. The military academy is under the immediate charge of a superintendent, an officer of the regular army, appointed by the secretary of war. Each cadet receives from the government an annual sum of money sufficient to pay all necessary expenses at the academy.

**Navy Department.**—The secretary of the navy presides over the navy department. He has control of all affairs relating to vessels of war, the naval forces, and naval operations. He has charge of the Naval Observatory at Washington, and of the United States Naval Academy at Annapolis. The naval department issues sailing charts, sailing directions, and other publications for the use of seamen.

**Bureaus.**—The naval department has numerous bureaus, which are in charge of competent officers detailed from the naval service.

The *bureau of navigation* gives out and enforces the secretary's orders to the officers of the navy, enlists sailors, keeps the records of the service, and has charge of the naval academy.

The *bureau of yards and docks* attends to the navy yards, docks, wharves, their buildings and machinery.

The *bureau of equipment* supplies vessels with fuel, sails, rigging, anchors, and other equipments, and with maps, charts, books, and other appliances needed in navigation. It has charge of the naval observatory, and of the nautical almanac used by navigators.

The *bureau of ordnance* superintends the forging

and testing of cannon, guns, and other military equipments, and the construction of torpedoes for naval warfare.

The *bureau of medicine and surgery* has charge of the naval laboratory, the eight naval hospitals, and the purchase and distribution of surgical instruments and medical stores for the naval department.

The *bureau of supplies and accounts* purchases and distributes provisions and clothing for the navy.

The *bureau of steam engineering* superintends the construction and repair of engines and machinery for the vessels of war.

The *bureau of construction and repair* has charge of all matters relating to the construction and repair of all vessels and boats used in the naval service.

**Naval Academy.**—The naval academy at Annapolis is maintained by the national government for the purpose of educating and training officers for the navy. It bears the same relation to the navy that the military academy bears to the army. Each member of Congress appoints two midshipmen to the academy, and the President appoints two from the District of Columbia and twenty from the United States at large. The academy is under the immediate charge of a superintendent, who is a naval officer appointed by the secretary of the navy. Each midshipman receives from the government an annual sum of money sufficient to pay all necessary expenses incurred at the academy.

**Post-Office Department.**—The postmaster-general presides over the post-office department. He has control of all questions relating to the management of post-offices and the carrying of the mails, and appoints all postmasters whose annual salaries are less than a thousand dollars each. Postmasters whose salaries exceed this sum are appointed by the President of the United States.

**Bureaus.**—The postmaster-general has four assistants, who, under him, are in charge of the various details of the vast establishment devoted to the postal service.

The *first assistant postmaster-general* controls the free delivery of mail matter in cities, and establishes rural free-delivery routes. He furnishes blanks and stationery to post-offices throughout the Union, has charge of the dead-letter office, and controls the post-office money-order business. By means of money orders people may deposit money in the post-office at which they mail their letters, and have it paid at the office to which their letters are addressed.

The *second assistant postmaster-general* attends to the letting of contracts for carrying the mails, decides upon the mode of conveyance, and fixes the time for the arrival and departure of mails at each post-office. He also has charge of the foreign mail service. The United States has postal treaties with all the other civilized countries in the world, by which regular mail lines are maintained.

The *third assistant postmaster-general* has charge of the financial affairs of the department. He provides stamps, stamped envelopes, and postal cards for post-offices, and receives the reports and settlements of postmasters. He also superintends the registered mail service.

The *fourth assistant postmaster-general* has charge of the establishment of new post-offices, and makes preparations for the appointment of all postmasters. He also has charge of the post-office inspectors, who investigate all complaints of losses or irregularities in the mails.

**Interior Department.**—The secretary of the interior is the chief officer of the interior department. The former name, *home department*, suggests the character of the subjects under its control. Its duties relate to various public interests which have been transferred to it from other departments. The department of the interior has charge of pensions, public lands, Indian affairs, patents, education, and the geological survey.

The *commissioner of pensions* has charge of the examination of pension claims and the granting of pensions and bounties for service in the army and the navy. There are about a million names on the pension rolls of the United States, and the annual payment of pensions amounts to about one hundred and forty million dollars.

The *commissioner of the general land office* superintends the surveys and sales of the lands belonging to the national government. The United States surveys divide the public lands into ranges, townships, sections, and fractions of sections. Ranges are bounded by north and south lines, six miles apart, and are numbered east and west. Ranges are divided into townships, each six miles square, numbered north and south. A township is divided into thirty-six sections, each one mile square, and containing six hundred and forty acres of land; and sections are divided into quarter sections.

The *commissioner of Indian affairs* has charge of questions relating to the government of the Indians. Its agents make treaties, manage lands, issue rations and clothing, and conduct trade with the Indians.

The *commissioner of patents* conducts all matters pertaining to the granting of patents for useful inventions, discoveries, and improvements.

A *patent* gives the inventor the exclusive right to manufacture, sell, and use the patented article for a period of seventeen years.

A *copyright*, which is somewhat similar to a patent, gives the author of a book the exclusive right to print, publish, and sell it for a period of twenty-eight years, with the privilege at the expiration of that time of renewing for fourteen years more.

An inventor or author may sell a patent or copyright, as well as other property.

The *commissioner of education* investigates the condition and progress of education in the several States and Territories, and collects information relating to schools, school systems, and methods of teaching. The facts collected are distributed among the people in annual reports published by the office.

The *director of the geological survey* sends out parties of scientific men, who explore various parts of the Union, trace the sources of rivers, measure the heights of lands, and gather other facts relating to the natural resources of the country. He publishes excellent maps of the regions that have been explored.

**Department of Justice.**—The attorney-general presides over the department of justice. He is the chief law officer of the government, and the legal adviser of all the departments. He is assisted by the solicitor-general, who is the second officer in rank; by four assistant attorney-generals, and by several solicitors for particular departments. The duties of the department of justice may be classified as follows:

1. To conduct before the supreme court all suits to which the United States is a party.
2. To conduct suits arising in any of the departments, when requested by the head thereof.
3. To give written advice and to render written opinions upon points of law, when requested by the President or the heads of departments.
4. To exercise supervision over the district attorneys and marshals of the United States district courts.
5. To examine the titles of lands proposed to be purchased by the United States, as sites for forts, arsenals, barracks, dockyards, custom-houses, post-offices, and other public purposes.
6. To examine and report upon applications for judicial offices and positions requiring legal ability.
7. To report annually to Congress upon the business of the department, and upon matters relating to the enforcement of the laws throughout the Union.

**Department of Agriculture.**—The department of agriculture was reorganized in 1889. Previous to that time it had been a bureau of the interior department. The secretary of agriculture is the chief officer of the department of agriculture.

This department collects and diffuses among the people useful knowledge relating to agriculture and agricultural products. Experiments are conducted upon farm and garden products, and the seeds of choice varieties are distributed among the people. Similar attention is given to stock-raising and the care of forests.

The department also includes the *weather bureau*, which collects and publishes telegraphic reports of storms and the condition of the weather, in the interest of agriculture and commerce.

**Department of Commerce and Labor.**—The secretary of commerce and labor presides over the department of commerce and labor, which was created in 1903. Its duty is to promote and develop commerce, mining, manufacturing, fisheries, and the interests of workingmen. It collects and publishes facts and figures on all these subjects; supplies exactly true weights and measures for any one to copy; controls stations for stocking waters with valuable fish; inspects and licenses steamships, rejecting any that are unseaworthy; surveys the seacoast of the United States, and maintains lighthouses at dangerous points.

The work of the department is divided among a number of bureaus, many of which were already in existence when the new department was formed. Among these is the *census office*, which takes a census of the United States every ten years, besides collecting other statistics at shorter intervals.

### SUGGESTIVE QUESTIONS.

1. **Why** does the Constitution require that the President shall be a native of the United States?

2. Who is now President, and of what State is he a citizen?

3. When was he elected?

4. Who is Vice President, and of what State is he a citizen?

5. Is the President's salary too large?

6. Should the President be eligible for reëlection?

7. Do you think he should have the veto power?

8. Read the last annual message of the President.

9. Of what use is a passport in traveling?

10. What is internal revenue?

11. What was the principal cause of the national debt?

12. For what are light-houses used?

13. Where is the nearest national bank to this place?

14. How many soldiers, including officers, in the army of the United States?

15. Give a full description of the national military academy?

16. Is there a signal service in this vicinity?

17. Of what value are the weather reports?

18. Of what use is a navy?

19. Give a full description of the naval academy.

20. Should postmasters be elected by the people?

21. How many post-offices in the United States?

22. Why is it right for the government to grant pensions?

23. Why should a census be taken?

24. What is the population of the United States, and what the population of this State, by the last census?

25. What is meant by conducting a suit before the supreme court?

26. Read the congressional act of 1862 granting public lands to the States for the establishment of agricultural and mechanical colleges.

### QUESTION FOR DEBATE.

*Resolved*, That the President and the Vice President should be elected by the popular vote.

# CHAPTER XIV.

## THE UNITED STATES—(*Continued*).

### JUDICIAL DEPARTMENT.

THE judicial department is one of the three great departments of the government, being coördinate with Congress, the legislative power, and with the President, the executive power. The principle of three coördinate departments of government is new, the United States being the first nation that ever embodied it in its constitution.

The judicial system of the United States includes the Supreme Court of the United States, the circuit courts of appeals, circuit courts, district courts, the supreme court of the District of Columbia, the court of claims, a territorial court for each of the Territories, and several commissioners' courts in each of the States.

**Jurisdiction of United States Courts.**—The jurisdiction of United States courts extends to the following classes of suits at law:

1. To all cases arising under laws passed by Congress.

2. Those affecting ministers, consuls, and other agents of the United States and foreign countries.

3. Suits arising on the high seas.

4. All suits to which the United States is a party.

5. Controversies between a State and the citizens of another State.

6. Cases between citizens of different States.

7. Suits between citizens of the same State claiming lands under grants by different States.

8. Cases between a State or its citizens and a foreign State or its citizens.

It will be seen that all cases at law to which a State is a party must be tried in the courts of the United States. A direct suit can not be brought against the United States except by authority of a special act of Congress; nor can a suit be brought against a State by a citizen of another State, or by one of its own citizens, except by the special permission of its legislature.

**Supreme Court of the United States.** — The Supreme Court of the United States is the highest judicial tribunal in the country. It consists of the Chief Justice and eight associate justices, nominated by the President and confirmed by the Senate. The country is divided into nine circuits, each represented by a justice of the Supreme Court. The justices hold their offices during life, unless impeached; but they have the privilege of retiring upon full pay, at seventy years of age, provided they have served in the court for ten years. A quorum consists of any six justices, and if four or more agree upon a decision it becomes the decision of the court.

The court holds annual sessions in the Capitol building at Washington, beginning upon the second Monday in October. The annual salary of the Chief Justice is thirteen thousand dollars; that of the associate justices is twelve thousand five hundred dollars each.

The Constitution of the United States creates and names the Supreme Court, and provides that the judicial power shall be vested in it "and in such inferior courts as the Congress may from time to time ordain and establish."

**Jurisdiction.**—The Supreme Court has original jurisdiction in all cases affecting ministers, consuls, and other agents of the United States and foreign countries, and in cases to which a State is a party.

Most cases tried by it are brought before it upon appeals from the inferior courts of the United States. They involve chiefly the questions of jurisdiction of the inferior courts, the constitutionality of laws, the validity of treaties, and the sentences in criminal and prize causes. An appeal from a State court can be carried to the Supreme Court only upon the ground that the decision of the State court is in conflict with the Constitution or laws of the United States.

The peculiar province of the Supreme Court is to interpret the Constitution, and in all conflicts between a State and the nation the final decision rests with the Supreme Court of the United States. It may, and does, modify its own judgments; but until it modifies or reverses a decision, it is final, and from it there is no appeal. Whether its decree be against a private citizen, a State, the Congress, or the President, that decree is "the end of the whole matter," and must be obeyed.

The Supreme Court is more admired and praised by foreign critics than is any other of our institutions.

It is conceded by all to be one of the strongest and best features in our system of government. In a free country like ours, such a tribunal is necessary to prevent the legislative and executive departments from trespassing upon the Constitution, and invading the rights of the people. Therefore the Supreme Court of the United States has been appropriately called "the balance-wheel in our system of government."

**United States Circuit Courts of Appeals.**—There are nine circuit courts of appeals, one for each United States circuit. The judges are the same as those of the circuit courts, but the circuit court of appeals is entirely independent in its jurisdiction. All appeals from the circuit and district courts must be made to the circuit courts of appeals, except in cases expressly provided by law to be taken direct to the Supreme Court; but provision is also made for appeal from the decision of the circuit courts of appeals to the Supreme Court in certain classes of cases.

**United States Circuit Court.**—Each United States circuit embraces several States, and has two or more circuit judges nominated by the President and confirmed by the Senate. One justice of the Supreme Court is also assigned to each circuit. The circuit court may consist of any one of the judges representing the circuit, or of all of them sitting together, or of either sitting with a judge of the United States district court. The circuit court has original jurisdiction in civil cases involving property worth five hundred dollars or more, and in all cases of crime against the United States.

In each State a large majority of the civil suits,

whatever the amount involved, and of criminal cases, whatever the offense committed, must be tried and finally decided in the State courts. In a vast majority of instances the people must obtain justice in the courts of the State in which they live.

**United States District Court.**—Each State has one or more United States district courts. The district judge presides in the district court, either alone or with the judge of the circuit court. The district court has both civil and criminal jurisdiction in all cases under the national law which are not required to be brought in the higher courts.

The United States circuit and district courts are commonly called federal courts. If the judges of these courts desire, they may retire upon full pay at the age of seventy, after ten years of consecutive service.

**Court of Claims.**—The court of claims holds its sessions at Washington, and consists of a chief justice and four associate justices. It hears and determines claims against the United States. No one could bring suit against the national government without permission from Congress; but a person having a claim against it may submit the claim to the court of claims for trial, and, if the claim is declared legal and just, it is usually paid by act of Congress.

**Other Courts.**—The *District of Columbia* has six supreme court justices and three justices of a court of appeals. Their jurisdiction is similar to that of the United States district courts and circuit courts of appeals, but is confined to the District of Columbia.

*Territorial courts* consist of a chief justice and two

associate justices, who hold their offices for a term of four years, unless removed by the President. A territorial court holds its sessions in the Territory for which it is constituted, and has jurisdiction of cases arising under the laws of Congress and the laws passed by the territorial legislature.

Appeals are taken from the courts of the District of Columbia and from the territorial courts to the supreme court of the United States.

A United States commissioner's court consists of a commissioner appointed by the judge of the district court. The chief duties of this court are to arrest and hold for trial persons charged with offenses against the United States, and to assist in taking testimony for the trial of cases. A judge of a State court or a justice of the peace may act as United States commissioner, but while engaged in such duties he is an officer of the United States, and not of the State.

**Term of Service.**—Justices of circuit courts, district courts, the court of claims, the courts of the District of Columbia, and of the territorial courts, are appointed by the President and confirmed by the Senate. The justices of these courts, except of the territorial courts, hold their offices during life, unless impeached. This life tenure of office, and the provision that a salary of a justice shall not be reduced during his term, render the courts of the United States independent of Congress and public opinion, and tend to preserve the purity and dignity of their decisions.

The salary of a judge of the circuit court is seven

thousand dollars; that of a judge of a district court is six thousand dollars; that of a justice of the court of claims is six thousand dollars, except the chief justice, who receives six thousand five hundred dollars; that of a justice of the court of appeals of the District of Columbia is seven thousand dollars, except the chief justice, who receives seven thousand five hundred dollars; and that of a justice of the supreme court of the District of Columbia is six thousand dollars.

**Officers of Courts.**—The United States district and circuit courts have grand juries and trial juries, who perform duties similar to those of juries in State courts. With the consent of the Senate, the President appoints for each district a United States district attorney and a United States marshal, who are also officers of the circuit court.

The *district attorney* represents the United States in all civil cases to which it is a party, and is the prosecuting officer in criminal cases.

The *marshal* is the executive and ministerial officer of the court, with duties similar to those of a sheriff.

The supreme court of the United States appoints a *reporter*, who reports—that is, edits and publishes— its decisions. This court also appoints its own *marshal*. The decisions of the circuit court and district court are reported by the judge, or by an attorney under the judge's sanction. Each court appoints a clerk, who keeps a record of its proceedings; gives a history of each case; notes all orders, decisions, and judgments; has charge of all money paid; and keeps and fixes the seal of the court.

The circuit courts of appeals appoint their own marshals and clerks. The duties of these officers are similar to those performed by the marshal and clerk of the Supreme Court. The circuit courts of appeals have no reporters.

## SUGGESTIVE QUESTIONS.

1. Who is chief justice of the United States, and of what State is he a citizen?

2. Why should a judge hold his position during a long term of years?

3. This State is a part of what United States circuit?

4. What justice represents this circuit in the supreme court?

5. Who is judge of the United States district court of this district?

6. Why can no person bring suit against the United States except by special act of Congress?

## QUESTION FOR DEBATE.

*Resolved*, That the jury system should be abolished.

# PART II.

## CHAPTER XV.

### GOVERNMENT.

GOVERNMENT is defined as *rule* or *control*. It is that which governs, and also the act of governing. In its political sense, it means the supreme authority of a State or other political community, or the act by which this authority is applied. It is sometimes said to be a system of institutions for the restraint of people living in the social state or social condition.

The word *govern* is derived from a Latin word which first meant *to steer the ship*, and then very naturally came to mean *to guide, to direct, to command*.

"The comparison of governing with steering is a very happy one," for the interest of him who steers is the same as that of the people in the ship: "all must float or sink together." So the interest of those that govern, of those that guide "the ship of state," as we often express it, is the same as that of the people.*

**Origin and Necessity.**—The origin of government is unknown; its beginning can not be traced. People

---

* Fiske's *Civil Government of the United States.*

everywhere, in all the varying degrees of civilization, recognize the necessity of a supreme authority, to whom all owe and render obedience.

Men can not long live in the same vicinity without some kind of political organization. Without some sort of government—that is, some supreme power to settle disputes—the people would be in continual warfare; there could be no security to person or property; each individual could look to himself alone for safety; "his hand would be against every man, and every man's hand against him."

Wherever men are found they live under some form of government, however rude and imperfect. In all parts and in all ages of the world they have seen the necessity of some power to protect the weak and restrain the strong, and have therefore set up a supreme authority for the common welfare.

A body of people living under government is called *society*, and the agreement existing between them, for their common welfare, is called the *social compact*.

Men are so constituted that society is necessary to their happiness. Therefore they seek the social state and join the social compact, thus agreeing to be governed by law and order.

**For the People.**—Government is for the people, and not for the rulers. Officers, the highest and the lowest, are merely the servants of the people.

All governments derive their just powers from the consent of the people, and are established and maintained for their good. All powers which are exercised without the consent of the people are unjust and tyrannical.

**Kinds.**—Government is of two kinds, civil and military.

*Civil government* is the government of civil society, or the government of the people in a peaceful state.

*Military government* is the government of men in a state of war. It prevails in the army and the navy, and sometimes in districts which are the scenes of military operations.

Military government is conducted by the rules of martial law, and in its penalties and exactions is much more severe than civil government.

### FORMS OF CIVIL GOVERNMENT.

There are many forms of civil government, but they may be reduced to three principal systems :

1. *Monarchy :* government by one person.
2. *Aristocracy :* government by a few persons.
3. *Democracy :* government by the people.

Every government is either one of these forms or is composed of two or more of them.

**Monarchy.**—A *monarchy* is a government whose chief authority is vested in one person, usually called king, queen, emperor, empress, or prince. Monarchies are absolute or limited.

In an *absolute monarchy* there is no limit to the power of the monarch ; his wishes are the laws of the people. The people are his property, and in his person are combined all the powers of government, legislative, executive, and judicial. Russia is the only civilized nation whose government is still an absolute monarchy.

In a *constitutional monarchy* the sovereign, or chief ruler, must govern by laws made by a representative body elected by the people. England and Germany are constitutional monarchies.

In an *hereditary monarchy* the sovereign inherits the ruling power, usually from his father.

In an *elective monarchy* the sovereign is elected for life, usually by the dignitaries of other nations.

A *patriarchy* is a monarchy in which the chief power is exercised by a patriarch, or father. The authority of the patriarch is confined to his tribe. This form of government was common in ancient times, before tribes were combined into nations.

A *theocracy* is a monarchy whose rulers claim to be under the direct guidance of God. The government of the ancient Hebrews was a theocracy.

**Aristocracy.**—An *aristocracy*, sometimes called *oligarchy*, is a government in which the supreme authority is vested in a privileged few, distinguished by their wealth and social position.

The privileged class are usually called nobles. They are above the common people in rank and bear titles of honor. These titles are mostly inherited, but are sometimes conferred upon persons by the sovereign.

An aristocracy never exists by itself; it is always combined with some other form of government, usually with a constitutional monarchy. The government of England is partly aristocratic; the House of Lords, one of the bodies of Parliament, being composed of nobles.

**Democracy.**—A *democracy* is a "government of

the people, by the people, for the people." It is a government by many, instead of by one or by a few. Hereditary titles are inconsistent with democratic government, and therefore never exist in a democracy.

A *pure democracy* is a government conducted by the people in person. It is practicable only in a political community so small that all the people may assemble at the seat of government. The New England "town meeting" is almost the only example of a pure democracy in the world at the present time; certainly the only example in the United States.

A *republic*, or *representative democracy*, is a government conducted by representatives elected by the people.

The United States, Mexico, France, Switzerland, and all South American nations are republics, and the republican principle of government is growing in popularity throughout the civilized world.

No form of government is equally good for all peoples. A certain form may be good for one country and bad for another country. A republic, which is the best government for a well-educated and virtuous people, is the worst for an ignorant and depraved people.

The excellence of a republican government depends upon the knowledge and virtue of its citizens. The people are the rulers, and, if they are wise and virtuous, they will rule well; if they are ignorant and depraved, they will rule ill. Therefore the hope of a republic like ours is, that its people will continue to grow wiser and better.

## SUGGESTIVE QUESTIONS.

1. Why is military government more severe than civil government?

2. Could society exist without law? Why?

3. Why is a republic a bad form of government for an ignorant people?

4. Are the people of the United States growing wiser and better?

5. Is this State improving in civilization?

# CHAPTER XVI.

## JUSTICE.

THE object of government is to protect the people, and to render justice to them. *Justice* is the security of rights. A *right* is a well-founded claim; that is, a just claim of one person upon other persons.

*Rights* are the most important things that a person can possess, because his happiness depends upon them. They are real things, for whose protection governments are instituted. The kind and extent of the rights recognized and protected in any country determine the form of its government. As a rule, there is more freedom among citizens of a republic than among those of other governments, because a republic guarantees more rights.

### RIGHTS AND DUTIES.

People have many rights, and they have equally as many duties. Each right given to a person is a trust placed in his hands for him to discharge. A right implies a duty, and a duty implies a right. Rights and duties go hand in hand. For example, children have a right to the protection of their parents, and this implies that it is the duty of children to obey their parents.

**Civil Rights and Duties.**—Rights and duties are civil and political. *Civil rights* are sometimes called *inalienable rights*, because they can not be justly taken away except as a punishment for crime. They are chiefly those rights with which we are endowed by nature. They are not conferred by any earthly power, but are given to every human being at his birth. They are called civil rights, because they belong to the citizen in his ordinary daily life. Among civil rights are:

1. *The right to personal security;* that is, the right to be free from attack and annoyance;

2. *The right of personal liberty;* that is, to go when and where he pleases, providing he does not trespass upon the rights of others; and

3. *The right of private property;* that is, the right to use, enjoy, and dispose of what he has acquired by labor, purchase, gift, or inheritance.

The greater part of these rights belong to men whether living in society, that is, under government, or living without government. Their natural rights are more extensive without society than with it, but are far less secure. Without government natural rights are unlimited; each person may lay claim to all land and to all it produces, provided he is strong enough to maintain his claim by force.

When men join the social compact, they agree to abandon some of their natural rights, in order to be protected by the government in those which they retain; that is, each person agrees that in making his own claims he will have due regard for the similar claims of others.

In entering the social compact, men also agree to submit their personal claims to settlement by the law, instead of going to war to maintain them. They agree to refer their disputes to courts established for that purpose. As a rule, under government, right prevails; without government, might prevails.

*Civil rights* are divided into *industrial rights, social rights,* and *moral* or *religious rights.*

**Industrial Rights and Duties.**—It is the right and duty of each person to provide in his own way, providing it is legal and honest, for himself and those dependent upon him. All business transactions; the search for homes, comforts, and wealth; agriculture, manufacturing, mining, and commerce; the conduct of all professions, occupations, and industries; the interests of farm laborers, operatives in factories, miners, clerks, and all persons engaged in mental or physical labor, are based upon industrial rights and duties.

The wages of people, the hours of labor, railway and telegraph lines, canals, express companies, other common carriers, the various kinds of employment, and the organization of men in different branches of industry to advance their interests, are questions affecting industrial rights. These rights underlie all efforts of people to improve their financial condition.

**Social Rights and Duties.**—Each member of society has rights as such, and these are called *social rights.* They include the rights of personal security and protection. They underlie all efforts for the improvement of the social condition of the people. Society is interested in better schools, in public health, in the reformation of criminals, in good highways and streets, in safe buildings, in well-lighted cities and villages, in the maintenance of charitable institutions, in the establishment of sources of harmless amusement, and in the preservation of peace and order.

The comfort and convenience of the public are even more important than the comfort and convenience of any person. Therefore, individual rights must yield to public rights when the two conflict. For example, the land of a private citizen may be condemned by the proper authorities, and be used for public highways or other public purposes. The government pays the owner of the property condemned, but usually less than his estimate of the value.

This right of society, existing above the right of any of its members, is called the RIGHT OF EMINENT DOMAIN. By it individual rights must yield to the rights of society, of the government, or of a corporation. A corporation is an association of individuals authorized by law to transact business as a single natural person. Railway companies, banks, chartered cities and villages, and the counties of some States are corporations.

**Moral Rights and Duties.**—Man is a moral being; that is, he is conscious of good and evil. Therefore he has moral rights and duties.

He has rights of conscience, with which it is not the province of government to interfere. He naturally worships a Being superior to himself, and feels the obligation to deal justly with his fellow-men. He has a right to do and say all things which are not unlawful or wrong within themselves. It is his right to worship when he pleases, whom he pleases, and as he pleases.

The moral rights and duties of the people are concerned in the maintenance of religion, the support of churches, in reverence for things sacred, in acts of charity and benevolence, in living an upright life, and in teaching lessons of morality, honesty, industry, and usefulness. Whatever is implied in the word *ought*, correctly used, is a moral duty.

**Political Rights and Duties.**—By the social compact, men also agree to abandon a part of their natural rights in order to participate in the government. They agree in part to be governed by others, in order that in part they may govern others. The rights of participation in the government, such as voting and holding office, are called political rights, because they affect the public policy of society.

Political rights do not belong to men by nature, but are conferred by government. Within reasonable bounds, they may be enlarged or restricted without injustice. Since they are conferred by the government, the power to vote and to hold office is a privilege to be enjoyed rather than a right to be asserted.

In the United States the political rights of the people are carefully set forth in the Constitution. The smallest functions of government, such as the size and color of a postage stamp, or the employment of a page in the State legislature, touch the political rights of the citizen. Appointment and elections to public office, the enactment of laws, and the performance of public duties are questions of political concern.

Good laws, good administrations, and the perpetuity of the government itself, depend upon the manner in which the people discharge their public duties. A man who habitually fails to vote and to take interest in the political affairs of his country may be a good man, but he is certainly a bad citizen.

To be a good citizen is to aid intelligently in giving the people good government. For a man to hold himself aloof from politics, unless his action is based upon conscientious scruples, shows his interest in himself, and his lack of interest in his country.

### SUGGESTIVE QUESTIONS.

1. Why does happiness depend upon the maintenance of rights?

2. How do persons *born* under government agree to be governed by the laws?

3. If the claims of people as to their rights conflict, how is the difference settled?

4. What is meant by the phrase "common carrier"?

5. Is it right for men to hold aloof from public affairs because there is corruption in politics?

# CHAPTER XVII.

## LAW AND LIBERTY.

THROUGH law rights are secured, and the performance of some duties is enforced. *Law* is a rule of action, prescribing what shall be done and what shall not be done. Laws exist for the purpose of securing the rights of the people. The enjoyment of rights is *liberty*.

As the enjoyment of rights depends upon their security, and as they are secured by law, therefore liberty is based upon law. Without law there could be no political liberty, and the civil liberty of the people would be narrow and uncertain. It may be said, therefore, that there can be no true liberty without law; but laws may be so many and so stringent that there can be no liberty. Liberty and *just* laws are inseparable.

Liberty and rights are of the same kinds, *industrial, social, moral* or *religious*, and *political*. The words "rights," "law," and "liberty" are full of meaning, and in a free country suggest ideas of the deepest reverence.

Origin.—The laws of the country are partly human and partly divine. They were framed by man, but some of them are based upon the laws of God. Some are of recent origin, and many are so ancient that their beginning can not be traced. When men began to live in society, they began to make laws, for laws at once became necessary. Laws are undergoing constant changes, as new conditions arise and new customs prevail.

## KINDS OF LAW.

The *moral law* prescribes our duties to men, and also to God. It is summed up and revealed in the Ten Commandments, and is the same as the law of nature taught us by our consciences.

The *common law* consists of the principles and rules of action applied by the courts in cases not regulated by express legislative acts. It is the *unwritten law* which has been practiced for ages in England and the United States. In all States of the Union, except Louisiana, cases not covered by the acts of the legislature are tried by the common law.

The *civil law* is the law that prevailed among the ancient Romans. It is still in use among most of the nations of continental Europe. In Louisiana it is applied to cases not covered by the laws of the legislature. The words *civil law* are sometimes used to denote the law governing civil suits.

*Statute law* consists of the acts passed by legislative assemblies. The words are used to denote the opposite of common law. The enactment of a statute by a State legislature repeals the common law previously in force upon the same subject.

*International law*, often called the *law of nations*, consists of the rules and customs prevailing between civilized nations in their relations with one another. It is based upon the law of nature, the law of right and wrong.

*Criminal law* is the law governing criminal cases. It is partly common law and partly statute law. "Ignorance of the law excuses no one."

*Parliamentary law* consists of the rules and customs governing parliamentary assemblies. It prevails in all law-making bodies, in conventions and deliberative meetings.

*Martial law* is the law which regulates men in military service. It prevails in the army and the navy. The courts which apply it are called *courts martial.* Martial law is noted for its severity.

*Maritime law,* or *marine law,* is the law especially relating to the business of the sea, to ships, their crews, and navigation. The courts of maritime law are *admiralty courts.*

*Commercial law* is a system of rules for the regulation of trade and commerce. It is deduced from the customs of merchants.

**Courts.**—Laws are administered, that is, explained and applied, by means of courts. A *court* is a body organized for the public administration of justice. A court may consist of a single judge or justice, or of a number of judges acting together.

A court can administer the laws only in cases which are brought before it. The highest court in the land can not make an order or render a judgment until the question comes to trial in a regular way.

**Suits.**—*Suits at law* are called *causes, cases,* or *actions.*

A *civil cause* is a suit between persons, brought to recover rights or to secure compensation for their infraction.

A *criminal cause* is a charge brought by a State or by the United States against a person for the commission of a crime.

The *plaintiff* is the person who brings the suit. The *defendant* is the person against whom the suit is brought.

In all criminal cases in State courts, the State is the plaintiff ; in other words, society prosecutes the offender in the name of the State. In criminal cases in the United States courts, the United States is the plaintiff.

**Judges.**—The judge represents the majesty of the law, and is often called the court. He maintains the dignity of the trial, determines the method of procedure, interprets the law, instructs the juries, renders judgment, and in criminal cases passes sentence upon the offender. Judges are presumed to be learned in the law, and to be perfectly just and impartial in their rulings.

**Juries.**—Most of the courts of this country have two juries, called respectively *grand jury* and *trial jury* (or *petit jury*).

The purpose of the grand jury is to investigate crime, and to present charges, called indictments, for trial by the court. The number of grand jurors to the court varies in different States, being not more than twenty-four and not less than twelve. The grand jury has a foreman, elected by it, or appointed by the judge of the court.

The grand jury inquires into violations of the law, and if, in the judgment of twelve jurors, the evidence in a particular case warrants a trial, a formal written charge is prepared, and the foreman indorses thereon, "*A true bill.*" Upon this indictment the offender is tried by the court.

In a few States grand juries are rarely if ever called, the indictment being found "on information" or on evidence presented to a court commissioner.

A trial jury usually consists of twelve men, but in some States a smaller number may be accepted by the judge of the court, in certain cases, by the agreement of the counsel upon the opposing sides. The trial jury hears the testimony and argument, and then decides upon the truth of the facts in dispute, and renders a verdict or decision in the suit, and in criminal cases convicts or acquits.

In some States all the jurors must agree, or there is no verdict. In other States the jury may render a verdict by the agreement of less than the whole number of jurors. Under certain regulations a party to a suit may *challenge*, that is, reject, a part or all of the jurors, and have others selected in their stead.

**Origin of Juries.**—Grand juries and trial juries are of great antiquity. It is thought that they existed among the Saxons in the north of Europe before they invaded and settled England, more than fourteen hundred years ago. The jury system and many other political institutions of the United States are derived from England.

Both the grand jury and the trial jury are firmly grounded in this country, being recognized in the constitutions of nearly all the States and the Constitution of the United States, and are regarded as among the strongest supports of a free government.

**Officers of Courts.**—Each court has one or more ministerial officers, variously designated as *constable, sheriff, tipstaff,* or *marshal.* Each court also has one or more *clerks,* and sometimes other officers. *Attorneys* are considered officers of the courts in which they practice. They usually represent the plaintiff and the defendant in court and are then called *counsel.*

**Legal Proceedings** in civil cases begin by the court issuing a writ, at the instance of plaintiff, summoning defendant to appear. The defendant responding, pleadings are filed—the claims of plaintiff, and answer or demurrer of defendant. If these disagree as to facts, the court subpœnas witnesses. In the presence of judge and jury, the plaintiff states his case and the defendant his defense, witnesses are examined and cross-examined, and the case is argued. The judge then charges the jury—summarizing the evidence and indicating points to be decided; the jury retire to prepare their verdict, which is announced and recorded as the judgment of the court.

In criminal cases the accused may be arrested on a grand jury indictment or a magistrate's warrant. Unless the crime is murder, the accused may be released upon bail until trial, which proceeds as in civil cases.

## SUGGESTIVE QUESTIONS.

1. Why does the State prosecute offenses, instead of leaving this duty to private persons ?
2. What is meant by passing sentence upon an offender ?
3. Do you believe in the jury system, or in the trial by several judges sitting together ? Why ?
4. Have you ever seen a court in session ?
5. In this State a grand jury has how many members ?

# CHAPTER XVIII.

## SUFFRAGE AND ELECTIONS.

**Suffrage.**—The most important political right is the right of *suffrage;* that is, the right to vote. As the government exists for the benefit of the governed, the purpose of suffrage is to place it under their control. It gives each qualified voter a voice in public affairs, and places the country under the rule of the people.

As the interests of the voters and their families are the same, and as the voters represent these interests, the whole people, including women and children, have an influence in the government. The whole machinery of the State and of the United States is in the hands of those who do the voting.

**Importance.**—The importance of this right can scarcely be overestimated. It constitutes the difference between a free country and a despotism. There can be no freedom unless the right to vote resides in the people; nor can there be good government unless this right is exercised with an intelligent regard for the public welfare. Yet vast numbers of voters never realize the power they wield or the great responsibility it entails upon them.

**Elections.**—The right of suffrage is exercised by means of elections. An *election* is the direct method of ascertaining the will of the people upon public affairs. They are held for the purpose of giving

( 175 )

the people opportunity to express their choice in the selection of officers, and thus to make known their will upon questions of public concern.

**Methods of Voting.**—There are two methods of voting—by ballot and *viva voce*. A man votes by *ballot* by handing to the election officers a slip of paper containing the names of the candidates voted for, and the office to which each aspires. The officers of the election deposit the ballots in a box called the *ballot-box*. A man votes *viva voce* by announcing to the officers the name of the candidate of his choice, and having it recorded upon the polling-list.

The *viva voce* method was once considered the better ; but voting by ballot is rapidly growing in favor, and bids fair to become general throughout the United States.

The Australian system provides at each polling-place a private apartment, called a booth, where each voter in private prepares his ballot from a printed list of all the candidates, and then hands it to the officers, who deposit it in the ballot-box.*

**Officers of Elections.**—The officers of elections at each polling-place are usually two or more supervisors, inspectors, or judges ; a clerk ; and a sheriff, marshal, or other officer of the peace.

The *supervisors* or inspectors decide who are entitled to vote under the law, and when the election is by ballot they deposit the ballots in the ballot-box.

The *clerk* makes a list of the names of voters,

---

* For details regarding this system see Chapter XIX.

and when the election is *viva voce* he records the votes.

The *sheriff* or other peace officer preserves order at the polls, has charge of the ballot-box and polling-list after the election closes, and delivers them to the proper authorities.

In most States, at the close of the election the officers *canvass*, that is, examine the votes cast, and certify the number of votes received by each candidate.

In some States the ballot-box is sealed at the close of the election, and delivered to the canvassing board of the county. In such cases the canvassing board of the county canvasses the vote, and in State and national elections sends returns to the canvassing board of the State at the State capital.

In some States election officers are appointed by the county officers, usually by the county judge or probate judge; in other States they are elected by the people.

**Bribery.**—Bribery in elections is one of the serious evils of politics. *Bribery* is offering or receiving a reward for voting. In most States, in addition to other penalties, persons convicted of giving or taking bribes are *disfranchised;* that is, are not permitted to vote thereafter. In ancient Athens a man convicted of corrupting a voter suffered the penalty of death.

The selling of a vote is regarded as one of the most infamous crimes that men can commit. Not even the conviction of theft so lowers a man in public esteem as a conviction of selling his vote, for bribery savors of both theft and treason. To sell his suffrage is to sell his manhood, his country, and his convictions. Most men who sell their votes do it through ignorance; they are not aware of the enormity of the crime. He who knows its infamy, and yet barters his suffrage for money, is unworthy of the smallest trust, or even of the recognition of honest men.

### SUGGESTIVE QUESTIONS.

1. In what way are voters responsible for the government of the country?
2. Do you believe in frequent elections? Why?
3. Do you believe in public voting or in secret voting? Why?
4. Why should election officers be fair and honest men?
5. What do you think of vote-buying and vote-selling?

# CHAPTER XIX.

## THE AUSTRALIAN BALLOT SYSTEM.

**Origin.**—The idea of the secret ballot system, now known under its various modifications as the Australian Ballot System, was first proposed by Francis S. Dutton, member of the legislature of South Australia from 1851 to 1865. At that time the vices frequently accompanying open elections had begun to flourish in Australia. Bribery, intimidation, disorder, and violence were the order of all election days. The plan was elaborated, and became a law under the name of the " Elections Act " in 1857.

The beneficial results of this method soon became evident to other countries, and the movement spread to Europe, Canada, and the United States.

**In the United States.**—A similar system to that originally adopted in Australia was first introduced into the United States by its adoption by law in the State of Massachusetts in 1888. The next year the legislatures of Indiana, Montana, Rhode Island, Wisconsin, Tennessee, Minnesota, Missouri, Michigan, and Connecticut passed laws providing for new systems of voting, more or less resembling the Australian system; and now their example has been followed by almost all the other States. In Kentucky the system was adopted for the city of Louisville in 1888.

**Principles.**—Although there are many modifications of detail in the statutes of the various States, there are two essential features of the ballot-reform system which are everywhere observed :

*First*, An arrangement of polling, by which compulsory secrecy of voting is secured, and intimidation or corruption of voters is prevented.

*Second*, One or more official ballots, printed and distributed under authority, on which the names of all candidates are found.

**Requirements.**—The following are the requirements of the system : Ballots must be provided by public expense, and none but these ballots may be used. On these ballots should be printed the names of all candidates who have been nominated previously to the election, with the names of the offices for which they have been nominated and of the parties they represent.

There are two forms of ballots : the *blanket ballot* and the *individual ballot*. The former is arranged in some States so as to group candidates by parties, and in other States by the offices for which they are nominated. In many cases the names of candidates are alphabetically arranged, so that there can be no accusation of giving one party or candidate precedence as to position on the ticket. In a few cases, the name of the party to which the candidate belongs does not appear on the ballot at all, but only the name of the office for which he has been nominated : but in most cases the name of each party is printed either at the head of the ticket or opposite the name of each candidate, or in both places.

Where *individual ballots* are used, a separate ballot is printed for each party or independent ticket.

**Voting.**—Special sworn clerks are engaged to distribute these ballots to voters at the polls.

The voter is allowed a limited time—say five or ten minutes—to retire into an election booth erected for the purpose, to make his choice of candidates or ballots. If the blanket ballot is in use, he does this by placing a cross opposite the name of the desired candidate or list of candidates; or by crossing out all others; or by means of pasters for the substitu-

ARRANGEMENT OF POLLING PLACE AS REQUIRED BY MASSACHUSETTS LAW.

tion of names. If individual ballots are provided, he selects the one he prefers, or corrects it to his liking by pasting upon it a single name or an entire ticket. If he prefers, he may write the names of candidates of his own nomination in place of those already printed. He, then, without communicating with any one, deposits his ballot as his vote. Only one man is allowed to enter a booth at a time, and none but the ballot clerks and the man about to deposit his ballot are allowed within the enclosure erected for the purpose.

In most States the booths are separated one from the other merely by partitions, as indicated in the cut; but in a few States each booth is a separate compartment with a door, which is closed to prevent even a suspicion of any external observation.

In many States, assistance is rendered to the illiterate or the blind. In some cases, in order to aid those who can not read, each party adopts a device, as an eagle or a flag, which is printed on the ballot. In most States a voter who declares that he can not read, or that by some physical disability he is unable to mark his ballot, may receive the assistance of one or two of the election officers in marking it.

Every ballot must be strictly accounted for. If any person in preparing a ballot should spoil it, he may obtain others, one at a time, not exceeding three in all, provided he returns each spoiled one. All ballots thus returned are either immediately burned or else cancelled and preserved by the clerk.

**Advantages.**—The advantages which have already accrued from the adoption of these laws are manifold:

*First*, A secret ballot offers an effectual preventive against bribery, since no man will place his money corruptly without satisfying himself that the vote is placed according to agreement.

*Second*, It secures the voter against the coercion, solicitation, or intimidation of others, and enables him to vote according to the dictates of his conscience.

*Third*, Bargaining and trading at the polls is prevented, and with these much tumult, riot, and disorder must of necessity disappear.

*Fourth*, Money is made less of a factor in politics, and the poor man is placed on a plane of equality with the rich as a candidate.

In addition to these obvious advantages, the ballot reform movement promises to have much wider effects, and to pave the way and lay the foundation for other political reforms.

**Forms of Ballots.**—On pages 185, 186, and 187 are given forms of ballots and other matter illustrating various methods employed in carrying out the ballot laws of the States. It will be observed that each of these three ballots is representative of a different method.

*First*, In the *Louisville* ballot, no party name appears, and the ballots are numbered consecutively to prevent duplication or fraud of any kind. On this form of ballot, which most resembles that used in Australia, the individual candidate is made prominent, and party connection does not appear at all.

*Second*, In the *Massachusetts* ballot, the names of the candidates are grouped according to office, but in addition to this, the party name appears opposite the name of each candidate. On this form of ballot, while the party connection of each candidate is indicated, greater prominence is given to the individual, and the voter is required to make choice of a candidate for each office separately. He cannot vote a straight ticket by a single mark.

*Third*, In the *Indiana* ticket, the names are grouped

according to party, not according to office, the party name appearing at the head of the ballot as well as at the side of each name. On this form of ballot, the party connection of the candidate is made most prominent, and while provision is made for voting for individuals representing different parties, still the voting of a straight ticket is made most easy.

Some one of these three forms is almost universally used wherever the ballot reform has been adopted.

A *fourth* form, namely, that of the *individual ballot* as used in the State of *New Jersey*, can not be here shown, as a separate ballot is required for each party or each independent nomination. These separate ballots are all *official*, and are furnished at public expense; but the use of an *unofficial* ballot is practically allowed, since the voter is permitted to take to the voting booth a paster ballot containing a complete party ticket, printed and furnished at party expense. This he can paste over the official ballot and deposit as his vote.

(285)

# BALLOTS USED AT ELECTIONS IN LOUISVILLE, KY.

**X** Indicates how the voter casts his ballot.

## FORM USED IN VOTING FOR CITY OFFICERS.

*(Ticket Deposited in Box.)*

| | Consecutive Number. |
|---|---|
| | 32225 |

For Mayor,
- [ ] P. BOOKER REED.
- [X] HENRY S. TYLER.
- [ ]

For Councilman,
- [ ] GUSTAV HENRY, Sr.
- [ ] SAMUEL MANLY.
- [X] MARTIN NORTON.
- [ ] THOMAS J. SCANLON.
- [ ]

For School Trustees,
- [X] JOHN T. FUNK.
- [X] E. G. WIGGINTON.
- [ ]
- [ ]

## FORM USED IN RATIFYING ACTS OF THE LEGISLATURE.

Consecutive Number, 9322

For the taking effect of an act of the General Assembly of the Commonwealth of Kentucky, entitled "An Act to provide for the establishment of Public Parks in and adjacent to the City of Louisville, Kentucky, and the improvement and management of the same," approved May 6, 1890.

[X] YES.

[ ] NO.

---

*(Stub Left in Book.)*

**CONSECUTIVE NUMBER.**

32225

NAME OF VOTER.

REGISTERED RESIDENCE,

---

Consecutive Number, 9322

NAME OF VOTER,

REGISTERED RESIDENCE,

# PART OF MASSACHUSETTS OFFICIAL BALLOT, NOVEMBER, 1889.

## To Vote for a Person, mark a Cross [X] in the Square at the right of the name.

| GOVERNOR. . . . . . Vote for ONE. | |
|---|---|
| OLIVER AMES, of Easton, . . . . Republican, | |
| WILLIAM H. EARLE, of Worcester, . . Prohibition, | |
| WILLIAM E. RUSSELL, of Cambridge, . . Democratic, | |

| LIEUTENANT-GOVERNOR. . . Vote for ONE. | |
|---|---|
| JOHN BASCOM, of Williamstown, . . Prohibition, | |
| JOHN Q. A. BRACKETT, of Arlington, . Republican, | |
| JOHN W. CORCORAN, of Clinton, . . . Democratic, | |

| SECRETARY. . . . . . Vote for ONE. | |
|---|---|
| WILLIAM N. OSGOOD, of Boston, . . Democratic, | |
| HENRY B. PEIRCE, of Abington, . . Republican, | |
| HENRY C. SMITH, of Williamsburg, . . Prohibition, | |

| TREASURER. . . . . . Vote for ONE. | |
|---|---|
| JOHN M. FISHER, of Attleborough, . . Prohibition, | |
| GEORGE A. MARDEN, of Lowell, . . Republican, | |

| REPRESENTATIVES IN GENERAL COURT. Vote for TWO. First Middlesex District. | |
|---|---|
| WILLIAM H. MARBLE, of Cambridge, . Prohibition, | |
| ISAAC McLEAN, of Cambridge, . . . Democratic, | |
| GEORGE A. PERKINS, of Cambridge, . Democratic, | |
| JOHN READ, of Cambridge, . . . Republican, | |
| CHESTER F. SANGER, of Cambridge, . Republican, | |
| WILLIAM A. START, of Cambridge, . . Prohibition, | |

| SHERIFF. . . . . . Vote for ONE. | |
|---|---|
| HENRY G. CUSHING, of Lowell, . . Republican, | |
| HENRY G. HARKINS, of Lowell, . . Prohibition, | |
| WILLIAM H. SHERMAN, of Ayer, . . Democratic, | |

| COMMISSIONERS OF INSOLVENCY. Vote for THREE. | |
|---|---|
| JOHN W. ALLARD, of Framingham, . . Democratic, | |
| GEORGE J. BURNS, of Ayer, . . . Republican, | |

(186)

# PART OF INDIANA STATE TICKET. NOV., 1890.

| | **Democratic Ticket.** | | **Republican Ticket.** | | **Prohibition Ticket.** | | **People's Ticket.** |
|---|---|---|---|---|---|---|---|
| **DEM.** | For Secretary of State, CLAUDE MATTHEWS | **REP.** | For Secretary of State, MILTON TRUSLER | **PRO.** | For Secretary of State, BRAZILLAI M. BLOUNT | **PEOP.** | For Secretary of State, LEROY TEMPLETON |
| **Dem.** | For Auditor of State, JOHN O. HENDERSON | **Rep.** | For Auditor of State, IVAN N. WALKER | **Pro.** | For Auditor of State, ABRAHAM HUNTSINGER | **Peop.** | For Auditor of State, JAMES M. JOHNSON |
| **Dem.** | For Treasurer of State, ALBERT GALL | **Rep.** | For Treasurer of State, GEORGE W. PIXLEY | **Pro.** | For Treasurer of State, ELI J. ROBB | **Peop.** | For Treasurer of State, ISAIAH N. MILLER |
| **Dem.** | For Judge of the Supreme Court, 5th District, JOSEPH A. S. MITCHELL | **Rep.** | For Judge of the Supreme Court, 5th District, ROBERT W. McBRIDE | **Pro.** | For Judge of the Supreme Court, 5th District, JOHN W. BAXTER, | **Peop.** | For Judge of the Supreme Court, 5th District, JOHN S. BENDER |
| **Dem.** | For Attorney General, ALONZO G. SMITH | **Rep.** | For Attorney General, JOHN W. LOVETT | **Pro.** | For Attorney General, SUMNER W. HAYNES | **Peop.** | For Attorney General, WILLIAM PATTERSON |

NOTE.—Persons desiring to vote a straight ticket, need only cancel the abbreviation before the name of the party, with the stamp provided in the polling booth, but those who wish to vote for special names on various party tickets, must cancel the abbreviation before each such name.

### SUGGESTIVE QUESTIONS.

1. What is meant by the Australian ballot system ?
2. Name some places in the United States in which a similar system of reform has been adopted.
3. What are the essential principles of the system ?
4. What are the necessary requirements for carrying out the law ?
5. What is the object in providing official ballots ?
6. Describe two kinds of polling booths used.
7. What are the obvious advantages of the reform ?
8. Describe the characteristic forms of ballot used in various States which have adopted the reform.
9. Name one place in the United States where each form is used.
10. Compare the Louisville ballot with the Massachusetts ballot, and note their differences.
11. Compare the Louisville ballot with the Indiana ballot.
12. In what respects do the Massachusetts and Indiana ballots differ ?

### QUESTION FOR DEBATE.

Which system of voting is likely to secure the best public officers: that represented in the Louisville ballot, in the Massachusetts ballot, or in the Indiana ballot ?

# CHAPTER XX.

## PARTIES AND PARTY MACHINERY.

WHEREVER the right to vote exists, the people naturally form themselves into political parties.

A *political party* is an organization of voters maintained for the purpose of impressing its principles upon the public policy of the country. Men have divers views as to the duties, scope, and proper measures of the government, and these divers views lead to the formation of opposing parties. In a free country the majority must rule, and parties are the means by which majorities are ascertained.

**Origin.**—Parties usually grow out of questions of legislation, rather than out of questions of executive management or judicial interpretation. In other words, a party is formed to influence the passage of laws, rather than their execution or their application by the courts. But, when parties are once formed, they usually extend their influence to the selection of officers of all grades and all departments, even the least important officials of a township or civil district.

The presidential election has come to be the most exciting and bitter of all political contests, because of the large influence which the President exerts upon national legislation, and because of the immense patronage of his office.

**Necessity.**—Parties appear to be a necessity in all free governments. They serve as check upon one another, as the party in power is responsible for the public policy of the country. If the people are dissatisfied with the party in power, they can displace it and elect another in its stead. Parties are therefore placed upon their good behavior, and made to feel their responsibility to the people.

If there were no party organizations, many of the views of a candidate would not be known, and there could be no assurance that he would be true to the interests of the majority electing him. The fact that a public man is a member of a certain party shows many of the views which he entertains and the principles which he may be expected to support.

Party government is often bad, but as the party is responsible for the conduct of all officers elected by it, party government, especially in legislative affairs, is better than personal government, in which no one but the officer himself is responsible for his official conduct.

**Party Machinery.**—The machinery of parties in this country is very complex, and is closely interwoven with our system of government. Each party must select candidates for the various offices in the gift of the people, in order that it may exert its greatest power in elections and in public affairs. The people in each party must have a voice in the selection of candidates for township offices, district offices, county offices, State offices, and President and Vice President of the United States. Therefore each party has a system of committees, conventions, primary elections, and caucuses, for ascertaining the choice of its members for these various offices.

Parties and party machinery are not generally provided for in the law, but they exist by a custom almost as old as the government, and are firmly fixed in our political system.

**Committees.**—Each of the great parties has a *national committee*, consisting of one member from each State and Territory, chosen by its national convention. The national committee is the chief executive authority of the party. It calls the national convention, fixes the time and place for holding it, and the representation to which each State and Territory is entitled. It appoints a sub-committee of its members, called the *campaign* or *executive committee*, which conducts the political canvass or campaign, for the party.

The campaign committee distributes pamphlets, speeches, newspapers, and other political documents among the voters of the country; selects public speakers; makes appointments for them to speak; arranges for party meetings; collects funds to bear the expenses of the campaign, and has a general oversight of the party work in all the States.

Each party also has a State committee in each State, usually consisting of a member from each congressional district, in some States consisting of a member from each county; a district committee in each congressional, judicial, senatorial, and representative district, consisting of a member from each county composing the district; a county committee, consisting of a member from each township or civil district; and in some States, various other committees.

Each of these committees performs for the division for which it is selected duties similiar to those which the national committee performs for the whole Union.

**Conventions.**—The usual method of ascertaining the choice of a party in the selection of candidates, especially for the higher offices, is by a convention.

A *political convention* is an assemblage of the voters of a party, either in person or by representatives called delegates. If the voters assemble in person, the convention is called a primary or mass meeting.

The purpose of a convention may be to select candidates for office, to send delegates to a higher convention, to adopt a declaration of principles, or to decide upon a party policy. It is common for two or more of these purposes to come before the same convention.

**Calling Conventions.**—In the year of the presidential election, the national committee calls a national convention, naming the time and place, and the representation of each State. The State committee calls a State convention to send delegates to the national convention ; and, if a State election is approaching, it may direct that the convention shall also select candidates for State offices. In response to this call, the county committees order county conventions in all the counties of the State to send delegates to the State convention, and perhaps to select candidates for county offices. In some States the township committees order township conventions in all townships for the purpose of sending delegates to the county conventions, and perhaps to name candidates for township offices.

It will be seen that the calling of the various conventions connected directly or indirectly with the selection of candidates for President and Vice President proceeds from the highest downward. The same order is observed in other conventions, the call always beginning with the highest committee concerned and proceeding to the lowest.

**Local and State Conventions.**—The order of holding a system of conventions reverses the order of their call. It proceeds from the lowest to the highest. The township holds a convention and sends delegates to the county convention. The county convention sends delegates to the State convention, and the State convention sends delegates to the national convention.

In case a convention is called in a district composed of several counties, the delegates from the counties assemble at a point selected by the district executive committee.

**National Convention.**—A national convention is an important assemblage. It contains many distinguished men, and exerts a great influence upon the political history of the country. A national convention usually consists of more than eight hundred delegates, there being four delegates from each State, two from each congressional district in the Union, and two from each Territory.

In the selection of delegates to the national convention, the State convention as a body selects four, representing the two United States senators, and the members of the convention from each congressional district select two, representing the lower house of Congress. For each delegate the State convention also selects an *alternate delegate*, who attends the national convention in case the regular delegate can not be present.

The national convention is called to order by the chairman of the national committee. It then elects a temporary chairman, and afterward a permanent president. The convention appoints the national committee, calling upon the delegation from each State to name its member; adopts a declaration of principles, called a *platform*, for the approaching campaign; nominates candidates for President and Vice President, and performs various other work connected with the party organization.

**Platform.**—The declaration of party principles adopted and issued by a convention is called a *platform*, and each separate statement of a principle is popularly called a *plank*.

The platform is an announcement of the policy to be pursued by the party if its candidates are elected, and is presumed to contain all the important principles upon which the voters of the party are agreed. Upon these principles the party claims the right to administer the public affairs of the country.

The platforms of State and local conventions are usually based upon the national platform of the same party, but also contain statements of principles upon local questions.

**Nominations.**—To *nominate* a candidate is to name him for office; that is, to place his name before the public. The person nominated is called the *nominee*, and all the nominees for a certain election constitute a *ticket*.

A nomination usually secures to a candidate the general support of the party. Voters may vote for other persons than the nominees, but the great body of voters usually support the tickets of their respective parties. Nomination serves to prevent a great number of candidates, and thus simplifies the election.

**Primary Elections.**—Candidates for township, county, and district offices are frequently chosen by means of primary elections.

A *primary election* is an election in which the members of a party express their choice for candidates for office. None but the members of the party holding it can vote in a primary election. Many persons prefer the primary to a convention, believing the former to be a fairer and more impartial method of ascertaining the choice of the party. The voting is sometimes by ballot and sometimes *viva voce*.

In some States primary elections are under the control of the law, and are guarded by the same restrictions that pertain to other elections.

**Caucuses.**—A meeting composed of the members of a legislative body who are of the same party, and assembled for party purposes, is called a *caucus*. *Ward conventions* in cities are sometimes called by the same name.

The usual purpose of a caucus is to nominate candidates for offices within the gift of the legislative body, or to consider questions of legislation. A caucus elects a chairman and other officers, but rarely if ever adopts a platform of principles. The great political parties of the country have caucuses in each branch of Congress, and usually in the legislatures of the several States.

## SUGGESTIVE QUESTIONS.

1. Name the great parties that have existed in the United States.

2. Who are the respective chairmen of the national executive committees of the two great parties?

3. Read the last national platforms of the two great parties.

4. Which do you like better, primary elections or conventions? Why?

5. Should a member of a legislative body be influenced in his vote by the decision of the caucus of his party?

# CHAPTER XXI.

## LEGISLATION.

**Legislation,** the act or process of making laws, is the most important function of government. It is the most important, because it is the first step, and the enforcement and interpretation of laws depend upon their enactment. The laws of a country should be as few in number, as simple in construction, and as uniform in their application, as will meet the needs of the people. It is a great misfortune for the laws to bear unequally upon the people; to grant special privileges to one class, or to impose special hardships upon another class.

The great variety and volume of laws made by the national and the State legislatures of the United States have led to a close study of legislation. In no other country is the process of making laws so thoroughly mastered, or parliamentary law so generally understood.

**Bills.**—The process of enacting a law, from its introduction to its final approval, is an intricate and interesting study. Until its passage and final approval, a measure is called either a *bill* or a *resolution.*

Bills and resolutions are very similar, the latter usually being simpler, and beginning with the words, " Be it resolved " or simply " Resolved," while the former begin with the words, " Be it enacted." A joint resolution as well as a bill requires the concurrence of both houses of a legislative assembly to make it a law.

**Introduction.**—The introduction of a bill is the first presentation of it to a legislative body for action. This is usually done by asking " leave " of the body, either orally or in writing, to bring the measure before it. This leave to present is rarely if ever refused.

The rules require that after its introduction it shall be three times read aloud before its passage. These three readings do not refer to readings for information as to its provisions. The constitutions of nearly all States require that the three readings shall be on three different days ; but in most of them this rule may be suspended by a two thirds, three fourths, four fifths, or unanimous vote, the requisite majority varying in different States.

**Committees.**—When a bill or resolution is introduced, it is usual to refer it to a committee for a critical consideration. A *committee* usually consists of from three to thirteen members, of whom the first named is usually chairman, presumably selected for their knowledge of the subjects to come before them.

A *standing committee* lasts during the entire session. Most legislative bodies have from twenty to forty standing committees.

A *special* or *select committee* is raised for a special purpose, and is usually adjourned when its report is made.

A *committee of the whole* consists of all the members of a body sitting as a committee. In committees of the whole the regular presiding officer usually vacates the chair, calling some other member of the body to act as chairman. The principal part of the work of a legislative body is perfected by its committees. They discuss the merits and demerits of bills, and perfect such as, in their judgment, should pass.

**Reports.**—The committee to whom a bill has been referred critically examines it, and usually reports it to the body, either *favorably* or *unfavorably*, recommending that it should pass or should not pass. If the members of a committee are equally or nearly equally divided as to the merits of the bill, it may be reported without an expression of opinion.

When important bills are reported by a committee they are usually discussed by the members of the body. The debate on the measure usually brings out the reasons for, and those against, its passage. Many bills are several times recommitted—that is, again referred to a committee—before their passage.

In some legislative bodies, especially in the Congress of the United States, a great many bills are *pigeon-holed* by committees; that is, are filed away and never reported. The reports of the committees, whether favorable or unfavorable, are usually adopted by the body, and therefore have an important bearing upon legislation.

**Amendments.**—In most legislative bodies a bill may be amended at the pleasure of the majority, before it is read the third time. Amendments are made for the purpose of perfecting the measure. A bill may be amended by striking out some of its provisions, by striking out and inserting, or by inserting.

A bill passed by one house of a legislature may be amended by the other house, but, if amended, must be returned with the amendment to the house in which it originated, in order that the amendment may be considered. If one house amends and the other refuses to accept, the bill is often referred to a *conference committee* of members of both houses. If this does not secure agreement, and both adhere to their original action, the bill fails.

**Passage.**—When a bill passes the house in which it originated, the clerk transmits and reports it to the other house for action. The house to which it is transmitted may pass it without commitment, but usually refers it to a committee, and, when reported, may pass it or reject it, or amend it and return it with the amendment to the house in which it originated.

When passed by both houses, the bill is engrossed —that is, rewritten without blots or erasures—and transmitted to the President or governor, as the case may be, for his approval. If approved and signed, or if not returned within a fixed time, the bill becomes a law. If vetoed, it must be again considered by both bodies, and is lost unless again passed by each, and in Congress and in many States by a two thirds vote.

### SUGGESTIVE QUESTIONS.

1. Obtain from any convenient source and present in the recitation a sample of a bill, and also of a resolution.

2. Why should a bill have three separate readings on three different days ?

3. Why is the report of a committee generally adopted by the body ?

4. Why are chairmanships of committees usually much sought after in legislative bodies ?

5. Present in the recitation a copy of the report of a legislative committee upon some subject.

# CHAPTER XXII.

## REVENUE AND TAXATION.

**Revenue.**—The regulation of revenue and taxation is one of the most important and difficult questions of government. One of the wisest of modern statesmen has said that the management of finance *is* government.

Government, whatever its form, is an intricate and expensive machine, and therefore sure and ample sources of revenue are as necessary to it as blood is to the human body. The necessary expenses of a local community, such as a village, a city, or a county, are heavy; while those of a State are immense, and those of a nation almost beyond conception. These expenses must be promptly met, or the government becomes bankrupt, lacking in respect, without power to enforce its rights even among its own people, and finally ceases to exist.

**Taxation.**—The chief source of revenue in all governments is taxation. A *tax* is a portion of private property taken by the government for public purposes. *Taxation*, the act of laying taxes, is regarded as the highest function of government. It is also one of the most delicate, because it touches the people directly, and is therefore frequently the cause of discontent among the masses.

The government makes no direct return to the

citizen for the taxes it exacts, and in this respect only does taxation differ from the exercise of the right of eminent domain. How much revenue must be raised? what articles should be taxed? what should be the rate of taxation? are questions that concern every government.

As a person may be at the same time a citizen of a village, a township, a county, a State, and the United States, so he may, during the same year, pay a separate tax to each of these five governments.

**Necessity of Taxation.**—Taxation is one of the necessary burdens of society. A government as well as an individual must have money to pay its expenses, and the principal part, if not all, of this money must be raised by taxation of one kind or another. Men may differ as to the kind and the rate of taxation, but taxes must be paid in order that government may exist. The tax payer receives no immediate return for his taxes, but has a *constant* return in the way of protection to life, liberty, and property, the enjoyment of public conveniences, and the improvement of society.

By means of taxes each person bears his part in the cost of maintaining the social compact. He gives up a portion of his property in order that what remains may be the more secure and valuable, and that he may enjoy many other blessings that would otherwise be impossible. Although the rate is often high, even higher than necessary, it is safe to say that every tax payer of the country receives from the government more than he contributes by taxation

Taxes are direct or indirect.

**Direct Taxes.**—A *direct tax* is levied directly at a given rate upon property or polls. Taxes levied by villages, towns, townships, cities, counties, and States are for the most part direct taxes.

A *poll tax* is levied upon the polls, or heads, of the male inhabitants who have attained a certain age, usually twenty-one years.

A *property tax*, as the name indicates, is levied upon property. Property is of two kinds, real and personal.

*Real property*, usually called *real estate*, consists of lands and buildings.

*Personal property* is that which can be moved from place to place, and includes everything that a person can own except real estate.

In all systems of taxation, much real estate, such as churches, cemeteries, tombs, colleges, universities, charitable institutions, and public buildings of the State and the United States, is exempt from payment of taxes.

Five times in its history—namely, in 1798, 1813, 1815, 1816, and 1861—the United States levied a direct tax upon the people, but in each case the law was in force but a single year. From 1861 to 1871 there was also an *income tax ;* that is, a tax of a given per cent. upon all annual incomes that exceeded a certain amount.

**Indirect Taxes.**—An *indirect tax* is assessed upon the property of one person, but is indirectly paid by another. The owner of the property at the time of assessment pays the tax to the government, but a part or all of the tax is ultimately paid by the consumer of the goods. All taxes now levied by the national government are indirect.

The indirect taxes levied by the national government are *customs*, or *duties*, and *internal revenue*.

**Customs, or Duties.**—*Customs*, or *duties*, are taxes levied upon certain goods imported from foreign countries. The Constitution prohibits the taxation of exports.

The schedule or list of articles taxed and of duties to be paid is called the *tariff*. Custom dues are collected by officers of the national government at the custom-houses, located at the ports of entry, usually, but not always, on or near the sea-coast. By far the larger portion of the national revenue is derived from customs.

**Internal Revenue.**—*Internal revenue*, sometimes called *excise*, is a tax levied upon certain articles produced in this country, such as tobacco and spirituous liquors. It is collected by officers of the national government, called collectors, stationed in different parts of the country.

### SUGGESTIVE QUESTIONS.

1. Name some of the items of expense in village government.
2. In township government.
3. In city government.
4. In county government.
5. In State government.
6. In national government.
7. What is the rate of property taxation in this **country?**
8. What is the rate in this State?
9. Where is the nearest custom-house?

# CONSTITUTION OF THE UNITED STATES.

## PREAMBLE.

WE, the people of the United States, in order to form a more perfect union, establish justice, insure domestic tranquillity, provide for the common defense, promote the general welfare, and secure the blessings of liberty to ourselves and our posterity, do ordain and establish this Constitution for the United States of America.

## ARTICLE I. LEGISLATIVE DEPARTMENT.

### SECTION I. *Congress in General.*

All legislative powers herein granted shall be vested in a Congress of the United States, which shall consist of a Senate and House of Representatives.

### SECTION II. *House of Representatives.*

*Clause 1.* The House of Representatives shall be composed of members chosen every second year by the people of the several states ; and the electors in each state shall have the qualifications requisite for electors of the most numerous branch of the State Legislature.

*Clause 2.* No person shall be a representative who shall not have attained to the age of twenty-five years, and been seven years a citizen of the United States, and who shall not, when elected, be an inhabitant of that state in which he shall be chosen.

*Clause 3.* Representatives and direct taxes shall be apportioned among the several states which may be included within this Union, according to their respective numbers, which shall be determined by adding to the whole number of free persons, including those bound to service for a term of years, and excluding Indians not taxed, three-fifths of all other persons. The actual enumeration shall be made within three years after the first meeting of the Congress of the United States, and within every subsequent term of ten years, in such manner as they shall by law direct. The number of representatives shall not exceed one for every thirty thousand, but each state shall have at least one representative ; and until such enumeration shall be made, the state of New Hampshire shall be entitled to choose three, Massachusetts eight, Rhode Island and Providence Plantations one, Connecticut five, New York six, New Jersey four, Pennsylvania eight, Delaware one, Maryland six, Virginia ten, North Carolina five, South Carolina five, and Georgia three.

*Clause 4.* When vacancies happen in the representation from any state, the executive authority thereof shall issue writs of election to fill such vacancies.

( 205 )

*Clause* 5. The House of Representatives shall choose their speaker and other officers, and shall have the sole power of impeachment.

## Section III. *Senate.*

*Clause* 1. The Senate of the United States shall be composed of two senators from each state, chosen by the Legislature thereof for six years, and each senator shall have one vote.

*Clause* 2. Immediately after they shall be assembled in consequence of the first election, they shall be divided, as equally as may be, into three classes. The seats of the senators of the first class shall be vacated at the expiration of the second year, of the second class at the expiration of the fourth year, and of the third class at the expiration of the sixth year, so that one-third may be chosen every second year ; and if vacancies happen, by resignation or otherwise, during the recess of the Legislature of any state, the executive thereof may make temporary appointments until the next meeting of the Legislature, which shall then fill such vacancies.

*Clause* 3. No person shall be a senator who shall not have attained to the age of thirty years, and been nine years a citizen of the United States, and who shall not, when elected, be an inhabitant of that state for which he shall be chosen.

*Clause* 4. The Vice-president of the United States shall be President of the Senate, but shall have no vote, unless they be equally divided.

*Clause* 5. The Senate shall choose their other officers, and also a president pro tempore, in the absence of the Vice-president, or when he shall exercise the office of President of the United States.

*Clause* 6. The Senate shall have the sole power to try all impeachments. When sitting for that purpose, they shall be on oath or affirmation. When the President of the United States is tried, the chief justice shall preside ; and no person shall be convicted without the concurrence of two-thirds of the members present.

*Clause* 7. Judgment in cases of impeachment shall not extend further than to removal from office, and disqualification to hold and enjoy any office of honor, trust, or profit under the United States ; but the party convicted shall, nevertheless, be liable and subject to indictment, trial, judgment, and punishment according to law.

## Section IV. *Both Houses.*

*Clause* 1. The times, places, and manner of holding elections for senators and representatives shall be prescribed in each state by the Legislature thereof ; but the Congress may at any time, by law, make or alter such regulations, except as to the places of choosing senators.

*Clause* 2. The Congress shall assemble at least once in every year, and such meeting shall be on the first Monday in December, unless they shall by law appoint a different day.

## Section V. *The Houses separately.*

*Clause* 1. Each house shall be the judge of the elections, returns, and qualifications of its own members, and a majority of each shall constitute a quorum to do business ; but a smaller number may adjourn from day to day, and may be authorized to compel the attendance of absent members, in such manner and under such penalties as each house may provide.

*Clause 2.* Each house may determine the rules of its proceedings, punish its members for disorderly behavior, and, with the concurrence of two-thirds, expel a member.

*Clause 3.* Each house shall keep a journal of its proceedings, and from time to time publish the same, excepting such parts as may in their judgment require secrecy ; and the yeas and nays of the members of either house, on any question, shall, at the desire of one-fifth of those present, be entered on the journal.

*Clause 4.* Neither house during the session of Congress shall, without the consent of the other, adjourn for more than three days, nor to any other place than that in which the two houses shall be sitting.

## Section VI. *Disabilities of Members.*

*Clause 1.* The senators and representatives shall receive a compensation for their services, to be ascertained by law, and paid out of the treasury of the United States. They shall in all cases, except treason, felony, and breach of the peace, be privileged from arrest during their attendance at the session of their respective houses, and in going to and returning from the same ; and for any speech or debate in either house, they shall not be questioned in any other place.

*Clause 2.* No senator or representative shall, during the time for which he was elected, be appointed to any civil office under the authority of the United States, which shall have been created, or the emoluments whereof shall have been increased, during such time ; and no person holding any office under the United States shall be a member of either house during his continuance in office.

## Section VII. *Mode of passing Laws.*

*Clause 1.* All bills for raising revenue shall originate in the House of Representatives ; but the Senate may propose or concur with amendments, as on other bills.

*Clause 2.* Every bill which shall have passed the House of Representatives and the Senate shall, before it become a law, be presented to the President of the United States ; if he approve, he shall sign it ; but if not, he shall return it, with his objections, to that house in which it shall have originated, who shall enter the objections at large on their journal, and proceed to reconsider it. If, after such reconsideration two-thirds of that house shall agree to pass the bill, it shall be sent, together with the objections, to the other house, by which it shall likewise be reconsidered, and if approved by two-thirds of that house, it shall become a law. But in all such cases the votes of both houses shall be determined by yeas and nays, and the names of the persons voting for and against the bill shall be entered on the journal of each house respectively. If any bill shall not be returned by the President within ten days (Sundays excepted) after it shall have been presented to him, the same shall be a law in like manner as if he had signed it, unless the Congress by their adjournment prevent its return, in which case it shall not be a law.

*Clause* 3. Every order, resolution, or vote to which the concurrence of the Senate and House of Representatives may be necessary (except on a question of adjournment) shall be presented to the President of the United States ; and before the same shall take effect, shall be approved by him, or, being disapproved by him, shall be repassed by two-thirds of the Senate and House of Representatives, according to the rules and limitations prescribed in the case of a bill.

## SECTION VIII. *Powers granted to Congress.*

The Congress shall have power—

*Clause* 1. To lay and collect taxes, duties, imposts, and excises, to pay the debts and provide for the common defense and general welfare of the United States ; but all duties, imposts and excises shall be uniform throughout the United States ;

*Clause* 2. To borrow money on the credit of the United States ;

*Clause* 3. To regulate commerce with foreign nations, and among the several states, and with the Indian tribes ;

*Clause* 4. To establish a uniform rule of naturalization and uniform laws on the subject of bankruptcies, throughout the United States ;

*Clause* 5. To coin money, regulate the value thereof and of foreign coin, and fix the standard of weights and measures ;

*Clause* 6. To provide for the punishment of counterfeiting the securities and current coin of the United States ;

*Clause* 7. To establish post-offices and post-roads ;

*Clause* 8. To promote the progress of science and useful arts, by securing for limited times to authors and inventors the exclusive right to their respective writings and discoveries ;

*Clause* 9. To constitute tribunals inferior to the Supreme Court ;

*Clause* 10. To define and punish piracies and felonies committed on the high seas, and offenses against the law of nations ;

*Clause* 11. To declare war, grant letters of marque and reprisal, and make rules concerning captures on land and water ;

*Clause* 12. To raise and support armies ; but no appropriation of money to that use shall be for a longer term than two years ;

*Clause* 13. To provide and maintain a navy ;

*Clause* 14. To make rules for the government and regulation of the land and naval forces ;

*Clause* 15. To provide for calling forth the militia to execute the laws of the Union, suppress insurrections, and repel invasions ;

*Clause* 16. To provide for organizing, arming, and disciplining the militia, and for governing such part of them as may be employed in the service of the United States, reserving to the states respectively the appointment of the officers and the authority of training the militia according to the discipline prescribed by Congress ;

*Clause* 17. To exercise exclusive legislation, in all cases whatsoever, over such district (not exceeding ten miles square) as may, by cession of particular states and the acceptance of Congress, become the seat of the government of the United States, and to exercise like authority over all places purchased, by the consent of the Legislature of the State in which the same shall be, for the erection of forts, magazines, arsenals, dock-yards, and other needful buildings ; and

*Clause* 18. To make all laws which shall be necessary and proper for carrying into execution the foregoing powers, and all other powers vested by this Constitution in the government of the United States, or, in any department or officer thereof.

## SECTION IX. *Powers denied to the United States.*

*Clause* 1. The migration or importation of such persons as any of the states now existing shall think proper to admit, shall not be prohibited by the Congress prior to the year one thousand eight hundred and eight ; but a tax or duty may be imposed on such importation, not exceeding ten dollars for each person.

*Clause* 2. The privilege of the writ of *habeas corpus* shall not be suspended unless when, in cases of rebellion or invasion, the public safety may require it.

*Clause* 3. No bill of attainder, or ex-post-facto law, shall be passed.

*Clause* 4. No capitation or other direct tax shall be laid, unless in proportion to the census or enumeration herein before directed to be taken.

*Clause* 5. No tax or duty shall be laid on articles exported from any state.

*Clause* 6. No preference shall be given by any regulation of commerce or revenue to the ports of one state over those of another ; nor shall vessels bound to or from one state be obliged to enter, clear, or pay duties in another.

*Clause* 7. No money shall be drawn from the treasury but in consequence of appropriations made by law ; and a regular statement and account of the receipts and expenditures of all public money shall be published from time to time.

*Clause* 8. No title of nobility shall be granted by the United States ; and no person holding any office of profit or trust under them shall, without the consent of the Congress, accept of any present, emolument, office, or title of any kind whatever, from any king, prince, or foreign state.

## SECTION X. *Powers denied to the States.*

*Clause* 1. No state shall enter into any treaty, alliance, or confederation ; grant letters of marque and reprisal ; coin money ; emit bills of credit ; make any thing but gold and silver coin a tender in payment of debts ; pass any bill of attainder, ex-post-facto law, or law impairing the obligation of contracts ; or grant any title of nobility.

*Clause* 2. No state shall, without the consent of the Congress, lay any imposts or duties on imports or exports except what may be absolutely necessary for executing its inspection laws ; and the net produce of all duties and imposts laid by any state on imports or exports shall be for the use of the treasury of the United States ; and all such laws shall be subject to the revision and control of the Congress.

*Clause* 3. No state shall, without the consent of Congress, lay any duty of tonnage, keep troops or ships of war in time of peace, enter into any agreement or compact with another state or with a foreign power, or engage in war, unless actually invaded, or in such imminent danger as will not admit of delay.

## ARTICLE II. Executive Department.

### Section I. *President and Vice-president.*

*Clause* 1. The executive power shall be vested in a President of the United States of America. He shall hold his office during the term of four years, and, together with the Vice-president, chosen for the same term, be elected as follows :

*Clause* 2. Each state shall appoint, in such manner as the Legislature thereof may direct, a number of electors, equal to the whole number of senators and representatives to which the state may be entitled in the Congress ; but no senator or representative, or person holding an office of trust or profit under the United States, shall be appointed an elector.

[*Clause* 3. The electors shall meet in their respective states, and vote by ballot for two persons, of whom one at least shall not be an inhabitant of the same state with themselves. And they shall make a list of all the persons voted for, and of the number of votes for each ; which list they shall sign and certify, and transmit, sealed, to the seat of the government of the United States, directed to the President of the Senate. The President of the Senate shall, in the presence of the Senate and House of Representatives, open all the certificates, and the votes shall then be counted. The person having the greatest number of votes shall be the President, if such number be a majority of the whole number of electors appointed ; and if there be more than one who have such majority, and have an equal number of votes, then the House of Representatives shall immediately choose by ballot one of them for President ; and if no person have a majority, then, from the five highest on the list, the said House shall in like manner choose the President. But in choosing the President, the votes shall be taken by states, the representation from each state having one vote, a quorum for this purpose shall consist of a member or members from two-thirds of the states, and a majority of all the states shall be necessary to a choice. In every case, after the choice of the President, the person having the greatest number of votes of the electors shall be the Vice-president. But if there should remain two or more who have equal votes, the Senate shall choose from them by ballot the Vice-president.*]

*Clause* 4. The Congress may determine the time of choosing the electors, and the day on which they shall give their votes, which day shall be the same throughout the United States.

*Clause* 5. No person except a natural-born citizen, or a citizen of

---

* Altered by the 12th Amendment. See page 217.

the United States at the time of the adoption of this Constitution, shall be eligible to the office of President ; neither shall any person be eligible to that office who shall not have attained to the age of thirty-five years, and been fourteen years a resident within the United States.

*Clause* 6. In case of the removal of the President from office, or of his death, resignation, or inability to discharge the powers and duties of the said office, the same shall devolve on the Vice-president ; and the Congress may by law provide for the case of removal, death, resignation, or inability, both of the President and Vice-president, declaring what officer shall then act as President ; and such officer shall act accordingly, until the disability be removed, or a President shall be elected.

*Clause* 7. The President shall, at stated times, receive for his services a compensation, which shall neither be increased nor diminished during the period for which he shall have been elected, and he shall not receive within that period any other emolument from the United States, or any of them.

*Clause* 8. Before he enter on the execution of his office, he shall take the following oath or affirmation :

"I do solemnly swear (or affirm) that I will faithfully execute the office of President of the United States, and will, to the best of my ability, preserve, protect, and defend the Constitution of the United States."

### Section II. *Powers of the President.*

*Clause* 1. The President shall be commander-in-chief of the army and navy of the United States and of the militia of the several states, when called into the actual service of the United States ; he may require the opinion in writing of the principal officer in each of the executive departments, upon any subject relating to the duties of their respective offices ; and he shall have power to grant reprieves and pardons for offenses against the United States, except in cases of impeachment.

*Clause* 2. He shall have power, by and with the advice and consent of the Senate, to make treaties, provided two-thirds of the senators present concur ; and he shall nominate, and by and with the advice and consent of the Senate shall appoint ambassadors, other public ministers and consuls, judges of the Supreme Court, and all other officers of the United States, whose appointments are not herein otherwise provided for, and which shall be established by law ; but the Congress may by law vest the appointment of such inferior officers as they think proper in the President alone, in the courts of law, or in the heads of departments.

*Clause* 3. The President shall have power to fill up all vacancies that may happen during the recess of the Senate, by granting commissions, which shall expire at the end of their next session.

### Section III. *Duties of the President.*

He shall, from time to time, give to the Congress information of the state of the Union, and recommend to their consideration such measures as he shall judge necessary and expedient ; he may, on extraordinary occasions, convene both houses, or either of them ; and in case of disagreement between them, with respect to the time of adjournment, he may adjourn them to such time as he shall think proper ; he shall receive ambassadors and other public ministers ; he shall take care that the laws be faithfully executed, and shall commission all the officers of the United States.

### SECTION IV. *Impeachment of the President.*

The President, Vice-president, and all civil officers of the United States, shall be removed from office on impeachment for and conviction of treason, bribery, or other high crimes and misdemeanors.

## ARTICLE III. JUDICIAL DEPARTMENT.

### SECTION I. *United States Courts.*

The judicial power of the United States shall be vested in one Supreme Court, and in such inferior courts as the Congress may from time to time ordain and establish. The judges, both of the supreme and inferior courts, shall hold their offices during good behavior; and shall, at stated times, receive for their services a compensation, which shall not be diminished during their continuance in office.

### SECTION II. *Jurisdiction of the United States Courts.*

*Clause* 1. The judicial power shall extend to all cases in law and equity arising under this Constitution, the laws of the United States, and treaties made, or which shall be made, under their authority ; to all cases affecting ambassadors, other public ministers, and consuls ; to all cases of admiralty and maritime jurisdiction ; to controversies to which the United States shall be a party ; to controversies between two or more states ; between a state and citizens of another state ; between citizens of different states ; between citizens of the same state claiming lands under grants of different states ; and between a state, or the citizens thereof, and foreign states, citizens, or subjects.*

*Clause* 2. In all cases affecting ambassadors, other public ministers and consuls, and those in which a state shall be party, the Supreme Court shall have original jurisdiction. In all the other cases before mentioned, the Supreme Court shall have appellate jurisdiction, both as to law and fact, with such exceptions, and under such regulations as the Congress shall make.

*Clause* 3. The trial of all crimes, except in cases of impeachment, shall be by jury ; and such trial shall be held in the state where the said crimes shall have been committed ; but when not committed

---

* Altered by the 11th Amendment. See page 216.

within any state, the trial shall be at such place or places as the Congress may by law have directed.

## Section III.    *Treason.*

*Clause* 1. Treason against the United States shall consist only in levying war against them, or in adhering to their enemies, giving them aid and comfort.   No person shall be convicted of treason unless on the testimony of two witnesses to the same overt act, or on confession in open court.

*Clause* 2. The Congress shall have power to declare the punishment of treason ; but no attainder of treason shall work corruption of blood, or forfeiture, except during the life of the person attainted.

## ARTICLE IV.

### Section I.    *State Records.*

Full faith and credit shall be given in each state to the public acts, records, and judicial proceedings of every other state.   And the Congress may, by general laws, prescribe the manner in which such acts, records, and proceedings shall be proved, and the effect thereof.

### Section II.    *Privileges of Citizens, etc.*

*Clause* 1. The citizens of each state shall be entitled to all privileges and immunities of citizens in the several states.

*Clause* 2. A person charged in any state with treason, felony, or other crime, who shall flee from justice and be found in another state, shall, on demand of the executive authority of the state from which he fled, be delivered up, to be removed to the state having jurisdiction of the crime.

*Clause* 3. No person held to service or labor in one state, under the laws thereof, escaping into another, shall, in consequence of any law or regulation therein, be discharged from such service or labor, but shall be delivered up on claim of the party to whom such service or labor may be due.

### Section III.    *New States and Territories.*

*Clause* 1. New states may be admitted by the Congress into this Union, but no new state shall be formed or erected within the jurisdiction of any other state ; nor any state be formed by the junction of two or more states, or parts of states, without the consent of the Legislatures of the states concerned, as well as of the Congress.

*Clause* 2. The Congress shall have power to dispose of, and make all needful rules and regulations respecting the territory or other property belonging to the United States ; and nothing in this Constitution shall be so construed as to prejudice any claims of the United States or of any particular state.

### SECTION IV. *Guarantee to the States.*

The United States shall guarantee to every state in this Union a republican form of government, and shall protect each of them against invasion ; and, on application of the Legislature, or of the executive (when the Legislature can not be convened), against domestic violence.

### ARTICLE V. POWER OF AMENDMENT.

The Congress, whenever two-thirds of both houses shall deem it necessary, shall propose amendments to this Constitution, or, on the application of the Legislatures of two-thirds of the several states, shall call a convention for proposing amendments, which, in either case, shall be valid to all intents and purposes, as part of this Constitution, when ratified by the Legislatures of three-fourths of the several states, or by conventions in three-fourths thereof, as the one or the other mode of ratification may be proposed by the Congress ; provided, that no amendment which may be made prior to the year one thousand eight hundred and eight shall in any manner affect the first and fourth clauses in the ninth section of the first Article ; and that no state, without its consent, shall be deprived of its equal suffrage in the Senate.

### ARTICLE VI. PUBLIC DEBT, SUPREMACY OF THE CONSTITUTION, OATH OF OFFICE, RELIGIOUS TEST.

*Clause* 1. All debts contracted and engagements entered into before the adoption of this Constitution, shall be as valid against the United States under this Constitution as under the Confederation.

*Clause* 2. This Constitution, and the laws of the United States which shall be made in pursuance thereof, and all treaties made, or which shall be made, under the authority of the United States, shall be the supreme law of the land ; and the judges in every state shall be bound thereby, any thing in the Constitution or laws of any state to the contrary notwithstanding.

*Clause* 3. The senators and representatives before mentioned, and the members of the several state Legislatures, and all executive and judicial officers, both of the United States and of the several states, shall be bound by oath or affirmation to support this Constitution ; but no religious test shall ever be required as a qualification to any office or public trust under the United States.

### ARTICLE VII. RATIFICATION OF THE CONSTITUTION.

The ratification of the Conventions of nine states shall be sufficient for the establishment of this Constitution between the states so ratifying the same.

Done in Convention, by the unanimous consent of the states present, the seventeenth day of September, in the year of our Lord one thousand seven hundred and eighty-seven, and of the Independence of the

United States of America the twelfth. In witness whereof, we have hereunto subscribed our names.

GEORGE WASHINGTON, *President and Deputy from Virginia.*

*New Hampshire.*—John Langdon, Nicholas Gilman.

*Massachusetts.*—Nathaniel Gorham, Rufus King.

*Connecticut.*—W m. S a m u e l Johnson, Roger Sherman.

*New York.*—Alexander Hamilton.

*New Jersey.*—William Livingston, William Patterson, David Brearley, Jonathan Dayton.

*P e n n s y l v a n i a .*—Benjamin Franklin, Robert Morris, Thomas Fitzsimons, James Wilson, Thomas Mifflin, George Clymer, Jared Ingersoll, Gouverneur Morris.

*Delaware.*—George Read, John Dickinson, Jacob Broom, Gunning Bedford, Jr., Richard Bassett.

*Maryland.*—James M'Henry, Daniel Carroll, Daniel of St. Tho. Jenifer.

*Virginia.*—John Blair, James Madison, Jr.

*North C a r o l i n a .*—William Blount, Hugh Williamson, Richard Dobbs Spaight.

*S o u t h Carolina.* —John Rutledge, Charles Cotesworth Pinckney, Pierce Butler.

*Georgia.*—William Few, Abraham Baldwin.

*Attest,*                    WILLIAM JACKSON, *Secretary.*

---

# AMENDMENTS TO THE CONSTITUTION.

### ARTICLE I.   *Freedom of Religion, etc.*

Congress shall make no law respecting an establishment of religion, or prohibiting the free exercise thereof ; or abridging the freedom of speech, or of the press ; or the right of the people peaceably to assemble, and to petition the government for a redress of grievances.

### ARTICLE II.   *Right to bear Arms.*

A well-regulated militia being necessary to the security of a free state, the right of the people to keep and bear arms shall not be infringed.

### ARTICLE III.   *Quartering Soldiers on Citizens.*

No soldier shall, in time of peace, be quartered in any house without the consent of the owner ; nor in time of war, but in a manner to be prescribed by law.

### ARTICLE IV.   *Search Warrants.*

The right of the people to be secure in their persons, houses, papers, and effects, against unreasonable searches and seizures, shall not be violated : and no warrants shall issue but upon probable cause, supported by oath or affirmation, and particularly describing the place to be searched, and the persons or things to be seized.

## Article V. *Trial for Crime, etc.*

No person shall be held to answer for a capital or otherwise infamous crime, unless on a presentment or indictment of a grand jury, except in cases arising in the land or naval forces, or in the militia when in actual service in time of war or public danger; nor shall any person be subject for the same offense to be twice put in jeopardy of life or limb; nor shall be compelled, in any criminal case, to be a witness against himself ; nor be deprived of life, liberty, or property, without due process of law ; nor shall private property be taken for public use without just compensation.

## Article VI. *Rights of accused Persons.*

In all criminal prosecutions, the accused shall enjoy the right to a speedy and public trial, by an impartial jury of the state and district wherein the crime shall have been committed, which district shall have been previously ascertained by law, and to be informed of the nature and cause of the accusation ; to be confronted with the witnesses against him ; to have compulsory process for obtaining witnesses in his favor; and to have the assistance of counsel for his defense.

## Article VII. *Suits at Common Law.*

In suits at common law, where the value in controversy shall exceed twenty dollars, the right of trial by jury shall be preserved ; and no fact tried by a jury shall be otherwise re-examined in any court of the United States than according to the rules of the common law.

## Article VIII. *Excessive Bail.*

Excessive bail shall not be required, nor excessive fines imposed, nor cruel and unusual punishments inflicted.

## Article IX.

The enumeration in the Constitution of certain rights shall not be construed to deny or disparage others retained by the people.

## Article X.

The powers not delegated to the United States by the Constitution, nor prohibited by it to the states, are reserved to the states respectively or to the people.

## Article XI.

The judicial power of the United States shall not be construed to extend to any suit in law or equity commenced or prosecuted against one of the United States by citizens of another state, or by citizens or subjects of any foreign state.

### ARTICLE XII. *Mode of choosing the President and Vice-president.*

*Clause* 1. The electors shall meet in their respective states, and vote by ballot for President and Vice-president, one of whom, at least, shall not be an inhabitant of the same state with themselves ; they shall name in their ballots the person voted for as President, and in distinct ballots the person voted for as Vice-president ; and they shall make distinct lists of all persons voted for as President, and of all persons voted for as Vice-president, and of the number of votes for each, which list they shall sign and certify, and transmit, sealed, to the seat of the government of the United States, directed to the President of the Senate ; the President of the Senate shall, in the presence of the Senate and House of Representatives, open all the certificates, and the votes shall then be counted ; the person having the greatest number of votes for President shall be the President, if such number be a majority of the whole number of electors appointed ; and if no person have such majority, then from the persons having the highest numbers, not exceeding three, on the list of those voted for as President, the House of Representatives shall choose immediately by ballot the President. But in choosing the President, the votes shall be taken by states, the representation from each state having one vote ; a quorum for this purpose shall consist of a member or members from two-thirds of the states, and a majority of all the states shall be necessary to a choice. And if the House of Representatives shall not choose a President, whenever the right of choice shall devolve upon them, before the fourth day of March next following, then the Vice-president shall act as President, as in the case of the death or other constitutional disability of the President.

*Clause* 2. The person having the greatest number of votes as Vice-president shall be the Vice-president, if such number be a majority of the whole number of electors appointed, and if no person have a majority, then from the two highest numbers on the list the Senate shall choose the Vice-president ; a quorum for the purpose shall consist of two-thirds of the whole number of senators, and a majority of the whole number shall be necessary to a choice.

*Clause* 3. But no person constitutionally ineligible to the office of President shall be eligible to that of Vice-president of the United States.

### ARTICLE XIII.

SECTION 1. Neither slavery nor involuntary servitude, except as a punishment for crime whereof the party shall have been duly convicted, shall exist within the United States, or any place subject to their jurisdiction.

SECTION 2. Congress shall have power to enforce this article by appropriate legislation.

### ARTICLE XIV.

SECTION 1. All persons born or naturalized in the United States, and subject to the jurisdiction thereof, are citizens of the United

States and of the state wherein they reside. No state shall make or enforce any law which shall abridge the privileges or immunities of citizens of the United States ; nor shall any state deprive any person of life, liberty, or property, without due process of law, nor deny to any person within its jurisdiction the equal protection of the laws.

SECTION 2. Representatives shall be apportioned among the several states according to their respective numbers, counting the whole number of persons in each state, excluding Indians not taxed. But when the right to vote at any election for the choice of electors for President and Vice-president of the United States, representatives in Congress, the executive and judicial officers of a state, or the members of the Legislature thereof, is denied to any of the male inhabitants of such state, being twenty-one years of age, and citizens of the United States, or in any way abridged, except for participation in rebellion or other crime, the basis of representation therein shall be reduced in the proportion which the number of such male citizens shall bear to the whole number of male citizens twenty-one years of age in such state.

SECTION 3. No person shall be a senator or representative in Congress, or elector of President and Vice-president, or hold any office, civil or military, under the United States, or under any state, who, having previously taken an oath, as a member of Congress, or as an Officer of the United States, or as a member of any State Legislature, or as an executive or judicial officer of any state, to support the Constitution of the United States, shall have engaged in insurrection or rebellion against the same, or given aid or comfort to the enemies thereof. But Congress may, by a vote of two-thirds of each house, remove such disability.

SECTION 4. The validity of the public debt of the United States, authorized by law, including debts incurred for payment of pensions and bounties for services in suppressing insurrection or rebellion, shall not be questioned. But neither the United States nor any state shall assume or pay any debt or obligation incurred in aid of insurrection or rebellion against the United States, or any claim for the loss or emancipation of any slave ; but all such debts, obligations, and claims shall be held illegal and void.

SECTION 5. The Congress shall have power to enforce by appropriate legislation the provisions of this article.

## ARTICLE XV.

SECTION 1. The right of citizens of the United States to vote shall not be denied or abridged by the United States or by any state on account of race, color, or previous condition of servitude.

SECTION 2. The Congress shall have power to enforce this article by appropriate legislation.

# INDEX.

# SUPPLEMENT.

## THE STATE OF NEW YORK.

**The Constitution.**—New York, one of the thirteen original States, has had four constitutions. The first was adopted in 1777, ten years before the framing of the Federal Constitution. It served the people for forty-five years. The next one, adopted in 1822, lasted about twenty-four years. The third, adopted in 1846, despite several attempts to change it, was the supreme law of the State for nearly fifty years. The fourth, adopted in 1895, is over us to-day.

As constitutions come and go, it has not seemed best, in this brief sketch, to say anything about such features of preceding constitutions as have had their day and ceased to be. But it is well for the student to know the constitution as it now exists, for it is the law of his citizen-life, and "ignorance of the law excuses no man."

Despite the necessary brevity of the following analysis, it is hoped that every great principle has been touched upon, in so far as it is named in the present constitution of the State of New York.

NEW YORK SUPPLEMENT—PETERMAN'S CIVIL GOVERNMENT.
Copyright, 1896, by AMERICAN BOOK COMPANY.

**Public Schools.**—The article of the constitution on education opens as follows: *The legislature shall provide for the maintenance and support of a system of free common schools, wherein all the children of this State may be educated.*

Thus brief is the authority on which rests the great common-school system of the Empire State. But, brief as it is, how strong! The legislature *shall* provide; the schools shall be *free;* they shall be for the education of *all* the children of the State. Moreover, by a recent law, called the Compulsory Education Law, provision is made by which all children not only "*may* be educated" but *must* be. Such a law the State has a right to pass, on the ground that it is for the good and welfare of the Commonwealth that all its citizens should possess at least the rudiments of an education.

By the same right to protect itself, the State has declared in this constitution that no State money shall be given to any school or institution of learning, "wholly or in part under the control or direction of any religious denomination, or in which any denominational tenet or doctrine is taught." To the end, also, that a free common-school system may be properly maintained and supported, the constitution commands that the common-school fund be used sacredly and solely for common-school purposes. It recognizes the constitutional authority of the University of the State of New York, a corporation created in the year 1784, and now possessing and exercising, in respect to secondary education, much of the power which the State Department of

Public Instruction wields over elementary or primary instruction. It will thus be seen that the educational system of the State is dual, or double-headed.

**State Department of Public Instruction.**—(Pages 21-26.)—The main officers of this department are a *State superintendent* and a *deputy-superintendent*. Under their supervision and control are more than eleven thousand school districts. These districts are under the immediate care of over one hundred school commissioners, whose duty it is to look after and take care of the varied educational interests of their respective districts. Various normal schools throughout the State are for the training of common-school teachers ; and, still better to equip them for their work, the State superintendent appoints Teachers' Institutes, from time to time, and in various places, presided over by trained and experienced conductors, who are expected to outline and develop the fundamental subjects taught in common schools.

**University of the State of New York.**—This is the name given in the constitution to an institution which exists only on paper ; that is, an institution not owning or occupying any buildings or doing any teaching, but whose work is that of supervision and control, of incorporation of colleges, academies, union and high schools ; of the distribution of the literature fund, based upon the results of examinations prescribed by the *regents*.

The *regents* are the executive officers of the University ; their number may not be less than nine, and they are chosen for life, by the legislature. They are not paid officials, and the office is largely honorary, the real work being done by a secretary and a corps of trained helpers. The board of regents numbers nineteen, exclusive of four *ex-officio* members; viz., the *governor, lieutenant-governor, secretary of state,* and *superintendent of public instruction.*

**The Town.**—(Pages 37-47.)—Although the town in New York State has not the power which has been so freely and fully accorded it in New England, it would be a great mistake to regard it as of little importance in our Commonwealth, or as possessing but little power. Where the chief references to the town are found in the constitution, the words "county," "city," "village" are used several times in connection with the word "town," the same privileges being accorded to each of the four, and the same prohibitions placed upon each. The main reference to the town is to its inability, under the constitution, to contract any debt whatsoever, except for town purposes. But the financial power and responsibility of the town being thus defined and settled, it is left largely to its own internal management and government, subject, of course, to certain legal restrictions needful for every community.

The most important officers of a town are a *supervisor* (representing his town in meetings of the county board of supervisors) ; a *town clerk* (secretary and statistician he might be called) ; *justices of the peace ; overseers of the poor ; assessors,* who make calculations of property, on the basis of which taxes are levied ; and *highway commissioners,* to whom the inspection and repair of highways and bridges are entrusted. To this list must be added such minor officers as *collector of taxes, constables, pound-masters,* etc. Town officers are paid, some by fees and others by the day; the term of office is in most cases one year.

**The County.**—(Pages 48–55.)—The first allusion in the revised constitution to the county is in connection with the division of the State into senatorial districts. And there the references are so many and so complex, that it seems best simply to say here, that out of the sixty counties in the State, the constitution carves fifty senatorial districts. But the use of the county as the basis for such districting will show its importance, both in a geographical and in a political sense. The constitution again shows the great importance of the county by making it the basis of representation in the Assembly, which, from January 1, 1896, is to consist of one hundred and fifty members.

It is made imperative upon the county to use its money, raised by taxation, for none other than county purposes; and the county is forbidden to become indebted, even for county purposes, for more than ten per cent of the assessed valuation of the real estate within its limits.

But in the case of the county, as in that of the town, the great question of indebtedness being settled by the constitution, a large degree of home rule is allowed by the State to the county. This is as it should be; for each county is far more concerned for itself and its own interests than the State at large could possibly be. The legislature, however, through laws of its own enactment, keeps a restraining hand upon the list of offices to be filled by the county.    Several officers are referred to specifically :

(1) The *sheriff* is elected every three years (except in the counties of New York and Kings, where the term is two or four years, as the legislature may direct).   He is the executive officer of the county, and really is the governor's representative there ; he is entrusted with the keeping of the peace, the care and custody of criminals, the summoning of witnesses, the watching of juries, and the execution of the commands of the courts.

(2) The *county clerk* is an officer entrusted with most important duties—the filing and protection of valuable papers, the registration of deeds and mortgages, and the careful custody of documents relating to the real estate in the county.

(3) The *district attorney* has the legal affairs of the county in charge ; is the legal representative of the grand jury in the matter of its indictments ; and the State's representative when trials are brought in its name and by its authority.

The *sheriff, county clerk, district attorney,* and *registrar* (in counties having such an officer for duties purely legal) are officers specifically named in the constitution.   In addition, the law provides for a *county judge ;* a *surrogate,* in certain populous counties; a *treasurer ;* one or more *superintendents of the poor ; school commissioners ;* and a *board of supervisors,* made up of one supervisor from each town and one from each city ward.   It is thus seen that the county government is quite complex and complete.

**Villages.**—(Pages 56–58.)—The allusion to villages is very slight, but significant ; for it is provided that the legislature shall not incorporate any village by a private or local bill. In other words, there is to be one general law for the incorporation of all villages. This is a very wise provision ; for, without it, some villages would manage to secure greater rights and privileges than others, and thus great inequalities and much injustice would prevail.

Another excellent provision is that which does not allow a village to loan its money or credit to, or in aid of, any individual, association, or incorporation ; nor become the owner of stock in, or bonds of, any association or corporation ; nor incur any village debt, except for village purposes. Certain other restrictions of a like sort, on taxation, borrowing, running in debt, assessing, etc., are tersely and clearly defined.

Of course the election of proper village officers is a very necessary thing, and the constitution provides therefor by ordering that such officers as are not named by the constitution shall be elected by the voters of the village, or be appointed by the authorities thereof, as the legislature may determine.

As should be the case in a form of government comparatively so primitive and simple, the main officers of a village are few—a *president*, as the executive officer, and, associated with him, three to nine *trustees*.

**Cities.**—(Pages 59–62.)—It is generally conceded that the cities present the gravest political problems that the State is called upon to solve. In 1895 there were thirty-six cities within the boundaries of the Empire State, and more than half of the entire population of the State was resident in those cities. These masses of pent-up humanity must, of course, be governed ; but to what extent shall they be self-governed, and how far governed by the legislature ? The best wisdom of the constitution-makers was not adequate for the solving of that dual question. But let us look at what they did.

In that famous section of the constitution which places certain restrictions upon the debt-incurring power of county, town, and village, the city is put under very similiar restraint. No use of city money, except for city purposes ! Even then there is great elasticity in the words "for city purposes." And, again, the city is confined in its tax-levying power to a sum not exceeding ten per cent of the assessed valuation of its real property ; nor, in any one year, in the case of cities of over one hundred thousand inhabitants, may the tax exceed two per cent of the assessed valuation of the real and personal estate of such city.

The constitution declares that it is the duty of the legislature to organize cities, and to restrict their power to tax, assess, borrow, and loan their credit. And why restrict ? it may be asked. In the express language of the constitution : "So as to prevent abuses in assessments and in contracting debt by such municipal corporations."

The old-time way was to give an individual charter to each separate city, on the plea that no two cities would have the same needs or use just the same corporate powers. But the makers of the new constitution, wiser than their predecessors, have divided all the cities of the State into three classes. Cities having a population of two hundred and fifty thousand or more constitute the *first class;* those having fifty thousand, and less than two hundred and fifty thousand, the *second class;* all other cities, the *third class.*

To each of these classes is given a charter, and over them are placed certain general city laws designed for the governance of all the cities of a particular class or classes. And yet, inasmuch as circumstances may arise, or conditions appear which are extraordinary in character, the constitution has provided for the passage of what it calls " special city laws," relating to a single city, or to less than all the cities, of a class. As the matter of the final disposition of such laws is somewhat curious, it may here be briefly noted :

As soon as a special law has been passed, relating to a city, a certified copy must at once be sent to the mayor of that city, who must return the bill within fifteen days, marked "Accepted by the city," or without such notice of acceptance. In the former case, the bill goes to the governor for his action ; in the latter case, the legislature may again pass the bill, endorsing it with the words, " Passed without the acceptance of the city," and send it to the governor. In cities of the first class, the mayor decides independently upon acceptance or non-acceptance; but in all other cities, the mayor must act concurrently with the legislative body of his city. [Students of civil government may be interested to study this special-city-law arrangement.]

The tenure, or time, of holding offices is so adjusted that in cities of the first and second class the time shall expire in an odd-numbered year; and the time of State officers, in an even-numbered year. Thus the municipal and the State elections will occur on different years. [Why was this plan agreed upon?]

It only remains, in this brief glance at the law and government of cities, to name the chief officers of the city, leaving it for those who are interested in the matter to study the general and special laws of the various municipalities of our many-citied State.

The city government has three divisions as well as the State and federal government. At the head of the executive board is the *mayor*, an officer by no means holding so responsible a position as the President of the United States, yet one more nearly touching the daily life of the urban citizen. The *board of aldermen*, or *common council*, is the legislative part of the city's political machinery. Its members are elected from the city wards, usually for two years. To it is entrusted, largely, the care of the city's financial interests and its valuable franchises. The judicial power is vested in certain *municipal courts*, varying somewhat in number and kind, in various cities.

To these must be added the officers of the board of health, the board of education, the police force, fire and excise commissioners, a city attorney, tax-collector, treasurer, assessors, a superintendent of police and of schools, and an ever-growing list as our cities multiply in number and in population.

**The State.**—(Pages 64–97.)—Now we reach, in this brief survey, that great political entity called the State. Let us, then, briefly examine the constitution —the palladium of our home liberty—in so far as it has to do with purely State matters, rather than with the lesser subdivisions of the State (like school district, village, town, county, city) already considered. And suppose we test the constitution upon some points mentioned in our text (page 71) as essential features of such a document.

1. PREAMBLE.—Here it is, brief, but all-comprehending: "We, the people of the State of New York, grateful to Almighty God for our freedom, in order to secure its blessings, do establish this constitution."

2. BILL OF RIGHTS.—(Pages 72 and 73.)—The very first article gives it : Without due legal process and impartial trial, no member of the State may be disfranchised, or deprived of any rights or privileges ; the right of trial by jury shall remain, in its essence, forever inviolate ; perfect religious liberty shall be accorded to every man, but may not be used to cloak licentiousness, or justify practices menacing the life or health of the body politic ; the writ of *habeas corpus* must not be suspended in peaceful times ; there shall be no excessive bail nor fines, no cruel and unusual punishments, no undue detention in duress of innocent witnesses in law cases ; no citizen may be officially charged with heinous crime,

save upon proper presentment of a grand jury, with due opportunity given him for defense; once freed, he cannot be jeopardized again for the same offense; he need not testify against himself; his life, liberty, property, are sacred by law; he is to be duly recompensed for any of his property taken by the State for public uses; he may freely speak, write, publish, taking care not to abuse the right; he may peaceably petition the State government, or any department thereof, for redress of grievances.

3. SUFFRAGE.—Here the constitution is very specific, as it must needs be. The right to vote belongs to every male citizen who is at least twenty-one years of age, has been a United States citizen for ninety days, an inhabitant of the State one year preceding an election, for the last four months a resident of the county, and for the last thirty days a resident of the election district in which he may offer his vote.

The proper election officers are commanded to reject the vote of any citizen who, if challenged, fails to swear or affirm that he has not received or paid, and does not expect to receive or pay, any money or valuable thing for " the giving or withholding of a vote " at the election, and it is made mandatory upon the legislature to enact laws excluding from voting any and all persons convicted of bribery or infamous crime.

But the voting law has yet another hold upon the citizen. If he lives in a city or village having five thousand or more inhabitants, he must register, in person, at least ten days before each election. Again, the constitution calls for that great safeguard, a secret ballot—a constitutional requirement now made practical and real by the enactment of an efficient ballot law, which proved its general efficiency and utility in the autumn elections of 1895.

The constitution requires those who register voters, or distribute ballots to voters, or who receive, record, or count votes at elections, to be chosen in equal numbers from the two political parties which respectively cast the highest and next highest number of votes at the election next preceding the one at which such officers are to serve. [What is the advantage of this provision?]

4. STATE DEBTS.—It may well be believed that the question of the financial affairs of a great State is a matter of prime importance. For there is a very real sense in which a Commonwealth is a great business corporation. The constitution, therefore, contains the declaration that the State's credit shall not be loaned for any individual or corporate purpose. Yet wisely it provides for any unlooked-for deficit, and for any special expense incurred by invasion, insurrection, or war. Moreover, a debt for some special work or object (say, for instance, the building of a capitol) may be incurred, provided that the proposition has first received the assent of a majority of the voting population of the State, and has also the sanction of the legislature. The sinking funds of the State must be separately kept and securely invested.

It is understood that a claim against the State may "outlaw," as the term goes, in the same way and in the same time limit as the claim of citizen *vs.* citizen. Thanks to the new constitution, certain lands called "the forest preserve" are forever to remain the property of the State; and the same is true of the Erie, Oswego, Champlain, Cayuga, Seneca, and Black River canals. Finally, as respects the canals, no tolls are to be imposed, and superintendence and repairs are to be at the expense of the State.

Moreover, the people at the fall election of 1895 authorized the expenditure of $9,000,000 for improvement of the canals, thus giving practical and speedy effect to that part of the constitution which says: "The canals may be improved in such manner as the legislature shall provide by law. A debt may be authorized for that purpose," etc., etc.

5. TAXATION.—Not much is said in a direct way in the constitution about taxes. The right of the State to tax is taken for granted. There is ample reason for this, and the necessity for it is very apparent. Practically, the State is free from debt, but it would not remain so for a day without the power to levy and collect taxes. And so the limit of taxation, the manner of it, the rate (a very important matter), the proportion of the total tax falling upon real estate and the proportion upon personal property —all these matters of detail and administration are to be found in the laws passed in pursuance of the right and need of the State to tax.

6. CORPORATIONS.—The constitutional definition of corporations is noteworthy. The word, or term, includes "all associations and joint-stock companies

having any of the powers or privileges of corporations not possessed by individuals or partnerships." They may sue or be sued. They are formed under general laws—very rarely under special act.

Under this same term, "corporations," come *savings banks* and institutions for savings. They possess a general charter, alike for all. Their trustees are simply holders in trust of the money deposited, and may not share in the profits, nor be financially interested in the loans of any money, or use of any property, of the bank of which they are trustees. The stockholders of any corporation for banking purposes shall be individually responsible to the amount of their respective share or shares of stock in such corporation, for all its debts and liabilities. Thus strongly hedged about by restrictions and safeguards are the banks that hold the savings or act as the financial agents of the people.

7. THE MILITIA.—The constitution does not stop to argue the need of a State militia, but it may be well for those who are studying into the philosophy of things to do so. It will prove a very interesting question. For the purpose of this brief analysis, however, it must suffice to say, that the possible militia force of the State is just equal to the number of able-bodied citizens between the ages of eighteen and forty-five; the real number must not be less than ten thousand men, divided into land, naval, active, and reserved forces, uniformed, armed, equipped, disciplined, ready for active service. At their head is the *governor* as the *commander in chief.* To him belongs the appointment of the chief officers; for

the residue, the legislature orders the choosing or appointing; and any officer may be removed for cause. The efficiency of the New York State militia has been proven many times and in crucial ways.

**The Legislature.**—(Pages 77–82.)—The portion of the constitution relating to the legislature is of extreme importance, for it tells the whole story of the organization and powers of the law-making branch of the State government. We find that the legislature is made up of two bodies, the Senate and the Assembly, divided, and yet one.

The *Senate* consists of fifty members, and the *Assembly* (or "lower branch" as it is sometimes called), of one hundred and fifty members. The fifty senatorial districts are carefully mapped out. An enumeration of the inhabitants of the State must be made every tenth year, and the distribution and quota of senators is to be according to population. The one hundred and fifty assembly districts are named specifically.

Among the most important of the provisions affecting the legislature are the following: The pay of each member of the legislature is $1,500 per annum, and an allowance of 10 cents a mile for one round trip, to and from home, each session; no senator or assemblyman may hold any other civil office in State or nation; no person is eligible to the legislature who for one hundred days previous to his election has held any military or civil office in State, nation, or municipality; and if after election he accepts any national office, that fact vacates his legislative seat. The senatorial and assembly elections are to be held on the Tuesday succeeding the first Monday of November—each year for assemblymen; every two years for senators. A quorum is a majority. Each house has its own rules, is its own judge as to the election, returns, and legal qualifications of its own members; chooses its own officers; keeps its own journal of proceedings, ordinarily published; its doors are generally thrown open to the public; neither house may adjourn for more than two days without consent of the other house. [Why?] Nobody may call senators and assemblymen to account for words uttered in debate. [Why?] Any bill may originate or be amended in either house. And here is an important provision—the enacting clause of all bills shall be: *The People of the State of New York, represented in Senate and Assembly, do enact as follows.* [Let the student study the language carefully; it is very suggestive.]

The legislature is enjoined by the constitution, in more than a dozen specific and comprehensive cases, from passing private or local bills, and, in all other cases where a general law will answer, must proceed under the general law. Again, the legislature itself cannot audit or allow any private claim against the State, but may appropriate money if the claim is established by legal proof; no public moneys or property can be applied by the legislature without concurrence of two thirds of its members, and no money can be expended, except *by law;* a yea and nay vote is necessary in all appropriations of public money.

The constitution creates boards of supervisors

and common councils (or aldermanic boards), giving power to the legislature to confer such local powers of administration and legislation upon them as it sees fit, and forbidding them to grant extra compensation to public servants.

Among the new items of the last constitution is the power conferred upon the Senate to choose a temporary president to act in case of the absence, impeachment, or refusal to act of the lieutenant-governor, or when he is acting as governor. Another new safeguard of wise legislation is the provision that no bill shall become a law (except when urgency is certified to by the governor) unless it has been in printed form on members' desks for three legislative days, at least, before final passage ; and on such final passage no amendment shall be allowed.

The most far-reaching and suggestive new constitutional legislation is that which forbids, after January, 1897, all "contract work" in the prison-houses of the State, leaving to the legislature the power to compel convicts to work for the State, and according permission to the State to purchase the work of its own prisoners. Students of penology will watch this experiment with great interest.

A bill becomes a law when it has been passed in both houses, and has received the assent of the governor ; or if he vetoes it, the bill must be repassed by a two-thirds vote in each house before it can become a law. Few bills survive the two-thirds ordeal.

Just here it may be well to add a few words concerning the making of bills into laws.

(1) If the governor fails to return a bill within ten

days, it becomes a law, by expiration of the time limit; but should the legislature adjourn before the ten days expire, it does not become a law without the governor's approval.

(2) The governor has thirty days after adjournment of the legislature in which to sign or veto. This gives him time to think calmly and decide coolly.

(3) The governor may approve some items in an appropriation bill; and disapprove others.

**The Executive Power.** — (Pages 84–91.) — The power to execute, or enforce the laws is entrusted to a *governor* (term, two years; salary, $10,000). Associated with him is a *lieutenant-governor* (term, two years; salary, $5,000). To be eligible to either office, a person must be not less than thirty years of age, and for five years, at least, a resident of New York State. If the governor, for any reason, such as impeachment, removal from office, death, or inability, becomes unable to discharge his duties, such duties thereupon devolve upon the lieutenant-governor; and after him in succession on the president of the Senate and the speaker of the Assembly.

Some of the *duties* of the governor are: To act as commander in chief of the military and naval forces of the State; to convene the legislature in special session; to send an annual message to the legislature, recommending certain things; to transact all necessary public business; and, especially, to see that the laws are faithfully executed.

Some of the *powers* conferred upon the governor

are : To grant "reprieves," "commutations," "pardons," except for treason and in cases of impeachment, in which the legislature has final authority; and each case of reprieve, commutation, or pardon must be reported to the legislature, although the latter cannot change the governor's action with respect to such cases. While the governor acts for the interests of the State at large, the lieutenant-governor presides over the deliberations of the Senate (though not a member of that body); and the speaker of the Assembly, who is a member of the Assembly, has a like duty to perform in that body.

The following officers are *also chosen by the people* for a term of two years each :

(1) The *secretary of state* (salary, $5,000) is the custodian of the valuable papers of the State, transcribing and attesting the correctness of the laws of the State.

(2) The *comptroller* (salary, $6,000) looks after the financial interests of the State, collects its taxes of all kinds, negotiates loans, and in general seeks to strengthen the credit and lessen the debts of the State.

(3) The *treasurer* (salary, $5,000) pays out money upon the warrant of the comptroller.

(4) The *attorney-general* (salary, $5,000) is the State's legal officer, and, as such, brings suit in the name of the people of the State of New York, or defends the State legally in case of need. To him other State officers look for legal opinions on controverted matters in their respective departments.

(5) The *State engineer and surveyor* (salary, $5,000) must be a " practical civil engineer," and, as the title of his office would imply, must care for the public waterways and highways of the State.

To the foregoing list of officers, chosen by the people, should be added the following, appointed by the governor, and specifically named in the constitution : a *superintendent of public works* (salary, $6,000), who really succeeds to the duties of the former canal commissioners and board of canal commissioners— that is, he has charge of all matters relating to the canals, except such as by law are given over to the State engineer and surveyor; and he has at his disposal much of what is called " political patronage."

A *superintendent of the State prisons* (salary, $6,000) takes the place of the former inspectors of State prisons. Like the commissioner of public works, he is appointed by and with the advice and consent of the Senate; but the term of office of the latter expires with that of the governor appointing him—the former holds the prison keys for five years. It goes almost without saying that the chief duty of this officer is the care of prisons and prisoners.

There are certain other officers, as *commissioners of the land office, commissioners of the canal fund,* and the *canal board,* who are neither chosen by the people nor appointed by the governor. These fill offices assigned by the constitution to various State officers. The land commissioners are the *lieutenant-governor, speaker of the Assembly, secretary of state, comptroller, treasurer, attorney-general, State engineer and surveyor.* And the first five constitute the commissioners of the canal fund, while the canal board consists of the canal fund commissioners, the State engineer and surveyor, and the *superintendent of public works.*

In addition to the executive offices thus far enumerated, there are very many others not mentioned in the constitution which are created by the statute law. And each of the many officers is supposed to stand in his appointed place, and do his part in executing the mandates of the State.

The Judicial Department.—(Pages 92–94.)—Upon no part of the new constitution was there expended so much thought and care as upon the judicial department, or the courts. The result is an entirely new article of twenty-three sections—too elaborate and technical to be discussed here. Even the judges are puzzled at some of the minor provisions and possible workings of the new judicial scheme. Let us confine ourselves, therefore, to a few main points and salient features.

By the abolition, after 1895, of certain courts— with the names of which we need not cumber our memory—and the retention of the judges (eighteen in number) of these abolished courts; by adding the forty-six justices of the old supreme court, and twelve new ones, making seventy-six in all, we get the *personnel* of the reorganized *supreme court.* A good tenure of office is theirs—fourteen years—and a salary of $6,000 per annum. This court has "general jurisdiction in law and equity." By the new constitution, also, there is formed an appellate division of the supreme court, having the jurisdiction formerly exercised by the "general terms" of the supreme court, and by the recently abolished courts.

The *court of appeals* is, we are glad to say, continued; for it has always been an honorable court. It consists of a chief judge and six associate judges (salary, $10,500 and $10,000, respectively). The tenure of office is fourteen years, and no judge of this court may hold a place upon the bench after he is seventy years of age. "The jurisdiction of the court of appeals, except where the judgment is of death, shall be limited to the review of questions of law."

Both as to the court of appeals judges and the justices of the supreme court, it is commanded that they shall hold no other office or public trust; furthermore, they may be removed by concurrent resolution of the legislature, two thirds of each house concurring.

The *county courts* are continued. This is well, alike for convenience and for disposal of many cases too important for the lowest courts, and yet often not of sufficient importance to warrant trial in the highest courts; yet to them appeal may be made. There is one judge for each county court (except Kings County, which has two); the length of term is six years, and a salary is established by law, and paid out of the county treasury. The old "court of sessions" went out of existence on the last day of December, 1895, and its pending actions and proceedings were transferred to the county court.

*Surrogate courts* are continued.   In small counties the county judge and surrogate are one person ;
in larger counties, different persons.   In all counties,
except that of New York, the surrogate's term is
six years ; in New York it is fourteen.   The salary is
determined by law.   The jurisdiction is much the
same as in county courts.

The voters elect justices of the peace for four
years, whose number, classification, and salary are
determined by law.   The *justices' court* has jurisdiction in cases of comparatively small importance,
in money value not exceeding two hundred dollars.
But any litigant not satisfied with the verdict of this
court may appeal to the county court.

Justices of the peace are the only judicial officers
who may receive " fees or perquisites of office "
(these in lieu of a fixed and sufficient salary) ; and
no judge of the appeals, supreme, county, or surrogate court may practice as attorney or counselor, or
act as referee in any court of record in this State.
[What is a court of record ?]

Finally, the chief courts of the State, leaving
out inferior and special courts, are four : appeals,
supreme, county, justices'.   By means of these four,
chiefly, the enormous legal business of the citizens
of the State is transacted.

The judges of the court of appeals have permanent
chambers at Albany, and the county, surrogate, and
justices' courts are permanent ; but the supreme
court judges hold court in various important places
throughout the State, so reaching every part of its
great domain.

**Supplementary.**—In our rapid survey of the most salient features of the constitution, a few points, well worthy of mention, have been omitted. Let us very briefly gather them together:

*Divorce* cannot be granted save by proper judicial proceedings. Any *lottery*, "or the sale of lottery tickets, pool-selling, bookmaking, or any other kind of gambling, shall not be authorized or allowed within this State." There shall be no limitation, hereafter, upon the amount recoverable for injuries resulting in death. For the purpose of *voting*, no person gains or loses a residence while in United States service, nor while engaged as a sailor, nor while a student in any seminary, nor while in an almshouse, or any institution kept by public or private charity, nor while a State's prison inmate.

The State treasurer, for suspected malfeasance in office, may be suspended, during the recess of legislature, by the governor. The power of *impeachment* is lodged with the Assembly. The impeachment court is composed of the president of the Senate, the senators, and the court of appeals judges.

The members of the court of impeachment are under oath, conviction requires concurrence of two thirds of the members present, and punishment is by simple removal from office, or added disqualification to hold any office of honor, trust, or profit under the State.

The legislature shall make due provision for the *education* and *support* of the blind, the deaf, the dumb, and of juvenile delinquents; "shall not prevent any county, city, town, village, from providing for the care, support, maintenance, and secular education of inmates of orphan asylums, homes for dependent children, or correctional institutions, whether under public or private control;" but payment for such services, if to private institutions, may only be authorized, not compelled, by the legislature, and the rules and regulations of such private institutions shall be such as are established by the State board of charities. Such a *State board of charities* the legislature shall provide for, and it shall be the duty of such board to look after and report upon charitable institutions, incorporated or not.

A *State commission in lunacy* is to inspect all institutions, either public or private, for the care and treatment of the insane ; and a *State commission of prisons* is to report upon such institutions as are " used for the detention of sane adults charged with or convicted of crime, or detained as witnesses or debtors."

Finally, we note the *civil service* regulations, a most important law, compelling appointments to, and promotions in, all of the civil divisions of the State to be by competitive examinations, " so far as practicable ; " provided, also, and furthermore, that honorably discharged soldiers and sailors of the civil war, citizens and residents of the State, shall have preference.

The *oath of office* is very stringent, yet most fair, requiring adhesion to the United States and the New York State constitutions; a promise to discharge faithfully all public duties; and utter denial of influencing, by any valuable consideration, the vote of any elector.

The attempt to *bribe* any officer of the State, or the reception of any such bribe by any officer, involves both the briber and the bribed in condemnation; if the bribe is rejected, only the tempter is responsible.

In regard to *passes* there is great and much-needed stringency. No public officer, either for his own use or benefit, or that of another, may ask or receive any "free pass, free transportation, franking privilege, or discrimination in passenger, telegraph, or telephone rates, from any person or corporation." If he does so, he shall give up his office at the demand of the attorney-general. And any corporation, through any officer or agent thereof, who shall offer such free pass, etc., shall be deemed guilty of a misdemeanor. The governor may remove a district attorney who fails to prosecute a person charged with the violation, in his county, of any provision of this plain-speaking thirteenth article. It is noteworthy that the cost of prosecution by the county is borne wholly by the State.

The "*political year and legislative term*" begin on the first day of January, the legislature assembling on the first Wednesday in January.

The constitution may be *amended* by a majority vote of two successive legislatures, followed by adoption by the people; and *revision* of the constitution may be made every twenty years, if such revision be in accordance with the expressed wish of the people.

## ORIGIN AND DEVELOPMENT OF GOVERNMENT.

**The Town.**—The foregoing part of this supplement is devoted to a brief but careful analysis of the constitution of the Empire State. By far the greater part of that document is sound and strong; the rest is worthy of a fair trial. And yet, the best constitution ever devised by the wisdom of men will avail but little for good government, unless sustained by loyal and law-abiding citizens.

A constitution cannot execute nor enforce itself; orderly government is necessary for the protection and peacefulness of mankind. Put, now, these two facts together, and it is not strange that little knots of families, early in history, came together into *clans;* not strange that these clans settled in little communities for mutual protection and defense. Each strip of land so inhabited was called a *mark;* and when encompassed by a wall, as a barrier against robbers and wild beasts, it was called a *tun*, our English *town*. No doubt the origin of the town goes back of English life; but the idea of the town as a kind of democracy agreed so well with the political genius of the Anglo-Saxon race, that it is in England we find the earliest and best development of the town idea. To that idea Englishmen clung; that idea they brought with them across the seas, in the beginning of the seventeenth century, to America.

That the idea assumed more nearly its native shape and power in New England than in Virginia is due to the differing types of Englishmen composing, respectively, the Jamestown and the Plymouth companies. The colony of New York came nearer to the New England ideal than did Virginia, and it had many town offices similar to those in the East. Still the Dutch colonists of New York were filled with the spirit of trade, and it takes something more than that to found an ideal town life; and the case was no better when the colony came under English domination.

And yet, wherever the town system of government came into use, even imperfectly, it gave voice to that cardinal doctrine of democracy, the principle of representation—a principle which a true American does not argue about, but feels; and as the town is a political unit, so the voice of the towns is a united one for representative government.

**The County.**—Not only is the town a political unit, it is also an integral part of another civil division, the *county*. As out of the clan came the town, so forth from the tribe came the shire—our county. In England the passing of the years has witnessed the development and the decay of a strictly county system of government; but this system was early transplanted to America, and took deep root here, flourishing at first, perhaps, because of its convenience, but now because of the great political power to which it has attained. And in no State of the Union is that power greater than in New York. Its wide scope is perhaps best seen in the county board of supervisors, made up of one supervisor from each town, and one from each city ward within the county borders. Its legislation is local, and yet supreme in many home concerns.    Well has it been styled "The County Legislature."

**The City.**—We have spoken of town and county, but what of the place of the *city* in our American life?   Historically it is true that the city, especially the English city, is the outcome of the borough, or perhaps it is truer to say it is kindred to the borough. Now a borough or a city—call it by whichever name you will—as related to English life simply meant the coming together in a natural way of a comparatively large number of people thus compacted into a comparatively small space.

But even though we grant that the American city had its genesis in the old city or borough of England, we must be very careful not to push the historic parallel too far.   For the essential character and life of a transatlantic and a cisatlantic city greatly differ.   Many offices of each are the same or similar. But in the cities of England there is greater watchfulness, responsibility, efficiency, and honor among municipal officers than in the cities of the United States.

**The State.** —Along the winding paths of the Dutch colonial settlement, dating from 1624, over the hard road of English colonial life, stretching from 1664 on for more than a century, New York marched, in 1776, through the gateway of independence to *Statehood*.   Remember the dates—from 1624 (about) to 1664 she was a Dutch colony; from 1664 to 1776, an English colony; since 1776, a State.

For nearly a century, also, this State, by common consent, has been accorded the *primacy* among the forty-five now comprising the Union. This is true of her population, and of her vast and varied commercial and manufacturing interests. *Educationally*, too, the State takes high rank. From a half-dozen funds, the public-school money aggregates $5,000,000 a year, and local taxation for common-school purposes amounts to three times that sum. By recent enactment the State has taken under its sheltering wing the helpless and insane, at a great, and as yet unknown, cost.

The State does not own the railroads within its limits, as it does the canals, yet upon the former it expends several thousand dollars annually, for inspection, to compel railroad corporations to a due respect for the rights and safety of the traveling public; nor does the State begrudge large amounts for needed internal improvements, for the maintenance of an effective militia force, and for such other police-like organizations as may be needed to keep the peace in the great Commonwealth of New York.

But the great public interests just mentioned, together with many others, call for a vast expenditure of money. This the State can get only by *taxation*, for it has no money of its own. The ordinary taxes levied upon the citizen are for town, county, and State purposes. Thus he becomes in a three-fold sense a citizen, responsible for the support of all three divisions of the body politic. The way in which taxes are assessed is somewhat like this: The town assessors make out a list of the value of all real and personal property subject to taxation (certain

forms of property, as schools, churches, public buildings, etc., being exempt). This list is submitted to
the citizens taxed, who may ask for a reduction, if
unfairly assessed. The list is then sent to the proper
State and county officers, whose duty it is to "ap-
portion," as the term is, the quota of each town,
based upon the valuation list, towards the expenses
of county and State.

Before the list becomes operative in a town, an
estimate of the expenses of the town for the current year must be made, and upon that estimate
the town tax is based. And so to town, county,
and State treasurers, respectively, the taxes of the
citizen finally are paid, in a grand total of $60,000,000
a year.

And yet the beneficent institutions and great
wealth of the State would soon perish were it not
for the *laws* which are over the citizen to preserve
the public welfare.

If A owes money to B, the latter can compel payment through the courts. That is called a "civil
case." If A attacks B with intent to do bodily
harm, a "criminal case" may grow out of that.
Now to state all the proceedings of the law in civil
and criminal cases would be a long task. It must
suffice to say this: The person suing is called the
*plaintiff;* the person sued, the *defendant.* By authority of the court, the plaintiff issues a summons
to the defendant, calling him into court. On both
sides witnesses are summoned; the trial comes on;
witnesses are examined and cross-examined; lawyers
plead; the case is decided by the court, or goes to a

jury for decision; and whatever that decision, either side may appeal to a higher court, if higher court there be.

**A Written Constitution.**—Thus have we given a few illustrations of the power wielded by the State for the good of its citizens. And when one thinks that this power is lodged in the written constitution of the State, one gets a better conception of the usefulness of such a document.

Moreover, it adds greatly to our regard to know and to remember that such documents—our various State constitutions—are the creation of American political genius and life. Grant that the germ of the constitution idea is in the charters of England, or in those given by her to our colonial ancestors, yet it is true that, even to this day, England has no written constitution, and that we have not a State in all our galaxy without one. " Let her be ruled by precedent;" we cry, " What says the law?" For the constitution of the State is its supreme law.

Yet it must not be forgotten that there is a law over the citizen higher than that of the State constitution. It is that of the Federal Constitution, to which every citizen in the land owes his first allegiance. And the general relation of the State to the Federal government cannot be summed up better than by the following quotation:

" This [Federal] Constitution . . . shall be the supreme law of the land; . . . anything in the constitution or laws of any State to the contrary notwithstanding."

### THE LAWS TOUCHING THE MORE IMPORTANT RELATIONS OF INDIVIDUALS.

**The Rights of Individuals.**—The rights to liberty, security, and private property, guaranteed by the State constitution (page 72), are secured by statute laws made by the legislature and by common law (page 170).

**Laws as to Persons.**—*Personal protection* is secured by laws which permit the individual to defend himself with all necessary force when assaulted, or, when he has reasonable ground to fear personal violence from any person, to cause that person to be placed under bond to keep the peace. There are also laws by which heavy damages may be collected for slander, that is, making or repeating false and injurious statements about another; and for libel, that is, the publishing by printing or writing of such false and injurious statements.

*Marriage.*—In this State it is illegal for a female under sixteen, or a male under eighteen years of age, to marry. Very near relations, as parent and child, brother and sister, or half-brother and sister, may not marry each other. A marriage contracted through force, deceit, or fraud may be annulled. It is a crime to have two or more wives or husbands at the same time, and all these marriages after the first are void. The ceremony of marriage is essentially a solemn declaration of the man and the woman that they take each other for husband and wife, and shall be solemnized by a clergyman or a magistrate, and in the presence of at least one witness. The husband is obliged to support his wife, and is liable for debts that she may contract for the necessities of life, but for no others. The wife may own property and make contracts independent of her husband, and at his death she has a life interest or estate, called her dower right, to one third of his real estate. The widow's dower right extends not only to the real estate the husband owns at his death, but to all that he has owned since his marriage, except such as the wife has expressly relinquished this interest in. Hence, in conveying real estate, the wife, as well as the husband, must sign the deed, and thus convey her dower right in the property. Divorce, or annulment of marriage, may be granted by the courts for certain causes, which differ somewhat in the different States.

*Parents and Children.*—The law gives to the parent the custody of his children and the right to their labor or wages until they are of age (twenty-one years old), but it requires him to support and educate them. In case a child has property of his own, the court appoints a guardian to take care of it until the child is of age; and if the child's parents are dead, the guardian takes their place toward the child, who is called his ward.

*Master and Servant.*—Occasionally a child is bound by a written agreement to serve a master for a period of years as an apprentice in consideration of being taught a trade. In such cases the master exercises in general the powers of a parent over the apprentice. In nearly all other cases, however, the servant is simply an employé of the master or employer, and the relations between them are those of principal and agent.

**Laws as to Property.**—*Title of Real Estate.*—Land is immovable and imperishable, and (together with its appurtenances, such as the buildings upon it, etc.,) it is therefore called real property, or real estate, or realty, in distinction to which all other kinds of property are classed as personal property, or personalty. A person's title to real estate may be absolute or qualified ownership. If absolute, he is said to own it in *fee simple.* It is absolutely his to do with as he pleases during his life, and to dispose of as he pleases at his death. Qualified ownership may be: (1) A *life estate*, in which case the tenant may use the property, or the rents from it, during his life, but may not sell nor mortgage it. A widow's dower is a life estate, and life estates are often created by a will. (2) An *estate for a term of years*, usually created by a writing called a lease, during the continuance of which the rights of the tenant in the property are much the same as if he were a life tenant. (3) A *trust*, in which the trustee holds and manages the property for the benefit of another.

*Transfer of Real Estate.*—When real estate is sold, the transfer is witnessed by a written contract called a deed, in which is set down the name of the purchaser, the consideration, a description of the property, and the interest conveyed. The deed is signed by the person selling, and by his wife, if he has one, and these signatures are witnessed and acknowledged before the proper officer. The deed usually contains also the maker's agreement to warrant and defend his title to the property conveyed. The document is then sealed, and delivered to the purchaser or his representative. The deed should then be sent by the purchaser to the proper officer for entry in the public records (page 53), that all persons interested may learn of the transfer.

*Mortgages.*—A mortgage has the form of a deed, and like it should be recorded. It is given to secure the repayment of a loan, and upon such repayment the mortgage becomes void. If the loan is not repaid, the mortgage may be foreclosed and the property may be sold to satisfy the debt.

*Leases.*—A lease is a contract, usually written, whereby the owner of real estate conveys to another the right to possess and use the property for a term of years, usually in consideration of a specified rental. During the continuance of the lease, the tenant is practically the owner of the property, and, unless the contrary is specified in the lease, he may assign his interest, or sublet a portion of the property, and is obliged to make ordinary repairs, as he must deliver the property back to the landlord at the expiration of the lease in as good condition as he received it, ordinary wear and tear excepted. The tenant is not obliged, however, to make extraordinary repairs, nor to rebuild houses destroyed by accidental causes. If the tenant fails to pay the rent, or otherwise violates the terms of the lease, he may be evicted or dispossessed before the expiration of the lease, by due process and by the officers of the law.

*Appurtenances.*—Appurtenances are the buildings, vegetation, springs, minerals, etc., on real estate and rights connected with it, which are considered part of it and are conveyed with it, although not specifically mentioned in the deed. Among possible appurtenances may be mentioned the right of way or passage over, or the right to lay pipes through or to get water from, or the right of pasturage upon, adjoining property belonging to another. Such rights are acquired either by direct grant from the owner of the adjoining property, or by twenty years undisputed use. A very common appurtenance in cities is a party wall built on adjoining lots. Both owners can use the wall as part of their houses, but neither can remove the part of the wall which stands on his lot ; it is an appurtenance of the adjoining property.

*Promissory Notes.*—A promissory note is a written promise to pay a specified sum on demand, or at a specified time, to bearer, or to the order of a person specified in the note. The person who signs the note is the maker ; the person to whose order the note is payable is the payee. Such notes are negotiable until their maturity (date of payment). The payee transfers the note by indorsing his name on the back of it, either with or without specification of the person to whose order it is to be paid. The person so specified may transfer the note by indorsing it himself, and so the note may be transferred indefinitely. If no person is specified by the indorser, the note becomes payable to bearer.

Upon maturity of a note the law holds the maker responsible for its payment, and the indorsers as well, provided the holder of the note immediately sends to them formal notification or protest against its non-payment by the maker. Unless the words "with interest" are specified, notes draw interest from the time they are due; demand notes, from the time payment is demanded. In some States three days of grace are allowed for the payment of the note after the date of payment named in it. Days of grace have been abolished, however, in New York and in several other States.

*Interest.*—The maximum rate of interest that can be charged for the use of money is fixed by law in nearly all of the States. In New York it is 6 per cent, but it varies in the different States. Heavy penalties are provided for *usury*, or the attempt to exact excessive interest.

*Wills.*—One may dispose of his property at death by means of a will, which must be in writing, and must, in general, be signed by the person making it, and by two witnesses in one another's presence. A will may be made at any time before death, and more than one may be made, in which case the latest supersedes the earlier wills. A codicil is an addition or appendix to a will, and is prepared with the same formalities as the will. After the death of the maker the will is entered for probate at the proper local court. This court empowers the executors to carry out the provisions of the will. If one dies intestate— that is, without leaving a will—the court distributes his real estate according to law among his children or relations, and appoints an administrator to distribute his personal property.

*Gifts and Bequests.*—Gifts of part or the whole of his property may be made by any person at any time, unless it can be shown that the object of the donor in parting with his property was to defraud his creditors. Gifts cannot be revoked after delivery is made, unless the gift is made when the donor believes himself at the point of death. In this case, if the donor should not die, he may revoke the gift.

*Contracts.*—A contract is an agreement between two or more people to do or not to do something. Some contracts must be in writing, as deeds, mortgages, and in general those which are to be executed at some future time, and those involving large sums of money; other contracts may be oral, while others may be simply implied. Thus, if the butcher supplies you with meat upon your order, the law construes your order as an implied contract to pay for the meat. All contracts to be valid must have a consideration; that is, something of value given or promised as a reason for the agreement.

The general object of all laws on the subject is to enforce the execution of valid contracts. Contracts are not valid if made by force or fraud; if one of the parties is a child, or not in sound mind; or if the subject of agreement is either a crime, or naturally impossible of execution. In case a valid contract is not carried out, the aggrieved party may obtain redress through the courts, which either force the other party to carry out his contract, or make him pay damages to the party aggrieved. A suit of this kind, however, must be brought within a reasonable time after the breaking of the contract. This time varies with the nature of the contract, and in different States.

A contract to sell personal property should be in writing if the amount is large, but this is not necessary if there is a delivery of part of the goods, or a payment of part of the price. If the time of delivery and payment is not specified in the contract, the seller has a lien on the goods, and need not deliver them until payment is made. He loses this lien, however, upon delivery of the goods. Lost or stolen property may be recovered by their true owner, although they may have been sold by the finder or the thief in the meantime.

*Common Carriers.*—Common carriers, such as railroads, steamboats, express companies, etc., are obliged to transport for all alike who tender the regular fee or charge, provided the vehicle is not already full, and the article to be transported is not of a character likely to injure the other contents of the vehicle. Common carriers are in general responsible for goods which they transport, and they have a lien upon them for freight charges until delivery, and they need not deliver them until the charges have been paid.

*Insurance Contracts.*—Such contracts, called policies, are in general void, unless the property belongs to the parties insuring and has been truly represented to the insurers.

*Principal and Agent.*—One employed to act for another is called an agent, and the one for whom he acts is his principal. In general the principal is bound by, and is responsible for, the act of his agent, if the latter is acting within his authority. If, however, the agent exceeds his authority, or if he does not tell who his principal is, or if he pretends to be himself the principal, he, and not his principal, is responsible.

*Partnerships.*—Partnerships are contracts between two or more people to carry on business and divide its profits and losses. In general the act of one partner in connection with his business binds the whole firm, and each partner is individually liable for the debts of the firm. If a partner withdraws from a firm, public notice must be given, in order to relieve the mutual responsibility for each other's acts of the withdrawn partner and the remainder of the firm.

*Limited* partnerships, in which the liability of one or more of the partners is limited to a certain amount, are permitted in New York and several of the States, provided the facts are fully stated in the partnership contract, and are recorded in the public records and duly advertised in the newspapers.

*Joint Stock Companies* and *Mutual Aid Associations.* —These are corporations formed and authorized, under the law, to transact business, under the company name, as a single person.

Members of such corporations are held responsible for debts only to the extent of their shares in the property of the company, except in the case of banks, where the stockholders are liable to the extent of twice their shares.

**Crimes.**—These are either *felonies* or *misdemeanors.* The graver crimes are felonies, and are punishable either by death or imprisonment in the State prison. Treason against the State, or murder in the first degree, that is, killing with malice and premeditation, are punishable with death. Murder in the second degree—killing without premeditation, or in a duel—is punishable with imprisonment for life. Other cases of unjustifiable homicide are manslaughter, and with all other felonies are punishable by imprisonment for varying terms, according to the gravity of the offense. Arson is the willful setting fire to buildings, railroad cars, vessels, or other vehicles. Bigamy, burglary, dueling, embezzlement or misapplication of funds, extortion or blackmail, forgery, grand larceny, or the theft of a sum of money over a certain amount, kidnapping, poisoning, receiving stolen property, rioting, robbery, are among the many crimes classified by the State laws as felonies. Misdemeanors being lesser crimes, are punishable by fines or shorter imprisonments, and the imprisonment is not in the State prison, but in the county jails, or in workhouses, or in houses of correction.

**International Relations.**—These do not ordinarily touch the individual. Travelers in general are subject to both the protection and the penalties of the laws of the country in which they are traveling. Ambassadors and ministers plenipotentiary, representing their own in a foreign country, are subject to and are under the protection of the laws of their own country only. Consuls residing in foreign countries, however, are subject to the laws of that country. Extradition treaties have been made between most civilized countries whereby they surrender fugitives accused of grave crimes for trial in their own country.

*Neutrals.*—A neutral nation may not, as a nation, aid either belligerent, and neither belligerent can use

the territory of the neutral nation for hostile purposes. The citizens of a neutral nation, however,
may continue their trade with either belligerent, and,
according to international law, neither belligerent
has a right to confiscate goods belonging to the
neutral citizen, even if captured by one belligerent
when in transit to the other, unless such goods be
arms or ammunition, or other commodities which
would directly contribute to the prosecution of the
war. If, however, one belligerent is able to blockade the ports of the other, the goods of neutrals
sent into that port may be captured and appropriated.

the territory of the neutral nation for hostile purposes. The citizens of a neutral nation, however, may continue their trade with either belligerent, and according to international law, neither belligerent has a right to molest such goods belonging to the neutral citizen, even if captured by one belligerent when in transit to the other, unless such goods be arms of ammunition, or other commodities which would directly contribute to the prosecution of the war. If, however, one belligerent is able to blockade the ports of the other, the goods of neutrals sent into that port may be captured and appropriated.

S0-BYP-624

WITHDRAWN
L. R. COLLEGE LIBRARY

CARL A. RUDISILL LIBRARY
LENOIR-RHYNE COLLEGE

# THE RISE AND FALL OF THE
# LUFTWAFFE

# THE RISE AND FALL
## OF THE

# 𝔏𝔲𝔣𝔱𝔴𝔞𝔣𝔣𝔢

### THE LIFE OF
### FIELD MARSHAL ERHARD MILCH

# DAVID IRVING

## LITTLE, BROWN AND COMPANY
### BOSTON – TORONTO

CARL A. RUDISILL LIBRARY
LENOIR-RHYNE COLLEGE

D
785
.I82
1973
Sept.1998

COPYRIGHT © 1973 BY DAVID IRVING

ALL RIGHTS RESERVED. NO PART OF THIS BOOK MAY BE REPRODUCED
IN ANY FORM OR BY ANY ELECTRONIC OR MECHANICAL MEANS IN-
CLUDING INFORMATION STORAGE AND RETRIEVAL SYSTEMS WITH-
OUT PERMISSION IN WRITING FROM THE PUBLISHER, EXCEPT BY A
REVIEWER WHO MAY QUOTE BRIEF PASSAGES IN A REVIEW.

*Published simultaneously in Canada*
*by Little, Brown & Company (Canada) Limited*

PRINTED IN THE UNITED STATES OF AMERICA

# CONTENTS

PART V      THE YEAR OF THE CLENCHED TEETH

PART VI     'CRASHED IN FLAMES'

tion'. Göring attempts to sort out the aircraft programme
his way. Führer demands the Me 262 *only* as jet bomber.
Göring 'discovers' the defence of the Reich. Milch is
shelved and aircraft production is taken over by Saur.
The fiasco of the first night of the flying-bomb (V 1)
offensive. Milch stands down as State Secretary and Director of Air Armament. The Heinkel 177 is cancelled.
Milch fades out of the war picture. Plans for manned
flying-bombs. Touring the western battlefields, Milch is
invalided in a severe car crash. Speer tells him of his plans
to return to power after the war.

PART VII    JUDGEMENT AT NUREMBERG

# ILLUSTRATIONS

# INTRODUCTION

Of the score or more field marshals created by Hitler three, and one grand-admiral, are still alive. Most of the others were killed in action, committed suicide, or were hanged by Hitler or their captors. To have written a biography of Milch, least famous of the survivors, requires some explanation. When I visited them, most of his contemporaries were surprised to learn that he was still alive. In the last years of his life he closeted himself behind an anonymous front door in suburban Düsseldorf, looked after by a niece, writing reports for a foreign aviation company of international repute. I was intrigued by the man when I first met him five years ago. Erhard Milch, Hermann Göring's deputy —his benefactor in time of poverty, his adversary in time of influence, his defender in time of trial—proved to be the repository of a thousand anecdotes of the war and its slow prelude.

He was the senior of the surviving field marshals, and the highest-ranking of the surviving Luftwaffe officers. The Luftwaffe was a force which he, more than any other German, created. But more than that: the dapper, florid businessman sitting upright in the stiff armchair next to me, preparing to narrate the three score years and ten of his life so far, had already created for himself a niche in history, quite outside the world of politics, by the time Adolf Hitler first entered the Reich Chancery in 1933. It was Milch whose administrative cunning and personal dynamism fashioned the German Lufthansa airline from its beginnings in local companies into an international concern, while at the same time secretly providing and nourishing the industrial roots from which a future Luftwaffe would spring.

This much is known. And yet the real story starts even earlier. During the First World War, Milch is to be seen with his hand camera, photographing Allied trenches from a German biplane; and if the wheel of time is allowed to spin, we catch a fleeting glimpse of the ex-Captain Milch, now commanding officer of a police air squadron in East Prussia, ordering a machine-gun to be turned on rioting strikers in Königsberg.

He describes it as though it were yesterday. Then, supporting himself on a walking stick, for he has sciatica, he walks stiffly across the drawing-room to an antique cupboard and returns with a yellowing sheaf of documents—the reports he wrote and some newspapers from Königsberg, a city name long vanished from the map of Europe.

When next I visited him I found he had retrieved from a local safe deposit a stained and heavy suitcase, which he unfastened to reveal some fifty diaries and notebooks. I leafed through one at random and found a young artillery officer trudging in streaming rain through the carnage of a midnight battlefield of the Russian front during the First World War. The language was simple, but written with great feeling for the suffering of the common soldier.

It is clear that Milch was no Prussian officer archetype himself. His conversation was studded with scornful remarks about the Prussian generals whose obstinacy and lack of vision caused the Hitler Reich's downfall, for he did not camouflage his enduring admiration of the Führer. He was a field marshal but never a true officer, if his First World War service be overlooked. From being managing director of Lufthansa he became managing director of the secret Luftwaffe. Only the rank and the uniform were new; the job was virtually the same. But it was the rank and uniform that antagonized his Prussian adversaries; and his competence infuriated them. The campaign they fought against him, with all the intrigues and tenacity the German general staff could muster, lasted the full eleven years from his appointment until his disgrace in 1944. When this biography was published in West Germany the controversy was renewed, with able commanders like General Student hastening to the attack and others, equally able, coming to his defence. Milch ruefully quoted Friedrich Schiller's lines on Wallenstein: 'Torn by the hatred and favour of each faction, his name merges unsteadily with the past.' (*'Von der Parteien Gunst und Hass verwirrt, schwankt sein Charakterbild in der Geschichte.'*)

Now that his personal papers and official records are open to inspection, we can reassess the role he played. The widow of another Luftwaffe field marshal, von Richthofen, has written to me:

Now I have read the biography, I must say I am simply appalled at the intriguing and bickering that went on between the ministries, while every airman was doing his utmost at the front—and I myself lost a son as a combat pilot. The accomplishments that were Milch's, and the opposition he had to overcome! I have wept bitter tears reading your biography—the tears of an impassioned soldier's daughter, of a soldier's wife, and of a soldier's mother. I have been shaken to the core.

My conversations with the field marshal for this book lasted four years. Subsequently he read and commented on the fifteen-hundred-page draft that I produced. The changes he suggested may interest the reader curious about Milch's character. Once he invited me to delete Göring's unflattering description of a minister at the time of the Röhm massacre ('pale as a sicked-up pea'), on the grounds that the man is now dead. (He was hanged at Nuremberg.) Again, a diary note where Göring disclosed a physical debility was removed at Milch's request, with regard to the widow's feelings. Nor was he devoid of sentiment himself: he was deeply upset when he read the chapter terminating in the suicide of Ernst Udet, his closest friend, and learned for the first time the hurtful anti-Semitic epitaph scrawled by Udet before he pulled the trigger. On occasions Milch argued powerfully for the moderation of critical passages founded on my reading of the primary sources of the time. Occasionally he told me a version of an episode he had clearly related so often that it had begun to live a separate, and often charming, existence of its own, almost wholly detached from the substance of what had really happened. I hope my knowledge of the man has enabled me to detect and prune these offshoots in good time.

Under the agreement whereby the field marshal surrendered his diaries, notebooks and papers for my use he retained a right to veto any passage. It is proper that I should state that he insisted on only one occasion, when I was unable to convince him to allow me to publish the whole truth about his real father (and in particular his identity), which I had meanwhile worked out for myself despite his wholly honourable effort to obscure it; he asked me not to disclose more than I have written in the narrative that follows, and although he has since died I am still bound by the undertaking I gave him in his lifetime.

# ACKNOWLEDGEMENTS

The list of people to whom this author is personally indebted is long, but first of all his gratitude must be expressed to Field Marshal Milch, who made available his papers for the first time, and read and commented on the manuscript at every stage; and to his family, who bore with the author's many visits with great patience. But the author wishes to make it plain that he alone is responsible for the statements made and the views expressed in this book, and that they do not necessarily reflect the opinions of Field Marshal Milch unless expressly stated.

Mention must also be made of Dr O. Puchner of the Staatsarchiv in Nuremberg, and of Dr Friedrich Bergold, the field marshal's erstwhile defence lawyer, for their assistance in providing much of the material on which the latter chapters were based. Professor Walther Hubatsch, Messrs Basil Collier, Albert Speer, Fritz Seiler and many others patiently read parts of the draft and suggested improvements; Gunner Archie Miller, who took Milch prisoner, described from his diary the capture and the looting that followed by other soldiers; Major E. W. Rushton, of the Marine Commandos, described at length the events at Neustadt as OC of the unit responsible for mopping up in May 1945, and confirmed that Milch was 'clobbered' by the Commandos (not Major Rushton) when taken prisoner.

Among the many others who assisted by granting interviews, writing letters, or reading the manuscript gratitude is owing to Major-General Hermann Aldinger; engineer G. B. Alpers; Colonel Nicolaus von Below; Dr Willi A. Boelcke; engineer Maximilian Bohlan; Mr Ernst Englander; Mr Richard Falke; Sir Roy Fedden; engineer Karl Frydag; Frau Irmingard Geist; Rear-Admiral Eberhard Godt; Mr Jacob Hennenberg—a former Jewish forced-labourer employed on Milch's estate near Breslau, who wrote unexpectedly to the author from Cleveland, Ohio, in defence of the field marshal; Mr Fritz Herrmann; General Walther Hertel; Frau Edith Hesselbarth; Mr Otto Horcher; Dr G. Hümmelchen; Professor Heinz Kalk; director Rakan Kokothaki; lawyer Dr Otto Kranzbühler; Count Lutz Schwerin von Krosigk; Colonel Viktor von Lossberg; lawyer Dr Werner Milch; Mr Fritz Nebel; Professor Lionel S. Penrose; Colonel Edgar Petersen; General Wolfgang Pickert; the late Dr Hjalmar Schacht; Major-General Friedrich Carl Schlichting; Mr

Hanfried Schliephake; Professor F. Seewald; General Otto Skorzeny; Professor Telford Taylor; Group-Captain Peter Townsend; the Rt Hon Lord Trevethin and Oaksey, who as Lord Lawrence presided over the Nuremberg Trials; Lieutenant-General Wolfgang Vorwald; test pilot Erich Warsitz; Frau Karin Weigel, secretary to General Koller; Major-General Karl-Eduard Wilke; and Mr Hans Karl von Winterfeld.

# PART I

# AIR POWER
# CONSERVED

# DEATH OF A RICH UNCLE, DEATH OF A RICH AUNT

## (*March 1892–January 1933*)

Europe first saw the shape of things to come on 15 March 1938, in a square in Vienna. To the sound of massed bands, the German army and its equipment was paraded through the newly occupied Austrian capital. All eyes centred on the knot of senior officers standing with Hitler in front of the Maria-Theresa monument. On one side stood Admiral Raeder and Colonel-General von Brauchitsch, C-in-Cs of the German navy and army; and on the other, not Hermann Göring's familiar resplendent figure, but a short, corpulent general in the blue full-length topcoat of the Luftwaffe, with round, youthful features and grey-blue eyes. It was proper that this general, Erhard Milch, should be there rather than Göring, for it was he who had recreated Germany's air power. Three years before neither the Luftwaffe nor the uniform he was wearing had formally existed; and two years before that, when Adolf Hitler had seized power, Milch was still a civilian airline manager, and the Luftwaffe nothing more menacing than a corridor in the Defence Ministry and an airfield outside Moscow.

Milch had been as surprised as anybody by the decision to enter Austria. On leave at a Swiss skiing village five days before this vast military parade, he had been called by the hotel porter to the telephone. It was Berlin on the line. He recognized the voice of his principal staff officer: 'Field Marshal Göring has ordered you to return to Berlin immediately!' Milch asked, 'What for?' The voice hesitated, then replied, 'Your aunt is dying.' Milch had no aunts, but he had been kept informed by Hitler of his plans to take over Austria ever since February. He pointedly asked, 'You mean—the *rich* aunt?' 'That's the one,' the voice replied.[1] Milch hurried back to Berlin that same evening. He flew into Vienna with the first wave of transports on the twelfth, and watched as his Junker 52s disgorged two thousand fully equipped and armed troops within the space of four hours.[2] The army followed more laboriously by road.

As the last echelons of the army parade passed the saluting base Hitler ordered his adjutants to bar the streets to prevent the more unruly Viennese populace from falling in behind his Wehrmacht troops. A few minutes would pass before two o'clock struck. General von Brauchitsch passed acid comment on the absence of the Luftwaffe, and Hitler turned an inquiring gaze on Milch. The latter pointed wordlessly to his watch. Half a minute before the hour the air began to tremble as the Luftwaffe's squadrons advanced across the suburbs towards them—over 450 aircraft, none of them more than 2,500 feet above the rooftops, with German and Austrian fighter squadrons in their van, and 270 heavy bombers bringing up the rear less than a thousand feet above the ground. As the leading aircraft—piloted, symbolically, by a German and an Austrian general—passed overhead Milch turned to Hitler, saluted and announced: '*Mein Führer,* I beg to report the commencement of the Luftwaffe's fly-past!'[3]

What was the making of this unorthodox field marshal, this uniformed 'managing director' of the Luftwaffe?

Along the North Sea coast of Germany, the folklore is that man is born on the rising tide and dies as it ebbs. This child was born on the afternoon of 30 March 1892 in the imperial navy port of Wilhelmshaven. The city's records show that one Anton Milch, apothecary of the Kaiser's navy, had registered 'a male child born to his wife, Klara Auguste Wilhelmine Milch, *née* Vetter, also of the Protestant faith'.[4] Of Anton Milch there is little that can be said, or needs to be, for he was not the real father of the child. His naval career tied the family to this undistinguished port, whereas his wife had grown up in Berlin. She was twenty-seven at Erhard's birth, a tall, well-formed woman with fair hair and luminous blue eyes. Anton was away from home for long periods and for about a quarter of each year she was also away for some reason, but the family was well served with housemaids despite the humble income of an apothecary. On the Kaiser's birthday she would purchase cream puffs with whipped cream and a cup of drinking chocolate as an annual treat for her family, and most summers their great-uncle Carl Bräuer would come from Berlin and invite them to patronize the ice-cream carts propelled by Italians through the streets of Wilhelmshaven. In this way the children grew up with equal admiration for the Kaiser and their Uncle Carl. On trial for his life fifty years later, the field marshal was to recall, 'Loyalty to the Kaiser and loyalty to my country were the only political doctrines I received, either as an officer or earlier in my parents' home.'[5]

Bräuer was one of the bigger building contractors in Berlin and his private fortune was large; when he died in 1906 it went entirely to Erhard's grandmother, and the Milch family were able to move into a fashionable villa in the Königsallee. On Bräuer's death the Berlin newspapers printed an obituary notice ('Our Beloved Uncle') from Milch's mother.[6] Her husband had by then left the navy and bought a struggling chemist's business at Gelsenkirchen in the Ruhr; Frau Milch took her children away from him and to Berlin, so Erhard moved from the Ruhr town's grammar school to the superior Joachimsthal public school in the capital, where he matriculated early in 1910.[7]

Much of his later nationalism must have stemmed from his childhood talks with his grandmother, who could relate fabulous details of the crushing of the revolution in Berlin in 1848. With the destruction of the monarchy in 1918 she lost all interest in life: 'I no longer want to live now that there is no King of Prussia any more,' she said, and she faded gracefully away soon after. When Erhard made known his intention of becoming an officer in the Kaiser's army it was she who offered to pay the money he needed to supplement the pittance that they paid.[8] The other early formative influence was Milch's neighbour in the Königsallee, Admiral Ludwig Schröder, the legendary 'Lion of Flanders' who later commanded the Naval Expeditionary Force in the First World War; Erhard looked effectively—if mistakenly—to him as a father, a powerful relationship that was to reach its maturity in the 1920s.

He volunteered in February 1910 and after eight months' training with the 1st Foot Artillery Regiment at Königsberg transferred as the youngest cadet to Anklam Military Academy, passing the officer's examination with the best marks out of 120 cadets and the military equivalent of a *summa cum laude*. This young, fair-haired dynamo remained firmly in his fellow lieutenants' memories.[9] In 1913 he transferred to the Artillery School at Jüterbog, where he was to stun his superiors during one paper exercise by ordering his heavy battery to 'cease fire', since he calculated that he had already run out of ammunition some days before. He applied for flying training, but was warned off by his CO after his return to Königsberg: 'My officers are too valuable for such tomfoolery!'[10]

At the outbreak of the First World War Lieutenant Erhard Milch, a robust artillery officer of twenty-two, was to be found at gunnery practice in West Prussia. As mobilization began he was ordered by telegram to return to Königsberg as battalion adjutant of the 1st Foot

—his battalion being in reserve—with orders to defend the fortress. He applied repeatedly for transfer to one of the front-line units, fearing that the war had left him behind; enviously he hung round the railway station, bidding *Auf Wiedersehen!* to his departing comrades—a vain injunction, for the regiment was to lose 65 officers and 1,600 men during the next few years. But after the first great battle was staged at Gumbinnen his battalion went to war for the first time, marching with steaming horses and groaning ammunition wagons as night fell through the Sackheim Gate in the east of the fortress—'Not a romantic exodus,' lamented Milch, 'the kind that one had dreamed of or seen depicted in the illustrated journals.'[11]

Their first battle station was on the River Deime. On the third day a Russian attack began against their lines and Milch's battery fired nine hundred rounds. How often in peacetime he had doubted whether one could entirely suppress the coward within oneself; he was very pleased with his own composure now the test had come. On the morning of 3 September 1914 a six-hour Russian barrage began and Milch's quarters suffered a direct hit. A corporal telephonist was badly injured, but continued reeling in the telephone cable as he had been ordered; Milch gently took the reel from him and led him to the dressing-station. As he left him there the corporal called out, *'Herr Leutnant,* may I write to you when they've put me together again, so that *Herr Leutnant* can ask for me back? Otherwise they might send me somewhere else.'* In the midst of this bombardment Milch received the first official mail, including an urgent letter from the General Inspectorate of Foot Artillery in Berlin with the battery's scorecards from their recent gunnery practice in West Prussia: two errors were pointed out, the cards to be corrected in duplicate and returned to Berlin. Milch returned the cards unamended with a covering note: 'We believe that war broke out on 1 August, which fact we obediently call to Berlin's attention.' 'Now you will never make it as Inspector General,' Milch's CO reproached him when he heard of this.

After East Prussia had been cleared of the enemy Milch's battalion was moved to the south-east of the province. Here the Russians had wrought frightful havoc in the villages and Milch was tempted to shut all compassion for the enemy out of his mind as the pursuit continued. He entered in his diary:

There, all at once, the highway was strewn with artillery-pieces and machine-guns, with dead horses and the corpses of men. One of our batteries or a machine-gun unit had surprised the enemy and literally shot him to pieces. Whole teams of horses had crumpled in a trice, and now they lay there, their legs stiffly in the air, in one large bloody morass. On top of this came the rain, pouring down in sheets. It was a hideous sight, and yet one was glad, because this was the hated enemy.

Having written these words he reflected, '. . . And yet even for him I have something akin to sympathy in my heart—he too has been driven to his death by his superiors.'

In October the German offensive came to a halt and turned into a slow, hard-fought retreat to East Prussia and the Angerapp Line where they spent the winter. In mid-February next year, to forestall a Russian evasive move to the east, Hindenburg ordered an attack, less with the intention of gaining ground than of destroying the enemy's attacking forces. So in Milch's sector two battalions of Pomeranian grenadiers stormed across the ice-bound River Angerapp and seized the Weedern, a famous East Prussian stud farm rendered seemingly impregnable by three lines of Russian trenches and barbed wire. As the German onslaught faltered something unforgettable occurred—one battalion commander, Major Langemark, drew his dagger, bellowed 'Follow me!' and battled his way through the entanglement while the assault troops followed on his heels, singing the German national hymn as they overwhelmed the Russian trenches.[12] Thus the Russians' fate was sealed. Milch later wrote, 'Of our two thousand assault troops over half lay on the battlefield. But the casualties of the equally valiant Siberian riflemen were by far the greater. It was an awful sight, the trenches heaped with the dead, most of them with their skulls caved in—a way of fighting as particular to our burly Pomeranians as the bayonet is to our East Prussians.'

Half the night they marched towards the East. There was no billet, for the Russians had burned everything to the ground in their retreat. The roads had been hammered into treacherous ice by the army centipede, and many a cannon and wagon skidded off the track, broke up and had to be abandoned. The weather changed, it began to pour with rain and the ice turned to slush. On the evening of 14 February they were ordered to capture Raczki. It was not a major action but again it left an indelible impression on Milch's memory. In one account he wrote,

At first light we began our advance, some way behind the advance party. To the right and left of us lay hundreds of infantrymen, sleeping as I thought at first, exhausted; but as it grew lighter I saw that all were dead. We came upon the battery we had silenced the day before, and then set out along a sunken lane leading to Raczki. The scene here was even more frightful, here the Siberians lay in their hundreds, their skulls beaten in, littering the whole path our troops had to follow.

And in his diary Lieutenant Milch recorded:

I will never be able to eradicate this memory of the road into the town; it was strewn with the corpses of our troops and those of the Russians. Most of them had hideous wounds, clubbed by rifle-butts, or torn by bayonets. Never had I yearned for peace so much as at that moment. The dead reached to the very market square of Raczki, and the filthy population just stood about, their hands in their pockets, staring insolently and without the least compassion for the horrors all about them. All this killing, even of the enemy, really hurts. But what is one to do about it? All the greater is my hatred for those responsible for this war.[13]

In July 1915 Lieutenant Milch was detailed to report for training as an aircraft observer. His aircrew training complete, he was transferred to the newly activated 204th Artillery Reconnaissance Unit on the western front, at an airfield between Metz and Verdun. His aircraft was the unarmed Albatros B, with a top speed of about eighty-five miles per hour. None of the normal accidents of flying in those days could dampen his enthusiasm; the wooden aircraft crashed, caught fire or came unstuck in the rain. There was a *camaraderie* among airmen of both sides that was wholly absent elsewhere. When a French Voisin was shot down in flames by a field-kitchen unit Milch considered this unsporting intervention by a ground formation unpardonable: 'The only things left were snapshots and letters, one of which began, *"Ma pomme adoreé!"*. I found I was very sorry for the poor chaps.' And when, a year later, a young Canadian airman called Douglas Weld was shot down in a Sopwith Camel near his airfield, Milch allowed the captive to live for three days in his mess and even to try out one of the German aircraft for himself, against a verbal undertaking not to escape; Milch sent a crew to drop a letter from Weld to his mother over his home airfield next day.[14] Not long after the British No. 5 Squadron wrote to Milch that one of his aircraft had been shot down and both its crew were safe; the note invited him to drop their personal luggage over the British airfield. Thirty years later, Milch's tender feelings for brother airmen had vanished.

On the Somme, in the summer of 1916, he met enemy air superiority for the first time. His crews were outnumbered twenty to one on this sector; here they had to fly three sorties a day, whereas at Verdun they had never needed to fly more than one. By the evening of the third day all four aircraft in his unit lay disabled upon the French countryside. It was the arrival on the same airfield as Milch of one man, Captain Boelcke, that saved the situation. He fought as a soldier, not as a sportsman; Milch was fascinated by his modesty and by his unforgettable eyes—the same blue eyes he found in Hermann Göring later. In the middle of June 1917 he was posted to No. 5 Air Unit as deputy commander, under the Sixth Army; it was well housed in luxurious villas near Lille. Their planes were faster, flew higher and had longer range, and they were hardly troubled as they photographed the Allied preparations for Haig's offensive in Flanders. As the battle reached its height the redoubtable army air commander Captain Wilberg had at one stage over seventy squadrons at his fingertips, including the ace fighter-squadron under Manfred, Baron von Richthofen.[15]

On 1 April 1918 Lieutenant Milch was selected as a candidate for the General Staff. As a preliminary he was posted to an infantry regiment holding a small sector near Arras. Here only the former churches and factories stood out as one-time artefacts of man—shallow pyramids of rubble among the treeless, grassless wastelands marking the front line. The German regiments had arranged themselves so that one battalion was always up front, a second about four hundred yards farther back and the third 'at ease' about two miles behind the front line. Milch was given No. 9 company of the 41st Infantry Regiment, a Memel company which had just lost forty men in a heavy British barrage; his predecessor had suffered a nervous breakdown and the survivors considered themselves doomed. It was a realistic test of any officer's powers of leadership. The soldiers had provided no trenches for themselves and were protected only by a few sheets of corrugated iron. Milch marked out a trench about sixty yards long, and ordered them to form up with spades and dig an eight-foot-deep trench. Nobody moved. He repeated his order, with the same effect. A young soldier muttered that there was no point in digging, as they were all dead men anyway. The lieutenant tore the spade from his hands and shouted: 'Either you start digging now, or I'll split your skull!' The digging started. Later the British opened up again with heavy cannon-fire, and the corrugated iron shelter was blasted to pieces. The soldiers appreciated the value of the trench they had now dug. Shortly afterwards one of the company's officers asked Milch to come over. The whole company stood at attention in a fine drizzle in the moonlight; and the man whom Milch had threatened the day before stepped forward and apologized in all his comrades' names, since it was obvious that without their lieutenant's stern action none of them would have survived the day.[16]

Spring turned to summer, but no grass grew and Milch and his troops became gaunt and dirty. He was posted to the field artillery and in July 1918 he returned to the Air Corps as an intelligence officer. A month later he was promoted to captain, to await a final posting to Staff College. Meantime he was given command of his old unit, the 204th Reconnaissance, under Captain Wilberg in Flanders. The unit had expanded to eleven aircraft, two of which were armoured (one of them being the slow but excellent all-metal aircraft built by the Junkers company); the armour enabled his unit to carry out reconnaissance missions at only 150 feet or so without losses. Milch's ability and inventiveness attracted the attention of his superiors, for on 1 October Wilberg gave him command of No. 6 Fighter Squadron, brushing aside the captain's objections that he could not fly himself; so Milch was obliged to command from the ground, an overwhelmingly uncomfortable experience for any commanding officer.[17] As the war came to its abrupt and dishonourable end five weeks later all the elements that were to characterize the later field marshal were already implanted within him—the vision and foresight, but also the unbecoming irreverence towards authority; the powerful nationalist and patriotic instinct, but also the seeds of a corroding xenophobia; the personal courage and ruthlessness in action, but also a strong humanity and sense of compassion even towards an enemy. To these features the next twenty years were to add only one— an outstanding ability to organize and administer.

On the last day of the First World War Captain Erhard Milch paraded his fighter squadron at dawn. As a final test of discipline he inspected them, handed out a savage dressing-down to a nonplussed flight commander for insolence, ordered the men to form up again properly, and stood them to attention for fifteen minutes. Only then did he read out the Fourth Army's order for the election of soldiers' councils. He ordered all the squadron's motor transport to be equipped with machine-guns and to set out for the German border.[18]

As the undefeated battalions marched back across the border into the Fatherland, their contempt for the revolutionaries was open. Before reaching the German border Milch ordered his convoy to halt and again paraded his men. He told them that they were now returning to their own country, and that they must march in with their heads held high; he asked them to do him one last favour, to fly the Kaiser's colours from their vehicles as they crossed the frontier. During the night they entered Aachen, the first German town. In his diary he wrote: 'Into

Germany. Not one of the swine welcomes us back—only the little children wave.'[19] At the town hall the local workers' council was in session with the Fourth Army's soldiers' council; about twenty sailors with red armbands milled about. The revolutionaries stared with some perplexity at Milch's uniform. Milch bluffed, 'I would advise you to get rid of your red armbands if you value your lives. There's a division loyal to the Kaiser not far behind, shooting every revolutionary they lay hands on.' He later regretted not having acted himself to restore order—the revolutionaries' fear of the front-line troops was enormous.

At Danzig he reported to the 17th Army Corps, and for the next months he toured the provincial cities nearby, taking over from the soldiers' councils, preventing the destruction or dumping of army property and disarming the bands of partisans that had formed.[20] All the time he yearned to return to the air. The Corps's chief of staff agreed to his suggestion that they should establish a volunteer flying squadron at Danzig's Langfuhr landing ground; the current occupants of the landing ground—a naval air school, now strongly revolutionary—did not approve, and it took a pitched battle fought with hand-grenades to eject them. When the Germans activated a border patrol along their common border with Poland in April 1919 Milch was appointed commander of No. 412 Volunteer Flying Unit, a motley collection of patriots, soldiers and mercenaries. In Posen and Upper Silesia there had been revolutions, exploited by the Poles to push their frontiers farther westwards, and Milch sensed keenly the disgrace inflicted on these eastern provinces. He proposed to the Army Corps a small private war, no less, to hound the none-too-powerful Poles out of Posen; but to his bitter disappointment the chief of staff rejected the idea. He did not dispute that they would enjoy a small victory at first and even liberate the province to its former frontiers. He later wrote to Milch, 'Nobody could be sorrier than I to have to subject your heartfelt plans to a sober criticism. Unfortunately I must. You must not let your emotions run away with you—cool reason must play its part, unfortunately. . . . Once and for all, the opportunities are long gone.'[21]

Originally the peace terms had been expected to permit Germany an army of two hundred thousand men including airmen, but the final terms of Versailles proved these hopes to be illusory; only a hundred thousand men were to be permitted in the Reichswehr, and none of these were to be airmen.[22] An additional police force was permitted, so the crafty Germans resolved to equip the police with air squadrons, seven in all, of which Milch was invited to establish one at Königsberg in September 1919.[23] He arrived there with his wife—he had married Käthe

Patschke in Berlin two and a half years before—and daughter Gerda, and selected a former Zeppelin airfield at Seerappen as his headquarters, far from the revolutionary influences of the provincial capital.[24] The barracks were currently occupied by four hundred and fifty soldiers; Milch's squadron appeared with nine aircraft on the afternoon of 1 November and fired machine-gun bursts into the air while a lieutenant and a trumpeter gave the squatters two hours to get out. In his diary Milch noted that the removal to Seerappen passed smoothly, 'despite a number of unpleasantnesses'.[25] With thought for the future, he collected there every aircraft and component he could lay hands on; soon there was not enough space in the Zeppelin hangar for this hoard, so the Social Democrat police-president of Königsberg allowed him to store valuable equipment in the police headquarters.

To Milch's surprise he found that he was expected to be not only airman but policeman as well, his squadron's personnel being ordered to put down a wave of gangsterism in the port. This exposed a ruthless streak in him that was to become fully developed when he was directing a war against more than just a few burglars in the streets of Königsberg, twenty years later. At first his men held back, until one of them was gunned down by an intruder; on each of the following nights, on Milch's orders, his squads shot dead a prowler. The break-ins halted dramatically as the gangsters fled to other provinces. In August 1920 his now toughly disciplined men held at bay an armed mob storming the Königsberg flour-mill; two of his men were clubbed to the ground before a third mastered the situation and opened fire with a machine-gun, holding the rioters at bay until reinforcements arrived. The factory's medical orderlies picked up the dead and injured.[26] A few months later the Allies exerted pressure on the Germans to abide by Versailles and even para-military flying was forbidden.[27] The police squadrons were obliged to surrender all their aircraft; Milch accordingly retired from the force at the end of March 1921 and took off his captain's uniform for the last time.

Temporarily unemployed, he looked to his future. Concealed in various parts of the country he had numbers of aircraft or their parts, but one by one these were discovered by the *Entente* officials and confiscated. 'Dear Captain Milch,' wrote one correspondent, 'it is my sad duty to advise you that your Fokker was discovered by the *Entente* yesterday and confiscated.'[28] 'Captain Milch, Right Honourable!' appealed another writer. 'There has been another unsuccessful search made here. May I now ask you to have the objects in question removed from here? I expect my farmstead to be rid of these things by 8 am tomorrow at the latest. I want no part of it.' On which Milch pencilled a lapidary comment: 'Never saw such cowardice in seven lines!'[29] Civil aviation seemed the only answer, while it lasted.

It had already existed in Germany for two years, a small company, the German Airline (Deutsche Luft-Reederei) having been granted a licence in 1919; but its aircraft were open, hazardous and primitive. A rival company, Lloyd Ostflug (Lloyd Eastern Airways), had been founded in 1921 by Professor Hugo Junkers and a former naval air service lieutenant, Gotthard Sachsenberg, to open up air routes in eastern Europe. Sachsenberg had crossed swords with Milch over Seerappen airfield a year before, and casting about him for an energetic manager for the new airline's Danzig office he remembered Milch and offered him the job; the latter accepted, and became the kingpin of the main route which was to run from Berlin through Danzig to Königsberg.[30] This marked the beginning of one of the most creative periods in his career—a period which was to end with him as chief executive of Lufthansa, the country's national airline.

He at once left for Danzig, leased the old airfield at Langfuhr and procured a six-year-old Rumpler CI reconnaissance aircraft, which the British high commissioner there allowed him to keep. The plane shuttled from Berlin to Danzig, with one passenger in the open observer's seat with a bag of mail on his lap. The mail to Berlin was often quicker by train, and the passenger air fare was certainly more expensive; but it was a beginning, if not an encouraging one. During the spring of 1921 the Junkers works delivered the first two F 13s—an all-metal, single-engined plane with a cabin for four passengers. Milch had advertising cards printed stressing the advantages of flying with Danzig Air Mail: 'Passengers are conveyed by the most up-to-date Junkers cabin aircraft. Special clothing like furs, goggles etc. are not needed.'[31] And what an innovation that was! Despite the Versailles decree that all German aircraft production should cease for six months, Junkers did not stop his factories; indeed in his Dessau drawing office a four-engined aircraft was already taking shape. In May 1921 the Western Powers delivered an ultimatum—if aircraft production did not cease, they would occupy the Ruhr. The German government capitulated and all F 13s manufactured to date were ordered to be surrendered to the Allies as well.

The manager of Danzig Air Mail knew nothing of these strictures, but he felt the effects. Two more F 13s had been delivered to him, and he and Sachsenberg had flown to Kovno and won a licence to open a route to that city far to the east of Königsberg; later that summer they concluded negotiations for the route to Riga.[32] But the French control officers dutifully pursued the little airline, with its Danzig-registered aircraft, and soon the company was running only one service and that was outside Germany, from Danzig onward to Riga; an adventurous game to conceal the forbidden F 13s had begun along the route.[33] The French had specific orders for the confiscation of each F 13 owned by the airline, but they knew them only by their registration numbers—DZ 31, 32, 35 or 38. They could not be in all places at all times and a paint-brush frequently reached the aircraft before the French officials did. This situation could not last for ever: towards the end of July 1921 three of Milch's aircraft were seized one after the other as they landed at Berlin; a few days later two French officers arrived on the Danzig airfield carrying sledge-hammers, to smash the rest. Their leader himself scratched at the registration number on one aircraft and exclaimed that there was another number painted underneath. Milch drily advised him, 'Keep scratching. You will find a lot more.'[34]

To add to his difficulties the four parent companies of Lloyd Eastern Airways began to break apart, and the airline was eventually divided between the contending major shareholders. Danzig Air Mail, which alone operated F 13s, fell to Professor Junkers and Gotthard Sachsenberg. At the end of October 1921 this company was forced to suspend operations altogether in the face of the continuing French harassment, an enforced idleness that was to last seven months.[35]

Ostensibly the Reich Defence Ministry abided by Versailles, but it maintained contact with the former officers of the Flying Corps; in January 1920 one Captain Kraehe circularized the more experienced of them to write reports on their experiences. Milch was asked to write on tactical reconnaissance and on 'the struggle for air supremacy'; it is worth mentioning that his two studies showed the fighter aircraft as the key to supremacy, while the 'workhorse aircraft' whose path it was to clear was of only secondary importance.[36] The Corps was formally dissolved in May 1920, and Captain Wilberg, now Kraehe's assistant, was seconded as 'air adviser' to General von Seeckt. His work continued unchanged, and on 1 November 1921 Milch was to be found in Wilberg's office; he wrote in his diary, 'Discussion on training school! Latest news on secret air force. . . .'

The military authorities were now casting thoughtful glances at Russia's territories: the Soviet Union had adopted none of the hostile measures towards German aviation favoured by Britain and France, and negotiated with both Danzig Air Mail and their rivals, the German Airline, over an air route from Königsberg onwards to Moscow and St Petersburg; at the same time the Reich Defence Ministry secured permission from the Russian government for Professor Junkers to erect a secret aircraft factory near Moscow, at Fili. Over the next four years the Reich provided nearly ten million gold marks in subsidies—a sum, as Ernst Brandenburg, Germany's head of civil aviation, later remarked, which would have sufficed during the inflation to buy up 'half Germany'.[37] Unhappily for the Fili venture, the parent Junkers company used the subsidies merely to meet domestic wage bills at Dessau; irritated by Russian complaints the ministry opened an investigation of Fili's affairs and the bubble was pricked. After the Locarno estrangement with Russia Germany stopped all further investment in Fili and an incurable crisis started for Junkers. Whether or not Professor Junkers was himself aware of the machinations of his colleagues—and particularly Sachsenberg—must remain obscure. Brandenburg later testified, 'I never knew what to make of him. Was it a childish ingenuousness or unscrupulous fraud?'[38] For the time being, however, at the beginning of 1922, the bubble remained unpricked; indeed, as if to drive Germany still further into the Soviet camp the Western Allies arbitrarily prolonged the veto on German aircraft manufacture a further six months, and in mid-April announced that new German aircraft were not to be designed to fly faster than 120 miles per hour, nor might they fly higher than 13,000 feet nor carry more than half a ton of payload. In high dudgeon the German delegation left the conference on postwar problems at Geneva and reached separate agreement with the Soviet Union at nearby Rapallo.

When the veto was lifted in May 1922 three large airlines—Junkers Airways, Lloyd Air Services and German Airline—dominated the scene; Sachsenberg envisaged a vast network of air routes operated by Junkers subsidiaries and flying Junkers aircraft, an airline network extending from London to Constantinople, and it was Milch who conducted the early negotiations with Swiss, Austrian and Hungarian airline representatives. His own interest centred on the east, and he drew up plans for a route from Danzig to Warsaw, Lemberg and Cracow, to be extended eventually to Bucharest, where it would pick up Sachsenberg's 'Trans-Europe Union' network.[39] He reached agreement with the Poles in the summer of 1922 and himself conducted the inaugural flights while Polish government officials jostled for a chance to board the Junkers 'limousines'. The new Polish company, Aerolot, opened on 1 September, the government paying sixty thousand Polish marks for every flight from Danzig through Warsaw to Lemberg, either in cash or fuel. It was, for Milch, a victory 'more satisfying than on any battlefield'.[40]

A year later he was promoted to Dessau as head of the company's management office. He was less happy here than at Danzig, and he found that he had personal opponents among Sachsenberg's loyal liegemen.

One of them was to say of him, when he was confined in Landsberg Prison, 'We all thought he was an opportunist, and we were convinced he could not be relied upon. In some strange way, he was not one of us. None of us was his friend.'[41] Above all Milch was a hard-headed businessman—he disapproved of the professor's futuristic plans and wanted more concentration on consolidating what had so far been achieved. The professor's reputation suffered a severe setback when an expedition he had rashly mounted to promote Junkers aircraft in South America met disaster: an American colonel who had advised him of the large market waiting there turned out to be an unemployed barber; the expedition had been despatched none the less. The first F 13 had crashed, killing its two-man crew (including the professor's son); the second had been forced down and sunk. Milch was sent out to pull Junkers's chestnuts out of the fire, with two more F 13s. In Buenos Aires he negotiated with big business and by April 1924 it was clear that he had turned the venture into a triumphant success; he flew demonstration flights with the aircraft to Montevideo and other cities, arranged for the sale of the aircraft to the military authorities and negotiated with the government on subsidies for a Junkers-controlled national airline. At one small town in Argentina an ancient, sunburned farmer approached the aeroplanes, walked round them, stroked their hot metal surfaces and finally inquired: 'Are these German planes?' Milch nodded that they were. 'Then Germany is not finished!' was the farmer's congratulation.[42]

The professor sent Milch to New York and then to tour the huge Ford automobile works at Detroit.[43] He never forgot the spectacle of the Ford factories at Highland Park, and dwelt in his diary on the awe-inspiring machinery of the foundry at River Rouge and the largely Negro manpower; above all he was astounded by the mass-production conveyer-belt techniques. He believed this ideal could never be attained in Germany, where the rival companies fought each other to the death in blissful ignorance of the industrial revolution happening across the Atlantic.[44] Milch was one of the few Germans to give warning of the mighty potential of the American war industries when the Second World War broke out.

When he returned to Germany in mid-August 1924 only two airlines were left of the thirty-eight that had sprouted in Germany since the First World War—the newly formed Junkers Airways under Gotthard Sachsenberg and the rival Aero-Lloyd. This concentration was the achievement of Ernst Brandenburg, who had seen it as his duty to allocate state subsidies only to these two companies.[45] But it was still not enough, for costly competition between the two companies continued and late in 1925 Brandenburg ruled that both must merge into one national airline—Deutsche Lufthansa. What astounded both companies was the directorship dictated by the State to Lufthansa—Otto Merkel and Martin Wronsky from Aero-Lloyd, and Erhard Milch (not Sachsenberg) from Junkers.

That Milch, at the age of thirty-three, should suddenly emerge with such a position was inexplicable to his enemies at Dessau; it was scarcely explicable to him. In prison he later wrote, 'It turned out to be a far more momentous step than I had ever guessed. Without it, I would have forfeited the most rewarding period of my life, the years from 1925 to 1933 with Deutsche Lufthansa; I would not have become a soldier again in 1933, and a field marshal in 1940; but nor would I now be sitting in a confined and gloomy prison cell. How inscrutable are the paths of man. . . .'[46] His acceptance of the ministry's offer evoked immediate Junkers accusations of disloyalty, but from his papers—which include transcripts of the vital conversations in Berlin—it is clear he acted in the professor's best interests throughout.[47] Sachsenberg, on the other hand, clearly stated: 'As a Junkers official my sole interest is to wreck the new company and enable our company to regain control of Junkers Airways.'[48] But Milch saw the coming of Lufthansa as inevitable, in which case it was vital for Junkers's interests to be equally represented in it; Professor Junkers should concentrate on building aircraft, not operating an airline. The professor himself eventually accepted this view, and Milch fought the company's case so well that while only 208 of Aero-Lloyd's former staff were taken on the Lufthansa payroll, 225 were taken on from the far smaller Junkers Airways.[49]

The Lufthansa organization plan showed three directorships. Aero-Lloyd had proposed four, of which they themselves wanted three—finance, technical and flying control; but Milch insisted that the latter must be a Junkers man. Eventually he himself filled the post. At a Junkers banquet held, coincidentally, on the evening of his appointment, powerful speeches were delivered against Milch; he endeavoured to defend his action, but it was not surprising that there were now those at Dessau who believed that their former director had stuck a dagger in their backs.[50] For Junkers, Ernst Brandenburg was to write, the new Lufthansa company was to become a red rag to a bull.[51] Sachsenberg waged war against it from the day it was formally established, 6 January 1926, shunning no method to bring it into disrepute and vilifying Milch as the traitor who had ruined Junkers Airways. Milch suffered deeply under this campaign.[52]

The new company's chairman was Emil-Georg von Stauss, an enlightened director of the Deutsche Bank. As his deputy directors Milch selected Karl-August, Baron von Gablenz and Joachim von Schröder —son of the admiral and a boyhood friend; flying was to be the life and death of both these men. His technical deputy was Dr Grulich, an Aero-Lloyd official blessed with neither Wronsky's diplomacy nor Merkel's intelligence; his relations with Milch were strained, as Wronsky and Merkel had hinted to him that the far younger Junkers man was only a temporary evil, whom Grulich would in due course replace.[53] The evil lasted longer than Grulich thought possible. Otto Merkel, the commercial manager, showed his strange talents at the very first Lufthansa board meeting. The entire capital of Junkers Airways and Aero-Lloyd had consisted only of aircraft and equipment; neither had liquid reserves. As however both companies had been assigned $27\frac{1}{2}$ per cent of Lufthansa's shares, each had to value its contribution at nearly seven million reichsmarks, which in effect meant dividing that sum by the number of aircraft each company turned in. To avoid adding cash, Aero-Lloyd's Merkel valued the obsolete Fokker F II and F III aircraft at grossly inflated prices. Milch protested immediately to Brandenburg about this millstone of insolvency being hung about the new company, but Brandenburg made it clear that for his ministry the success of the merger was more important than the prospects of the company.[54]

Thus the airline's first fleet consisted in all of some 150 aircraft of a score of different makes and types, a technical director's nightmare. The root problem of German aircraft design at that time, and for the next two decades, was the lack of powerful aero-engines. In 1926 the biggest was the Bavarian Motor Works' BMW VI, rated at about 500 horsepower, but it was still suffering teething troubles and Milch preferred the Junkers LV, a 350-horsepower engine, as the more reliable. In the first few months he repeatedly asked himself whether one could accept the risk of carrying passengers at all.

To his fellow directors he was still an unknown quantity, a man of whom they expected little because of his youth. From all but von Stauss and the two ministry nominees on the board, Willy Fisch and Friedrich Heck, the Junkers man experienced a certain hostility for the first year. His early efforts were devoted to increasing the numbers of long-distance routes and reducing the short city-to-city hops. But he fought alone: Merkel was interested only in flying as many miles as possible, to get as big a return on his aircraft as he could; and Wronsky was concerned only with the size of the network he could parade before his foreign counterparts at the annual meetings of the IATA, the International Air Transport Association. A look at the Lufthansa board assembled in the Great Hall of the Deutsche Bank in Berlin showed the opposition Milch could expect: of the sixty-six board members the majority were local mayors like Bracht of Essen, Adenauer of Cologne, Landmann of Frankfurt, Scharnagl of Munich and Lehr of Düsseldorf.

But gradually the long-distance routes were extended. He flew to Moscow and renewed the agreement on the subsidiary company 'Deruluft' for a further five years, and that summer he promoted Lufthansa's first transcontinental expedition to explore an air route across Russia to the Far East. Two Junkers G 24s were despatched from Berlin in July 1926, following the old Danzig Air Mail route as far as Kovno, then to Moscow and onwards across the Urals and Siberia to the Pacific Ocean and Peking; at Peking crowds waited on the beaches as the two aircraft, giants of their day, passed overhead, their German insignia clear to all the watchers in the August sun. The wife of one Hanover businessman wrote home: '. . . And there I stood, gazing as they flew on like enormous birds towards the lilac-coloured mountains in the west. I scarcely noticed the tears running down my cheeks. I was back home again! This was Germany calling and beckoning us from the Fatherland.'[55] Not long after Milch sent a Lufthansa 'Whale' flying-boat to Brazil to prepare a transatlantic service, and a Lufthansa offshoot, the Condor Syndicate, was awarded a Brazilian licence to operate along that country's seaboard.[56]

During its first year, 1926, Lufthansa carried 93,000 passengers, and its aircraft flew a daily average of 25,000 miles, a figure which was to increase to 46,600 in 1927. Lufthansa planes carried gold bullion, shipments of stocks and shares, fresh flowers from Holland, furs and caviar from Russia, gowns from Paris and Vienna and the latest table delicacies for hotels and restaurants.[57] Milch pioneered blind-flying schools for his pilots and prevailed on German industry to supply the special instruments that this needed.[58] On Brandenburg's initiative he opened half a dozen regular pilot-training schools. Thanks to his insistence on proper servicing and frequent overhauls, the airline flew with ninety-seven per cent regularity and with ninety-eight per cent safety.

Occasionally Lufthansa aircraft made unscheduled landings, but the loss of life was small. In March 1927 Milch flew on the inaugural flight from Berlin to Vienna, via Dresden and Prague; the flight went off perfectly and great was the celebration in Vienna before their return. This may have proved the pilot's undoing, for after two attempts at flying over the mountains outside Dresden, on the third their aircraft came to rest in a pine forest on the very crown of one of them. The heavy plane snapped a score or more trees like matchwood before stopping. While Milch marshalled the passengers in the snow the pilot stood, head in hands, staring at his machine; the airline director invited the passengers to sit along one wing-edge in the sun, and led them in singing an old flying song:

> If you touch down in a leafy glade,
>     And the point of your journey is gone,
> Then twitter about and sample the shade
>     Of the branches the birds cluster on.

Soon a handful of local villagers arrived and carried their baggage to the nearest village. Milch summoned a car from Dresden and there he invited the passengers to sample a 1921 Rhine wine with him. Lufthansa could hardly have looked after its passengers better in those days.[59]

That was the spring in which an American airman, Captain Lindbergh, flew non-stop across the Atlantic. No German aircraft could match the achievement yet, but Lufthansa still intended to establish the first regular transatlantic service. The Condor Syndicate had been the first step and the second was the completion of part of the European end of the route by the establishment of a German–Spanish airline, 'Iberia', on 14 December; three weeks later the whole section from Berlin to Madrid was opened by Lufthansa. In May the following year Milch was prophesying, 'Regular transatlantic flights, non-stop, are today within the realms of reality.'[60] But the dream was a distant one, and in the meantime he opposed any Lufthansa involvement in spectacular overseas flights like Lindbergh's; overland flights were within sight of becoming self-supporting enterprises, and these were the only answer to growing left-wing criticism of the State subsidies for Lufthansa in the Reichstag.[61]

The criticism was further nourished by Junkers and Sachsenberg, who had gone to some lengths to curry Socialist support and who were paying regular sums of money to at least three Reichstag deputies to attack Lufthansa;[62] these deputies demanded that Lufthansa's subsidies be halved, and when the airline's directors privately appealed to Ernst Brandenburg to defend the subsidies, the civil servant could only point helplessly to the powerful opposition and recommend Lufthansa to purchase a number of Reichstag deputies for itself.

At the Reichstag elections in May 1928 twelve extreme right-wing NSDAP deputies were elected. Among them was Hermann Göring, one of the more socially acceptable of the Nazis. Like Milch he had attained the rank of captain in the Flying Corps, serving first as an observer, and then as a fighter pilot, winning the *pour le mérite* medal on the western front. For Lufthansa he was one of the more attractive deputies, having maintained his contacts with civil aviation after the Armistice by acting as an exhibition pilot and then as a parachute salesman in Sweden.[63] There can be no doubt that even before his election Göring was financed by Lufthansa. Among Deutsche Bank archives now in East German hands is a letter written by Milch in 1930, explaining: '. . . As far as the Deputy Göring is concerned, he did have an advisory post in Deutsche Lufthansa before his election to the Reichstag—i.e. while he was not an employee in the strict sense of the word, he was an "expert consultant" in the American sense.'[64] The bank's records also show at least one cheque for ten thousand reichsmarks paid to Göring in June 1929, charged against Lufthansa's account;[65] the company also bought the Social Democrat deputy Keil and the German People's Party deputy Dr Cremer.*[66]

Junkers struck his most serious blow at Lufthansa in the summer of 1928: he declared that his own three-engined G 24 aircraft, which formed the backbone of the airline's fleet, was unfit for flight unless its all-up weight could be reduced by a thousand pounds.[67] The airline faced ruin until Milch himself thought of an ingenious solution—they could take out the two wing engines and use just one more powerful central engine, for example the improved BMW VI. 'Out of the question!' was the old professor's astounded reaction. In 1943 Milch was to recall with evident relish, 'So I told Schatzki to go over all the calculations. He did so and told me immediately, "It will work!"' Dr Schatzki was one of Grulich's senior engineers. 'It was I, a complete layman, who had this idea, and that's how we saved Lufthansa's fortunes. . . . And when I as Technical Director went up in it with our Flight-Captain Pieper, my own technical deputy Grulich exclaimed out loud: "I hope it crashes. Then we'll be rid of our Technical Director at long last." '[68] All Lufthansa's G 24s underwent this drastic modification, to the rage of Professor Junkers. Milch demanded the dismissal of Grulich, but Otto Merkel brusquely refused.[69]

Learning that Merkel was collecting material against him, Director Milch accordingly opened a dossier on Merkel. Later he was to give the impression that his rival's downfall was as much of a surprise to him as it was to the victim,[70] but Milch's private papers show that as

---

* Lieutenant-Colonel Killinger told the same story under British (CSDIC) interrogation: 'Even before 1933 in his capacity as Nazi Reichstag deputy [Göring] received about 1,000 Reichsmarks monthly from Milch and Gablenz, directors of Lufthansa, in return for which he vigorously defended Lufthansa's interests in the Reichstag.' It is furthermore known that the records of the Bavarian Aircraft Works show at least one payment to Göring at this time, amounting to 2,800 Reichsmarks and entered in the firm's books as 'a one-time cash allowance to "G".'

early as the spring of 1928 he had begun collecting damaging material, while at the same time cultivating his own relations with his chairman and vice-chairman; Milch became a frequent guest at Stauss's home, went yachting with him, carefully entered Stauss and his wife (along with Göring) on his expanding birthday-present list and chronicled the progress he was making: 'Midday, called on von Stauss: trouble with Merkel, etc.' 'Afternoon, Heck reports to me Stauss favours Milch, opposes Wronsky and Merkel.' 'Stauss telephones: satisfied with me, but not with Merkel or Wronsky.' And, 'Von Stauss dresses down the directors on their commercial policies.'[71] His most effective weapon was a pocket notebook in which he entered each month Lufthansa's precise financial position.[72] Evidently the company was accumulating a huge deficit under Merkel and was about to meet disaster. From early 1929 onwards the threat of reduced services and redundancy loomed over the airline. Lufthansa increased its financial support for Göring and his fellow deputies, but the opposition successfully forced an investigation of the airline's accounts.[73] Lufthansa's subsidy was halved for the coming year.[74]

Göring did what he could to fight the cuts. In mid-June 1929 when the transport budget received its second reading in the Reichstag he demanded that the Reich should expand German civil aviation, not restrict it, as a great patriotic task: 'Because if you don't you will live to regret it.'[75] The government would not reconsider its decision. Redundancy was inevitable; Lufthansa would have to cut its staff by about thirty-five per cent.[76] The government audit committee recommended that the cuts should start at the top. The obstinate Grulich went, and Milch promoted Grulich's assistants, Dr Stüssel and Dr Schatzki.[77] On 1 July the committee asked Milch to take over Merkel's office as commercial director as well. He later wrote, 'This decision flabbergasted me. I did not even know how to read a balance sheet.' Unaware of this decision, Merkel mentioned to him three days later that Stauss was expecting one of them to resign to set a good example; Milch 'volunteered' to resign himself, aware as he was by then that Merkel had already drawn the short straw.[78] On 5 September Milch took over the commercial management, making him effectively 'chief executive' of Deutsche Lufthansa.

After the Nazi seizure of power he procured a well-rewarded position for Dr Grulich out of compassion for the ageing engineer's family.[79] He bore no grudge against defeated rivals, but it will be appreciated that in his upward path he had trodden heavily on many allegiances and had collected many enemies. 'I am not surprised that the air is thick with stupid rumours about Lufthansa,' he wrote to a company official in

Shanghai in November. 'Most of them can be ascribed to the fury of all those liars who have proved themselves incapable of putting their vile and selfish plans against us into effect. . . .' And he added, 'If you like to think of me as having once been energetic, I suggest you now add the word "ruthless"—or multiply by it, whichever is easier with your slide-rule!'[80]

Much had occurred to bolster Lufthansa's public reputation. The Lloyd liners *Bremen* and *Europa* had been fitted with catapults, from which mail-carrying aircraft were launched several hundred miles out in the Atlantic towards New York.[81] The company had also supported a spectacular transatlantic seaplane, the 56-ton, twelve-engined Dornier X, which had flown for the first time in mid-July 1929.[82] Late in October Joachim von Schröder flew non-stop to Constantinople in eleven hours, involving many hours of blind flying. But for the time being Milch did not anticipate any transatlantic service with land-based aircraft. 'As you see, we are concerned not with outward effect but with the steady development of air transport.'[83]

Lufthansa's staggering deficit was currently running at 19.8 million reichsmarks when Milch took over, of which six millions were in the form of short-term bank drafts valid for only three months at a time. His financial assistant, Walter Luz, called on him each evening and patiently went over the accounts with him. Red figures dominated every page. When the major banks almost immediately threatened to withdraw their credit Milch asked them to convert the credit to long-term; they declined, so he advised his chairman that, since Lufthansa must regard half its capital as lost, it must declare itself bankrupt under German company law (the only clause known to him at that time!). At this the banks precipitously changed the debt to a long-term one, to be redeemed at the rate of two million reichsmarks a year. One year later he paid back the first two million on time; and when after only eight more months he tried to repay the entire balance, the banks at first refused because of the interest they would now lose.[84]

Good husbandry alone had changed the airline's fortunes. Milch ordered a ruthless clearance of spare parts at airfield level; instead of insuring the company's aircraft with an outside firm he devised a system of self-insurance, and saved the premiums; he subjected the fleet to a thorough weeding-out process, too. The profits were invested in an Equipment Replacement Fund, for one day the wonder aircraft he was dreaming of must come, and by then Lufthansa must have accumulated so much money that they could convert their entire fleet within two years at most. Significantly, he saw his airline's role as being to revitalize and modernize the German air industry. In a lecture in May 1928 he had openly admitted this: 'We are prepared to accept the extraordinary diversity of aircraft and engine-types, in order to give the entire German industry involved a means of surviving.'[85] In September 1929 he repeated this, in his first business report to the airline's bankers: 'Germany's special position compels special consideration for the maintenance of a viable aircraft industry, particularly as it must be borne in mind that *civil* aviation is its only customer.'[86] This was the reason for Lufthansa's costly and unusually well-endowed Technical Development Division, with its scores of outstanding engineers; and this was the reason for fitting their aircraft with the most modern wireless and navigating equipment; and this was why sometimes their aircraft were even flying on IG Farben's new experimental synthetic petrol. Erhard Milch was providing for an air force of the future.

Politics were a closed book to Milch from the very outset. He had never belonged to a party, since they all seemed to make very much the same promises, before they broke them. He had at first remained unimpressed by the gradual rise of the National Socialists, although his brother Werner had evidently been one of the earliest members, for back in November 1923 he had received a hasty letter from him excusing his sudden absence from his Danzig Air Mail job: 'Dear Erhard! I received urgent letters from Munich yesterday, summoning me there. I know you would have acted the same if you were twenty, but please forgive me if this upsets any of your plans for me . . . I will let you know more from Munich.' In Munich, the Nazis had just begun their abortive revolution, and thousands of party members had been summoned to the Bavarian capital to assist.[87] Over the years since Versailles, however, Erhard Milch had watched the government's growing estrangement from the people, and particularly from the working classes; he reflected that something must have been wrong if even in the Kaiser's time the workers were in opposition and even a Social Democrat republic could not cure the growing unemployment. 'We all waited for leadership,' he wrote at Nuremberg, 'we waited for someone who would create work and nourishment, who would solve our social problems and would win the workers back for the nation. We waited as the Jews once waited for their Messiah.'[88] He found himself fascinated by the marked shift in allegiance of Lufthansa's salaried staff and workers from their previous acceptance of inevitable communism to an increasing support for Hitler's party.

His first personal contact with the National Socialists was Hermann Göring and he was undoubtedly captivated by the elegant Reichstag deputy. Göring was about five foot nine inches tall, energetic and dazzlingly handsome, with ice-blue eyes and great personal presence. He spoke well, and Milch was impressed by his adroit and persuasive manner during the debates on the civil aviation budget and by his expert knowledge and grasp of difficult subjects.[89] He was a year younger than the Lufthansa director and had been wounded in the stomach in the November 1923 *putsch* when government forces had opened fire; he had fled abroad and undergone medical treatment, as a result of which he had become a morphine addict, finally curing himself by the will-power of which at that time he had still been capable. He always spoke of Hitler in tones of awe and reverence; otherwise he never mentioned Party affairs.

The manner in which Milch joined the Nazi Party reflected the manner in which it worked. The Party files retained under close American custody in West Berlin contain a letter from Milch to the local branch, written after the seizure of power, justifying his plea for a rare, early membership number:

. . . Early in 1929 I declared to [the now] Reichsminister Göring my readiness to join the NSDAP. Reichsminister Göring asked me to wait until he could discuss with the Führer whether it would be in the Party's best interests for me to join then. Reichsminister Göring told me the Führer had decided I might regard myself as a Party member already, and a number would be reserved for me, but that the Party's purposes would be better served by my not officially joining, so that I could continue my work within Deutsche Lufthansa as laid down by Reichsminister Göring.[90]

He was first introduced to Hitler in Göring's apartment on the evening of the Reichstag's tumultuous reopening after further Nazi election victories on 13 October 1930. Josef Goebbels, Rudolf Hess and about a dozen members of the nobility were also there.[91] Hitler inquired about his previous career and work with Lufthansa and they spoke briefly about the development of Germany's civil aviation. Milch was captured by the Party's programme as Hitler unfolded it.[92] In retrospect it is likely that Göring's invitation of Milch to the gathering was not a casual courtesy: Hitler was preparing a fitting position for the Lufthansa director and clandestine Party member to occupy.

The airline was already paying out substantial sums of money. Early in 1930 it had issued contracts to the air industry for 8.6 million reichsmarks. For any major aircraft factory to survive it had to do as Milch directed. This brutal fact was brought home to the intractable Professor

Hugo Junkers during the year. To Milch's consternation the Dessau engineer Ernst Zindel had built an aircraft powered by a 650-horsepower BMW engine of which only prototypes were so far available; this was offered to Lufthansa. Milch had high praise for the cabin and general construction of the fuselage, but indicated to Junkers that he would prefer a three-engined version. The professor flatly rejected the idea, but the manager of BMW was on his way to America in any case and agreed to look out for a suitable engine of about five hundred horse-power.[93] He discovered there the Pratt and Whitney 'Hornet' engine, and secured manufacturing rights for BMW. Lufthansa's Dr Schatzki redesigned the aircraft—none other than the famous Junkers 52—to carry three Hornet engines. Professor Junkers still refused to co-operate, exclaiming: 'We don't have to toe Lufthansa's line!' Fortunately the usual financial crisis descended on Dessau, and Milch agreed to bail the company out only on condition that they manufactured the three-engined Ju 52 for his airline. With many misgivings the old professor gave in.*[94]

Lufthansa technicians moved into the factory and controlled the new plane's production. Milch sent his best pilot to test-fly it a few months later, on 15 June 1932.[95] His report was so enthusiastic that Lufthansa promptly entered the Ju 52 to the Zürich Air Meeting a month later. The new aircraft displayed the shortest take-off run, the best speed and the fastest climb, and it carried the greatest payload. It won a great victory in the round-the-Alps competition, although forced to fly blind with heavy icing much of the time.[96] Milch decided to convert his entire fleet to the Junkers 52. With the coveted Chavez-Bider Cup and the first prize of eleven thousand francs in his luggage he flew back to Munich; after lunch he took off for Berlin in the same aircraft. A thousand feet up an explosion tore the port-engine, landing wheel and part of the wing away. The ground rushed up towards them, but the pilot gave the two remaining engines enough power to clear some trees, levelled out and brought the heavy aircraft down in a field of uncut corn.[97]

It seemed the end of the dream: to lose an engine and half its wing the aircraft must have some basic design fault. Milch staggered clear of the maimed aeroplane and lit a cigar, blood soaking into his Lufthansa uniform from a gash in his neck. He was startled by a shout from one of the crew, inspecting the wing. There was a strange engine and a mangled propeller embedded in it—and a pair of human legs. They

* Milch again related this at an Air Ministry conference in December 1942, and added that it was documented in the files of Lufthansa: 'It won't have been the first time a bouncing baby was born to somebody quite without his wishing it!'

had survived a mid-air collision. A Flamingo trainer had rammed them head on from out of the sun. This incident, with the aircraft's relatively smooth emergency landing, was final proof of the plane's amazing robustness. Milch took the night express to Berlin, his last doubts about the plane removed. The Junkers 52 was a significant aviation success. The sturdy aircraft became the staple equipment of the later Luftwaffe's transport squadrons; altogether 4,845 were manufactured up to the end of the war, and thirty airlines in twenty-five different countries made it their standard medium-range airliner.[98]

In the meantime, the world economic crisis had struck the airline just as Milch had paid off its last debts. The depression was to last for the next two years in Germany and by the end of 1931 there would be 5.66 million unemployed.[99] For the second time he had the heart-breaking job of dismissing large sections of his staff, about 1,200 all told. He arranged some compensation for them this time—the older workers, and those with families, would get more cash and longer notice than the younger ones. Nor did he take the easy way out: on 16 September 1931 he himself assembled the one thousand aircraft-overhaul workers in a big hangar at Staaken airfield, stood on a table and broke the bad news to them.[100] When he finished, a workman asked if he might speak. He wanted to thank the director for coming in person with the bad news and not just pinning up a notice announcing the dismissals. The other workers murmured their approval. After Milch left the hangar the entire assembly signed a statement to the effect that should times improve they all wanted to return to Lufthansa. This was the spirit he had created.

Initially his loyalties had lain unconditionally with Hindenburg. In the presidential election of mid-March 1932 Hindenburg still enjoyed a huge majority over Hitler; Hitler was persuaded to stand again, and a second election followed in April. Deprived of the use of the mass news media, Hitler chartered a Rohrbach Roland from Lufthansa so that he could appear in two or three cities every day. Milch now met him more frequently, and when he attended Hitler's great meeting at the Sport Palace in Berlin on 4 April he was convinced that this was the leader Germany had been waiting for.[101] On the twenty-eighth he met Hitler again at Göring's new apartment in Badische Strasse, and found himself being asked remarkably pertinent questions on civil and military aviation.[102] Hitler openly told him that as soon as he seized power he would found a powerful air force in defiance of Versailles; did Milch believe this would be possible with four hundred million reichsmarks a year to start with? Milch replied that this sum was eight times the entire civil aviation budget, including the pilot training schools, research bodies and airfield construction.[103]

Milch now states, 'Hitler then spoke at length on the ideas of General Douhet.* As early as this he was principally interested in bombing warfare as the best means of deterring an aggressor. He talked of the importance of powerful armed forces, in which he saw the air force as occupying a position equal to the army's (at that time a totally novel concept); this was the only way for Germany to rid herself of the shackles of Versailles short of war itself.'[104] Never before had anybody spoken so vehemently to him, and of such grand plans.

In August Hermann Göring telephoned that Hitler was negotiating with Hindenburg on a coalition government in which he, Göring, would be setting up an 'Air Ministry'; and next day he asked Milch if he would leave Lufthansa and accept the position of state secretary in that ministry.[105] Milch asked for time to think it over. As things turned out, Hitler and Hindenburg failed to agree and Göring's plan fell through. Milch met Hitler socially twice more before the Nazis came to power: once on 31 August at Göring's Berlin apartment, surrounded by a dozen men later to occupy key positions in the Hitler government; and again a week later over a private luncheon at the Kaiserhof hotel, Hitler's headquarters in the capital.[106] In the general election of 6 November he voted for the first time in his life: along with fourteen million others, he voted for Hitler's party.[107] The election went badly for Hitler, but Göring turned to Milch again on the twenty-eighth and offered him the state secretaryship in the government of Prussia. Milch declined the offer.[108]

He was supremely content to be chief executive of Lufthansa. The credit for the airline's reputation was his alone. From China to South America the network of air routes controlled by his Berlin office was beginning to extend. At a postwar session of the Federal Chancellor's office, when it was diplomatically suggested that others had played a greater role in the airline's fortunes than Erhard Milch—by now discredited and convicted as a prisoner of the Allies in Landsberg—Konrad Adenauer interrupted the debate and stated: 'Ladies and gentlemen . . . What you are saying is just not true. Those other people, Stauss and Weigelt, they were just the bankers; the real architect of Lufthansa was Herr Milch.'[109]

---

* General Giulio Douhet was an Italian strategist of the twenties; in his study *The Command of the Air* he had predicted that future wars would be determined by ruthless bombing operations alone.

# THE LUFTWAFFE REBORN

## (*January 1933–May 1937*)

Two nights before Hitler's seizure of power on 30 January 1933 Göring appeared at Milch's modest Berlin flat with his state secretary, Paul Körner, and told him that Hitler proposed to create an Air Ministry in the new government with Göring as minister, and again appealed to him to accept the post of state secretary there.[1] That evening Milch was already host to a dozen guests, mostly Lufthansa directors; he suggested to his visitor two other names for the post, those of Brandenburg and Admiral Lahs, president of the Society of German Aircraft Manufacturers.[2] Göring rejected them out of hand: 'Make no mistake,' he said, 'I will not take no for an answer.' He gave Milch until Monday the thirtieth to decide.

On the Sunday afternoon Körner telephoned the still-unresolved Milch that Göring was saying he would make a perfect state secretary. Milch reminded him that he had not yet agreed.[3] On Monday the Lufthansa chairman and vice-chairman recommended him to accept the offer, provided he could remain honorary director of the airline as well.[4] For Milch one personal objection still remained; recalling that Göring had told him about becoming accidentally addicted to morphine in 1923, he delicately broached the subject again. Göring assured him that he had overcome the affliction.[5] He took him to see Hitler, newly appointed as Reich Chancellor, next day.[6] Hitler adroitly conquered Milch's last compunctions: 'I may not have known you for very long, but you are an expert in your own field, and we have nobody in the Party who knows as much about aviation as you. You must accept! It is not the Party calling you, it is Germany—Germany needs you in this office!' 'Thereupon,' Milch explained at his trial, 'I accepted.'

Initially there was no Air Ministry as such. Göring was appointed 'Reich Commissioner for Aviation' and Milch was his deputy.[7] They immediately began work on the enlargement of the existing secret air force. Since 1931 flying training had been carried on at the 'commercial pilot' training schools on behalf of the Reichswehr. Milch was aware of the German fighter and reconnaissance training school set up some years before on Russian soil at Lipezk, and as recently as September 1932 he had flown to Moscow and inspected the establishment built by the German Aeronautical Research Institute at Yagi for the secret development of new aircraft and aero-engines. Although about 120 fighter pilots and 100 observers passed through Lipezk, these beginnings in Russia had more political than military significance. It was in Germany itself that the dramatic expansion now took place.[8]

Hitler's policies centred on regaining Germany's strategic position, as he confided to the Reichswehr commanders within a few days of taking office.[9] This meant rebuilding the Wehrmacht as an instrument of foreign policy. Clearly, he said, 'the most dangerous time will be while the Wehrmacht is being built up. Then we shall see whether France has any statesmen, for if she has, she will not give us the time we need, but will fall upon us, most probably in concert with her satellites in the east.' Hitler's policy of rapid, concealed rearmament was transmitted to Milch in the shape of two basic dicta. Göring told him, 'I collect planes like others collect postage stamps'; and not unrelated to this, 'Money is no object'.* Otherwise Milch had a free hand. At a cabinet meeting on 9 February 1933 he was advised that forty million reichsmarks would be made available for aviation; in fact, encouraged by the new Defence Minister von Blomberg and Göring, he was soon dispensing sums of money far in excess of that budget.[10]

The War Office still believed that it would control the secret air squadrons. Milch and Göring knew differently. Milch shunned the office space offered him by the Transport Ministry as well—with its scent of centuries of mouldering documents and cobwebs of red tape—and moved instead early in March 1933 into the empty head office of a bank ruined in the Wall Street crash of 1931.[11] There, in Behrenstrasse, he occupied the former desk of Dr Hjalmar Schacht, who was now President of the Reich Bank; he had the old boardroom furnished for Göring, but Göring officiated there only twice.[12] A German Flying Sport Association, which had long existed to provide a legal basis for pilot training of 'amateurs', was absorbed into the embryo ministry later that month and a uniform designed for it—international air force blue, with one shoulder-lanyard.[13] The otherwise identical uniform of the State flying schools, training future military airmen, was distinguished by having two lan-

---

* The Defence Minister von Blomberg had a similarly generous attitude towards the financing of the Luftwaffe. On 18 October 1935 Milch noted him as saying, 'There is no ceiling on credit for the financing of rearmament!' By 1937 the ceiling was none the less found, as a raw materials crisis set in.

yards. Blomberg, an officer of considerable vision, furthered the new air force's cause with great impartiality—he was himself an infantry general—giving up some of his best army officers to fill the secret force's ranks. About 550 trained airmen were immediately transferred from the army and navy, followed by about four thousand young officers and NCOs volunteering for the new force.[14] Indeed Blomberg proved to be a more zealous visitor of air force units than Göring, and the most important orders of the following months were issued over Milch's name alone.

This was not surprising. Göring was constructing a new police state and was enmeshed in internal politics. It was not until 29 March that he realized the advances that had been made in aircraft and equipment design, when Milch took him to see Rechlin air station. He trusted Milch implicitly, and it was the state secretary who decided on the contours of the air force he was building. Instinctively, or perhaps from his talks with Hitler, he recognized that only a predominantly bomber force would deter Germany's neighbours from interfering in the rearmament programme. When Göring took him to Rome in April he made this point to the Italians. Mussolini agreed with this risky strategy. But General Balbo, his Chief of Air Staff, warned him urgently against defying Versailles: an all-fighter, all-reconnaissance force would be both safe and adequate, he considered. Later Milch was forced to reflect, 'Nowhere was the strategy of air warfare less heeded than in the native land of General Douhet.'[15] In their hotel that evening Göring thoroughly approved Milch's decision: 'Do as you think best,' was his only comment. The Italians promised to supply fighter aircraft and provide training facilities, but perhaps for political reasons the aircraft were never delivered.

Upon their return to Berlin the last army opposition to a separate Air Ministry had been overcome.[16] On 6 May Milch commissioned studies for a thousand-aircraft programme, a significant number of which was to be bombers.[17] Lufthansa's traffic manager submitted to him a detailed memorandum in which the concept of a provisional 'deterrent air force' (*Risiko Flotte*), with which any potential aggressor must reckon, was set out; Milch arranged with him that in the event of an emergency the airline should provide aircraft for five bomber *Staffeln* —flights of about nine aircraft.[18] On 10 May Blomberg directed that the air operations staff recently set up in his Defence Ministry under Colonel Bohnstedt—a monocled army officer of the old guard—should be transferred to the Air Ministry upon its formal activation on 15 May.[19] This order is rightly described as the 'birth certificate' of the Luftwaffe. Milch left Bohnstedt to his own devices. Blomberg's chief of staff, Reichenau, later told him that in appointing Bohnstedt, the then Chief of the Army Command General Kurt von Hammerstein had sardonically pronounced him 'the stupidest clot I could find in my General Staff'. This would ensure that nothing would ever come of the Luftwaffe.[20]

Hitler publicly announced his rearmament intentions in the Reichstag a few days later, justifying Germany's demand for at least token forces of the same types of weapons as in the hands of her neighbours.[21] At the Geneva disarmament conferences meantime the German representatives modestly requested permission to operate a force of five hundred fighter and reconnaissance aircraft. No mention was made of bombers.[22] As Blomberg stated to his commanders early in June 1933, it was illusory to expect any concrete concessions towards German military sovereignty at Geneva. Illicit rearmament was the only way. 'Over the next few years the Wehrmacht must devote itself wholly to the task of creating the reserves denied us until now. A Panzer army and an air force are to be established. The Officer Corps of the latter is to be an élite, fired only by the will to win. It will be necessary to give it preference over everything else, and this must be understood by the other branches of the Wehrmacht.'[23] When unidentified aircraft showered communist leaflets on Berlin on 22 June it was Milch who took this opportunity of drawing attention to Germany's impotence to defend her air space; he issued a public statement that their neighbours had ten thousand armed war planes, and demanded German equality.[24] At a meeting with Blomberg, Schacht and Raeder—commander-in-chief of the navy—Hitler openly praised the absent Milch's efficiency.[25]

Financing this rearmament was a problem of its own. Hitler put the complete programme's cost at thirty thousand million reichsmarks.[26] Milch was at the crucial cabinet meeting where the matter was resolved.[27] The Finance Minister, von Krosigk, told Hitler it would be impossible to raise funds for any grandiose armament programme, and the Prussian Finance Minister Popitz echoed his pessimism. At this juncture Schacht suddenly interjected, *'Herr Reichskanzler,* I have an idea how we could raise the money.' Hitler asked how much and the banker answered coolly, 'A few thousand millions.' Hitler asked Schacht what he would need, and the latter replied, 'The assistance of Herr Milch.' Milch was as speechless as his minister, as his contacts with Schacht had previously been minimal.[28] He went next day to see Schacht: the banker's proposal was a classic example of Keynesian economics. An old skeleton company—eventually the Metal Research Company 'Mefo' was chosen—should be guaranteed by the Reichsbank and used to cover the financing of industry with its own bills of exchange, of nominal validity of three months, automatically extended each time. These Reich-backed 'Mefo-bills' could be discounted at the Reichsbank at any time, and would go to selected big industrial concerns as payment. Milch and Schacht were the directors of the company. It was a neat economic trick, but not an illicit one.

The air force's armament over the next six years cost an average of three thousand million reichsmarks each year; thanks to 'Mefo' and the Air Ministry's insistence on the expanding air industry's finding its own capital for expansion, these figures were successfully concealed from public scrutiny. By the end of 1933 the air force was employing two million workers on airfield and factory construction.[29] Milch's target for late 1935, as discussed with Blomberg's chief of staff on 19 June 1933, was a force of six hundred front-line aircraft including nine bomber wings (taking Lufthansa's contribution into account). Both Milch and Reichenau opposed the allocation of any bomber or fighter units to the navy—a major error, vehemently opposed by Raeder, and subsequently regretted by Milch. The conference note concluded, 'This programme is to be carried out under camouflage as far as possible.'[30]

The camouflage was a necessity for the next two years. On 25 July Milch issued orders designed 'to make it impossible for foreign powers to prove actual violations of our existing foreign commitments' and 'to prevent foreign powers from deriving any clear picture of the rate of growth, or of the actual size and organization of the Luftwaffe we are founding'.[31] After confidential talks with the Transport Ministry, the Reichsbahn became the first railway concern in Europe to own an airline, conveniently operating only by night between two distant points, Berlin and Königsberg—the old Danzig Air Mail route.[32] These 'RB-routes' served only one purpose, the training of aircrews in long-distance overland night flying in multi-engined aircraft; the Reichsbahn airline was an offshoot of Lufthansa's auxiliary bomber wing. At the head office in Berlin a locked door barred access to the harmlessly named 'Traffic Inspectorate'; but its staff were in reality civilian-clothed Reichswehr officers organizing the airline for war mobilization and training its personnel in war tactics at courses known simply as 'navigation courses'.[33]

Colonel Bohnstedt eventually approached Milch with his own plans for the future Luftwaffe. He envisaged 144 fighters, twelve bombers and some reconnaissance aircraft, some two hundred aircraft in all. Milch told him that he was planning to have six hundred aircraft for his front line by 1935, predominantly bombers; Bohnstedt's jaw sagged and he had to sit down. Eventually he gasped, 'But this is terrible! Poor Germany!' Bohnstedt was retired in August, and a few days later a new organization came into effect which was to remain substantially the same for the next four years.[34] Soon Milch was considering a programme far in excess of the thousand-aircraft programme he had been thinking of in May, increasing the aircraft industry by twenty or thirty times to that end.

He had started this aspect of his work in March 1933, in tough negotiations with Junkers. The chief difficulty was the old professor himself, by now seventy-four years old, a convinced democrat and pacifist.[35] Both Göring and Milch insisted that he transfer his key patents on aircraft designs to the Junkers Aero-Engine and Junkers Aircraft companies before the Reich would issue contracts to them. Milch went one stage further and insisted on the dismissal of a number of Junkers's senior staff who had been identified as security risks.[36] The professor regarded it as a political vendetta and wrote a tragic commentary in his personal diaries. 'Political hatred is a bad coachman—it whips the horses until they bolt and the carriage ends up in the ditch.'[37] Early in April Milch summoned Junkers to his ministry and issued the first of many ultimatums to him, but the old man dug his heels in further; so he was forbidden to leave Dessau and this restriction was raised only at the end of May when he finally agreed to Milch's terms. This by no means marked the end of the affair, however.

With the Dornier and Heinkel aircraft companies the Air Ministry was on a surer footing. In June Milch sent Colonel Albert Kesselring, the brilliant administrative and financial expert provided for him by the army, to inspect the Heinkel works on the Baltic coast; the outcome was that Heinkel was invited to establish a big new factory at Rostock, a few miles away.[38] At the same time Milch issued to Messerschmitt's Bavarian Aircraft Company a contract for the construction under licence of Dornier 11 bombers. As each month passed his plans grew larger. In mid-August 1933 he ordered the establishment within twelve months of a dozen specialized air-training schools, for observers, bomb-aimers, air gunners, fighter pilots, mechanics and navy co-operation airmen.[39] He drew up a still larger aircraft production programme, reflecting the new emphasis he was properly placing on training. It provided for the manufacture of more than *four thousand* aircraft in the next twenty-one months, of which no fewer than 1,760 were to be turned over to the training units.[40] He converted factories manufacturing railway-locomotives, rolling-stock and shipping to the manufacture of aircraft and components; without Professor Junkers's knowledge, as early as 24 March he had entered into talks with the ATG railway-wagon factory, owned by his friend the wealthy industrialist Friedrich Flick, for the manufacture of Junkers aircraft.[41]

No industry had ever seen a revolution like it. Before Hitler's seizure of power the entire aircraft industry in Germany had employed less than four thousand workers; Junkers, with 2,200 employees, could construct only eighteen Ju 52 aircraft a year, provided all other types ceased production. Milch changed all that.[42] On 22 August he disclosed to Klaus Junkers, the professor's son, that the factory was to be given a contract for roughly one thousand Ju 52s and a number of the older W33 and W34 types to serve as trainers. Of these the first 178 Ju 52s and 45 of the others were to be delivered in 1934. It would mean a revolutionary new production system.[43] At the same time Milch ordered a thousand Dornier 11 and Dornier 13 aircraft from other factories. These planes were already obsolete, but he intended to instil into the money market confidence in the air industry as such, and give tens of thousands of workers vital experience in the newest techniques involved in aircraft and aero-engine manufacture.[44] By 1937, under Milch's leadership the air industry would be employing 230,000 men, of whom 121,000 were manufacturing airframes and 73,000 engines; and still the expansion would not be complete.[45]

Of all the departmental heads now officiating under Milch and Göring —Colonels Wimmer, Kesselring and Stumpff and the civil servant Fisch —none was to be rated so highly in retrospect as the man Milch selected to succeed Bohnstedt as the first real Chief of Air Staff. Originally the choice lay between two army colonels—von Manstein and Wever, but the Defence Minister assessed Manstein as somewhat old-fashioned, hostile to technological advance and certainly no admirer of aviation, so Milch asked for Wever, a level-headed officer who, though only a captain, had been Ludendorff's adjutant in the First World War. Blomberg released Wever only very reluctantly, saying he was losing a future C-in-C of the Army in doing so.[46]

Milch encouraged Wever, like all his senior staff, to learn to fly, and gave him Douhet's book to read. But Wever already had a mind of his own—he pondered night and day on the tactical and strategic problems of air power and in a short time had conjured up more bright ideas than all the professional airmen had between them. Late in August Milch had inspected the blueprints of the Heinkel 111 bomber at Heinkel's factory; this was a medium-range aircraft, suitable for hostilities with France or Germany's other neighbours.[47] He and Wever agreed that the next immediate requirement was for a heavy bomber, with a range characterized by Milch in the following words: 'It must be able to fly right round Britain under combat conditions.' This was principally for attacking Britain's shipping lanes. A specification was put out for a four-engined bomber for Dornier and Junkers to develop.[48] Not long after an excuse was found to give Göring an army general's uniform (he had refused any lower rank), and Blomberg settled that Milch should be appointed colonel, with just sufficient seniority to issue orders to his Chief of Air Staff. No use could yet be made of the Luftwaffe's real uniform, which Milch secretly demonstrated to Göring on 4 October.[49]

Hitler meantime withdrew Germany from the League of Nations and the Geneva Conference in mid-October 1933. While Hitler made cynical offers to the separate governments on the limitation of air forces and the prohibition of bombing, Milch issued the first firm production contracts for exclusively military aircraft.[50] Weeks of internal crisis followed the German withdrawal; Hitler played for time by asking the British to allow Germany a three-hundred-thousand-man army with no offensive weapons like tanks, heavy artillery or bombers, and he again proposed that poison-gas warfare and bombing of civilian targets should be absolutely prohibited.[51] All these suggestions were flatly rejected. Two days after the withdrawal Milch began a series of conferences on increasing aircraft production.[52] For several weeks Berlin expected military intervention by her neighbours: Göring was moved to deep depression,[53] and Milch's diary shows even old Gustav Krupp to have been flatly opposed to any action contrary to the spirit of Versailles, refusing to allow any participation of his armament works in the rearmament of Germany.[54] In Göring's absence in Sweden Milch began discussions with Blomberg on a secret Wehrmacht last-ditch directive for defending Germany if the worst came to the worst. It spoke of the Reich's resolve to resist, 'regardless of the prospects of success'. The secret air force was to defend Berlin and the mid-German industrial towns as best it could; Milch considered the time ripe to reread Douhet himself, and did so.[55]

Under this fearful prospect of foreign intervention he summoned an industrialists' conference on 20 October. One of Flick's directors, Dr Heinrich Koppenberg, wrote:

In addition to the ministry's top officials I saw not only aircraft and engine factory chiefs but also senior directors of the industry producing light-weight and heavy raw materials. The assembly was presided over by State Secretary Milch. He appealed to the dependability, loyalty, ardour and patriotism of those present, and indicated that for Germany the hour had struck for the construction of a new air force. The climax of the meeting was when Hermann Göring entered, silently greeted by all present with arms raised in salute. He announced that the Führer has ordered him to establish Germany as an air power *'within one year'*.[56]

The principal factory was Junkers. The process of removing the obstinate professor from his autocratic control of the factories and patents was not a gentle one. Weakened by old age, he had withdrawn to Bavaria and surrounded himself with lawyers to fight off the Air Ministry's claims. Milch had no desire to hinder his former chief's valuable pure research, but the Reich considered that it had a strong claim to the factories, having alone kept the company afloat by subsidies and inflated Lufthansa orders.[57] The professor was told bluntly that unless he agreed to sell control of his two companies to the Reich he would be banished from Dessau for ever;[58] in addition, the long-postponed criminal investigation of the Fili affair* would begin, and prosecution for treason (on a technicality) would be put in hand.[59] The professor still hesitated; he was thereupon fetched under police escort from his Bavarian retreat and flown to Dessau, where a public prosecutor repeated the threat of criminal proceedings. At 2 am on 18 October, after six hours of interrogation, the old man gave in and signed over fifty-one per cent of his companies to the Reich. Milch was informed of this at midday.[60] On the thirtieth he indicated to Koppenberg that he was going to appoint him chairman of both companies. Kesselring asked the Dessau criminal authorities to continue their investigation.[61] Faced with this persisting threat, Junkers relinquished his chairmanship of both companies on 24 November, and Koppenberg replaced him.[62]

On Party instructions the ailing professor was banished to Bavaria and never saw Dessau again. Milch undertook to lift the house arrest if he agreed to sell off his remaining shares to the Reich, and in mid-February 1934 the professor gave way here too, but even then he prolonged the actual negotiations and a new ultimatum had to be issued over Milch's name. It expired at 10 am on 30 August, but on Hitler's instructions Milch refrained from allowing any further measures against Junkers. In any case the latter's old age was about to put a natural end to the whole distasteful affair.[63] The ministry sent a party with a wreath to the funeral, but the family were so incensed that they threatened to stage it elsewhere. Milch's officers were fetched off the train half-way and ordered back to Berlin. From this time on there were few troubles with what Milch was to make one of the biggest industrial combines in the world.[64]

The new Junkers general manager was one of the most forceful personalities to break into the German air industry: robust, bull-necked and choleric, Koppenberg was a former mechanic who had made his name building a new steelworks for Flick. He expanded the Junkers

* See page 14.

companies with 'literally American bustle'.[65] On the day after his appointment he rented a railway locomotive repair factory at South Dessau; within six weeks he was producing fuselages for the Ju 52 aircraft there. In December 1933 he and Milch reached agreement on the construction of a modern factory next to the old one at Dessau, concentrating on conveyer-belt production methods; while in February 1934 the site was still an open field, three months later the buildings were complete and production had already begun. His ultimate target was the assembly of two hundred aircraft and one thousand engines a month, with other factories acting as component manufacturers.[66] By the end of 1934 the firm was employing four times as many workers as twelve months before. The fate of Professor Junkers, outlawed from his own home town and factory, remained an awful warning to all the other aircraft manufacturers.

Towards the end of January 1934 Poland signed a non-aggression pact with Hitler. Blomberg advised his commanders that after fifteen years of tension along their eastern frontier Germany could devote all her efforts to expanding the Wehrmacht. Hitler's aim was to keep this peace for a number of years, and even then he had no intention of attacking anybody, or at least so Blomberg emphasized. 'But at the end of that time the Reich is to be in a position to intervene actively in foreign affairs.'[67] Milch's papers show that he currently planned that by the autumn of 1938 they would be producing 525 bombers, 120 fighters and 127 other types of aircraft every month.[68]

Attention now turned to the threat of a French attack on Germany. As early as the summer of 1933 Milch had begun extensive air-raid shelter construction in Berlin.[69] His 1934 notes chronicle his growing concern with the west: one French bomb would suffice to immobilize Cologne's huge power station; they must have smoke-screens for the Ruhr; he recorded a demand from Hitler for 'special towers for flak, heavily armoured, rearing 100 feet above a city's skyline as a protection against low-level attack'; he was authorized to start building a vast new Reich Air Ministry building and a modern underground operations centre near Potsdam.[70] At the end of January he also studied ways of meeting the air force's needs for scarce materials under wartime blockade conditions. IG Farben was to investigate the large-scale production of synthetic fuels, with a twenty-million-reichsmark grant from Air Ministry funds. A similar grant was paid for research into synthetic rubber. AEG received three million reichsmarks to develop means of running power lines underground near airfields.[71] Money was still no object.

On 7 November 1933 Milch had obtained from Schacht a guarantee of over a thousand million reichsmarks for the financial year 1934–5.[72] The government budget publicly disclosed at the end of March 1934 revealed barely a fifth of this true amount, 210 millions, but even this was three times the amount of the previous year.[73] The German Foreign Office answered alarmed British official inquiries that the increase was largely necessary for the expansion of Lufthansa—the modernization of its aircraft fleet and establishment.*[74] The French were not deceived and protested to Britain that it was obvious that Germany was snapping her fingers at Versailles. When Milch, now a major-general, discussed this increasingly threadbare deception with Hitler, the latter replied: 'I could not tell a lie to benefit myself, but for Germany there is no lie I would not utter.'[75]

Seldom can deception have been practised on a larger scale: all over Germany the scars left by the air force construction programme were to be seen. Two million workers were building new airfields, emergency landing grounds and the ground control stations, flying schools and barracks that the new force would need; hundreds of men were being recruited every week. The new buildings sported nameplates like 'Air transport office of the Reich autobahn', 'Central German Display Squadron', 'Air Depot of Volunteer Labour Service' and 'South German Lufthansa Co.'[76] Lufthansa's commercial manager almost collapsed when he mistakenly received an astronomical bill for a new building for the latter company, an almost defunct subsidiary.[77] Word reached President Hindenburg and he sent for Milch: 'One hears so much these days about a "strategic air force". I'm an old army man myself and I don't understand much about this new-fangled idea. Would you like to explain it to me?' Milch asked him how much time he could spare, and Hindenburg replied, 'It depends how much time you need—I am an old man and can't spare long.' Offered a quarter of an hour, Milch diplomatically suggested eight minutes and was finished in seven. 'The way you explain it,' Hindenburg complimented him, 'I now understand it perfectly. Your ideas are well founded, even if somewhat unfamiliar to me at first. Keep on the same track even if others should not agree with you.' Twenty years later, Milch could still hear the deep, melodious voice of the president in his ears.[78]

By now his support for Hitler was unconditional. He understood nothing of Hitler's programme; he had begun to read *Mein Kampf* but had given up after the first twenty pages.[79] But he recognized the Nazis as

---

* When war broke out in 1939 Lufthansa contributed 116 aircraft for transport and training purposes.

the first party to succeed in fighting unemployment. Just after the seizure of power he had once accompanied Göring to Dortmund and been shocked by the starving and ashen-faced children clustering in the working-class streets; in mid-March 1934 he returned to the Ruhr with Göring and rejoiced at the change that had come about. At Nuremberg he was to say, 'It was small wonder that all of us believed in the man, after that, and that we would have said that anybody who predicted Hitler would lead us into a world war and would not stop until Germany was in ruins was a lunatic.'[80]

Yet the warning signs were there by 1934, and Milch was a first-hand witness of them, and particularly of the ruthlessness with which Hitler purged the SA, Ernst Röhm's brownshirt Party army. That Hitler was disturbed at the SA's military ambitions became evident to Milch early on, and was confirmed by a macabre incident involving the notorious Berlin SA commander, Ernst, and one of Milch's officers: after an exchange of insults outside a bar, fists had flown and Ernst's adjutant had threatened the officer with a drawn pistol; the Luftwaffe officer, one Lieutenant Schalke, had formally challenged him to a duel. The whole matter was chased up through official channels until the files landed on the desks of Milch and Röhm themselves, and Hitler also heard of the imminent duel; he sent for Milch and expressed his approval. Seeing the general's astonished expression, Hitler added, 'Ernst has been asking for this for some time!' He was visibly downcast when Milch explained that it was only Ernst's adjutant who was involved.[81] The duel took place and the brownshirt officer was adequately injured by the first fusillade. He was removed to hospital and he alone escaped the massacre which awaited all his colleagues a few days later.[82]

Among the indications that Röhm was planning to overthrow Hitler was a statement to Göring by the SA officer Theodor Croneiss, vice-chairman of Messerschmitt's aircraft factory and a life-long enemy of Milch, to the effect that he knew of the plans and had, moreover, been designated Göring's successor; that Röhm saw in Croneiss his future Air Minister is also known from Messerschmitt sources.[83] On 29 June Göring told Milch that the revolution was likely in the next few days; Milch was to take all necessary steps to defend air force installations.[84] He already had four companies of airmen, a total of about eight hundred, undergoing basic training under Colonel Kurt Student at Jüterbog airfield ('German Glider Research Institute, Spare Parts Depot') outside Berlin; he sent them to guard Berlin's airfields and the Air Ministry building in Behrenstrasse, and he ordered fighter planes, such as they were, to stand by. Körner later told Milch that Göring sent him that afternoon to Hitler in the Ruhr, with the final proof of Röhm's guilt—evidently telephone conversations intercepted by Göring's efficient *Forschungsamt*.\* Hitler flew south to root out the conspirators.

Next morning was 30 June. While flying in his trainer over Berlin Milch was recalled and ordered to report at once to Göring. At Göring's villa he found General von Fritsch, the new Army C-in-C, with Reichenau, Wever, Körner and the head of the SS, Heinrich Himmler.[85] 'My house looked like a castle of refuge,' Göring later said. 'They all felt safe in my house, so they came to me for protection. Even Herr Frick [Minister of the Interior] came slinking in, pale as a sicked-up pea!'[86] Körner told Milch that the Gestapo had captured execution lists drawn up by Röhm, on which were the names of Göring, Milch and many others. Göring personally forced his way into the SA's Berlin headquarters and arrested the lot of them; Ernst himself had fled to the north.[87] Hitler was in southern Germany, stamping out the wasps' nest there; a wave of executions was sweeping the Reich.

Milch was shown into a small inner room in Göring's villa. For the next half hour he was the witness—and the only surviving one who talked—of the execution council in session. Himmler was slowly reading out a list of names, none of which Milch recognized. Göring and von Reichenau were nodding assent or shaking their heads to each name in turn. If all were in agreement, Himmler dictated the name to Körner, adding curtly: 'Confirmation!' The singular atmosphere of this dark conclave is well illustrated by the moment when one of the three suggested a name evidently not on the list, a certain diplomat's aunt who had attracted much displeasure in Party circles for her excessive Nazi zeal ('A thousandfold *Sieg Heil!*'). All heaved with nervous laughter at the thought of including her. From time to time Paul Körner took the lengthening scroll of names outside, where others telephoned the instructions to trustworthy officers on the spot. It was obvious to Milch that the men listed were not being singled out for promotion.[88] Other authors have effectively quoted *Julius Caesar*: 'These many then shall die, their names are prick'd. . . . He shall not live. Look, with a spot I damn him!' From the evidence of Erhard Milch we know now that that was just the way it was. By the time he wrote his diary that night, about a hundred of the *putschists* had been shot.

That evening they drove in a fleet of black Mercedes limousines to Tempelhof airport to await Hitler's return. A Ju 52 arrived from the north, bringing back the SA commander Ernst, heavily manacled, from Bremen. Hitler landed not long afterwards, looking pale as death and

\* Literally 'Research Office'; the telephone-tappers were called 'researchers', but otherwise this name was purely camouflage.

graver than Milch had ever seen him. He greeted the waiting officials and SS and Party units paraded on the tarmac. Then orders rang out and four hundred airmen smartly presented arms—the two companies detailed by Milch to guard the airport. Hitler's face reflected his astonishment. He asked Göring who these uniformed men were; Göring asked Milch, and Milch replied that this was the new air force. Hitler complimented Göring: 'This is the first welcome sight today. The men have been well chosen for their race!'[89]

Within a few weeks the state secretary was mentally cataloguing a number of inconsistencies about the official version of the *putsch* given by Hitler in cabinet and in the Reichstag. All his endeavours to inspect the 'black list' said to have been drawn up by Röhm were unavailing.[90] Röhm himself had been executed. As for Croneiss, the informant, Göring took him under his wing after the bloody purge; he emerged with high rank in Himmler's now independent SS and was allowed to retain his very sensitive position in the German aviation industry until his death in 1942.[91]

Well-balanced though Milch's plans for the size and composition of the future air force were, the actual striking power would inevitably remain meagre for some years. At the beginning of July 1934 the ministry adopted a new aircraft construction programme under which 4,021 aircraft would be built during the next fourteen months, including 822 bombers; the rest were predominantly trainers and fighters.[92] Hitler, however, demanded that they set their sights still higher and summoned Göring, Milch and Wever to see him at Bayreuth at the end of July. Wever had long urged Milch to resist such demands, but Göring willingly complied with them and actually insulted Milch in front of Hitler when he raised practical objections. Wever weakened and sided with Göring, an act for which he apologized to Milch during the flight back to Berlin: he admitted that with the best will in the world Hitler's new target was impossible.[93] Milch knew that they could not train aircrew or squadron commanders, or build airfields, fast enough. In his opinion Göring wanted only a propaganda air force. Milch—by now a general—wanted the real thing.[94]

His relations with the Air Minister were already see-sawing sharply. Next time they went to see Hitler together, at Berchtesgaden in August 1934, Göring brushed him aside and said he would not need him to be present; Hitler overrode Göring's objection. Next day Göring apologized to Milch and at the end of the month confided to him that he had asked Hitler to approve him as the next Air Minister, should anything ever happen to himself.[95]

Despite the claims by Mr Winston Churchill that Germany's illegal air force was 'rapidly approaching equality with our own', the Luftwaffe was still weak, and it was tactically aligned not against Britain but against France.[96] We know from Blomberg's and Hitler's secret speeches of this period—particularly from a secret conference held by Blomberg on 9 October—that Germany's intention was to secure air parity with France, whose intentions Hitler suspected.[97] And there is a telling passage in General Milch's private notebook for the first months of 1935, in which he recorded—evidently after discussion with Hitler—what was to be Germany's future strength and political alignment. The German navy was to be thirty-five per cent of the British Royal Navy's size; the army was to be as big as the French army, and the Luftwaffe as big as the RAF or the French air force. No hostilities were envisaged with Britain at all; indeed, should armed conflict with the Soviet Union break out, as Milch quoted Hitler, 'We must fasten our hopes on Great Britain'.[98] In a further secret speech noted by Milch on 12 January 1935, Blomberg explained to his commanders: 'We must feign as much armed strength as we can, in order to look as powerful as possible to the western powers.' And he added, 'We are only putting together the scaffolding at present. The Führer gives us full credit for this—but he expects more.'[99]

In the same month Milch laid the foundation stone of the new Reich Air Ministry building in Leipzigerstrasse, Berlin. He cleared the site with characteristic inflexibility; when Hitler and Göring ordered the old Royal Prussian War Ministry on that site to be preserved as a historic example of the work of the Prussian architect Schinkel, Milch secured an expert opinion that it was not, and settled the dispute arbitrarily one night with five thousand demolition workers. Ten months later the new building was 'topped out', and a few weeks after that the first one thousand of the huge edifice's 4,500 rooms were being occupied.[100] All over Germany the still secret air force's new barracks and other installations were springing up, designed by some of the country's finest architects.[101] Milch issued orders for the construction of scores of 'caretaker' airfields—unmanned landing grounds about 500 yards wide and 1,100 yards long, already provided with the necessary underground fuel dumps and flarepath equipment, to be completed by the autumn of 1938.[102]

When Milch reported to Party leaders in Berlin in mid-February 1935 one of them, Reichsleiter Alfred Rosenberg, marvelled at 'the fact that within two years there has emerged from a completely naked country a Reich to be reckoned with, a Reich that even now nobody can affront with impunity'. And Göring—who had not bothered to visit the first secret units until 1 November the previous year—boasted at the same gathering, 'Apart from Russia, whose strength is somewhat obscure, Germany will have the biggest air force in the world by this autumn.'[103] Quantitatively this was not true, but qualitatively there could be no doubt: Junkers draughtsmen were already designing a fast medium bomber which was to become the famous Junkers 88, and Dr Koppenberg reported in the same month that preliminary work on the four-engined Ju 89 heavy bomber was complete.[104] Simultaneously Milch fashioned the mould for the new Luftwaffe's officers in a basic directive: 'It is a fundamental requirement for staff and technical officers of the higher echelons to have had practical operational experience,' he laid down. And, conversely, 'The paths to the very highest positions of command are open to every officer suitable for them.' He wanted the best men for the job, without favouritism and without fear.[105]

„Und siehe eh' der Morgen graut,
hat er die Luftwaff'aufgebaut!"

Göring builds the Luftwaffe: 'And look as morning dawns afar,
our man has built the Luftwaffe!'  (*Sketch by Ernst Udet*)

The existence of a German air force was by now an open secret. At the Berlin funeral of an airman Milch saw one boy pointing to the uniformed airmen present and whisper loudly to his friend, 'The ones with the two shoulder-straps are the real ones; the others are just pretending!'[106] During February 1935 Hitler signed a decree that on 1

March the 'Reich Luftwaffe' would be founded, as a third service next to the Reich army and the Reich navy, with the present Air Minister Göring as its first C-in-C.[107] At the same time Blomberg authorized Göring to uncamouflage the air force, 'step by step', while carefully avoiding any measure which might provoke public comment.[108] In executing these orders Wever decreed that the size, type and composition of the Luftwaffe's units were to remain as secret as before.[109] In the event Hitler's nose was put out of joint by a premature British government announcement of a significant strengthening of the RAF, and the formal and somewhat circumlocutory disclosure of the existence of a Luftwaffe was made at attaché level on 10 March.

In Milch's eyes this violation of Versailles, and the introduction of conscription a few days later, was the most critical moment, when the Versailles signatories would have been justified in intervening. Nor could Germany have offered much resistance: of the 2,500 aircraft in the new Luftwaffe only some 800 were of front-line types and these were distributed among the training school as well as the operational squadrons. When Hitler, Göring and Milch inspected the new service on 28 March, the fighters mustered by the 'Richthofen' squadron for its fly-past were still diminutive Heinkel 51 biplanes. By the autumn of 1935 the Luftwaffe had reached the target of 1,800 first-line aircraft set by Milch in July the previous year, but on 7 October Göring informed him that the uncertain political situation called for even faster rearmament, and Blomberg also appealed to him to increase aircraft production.[110] The industry currently numbered fourteen major factories, including Junkers, Arado, Messerschmitt, Dornier, Focke-Wulf and Heinkel. On the twenty-fourth Milch asked for 616 million reichsmarks more to cover the expense of this acceleration of the programme.[111] Within two years the list of major factories had swollen to thirty-six.

General Wever's Air Staff had meanwhile prepared specifications for some of the world's most advanced aircraft. At Rechlin research station in March 1936 test pilots were already flying prototypes of the Messerschmitt 109 fighter aircraft, of the Me 110 twin-engined long-range fighter, the Ju 87 and Henschel 123 dive-bombers and of the Do 17 and He 111 medium bombers. There was even an early Ju 88 bomber undergoing trials. The Dornier company had built three prototypes of the important Do 19 four-engined heavy bomber, and Junkers had built two Ju 89s—these in a year when the specification for a four-engined bomber was only just being issued in Britain.[112] Of all these the Heinkel 111 seemed to be the standard bomber of the future; it could carry a ton of bombs and was fast by modern standards. The

Air Ministry invited Dr Heinkel to construct a large new factory at Oranienburg outside Berlin, capable of producing no fewer than a hundred of these bombers a month; Heinkel accepted and the first turf was cut on the empty site in May 1936. One year later he handed over the first He 111 manufactured there.[113]

Politically, the Wehrmacht considered that it was not rearming in a vacuum. In a document issued late in 1935 the Luftwaffe summed up: 'France has evidently determined on war, if her extensive military preparations are anything to go by'; it was furthermore accepted that should such a conflict break out, Lithuania and Czechoslovakia would remain neutral only so long as this served their own interests.[114] Early in November Blomberg invited the three services to develop a working basis for joint strategic planning; after a meeting of the principal Luftwaffe commanders presided over by Milch on the sixteenth Wever signed the Luftwaffe's part of the 'Wehrmacht Study', as the planning document was called, two days later.[115] France and Czechoslovakia were seen as the only potential enemies. For political reasons, the Luftwaffe was to avoid the role of aggressor at all costs. Without Göring's express orders no frontier was to be crossed and there was to be absolutely no entry into the demilitarized Rhineland—or even overflying of it by Luftwaffe aircraft—until a deliberate violation of German frontiers had been established by the enemy. The Luftwaffe assumed that the French air force would begin any French attack with a surprise air raid, 'probably without any declaration of war'. The Luftwaffe's primary task would be the destruction of the French air force and its bases, followed by a rapid switching of most of the bomber squadrons to the east and the destruction of the Czech air force. Considerable importance was attached to air reconnaissance, but little to strategic air warfare—a number of French and Czech arsenals, munitions factories and wireless stations were listed by name as targets, but curiously reserved for 'reprisal attacks for raids on German towns'.

Both Göring and Milch were taken by surprise by Hitler's sudden decision to march into the demilitarized Rhineland in March 1936. The state secretary was away on a month's leave when the Führer first mentioned this new intention to Blomberg on 13 February—a result of the imminent ratification of a Franco-Soviet treaty.[116] No word reached Milch until the eve of the day chosen, when General Wever telephoned that he was required immediately in Berlin.[117] As he entered his aircraft at Munich airport next morning, 7 March, he heard loudspeakers relaying Hitler's announcement that at that moment German troops were marching into the Rhineland. In all Germany, as Milch knew, there were only three fighter squadrons, and since the eastern frontier could not be left denuded only one of these could be spared for the west; this was divided between airfields at Cologne and Düsseldorf and a dive-bomber squadron was also transferred to the Rhineland that day. The fighters carried a thousand rounds of ammunition each, but their machine-guns had not been adjusted. With this small cast the Luftwaffe laid on a great spectacle—it was like the Danzig Air Mail all over again, only this time the paint-pot and brush were used to multiply the number of aircraft in evidence, not reduce them.[118] The fighter squadron was flown round from one airfield to the next, changing its insignia between each demonstration. Freshly painted nameplates were displayed outside harmless training schools, proclaiming them to be fighter or bomber wings. Not for the last time, the French were taken in.

The first Luftwaffe training manual on air strategy was issued by General Wever in May 1936. It was remarkable proof of Wever's and Wilberg's farsightedness, for although both officers were rooted in the traditions of the army, and of army air support, the manual set out a clear blueprint for the Luftwaffe's lightning successes three years later in Poland and France. It became the basis of all staff training at the Air Staff College at Gatow. 'Air power carries the war right into the heart of enemy country from the moment war breaks out,' ran one paragraph. 'It strikes at the very root of the enemy's fighting power and of the people's will to resist.' The Luftwaffe's duty was to fight for air supremacy; that achieved, it was to support the land and sea battles where necessary, or attack the enemy's resources—his industrial potential, his food supplies, his vital import routes, his transport and governmental centres. But the manual expressly ruled out attacks on civil populations in paragraph 186: 'Attacks on cities for the purpose of terrorizing the civilian population are absolutely forbidden.'[119]

All the greater was the tragedy which overtook the young air force on 3 June when Wever was killed piloting his own aircraft. His successor was General Kesselring, the tall, happy-go-lucky Luftwaffe chief of administration, who had played an important part in the growth of the air industry and the construction of the ground establishments. Milch felt that his knowledge of strategy and air tactics was very limited, however, and Kesselring's appointment caused widespread controversy; the two generals worked together for barely a year—with Kesselring overwhelmed by the contempt of the career officer for the 'managing director' who was state secretary, and Milch magnifying every error committed by the newcomer to create incidents of almost diplomatic magnitude. Milch marshalled the aircraft industry on his side and Kesselring was replaced in 1937 by General Stumpff, a more satisfactory candidate in Milch's view; Kesselring joined Göring's camp.

Kesselring's appointment in June 1936 was accompanied by another, seemingly minor reshuffle of the ministry's officers. The head of the technical department, General Wimmer, and his two chief assistants, Colonel Loeb and Colonel Wolfram von Richthofen (cousin of the famous air ace), were the architects of the Luftwaffe's technical advance; unhappily, Göring found Wimmer somewhat mulish and pedantic and decided to replace him.[120] As a successor he selected Ernst Udet, a popular First World War fighter pilot who had rejoined the Luftwaffe twelve months before with the rank of colonel. Udet—Bohemian, boisterous and likeable—had formed an intimate friendship with Milch and had joined the regular company at Milch's table at Horcher's, the leather-panelled gourmet's restaurant in Berlin. He was a virtuoso pilot, used to thrilling interwar crowds with his act at air displays, picking up pocket handkerchiefs with a hook fastened to the wingtip of his plane. He had taught Milch to fly, and on their sixth flying lesson had shouted

Ritter von Greim, Chief of Luftwaffe personnel (and Göring's 1945 successor).    (*Sketch by Ernst Udet*)

to him that he now had complete faith in him and threw his control-column overboard—a wooden dummy he had smuggled aboard especially for the purpose.

Udet was not at that time Göring's friend—quite the contrary, for in 1918 it was Udet who was elected chairman of the Richthofen Veterans' Association, although Göring had been the squadron's last commander; Udet had moreover challenged the authenticity of many of Göring's 'kills' as a fighter pilot, hinting that he had cheated by claiming for himself the unclaimed enemy aircraft credited to his squadron; eventually Udet had thrown him out of the Association altogether. Knowledge of this was the hold that Ernst Udet had on the minister, and Göring admitted this privately to Milch.[121] Milch for his part suspected that Udet's appointment was Göring's shrewd attempt to silence someone who had Hitler's ear on air matters. He later wrote, 'Hitler recognized in Udet one of the greatest pilots, and he was right. But he also saw him as one of our greatest technical experts, and here he was very mistaken.' As an inspector of fighters or of dive-bombers Udet would have been in his element; but now he was put in charge of the Luftwaffe's technical department, a desk job requiring concentration, hard work and vision. He was neither a beaver like Milch, nor an administrator like Kesselring; easy-going and increasingly dissolute, Udet allowed the Luftwaffe's technical lead to wither away, and in time he was to prove Göring's own undoing.[122]

In the Spanish Civil War the Luftwaffe found its first active involvement. General Franco appealed to Hitler to help him transport his insurgent forces from Tetuan in North Africa to the Spanish mainland. Hitler was at Bayreuth when the Spanish delegation arrived in Berlin; Milch referred them to Blomberg, and Canaris, Blomberg's foreign intelligence chief, introduced them to Hitler and Party officials at Bayreuth on 25 July 1936, Göring summoned Milch to Bayreuth with Stumpff next morning and reported that Hitler was in favour of German intervention on Franco's behalf, without actual participation in the fighting. Milch flew back to Berlin for an immediate meeting of his departmental heads with the Spanish officers and Stumpff; their first action was to set up a special unit (*Sonderstab*) 'W' under Wilberg, to coordinate the airlift of Franco's troops to Seville in southern Spain.[123]

The first Ju 52 transport plane left Tempelhof on the very next day for Spanish Morocco, transferred to a hastily registered 'Hispano-Moroccan Transport Company (Tetuan-Seville)'; a score more followed, crewed mostly by Luftwaffe reservists. On 31 July Milch took leave of the first eighty-five volunteers, who were formally discharged from the Luftwaffe and equipped with plain clothes; six He 51 biplane fighters accompanied them on the voyage to Cadiz. A week later this advance party, camouflaged as the 'Union Travel Association', was in

Seville. About 270 tons of assorted equipment and ammunition joined them there.[124] During August the transports ferried about ten thousand Moroccan troops to Spain. Milch kept Blomberg, Neurath (the Foreign Minister), Raeder and Göring regularly briefed, for at this stage he was in charge of the entire German intervention.[125] The He 51 proved surprisingly inferior to the Russian-built aircraft opposing them, so on 29 October the decision was taken to send more modern equipment, backed up by bomber and fighter squadrons; the new Me 109 would have to be rushed to Spain as soon as possible. When proof was found that Russian-made bombs were being used against Franco's troops, Hitler on the same day approved full-scale military intervention by the Luftwaffe (as Mussolini had said to Milch in Rome two weeks before, 'Communism *is* war!').[126]

Under the code-name 'Rügen Winter Exercise', the Luftwaffe embarked a large force of volunteers under Major-General Hugo Sperrle for Spain; a similar force of army volunteers would be commanded by General Walter Warlimont. This new force fought in Spain as the 'Legion Condor'. On 6 November the first bomber squadron of KG 88 left German soil; Milch saw the unit proudly off at Greifswald airfield, Göring having written, 'Milch is to stand in for me' on the bomber squadron's invitation to the ceremony.[127] Thus the Luftwaffe was now embroiled in war on foreign soil. Altogether the Legion Condor was to achieve a strength in Spain of about five thousand men, with two hundred assorted aircraft. In mid-November word reached the state secretary of the first Luftwaffe 'kill' in Spain, and at the same time of the death of one of his friends in action.[128]

The international reaction to these German 'volunteers' was immediate and hostile. Göring told Milch that Britain had lodged a formal protest. At a meeting with Milch and his departmental heads early in December he reflected that Germany had strictly 'wanted peace until 1941'; now anything might happen: 'We are already at war, if not a shooting one.' It seemed that Russia wanted war, and it was obvious that Britain was rearming very fast. His familiar demand was that the Luftwaffe expand still faster, 'without regard for financial difficulties'. From the New Year all his factories were to operate on a wartime basis, geared to the production of aircraft, weapons and equipment rather than to putting the finishing touches to barracks and airfield accommodation.[129]

Once Göring had bragged to the Finance Minister, 'You know, when I want to expand the Luftwaffe, I send for Milch. Then he always says, "We can't exceed such-and-such a limit, as that would dilute it too much." So I kick him up the arse and he multiplies the front line in a matter of weeks!' Milch heard of this vulgar appraisal and contradicted Göring: 'The only one to get his backside kicked is the one who offers it. And don't expect that from me!'[130] It is impossible to put a firm date on the final freeze in Göring's relations with his state secretary; the jealous career officers surrounding the minister will have done little to defend Milch, the ambitious executive, the civilian in uniform (and a general's uniform at that).

The cooling off was at first perceptible only in minor details, which even then the sensitive Erhard Milch might have been exaggerating were it not for the subsequent undeniable decline. Göring no longer invited him to share his foreign leaves or be his guest at his hunting lodge during the annual Nuremberg Party rallies; Milch's name disappeared from Göring's Christmas list; when the minister himself designed a Luftwaffe brooch it seemed that every other ministry lady from the most humble clerk's wife upwards received one, but not Frau Milch. For Göring, the last straw came when Hitler said in a public speech, 'Two names are ineradicably linked with the birth of our Luftwaffe— Göring and Milch. . . .' The minister took to interviewing Milch's subordinates over his head. ('There is no need to tell your chief of this,' he would assure them.) Thus we are no longer surprised to find that while Milch was in Berlin one day in November 1936, Göring was conferring with Udet at the minister's new opulent forest palace, Karinhall, about far-reaching plans for the standardization of airframes and aero-engines.[131] The minutes of these discussions were not shown to Milch. Göring was wont to explain, 'That's the way the Führer works, as well.'

The ministry's telephone operators heard increasingly caustic exchanges between the two. More than once Milch slammed his receiver down, and when Göring once rang back to apologize for their having been cut off, Milch retorted: 'We weren't cut off. I hung up on you. I don't want my switchboard staff getting the impression our minister has no manners!' It was like a marriage going hopelessly wrong, but neither was in the position to end it. Göring dared not dismiss Milch, for he was still creating the Luftwaffe, and Milch had Hitler's confidence; Milch for his part was enthralled by the task and by the power he wielded as the force grew in his hands. But he suffered deeply under Göring's humiliating actions. On 26 November he threatened to resign, and when this was brushed aside he stubbornly indicated that he was not the minister's slave and hinted that a German officer always had one way out of an impasse. He motioned towards his revolver.[132] Göring reproached him that people were beginning to speak of Milch as though *he* were the C-in-C and minister: when the first bomber squadron had left for Spain, it was Milch who had taken the salute at Greifswald. Milch hotly reminded him of his own words on the margin of the invitation, 'Milch is to stand in for me'. Göring denied having written any such injunction; Milch sent his elderly Central Office chief, Witzendorff, to bring the letter out of the files, but Witzendorff apologized and said that there was no such letter there.

Not until six years later was that particular mystery resolved. Witzendorff retired and confessed, weeping, to Milch that he had been ordered by Kesselring to destroy the letter so as to damage the state secretary. Other officers on the Air Staff also admitted to Milch that they had had a hand in the intrigue. As the New Year, 1937, dawned, we can accept that the Seven Years' War between the Air Staff and General Milch, the outsider, was only just beginning.

The increases in the Luftwaffe's production planning were followed with growing alarm by the British government. The German authorities confidentially imparted to the British authentic details, late in 1936, of their intentions.[133] In Hitler's view such exchanges were to be welcomed; still fired by his dream of a great Anglo-Saxon alliance, uniting Germany's powerful armies, Britain's command of the seas and the RAF and Luftwaffe in joint domination of the skies, he authorized Milch to invite senior RAF officers to study the Luftwaffe's secrets.[134] Milch believed this very necessary in view of the enormous exaggerations appearing in the British press.[135] The outcome was a unique exchange of information between two rival air forces which only three years later were locked in combat in each other's skies. The RAF sent to Berlin two air vice-marshals, Courtney and Evill, and two intelligence officers; Milch showed them every Luftwaffe establishment of importance during the next few days. They saw the Richthofen fighter wing, the Air Staff College and the original Heinkel production line on the Baltic coast; Germany's most advanced aircraft, like the He 111, the Ju 86, the Ju 87 and the Do 17 bombers were demonstrated to them, and they were verbally informed of their performances to enable them to make precise comparisons.[136] Milch requested the British party not to take written notes, and expressed anxiety that none of the secret information should go beyond the British Air Ministry, and certainly not to the Foreign Office which would channel it directly to Paris if it could. Courtney undertook that, when he reported to the Air Ministry, he would pass on these wishes. At Courtney's request General Milch set out the bare facts of the Luftwaffe construction programme initiated in 1934; it was due for completion in 1938, by which time Germany would have thirty bomber squadrons, six dive-bomber squadrons and twelve fighter squadrons—a Luftwaffe first line of about 2,340 aircraft including immediate reserves. He enlarged at length to the British air marshals on his political views as a soldier, and stressed that Germany desired nothing more than rapprochement with the principal western Powers. The information he gave broadly was complete, honest and accurate (indeed, Kesselring denounced him to Göring for high treason, for disclosing as much as he had).*[137]

Two weeks later Major-General Wenninger, the German air attaché in London, was called to the Air Ministry there and given similar details on the RAF: 'according to current planning' the RAF would dispose of 1,736 aircraft in its first line, plus one-third more 'immediate reserves' without pilots, by the end of 1938; this force would comprise 1,022 bombers and 420 fighter aircraft, plus a number overseas. The British intimated that the RAF would welcome even closer contacts with the Luftwaffe and invited an official German delegation to visit London that autumn.

From Douhet's writings Milch knew that the Luftwaffe could never be big enough to meet every strategic demand—the multiplicity of possible targets was daunting. After the British officers had left Berlin he wrote for Göring a long confidential study, reminding his minister that by mid-1937 they would have a total of 36 bomber- and dive-bomber squadrons, but that Germany alone now had over two thousand industrial plants classified as 'vital' for war production, while her 'largest neighbour' (France) had over ninety explosives factories, thirty poison-gas factories and fifty aircraft production plants. Since the Luftwaffe would be occupied with tactical operations and with the destruction of the enemy air force, some time would pass before it could turn to true strategic air war. The quicker the enemy air force was destroyed the better. 'The Luftwaffe's ideal is therefore to cross the frontier simultaneously with the declaration of war, or even better, to launch its attack on the enemy's air bases *in lieu of* a declaration of war.'[138] The lengthy study could with profit have been read by Göring, but Bodenschatz returned it to him with a note reading, 'The colonel-general [Göring] has taken note of it, but asks you to send it to him again some time.' The initial surprise air attack on the enemy's air force became

* Air Chief-Marshal Courtney informs the author that doubt was left on one point: according to Milch this programme was 50 per cent complete, but this did not tally with the figures secured by British Intelligence. The Germans subsequently admitted that the half-way mark had been reached in the spring of 1936, nine months earlier.

the Luftwaffe's trademark however, opening the campaigns in Poland, France, Yugoslavia and Russia; and it was imitated with equally devastating effect by Israel in the Six-Day War.

Of the three Wehrmacht branches, Milch considered only the army fortunate in its C-in-C, von Fritsch. Raeder he classed in the same category as Göring: 'Stupid lecture by Raeder at Defence Ministry in presence of Führer and others,' he recorded at this time; Raeder had expounded the possibilities of naval war against the United States, based on ports in Mexico and South America.[139] Raeder for his part could not stand Milch, and when the Reich dedicated a Jutland memorial in 1936 he announced that if Göring's state secretary were invited to stay aboard the Führer's yacht, *Grille,* then he, Raeder, would not.[140] But Milch's loyalty towards Hitler was still inalienable. On 30 January 1937 Hitler presented the golden Party emblem to him at a special cabinet meeting.[141]

Göring recognized that he could not wholly dispense with Milch. He needed the dynamo to power the ministry, and to strengthen his own position with Hitler. The Reich's strong men—Blomberg, Himmler, Hess and Goebbels—were frequent guests at Milch's table, seeing in him perhaps a future Air Minister.[142] By the spring of 1937, however, Göring's satraps were hinting to him that Milch was no longer indispensable. Udet was looking after the technical side, assisted now by Major Hans Jeschonnek, the youthful former staff officer to Milch who now commanded the Operational Development Wing at Greifswald; Kesselring had tactical matters well in hand. As ill-fortune would have it, Milch was stricken by appendicitis at this time. The Air Staff and Göring were conspicuous by their lack of sympathy for him.[143] Upon his recovery he called a departmental conference; Kesselring stayed ostentatiously away.[144] Milch convalesced in Italy. Upon his return Göring had no time to see him, so he left Berlin again for a mountaineering holiday in the Alps. In mid-April 1937 Milch at last had a 'scarcely satisfactory' debate with his minister. Göring broke it to him that now that his internal political duties were less arduous he intended to take over direct control of the Luftwaffe himself. Two days later he departed himself for Italy.[145]

Weeks before, in Milch's absence, he had already taken a crucial decision.[146] He had ordered the scrapping of both the four-engined heavy bomber prototypes developed by Junkers and Dornier to meet the requirement issued by Milch and Wever four years before. The Ju 89 and the Do 19—the latter with its 110-foot wingspan and 19 tons take-off weight—were generally considered to be far ahead of their time.

Only later did Milch learn of this arbitrary decision and how it had come about: Kesselring and Jeschonnek had suggested to Göring that it would be better to drop the heavy bomber projects in view of the pressure on scarce raw materials.[147] The records do indeed show that of the 4,500 tons of aluminium required monthly for aircraft manufacture, only about half was currently available.[148] Göring had inquired, 'How many twin-engined aircraft can we make for each four-engined one?' The reply was 'About two and a half.' 'The Führer,' concluded Göring, 'does not ask me how big my bombers are, but how many there are.'[149]

The Luftwaffe reorganization decided on by Göring at the same time had equally disastrous effects, in Milch's eyes. Göring revealed it to him in broad outline during May 1937. He intended to carve the whole ministry into two establishments—a ministerial side, under Milch, and a command side as a separate entity under the Chief of Air Staff, who would be equal in status to Milch and responsible only to Göring; Milch would 'inspect' the Luftwaffe, but nothing else. 'Only half a solution,' was how Milch described it.[150] He doubted whether Göring —in whom Hitler had some months before vested the enormous Four-Year Plan undertaking—would really have the time, energy or inclination to devote himself to linking these two entities. On the last day of May he was shown Göring's final draft for the reorganization: 'Now that the construction of the Luftwaffe has reached its provisional conclusion,' Göring wrote, 'I intend to apply to the Luftwaffe's structure a form relevant to command problems in war as well as peace.' In future he would exercise 'sole and immediate' command over the Luftwaffe. Milch would no longer act as his permanent deputy. The pious hope was expressed that although Milch and the Chief of Air Staff would now be equal in status they would keep each other informed on all basic matters. This order Göring signed in person.[151]

A few weeks later Göring removed both the Personnel Department (under von Greim) and the Technical Department (under Udet) from Milch's control and elevated them to equal status with Milch and the Chief of Air Staff. He promised to invite Milch to join all their discussions, but broke this promise within a few days as both Udet and Greim were summoned to confer with him without Milch learning of it until afterwards.[152] In this period Milch saw all his worst fears confirmed. Göring took only sporadic interest, discussed problems with his departmental heads alone as before, asked nobody's advice, tolerated no contradiction, cursed people in their absence and extolled his own virtues. 'And all the time,' described Milch, 'he scribbled little notes, usually in a different book each day, without anybody being able to see the point of it all, since he invariably forgot or distorted what had been under discussion.'[153]

Reviewing the causes for the Luftwaffe's eventual defeat, Milch was to list this 1937 reorganization first and foremost. One minor episode serves to illustrate the Byzantine art of Hitler's paladin: several times Göring warned Milch to watch out for General Stumpff's intrigues; Milch at once mentioned Göring's warning to the Chief of Air Staff himself, and Stumpff replied in astonishment, 'But that is precisely what the colonel-general said to me about you only a few days ago!' At the beginning of the war that was to follow Milch cornered his C-in-C in a quiet moment and rebuked him. 'The ancient Romans had a motto: *divide et impera,* divide and rule. But the Romans applied this only to their enemies, while you seek to do so against your friends. I cannot anticipate much success for you.' Göring made no comment.

# MORE BLUFF THAN BLOOD

## (*July 1937–September 1939*)

In his 1937 directive on combined Wehrmacht planning for the contingency of war, the Defence Minister, von Blomberg, stressed that it was of continued urgency to secure Britain's friendship. Should France decide to attack Germany, or should Germany first decide to attack Czechoslovakia—France's ally in the east—Britain's neutrality would be of paramount importance to Hitler; because if Britain sided with his enemies she would undoubtedly try to win the Low Countries as bases for her air force to attack Germany's industrial centres in the west.[1]

These fears led to further exchanges between Britain and Germany. Ernst Udet was sent to participate in the British air display at Hendon; the chief designer of the Bristol Aircraft Company was shown round German aircraft factories and opened negotiations for the sale of Bristol aero-engines to Germany.[2] On 1 July 1937 Lord Trenchard, the founder of the RAF, visited Berlin. He asked whether Germany would ever use poison gas; Milch gave him a solemn undertaking that Germany would not initiate such warfare.[3]

At the end of July Hitler allowed the new Luftwaffe to flex its muscles at the fourth international air meeting at Zürich. Milch captained the German team. Udet flew a special Me 109 fighter, but the principal event was the bomber competition: the Dornier 17, the latest German bomber, proved to be faster than any foreign *fighter* taking part, an unwelcome surprise to many countries present. The RAF did not compete, but Milch willingly allowed the British experts to inspect the new German equipment, particularly the advanced Daimler-Benz 600 and 601 engines.[4] Back in Berlin he tried to report all this to Göring; the minister received Udet but did not grant Milch an audience until September, when he quietened the mutinous state secretary by reminding him he was the one he had nominated as his successor, in his will.[5]

The increase in the Luftwaffe proceeded, but not as planned. In September Göring approved Milch's estimate of three thousand million reichsmarks for this programme in 1938; but money alone was not enough, as raw material shortages had become increasingly apparent, particularly in the supply of iron and steel as the Services competed for them.[6] Early in June Hitler had asked Blomberg to report on the effect of these shortages on rearmament, and late in August the Air Ministry had to warn that because of them there would have to be 'a significant reduction in the Luftwaffe's rate of expansion'.[7] The complete equipment of the squadrons would not be achieved until April 1939, a delay of six months on their original target. By the end of October 1937 even this prediction was recognized as over-optimistic, and Milch advised Göring that the iron and steel deficit was such as to set back some elements of the next five years' production programme by as much as another five years.[8]

Even as it was, the Luftwaffe was already a formidable weapon, as it showed in full-scale Wehrmacht manoeuvres late in September 1937. It contributed over 62,000 uniformed Luftwaffe officers and men and 22,500 civilian officials and workers; and it fielded 1,337 aircraft, 639 flak guns, 160 searchlights and 9,720 motorized vehicles.[9] The manoeuvres began with a simulated surprise air attack on Berlin early on the twentieth. Large-scale army movements followed across open countryside between Berlin and the Baltic, witnessed by Hitler with Mussolini as his guest. In the Luftwaffe's new communications aircraft, the diminutive Fieseler 'Storch', Milch visited the battlefields, alighting without difficulty in pocket-handkerchief areas among the astounded troops. He had issued the 'Storch' specification in 1933, strongly opposed by Richthofen who saw no future for such a plane. It was to perform incredible feats during the war, including the rescue of the bulky Fascist leader Benito Mussolini from a mountain prison in 1943.[10] From the slowest to the fastest aircraft the Luftwaffe now dominated the skies of Europe—or so it seemed.

Erhard Milch's reputation climbed rapidly in foreign diplomatic circles. He paid official visits to Germany's neighbours, collecting honours ('all good for decking out the coffin lid,' he used to wisecrack) and distributing goodwill.[11] The climax came in October 1937, with visits to Paris and London.

Early in October he flew to Paris with Udet and his staff, together with the French ambassador François-Poncet. He deliberately chose the Luftwaffe's most modern aircraft, the Heinkel 111, landing on the military side of Le Bourget airport. As he stepped to the ground a French military band struck up the German national anthem and a considerable guard of honour was drawn up for his inspection. General Vuillemin, the French C-in-C, impressed upon him that this was the first time a French guard of honour had presented arms to a German officer since the late 1860s. That the invitation to Paris had an inner political objective was further underlined at a private meeting with the French Foreign, Air and Navy Ministers, who asked Milch to stress to the Führer their wish to establish 'closer relations' with Germany. The German ambassador saw Milch's quizzical look and hurriedly explained that Hitler no longer received him in person: 'But when you, as a soldier, go to see him, he listens to what you say. It's the soldiers who count now in Germany.' As Milch departed from Paris the elderly French commander of the Paris air zone delivered a tearful speech, describing this as the most moving moment of his life—that 'after a thousand years of war' Germany and France had finally buried the hatchet.[12] Next day, on 10 October, Hitler received Milch and Udet for two hours on the Obersalzberg. Milch outlined the French desires for some kind of alliance, but Hitler showed in one sentence what his real sentiments were: 'I am going to teach them a lesson they will never forget.'[13]

A few days later General Milch headed an influential Luftwaffe delegation to London. Here the reception was perceptibly cooler than in Paris. Although the speeches delivered by Lord Swinton—the Air Minister—and the Chief of Air Staff were warm enough and the RAF band even played Nazi marches like *Badenweiler* and *Comrades of old,* and even a Hitler Youth ballad (*In front of us flutters the German Flag . . .*), the guided tours of RAF bomber and fighter squadrons were perhaps coincidentally intimidating in effect. For a whole day he was shown over the unique 'shadow factories' in the Midlands—producing motor-cars and engines in peacetime, but ready for instant conversion to aircraft production in war. He also met the air chief marshals who were to direct the fight against Germany and the Luftwaffe in two years' time, Ludlow-Hewitt and Dowding. No doubt he also shook hands with many another, incognito, whose existence he was later to regret.[14] He livened up one formal luncheon held in his honour at Fighter Command headquarters when in his own blunt way he appealed unprompted to his hosts, 'How are you getting on with your experiments in the radio detection of aircraft approaching your shores?' Glasses clattered to the floor and a very red-faced air vice-marshal tried to laugh the question off. But Milch persisted that there was no need to be coy. 'We have known for some time that you are developing a radar system,' he said. 'So are we, and we think we are a jump ahead of you.' Word of this must have reached Hitler, for years later he was to complain that Milch had betrayed the secret of radar to the British.[15]

Back in London Lord Swinton introduced him to another formidable future opponent, over cocktails in a secluded ring of leather armchairs in a club. Milch found himself cornered between Mr Winston Churchill and his supporters Duff Cooper, Lord Camrose and Leo Amery, while Trenchard and Swinton urged him into battle. In prison later, Milch wrote of Churchill as an enigma. Of the young Churchill portrayed in his own autobiography *My Early Life* Milch summarized that as a child he had evidently played only with tin soldiers, that as a youth he had hastened to become an officer, sought out every scene of hostilities and bloodshed from Cuba, India and Egypt to South Africa, and that everywhere he had obviously found great pleasure in the adventure of fighting and killing: 'I know of no such enthusiasts amongst my own acquaintances,' he wrote in his private Nuremberg diary;[16] and when one considers who Milch's acquaintances had been by that time, the sting of the judgement is recognized.

After the chatter had subsided Mr Churchill, who had been contemplating the German through their combined wreaths of cigar smoke for some time, began an encirclement action. 'What do you think of gliding as a sport?' he asked, and 'Do you think I could pick it up, if I tried to, at my age?' Milch courteously offered him the opportunity in Germany (where the Luftwaffe maintained extensive gliding schools, for reasons which were to become apparent in 1940). So Churchill said, 'If you value gliding so highly, could you not with profit dispense with powered flight entirely? That would eminently solve all our difficulties!' This brought delighted chuckles from his party, but Milch responded: 'I am convinced that our Führer would accept such a proposal.' Churchill removed his cigar and said, 'Oh, really?' Milch explained that there was one small condition—'That the Royal Navy revert to those beautiful old sailing ships!' Lord Swinton loudly proclaimed, 'One-nil to Milch!' The party broke up in the small hours of the morning.[17]

The events in London interested everybody of importance in Berlin except Göring. Milch reported fully both to the Foreign Minister, von Neurath, and to Blomberg upon his return, but the Defence Minister was already growing aware of his inability to moderate Hitler's foreign aims and Milch found him more despondent than ever before. He recorded Blomberg's pessimism: 'He is gravely worried.'[18] Hitler received him for two hours the next afternoon, 2 November, and listened intently to the description of the British shadow factories and the magnificent officer-material seen at the RAF College at Cranwell. The state secretary particularly warned against writing off Churchill just because of the Dardanelles fiasco in the First World War; Churchill was undoubtedly the submerged iceberg on which Germany might founder.

His faction seemed bent on war, the grounds for which could not yet
be foreseen and perhaps did not yet exist. In reply Hitler outlined his
grand strategy and stressed that he was interested only in collaboration
with Great Britain and the Empire.[19] Of course, we have only Milch's
word for this. His diary records simply, '3.15 to 5.15 pm with Udet to
see Führer about journey to England! (Grand strategy).'[20] The words
'grand strategy' ('grosse Politik') also appear on other occasions in
Milch's diary, but always with a somewhat sinister connotation.

Of the Armistice concluded at the end of the First World War on 11
November 1918 the young Captain Milch had written on the day it was
signed: 'The terms are the best possible cause for a future war.' But it
was less the terms of the Armistice than the conditions and frontiers
created by Versailles that incited Hitler. After Austria's *Anschluss* to
Germany in March 1938 Czechoslovakia was surrounded on three sides
by his armies; the Austrian air force was modernized and incorporated
as a body into the Luftwaffe—keeping General Alexander Löhr, at
Milch's suggestion, as their commanding-general; Austrian factories began the manufacture of German aircraft types; and the Luftwaffe gained
important strategic bases from which to menace Czechoslovakia.

Behind all German military planning lurked the traditional ideological
fear of Russia, the unknown quantity in all their calculations. In 1935
word had reached Berlin of negotiations between France and Czechoslovakia to add Russia to their alliance.[21] There were indications that
Russian air force officers were already stationed in Czechoslovakia,
and that twenty-five large airfields were under construction there—far
beyond the needs of such a small territory. The fear that these might
be used by Russia to launch a surprise attack on Germany resulted that
spring in the very first warlike contingency plans drawn up by the Luftwaffe.[22] Milch represented the Luftwaffe at the Wehrmacht consultations. Von Fritsch described the Russian–French–Czech alliance as
acutely dangerous for Germany. On 2 May Blomberg personally handed
the C-in-Cs a secret directive to prepare an unidentified operation code-
named *Schulung* ('Training').[23] Milch's notes leave no doubt that they
were being asked to prepare a blueprint for a surprise attack on Czechoslovakia, combined with a defensive campaign in the west should
France intervene. By 15 May the Luftwaffe study was complete and
on the following day Milch reported, 'Training exercise completed', to
Blomberg's chief of staff.[24] The Wehrmacht's Czech study was updated
periodically until the issue was finally resolved in 1938. As recently
as January 1938 Milch presided over a discussion on the operation,
now code-named *Fall Grün*.[25]

Hitler's decision to destroy Czechoslovakia left no mark on General Milch's conscience. On 21 May 1938, as he was attending a large conference with Göring on the very relevant matter of strenghtening Germany's eastern and western fortifications, the first news of alleged Czech outrages against German nationals in the Sudeten territories bordering on Germany reached him.[26] On the twenty-eighth Hitler announced to his C-in-Cs his intention of dealing with this troublesome neighbour, and Göring forwarded the Führer's orders to Milch and the other Luftwaffe commanders next day.[27] The deadline for the attack was 1 October. It was of great concern to Hitler that French intervention be resisted while he was rapidly destroying Czechoslovakia, and this he proposed to achieve by buttress and by bluff. On 1 June Milch decreed the formation of an Air Defence Zone 'West' under General Kitzinger —a secondary line of fortifications and associated flak positions along the western frontiers.[28] Travelling by Göring's magnificent special train Milch and a large party of Luftwaffe generals inspected the fortifications constructed so far by the army, and back in Berlin again he busied himself with the minutiae of air warfare against Czechoslovakia. Of particular interest is the evidence that he discussed with Dr Plendl the use of radio beams for the blind bombing of Czech targets.[29]

During June 1938 the air industry factories were converted to ten-hour shift working.[30] Göring, a field marshal now that Defence Minister Blomberg had been deposed, called his major industrialists to Karinhall on 8 July and warned them that war with Czechoslovakia was imminent; he concealed his knowledge of Hitler's initiative, but portrayed their neighbour as the one seeking to provoke a general European war. 'You may know,' he declared, 'that at the present moment it is by no means dependent only on Germany whether or not the peace can be kept. The sword of Damocles threatening this peace is Czechoslovakia. . . .' On the other hand, he promised the industrialists, there was something in a war for everybody: 'If we win the fight, then Germany will be the greatest power on earth; the world's markets will belong to Germany, and the time will come for abundant prosperity in Germany. But we must venture something for this; we have to make the investment. . . .'[31]

Three days later the First Air Group circulated a top secret study on *Fall Grün* as a basis for the operations of the four hundred fighters and six hundred bombers (plus two hundred dive-bombers and ground-attack aircraft) being concentrated for the attack on Czechoslovakia in October. The First Air Group would attack from bases in central and eastern Germany, while the somewhat smaller Third Air Group would attack from Bavaria and Austria.[32] About 250 Junkers 52 transport aircraft would discharge the paratroops of Göring's Seventh Airborne Division over vital Czech strong-points. At Jüterbog artillery range outside Berlin full-scale concrete mock-ups of the Czech fortifications had been erected; on 15 August Milch watched with Hitler as heavy artillery and 88-millimetre flak pieces pounded these targets to demonstrate to von Brauchitsch, Fritsch's successor as army C-in-C, and his worried generals that the fortifications were not impregnable. From 2.45 pm that day Hitler opened his mind to the generals about the future and the superiority of the German military position. It was on bluff that he placed most reliance. At one stage he described it as a war on Czechoslovakia's nerves: 'Imagine how it must feel to watch your neighbour sharpening up his knife for three months!'* After ninety minutes Milch noted uncritically in his private diary, 'Speech by Führer. Insight into his thoughts. *His mind is made up!!*'[33]

It was clear that a German attack on Czechoslovakia might result in a declaration of war by France, followed almost at once by Russia and Britain, the latter with the clandestine support of America. All these risks Hitler was prepared to take. The Luftwaffe obediently developed a plan of operations, which they aptly code-named *'Fall Grün,* Enlarged', in which they assumed that the RAF would impinge on neutral Belgian and Dutch air space to strike at the Ruhr, while Russia would be restricted by Poland's more genuine neutrality to air attacks on East Prussia and Berlin.[34] Milch had been aware since late April that Anglo-French staff talks had been resumed at the instance of the new French premier, Daladier, and that a French military mission headed by General Vuillemin had visited London at the end of May. But for the time being neither the British nor French bomber forces was taken seriously: on 1 October the former would probably consist of only 640 bombers, all but 120 of them obsolete, and the RAF were understood to have 859 bombers, all but 350 being obsolete. In May 1938 Milch had learned that a British mission had been sent to America to purchase aircraft and organize the expansion of the Canadian aircraft industry; the Air Staff's August planning document put British production at 200 of all types per month, and North American production at 250. General Milch initialled the first page of the document, and there is no indication that he expressed pessimism in any form as to the outcome of such an enlarged conflict.[35]

Boundless optimism and a degree of bluff were his *forte* for the next

* The only surviving contemporary note on Hitler's secret speech that day is in the diary of Captain Wolf Eberhard, Keitel's adjutant, in the author's possession.

six years—confounding his critics and enraging the despondent. When Hitler held a banquet on 24 August in honour of Admiral Horthy, the Hungarian Regent, the Army General Curt Liebmann buttonholed Milch afterwards in the smoking-room and poured out his woes about the inadequacy of the West Wall. Milch refused to be infected by his mood. Liebmann angrily accused him, 'You may well be a brilliant airman, General, but about army tactics you obviously haven't got a glimmer!' Milch spoke to Göring, and Göring arranged to have Liebmann ('another of those grousing generals') removed from his command.[36]

The chance for grand bluff came in August 1938, when General Vuillemin arrived in Germany for a five-day tour of Luftwaffe installations. Forewarned about Vuillemin's liaisons with the British, Milch staged a spectacular display, conducting him and his mission round the Messerschmitt, Junkers and Heinkel factories and several operational units. Every fighter aircraft in Germany was flown to one airfield in southern Germany, where Vuillemin's plane was scheduled to make a casual stop; at Augsburg he was shown Messerschmitt's latest fighter, the Me 109E, and an Me 110 twin-engined long-range fighter firing cannon into the butts. At the new Heinkel aircraft factory at Oranienburg—not even shown to the British the year before—an He 111 bomber demonstrated its really astounding manoeuvrability, even on one engine, and the French general was allowed to glimpse scores of brand-new bombers in the despatch hangar. He was shown the modern air-raid damage-control centre, and found everything ready, down to a dozen sharpened pencils. He expostulated, *'Je suis écrasé!'*[37]

But the *pièce de résistance* was to come. Udet lured him up in a Fieseler 'Storch', to show him Oranienburg from the air; on Milch's instructions a Heinkel 100 fighter—in which Udet had just smashed the world speed record—flew at full throttle over the 80 m.p.h.-Storch just as it was landing. Vuillemin and the air attaché went momentarily white. On the airfield tarmac Milch blandly asked Udet how the He 100's mass production was coming along, and the latter replied with poker face, 'The second production line is just starting up, and the third in two weeks' time.' In fact only a handful of He 100s was ever manufactured; Udet waved aside Dr Heinkel's amazement at the strange conversation, 'You have to blow your own trumpet sometimes!' In the factory gymnasium Milch challenged the French air attaché to a race up the ropes. After the French colonel had manfully hauled himself up with his arms alone, Milch scrambled up in half the time using his legs as well and proclaimed himself the winner.[38] General Vuillemin privately notified his government that the French air force would not last a week against what he had seen in Germany.[39]

The RAF was another proposition.

If Göring had always hoped there would be no war with Britain this had not prevented Stumpff in February 1938 from commissioning General Felmy, the north-western tactical commander (Second Air Group) to investigate what war with Britain would mean.[40] After the *Anschluss* the Anglo-German exchange of information dried up. When the British Chief of Air Staff asked in April for further information the German air attaché admonished him, as he reported to Milch, 'If we are to hand over secret data to you, then we expect to receive in exchange something that we have not already read for ourselves in the British press and other journals. . . .'[41] By August air war with Britain had advanced from 'possibility' to 'probability'. It was only now that Göring recognized that he had no suitable aircraft for such a war; at Karinhall on the twenty-third he instructed Felmy to assemble information on targets in Britain and suitable tactics for attack. Since Felmy had only two bomber wings he was to prepare to accommodate three or four more bombers as soon as Czechoslovakia had been crushed. Until then, with its two existing wings the group could do little more than support ground operations in the west and provide for air raids on London and Paris on a reprisal basis should the need arise. Other British targets particularly mentioned were the London docks, the capital's armament factories, the Channel ports and airfields in eastern England. Should the bomber forces prove adequate, an extensive campaign against Britain's seaborne food supplies should begin.[42]

Adequate was the key word. Felmy, appointed on 17 September to head a *Sonderstab* (Special Unit) England, reported on the twenty-second that the Luftwaffe was incapable of effectively attacking Britain.[43] 'With the means available,' he wrote, 'we cannot expect to achieve anything more than a disruptive effect. Whether this will lead to an erosion of the British will to fight is something that depends on imponderable and certainly unpredictable factors. . . . A war of annihilation against Britain appears out of the question with the means at hand.' Yet war with Britain was a 'probability' now: on 21 September Milch toured the loading airfields, haranguing the paratroops; on the twenty-second he attended a war conference with the Air Staff; on the twenty-third Hitler issued his ultimatum to Prague, to provide the pretext for his attack a week later.[44] This was no time for Göring to learn that the Luftwaffe had been supplied with inadequate aircraft.

As Felmy warned, unless forward airfields could be established in Belgium and Holland there was no German aircraft that could operate effectively against Britain. The Luftwaffe's existing bombers could not penetrate farther than 430 miles with a half-ton bomb load. The four-engined bombers ordered by Milch and Wever had been scrapped in 1937. Recognizing that there *was* a need for them, Udet had decided in mid-1938 to order a different four-engined aircraft, the He 177, that would be capable of dive-bombing—a requirement that would involve coupling the engines in pairs to avoid weakening the wing structures.[45] Clearly the He 177 could not fly for at least a year, let alone enter mass production. It was in this situation that Göring was persuaded by Junkers's general manager, Koppenberg, to order the mass production of an as yet untested aircraft, the Junkers 88 dive-bomber, with the highest priority.[46]

Designed by Junkers to meet a 1935 requirement by Wever for a conventional high-speed bomber, the straight Ju 88 had first flown in 1936. Powered by two Jumo 211 engines, it promised to carry over two tons of bombs, fly nearly two thousand miles and reach speeds faster than 300 mph. In December 1936, however, Udet had stated a fatal further requirement—that the Ju 88 should be capable of dive-bombing, in view of Germany's disheartening experiences with conventional bombing in Spain. Junkers redesigned the aircraft and the new prototype first flew on 1 June 1938.[47] Production began at the Dessau parent factory early in September. Göring was persuaded that this was the aircraft he needed. He would hear no evil of the Ju 88, despite a warning from the independent air industrialists that Junkers, as a State-owned company, might well be pulling the wool over his eyes about the aircraft's performance.[48] Late in September Göring proposed to Milch, Udet and Koppenberg that they should nominate the Ju 88 the Luftwaffe's standard bomber of the future, manufacturing 250 a month in half a dozen different factories. Udet was in favour, as was Jeschonnek, but Milch felt uneasy—not, as he stressed later in the war, out of personal antipathy towards Junkers,[49] but because the dive-bomber's performance would suffer severely from the heavy air brakes and structural strengthening; he questioned whether it would be any improvement on the He 111 now being manufactured in large numbers.[50]

He was overruled. Years later Göring tacitly acknowledged that Milch's prognosis was correct. 'I recall the marvellous circles they drew on their charts for me,' he said in 1943, 'showing the radii—how this aircraft could cruise up and down the west coast of Ireland attacking the enemy shipping lanes. But we *still* have not got any such aircraft!'[51] All too trustingly the field marshal took the fateful step and appointed

Koppenberg conjures Junkers 88 out of his hat          [*Sketch by Ernst Udet*]

Koppenberg overlord for the manufacture of Ju 88 bombers, charged with dramatic powers to issue orders and take over the production of the participating companies—'even those outside the Junkers group'.[52] The field marshal sent this unique document to Koppenberg on 30 September, and enjoined him: '. . . Now let the signal be given, and create for me in the shortest possible time a mighty armada of Ju 88 bombers!' The first production model emerged from the assembly line early in January 1939; but in the months of tests that followed, considerable design faults in the dive-bomber version came to light.

By the time he signed the letter Göring was at Munich for Hitler's talks with the British, Italian and French leaders, and a breathing space had been gained. Milch had also been ordered to fly there—perhaps Hitler had intended to amass even more *dramatis personae* than he had for his confrontation with the unfortunate Austrian chancellor Schuschnigg in February; (on that occasion he asked both Sperrle and Reichenau to be present, 'my two most brutal-looking generals', as he confessed with a laugh to Milch).[53] A month after Munich Hitler summoned his military commanders to Berchtesgaden and rewarded them as though it had been a military victory—promoting Udet to Lieutenant-General and Milch to Colonel-General (four-star rank). Field Marshal Göring warned Milch that he need expect no further promotion from now on.[54]

The spirit of Munich did not last long. War with Britain had been postponed but not averted. In mid-October 1938 Hitler ordered Göring to 'execute a gigantic production programme, against which previous efforts would pale into insignificance'; in particular the Luftwaffe was to be 'expanded fivefold' forthwith.[55] On the fifteenth Göring and Milch conferred on the related problem of increasing the Luftwaffe's training capacity and on plans for a future air war with Britain, and on the twenty-sixth there was a further large conference at Karinhall on the Luftwaffe's requirements for air warfare against Britain and her shipping.* Here Jeschonnek, Stumpff's deputy, persuaded Göring to authorize the manufacture of 'as many He 177s as possible, and at least four wings'—indicating an establishment of a formidable force of five hundred of these four-engined long-range bombers—by the autumn of 1942, the completion date for the new 'concentrated aircraft production programme' under consideration.[56] Clearly it was hoped to postpone war with Britain until then.

---

* German naval archives contain (in file PG/33046) an important exposition by Jeschonnek of the Luftwaffe's plans for the next two years, at an inter-service conference on 24 November 1938. The 'common enemy' of both navy and Luftwaffe was now recognized to be Britain.

The new programme did not escape controversy. Udet's department opposed it because the mere fuelling of over a hundred wings of aircraft —altogether about nineteen thousand aircraft—would require Germany to import about eighty-five per cent of the world's current output of aviation spirit.[57] The chief of the organization branch, Colonel Josef Kammhuber, drafted a more moderate programme and Stumpff suggested that they should adopt this as an interim target. Milch apparently supported him and proposed in conference that they put it up to Göring, but to this Colonel Jeschonnek objected: 'In my view it is our duty not to betray the Führer's ideals like this!' So Milch took Jeschonnek to Göring instead. When they returned he announced, 'Gentlemen, the field marshal has decided that the Führer's programme is capable of execution.'[58] That settled the matter. Milch agreed the final programme with the Air Staff at the end of November 1938: its weakness, as we can see in retrospect, was that it relied heavily on as yet completely unproven aircraft. Of the 31,300 aircraft to be manufactured under the programme by April 1942, 7,700 were Ju 88s and He 177s, the troubles of which will be related at length in later chapters—suffice it to say that the Ju 88 was not satisfactory until 1943, and the He 177 had not even entered squadron service by the end of 1942.[59] In another respect an opportunity was also missed: by 1942 Udet planned to produce about one hundred fighter aircraft per month; this target compares strikingly with the peak output of 3,500 fighters per month achieved by Milch in 1944.

The stars of both Udet and Jeschonnek were firmly in the ascendant. On 1 February 1939 Göring founded a formidable new bureaucratic structure, the Office of Air Armament, whose director (General-Luftzeugmeister or GL)—incredibly to all who knew him—was to be Ernst Udet.[60] He was already head of the Technical Department, and this he had reorganized from its simple horizontal structure (research, development, procurement and budget) into a hopelessly complex vertical structure (airframes, aero-engines, etc.); but with this new post of GL came five research establishments like Rechlin and Peenemünde and a host of other offices. Udet would now control directly twenty-six subordinate offices; even Milch, who positively relished desk work, had never tried to control more than four. Göring exercised no supervision, either: when inevitably the whole fragile structure crashed in 1941, the legal officers appointed to investigate established that with Göring, Udet talked only of old times.[61]

The final blow to Milch's active authority was delivered by Göring on the same date, 1 February 1939: he replaced Stumpff as Chief of Air Staff by Colonel Jeschonnek. Jeschonnek, son of a schoolmaster from Allenstein, was seven years younger than the state secretary, but a recognized prodigy ever since childhood. An army lieutenant by the time he was fifteen, he had served in the same fighter squadron in the First World War as Milch, and had subsequently been associated with the work of the secret air force in Russia. For the first years of Milch's office Jeschonnek had been his principal staff officer, and General Wever had predicted that he would succeed him as Chief of Air Staff. As recently as the autumn of 1938 Jeschonnek had reminded Milch of this and asked when he might expect to replace Stumpff; Milch had sent him away with a flea in his ear, for out of their earlier father-and-son friendship had blossomed an ugly mutual contempt. The real reasons are obscure, but Milch himself has mentioned two: the first was an odd incident in 1934 when his car was flagged down by an SA officer who asked him if he would transport an injured storm-trooper to hospital after a motor accident; Milch had taken one look at the trooper's severe skull injuries and instructed that nobody move him until proper medical aid arrived. Jeschonnek denounced Milch to Göring for 'refusing to assist', and declined to recant even when all the authorities, including the SA officer concerned, bore Milch's version out. The second affair, irrevocably clouding their relations, was about two years later: Jeschonnek, now commanding the Operational Development Wing at Greifswald, was accused of causing the deaths of two crews by ordering that in practice low-level attacks on shipping their planes' airscrews had to touch the tops of the waves. Milch flew to Greifswald and advised the youthful wing commander that he would let him off the court martial he deserved and delivered a verbal reprimand, to save his career. Jeschonnek resented even the reprimand. Milch later wrote of him as 'a plucky, intelligent officer but narrow-minded and headstrong, and contemptuous of other walks of life'.[62] Their feud became notorious throughout the Luftwaffe and was ended only by Jeschonnek's untimely death in 1943.[63]

In mid-February 1939 Milch departed for his annual skiing holiday in the Austrian Alps. He had despatched to Göring the final plans for financing the large new aircraft programme and the necessary factory expansion, and motored down to Austria in his BMW. It was several weeks before the inevitable telegram arrived, at 1 am on 12 March: his principal staff officer was hastening to a nearby town with an urgent memorized message for him. Milch met him a few hours later. The message was: 'The Czechoslovakian state is breaking up. It may become necessary for the Wehrmacht to intervene within the next few days. The Führer has requested your immediate return to Berlin.' Milch telephoned Hitler's Luftwaffe adjutant that he was on his way and arrived in Munich early on the thirteenth.[64]

Not only he had been caught unawares. Göring was still on leave at San Remo, and some high army officers were equally distant from Berlin.[65] In Munich Milch learned from Jeschonnek and General Sperrle that Prague had dismissed the autonomous Slovak separatist government and was planning to enter Slovakia. Hitler therefore intended to act now to 'destroy' Czechoslovakia. The role of the Luftwaffe was obvious.[66] The warlike preparations were continued all day in Berlin, with Milch presiding over further conferences with Jeschonnek and Stumpff. This time there was a marked lack of enthusiasm from the public, which was usually so proud of its armed forces. During the afternoon Milch collected Göring from the station and in the evening the Czech President arrived from Prague. In the face of the Luftwaffe's very real preparations to destroy the city, which Göring earnestly described to him, President Hacha capitulated and agreed to the entry of German troops into his country next morning. Milch toured the airborne division and fighter squadrons, and the flak batteries hurriedly stationed within Berlin, in his capacity as 'Inspector-General';[67] but the Seventh Airborne Division was grounded by bad weather so the Luftwaffe took little active part in the occupation. By its very existence it had done enough.

So once more a newly occupied European capital vibrated to a thousand German aircraft engines, as the Luftwaffe paraded over Prague on 17 March. In a hotel off Wenceslas Square the Czech Chief of Air Staff formally surrendered his air force and handed the document to Milch.[68] Udet and his experts toured the newly acquired factories and airfields and were astonished at the quantity and quality of the aircraft and equipment on hand.[69] All of it was absorbed by the Luftwaffe. On the seventeenth Göring accepted Milch's proposal for a fourth air force headquarters, *Luftflotte* 4, to command the new south-eastern sector, under the Austrian General Löhr, and four days later he returned to his holiday at San Remo. When the territory of Memel was returned to the Reich and Hitler formally entered the city on the twenty-third, Milch exercised his newly granted status as Göring's deputy for the first time, awaiting Hitler at the gates of that ancient German city.[70]

In Poland the transfer of Memel roused apprehensions lest a coup might be imminent against Danzig. The Polish government ordered partial mobilization and upon his return to Berlin Milch quoted the latest intelligence reports in his diary, on 25 March: 'Fighting between Hungary and Slovakia; Poland is mobilizing against us, Rumania against Hungary, France against Italy. Sheer confusion amongst the rest.' On the same day Hitler disclosed to von Brauchitsch that he might well force a solution of the Danzig and Polish Corridor problems in the future; and when the German High Command (OKW) issued its annual directive on 3 April one section accordingly dealt with the possibility of an attack on Poland.[71] The earliest date for this operation, *Fall Weiss,* was named as 1 September 1939. The OKW asked each Service to submit a draft timetable of operations.

Of all this Göring remained happily unaware until his return from San Remo on 18 April. Then, over dinner one evening, Hitler suddenly said that Danzig must become German again and that there must be a solution to the Corridor problem. He would resort to war if all else failed, and he reminded Göring that he had prepared other situations skilfully, and this would be no exception.[72] On the twenty-seventh Jeschonnek disclosed the Luftwaffe's plans within *Fall Weiss* to a large circle of officers including Milch: the Luftwaffe was to destroy the Polish air force first, then turn to the disruption of Polish mobilization efforts and tactical support for the German army.[73]

The spectre of war with Britain was again raised, the more so since Britain had now offered a treaty to Poland, guaranteeing her assistance in the event of war. General Felmy conducted a three-day war exercise at the Second Air Force's Brunswick headquarters during May, based on a war with Britain; Milch flew to Brunswick on the thirteenth to hear the outcome.[74] Felmy concluded that the Luftwaffe could not possibly be ready for a major war in 1939, a view echoed a week later by the Air Staff's operations division in a study on 'Tactical Aims for the Luftwaffe in the Event of War against Britain in 1939'. The latter study emphasized right at the beginning, '. . . the equipment, state of training and strength of the Second Air Force cannot bring about a quick decision in any war with Britain in 1939.' In particular the He 111 bomber was inadequate in range and numbers, suitable anti-shipping tactics had yet to be developed and the standard of blind-flying was not high enough.[75] All this was precisely what Milch had been warning of all along. In 1933 he had asked for ten years to build the Luftwaffe into an efficient fighting service. But Göring was apparently unconvinced by the threat of war with Britain and departed from Berlin to resume once again his interrupted holiday in Italy on 3 May.

This easy lack of concern reassured Milch that war was still a distant prospect. Like Göring he had much to live for, and much to lose if war broke out. Some of his minister's luxurious inclination had rubbed off on him; while he never gave up his modest Steglitz flat, he too had become a keen huntsman and had built a hunting lodge in idyllic surroundings outside Berlin. Much of his time was consumed in furnishing this new home, and in family affairs. His elder daughter had married a Luftwaffe officer. Late in May, however, he attended a secret conference with Hitler which left him with the impression that this time war might not be averted. On the morning of 23 May 1939 Bodenschatz telephoned him and said that Hitler was going to address his C-in-Cs at four o'clock that afternoon; could Milch go in Göring's place? In Hitler's study in the Reich Chancery Milch found about a dozen chairs facing a small lectern. On the middle chair was a card with Göring's name and here he took his place flanked by Raeder on one side and Brauchitsch and the OKW's General Keitel on the other.[76]

It is impossible to state with certainty what Hitler disclosed to them. A memorandum exists by Hitler's chief adjutant, Schmundt, but it was probably written long afterwards for it lists as present both Göring and another officer who was absent, and the contents are in no way germane to the military situation of May 1939.[77] All the witnesses questioned about the conference seven years later at Nuremberg had been shown Schmundt's record first; most of them emphatically questioned its accuracy. Milch later wrote that Hitler's purpose was to warn his C-in-Cs against complacency, the belief that this time too he would solve Germany's problems without war; they should apply themselves more urgently to the armaments problem. In Nuremberg Prison Milch privately asked Raeder for his recollection; the admiral stressed at once that it was not an active preparation for war, but just Hitler 'letting his light as warlord glow a little'.[78] Whatever was said, Milch's documents and the surviving records of the Reich Air Ministry betray no evidence consistent with active preparation for war until the beginning of August 1939.

There are certainly tokens of contingency planning. 'Can the Volkswagen works manufacture aero-engines in the event of war?' Göring asked of Udet on 21 June.[79] And on the twenty-third he pointed out to the Reich Defence Council that the disguised methods hitherto employed to move troops would be useless if a military operation should be launched 'unexpectedly and at short notice'.* The Luftwaffe's expansion was due for completion in 1942, and as late as the end of July 1939 Göring calmly accepted the assessment by Milch and Udet that the ultimate strength of five thousand Ju 88 bombers would be reached in April 1943.[81] On 22 July 1939 Raeder confirmed to his officers that the Führer had given him an undertaking that no war was at hand.[82] Hitler made similar statements to Milch, when the latter reported that

---

* Göring warned, 'In the field of transport, for example, Germany is still not ready for war. There were no real troop movements involved in the three operations of 1938 and 1939.'[80]

recently in Rome Mussolini had also stated, 'War is inevitable, but we shall try to postpone it until 1942.' Hitler reassured Milch that the Duce's fear of war breaking out even then was quite mistaken.[83]

None the less, on 8 June Milch and Udet took their anxieties about the continued shortage of raw materials for the Luftwaffe to Rudolf Hess, to prod him into interceding with Hitler on the Luftwaffe's behalf; currently the warship construction programme had the highest priority for materials and manpower.[84] Milch knew, perhaps better than anyone else, how unprepared the Luftwaffe was. They still lacked trained commanders at every level. They had fuel stores sufficient for war operations for six months at most.[85] The bomb dumps held enough bombs for about three weeks' hostilities against a small enemy and most of these were 10-kilogramme bombs secretly purchased by the Reichswehr a decade before; sample quantities of 50- and 250-kilogramme bombs and a very few 500-kilogramme bombs had been manufactured for the Spanish War, but all larger sizes were still on the drawing board.[86] Hitler forbade the manufacture of more, explaining to Milch, 'Nobody inquires whether I have any bombs or ammunition, it is the number of aircraft and guns that count.' Only 182,000 tons of steel had been allocated to air force equipment and ammunition in the year ending 1 April 1939, compared with 380,400 tons for the expansion of the industry and civil aviation. Hardly can a nation have planned for world war within one year with less foresight than Germany in 1939.

The only lasting solution was to impress Hitler with the Luftwaffe's potential. In mid-April 1939 Milch had already proposed to Göring that they should lay on a display to show Hitler their most advanced weaponry: 'The Luftwaffe must make use of such a display to win support for its expansion programme, since if war does break out it will have to bear the brunt of the fighting in the west virtually alone for the next few years.' Göring agreed, and a dress rehearsal was laid on for the Italians towards the end of June, at Rechlin.[87]

The special display for Hitler was arranged on 3 July, a fine summer afternoon. It was to have significant effects on Hitler's thinking, for he evidently drew conclusions about the Luftwaffe's operational readiness which would have been better drawn from a visit to operational squadrons, not to a research establishment. The equipment at Rechlin was beyond doubt the most advanced in the world: there was the He 100 fighter and its rival, the Me 109, which had just smashed the Heinkel's world speed record; there was the world's first rocket-propelled interceptor aircraft, the He 176; the Führer was also shown the new 30-

millimetre aircraft cannon, the MK 101, a weapon of annihilating effect, mounted in an Me 110 twin-engined fighter jacked up in the firing butts. Hitler saw a heavily overloaded He 111 bomber thunder into the air with rocket-assisted take-off units. In the laboratories he inspected a high-altitude pressurized cockpit and a new Luftwaffe procedure for starting aero-engines in sub-zero temperatures.[88] General Milch was undoubtedly pleased at the impression made on Hitler and there is no evidence that he recognized the damage that had been done.* The display did not better the Luftwaffe's raw materials position, but now Hitler, like the French War Minister Ferdinand Leboeuf seventy years before, believed that his forces were *archi-prêts* for war.

Four years later the squadrons were still waiting for most of the equipment he had seen in 1939. The Führer never forgave the Luftwaffe for this. In 1942 Göring was to complain, 'Do you know, I once witnessed a display before the war at Rechlin, compared with which I can only say—what bunglers all our professional magicians are! Because the world has never before and never will again see the likes of what was conjured up before my—and far worse, the Führer's—eyes at Rechlin!'[90] He resolved never to set foot inside Rechlin again, and when none the less he did in May 1942 he again recalled with bitterness that July day in 1939: 'The Führer reached the most serious decisions as a result of that display,' he said. 'It was a miracle that things worked out as well as they did, and that the consequences were not far worse.'[91] Hitler himself expressed similar recriminations to his acting Chief of Air Staff in the summer of 1944.[92]

The non-production of the equipment was not Göring's fault alone. Both verbally and in writing Göring stressed to his staff Hitler's interest in the 30-millimetre cannon (Hitler had emphasized, 'We just can't have too many heavy-calibre weapons') and the high-altitude cockpit.[93] On 20 July Udet was informed, 'The field marshal [Göring] emphasized the significance of the high-altitude bomber and demanded that the trials should be speeded up by all means at our disposal. In this connection he also mentioned the development of a high-altitude fighter aircraft.'[94] Göring also ordained the rapid manufacture of three thousand 30-millimetre cannon. None of these orders was followed up. Four years later Milch was forced to reopen the long-closed file on high-altitude fighter and bomber aircraft; and as for the 30-millimetre cannon, by 1943 only 220 had been manufactured, none of which had

* This is disputed by the field marshal in postwar accounts, where he has claimed that he warned Hitler that none of these new weapons would be in service for five years at least.[89]

reached the front-line squadrons. Udet's office actively blocked some of the most advanced research undertaken by independent aircraft designers. Göring's request for research into building aircraft from wood laminates was ignored. The He 100 was dropped although 50 mph faster than the standard Me 109, and when Heinkel protested Udet's chief engineer wrote on 12 July forbidding him to pursue the matter.[95] Udet adopted the same half-comic attitude towards all new inventions. Of Heinkel's rocket-propelled interceptor, the He 176, he jested, 'Every take-off that prospers is a crash that miscarries, in that thing', and he ordered the prototype to be shipped to a Berlin aviation museum; here it was destroyed in an Allied air raid in 1943.[96] When, a few weeks later, the world's first pure jet aircraft, the He 178, flew no contract was forthcoming; Udet had already promised jet-fighter development to Messerschmitt. Certainly Milch—who saw the Heinkel jet flying in November 1939—should have intervened, but Udet continued to confer alone with Göring, and kept him in the dark.

During these weeks Milch had only one personal conversation with his minister, on 21 July; Göring's yacht *Karin II* was moored in a Westphalian waterway. Milch reported his impressions of a recent visit to Brussels and of the respects paid by King Leopold to a young Luftwaffe officer killed in the air display there; but the Belgian public had displayed open hostility, and the RAF officers who had been friendly towards him in London were now cool and aloof. RAF Battles and Blenheims had carried out mock attacks on the crowds at the display. In Brussels, reported Milch, their London air attaché had left him in no doubt that Britain would honour her obligations towards Poland. He reminded Göring that their young Luftwaffe had so far experienced five different Chiefs of Air Staff, and its latest was but a colonel; for the sake of continuity he begged Göring to make more use of him. Göring readily agreed, but as readily forgot about it afterwards.[97]

By August 1939 it was plain that the important Ju 88 programme had gone wrong. Although being mass produced at half a dozen factories under Koppenberg's impetuous overall direction, it had still not reached the operational squadrons. Milch's own enthusiasm for Koppenberg had long waned, but not Udet's: the GL, who was an outstanding cartoonist, had drawn admiring caricatures of his friend 'Koppenbergini' conjuring multiple Ju 88s out of a hat; and of Koppenberg as a bull in the industry's china-shop, putting his indolent and contrary rivals all to flight. But the early test flights at Rechlin were costing lives and precious time. The eventual peak output was set at 172 per month, but Udet advised Hitler at Rechlin that this was impossible because of the aluminium shortage; Göring reluctantly approved cuts in the other aircraft types to allow the Ju 88 target to be met. On 20 July Udet admitted to Göring that the design faults now showing up would set them back three months. While in April Göring could boast to Mussolini, 'Such is the range of this bomber that it can not only attack Britain but also carry on to the west and bomb the shipping lanes across the Atlantic!', by March 1943 he would know better: 'The plane has so far not even flown as far as Ireland,' he raged. 'Now can you understand my boundless exasperation! What you people have been turning out is the product of a pig-sty!'[98]

Milch watched the project's difficulties with the mixed feelings of one whose predictions have been proved correct, but whose country will suffer the consequences. Originally planned as a super-fast bomber weighing only about six tons, the Ju 88 had rapidly put on weight as the list of Air Staff requirements grew. A vicious circle had developed— being heavier, it was slower; and being slower, it needed heavier armament after all; and all this drastically reduced its range. By mid-1939 the plane's all-up weight on take-off was over twelve tons. Small wonder that Milch termed it a 'flying barndoor'. Udet hotly disputed that its speed had suffered, but to his intimates he showed a marked uneasiness. 'The main thing is, the plane does fly', he pointed out to Ernst Heinkel. 'Only Milch still has any objections—but he always was a stick-in-the-mud in my view. He never commits himself, so that it is impossible afterwards to pin anything onto him should things go wrong.'[99]

On 5 August Göring urgently ordered Milch, Udet and Jeschonnek to discuss a radical change in the 'concentrated aircraft programme' next day; they met on the sixth in the stateroom of *Karin II,* as it steamed the twenty miles from Lüneburg to Hamburg. Göring now demanded a Luftwaffe of attack—he was going to activate thirty-two new bomber wings by 1 April 1943—4,330 aircraft of which 2,460 were to be Ju 88s; this colossal expansion of the bomber force was to be effected at the expense of every other kind of aircraft, such as transporters and training aircraft. It was to be a *Blitzkrieg* Luftwaffe. Jeschonnek duly rephrased the Air Staff's requirements three days later: the aircraft industry was to concentrate on the He 177, Ju 88 and Me 210—the latter, a twin-engined dive-bomber and ground-attack plane, being an extended version of the Me 110 yet to be built.[100] In terms of totals, the Air Staff asked for 2,460 Ju 88s, 800 He 177s and 3,000 Me 210s by April 1943; it is a measure of the disaster that was to come that by that date the Luftwaffe had in fact only one *squadron* with less than a dozen He 177s in service, while the Me 210 had been scrapped as useless in the spring of 1942, leaving acres of storage space crammed with useless, corroding wings, fuselages and components. Göring ordered Koppenberg to report with the others to him again on the fifteenth, to discuss the feasibility of producing 300 Ju 88s a month; Udet demanded a Führer decree equivalent to that secured by the navy in January, and this was signed by Hitler on 21 August.[101]

By that date the political situation had sharply altered. On 14 August Hitler summoned Göring and the other C-in-Cs to Berchtesgaden and informed them of his decision to attack Poland; Göring immediately ordered Milch to join him there, and Milch flew down on the fifteenth from Prague, where he had been inspecting Luftwaffe units. At 11 am Göring told him of Hitler's resolve—the Führer considered the coming crisis a test of nerves, and he would show the Poles his were the stronger. This could not be said of Göring, who seemed to Milch particularly apprehensive of the future. Milch flew back to Berlin and briefed the departmental heads and Jeschonnek along the guidelines Göring had given him. For the next three days his principal task was issuing the directives for war, in Göring's name.[102]

He took it all at a leisurely pace, retiring from the heat of August Berlin to the cool of his forest hunting lodge each evening, while the Luftwaffe machine slowly wound up for Armageddon. On the twenty-first he was recalled to Göring's Obersalzberg villa, to confer with the four *Luftflotte* commanders, Generals Kesselring, Felmy, Sperrle and Löhr; Udet had brought the latest figures on British, French and Polish fighters and bombers. At that moment eleven production Ju 88s were on hand at Rechlin, and four more would become available before the twenty-eighth, 'provided no unforeseen technical problems occur. . . .' This was hardly the armada of Ju 88s Göring had called for a year before. At this final Luftwaffe conference Göring disclosed that Hitler planned to attack Poland early on the twenty-sixth. Luftwaffe operations would be controlled by the First and Fourth Air Forces (Kesselring and Löhr). Göring was a different man from the nervous apparition of six days before; he announced that Stalin had telegraphed Hitler his agreement to an immediate pact with Germany.[103] 'Russia will not march against us now,' he beamed. Russia and Germany as allies? At that moment, Milch must have recalled the admiring suggestion of a Russian NCO he took prisoner in March 1915: *'Russki soldier und Prusski officer—whole world kaput!'*[104]

Hitler summoned fifty of his senior commanders to the Berghof next day and delivered a harangue in the tradition of Caesar and of Hannibal. In effect he proclaimed that there was to be a short war, a just war and a war which Germany could not lose. 'It is a matter of war and victory, not of law and justice!' Poland now stood alone. The Luftwaffe would 'grind away' the enemy, and—an evident echo of his visit to Rechlin—'our technical superiority will mangle every Polish nerve'. Britain had only 150 flak guns in the entire country—equivalent to one month's output in Germany. No discussion followed the lengthy speech.[105] Göring had his closer relatives withdrawn from front-line units and posted to the rear; and perhaps to camouflage his action he withdrew Milch's relatives as well. Milch, more honourably, casually despatched his own family from Berlin to a holiday on the Baltic coast. He himself camped in the Air Ministry building each night. On 25 August Hitler ordered the attack to begin at 4.45 am next morning.

Scarcely was this order issued, however, than it was countermanded. Early on the twenty-sixth Milch was summoned first to Karinhall—where he found Göring had already left—and then to the Reich Chancery. In Hitler's study he found an atmosphere of gloom. Hitler was vehemently cursing Italy; Ribbentrop and Keitel were nodding their agreement. Hitler said the Italians were finding excuses not to join the attack on Poland and the British had accordingly ratified their pact with Poland. Milch read the latest Italian communication and exclaimed, 'Mein Führer, this is the best thing that could have happened! For if the Italians were to march against us, then we should have to divert troops against them; if Italy joins forces with us, then the enemy will always know precisely where the chink in our armour is; but if they stay benevolent neutrals, we can obtain all manner of goods from them—raw materials, oil and war supplies.' This was an aspect Hitler had evidently not considered and over lunch he brightened considerably. He believed that Britain was counting on Poland to give way.[106]

That night Milch slept at the Luftwaffe underground operations centre outside Potsdam. Göring's special war train, a collection of purpose-built conference cars, wireless rooms and flat tops with 20-millimetre flak mountings, had also been shunted into the compound; here Milch and Jeschonnek were summoned at 3.30 am on the twenty-seventh, as Göring drove up from Berlin. He announced that King Victor Emmanuel III of Italy was responsible for Mussolini's refusal to honour his Pact of Steel commitments. Later that day the four *Luftflotte* commanders were given their final briefing and on the twenty-eighth Milch toured the airfields of General Grauert's First Air Division, from which the main attack would be launched.[107] On the afternoon of 31 August the executive order was issued to the Luftwaffe to open the attack on Poland next day.[108] Göring still believed that hostilities could be localized to Poland, but Milch did not share this illusion: everything he had seen in Britain pointed the other way. On 3 September 1939 Britain and France declared war on Germany; and within a year the Luftwaffe was to be locked in combat with an adversary to whom Douhet's principles could not so easily be applied.

# PART II

# WORLD WAR TOO SOON

*'The war is to continue!'*
—Hitler to Milch, 12 October 1939

# THE RAINMAKER

## (*September 1939–May 1940*)

At the outbreak of the war, the Luftwaffe was formidable in size, but suffered from a weak substructure. Its basic strength before mobilization in August 1939 was some 370,000 men, of which 208,000 were in the air force (including 20,000 aircrew and 1,500 paratroops), 107,000 were in the flak and 58,000 were in the air signals units.[1] Its basic weaknesses, in Milch's view, looking back after the war, were the following: its vertical organization in four territorially determined *Luftflotte* commands was proper for home defence, but unsuitable for carrying the attack far beyond Germany's frontiers. There was too little consultation between the three Services, and only the most inadequate joint manoeuvres. Milch would have preferred a horizontal organization, with all-Reich commands for fighters, bombers and the ground Observer Corps, on the British models. The airfields had not been built with an eye to the size of the new generation of aircraft that was to come; indeed the Luftwaffe still lacked a long-range strategic bomber aircraft (the He 177, designed to fill this gap, would not fly until November), it lacked night bombers, bombs larger than one thousand pounds, air torpedoes, modern mines, modern armament and bombsights. Many of the shortcomings, such as the absence of air-to-air communication facilities between bomber formations and their escorting fighter groups, were to become evident only in 1940; others, such as the Luftwaffe's inadequate investment in ground-to-air guided missile development, not until 1943.[2]

As war now broke out, the Luftwaffe did still field the largest air force fleet in the world: 4,093 first-line aircraft (of which 3,646 were operational) were available, including 1,176 bombers, 408 twin-engined and 771 single-engined fighters and 552 Ju 52 transport aircraft (mostly still on loan to training schools).[3] But there were wholly inadequate reserves and the air industry's capacity was only a quarter of what it was later to become under Milch's direction. Germany had no significant stockpiles of materials such as aluminium, magnesium or rubber. In short, the indications are that world war came three years sooner than Hitler expected.

The local conflict in Poland lasted less than a month. Each evening Milch reported to Göring at his Potsdam headquarters and each morning he set out early in his fast Dornier bomber and toured the battlefields of east Prussia and Silesia, or climbed into a Fieseler Storch and dropped in on local air commanders; in this way he gained insight into their requirements and the course of the battle.

On 13 September Milch accompanied a Luftwaffe dive-bomber attack. He took off with about 180 Stukas; Kesselring was relying on dive-bombers for the main attacks on Warsaw, to ensure that at this stage only the strictly military targets were hit.[4] The Polish capital put up a wall of flak as the Ju 87s peeled off and dived on their targets, their 'Udet sirens' screaming in the slipstream: from his Do 17 Milch could see every bomb blast, and he reported the results of the attack to Göring afterwards. With the possible exception of the saturation attack on the Polish capital at the end of the campaign, no strategic bombing was attempted during this phase; the Luftwaffe restricted itself to army support operations.[5]

After twenty-two days the main fight was over, but the air force had exhausted over half its bomb supplies.[6] Compared with the army's losses, however, the Luftwaffe's casualties were very low: they had lost 285 of the 1,939 aircraft in the Polish theatre; and Milch's private papers show that the air force had lost 239 airmen, with a further 88 missing, one-fifth being officers. By comparison, the Luftwaffe lost a further 520 airmen killed and 298 missing during the 'phoney war' operations from 1 September 1939 to the end of March 1940 on the western front, for no subsequent gain.[7]

On 27 September Hitler instructed his C-in-Cs that he intended to open an offensive against France as soon as possible.[8] The Luftwaffe's most serious problem was that the bomber force would exhaust its remaining supply of bombs within the first two weeks of any new campaign. At first Hitler refused to allow the Luftwaffe to resume bomb production, but by 12 October 1939 he had to accept that both Britain and France had rejected his terms. He summoned Göring, Milch and Udet and announced 'You may now manufacture bombs again. The war is to continue!'[9] He held them personally responsible for ensuring adequate stocks when he opened his campaign in the west. Milch proposed to

Göring that he should be given dictatorial powers, above Udet's head, to organize an urgent bomb-production programme. Göring agreed. It was now that Milch remembered a visit he and Udet had paid two years before to a Swiss factory specializing in the manufacture of concrete bombs filled with shrapnel.[10] He ordered a factory outside Berlin to start churning out concrete bombs at once, and on his return from Norway in April 1940 learnt that a stockpile of several million concrete bombs had been produced, which he considered enough.*

The prolongation of the war took Ernst Udet, as Director of Air Armament, by surprise. When he and Milch visited the Heinkel factories on the Baltic coast at the beginning of November to see the He 177 heavy bomber and the He 178 jet aircraft (the latter in flight), Udet took Heinkel aside and murmured to him, 'I never really thought there would be war with Britain.'[12] Increasingly it was now Milch who had to step into this breach left by Udet, giving advice on the maze of technical problems facing them.

Meanwhile, in Berlin Göring prepared for the new campaign with frequent nervous conferences—in Milch's view to indicate to Hitler how alert he really was. On 5 November Hitler fixed the new date as the twelfth, but he bowed to the Luftwaffe's requirement of five days' fine weather so that the French air force could be destroyed. Göring presided over daily meteorological conferences and took frequent counsel of his chief weather expert, Diesing.[13] The one thing Göring feared most was fine weather, with the Luftwaffe as unready as it was. Milch could see the various pressures that Hitler and Göring brought to bear on this expert, but Diesing would not give way. *'Mein Führer,'* he said once, 'I will gladly be bold and predict fine weather for three days; but not foolhardy—not five days!' Göring even consulted a 'rainmaker', a certain Herr Schwefler who professed to influence the weather; he was paid a hundred thousand marks, but whether Göring instructed him to make five days' good or five months' bad weather proved immaterial, for his equipment later turned out to be a broken domestic wireless set.[14]

Both Hitler and Milch were aware that time was working to Germany's disadvantage; Intelligence put the combined British and French

---

* At the time he even believed the fifty-kilo concrete bombs superior to the small H.E. steel-cased bombs. Later he changed his opinion. In a conference in November 1942 he admitted, 'The tests carried out here quite clearly establish the opposite. I am obliged to change my view. The others (the concrete bombs) are thus only of use as a stop-gap, as was intended at the time.' But he added, 'I am no champion of the concrete bomb, but if the French campaign had started right after the Polish one, we in the Luftwaffe would probably have been relegated to the sidelines. The war would have been over for us on the fifth day.'[11]

air strength at 1,782 bombers and 1,823 fighters on 1 January 1940, of which perhaps sixty per cent were operational; Milch knew that both Britain and France were purchasing aircraft from America—he even knew the precise figures—so it was only a matter of time before the Luftwaffe found itself confronted by a numerically equal enemy.

Hitler now fixed the date for the attack on Belgium, Holland and France for 17 January. Belgium and Holland had been particularly included at Jeschonnek's request, to provide advance Luftwaffe bases from which to attack Britain and defend the Reich's airspace.[15] But a week before—even as Milch was accepting a high decoration at the hands of the Belgian ambassador—a light aircraft from General Felmy's Second Air Force strayed over the Belgian frontier and crash-landed; the aircraft had been carrying an unauthorized passenger, and he in turn had been carrying the entire operational plans for an airborne unit in the attack on Belgium due a few days hence. When Milch went to Karinhall next day to congratulate Göring on his birthday the field marshal was still in agonies of uncertainty about the incident.[16]

The news was the blackest mark so far against the reputation of the whole air force. Göring later said, 'The Führer rebuked me frightfully, as the C-in-C of the unfortunate courier, for having allowed a major part of our western mobilization and the very fact of such German plans to be betrayed. Look what a ghastly burden on my nerves it is to know that in the Führer's view my Luftwaffe officers have thrown this, the German people's mortal struggle, into jeopardy!'[17] The episode nearly finished Göring, so seriously did Hitler view this security lapse; Göring sacrificed Felmy and his chief of staff, Colonel Kammhuber, and dismissed them immediately *pour encourager les autres*.[18] Opportunist that Milch undoubtedly was, and glimpsing a chance to escape Berlin, he urged Göring to give him the vacant Second Air Force command. Göring was not averse to this, but Jeschonnek flatly objected. Göring gave the post to General Kesselring.[19]

The German legation in Brussels made discreet inquiries to find out whether the documents had been safely destroyed. That evening Milch found Göring somewhat more relaxed since word had arrived from General Wenninger, the attaché in Brussels, that the officers were claiming to have burnt them. Göring tried to burn a comparable bundle of documents himself, but the result was inconclusive. At his wife's suggestion he consulted clairvoyants and they sagely—though inaccurately, as we now know—pronounced that no trace of the incriminating documents had survived.[20] In any event, as Milch noted in his diary next day, the 'big event' had been 'postponed for some days because of the weather (thaw)'. Three days later Hitler postponed the operation until the spring.

The winter was exceptionally severe. The canals froze over and raw material movements inside Germany came to a standstill. The aircraft in squadron service were found to be unequal to the cold: the oxygen equipment of the fighters failed at high altitudes and the guns jammed, and several lives were lost through causes like these.[21] But gradually the *Luftflotte* commanders were able to report that their bomb dumps were filling up; a number of 2,200-pounders had reached them by the end of January and they had about two hundred thousand of the scarce 110-pounders by the end of March.[22]

Aircraft production itself was still falling short of expectations; for this the shortage of steel and duralumin was partly to blame. Early in February 1940 Göring ordered that as an economy any Wehrmacht project which would not bear fruit until after the war was over was to be ruthlessly cancelled, with the exception of the plan of Professor Krauch, director of IG Farben, for the synthetic production of fuel. But how long was the war to last? The official record of Göring's conference gave a clue: 'Those projects are considered vital which will be completed in 1940 or will be bearing fruit by 1941 at the latest.'[23] Ernst Udet accordingly cancelled the Jumo 004 jet engine until further notice, and the Me 262 jet airframe; other important fields of research like ground-to-air missiles were also set back.[24] When voices were raised in protest Udet brushed them aside: 'Now that I am a full general,' he told aircraft manufacturer Ernst Heinkel, 'the squadrons will just have to accept the aircraft I give them.'[25]

Outwardly Milch and Udet were still the closest friends, but Milch was increasingly irked by the other's direct access to Field Marshal Göring. One day in March 1940, as they were all three returning from a tour of the operational squadrons in the west, Göring began to praise the Director of Air Armament for all they had seen. Milch angrily pointed out that not all the credit was due to Udet: the He 111 had first been ordered by Lufthansa and the other aircraft and engines had been ordered long before Udet's appointment.[26] Since war had broken out there had been no increase in aircraft output (in the first four months only 1,869 aircraft had been delivered—less than the output of one month after Milch took over). Milch later learned that whereas crankshaft output from two factories had been 6,700 a month in 1938 and 1939, a year later the output was only 7,900 ('as though war had not broken out on 1 September 1939').[27] Some of Milch's words must have sunk into Göring, because next time he held a conference on aircraft production with Udet he asked Milch to be present as well.[28] These developments undoubtedly gave Udet food for thought.

After the *Altmark* incident, Hitler accelerated planning for a possible German invasion of Norway.[29] At the beginning of the year he had circulated a Wehrmacht study to the three Services, providing for a planning staff under a Luftwaffe general to devise possible invasion plans for Norway. Erhard Milch was the general selected to head this small staff, code-named 'Oyster', and it held its first and last meeting on 14 January.[30] But he also fell victim to the Felmy incident. The more the Führer had pondered the less satisfied he was of the Luftwaffe's ability to keep secrets. In any campaign against Norway—where the German navy would be at huge disadvantage—surprise was of the essence. He ordered the study to be recalled, 'Oyster' to be dissolved and all further planning to be confined to the cloisters of the High Command.[31] Here the preparations were co-ordinated by a navy captain, while an army corps commander, General Nikolaus von Falkenhorst, was appointed to direct the actual operation. Initially air operations would be conducted by General Hans Geisler's Tenth Air Corps, consisting of a number of bomber and fighter squadrons.

The Wehrmacht invaded Norway and Denmark on 9 April 1940, in a lightning coup a few hours before British forces, which had already been embarked, could undertake a similar operation of their own for the occupation of Norway. The Special Transport Squadron 172, established from Lufthansa crews under the company's traffic manager, ferried hundreds of troops in Ju 52s to the airfields seized by paratroops in Norway.[32] The Luftwaffe's first preoccupation was to consolidate its hold on the airfields, from which General Geisler's bombers could attack the Royal Navy's units that now hastened to Norway's aid.

Göring told Milch that he was to be given an operational command at last: he was to establish a Fifth Air Force command in Norway, to control the Tenth Air Corps's operations there. He would not lose his jealously guarded rights as state secretary and Göring's representative in Berlin, but Norway was to come first, as a prologue to the main air war against Britain; in addition to directing Luftwaffe support of Falkenhorst's operations—now increasingly hampered by the Norwegian resistance—Milch was to expand, modernize and increase in number the airfields in Norway and Denmark. As soon as the attack on France became imminent he would be recalled to Berlin at once.[33]

It seems in retrospect that Göring had two reasons for putting Milch in charge of the new air force. If the Norwegian campaign went against the Germans Milch would get the blame; and he wanted to get him away from Berlin and his troubled protégé Udet. Significantly, when Milch suggested locating Fifth Air Force headquarters in Hamburg, because of communication problems inside Norway, Göring insisted on Oslo; the result was that Milch had inadequate communication with the most important airfield, Stavanger, and with the (totally unsuitable) emergency airfield at Trondheim, as there were no cables or telephone lines and the wireless signals were screened by high mountains.

Milch attacked the new task with vigour. In southern Norway the Luftwaffe was operating about six hundred fighters, bombers and reconnaissance aircraft, and over six hundred transporters had airlifted the German troops to this theatre. It was vital to consolidate their hold on the main airfields—Stavanger (Sola), Oslo (Fornebu and Kjeller) and Trondheim (Vaernes)—as air superiority was to be the key to the struggle. In the south it would be virtually complete, as the enemy had no airfields at all; but near Narvik the British managed in time to establish two fighter squadrons and these made long-range Luftwaffe support operations extremely hazardous. Milch flew to Hamburg to await a chance to set up his headquarters in Oslo; by 13 April Göring was already telephoning repeatedly from Berlin, urging the Luftwaffe to launch full-scale air operations in support of the beleaguered forces at Narvik.[34]

Bad weather now kept Milch grounded in Hamburg for several days. He attended four days of conferences with the Air Staff and Hitler on the crisis in northern Norway, complicated by a British seaborne landing at Namsos, 125 miles by road north of the major port of Trondheim, which was obviously the objective; there were also reconnaissance reports of an imminent British landing at Åndalsnes, 200 miles by road to the south. (The latter operation did not in fact take place until the seventeenth.) The Namsos landing was unopposed and in considerable strength; if Trondheim were captured by the British it would make the relief of Narvik impossible and would jeopardize the whole operation. When the first reports of the landings near Trondheim reached Hitler he sent for Göring, Milch and Jeschonnek to confer on means of containing the British forces believed to be at Åndalsnes: he recommended that with even more urgency than the support operations for General Dietl's men at Narvik, the air force should rush paratroops to the endangered area, strafe armoured trains and employ what he called 'Udet bombers'—i.e. dive-bombers—to sink the British warships offshore. The small harbour of Åndalsnes itself should be destroyed by KG 4's bombers, together with the invading troops it contained. Hitler also directed that the railway lines near Åndalsnes should be cut, but only temporarily (the important viaducts should be left intact). If the German-controlled railways elsewhere were sabotaged the nearest villages were to be wiped out.[35] Milch was urgently to improve Vaernes airfield, about twenty miles east of Trondheim, and to enlarge a second landing ground there, for Stuka and transporting squadrons. Milch telephoned these instructions to General Geisler in Hamburg at once.

He flew to Stavanger on 16 April. Geisler's squadrons there were heavily committed to operations against British naval units. The British found it almost impossible to attack Trondheim's Vaernes airfield and instead bombarded ships and aircraft on Stavanger's airfield, starting on the seventeenth.[36] By 18 April the British had landed thirteen thousand men at Namsos and Åndalsnes and von Falkenhorst had the gravest fears for the German campaign's future. Milch ordered the Luftwaffe's twin-engined fighters and bombers to maintain their attack on the enemy troops. On 19 April the Luftwaffe delivered a devastating attack on the harbour and town of Namsos and left it in ruins. A few days later the British commander advised London, 'I see little chance of carrying out decisive, or indeed any, operations, unless enemy air activity is considerably restricted.'[37]

Towards the end of April the Germans' situation in northern Norway further worsened, causing recrimination between the army and the Luftwaffe. Göring sent his staff officers to Oslo in order to report on Milch but the latter kept his nerve throughout, even when the besieged Dietl's position at Narvik seemed quite hopeless. Von Falkenhorst visited Milch, thoroughly dejected, and advised him, 'We will all have to get back on the ships—we are just not getting anywhere.' Their only hope was still more air support.[38] Milch did what he could. Two giant ex-Lufthansa Do 26 seaplanes were loaded with mountain troops and flown to Narvik (where they met a sticky end). At the same time a final effort was made to dislodge the Allied troops fighting their way towards Trondheim. Göring continued to intervene with 'idiotic telegrams' from Berlin. The breakthrough at Bagn on the twenty-seventh, greatly aided by dive-bomber support, spelt the end of Norwegian and British resistance in central Norway. On the twenty-eighth the evacuation of all troops at Namsos and Åndalsnes was ordered by the British; they left on 3 May, the transporters and escorts pursued by the Luftwaffe's bombers all the way. All of Norway, except for Narvik, where Dietl's mixed force of six thousand soldiers and sailors were holding twenty thousand Allied troops at bay, was now under German control.

For the Norwegian operation, Erhard Milch's only field command in the Second World War, he was awarded the Knight's Cross. Hitler was later to utter high words of praise for Milch's contribution to the campaign. In conference with Speer and others he recalled how the colonel-general had taken control of the situation as soon as he arrived in Norway, a situation which to others had appeared all but lost: 'And why? Because here was a man like me, who just did not know the word "impossible".'[39]

# A QUESTION OF TIME

## (*May–July 1940*)

In the first days of the attack on France and the Low Countries the Luftwaffe lived up to its reputation. Despite the recent diversion to Norway, Göring had marshalled nearly four thousand aircraft for the new offensive, including 1,482 bombers and dive-bombers, 42 ground-attack aircraft, 248 twin-engined and 1,016 single-engined fighters; the Allies had mustered 1,151 fighters in France, but very many fewer bombers than the Germans. At dawn on 10 May 1940 wave after wave of German aircraft crossed the frontiers and attacked over seventy of the enemy's airfields, destroying large numbers of aircraft on the ground. Göring's airborne troops seized key targets like the Moerdijk bridge in Holland and the Rotterdam strongpoints, while gliders silently landed on the fortresses of Belgium and took them by surprise. With almost complete air superiority achieved, the Luftwaffe changed to close support of the army's operations, battering a way for the columns of tanks and field-grey infantry storming in their wake. Thanks to Milch's early insistence on mobility, the Luftwaffe's squadrons were able to leapfrog forward from one captured airfield to the next, so that close air support was never lacking. By the evening of 11 May there were reports that the enemy's air forces had lost up to a thousand aircraft already.

Milch flew his Dornier over the front line almost every day of the French campaign, witnessing every major battle; not without reason Ernst Udet sketched a winged Milch, camera in hand, hovering above the battlefields. Late on 15 May Göring's special train, 'Asia', left Potsdam for the western front; at 11 am next morning it reached its specially prepared site outside a railway tunnel near the French border. Every morning Milch attended Göring's war conference to report on the most advanced squadrons and armoured spearheads, then set out for six or seven hours in a Dornier and a Storch. In the evening he again reported on what he had seen and Göring retailed Milch's reconnaissance report —sketched on a chart just as he had taught his airmen in the First World

War—to Hitler's headquarters not far away. Milch's reports were both more accurate and swifter than the routine army reconnaissance reports. The rate of advance was spectacular; the Luftwaffe's squadron flags fluttered from airfields farther and farther to the west. It was clear that the first battle for France was nearly over. As the British Expeditionary Force—over a quarter of a million soldiers—withdrew to the Channel ports, the German armour poised to cut them off.

It was Hermann Göring who persuaded the Führer to concentrate his army on other more immediate tasks than the capture of Dunkirk.[1] He saw it as an opportunity of scoring over the army and emphasizing the Luftwaffe's prowess; after the war one of his adjutants was to state, 'He used to look down on the army as a pitiful, obsolete branch of the armed forces.'[2] On 23 May Göring telephoned to Hitler his view that the Luftwaffe's 'finest hour' was at hand; single-handed it would destroy the British forces in France.[3] Against furious army opposition Hitler welcomed the offer (General Jodl, Hitler's principal strategic adviser, sarcastically observed to an adjutant, 'There goes Göring shooting off his big mouth again!'). When Göring and Jeschonnek returned to Luftwaffe headquarters the former triumphed to Milch, 'We have done it! The Luftwaffe is to wipe out the British on the beaches. I have managed to talk the Führer round to halting the army.' He waved aside Milch's misgivings: 'The army always wants to act the gentleman. They round up the British as prisoners with as little harm to them as possible. The Führer wants them to be taught a lesson they won't easily forget.'*[4]

Having made his promise Göring departed on his travels, flying to Amsterdam. But now there were new conditions. Not only were the Luftwaffe's bomber airfields too far from Dunkirk, but for three vital days they were blanketed in fog. Thus on 30 May, although three hundred bombers stood by all day, with fighter cover promised, they were unable to take off because of ten-tenths cloud cover at three hundred feet. Meanwhile the brave shoals of British small craft embarked the fleeing British Expeditionary Force, while the French army fought a costly rearguard action. The small vessels presented poor targets for the Eighth Air Corps's dive-bombers, accustomed to attacking tanks and airfields; the bombs buried deep in the sand before exploding, with little anti-personnel effect. The German tanks remained at a standstill, on Rundstedt's orders.

More potent as an augury of future events was the local daylight air superiority achieved over the Me 109 by the British Spitfire fighter,

---

* Hitler's army adjutant wrote soon after, 'The impression is that Göring has been actively stirring things up against the army. Führer keeps harping on how reliable the Luftwaffe is ideologically, in contrast to the army. . . .'[5]

operating at short ranges over Dunkirk. All German calculations had assumed that Professor Messerschmitt's plane would prove the better of the two, but now the Spitfire wrought havoc on the German fighter squadrons and the bombers approaching Dunkirk were easy prey. One Ju 88 squadron was mauled almost into oblivion as it flew in from its distant airfield in Holland. Göring's confidence, in short, remained misplaced: by 4 June, when Dunkirk was finally captured by the German army, the British had rescued 338,000 men from France. At the time the long-term lessons, and even the fact of the miscarriage of German plans, were not recognized by Göring.

Milch flew to Dunkirk on 5 June. The chaos left by a whole army in full flight made an awesome spectacle. The fields were full of untended cattle, and thousands of unguarded prisoners—mostly French—were trudging into the dead city, which had been reduced to ruins by the devastating Luftwaffe attacks. About fifty thousand abandoned vehicles were choking the streets converging on the beach and the hulks of a score of large ships could be seen half-submerged off-shore; 235 vessels, including nine destroyers, had been sunk here by the Luftwaffe.*[6]

The sandy beaches were strewn with shoes, weapons, bicycles, lorries, food and abandoned property—linen, books and photographs scattered in confusion. It reminded Milch of the scenes in east Prussia after the rout of the Russian invaders twenty-five years before.

The fact that the army itself had escaped almost intact dawned on Göring only slowly. When Milch flew back to 'Asia' that evening to report what he had seen Göring was still congratulating himself on the frightful débâcle that the British army must have suffered. Milch disillusioned him: 'The British army? I saw perhaps twenty or thirty corpses. The rest of the British army has got clean away to the other side. They have left their equipment and escaped.' He agreed that being thrown out of France after only three weeks was a tremendous reverse for the British, but, 'The fact remains that they have succeeded in bringing out practically the whole of their army, and that is an achievement which it would be hard to beat.'[7]

Göring asked what conclusions he would draw. 'I would recommend,' said Milch, 'that this very day all our air units—of both the Second and Third Air Forces—should be moved up to the Channel coast, and that Britain should be invaded *immediately*.' The navy would eventually have to be brought in to transfer the ground forces to southern England, but

---

* A similar description of the chaos left by the British army on the approaches to Dunkirk will be found in the diary of General Fedor von Bock, the German army group commander.

the highly mobile Luftwaffe could go over as they were. Their paratroops would have to capture a few vital airfields in southern England
and the Luftwaffe would then immediately fly in fighter and Stuka squadrons to operate from them—just as they had in the Norwegian campaign.
They had several hundred transport aircraft available and these could
ferry over two or three divisions of troops with fighter escort. Obviously,
Milch continued, it would be a great gamble without armour or heavy
artillery for this spearhead; but he was convinced that for the next few
days the British army would be incapable of combating a really determined landing. He warned Göring, 'If we leave the British in peace for
four weeks it will be too late.'

But Göring thought it could not be done. He may well have been
right. He later explained, 'I had only one paratroop division, and even
that I had had to work up almost clandestinely, as I could make no
headway with my demand for four such divisions against the demands
of the army. Had I had these four divisions at the time of Dunkirk, I
would have gone across to Britain immediately.'[8]

Milch saw in this hesitance the High Command's first decisive mistake,
and he laid most of the blame on his old enemy Admiral Raeder. He
had gained the impression that Raeder had made no preparations for an
invasion of England, and that to stall for time he now insisted that air
supremacy must first be won by the Luftwaffe. And only as he raised
this demand, Milch thought, had Raeder begun feverish activity to make
up for the delay. By the summer of 1940 the German air force was to
be involved in a costly war of attrition at extended range against the
British fighter squadrons; when the onset of autumn finally killed all
hope of an invasion in 1940, the German navy was still unready but
could now blame the Luftwaffe for not having fulfilled the main
requirement.

Visiting the various captured airfields and headquarters as Inspector
during June 1940, Milch could see that in the absence of a Führer decree to that effect no preparations *at all* were being made for air war
with Britain.

The end of June 1940 brought respite to the German air force. No
decision had yet been reached on the future of the war. Hitler believed
it was over and considered the appeal to Britain's reason only a formality. It was time to reward his commanders: on 19 July Milch was
among the new field marshals created by Hitler in a major Reichstag
speech; for Göring an even more exalted rank was created, *'Reichsmarschall* of the Greater German Reich'.[9]

Milch recognized the artificiality of a promotion which now ranked him equal to a von Moltke or a Hindenburg; and for a born climber there was a certain sense of denouement upon reaching a rank beyond which no mortal could mount, with any amount of energy, diligence or ruthlessness. And yet, 'Be that as it may, my pleasure was enormous and unforgettable.' Under the old ordinance of 1878 field marshals took precedence over both the Reich Chancellor and the Reich ministers; they had a rank of which they could never be deprived and from which they could never retire. Milch wore the new insignia proudly until the day of his capture, a gesture which attracted the fury of the more anonymously clad commandos into whose hands he was delivered at the end of the war. And he greeted with derision the American attempts to strip him of his rank ('You did not appoint me, so you cannot dismiss me!').[10] The German field marshal traditionally enjoyed the right to full pay, with an office, a clerk, a staff officer and motor vehicles or horses to the end of his life. But these were the privileges of a field marshal in victory; the lot of a field marshal in defeat will be the subject of a later chapter.

# 'IF EIGHT MILLION GO MAD...'

## (*July–December 1940*)

'The ultimate German victory of arms over Britain is only a matter of time,' General Jodl confidently concluded at the end of the French campaign. 'Large-scale enemy operations are no longer possible.'[1] These were not unreasonable prophesies. Hitler commanded strategic positions which even he had not ventured openly to predict a year before. From northern Norway down to the Spanish frontier the entire European coastline facing Britain was in his hands. The Luftwaffe's airfields were but an hour's flight from London, while Berlin was virtually unattainable for the RAF. Having gained this position, however, Hitler proceeded to squander it, for he still had no intention of humiliating Britain; he considered the British a kindred race, perverse but not without intelligence, and his eyes were already straying eastwards towards his eternal, restless enemy, the Soviet Union. Until the end of 1940 he still dreamed of peace with Britain; and this alone explains why the man who nine months later was to show in the bombing of Belgrade with what ruthlessness he could invade a nation of Serbs stayed the hand of his Luftwaffe for two long months above London's streets, and even then displayed traits of sentimentality—for example on Christmas Eve —wholly unprofitable in modern warfare.

His staff were more old-fashioned and wanted to see Britain defeated, rather than coming to terms. Jodl reasoned, 'First of all must come the fight against the British air force.'[2] If they could destroy the British aircraft industry the RAF could no longer be replenished, and this in turn would preempt Britain's only means of attacking Germany, since naval blockade could no longer spell the end for the Reich. Indeed now the Luftwaffe could blockade Britain: 'In conjunction with propaganda and terror-raids from time to time—announced as "reprisals"—a cumulative depletion of Britain's food stocks will paralyse the will of the people to resist, and then break it altogether, forcing the capitulation of their government.'

Whether Jodl's views would have proved true had they been put into practice at this point, one month after Dunkirk, may seem a moot point, in the light of later events. But it was certainly the most advantageous time: there were still three clear summer months ahead for Luftwaffe operations, and with every week that passed the Royal Air Force's defences were growing stronger, and at a faster rate than the comparable Luftwaffe expansion. On 30 June 1940 the Luftwaffe had 841 serviceable bombers and rather over seven hundred fighters against a similar number of RAF fighters; the latter, Milch knew, were being replenished at over four hundred a month—over twice as fast as the production of the sole German single-engined fighter, the Me 109.[3] This made nonsense of any policy of conservation on the part of the Luftwaffe. Yet such a policy instruction was issued,[4] while the German armies ostentatiously regrouped on the Channel coast and hundreds of ships, barges and boats were massed in full view for an invasion of southern England—an invasion which Jodl anticipated would not take place before early September, and even then only as the *coup de grâce* for a Britain with her economy paralysed and her air force beaten, 'should such a *coup* still be necessary'.

For the first three weeks in July this directive effectively tied the Luftwaffe's own hands, permitting them to execute only harassing raids in addition to an anti-shipping campaign. Under Kesselring and Sperrle the Second and Third Air Forces, with a common boundary on the River Seine, were allocated spheres of operations in western and eastern England respectively; eventually the Fifth Air Force (Stumpff) would take in northern England from Norwegian airfields. There was one organizational innovation, the introduction of two tactical fighter commanders on the ground, *Jagdfliegerführer 2,* subordinated to the Second Air Force, and *Jagdfliegerführer 3* to the Third.[5] These controlled respectively 460 single- and 90 twin-engined fighters, and 300 single- and 130 twin-engined fighters. Their disadvantage over the comparable RAF Fighter Groups was that these improvised *Jafü*'s could not plot the enemy squadrons' movements; nor had any provision been made for them to control their fighter squadrons by radio telephone once they had left the ground. Not surprisingly, Göring asked Kesselring and Sperrle 'to inform him how they envisaged controlling their fighter escort squadrons', and stated the need for 'information centres for the Air Corps during our attacks, so that we keep a clear picture of what the enemy's up to'; these centres were to work in close co-operation with heir wireless monitoring service.*[6] These technical shortcomings came to Milch's attention only after the Battle of Britain had begun.

Initially Hitler had been thinking of an invasion of Britain in mid-August. The orders issued by the Luftwaffe operations staff in mid-July set out their twin objectives in the 'final phase' before the invasion as the destruction of Britain's air force and the disruption of her supplies by attacks on her ports and shipping. To this latter end the Fourth Air Corps was transferred to north-west France, to tread on Britain's corns –her shipping lanes. The Eighth Air Corps (von Richthofen's dive-bombers) was assigned to closing the English Channel by day, and other units were to attack Britain's shipping and close her ports with minefields by night.

The former objective, the attack on the RAF, would be completed in two stages: first the fighter defences and defence organization in southern England only would be annihilated; then daylight operations would roll northwards until complete air supremacy had been achieved, while at the same time a complementary assault on the British aircraft industry would take place. From 'Eagle Day', the initial day of this second phase, four weeks would probably elapse to the day on which an invasion could take place; and 'Eagle Day' itself could come as soon as four days after the start of this intensive campaign. So much for the Luftwaffe plan; there is no evidence that Milch disputed it.

On 16 July Hitler issued a directive for the planning of an invasion 'if it should prove necessary'; on the seventeenth the Luftwaffe squadrons were placed on maximum readiness, and a crescendo of attacks on the supply lines began as part of the softening up. On the nineteenth Hitler issued an open appeal to the British, which was rejected on the twenty-second. Hitler believed that Britain's otherwise inexplicable attitude could be attributed to her hopes of a change of heart in currently isolationist America, and a change of alliance in Russia.[7] In a conference with Jeschonnek and the army and navy C-in-Cs on the twenty-first, he described an invasion threat as the best means of forcing Britain to see reason, and he asked them to discover whether such an invasion could be executed by 15 September—the last possible date, it seemed, for reasons of tide and weather. The navy at once indicated that they could commence 'practical preliminaries' only when the Luftwaffe had secured air supremacy.

* Milch had first demanded radio to enable ground controllers to communicate with fighter pilots and escort fighters with bombers back in 1934. In September 1943 he reflected, 'I never found out why our bombers were unable to communicate with their escort fighters in the attacks on Britain.'

On the same day, 21 July, Göring called all his senior commanders and Air Staff officers to Karinhall for a luncheon and conference. Göring predicted that the current interim series of scattered night attacks on ports and the British aircraft industry would be replaced by the 'final phase', starting in a week's time. In the meantime he asked for more determined attacks on Britain's shipping and ports. He wanted to see the 'convoys swept up, starting with the merchant ships', and extensive minelaying operations to block the western approaches, camouflaged by simultaneous bombing attacks on nearby ports. When the main attack on land targets began, these would be 'violent attacks to unsettle the whole country'. The bombers were to drop bombs fitted with anti-disturbance and time fuses, set for several hours' delay. Primary targets like the ports of the south coast were to be spared from attack as yet, 'particularly the unloading facilities in the ports along the coast from the Isle of Wight to the south-eastern corner'—for this was where in September Germany would need unloading facilities the most.[8]

Before they left Karinhall both of the *Luftflotte* commanders in France were asked to submit to Göring within one week their own views on achieving air supremacy. Göring himself believed that this could be achieved only by destroying the RAF and its supporting aero-engine industry—an industry the enemy would be forced to defend. The theory was that the RAF's fighter squadrons would be hammered on the anvil of swarms of superior Me 109s and Me 110s escorting the bombers. The selection of the British aero-engine factories was a significant reflection of the most vulnerable target system in the Luftwaffe's industrial base. As to their tactics, Göring suggested they make these factories the target for 'nuisance raids' by night at once: 'Leave the enemy in constant doubt as to time and place,' he suggested, 'so that he cannot concentrate his defences.' In fact these crucial factories were beyond the range of the Me 109 escorts, and there were far too few of the heavier Me 110s for such a purpose.

A number of points must be borne in mind before the narrative of the battle commences. Firstly, Hitler had not yet decided on an invasion at all (as late as 31 July he advised the other C-in-Cs that he would decide between the alternatives, September 1940 and May 1941, only after a week's trial of the Luftwaffe's main attack).[9] Secondly, until mid-September Hitler refused to authorize any kind of attack on London's inhabitants, and this in General Jeschonnek's view seriously blunted the edge of the Luftwaffe's weapon. Thirdly, Göring had based his undertakings about the length of time needed to destroy the RAF on a number of assumptions which were to prove very wrong indeed.

It was only now, for example, as the attack began, that the Germans realized from intercepted wireless orders that the RAF fighter squadrons were radar-controlled from the ground; and it was only now that Göring discovered that the Me 110 twin-engined fighter (of which he had no fewer than two hundred) was useless as a daylight escort for the bomber forces since it was inferior to the agile Spitfire and Hurricane. But the

Field Marshal Kesselring (right) and Sperrle, commanding *Luftflotten* 2 and 3 respectively in the Battle of Britain.   [*Sketch by Ernst Udet*]

Me 109 single-engined fighter could barely reach London and Milch's early recommendation, made many months before, that cheap drop tanks should be fitted to extend the Me 109's fuel endurance had been followed up too late, with the result that the crews were untrained in their use and reluctant to employ them.

This was a very late hour to make such discoveries. The battle could not be called off, but its tactics should have been amended to allow the Luftwaffe a task of which it *was* capable. The objectives remained the same, however; in the Führer's directive of 1 August the force's objective was still 'to subdue the British air force', followed by attacks on the air industry and anti-aircraft gun production. Hitler still prohibited 'terror raids as reprisals', and London was still a prohibited area.[10] With hindsight, it can be seen that in this first phase the Luftwaffe should have concentrated on destroying the fighters' radar and

CARL A. RUDISILL LIBRARY
LENOIR-RHYNE COLLEGE

ground-control organization, but only the general strategic objective
were reflected in the directive issued to the *Luftflotten* on 2 August.[1]

Hitherto the Germans had sent short-range fighter squadrons in strength
over southern England to lure the RAF into a battle in which they would
be outnumbered: recognizing that this was the tactic, the British fighter
commanders wisely refused to accept battle unless actual bomber attacks were in progress. Subsequently the Luftwaffe had sent small formations of bombers, heavily escorted by fighters, to provoke the defence
by harassing ports and shipping. It was soon obvious that the RAF
losses were not of such a rate as to weaken Fighter Command enough
for the 'second phase' of the attack, the rolling-up of the defences north
of southern England. All this time the British air industry was producing
fighter aircraft at twice the German industry's rate.

Nevertheless, Göring launched the second phase with 'Eagle Day',
a day for which he worked out a precise plan of attacks. The details
were dispensed to Milch and the three *Luftflotte* commanders (Stumpf
having been brought in from Norway) at Karinhall at noon on 6 August
in the new offensive heavily escorted bomber formations would attack
the 'vicinity of London' in broad daylight, as a tactic to overpower
the fighter defences.[12] London itself would not be touched. If during the
first days of this new phase the German losses proved too high, or the
returns in RAF losses too uncertain, then Göring was ready to call
the whole operation off. 'Eagle Day', the start of the full air assault on
the RAF, would be 10 August, Göring announced. This would be consistent with a final invasion in mid-September.

For three days bad weather prevented the Luftwaffe from opening
the assault. On 11 August Göring promised Hitler he would begin as
soon as he had a forecast of three days' fine weather; and on the afternoon of the twelfth he announced 'Eagle Day' for next day.[13] Since
effectively it was to be a duel between fighter forces the opposing sides
were quite evenly matched in numbers: the Luftwaffe disposed of 702
single-engined fighters on 10 August (with an additional 227 twin-
engined Me 110s, which were soon taken out of the battle); the RAF
commanded a force of 749, mostly single-engined Hurricanes and Spitfires, being replenished at considerable speed (490 had been manufactured during July alone). The Luftwaffe also disposed of 875
serviceable bombers and 316 dive-bombers.[14]

The attack opened early on 13 August, but went off at a tangent
since Göring ordered the recall of the entire Second Air Force as the
weather worsened: 'Grand slam opens with only Third Air Force because of weather,' Milch recorded.[15] Nearly five hundred bomber sor-

ties, with twice as many fighters as escorts, were made against airfields and fighter defences in southern England, however, and fierce air battles developed. Two days later the Fifth Air Force joined in, with diversionary attacks against northern England. Far from heralding the final defeat of the RAF, the offensive brought mounting German losses: on the thirteenth the Luftwaffe lost forty-five aircraft, for thirteen RAF fighters (six of the RAF pilots survived to fight again); on the fourteenth the Germans lost nineteen, the RAF only eight (the Luftwaffe claimed eighteen).

It was obvious to Göring that no real headway was being made. At noon on the fifteenth he called his three *Luftflotte* commanders back to Karinhall, together with Milch and Jeschonnek, to express his dissatisfaction with the *Luftflotte* commanders' tactics and achievements.[16] He mentioned many technical shortcomings: there were not enough He 59 ambulance floatplanes; the fighters were refusing to use the drop tanks unless they were armour-plated; and most important of all: 'How can we establish radio-telephone contact between the bombers and their fighter escort?' he asked. Göring now accepted that the Me 110s were inadequate when confronted with Spitfires and Hurricanes, and that they must be withdrawn from the battle; he also suggested that they should treat the British radar stations only as 'alternative targets'. The radio-beam squadron, K.Gr 100, might be used to attack the aircraft industry at Birmingham, he proposed; but he warned, 'Cities as such are not to be attacked yet—particularly not London.'

That day the RAF lost only thirty-four aircraft compared with the Luftwaffe's seventy-five. Within three days what should have been the Luftwaffe's hour of triumph was instead the beginning of a rout: during 16 August all three air forces had operated, losing forty-five aircraft, while the RAF lost only twenty-one (the Luftwaffe claimed 108).[17] In extensive operations on the eighteenth the dive-bombers mislaid their escort and were almost annihilated: seventy-one Luftwaffe aircraft were destroyed, compared with twenty-seven RAF fighters. On the nineteenth bad weather brought the offensive to a standstill, with the objective even further away than when it had started.

Göring summoned a new meeting of every commander down to squadron level on 19 August, to tell them of his disappointment at the fighters' performance and to explain their new strategy: for the time being, the costly daylight attacks on aircraft factories and similar targets must be replaced by night attacks. Henceforth major daylight operations would aim only at provoking fighter battles, with just enough bombers provided to act as bait. The campaign against fighter airfields would continue, but the more vulnerable aircraft like the Ju 87s and the Me 110s were to be held in reserve until the 'grand slam' which would spell the RAF's final defeat: 'The main task of the twin-engined aircraft will come when the fighters reach the limit of their range.' In bad weather they would attack targets like Norwich, but 'primarily RAF targets', to force the fighter defences to come up; when the weather improved they were to destroy the RAF fighters in the air by *Schwerpunkt* formation: all single-engined fighters of both *Luftflotten* should escort the bombers of one *Luftflotte,* followed up by the twin-engined fighters as a last wave of reinforcements.

Göring angrily appealed to the fighter pilots for a sense of responsibility: 'Neither type of fighter is allowed to break off its escort mission because of weather,' he instructed, and warned that any pilot found guilty of this misdemeanour would face a court martial—a sure indication of the increasing nervousness of the bomber pilots. He ordered the bombers to keep 'grimly in formation' to give the escorts a chance of doing their job. He also recommended that each bomber formation should always have the same escort squadron, and that the respective commanders should get to know each other, in order to cultivate a personal sense of responsibility. (In the event, the rigid binding of the fast fighters to slow, lumbering bombers gave the RAF just the edge it needed over the Luftwaffe.)

Mass attacks on cities, as opposed to nuisance attacks, were still forbidden. But to give credibility to the diversionary attacks from Norwegian airfields, Göring authorized General Geisler's Tenth Air Corps to make a heavy attack on the Glasgow city area in the far north. Nuisance raids on British industry were to continue, 'but not yet on London'. The primary object was still to induce the RAF to offer battle on the Luftwaffe's terms.[18]

The Germans believed that the RAF had managed to stock up about 350 fighters, assisted by the bad weather respite, after being down to their 'last hundred'. (In fact on 23 August the RAF had over 700 fighter aircraft serviceable). When the weather lifted and the Luftwaffe were able to resume the offensive on the twenty-third an important second phase of the RAF's defence also began: recognizing that the Germans lacked a long-range escort fighter the British had withdrawn their southern fighter squadrons to airfields around London where the Me 109 would be at the limit of its fuel endurance. To the Germans, the only way to destroy what seemed an importunate few was to provoke them *en masse* (*Schwerpunkt* formation) and that seemed to indicate daylight attacks on London itself.

On 25 August the RAF bombed Berlin (after one flight of Luftwaffe aircraft had strayed over London, killing nine civilians there). Within the next ten days four more RAF attacks were aimed at Berlin. This was what Hitler had hoped to avoid; on 4 September he warned, 'If they continue to attack our cities, then we will wipe out theirs. . . .'

Of the Luftwaffe commanders it was General Jeschonnek who expected most from mass daylight attacks on London.[19] Göring challenged him, after dinner in his dining car, 'Do you think that Germany would give in if Berlin were in ruins?' 'Of course not,' replied Jeschonnek. He clearly assumed that British civilian morale was more fragile than German. 'That,' concluded Göring, 'is where you are wrong.'[20] Not for the last time, he showed that he assessed the true position more accurately than he was prepared to admit to Hitler.

Milch had begun an extended series of inspection trips on 20 August and these spread over several weeks. Travelling by fast plane or black Mercedes saloon he sprung himself on fighter and bomber commanders without warning, checking squadron morale and equipment performance, testing their camouflage and watching their operations. 'If the last war taught us how to dig in, this war has taught us camouflage,' he reported to Göring on 26 August.[21] Page after page of a green 1936 'Collins Paragon Diary' he filled with notes—complaints about medals, tactics, guns, ammunition, aircraft and engines; he prodded the reluctant with his interim baton and rewarded the brave with decorations or boxes of Brazil cigars.[22]

The taut morale of the highly-disciplined Luftwaffe squadrons was still largely intact, but some of them, particularly the Stuka and Me 110 squadrons, were showing signs of strain. The Me 110's depth of penetration was only about 160 miles and allowed only fifteen or twenty minutes' combat endurance on top of that. All the fighter squadrons he inspected favoured freelance fighter operations rather than the murderous close-formation escort work. 'It is unfortunate for close cooperation between fighter and bomber squadrons,' he reported to Göring afterwards, 'that the units escorting the bombers are constantly changed; two squadrons consistently working together and able to discuss their missions in person with each other beforehand are far more likely to be successful.'

After *Luftflotte* 2, Milch turned his attention to Field Marshal Sperrle's *Luftflotte* 3; since 27 August it had been principally engaged in night attacks, including four heavy raids on Liverpool and Birkenhead mounted at a cost of only seven bombers.[23] When he flew back to Berlin on 3 September he saw Hitler, who had also hurried back to

Milch photographing battlefield hotspots in 1940     [*Sketch by Ernst Udet*]

ιe capital as soon as the RAF attacks began. Hitler asked him to in-
rease the output of 2,200-pound bombs—a sure indication that the
ιr war was now to turn to Britain's cities.[24]

On the same day Hitler removed his embargo on night attacks on
ιngland, in view of Sperrle's success, but London itself was still a
rohibited area. The Luftwaffe now accepted that, despite the desperate
ιr battles that had taken place, the RAF still had about 420 serviceable
ghters left.[25] Hitler recognized that the requirement for the invasion
f England ('achievement of air supremacy') had still not been met,
ut was withholding the final order for the present until he saw the
esults of the continued attack on the RAF.[26] The earliest possible date
or the preliminary invasion order was understood to be 21 September.

ουring August the RAF had lost 359 fighter aircraft and the German
ιr force 653; the Luftwaffe believed that their victories were very much
ιore substantial. Their recent tactics of concentrating some effort on
ιe fighter airfields were indeed proving an embarrassment to the RAF.
ωn 1 September the German squadrons for the first time reported a
ωeakening in the defences, and on the sixth the OKW was told that
ιverage RAF fighter squadron strength had sunk from twelve to only
ιve or seven aircraft.[27] It was now—stimulated by another raid on
ιerlin—that Hitler ordered the attack on London to begin at last, and
ωith the abandonment of the attack on the fighter airfields in southern
ιngland the Battle of Britain passed its turning-point.

Göring had already informed Milch that to exert a greater influence
ιn the battle he was going to Holland on 6 September and Ghent on
ιe seventh, and that he intended to stay in the west for about two
ωeeks, directing the battle. (Milch was to deputize for him in Berlin.)
ιow that the final assault on London itself was to begin, Göring told
ιe German nation by wireless, 'I myself have taken command of the
ιuftwaffe's battle for Britain.' By attacking London by day he hoped to
ιrce the British to sacrifice 'the tiny remainder of their fighters'.

On the night of 5 September, as Milch was relaxing in Berlin after a
ιay's hunting and drinking with Udet, Kesselring's bomber squadrons
ιarried out their first attack on London's dockland. On 7 September,
ιs Göring stood with Kesselring and Bruno Loerzer, one of the Air
ιorps commanders, on the cliffs at Cap Blanc Nez, training binocu-
ιrs on the English coast, wave after wave of aircraft—three hundred
ιombers and six hundred fighters—thundered northward in tight forma-
ιon towards London; all afternoon and all night long after that the
ιttack on docks and oil targets along the Thames continued. Twenty-

three RAF fighter squadrons were thrown into the battle, but the victor was with Göring that day, even though the Luftwaffe lost forty aircraft to the RAF's twenty-eight.

For Hitler these results were still too uncertain to justify issuing the preliminary order for the invasion.[28] The most favourable date, 2 September, was barely two weeks away, and since the planning called for ten days' notice he must make up his mind on the fourteenth. Twice in mid-September, on the thirteenth and fourteenth, Hitler called Milch to hear his deliberations on invasion, since Göring was still directing the battle in the west.[29] Milch took a lengthy note of the Führer's remarks on the fourteenth. They began with a survey of Germany's strategic position, in which Hitler's disquiet about Russia's intentions was evident. Moscow was obviously dissatisfied with events, having hoped that the Reich would bleed herself to death, and was now turning its attention to Rumania and Finland. Germany needed Rumania for oil and Finland for the balance of power in the Baltic. Hitler hinted at the possibility of 'new conflicts', but he was inclined to view them with equanimity: 'We have attained our objectives already,' he told his commanders on the fourteenth. 'That is why we have no interest in dragging this war on.'

The question was, how to write the final chapter. Hitler now saw an invasion of Britain as a means of accelerating the end, rather than as an end in itself. The navy was ready, it seemed, and while in its fight for air supremacy the Luftwaffe had achieved the near impossible. Göring had always warned that he needed several consecutive days of fine weather to destroy the RAF, and this had been denied him. The RAF had recuperated. Nobody knew how many fighter aircraft the British still had, but they must have 'suffered badly'. The brutal truth was that air supremacy had not been achieved. 'Should we call it off altogether' Hitler asked. He answered this question himself: their earlier option of a conventional invasion with massive air superiority, had been thwarted; so he now intended to try an alternative method, which was less certain, but also less harmful to prestige than a total cancellation of the invasion—a war of nerves, supported by crushing air attack and the persisting *threat* of seaborne invasion. 'Our attacks so far have already been enormously successful,' he pointed out. Such a war of nerves would force the RAF to reserve bombers to combat an invasion; this would take the pressure off Germany. And the bombing of London alone might bring about the final collapse. 'If eight million people go mad, it might very well turn into a catastrophe! If we get the fine weather, and we can eliminate the enemy's air force, then even a small invasion might go a long way.' Therefore he was against cancelling invasion preparations altogether. 'The cancellation would come to the ears of the enemy and would strengthen his resolve.'[30]

Milch recognized that neither army nor navy was enthusiastic about the invasion. Jeschonnek suggested that the Luftwaffe had now brought about a grave food shortage in England and asserted that 'the British public have still not been hit' in such a way as to cause real panic. (In fact, in the first half of September alone two thousand London civilians had been killed in the bombing.) Hitler still refused to authorize attacks on London's residential areas, but agreed to consider such a policy in future: 'You see, it is our ultimate reprisal. That's why we have to keep to military targets for the time being.' By these he meant London's stations, water, gas and other public utility works and similar targets. 'That's why we can't attack the public.'*

The next day's air operations proved that German air supremacy was still a ghostly chimera: on 15 September the biggest raiding force yet— both *Luftflotten*—was sent to raid targets in London, still defended by three hundred RAF fighters; sixty German aircraft were destroyed for twenty-six RAF losses. Next day at a conference in Göring's train near Beauvais in France Göring fulminated about the failure of his own fighter escorts, while Milch stoutly defended them. The source of the RAF's strength was a mystery: assuming that on 8 September the British had had 465 fighters (three-quarters of them serviceable) and allowing for the 288 claimed destroyed since then, then the RAF could not have more than 177 left to defend the whole of Britain. Göring believed the last British reserves to have been scraped together.[31] That the RAF's real shortage was of trained pilots, not aircraft, was not considered.[32]

Göring ordered that the night attacks on London were to continue, with both *Luftflotten,* on every possible occasion; Sperrle's bombers were also to attack Southampton by day, while Kesselring—to whom most of the fighters had now been transferred—should engage the RAF's fighter force. Göring mentioned that there was evidence that British pilots had been encouraged to ram the German bombers, so harsh was their position now. He proposed a new tactic to destroy the remaining fighters: they should operate formations of up to thirty Ju 88 fast bombers three times a day over Britain, with very heavy fighter escort; given three consecutive fine days, the ensuing air battles would so deplete the

---

* From the lengthy notes taken by Milch during Hitler's conference; broadly similar versions will be found in the diaries of Halder and the German naval staff (14 September 1940). Keitel's version is in Nuremberg document 803-PS.

RAF defences that the main force of bombers could again operate at
will. In the meantime, London's night ordeal was beginning with a
vengeance, for at night there was little the defences could do to stop the
bombers.

On 17 September 1940 Hitler decided on the indefinite postponement
of the invasion.[33] In effect, the Luftwaffe had borne the fighting alone
since July, while the other Services had relaxed, refitted and regrouped.
Now it was the Luftwaffe at whose door the blame was laid. Much of
the blame is in fact Hitler's: the campaign should have been started
earlier, when fine weather still prevailed and the RAF defences were
still weak, and the Luftwaffe regarded themselves as hampered by
Hitler's prohibition against mass attacks on the London population. As
it was, mid-September 1940 found the Luftwaffe still searching for a
strategy, with the bomber and fighter arms engaged in growing recrimination against each other.

Göring's new daylight strategy of small fast Ju 88 formations, escorted by sometimes ten times as many fighters, came into operation
on 27 September; on other occasions single fighter-bombers operated
singly over London and southern England. It was all very different
from the mass attacks envisaged as a prelude to invasion. Early in
October 1940 Göring seized the excuse of deteriorating weather to call
off daylight operations over Britain; all hope of destroying RAF's fighters in the air receded.

Above all, the Luftwaffe's equipment had proved inadequate. As Director of Air Armament Udet felt, not without reason, that the finger of
guilt was pointing at his office. He stayed away from Göring's conferences and cracked wan jokes with his friends about the future. His
friends shielded him, while his rivals multiplied.[34] Whispers of the
coming technical deficiencies reached Göring. One day that autumn
when he was walking in the woods near Beauvais, Major Storp, an
experienced squadron commander, shocked him with a gloomy prediction of things to come.[35] 'The time will come when you witness a
situation which seems unimaginable to you now,' the major warned,
and he related details of the negligence of Udet's senior advisers. Of
one aero-engine project, probably the Daimler-Benz 603, Storp prophesied: 'You won't ever get it. You *could,* and it should have been in
service long ago; but if you don't act now you still won't have it three
years from now.' Göring did not act, and he was to recall this conversation ruefully to Milch three years later when the predictions were fulfilled.[36]

The controversial Junkers 88 high-speed bomber, on which Udet and Jeschonnek had set great store, was the most problematic of Udet's protégés. Erhard Milch was torn between two conflicting duties: he was a long-standing friend of Udet; but he was also Inspector-General, and profoundly patriotic. Throughout the summer of 1940 he collected the squadron's complaints against the Ju 88: it was slower than the obsolescent He 111, its dinghy could not be released in an emergency, there were insufficient Ju 88 workshops, take-offs at night were difficult with full tanks, there had been frequent cases of Ju 88s catching fire in mid-air, and so on. Altogether he listed thirty-two complaints in a report to Göring; early in October the Reichsmarschall ordered him to tour the Ju 88 squadrons and report even more fully.[37] Milch's report was a devastating indictment of the Ju 88 and its effect on squadron morale; in particular he concluded that its present armament was so inadequate that it could not be operated without fighter escort. Of one Ju 88 squadron's twenty-six crews, only five were ready to continue flying, so badly had the aircraft affected crew morale; indeed General Loerzer's Second Air Corps had sent a medical officer to examine the others, suspecting malingering. Milch's scathing comment on this to Göring was, 'It's not the enemy the squadron's frightened of—it's the Junkers 88!'[38]

These criticisms were tactfully laid before Junkers's general manager, Dr Koppenberg; Göring told him the aircraft 'has not fully come up to our expectations', especially those concerning air safety. He reassured the industrialist of his confidence in him ('these unseemly and carping critics get a deaf ear from me') but hinted that perhaps they should be concentrating more on the old He 111 under present war conditions. Koppenberg for his part talked of the Ju 88 Mark A4 now coming off the production lines, which was indeed a commendable improvement, and he described the new generation of bombers, particularly the Ju 288, powered by the revolutionary new engine, the Jumo 222, coming in 1942.[39] A high-altitude, high-speed bomber, with internal bomb racks and a dive-bomber capability, it would carry five tons of bombs over 1,250 miles or two tons over 3,100 miles; with its pressurized cockpit it would have a service ceiling of some 28,000 feet, extending to 38,000 feet once the engine had been fitted with special superchargers. From the way Koppenberg talked there seemed to be no problems with either the engine or the aircraft; but there were, and we must return to both in later chapters.

Despite their official differences Milch encouraged Udet not to forget their personal friendship. In Paris they joined forces on shopping expeditions to Cartier's; in Berlin they shared a table at Horcher's at least half a dozen times that autumn.[40] But the general's condition over the last few weeks had been worsening rapidly, and it pained Milch to see how little he was applying himself to his duties. Udet was drinking and smoking to excess, and eating only meat.[41] He was also relying extensively on a narcotic to overcome his growing depression and the chosen drug, 'Pervitin', brought after-effects which made him morose and suspicious.

A week after reporting to Göring on the Ju 88 Milch took the opportunity of a Sunday afternoon stroll near Karinhall to have a long fatherly talk with Udet about the aircraft.[42] This unrelenting pressure only intensified Udet's suspicions. Two days later, his constitution weakened by his unhealthy mode of life, he was taken ill, and Milch committed him to the care of his personal physician Professor Kalk; but within a week the ailing general had discharged himself from hospital, fearing, as he told his friends, that Milch was exploiting his absence to trespass on his office.[43] And yet it was possible for this strange, schizophrenic general to sit at Milch's favourite table at Horcher's not long after, as though there was not a single source of disaffection between them.[44]

The German public's retina still retained the image Göring had offered in his radio broadcasts at the time of the mass daylight attacks on London —the Reichsmarschall, striding the Channel coast, personally directing the battle. Indeed so pleased was Göring with this image that once his signals officer surprised him in his Ritz suite in Paris (the hotel was largely populated by the Luftwaffe), dressed only in a blue silk dressing-gown, describing by telephone to his wife how at that moment he was on the cliffs at Calais while his squadrons thundered overhead to England.[45]

The reality was different. Since mid-September the air force had appeared in strength over England only by night, and a further complication of this unexpectedly continuing war was that Germany would now have to provide a realistic air defence against British bombing raids. On the night of 23 September 1940 over a hundred RAF medium bombers attacked Berlin and twenty-two civilians died. At the beginning of October Milch inspected the first squadrons of the night-fighter organization established under Colonel Josef Kammhuber in Holland at a staff conference on the third Göring called for better flak for Berlin, a swifter air-raid alert system, stronger shelters and more decoy sites.[46]

October marked the beginning of the long war between German concrete and British bombs. The Reichsmarschall decided to put Milch in charge of civil defence again. It had been his province long before—the

instruction posters pinned up in every basement bore Milch's signature
—but it had been taken away from him before war broke out; now that
the damage was beginning, Inspectorate No. 14 (Air Defence) was
returned to him.[47]

The Germans were beginning to experience the costly inconvenience
they had hoped to inflict only on their enemies. Thousands of children
had to be evacuated from the big cities; hospitals, factories, schools—all
had to have special air-raid warning systems; millions of homes throughout the country had to have shelters; hundreds of thousands of tons of
concrete and steel were needed for public shelters. All this was discussed by Göring and Milch on 12 October. Udet was told admonish-
ingly that the only long-term answer was to build more aircraft; these
were 'far more important than air-raid shelters'.[48] The wisdom of this
is obvious from Milch's notes—they would need two hundred thousand
workers and four thousand lorries for the Berlin shelter programme
alone.[49] On the fifteenth Milch had a long private talk with Hitler on
the psychology of air-raid alerts.[50]

The state secretary remained responsible for passive air defence measures until 1942, when the Reich Propaganda Minister Dr Goebbels was
nominally put in charge, 'which led,' wrote Milch, 'only to an improvement in the propaganda about what had been done.' In 1944 the task
was transferred to Speer's Armaments Ministry and all public shelter
construction came to a halt.[51]

With the failure of the Battle of Britain Göring lost interest in the war.
At a conference at Deauville on the last day of October 1940 he mentioned casually to Milch that soon he planned to take six weeks' leave;
the state secretary was to stand in for him.[52] At headquarters a few
days later Hitler for the first time openly criticized Göring over the
Luftwaffe's failure, which was having widespread repercussions in foreign policy. Citing foreign press reports he queried the success of the
raids on Britain and spoke sceptically of the Luftwaffe's claims of great
air victories; Göring was saved by General Jodl, who said he also believed that the RAF was at its last gasp—it must have thrown its last
aircraft, piloted by a handful of training officers and the squadron commanders themselves, into the battle.[53]

Milch had warned long ago that the current series of night attacks
was useless without special radio-beam devices, like the new
X-equipment. (A radio receiver in the bombers followed a main beam
laid over the target, and was alerted by two cross beams a set distance
from each other and from the target.) It was all too easy to bomb British
decoy sites, since most bomber crews were happy to release their loads

somewhere between the searchlights, whether they saw a target or not: 'On dark nights only the largest targets can be effectively found; in my view the effect on all other targets is about a fifth of a daylight attack.'[54] Milch recommended that the special radio-beam squadron, *Kampfgruppe* 100, should receive priority in personnel and aircraft. He advised Göring that if radio-beam techniques should prove satisfactory then they could attack even on the darkest nights, or through cloud, or they could fly with accuracy by day to the neighbourhood of the smallest targets.

On 14 November Göring called Milch over to Karinhall and formally handed over command of the Luftwaffe to him; he then departed on leave to his hunting lodge on Rominten Heath in East Prussia.[55] He did not resume command until late January 1941, although he was never far from his telephone. His departure coincided with one of the most destructive Luftwaffe attacks of the war: 450 bombers attacked Coventry, spearheaded by a fire-raising force from *Kampfgruppe* 100 using X-equipment for the first time.

Field Marshal Milch's arrival at 'Robinson I'—the Air Staff's headquarters at La Boissière-le-Déluge, near Beauvais—caused something of a crisis.

General Jeschonnek waited for Milch to arrive, then ostentatiously departed to join the Reichsmarschall at his hunting lodge, leaving his deputy with Milch; the latter, von Waldau, found the newcomer easier to accept than the situation caused by Göring's departure. 'About our commanders I have my own views,' Waldau wrote, 'and these lead me increasingly to the view that the end is not in sight. We must clench our teeth.' In the afternoon he added, 'Jeschonnek still in Berlin. Thus there is much to be done—and done independently in default of the Reichsmarschall.'[56]

Göring had withdrawn his special train 'Asia' to Rominten as well and with it had vanished Milch's coach. Since there was no question of his occupying Jeschonnek's train his staff assembled a special train of sorts at the Gare St Lazare in Paris: it was put together from Marshal Pétain's dining car of the First World War, which included an opulent bathroom and a dining-room upholstered in corduroy and green baize; the dining-car of President Lebrun's special train with two of his best chefs; and several less august items of rolling stock. The heating system was so erratic that while the adjutant's room was permanently filled with metallic knocking, steam and heat, at the other end of the train Arctic conditions reigned. From the temperate regions of the dining car Milch now conducted the air war against Britain's cities while

Göring—and, on one memorable occasion when Plymouth was the target, even his nurse Sister Christa—dictated orders down the telephone from Rominten.

A second theatre of operations was now opening for the Luftwaffe.

Late in October Mussolini—piqued by German military intervention in Rumania—had launched an attack on Greece. But his armies were already severely extended in North Africa and the new adventure brought him nothing but misfortune. The British occupied Crete, a key Mediterranean island from which RAF bombers were within range of the Rumanian oilfields. The Greeks launched a plucky counter-offensive and pursued the Italian invaders into Albania. Hitler decided to relieve the Italians by attacking the British forces in the Mediterranean; he sent for Milch to discuss means of doing so.[57]

Hitler explained that as a consequence of the Italian attack not only was Germany now obliged to provide flak for Rumania and southeastern Germany, but the Italians themselves were in danger. The Luftwaffe should prepare to attack the Suez Canal and the Royal Navy's bases both at Gibraltar and at Alexandria; meantime Milch was to go to Mussolini and explain how far the Luftwaffe could help him directly. The Italians should be given three clear objectives—to hold their front line, to tie down the Greeks until the German army itself could intervene in the spring, and to improve their supply lines. Meantime the British should be demoralized by a number of heavy air raids on London, Liverpool and Manchester. Göring, meanwhile, continued his extended leave at Rominten, jogging pleasantly from one hunting preserve to the next in his landau.[58]

The Luftwaffe proposed deploying what was virtually a *Luftflotte* in Italy, made up of Geisler's Tenth Air Corps from Norway and a number of Ju 88, He 111 and minelaying squadrons and a long-range fighter squadron.[59] While von Waldau directed these preparations—by January 1941 there was a force of 330 first-line aircraft in this new Luftwaffe theatre—Milch returned to Air Staff headquarters in France to resume his direction of the night blitz against Britain. Since November it had been aimed generally at crippling the British industrial effort, spearheaded by *Kampfgruppe* 100, the Pathfinder squadron, using the X-equipment and another unit, KG 26, using the new Y-beam system whereby the bomber aircraft, carrying special repeater-transmitters, were precisely plotted even at great range by German ground stations and given course and bombing instructions by them.

On balance the Luftwaffe was still winning this cruel war of the cities. Measured in terms of human life, compared with over fifteen thousand

Churchill's Battle of Britain, Luftwaffe view.　　　[*Sketch by Ernst Udet*]

British dead by mid-November 1940, the entire six months of the RAF attack on Germany had so far killed only 975 Germans; Milch established to his own satisfaction that twice as many Germans had been killed in the same period in road accidents.[60] In Britain's cities the ordeal was only just beginning—although the Luftwaffe aiming points (like the RAF's at this stage) were invariably the large factories. Mixed loads of high explosive and fire bombs were scattered round them night after night, with the RAF night-fighter defences almost powerless to intervene, the necessary radar equipment still being under development. Britain's industrial centres were the hardest hit: on 11 December we see Sperrle reporting to Milch on his night's raid on Birmingham; on the twelfth we find Milch on the runway at Villacoublay watching a squadron of KG 55's Heinkels taking off for the night's attack on Sheffield.[61] On the fifteenth the Luftwaffe again attacked Sheffield, and next day the RAF delivered the war's first 'area attack', with its aiming point the residential heart of Mannheim.* Five days later Milch himself witnessed the British attempt to raid Berlin, but it was a puny effort compared with the Luftwaffe's spectacular fire raids. In three operations between then and Christmas Eve the Germans inflicted catastrophic damage on Manchester and Liverpool. But after this holocaust came respite. From the early morning of Christmas Eve, the Luftwaffe airfields were silent; on Hitler's instructions all air operations against the British Isles were prohibited during the Christmas festival.†

On Christmas Eve Hitler's special train arrived alongside Air Staff headquarters at Le Déluge, and early next morning Milch and Jeschonnek were ordered to see the Führer.[62] After the field marshal had reported on the Blitz word arrived that an emissary of the French president had arrived, so the discussion had to end; but as Hitler accompanied his guests to the door of the compartment he mentioned for the first time to Milch his fears of a Russian campaign against Germany, and he hinted that he intended to get in an attack on Russia first.

* As the official history, *The Strategic Air Offensive against Germany 1939–1945*, vol. I, points out (p. 215), 'It was not until after the German attack on Coventry that Bomber Command was deliberately given the centre of a town as its target. This, the first "area" attack of the war, was carried out against Mannheim on the night of 16th December 1940.'

† Milch's diary 26 December 1940: 'At *Robinson*. From 24 to early 26 December no air attacks on Britain on Führer's orders.'

# A NEW CAMPAIGN

## (December 1940–June 1941)

When Hitler mentioned to Milch in September 1940 that Moscow was 'evidently dissatisfied' with the way the war was going this was his first indication that there was an element of cynicism in the twelve-month-old pact with the Soviet Union.

From the several conferences on German deliveries to Russia he had attended Milch knew just what this pact had cost them. In addition to scarce equipment and machine tools the navy was supposed to hand over the modern cruiser *Lützow* and the Luftwaffe some of its most secret armament, including the new 105-millimetre heavy flak battery. A Russian general had arrived to test-fly the Heinkel 100 record-breaking fighter prototype, and then that had been crated up for Russia too. The Russians were even demanding the blueprints for every item they were given. In return they were supplying oil and raw materials to Germany.[1]

This cooperation ended after Germany's staggering *blitzkrieg* victories over Norway and France. Göring later said, 'The Soviet Union thereupon increased the scale of its own arms programme and redoubled its preparations in the territories it had newly occupied, particularly in the Baltic states, in eastern Poland and Bessarabia, where numerous airfields were constructed and troops were concentrated.'[2] Luftwaffe experts who toured the Russian industrial region reported to Göring that the aero-engine factories at Kuibyshev alone were bigger than Germany's six main assembly factories.[3] None the less, when Hitler told him during the autumn that he would probably attack Russia, Göring objected—on grounds of expediency rather than of morality. He argued that it would be strategically wrong to break off the air offensive against Britain now; furthermore, he considered that operations against Gibraltar, French North Africa, Malta or Suez rated more attention than opening up voluntarily such an immense new theatre. He believed the Russian rearmament programme would not be complete until 1943.[4]

The visit of the Soviet Foreign Minister Molotov to Berlin in mid-November 1940 revealed to the Germans the edge of the abyss; from these conversations Hitler realized that the 'honeymoon', as he termed it, was over. He had already ordered that preparations for a Russian campaign should continue without remission; now he tentatively set the date for mid-May 1941—the date he had previously earmarked for the invasion of Britain. This new contingency was the subject of a select conference at the Air Ministry on 13 January 1941; Milch recorded in his diary only, 'Afternoon, major conference with Göring, Jeschonnek, Bodenschatz re: the East.' The same day Jeschonnek flew to his head-quarters and briefed the Air Staff for the first time on the planning for 'Barbarossa', the Russian campaign.[5] Two weeks later Göring's special train returned and the Reichsmarschall resumed command, his two-month leave at an end.[6] His state secretary, Milch, now went on leave himself and it was in his absence, on 20 February, that a special unit (like those earlier established for the campaigns in Spain and Norway) was set up at the Air Staff College under Colonel Löbel, to coordinate planning for 'Barbarossa'.[7]

Milch went on leave and heard no more about Russia. On his return a bombshell burst: General Otto Rüdel, Chief of Air Defence, who had been deputizing for him, appeared in his room at the ministry with an officer from the administration department and inquired whether Milch approved the directive that no winter clothing be ordered for the new campaign.

'New campaign?' Milch asked. Rüdel explained, 'The campaign in Russia.' Milch leapt out of his chair, overcome with surprise. Visions of the eastern front—of the slaughter he had witnessed at Gumbinnen, Ossowiez and Raczki in the First World War—crossed before his eyes. 'We have been ordered to prepare for a campaign against Russia,' Rüdel continued. 'But it will all be over before winter sets in.' Milch retorted, 'Whoever said that must be mad.' Rüdel warned in some embarrassment, 'It comes on very high authority.' The field marshal replied that even so they must assume that any war with Russia would last at least four years; and that could mean four winters.[8]

The Air Staff, and in particular the Quartermaster-General, von Seidel, refused to accept responsibility for violating Hitler's edict; but Milch knew no scruples, accepted full responsibility and personally ordered the manufacture of extra woollen underwear, five pairs of stockings, big fur boots and sheepskins for each of a million Luftwaffe men on the eastern front; he also ordered the urgent provision of winter equipment for the squadrons. The winter clothing was manufactured, as usual, by the army's clothing office. There was no reason why the army could not have taken the same precautions for its own men; but to the General Staff, too, Hitler's edict was law and only the sixty divisions foreseen for the army of occupation in a defeated Russia had been provided with special winter clothing by the time the campaign began.[9] When the terrible winter came the army suffered more casualties from frostbite than from action, and the Luftwaffe's eight hundred thousand men were ordered by Hitler to relinquish some of their own winter clothing to the army.[10]

After the winter was over von Seidel accepted Göring's congratulations ('We have been issuing winter orders and directives ever since 22 June 1941,' he said—as though these could have any real effect by the coming winter;[11] the evidence is that the Air Staff did not itself issue such orders until late August). Through Milch's foresight the Luftwaffe was spared the worst.

All this did not mean that he approved of the Russian campaign. He argued strongly against it, reminding Göring that the Führer had so far avoided the perils of a war on two fronts; the formation of a western front must surely only be a matter of time, and sooner or later America would also enter the war, as was evident from the secret American arms production figures he regularly noted in his pocket-book. Göring answered that since there could be no western front until 1942 the Führer had a year to fight himself free in the rear. When Milch rejoined that he doubted that one summer campaign would suffice to finish off Russia Göring reassured him, 'If we strike hard enough, Russia will collapse like a pack of cards, because the communist system is despised by the masses in Russia.' The Führer, he added, was a unique leader, granted to the German nation by Providence: 'The rest of us, we lesser mortals, can only march behind him with complete faith in his ability. Then we cannot go wrong.'[12]

The existence of a God and Providence was not disputed by Milch. None the less he appealed to Göring to try again to dissuade Hitler. 'Herr Reichsmarschall—this is your great, historic hour. You must prevent this attack on Russia—you are the only one who is in a position to bring the Führer round to accept your view. If you can prevent this war in the east, then you will have done your Fatherland the greatest service of your life.' Göring replied that it was hopeless: 'The Führer

has made up his mind. There is no power on earth that can change it
for him now.'

Even now there was an unexpected series of interludes. At the end of
March 1941 Milch was committed to a one-week tour of Germany's
major towns to check on the progress of his air-raid defence programme.
As he was flying to Hamburg news arrived in Berlin of an anti-German
revolution in Belgrade. Hitler called his C-in-Cs to the Reich Chancery
and announced his decision 'to destroy Yugoslavia both as a military
power and as a nation'. For some weeks he had been planning a lightning war in Greece to rescue the Italians; the attack on Yugoslavia
would be synchronized with that on Greece, starting early on 6 April.[13]

Milch was ordered back to Berlin with other senior generals to hear a
fresh harangue from Hitler. For three hours Hitler argued that the
western theatre—and that meant Britain—was still the vital one, but that
an attack on the Balkans was now a regrettable prerequisite to the
defeat of Britain.[14] Justifying his decision to attack Russia too, he
stated that only by destroying the Soviet armed forces could Germany
maintain her position in the air and on the seas in two years' time. But
he also spoke in unmistakable terms of his intention of destroying
Bolshevism and all its panoply—'liquidating the Bolshevik commissars
and the communist intelligentsia'.[15]

Within ten days the Luftwaffe had completed its rapid regrouping for
the Balkan campaign—about six hundred aircraft having been moved up
from bases in France, Sicily and Africa and added to the five hundred
German aircraft already in this new theatre. The offensive opened on
6 April with a heavy air attack on Yugoslav airfields and the capital: in
Belgrade seventeen thousand people were killed and the government
quarters paralysed within hours of the war breaking out. Yugoslavia
was defeated within a week.[16] In Greece, despite the support of General von Richthofen's Eighth Air Corps, the Germans met more determined opposition. Milch marvelled at the heroic resistance offered
by the Greeks at the crossing of the Struma river.[17] On 21 April Greece
too laid down her arms. It was to be the last occasion on which the
Luftwaffe could claim an unqualified victory.

General Rieckhoff, in the earliest postwar history of the Luftwaffe,
wrote: 'Of all the senior officers in the Reich Air Ministry there was
nobody who saw the coming technical débâcle and interpreted it better
than the state secretary, Milch.'[18] Because of the lack of adequate
development control the new aircraft on which the Air Staff had been

relying for 1941 were still not there; indeed those bearing the main burden—the Me 109, the Me 110, the He 111, the Ju 52, the Ju 87, the Do 17 and the FW 200—had all been developed in the pre-Udet era, before 1936. They had entered mass production only after completion of a three-year sequence of four preliminary stages: first had come the construction and design of the prototype and then had come three carefully overlapped intermediate stages—test-flying, preparation for serial production and pilot series. Udet had attempted to concertina these three stages to cut a year off the total time; the mass production had begun before test-flying was complete, leading to repeated breakdowns and stopping of production. The Ju 88 had been the first casualty; now, in early 1941, several more became apparent—the Me 109F, the Me 210, the He 177 and the FW 190.[19]

After the Luftwaffe's more experienced fighter commanders, Galland and Mölders, had complained in the autumn of 1940 to Göring that the Me 109E was inferior to the Spitfire, Udet had told them about the Mark F, with its DB 601E engine, which would arrive early in 1941 at the squadrons. By the spring, however, it was still not coming out of the Messerschmitt production plants.

Far more serious was the case of the Me 210 twin-engined fighter-bomber. The Air Staff had asked Professor Messerschmitt to update the Me 110 by minor aerodynamic changes and by fitting a bigger power plant, the 1,900-horsepower Daimler-Benz 603; the revised aircraft was to carry better defensive armament and bombs up to 500 kilos on internal racks, as a dive-bomber. Udet's intention was that the modifications should be made without interrupting the Me 110 production schedule. Without informing him, however, Professor Messerschmitt seized the opportunity of designing a completely new aircraft, the Me 210; he did not seek to amend the delivery date, and the Air Staff believed the first one thousand would have been delivered by the spring of 1941. In view of the coming offensive, Jeschonnek attached great importance to this aircraft.[20]

By April 1941, however, not one Me 210 had been delivered and there was growing consternation at the ministry. Kokothaki, Messerschmitt's business manager, disclosed to a ministry investigator that the aircraft had gone into mass production not only at Augsburg but also on a licence basis elsewhere, even though the prototype's test-flights were not complete. He depicted this action of his master as 'irresponsible'. Messerschmitt took him aside and threatened him with dismissal but Kokothaki stood his ground. The ministry had no alternative but to pour manpower and effort into the factory in an effort to save the aircraft; but deliveries of the Me 210 did not commence until 1942, and even then its troubles were only just beginning.

Of all this Milch had been unaware, as he had long been excluded from Udet's consultations. Until 1941 nobody ventured to injure the sensitive Director of Air Armament, although many recognized where the blame lay. General von Witzendorff described Udet as 'a sparkling society man, full of wit and humour'; but he disliked desk work and had relied so heavily on his staff that their power had outgrown his own. The Luftwaffe's chief judge advocate wrote of Udet, 'He had none of the qualities needed for a high office. Above all he lacked real knowledge, he lacked moral rectitude and he lacked a sense of responsibility.'[21] And Heinkel's Berlin representative minuted in February 1941 that Milch was blaming Udet for their equipment shortcomings in the Battle of Britain: 'Everything turns to dust in Udet's hands.'[22]

At the ministry Udet's staff had swollen to encompass over four thousand—a rabbit warren of colonels, bureaucrats and engineers, responsible for everything but responsible to nobody. After this unwholesome heritage had fallen to Milch Göring warned him: 'There's still many a scoundrel there. . . . There are departments you've never heard of. But suddenly they come to life—suddenly there is some foul-up and the shout goes up: "Air Ministry!"—"Not us!" you say. *"And how!"* is the reply. And all of a sudden you find there is this department that has been ticking away there for a dozen years and nobody knew about it.' Göring even claimed, 'You'll find people there who've been thrown out on their ears three times already, and they come to light in some other department again, only bigger and stronger than ever.'[23]

Of Udet's chief of staff, Major-General Ploch, Milch had already made an implacable enemy. He had lost heavily gambling with Milch and Sperrle at Deauville some months before and could not pay the debt; Milch had given the general a stern dressing-down, and Sperrle insisted on payment and used the money to buy clothes and food for Ploch's wife. Ploch was found to have played a crucial role in Udet's final collapse.[24] To his friends Udet began to complain of the interest Milch was showing in his affairs. He declared that Milch was a foe in his absence and a friend to his face. The field marshal was too much his opposite—too much of the 'able and energetic US businessman', as *Time* magazine had recently described him. Moreover even Udet, the antiseptic hero of the pre-1933 German film industry, had become infected with Nazi propaganda, and he did not remain unsusceptible to malicious rumours which were circulating about Milch's non-Aryan origins.

Early in April 1941 Udet was called upon to explain discrepancies discovered by Jeschonnek in the aircraft production figures. The resulting scrutiny exposed the weaknesses of the 'sliding programmes' which characterized the Udet era—programmes constantly altered to fit the results.[25] Throughout the spring the growing shortage of aero-engines and fighter aircraft featured regularly on Udet's agenda for discussion with Göring, but there is no evidence that these topics were ever discussed. 'When he met Göring,' the judge advocate later wrote, 'they just spoke of the old days. All talk of shop was painfully avoided.'*[26]

On 6 May 1941 Göring again went on leave for a month, staying at his tenth-century family castle outside Nuremberg. In his absence Milch intervened more firmly in Udet's department, calling him to his hunting lodge one afternoon and ordering him to pull himself together.[27] The field marshal could be very tough indeed—one of Göring's other state secretaries once claimed: 'That Milch—he pisses ice!'—and there is no doubt that Milch used his authority on this occasion. For the first time he learned that Udet had, as we have seen, no fewer than twenty-six departmental heads reporting directly to him; he advised him to regroup his organization into three or four main sections, but the advice fell on deaf ears.[28]

Meanwhile the Luftwaffe had mounted a major airborne invasion—its last—to capture the Mediterranean island of Crete. In costly fighting the German paratroops forced the British defences out; by the end of the operation 4,500 of the thirteen thousand of Göring's troops who had taken part were dead or missing, and the Ju 52 transport fleet had been halved (271 Ju 52s were destroyed or damaged beyond repair.) On 22 May, with this battle still at its height, Göring summoned Milch to his castle to hear the news about Crete. Evidently Milch lost no time in outlining the chaotic production position—Germany was to enter the Russian campaign with 2,770 first-line aircraft in the east, compared with the 2,600 she had marshalled against Britain one year before— since on the very next day, 23 May, Udet was subjected to a blistering attack by Göring, probably for the first time.[29] Udet in turn vented his feelings privately on Milch, telling Heinkel in Berlin: 'They're all against

* Udet's agendas are preserved among Milch's documents in Freiburg. They make interesting reading. In the notes for 6 March 1941, 'Supply position and conference with Air Staff on increasing fighter production' is Item 10, after such items as 'War Service Medal with Swords for Hanna Reitsch'; item 10 was not reached, for it appears again as item 17 on 12 March and again on 18 March 1941. Study of the whole series of notes suggests that most such items remained permanently undiscussed. The list of notes for 29 April is decorated by Udet with a cluster of thirty brightly coloured balloons on a string, held by nobody.

me. The "Iron Man" [Göring] has just gone on leave and he has left me at Milch's mercy. Milch deputizes for him at the Führer's headquarters, and will see that every error I have ever made is served up for the Führer's edification.'[30] A few days later Udet was to be seen in the same restaurant, at Milch's table, laughing and drinking with his friend as usual.[31]

Göring sent Milch to France to scrutinize Sperrle's Third Air Force, but within a few days the field marshal was back in Berlin, resuming his investigation of Udet's office. The latter's adjutant recorded 'considerable arguments' with Milch; Milch just noted, 'Hopeless', in his diary.[32] It proved impossible to extract firm statistics from Udet's staff. 'What they dished up there was just rubbish,' Milch recalled two years later. 'Nobody understood it, least of all the people who had prepared the figures.' And Göring shared his mistrust: 'If they come to me with graphs, then I know from the outset that it's a swindle; and if they want to multiply the swindle, they do it all in three colours!'[33]

Milch knew enough to spot the fallacies: a new aircraft took nine months or more to manufacture; yet on average Udet's staff had drafted a new programme every six weeks. He was beginning to suspect that Udet's whole four-thousand-man office was based on nothing but self-deception and fantasy.[34] This was a view which Göring also adopted in time: 'Never have I been so deceived, so bamboozled and so cheated as by that office. It has no equal in history.'

In mid-June Milch saw Hitler again, in company with over forty other senior officers in Berlin for a final discussion before the invasion of Russia began eight days later.[35] Hitler spoke to them on the justification for his attack. The principal enemy was still Britain—she would keep fighting as long as this had any point. It was a British national characteristic illustrated as much by the individual soldier's demeanour at Flanders and Dunkirk as in Greece and Crete.[36] But Britain's fight made sense only so long as there was a prospect of effective American aid and Russian intervention, and American aid could have no effect before the summer of 1942; and only then if the volume of traffic across the Atlantic could be maintained in face of mounting Allied shipping losses. Russia's attitude had always been one of opportunism: even if Germany were to make peace with Britain, the size of Russia's armed forces would preclude any German demobilization.

An early conflict, at a time of Germany's choosing, was the only solution. As Russia had concentrated the bulk of her armed forces on their common frontier there was every prospect of defeating her right there.

Hitler had set out the Luftwaffe's task as being 'to release such power-ful forces for the eastern campaign that a rapid conclusion of the ground operations may be anticipated'. At the same time it was to ensure that 'offensive operations against Britain, and in particular against her supply lines, do not come to a total standstill'.[37] On the day after Hitler's con-ference Göring summoned his own commanders to Karinhall for a similar discussion. Milch gained the impression that Göring was un-certain of the future, and the general atmosphere was not one of elation.

The campaign opened shortly before dawn on 22 June, with heavy air attacks on three-score Russian airfields and on selected cities within aircraft range. The Russians were evidently taken by surprise and Milch ascribed this to the probability that the enemy had 'overestimated our intelligence'.[38] In fact, the Germans had underestimated the Russians' strength—the strength of Soviet industry and the blind courage of the Soviet soldier. Most of Hitler's commanders had served on the western front in the First World War and had no concept of the endlessness of the Russian expanses; this was certainly true of Göring and Jeschonnek. But Milch knew the Russians: he had himself flown across the steppes, and above all he had cause to know the willingness with which the Slavs sacrificed themselves in a patriotic struggle; he was still haunted by memories of the bloodbaths he had seen on the Russian front a quarter of a century before.

General Jeschonnek approached the new war with enthusiasm ('at last a proper war!') and even Milch shared this momentary fervour: he recorded 1,600 Russian aircraft destroyed on the first day, a figure he amended before nightfall to 1,800.[39] About 800 more were reported destroyed on the twenty-third, 557 on the twenty-fourth, 351 on the twenty-fifth and a further 300 next day. Exaggerated though these early reports probably were, the Luftwaffe's own losses were nothing in comparison.[40]

Only later did it become clear that the 'army support' role assigned to the Luftwaffe would last longer than just the first few weeks. Inevitably the temporary prohibition on attacking strategic targets in the Soviet hinterland continued in force, because the initial war of movement did not come to an end. In the meantime the enemy's industrial plants were evacuated along still intact railways to far beyond the Urals, where the German bombers could not reach them, and soon the stricken Soviet air force was being re-equipped with new aircraft. After the first weeks of triumph, a night without end closed upon Hitler and his grand strategy.

# EXIT A HERO

## (*June–November 1941*)

Seen in the perspective of war, the passing of one man may seem of little interest in the biography of another. Yet no event was to have a more profound effect on Erhard Milch than the death of Ernst Udet.

The long final phase of this personal tragedy began two days before the invasion of the Soviet Union. Anticipating swift victory, Hitler commanded a reduction in the level of army armaments production and high priority for the production of aircraft for the subsequent fight against Britain.[1] Göring issued orders for the quadrupling of the Luftwaffe's front line, and to this purpose he gave Milch a special commission to carry the new programme through; Milch was to discuss everything with Udet over the next few days and find out what the true capabilities of the air industry were.[2]

Udet, however, knew of no way of increasing aircraft production. He was already very ill—apathetic, afflicted with blood disorders and terrible headaches; all day long he heard a buzzing in his ears and no doctor could help him.[3] He feared the bustling field marshal more than he feared any other. Now Milch came to him with instructions from Göring that he was to be told all. Milch later said, 'Udet told me all his woes—not enough raw materials, not enough workers.' In other ways too the Luftwaffe was the Cinderella of the war economy, said Udet: 'Nobody stands up for the Luftwaffe. Minister Todt has far greater influence on the Führer than Göring.'[4] Todt had headed the army's munitions procurement since the spring of 1940; as such his authority over the allocation of raw materials and manpower was formidable.

Milch told Göring that the Führer's new command would result in an increased front line only if it was supported by a powerful written authority for 'either Udet or me', an authority 'with which we can make headway against the army's armament'. Göring asked him to draw one up and he would sign it.[5] It was ready a few hours later and Milch's was the name entered in it.[6]

The document authorized Milch to close down and confiscate factories, to erect temporary buildings regardless of industrial regulations, air-raid precautions, social amenities and the like; it empowered him to draft German manpower by force into factory construction and aircraft manufacture; he could cancel contracts, 'dismiss and transfer leading personalities of the entire armaments industry without regard to existing private contracts of service', create new limited companies and hive off old factories operating inefficiently. The document was addressed to every Reich minister, to the military economics officers and to the High Command.[7] Göring signed it without hesitation.[8]

Milch immediately set the revolution in motion: on 23 June he charged Albert Speer, Berlin's chief architect, with the rapid erection of three huge aircraft factories—each as big as the rambling Volkswagen works—at Brünn, Graz and Vienna. Speer noted, 'Each building is to be put up in temporary form only, and is to be pulled down without question at the end of the war.'[9] Speer completed these three buildings within eight months. Next day Milch discussed with the industrialization expert, William Werner, the radical reorganization of the industry under an 'industrial council' as supervisory body: the factories were to be encouraged to work more on their own initiative, but the industry would be divided up into slabs according to product, not according to the factory's name or the aircraft type. Each such slab, termed a 'production ring', would have a 'controller' responsible to the council, of which Milch was chairman; the controller would be the most outstanding industrialist in that particular field. If crankshafts were produced at twenty factories all would now be controlled by the one man; it meant the end of trade secrets, but an obvious increase in efficiency.[10] In Milch's view only the industrialists—whom he knew and respected from his Lufthansa days—could meet the new challenge.

Milch called a major conference at the Air Ministry to unfold the 'Göring Programme'.[11] He announced that the present production of the air industry was not enough to keep pace with their losses; they would probably lose eight or nine hundred aircraft during June. During the Russian campaign, moreover, British aircraft production would be undisturbed by air attack, and soon the Germans must reckon with American aircraft production being added to the scales as well. 'The Luftwaffe is therefore to be quadrupled,' he explained. The name 'Göring Programme' was Milch's own idea: 'I wanted the programme to carry the Reichsmarschall's name,' he candidly told industrialists later, 'so that he would feel some close connection with it.'[12]

The first target Milch set was to double production of war aircraft—an increase of 1,200—by the late spring of 1942. The three bottlenecks—

aero-engine production, manpower and aluminium supplies—would each be settled in a different way: a plant with a capacity of a thousand engines a month was under construction; its completion would be brought forward by one month to four months. Speer was building three aircraft assembly factories. To meet the huge labour requirements —assessed by Udet at a minimum of 3,500,000 new workers to add to the existing 1,300,000 in air armament—Hitler ordered the immediate disbandment of three divisions in the east as one contribution, while the bulk of the rest were 'to be withdrawn from army production'. To curb the growing problems of absentees (*Bummelanten*) Milch announced, 'I have reached agreement with the Reichsführer SS Himmler, that anybody who changes jobs more than three times a year is to be drafted to a forced labour battalion; and anybody who refuses to work even there will be shot.'

Udet did not attend these Air Ministry conferences. His engineers advised Milch that the whole aircraft programme was hamstrung by the supplies of aluminium and copper available. The existing airframe industry could use only eighty per cent of its production capacity as it was, because of the aluminium shortage; what was the point of expanding the capacity?*

There seemed no way round this. Milch pondered the aluminium problem for several days and finally sent a score of young engineers to examine every aircraft factory for ways of reducing aluminium and copper consumption. They reported to him not only on wasteful metal-working practices—for example better machining methods would save 1,500 pounds of aluminium in one aero-engine alone—but on downright abuses of the Reich's aluminium resources. At Messerschmitt's factory his engineers chanced upon workers manufacturing tropical huts from the Luftwaffe's aluminium stocks, for a navy contract in connection with Germany's future colonial programme; other Messerschmitt workers were turning out aluminium ladders for vineyards. All the inspectors reported finding secret stocks of aluminium hoarded for emergencies.[14]

In Milch's view the emergency had now come. Above all he was alarmed by the resources of the United States. By 1 May combined Anglo-American aircraft production was greater than that of the Axis countries, and if Germany was content with the present rate the im-

---

* So Milch said on 26 June 1941. In August 1943 he recalled, 'At that time the experts calculated that we needed 16,000 tons of copper a month, otherwise the industry would never manage 800 aircraft. Today we are not even getting 4,000 tons of copper but we have not manufactured one single aircraft or aircraft component fewer because of any copper shortage.'[13]

balance would be twice as great by the end of 1942. From Intelligence
sources Milch knew that in June the American industry had manufactured 2,800 high-grade aero-engines. By the summer American production was 1,400 aircraft of all war types (including trainers) every
month; in 1942 America would probably produce sixteen thousand
military aircraft.[15] 'Britain would have hauled the flag down long ago
if it had not been for America's support,' Milch was to say later in the
summer. 'The Americans can manufacture in peace; they have enough
to eat, they have enough workers (with still over five million unemployed) and they do not suffer air raids. American war industry is mag-
nificently organized by a man who really knows his business, Mr
Knudsen of General Motors.'[16]

Against this firm intelligence on the British and American aircraft
production programmes Milch could set only the vaguest information
on German production. He knew that Udet was running down production of all the currently used engine types and most of the bombers,
except the improved Dornier (the Do 217), which would rise to sixty
a month from February 1942; but he could extract no firm promises
from Udet on what bomber was to replace the Heinkel 111 and the
Junkers 88 from early 1942. There was talk in Udet's office of a
Bomber 'B', but when Milch, suddenly alarmed for the future, pressed
for information it became apparent that no decision had even been
reached on which of two contenders—a Junkers 288, or a Focke-Wulf
191—was to be the Bomber 'B'.[17]

At Nuremberg Milch was to testify, '. . . and now I wanted to see
this new aircraft; and in doing so I found out that this aircraft could
never start production in 1942, but in 1944 at the earliest.'[18] It was
generally agreed that 'B' would be powered by the Jumo 222, with a
take-off power of 2,000 horsepower; it had originally been designed to
succeed the 1,500-horsepower Jumo 213, the hoped-for successor to
the Jumo 211 powering the Junkers 88; in 1940, when the more powerful (1,450 horsepower) Jumo 211J had been developed using special
air cooling, the ministry had decided to use it to power the next generation of Junkers 88s instead of the Jumo 213 which was not much better,
and then proceed straight to Bomber 'B'—probably the Junkers 288—
at the beginning of 1942. The trouble was that the Jumo 222 was causing difficulties: the airframe of the Ju 288 had first flown at the end of
1940, using the BMW 801G engines as stand-ins, but it had still not
flown using the Jumo 222s.[19] This was the problem to which not only
Udet but his entire staff had shut their eyes; production of their existing
bombers was being run to a standstill; but the replacement was hopelessly delayed. From the spring of 1942 the Reich would be producing

less than one hundred bombers a month. It spelt certain death to the bomber arm.

Even worse was the fighter aircraft situation. Average fighter production had never exceeded 220 a month, but now Udet had stopped production of the old fighters and was retooling for an advanced Me 109 powered by the DB 605 engine; the trouble was that this engine was overheating and neither the industry nor Udet's engineers had solved the problem. Similarly, the replacement for the Me 110 twin-engined fighter, the Me 210, was demonstrating serious design faults: it tended to go into a flat spin, and many brave test pilots had already lost their lives.[20] Finally, they were also experiencing trouble with the engine for Kurt Tank's remarkable fighter, the Focke-Wulf 190; the double-row radial engine—the BMW 801—was a departure from the in-line liquid cooled engines previously favoured by German designers. In short, a daunting task confronted Milch.

'I wanted this job like the devil,' wrote Milch in his memoirs, 'because I had no wish to make things more difficult for my friend Udet, who allowed himself to be talked into things by his staff, unfortunately. On the other hand, it was a matter of life and death.' By early July it was clear to him that a quadrupling of the Luftwaffe, the 'Göring Programme' was an unrealistic ideal, as they would have neither the aluminium to build the planes, nor the fuel to fly them. The High Command's General Thomas and Ernst Udet agreed with him on an interim target of doubling the front line, beginning in the summer of 1942; Milch asked Udet to draw up an interim production programme, reflecting this. 'Give me until tomorrow,' was the general's reply. (Milch later found that there was a special department which did nothing but draw up programmes in multi-colored graphs and diagrams.) But he advised Udet to take rather longer to draw up this one, and to bring the draft to his office on 8 July.[21] He reported to Göring on the fourth on the steps he had taken, and departed on his first tour of the units fighting on the eastern front.

Udet did not appear on the eighth. His staff said that he had flown independently to headquarters to show Göring the new 'Moose' programme. (This was evidently the embryo interim programme.) Milch angrily cabled the Director of Air Armament, 'care of Reichsmarschall Göring', instructing him to return to Berlin before showing the 'Moose' programme to the Reichsmarschall.[22] How could he carry out Göring's special commission if Udet continued to act as if it did not exist?

Neither Göring nor Udet saw the incident in this light. Udet complained about the telegram, and on 9 July Milch received a letter from Göring, berating him for putting pressure on the colonel-general; he,

Udet and the vain dream of a Department Head.    [*Sketch by Ernst Udet*]

Göring, would discuss his programme with anybody he liked. Udet returned to Berlin that evening, but for many days declined to call on Milch. Eventually Milch cabled Göring that he wished to be released immediately from the special commission. After several more days he was instructed to fly to headquarters on the sixteenth, here Göring abused him for his lack of cooperation with Udet.[23] The state secretary replied that he had good cause: much against his instincts, he had accepted Göring's commission, yet Udet was acting as though it did not exist. Shown Udet's new 'Moose' programme, he told the Reichsmarschall it was as impossible as its predecessors. There could be no effect on finished aircraft production for at least nine months—that being the length of the production pipeline, yet the 'Moose' programme showed a huge increase within ten months. Udet could only apologize that these were his experts' figures—he could not check them himself. 'The main thing is that we are of one accord,' Milch said, and Udet and Milch flew back to Berlin together.[24]

For the next weeks the new harmony was maintained. It was the harmony of doctor and patient. But over them hung the knowledge that production was still not keeping pace. By 5 July the Luftwaffe's first-line strength on the eastern front was down to 1,888 fighters and bombers.[25] Milch and Udet toiled round from BMW to Daimler-Benz and from Dornier to Messerschmitt. The state secretary tried hard to overcome his antipathy towards the latter—it was he who had recommended Messerschmitt (and Heinkel) for the National Prize some years before. Yet Professor Messerschmitt was only interested in designing *new* aircraft. Altogether there were currently no fewer than forty different German aircraft types under production, of which Messerschmitt was working on eleven (Heinkel had designed ten aircraft, of which only one was in mass production). Milch attached particular importance to the undisturbed production of the Me 109 fighter, particularly the Mark F, as soon as possible.

On 7 August he flew to Bavaria with Udet to tour the Messerschmitt factories. When they landed at Augsburg they found the Messerschmitt staff lined up for a great parade; this was the first irritation Milch encountered. The second was that he found surprisingly little activity when he toured the Me 109 production line. The professor guided him into a development building and proudly showed him the prototype of the Me 262 jet fighter; but it had only wooden engines, and Milch knew that the first Jumo 004 jet engines were not nearly ready (the engine's flight trials did not begin for seven months).[26] He suspected that Messerschmitt was trying to distract attention and angrily ordered the ministry's inspector at the works to see that no work whatsoever was done on the Me 262 mock-up until the Me 109F was coming off the production lines.

But Professor Messerschmitt remained unconvinced by Milch's hard language. He now recalls, 'As soon as my visitors had flown off, I sat down with the ministry inspector—Engineer-Colonel Meyer—and his people and persuaded them to let me carry on with the jet on the quiet. They granted me twenty engineers, and we went on as though nothing had happened.'[27] Milch soon concluded that he could not rely on Messerschmitt, and when he promulgated his new production programme it showed an increase in the Me 109, but a demand for two and a half times as many Focke-Wulf 190s as Me 109s.[28]

Setbacks in the Russian campaign in August resulted in a recasting of priorities. The army could no longer demobilize manpower for Milch, and now had a requirement for six hundred medium and fifty heavy tanks a month. In mid-August Milch none the less argued with the other Services for the provision of sufficient workers for the air industry: 'The production and wastage of aircraft are just about balancing each other out at present,' he said. 'So there will not be any overall increase in our fighting strength—indeed, there will be a decrease, since we cannot expect to get the aircraft back from the eastern front in perfect condition for the western front, when the war in Russia is over.'[29] He urged the adoption of total war measures (like prohibiting any construction work of purely postwar interest, for example the reconstruction of Munich station) before it was too late.

He did what he could to alleviate the most pressing needs of the squadrons. On 21 August he flew to the eastern front and toured the units. On every airfield there were scores, and sometimes hundreds, of damaged aircraft immobilized by the lack of proper spares. He organized squads of engineers to fly from squadron to squadron, cannibalizing the damaged aircraft to produce fit ones again.[30] As in one of Lufthansa's crises many years before, Milch scrutinized the stocks of useless spares held by the squadrons. 'When I recall what an idiot I was myself as a squadron commander in the Great War!' Milch said some weeks later. 'For just nine aircraft we had several hundred Bosch magnetos and five hundred rubber tyres in our stores.'[31] A typical absurdity permitted by Udet now was that while the most frequent requirement was for new undercarriages for Ju 52 transporters damaged by the rough landing grounds, a complete set of Ju 52 spares costing 120,000 marks had to be purchased each time. On his return from the front Milch dictated a blistering letter to Udet's chief of staff: 'Our current contracts for supply of spares run to 1.9 billion marks.

This sum is to be cut radically and immediately, and by that I mean at least one billion marks before further investigation!'[32]

Inevitably his first major *casus belli* was the Bomber 'B'. Since the Focke-Wulf 191 was a year behind the Ju 288 Milch could narrow the choice down immediately to the latter. But by August 1941 it was plain that a not unfamiliar problem had arisen: the all-up weight of the Ju 288 had increased as the Air Staff continually added to their specification; and the prototype Jumo 222 power-plant was not only now too weak, but was plagued by malfunctions.[33] Yet Udet's Bomber 'B' was the pivot of 1942's aircraft production, rising to a production of three hundred a month by the end of that year. Milch asked Junkers's general manager Dr Koppenberg whether he could start manufacturing Bomber 'B' *at all* in 1942. He replied emphatically that he could, but mentioned a possible delay because of the engine. Milch had obtained a graphic lay-out of the history of the Ju 52 from design through development and pilot series to mass production; and the Ju 288 was far more complex: 'If I use this as a basis of comparison,' he pointed out, 'and assume that the Bomber 'B' can be completed just as quickly as the Ju 52, then you see we will get it not in 1942, but in 1944!' He dismissed Koppenberg from Junkers on the spot.[34]

At the end of August Milch's staff were told that there were indeed fundamental problems in the Jumo 222's piston-rod bearings and cylinder-heads, but that mass production was envisaged for mid-1942. The Ju 288 would start production in August 1942. Milch instinctively mistrusted this aircraft; far better to rely on the most modern version of the Ju 88 for another year. On 6 September, Göring approved this reasoning: it was the numbers of aircraft alone that counted. He authorized Milch to cancel the Jumo 222 engine contract, and to postpone the Bomber 'B'.[35] It was clear that Koppenberg's was just the first head to roll.

When Milch had returned from his tour of the Russian front, on 27 August 1941, he found Udet gone: he had at last departed on sick leave on Göring's insistence, and became a patient in a sanatorium.[36] Even here Udet had little respite, for many measures required his signature—the reorganization of his office, the reversion to the older aircraft types, new programme schedules and the like. Milch had to visit him at his bedside to ask him to reinstate the previously cancelled aircraft in the production programme: more than 240 Ju 88s, 160 He 111s and 65 Do 217s would have to be produced with the requisite engines each month until such time as the replacement types were ripe for production.[37] Milch later explained, 'I visited him and procured his signature, though not without some pressure. Had we not done so on 1 September, we would have seen no new bombers and scarcely any new fighters in 1942.'[38]

A few days later Milch also dismissed Udet's planning chief, Engineer-General Tschersich, and at the same time removed Koppenberg from the Industrial Council and stripped him of the special powers for Ju 88 production.[39] He already had new men lined up for the vacancies—big names from Lufthansa and industry. As a shrewd move for the future he invited Dr Albert Vögler, one of the most respected names in the steel industry, to join his Industrial Council; on it Milch rested his hopes for increasing output. He planned to fight American conveyer-belt techniques, like those he had himself witnessed at Detroit in the twenties, and Soviet slave-labour with the capitalist profit incentive. To set against Russia's vast losses ('she has lost 1.2 to 1.3 million dead already') there remained one inescapable fact: 'In 1941 we manufactured fewer aircraft each month than we did in 1940!'[40]

There was no problem associated with increasing production which the state secretary did not consider. With Rautenbach he organized extra foundry capacity; with Porsche he arranged for the incorporation of part of the Volkswagen works; recalling that the Luftwaffe maintained large sawmills in the east, he ordered mass production of sixty thousand wooden chalets to help house the hundreds of thousands of extra workers to be injected into the industry.[41]

All of this had been put in hand by 25 September, when Colonel-General Udet—healed in body but still haunted by fears—returned two weeks early from his convalescence.[42] Milch told him of the reorganization of the office and proposed Lufthansa's Karl-August von Gablenz as the new planning chief; Udet reacted violently against the suggestion, but he agreed to appoint Colonel Edgar Petersen—who had commanded KG 40, a wing of FW 200s—as the new Commander of Research Establishments, with Colonel Wolfgang Vorwald taking over Udet's second office, head of the Technical Department.[43]

Göring persuaded Udet to accept even von Gablenz, emphasizing with a sidelong glance at Milch, 'That's the very best man I have!'[44]

Milch had also recommended that Udet's chief of staff, Ploch, should be honourably posted away from Berlin, but Göring was in no mood for half measures. On 28 September Udet ordered him to report to the Reichsmarschall. The leave-taking cannot have been a friendly one, for Göring still spoke of him years later with the utmost distaste: 'There was a case when an inventor of some standing came to us with an idea. As Udet was busy he was referred to the chief of staff [Ploch]. Ploch sat up and said, "Yes? So you are the crackpot with yet another invention for us! Well, I've got an invention too. It's called a door. You came in by it. Get out!" ' Göring sacked Ploch and banished him to the eastern front.[45]

From that time Ernst Udet could only assume, despite all Milch's assurances to the contrary, that his own career was at an end. Inevitably he sensed the ease with which Milch invested the new programme with momentum and urgency. At Opel's production line near Frankfurt they inspected Ju 88 manufacture and Milch called Udet's attention to the mass-production techniques employed and the firm's avoidance of bureaucratic methods.[46] By the twentieth the new aircraft programme was drawn up in final outline and approved by Göring.[47] Altogether Milch and Udet were together a dozen times during October, and tried to pick up their old friendship at Horcher's again. Before the war Udet had once told the author Carl Zuckmayer that he would never go to Horcher's again: 'That's where the top Nazis hang out now. . . .' But now he was a top Nazi himself, and he had enjoyed the fruits of power too long to be able to abdicate painlessly.

On 21 October 1941 Milch announced details of the aircraft production programme—Udet's last—to two hundred representatives of the industry at the ministry.[48] One feature was very new: whereas the old ratio of Me 109s to FW 190s had been four to one in Messerschmitt's favour, it was now three to one against. It seemed that Kurt Tank's new fighter was proving more reliable in the squadrons than the Me 109, whose fragile landing gear was a constant source of trouble. Many factories currently assembling the Me 109 under licence were to change over to the FW 190.

This shattering news was reported to Messerschmitt's board next day. The company's deputy chairman and banker, Fritz Seiler, who had devoted eight years to making Messerschmitt independent of ministry finance, was stunned by the landslide; after the Me 210 fiasco it was a terrible blow to company prestige. When he pointed out to Milch that the conversion to FW 190s would cause a considerable production loss, the state secretary observed that the particulars had been assembled for him by Udet's office. Seiler gathered that Messerschmitt's objections came at 'anything but an inconvenient moment' for Milch. The latter gave him two or three weeks to prove his case.[49]

Seiler soon learned that the Me 109's superiority was *not* enough to warrant reverting to the old ratio by itself; but from one of the biggest aircraft repair plants he obtained proof that one of Udet's staff had supplied falsified test data favouring the FW 190. And from one of the

Me 109 factories—the first due for conversion to FW 190 production—Seiler received statistical evidence that the conversion would cost a production loss of six hundred fighter aircraft there alone. On Professor Messerschmitt's suggestion this production loss was marked as a red shaded area on a graph for Milch.

This ammunition was ready in time for Milch's conference on 12 November. The state secretary explained that Messerschmitt's banker had claimed that converting factories to FW 190 production was not only an unjustified repudiation of the Me 109, but would also set back total fighter production for many months. He invited Seiler to explain why his test findings on the two aircraft differed from the reports supplied by Udet's office to both Göring and himself. By way of reply, Seiler handed him the photocopied documents establishing the falsification of the test reports. Milch studied the papers and handed them to Udet; Udet looked at them and turned to Seiler, saying: 'Not a very comradely action, Herr Seiler. The decent thing would have been to tell me of this beforehand.' Seiler retorted that nobody had warned Messerschmitt's of the impending programme change: 'It's a game of chess, Herr Udet. I am making the second move.'

Now Seiler announced that, as we have seen, the fighter production loss from just one factory he had investigated would be six hundred aircraft. Milch studied the red-shaded diagram and complained, 'Why was no such chart prepared by the Office of Air Armament?' Udet made no reply. In the circumstances, Milch announced, he would do what he could to restore the original ratio of Me 109s to FW 190s, although he could not promise more than three to one, as one factory was already being converted. It was the ultimate humiliation for Udet and his staff.

Perhaps Udet felt he had been ambushed by his friend. Detecting his bitter expression as they left the room, Milch called him aside and said, 'Udet, I have the impression that our relationship has taken a beating. We must straighten things out again. Let's go to Paris for a few days' relaxation. We both need the break.' Udet accepted the invitation.[50] As Milch had arranged to go hare-coursing outside Breslau over the coming weekend he suggested that he should collect his friend at Tempelhof airport at noon on Monday. They would fly to Paris together in Udet's small Siebel 104 passenger plane.

With that they parted. Udet spent the weekend with his mistress, a rich divorcee, and with Major-General Ploch, who had returned to Berlin from the eastern front, whither he had been banished by Göring some weeks before. Milch flew to Breslau. On 17 November dense fog stopped him flying back, so he drove the two hundred miles to Berlin

along the autobahn. At the ministry he was about to set out for Tempelhof when Udet's adjutant telephoned: Udet had shot himself that
morning.[51]

In his last long talk with his mistress the previous day Udet had mentioned some of the problems in which he had become enmeshed—
problems of supply, bottlenecks and material shortages. 'I am sitting
at the wrong desk,' he had kept repeating. That morning her telephone
had rung and she had recognized his troubled voice. She offered to
come round, but he had interrupted, 'No, it is too late! Tell "Pili"
Körner that he is to execute my testament . . .' (Körner was one of
Göring's other state secretaries). A shot had sounded in the receiver.
Aghast, she rang Udet back on another line; the phone was not answered. By the time she and Körner reached the house the housekeeper
had forced open the bedroom door. Two empty cognac bottles lay near
the revolver on the floor; the body was on the bed.[52]

She told Körner that Udet had said that 'they' were after him. Whom
Udet meant by 'they' was evident from two red-crayon phrases scrawled
on the grey wall above the bed. One was directed against Reichsmarschall Göring: 'Iron Man, you left me!' In the other he turned on
Milch, his best friend, asking Göring why he had surrendered him to
'those Jews' Milch and von Gablenz.[53] While the lifeless body was
carried into the bathroom Udet's adjutant scrubbed the writing from
the wall. Körner opened the dead man's safe and while the adjutant
cleared out the official papers Körner removed an envelope addressed
to him. It contained Udet's last letter to Göring. Körner decided he
could not send it on. It amplified the wall graffiti with some venom—
in one sentence Udet had described himself as a victim of 'the Jews'
Milch and von Gablenz.[54]

By midday Milch himself had arrived at the house. Together they
reconstructed Udet's last hours. His heavy recourse to narcotic stimu-
lants and all the ugly side-effects of addiction on his personal appearance
had finally proved too much for his mistress and she was leaving him;
his difficulties in the ministry, and the sudden return of Ploch from the
eastern front, had pushed him over the brink. Ploch had spent the
small hours drinking with him and was found by the official inquiry to
have hinted that Milch was planning to dismiss Udet altogether; learning of all this from Göring six months later, Milch wrote in his diary,
'The swine was Ploch!'[55]

Not since the death of a boyhood friend in a Lufthansa crash eleven
years before had one man's death affected Erhard Milch so much. He

telephoned Göring that evening and discussed the implications. The Reichsmarschall was in no doubt that the scandal had to be hushed up. Next morning his physician cabled to the ministry a press notice Göring had dictated:

While testing a new weapon on Monday 17 November 1941, the Director of Air Armament Colonel-General Udet suffered such a severe accident that he died of his injuries on the way to hospital.

The Führer has ordained a State funeral for this officer, who has departed this world so tragically in fulfilment of his duty.[56]

In Berlin the mortal remains of the man—a failure in his lifetime, and a hero again with his death—were returned to the Air Ministry. With solemn face Milch awaited the arrival of the cortège. As the pall-bearers slow-marched into the Great Hall the flags went to half-mast on every building in Berlin. The leading bearers of the Knight's Cross were summoned from every corner of the Reich to mount guard on the coffin during the funeral service.

That morning was overshadowed by still further tragedy. General Wilberg, one of Milch's earliest commanders and a father of the secret Luftwaffe of the twenties, had been killed in an air crash, and Werner Mölders died as his aircraft hit a factory chimney on the way to the funeral. Hitler remained silent throughout the ceremony (years later he was to comment on the circumstances of Udet's departure, 'How easy he made it for himself!').[57] As the Great Hall slowly emptied Hitler took Field Marshal Milch aside and said pointedly to him: 'Now there is another grave burden for you to take upon yourself.'

After four years of enforced inactivity, watching as incompetent men —some well-meaning, some evil—had destroyed the future of the German air force, Erhard Milch, the state secretary in the Air Ministry, was to become Director of Air Armament as well; he was to preside over the Luftwaffe's rebirth.

# PART III

# THE AUGEAN STABLES

*'Perhaps I look a sight to you today: but I guarantee I won't still look a sight in three months' time'*
—Milch to his staff, early 1942

# NEW BROOM

## (*November 1941–March 1942*)

Asked by an Allied interrogator to describe the Luftwaffe's cardinal errors in the Second World War, Field Marshal Milch replied that he knew only one: 'One hundred and forty thousand unbuilt fighter aircraft!'[1] More clearly than any of his contemporaries he had foretold the coming apocalypse. From Intelligence sources the Germans knew that America—now at war with Japan and Germany—was planning to manufacture sixty thousand aircraft in 1942 and twice that number in 1943.[2]

Milch had inherited a veritable clinic of ailing projects, ill-planned industry and corrupt organization. In the spring of 1944, when air superiority was finally lost to the Allies, a Luftwaffe expert was to write, looking back over the years of Udet:

Were one to pen a faithful account, an objective history of the Luftwaffe's technical development since 1934, then any outsider today—or better, any of our descendants—would take the whole thing as satire, dreamed up by some diseased imagination. Who could seriously believe that in real life there would be so much inadequacy, bungling, entanglement, misplaced power, lack of appreciation of the truth and overlooking of intelligent ideas . . . ?[3]

Milch proved himself equal to the situation. In the twenty months before the appearance of the American air force in earnest in July 1943 he increased German aircraft production 2.7 times.[4] By the time he was forced to stand down in June 1944, the industry was manufacturing *fifteen* times as many fighter aircraft as in the summer of 1941. Milch achieved this by ruthless rationalization of the industry, and by a seemingly immiscible amalgam of brutality and humanity; important posts were filled with capable officers, paper work was halved, efficient contacts were established between industry and squadron, and eccentric and useless aircraft projects were struck off the programmes. By early 1943 he had reached the supreme pinnacle of his career. The story would take a dozen volumes to tell with justice.

His relations with the principal aircraft designers, and particularly with Willy Messerschmitt, had always been marked by an animosity for which there was probably no sound reason; but once it was there it could not be dispelled, and each discovered added cause to dislike the other. The feud with Messerschmitt dated back to 1928. At Nuremberg —and indeed during the war—Milch alleged that the tall, balding designer had not built his aircraft with the necessary safety factors. In 1928 he had ordered six Me 20 passenger planes for Lufthansa, of which three had crashed because of a design fault, killing among others a lifelong personal friend and assistant of Milch. Milch had cancelled the airline's remaining contract with Messerschmitt, forcing his company into near bankruptcy. As will be seen in a later chapter (*see* page 332), it was Messerschmitt's vice-chairman, the 'brownshirt' SA general Theo Croneiss, who had spread the rumours of Milch's Jewish blood in 1933, and he had even produced for Göring a dossier including a photograph of a tombstone in a Jewish cemetery in Breslau bearing the name 'Milch'. When, in June 1933, Messerschmitt approached the new Air Ministry for fresh contracts, Milch had required the banker Seiler to sign a two-million-mark bond, to be forfeited the day any new Messerschmitt aircraft crashed because of design failure; and when the banker accepted this almost outrageous demand, Milch warned him, 'You are bailing out a would-be industrialist who will never make the grade. And the moment you are down, Messerschmitt won't help you up. He'll kick you in the teeth!'[5]

When Milch in turn was powerless, in Landsberg Prison, the sensitive and gifted professor secured his revenge by spreading malicious half-truths about how Milch had 'rejected' the Me 262 jet fighter. ('Again and again the vengeance of this scoundrel,' fumed Milch. 'Just because I declared 360,000 marks a year too high a salary for him and four or five of his directors!')[6]

Professor Heinkel was another *prima donna* Milch did not believe he could trust in the drawing office. The He 177 long-range bomber and reconnaissance plane was still not in service. Its promised performance was better than any bomber in the world, carrying two tons of bombs to targets 1,400 miles inside enemy territory at 225 miles per hour, with a top speed of 325 miles per hour and a service ceiling of over 25,000 feet. Milch's programme included 120 He 177s a month, but many had crashed or caught fire in mid-air and a dozen test-pilots had already been killed. The tail-plane and rudder had had to be enlarged and there were serious difficulties with the huge airscrews and with the coupled engines. The engines were water-cooled, and the water-circulation was inadequate.[7] Göring was to ask why this strange engine design had been chosen, with the two engines fitted into the same casing side by side: 'I was told at the time that the two would be coupled in tandem, and now suddenly we find this monstrosity with the two engines welded together side by side, so that you just can't get at them.'[8]

Engine design had been Germany's weakness for some years.[9] Under Udet's stewardship airframe design alone had made great advances. Despite Göring's express orders in 1938 work had still not even started on a thousand-engine factory. Daimler-Benz's DB 601 production was running down, but the new generation of engines was plagued by problems and delay. For three years between 1937 and 1940 Udet had stopped all work on the further development of the DB 603, and had carefully policed the factories to ensure that his order was obeyed. The DB 603's rival, the Jumo 213, had been put into abeyance in anticipation of the Jumo 222, but now that Milch had forced from Junkers's general manager an admission of the latter engine's tardiness, he was forced to put that on to a caretaker basis, and reopened the whole question of the somewhat smaller DB 603's advantages over the Jumo 213; in any event, neither could enter mass production before 1943.[10] Meantime, the DB 605 had encountered technical problems: it was overheating and catching fire, and some of Germany's best pilots, including the legendary Marseille, had been killed flying it in the Me 109G;[11] but the mass-production lines had already been retooled, so there was no going back. 'The entire fighter aircraft programme depends on it,' Milch was to tell Göring.[12]

Reichsmarschall Göring ordered a full inquiry into the scandalous situation; the principal defendants were Ploch, Tschersich and Reidenbach; Udet himself was beyond mortal judgement.[13] Months of interrogation of everybody, from Göring through Jeschonnek and von Seidel to the lowest clerks, began. Perhaps mercifully the records of what became known as the Udet Case have not been preserved; occasionally among the captured German files we come across the scars it left.[14] The judge advocate finally reported to Göring that Udet had failed to provide any leadership and had neglected his duties in almost criminal fashion. He further proposed that no charges should be brought against Udet's three lieutenants, as nobody would now benefit except perhaps the enemy. Göring was shattered by the report, broke into tears and told Hammerstein, head of his legal department, that he was grateful for the fate which had pressed the revolver into Udet's hand.[15]

For many months afterwards he continued to curse Udet and his staff. It was Reidenbach, one of Udet's chief technical advisers, who had prevented Germany from owning a wooden aircraft like the superb RAF Mosquito; Göring had himself issued such a specification before the war at a technical conference. 'Then the conference ended,' Göring recalled to Milch, 'and they left. And scarcely were they all outside than this fine gentleman, Reidenbach, announced, "Of course there's no question of manufacturing such rubbish!" '[16] The records of the Udet Case were full of similar episodes.

Over the winter of 1941–2 the hopes of a *blitzkrieg* victory over Russia were finally dispelled. The Luftwaffe's plans for postwar occupation of a defeated Russia were shelved for the time being.[17] In January Hitler cancelled the absolute priority accorded six months before to aircraft production, and reverted to the rearmament of the army in depth.[18] In the east his armies waged a desperate battle with the Russian winter. Frequently the Führer drew comfort from the knowledge that Frederick the Great had extracted himself from worse predicaments than these, and he ordered Milch to lecture the Party and Wehrmacht on the great Prussian's exploits. 'When one reflects that Frederick the Great held out against forces twelve times greater than his own,' reflected Hitler, after reading Milch's speech, 'one looks a proper dunce in comparison. And this time it is *we* who have the supremacy! Isn't that a disgrace!'[19]

Of course the greatest supremacy in the world was inadequate when channelled through the bureaucracy of the German higher commands. Milch's own efforts in March 1941 had spared the Luftwaffe the worst injury; at least the airmen and ground personnel were well clothed for the Russian winter.[20] But thanks to the neglect of the Quartermaster-General a major disaster had overtaken their equipment: of a hundred thousand Luftwaffe vehicles in the east, only fifteen per cent were still functioning early in January 1942.[21] The complicated cold-start equipment had proved too delicate for Russian conditions, and the army, SS and Luftwaffe had all ignored the simple cold-start procedure (thinning the oil with a little petrol, while the engine was still warm) which the Luftwaffe had itself demonstrated at the great Rechlin display in 1939.[22] Twice since Rechlin the army had been reminded of the cold-start procedure; but only on 10 November 1941 had the German War Office ordered the procedure to be introduced.

Learning of this, Milch exploded: 'If a regulation for winter-starting is issued by an authority on 10 November, it takes eight weeks for it to circulate *in Germany*. So think what it will take on the eastern front!'[23] He ordered a further investigation and learned that von Seidel's department had not published the Luftwaffe pamphlets on winter precautions until October, with revisions and further leaflets still being issued in January and February 1942. The losses of military equipment were enormous by the time the winter ended. 'I have always hated snow,' Hitler said when Milch was invited to dinner during February. 'Now I know why. It was a presentiment.'[24]

During January 1942 a number of Dr Todt's rivals came together and decided that 'an armament overlord' should be appointed, superior to Todt and to themselves; by the end of the month the choice had fallen informally on Milch, who had the support of Göring as head of the Four-Year Plan.[25] 'We did not apprise Todt of this,' Milch later said. 'We wanted to present him with a *fait accompli*.'[26] In the event, it was the plotters who were taken unawares: Todt was killed early in February when his plane crashed on take-off at the Führer's headquarters.[27] Göring, who hurried over, was stunned to be told by Hitler that he had appointed thirty-six-year-old Albert Speer to succeed him.[28]

Speer successfully warded off every attempt made during the coming week to carve up Todt's former responsibilities.[29] On 12 February Milch put to Speer the *fait accompli* which had been intended for his predecessor: a conference of industrialists had been summoned for next morning and Speer might like to attend; Milch took Speer to Göring, who emphasized that Speer's job was 'purely army production'.[30] He would learn the rest at Milch's big conference next day. Speer immediately reported his apprehension about this to Hitler, who assured him of his support: 'Should any attempt be made to gang up against you,' he said, 'close the meeting and invite all the industrialists to the Cabinet Room. I will then address them in person!' Next morning at the Air Ministry the steel magnate Albert Vögler announced to the industrialists the need for one overlord over all Services, to decide on priorities; the Economics Minister, Funk, rose and proposed, to general acclaim, that this overlord should be Milch.[31] Before the field marshal could speak Speer leaned across to him and whispered softly that he had just asked for, and been given, this very job by Hitler. Out loud, he announced that the Führer wished to address them all that afternoon in the Cabinet Room; in future, any such meetings would take place at *his* ministry, the Ministry of Munitions.[32]

This was the beginning of the remarkable Speer–Milch partnership. It was remarkable for the completeness with which Erhard Milch now urged obedience to Speer's requirements, even though he saw as the months passed that the army's production was being favoured as never before under Todt. And it was remarkable too for the cynicism with which it was exploited by Speer to his country's ends. Tall, high-cheekboned and handsome, Speer was Henry Fonda to Milch's James Cagney. A healthy admiration and respect sprang up between them—like a tiger and a lion cub. But while Speer's private chronicle recorded, 'Attempted raids on the Minister's provinces, carried out by various factions (Funk, Ley and Milch) during the first days of his office were immediately identified and nipped in the bud', thoughts continued to linger in Milch's mind about this new—and evidently highly protected —opponent, as his private papers show. Was Speer just 'driven by pathological ambition and hunger for power'?[33] He liked the young man personally, and was genuinely impressed by his achievements in expanding the aircraft industry's floorspace; yet his friendship with Speer was never to be understood. Vorwald, Petersen, Göring's chief adjutant von Brauchitsch—all warned against him. After hearing one inexplicable conflict of evidence over Speer's actions towards the end of the war, Milch, at a time of his own black despair, was to write: 'Seldom have I expected too much of anybody, but this time I have been sadly disappointed. I am still fighting off this feeling, and hoping for some favourable explanation, but this hope springs only weakly. . . .'[34]

On 13 February 1942 Hitler introduced Speer to the industrialists he was to govern.[35] He said that this was an instance where prestige must take a back seat, and assured them that he did not intend Speer to remain in charge for ever; when the war had been won he would need him for finer things. In his closing words Hitler asked them all to work together, in good heart; and he appealed to their 'sense of decency' in easing Herr Speer's task.[36]

Reichsmarschall Göring was already retiring from the war effort and devoting himself increasingly to extensive purchasing missions abroad for the art gallery he was assembling at Karinhall. His extensive knowledge of art benefited from his contempt for the rule of law, and his complicated financial transactions boiled down to thievery on a grand scale. While his attitude towards enemy persons was humane and soldierly, and the Luftwaffe itself prosecuted cases of rape and similar felonies among its ranks with unparalleled ferocity, this awe did not extend to enemy property, and Karinhall gradually filled with priceless objects culled from every corner of Germany's expanding domains.

His state secretary did what he could to step on this thievery. Late in February 1942 two crates labelled 'Glass—with Care' were found, addressed on printed labels to Göring's office, on the courier aircraft from Athens; Milch ordered legal officers to investigate and seized the crates

and contents. When Göring's office asked about the missing cargo the
egal department replied: 'Field Marshal Milch suspects that, as has
often happened with his own name, some unauthorized person is mis-
using the good name of the Reichsmarschall.'[37] But it was Göring
himself who was the smuggler, and he tolerated similar behaviour only
among his cronies. General Bruno Loerzer could send trainloads of
stockings and oranges from Italy and get away with it; others were
less fortunate. The Austrian Luftwaffe General Waver was found to
have appropriated a bracelet belonging to a female spy, and summarily
shared her fate; and when another was found to have used Luftwaffe
trucks to transport his private booty back to Germany during the Third
Air Force's headlong evacuation of France he was thrown into a concentration camp and dismissed from the Luftwaffe.[38]

Once when the judge advocate, Kraell, reported on sabotage in a
squadron in Crete, he made the mistake of describing to Göring in moving terms the beauty of the Palace of Minos there. 'That's coming to
Karinhall after the war,' Göring promptly declared. Kraell humbly
pointed out, 'That will pose some problems, Herr Reichsmarschall: it
measures two miles by one-and-a-half!' Unabashed Göring retorted,
'Have you any idea how big Karinhall's going to be after the war?'[39]
Reichsmarschall Göring was above the law.

On Milch's desk there were already the most alarming reports, not only
of the gathering RAF bomber strength, but of bomber production in
America too. To him, air defence rested primarily on the fighter squadrons, but at present the Air Staff was calling for only 360 fighter aircraft
to be produced a month. Fighter production had averaged 250 single-
and 64 twin-engined aircraft a month during 1941; Milch and his new
planning chief von Gablenz wanted far greater numbers, and with more
bombers as well—not only the 200 He 177s but 750 Ju 88s of the latest
type as well.[40]

Unhappily, Milch also had to fit in the Bomber 'B'. At the end of
February 1942 he and Jeschonnek, the Chief of Air Staff, jointly re-
affirmed that the Junkers 288 should eventually be adopted as 'B'.[41]
Göring initialled the recommendation: 'Ju 288, agreed. Göring'; but
there was more to the problem than a simple green-pencil note on a
letter margin. 'In my view the whole Bomber "B" is a misfit,' Milch was
to say in June.[42] But although he regarded the project as still-born, he
was forced to allow it to stay alive: 'The aircraft will make sense only
if its power plant is the [Jumo] 222. I have no idea what kind of aircraft
it's supposed to be: it's not a plane that carries very much; and it

doesn't fly very far.'⁴³ Already his heart was with the fighter production programme.

Milch took his ambitious plan for 'an umbrella over Germany' to Göring and Jeschonnek late in March. 'Herr Reichsmarschall,' he said, 'your total demand is for 360 new fighter aircraft per month. I fail to understand. If you were to say *3,600* fighters, then I would be bound to state that against America and Britain combined, even 3,600 are too few! You must produce *more*. But to demand only 360 fighters . . . !' He turned a contemptuous gaze on Jeschonnek, but the Chief of Air Staff objected violently: *'I do not know what I should do with more than 360 fighters!'*⁴⁴

This brief reply encapsulated the Luftwaffe's ultimate downfall. It remained rooted in Milch's memory for many years, incredible but true. He returned to it in January 1943: 'I just can't get over the fact that no more than ten months ago 360 fighters were required as maximum.' (By 1943 Milch's planning was already envisaging three *thousand* fighters a month.)⁴⁵ Five months after that, with the Ruhr's great towns in ruins after the RAF's devastating assaults and with the American daylight offensive just beginning, Milch again recalled Jeschonnek's remark: 'If I had said then, "My plan is that in one and a half years the programme will be what it is today—in 1943—to manufacture around 900 or a thousand fighters a month", then everybody would have said, "It's impossible!"' Milch had achieved this impossible, but he was still not satisfied: 'Even if we were turning out two thousand fighters, they would still be greedily snatched up by the squadrons, and there would still be enough work for them and for everything that goes with them—armament and fuel. Then things would look bloody different in Germany today; these daylight raids would be quite impossible.'⁴⁶

In the spring of 1942, however, this ordeal was only just beginning. After a very heavy RAF night attack on Paris in which eight hundred civilians had been killed, Hitler demanded a heavy reprisal attack on London as soon as the weather was suitable.⁴⁷ As his anger subsided, however, he cancelled the operation. In reply to a question from Göring, Jeschonnek explained: 'The Führer wishes to avoid provoking an attack on Germany's cities as long as the British keep to their present small scale of operations, and we for our part are unable to deliver annihilating blows in the west.'⁴⁸

Precisely a week later, on 28 March, the RAF sent 230 bombers to attack the North German medieval town of Lübeck by night, setting it on fire from end to end. Milch's first reaction, when he studied the reports, was that once again he had been proved right. The public had done nothing to prevent the spread of fires: 'They all got the hell out of it. Lübeck opposed our civil defence measures from the very outset and refused to join in. They kept saying, "Nobody's going to attack us." This is the result—256 people killed in one raid, with another hundred missing and fifteen thousand evacuated. That's the pay-off for their negative attitude.'[49] He had no doubt that worse was to come.

One episode throws light on the strained relations between Milch and his sole superior. Two days after Lübeck he celebrated his fiftieth birthday and noticed with pleasure that for the first time ever Göring congratulated him in person. But a document from Göring's files reveals the hollowness of the greetings: Göring's personal assistant had noted that whatever orders to the contrary Milch might have given, the press was to devote special attention to the birthday. 'Photographs showing the Reichsmarschall with Field Marshal Milch should be used in this connection. The Reichsmarschall will himself personally congratulate Field Marshal Milch in his office at the Air Ministry at 1 pm. This fact is also to be given prominence in the next day's press, and particularly emphasized in the photographic and newsreel coverage. . . .'[50]

And so, while the General Göring regiment played a serenade outside the windows and the newsreel cameras whirred, Göring presented to Milch a priceless three hundred-year-old Gobelin tapestry. He whispered that it was worth twenty-five thousand marks, and the field marshal replied, equally *sotto voce,* 'Where was it snitched?'

In a personal letter Hitler wished Milch a long life to expand the Luftwaffe: 'In this war I myself have come to value your presence at times when even a soldier must somehow keep faith—at times of tension, crisis and anxiety.' He said that he included Milch in that select band of men for whom the word 'impossible' did not exist.[51] There was also a cheque for a quarter of a million marks to purchase an estate; Milch used it as the deposit on a 740-acre property in Silesia. There was inevitably criticism of this gift from his American prosecutors at Nuremberg, but Milch replied that such donations were commonplace in other countries. Britain gave great estates to the Duke of Marlborough and Wellington. But several other gifts he did refuse. He declined two honorary doctorates, and when the President of the Aircraft Manufacturers' Association approached him with a gift of fifty thousand marks he politely turned it down.[52] The odour of corruption, which had lingered unchecked in the Office of Air Armament for so long, had finally been dispelled.

# NO SUCH WORD AS 'IMPOSSIBLE'

## (*March–June 1942*)

At fifty years of age Erhard Milch had retained his features well. He spoke emphatically, his mobile sky-blue eyes were still eloquent, and he flushed easily and often when his feelings were aroused. He liked good food and wines and smoked cigars endlessly. He was energetic and handsome and a moderate success in Berlin society. He did not neglect his family (although he was now separated from his wife, whom he had married as a young lieutenant in East Prussia); but nor did he entirely withstand the attentions of other ladies of his immediate society. One particularly persistent lady, a golden-haired beauty with the blue eyes of Germany's Baltic provinces, had finally despaired that the field marshal would ever gather the fruits while he could and had sent him a book about a Hungarian countess, the mistress of a man sharing her passion for horses, among other things. On the book's last breath-taking page Milch's admirer had written, 'All that could be yours as well!'

There was, as Hitler said, no such word as 'impossible' in Milch's vocabulary. Nothing pleased him more than to be given a great task where other men had failed, and to astound all the opponents who predicted that this time he must surely fail. One of his best friends, von Gablenz, once described how when he reproached Milch for setting unrealistic targets the state secretary replied that nothing would shake his faith in the Führer: 'Even if he commanded me to walk across the waves to him, I would unhesitatingly obey.'[1]

If there was one German aircraft designer who contributed to the change in Germany's fortunes in 1942 it was Messerschmitt. Hitler thought highly of him and commented to Milch more than once that the professor had 'the skull of a genius'; Milch did not share this enthusiasm and remained bitterly prejudiced against the Bavarian despite every attempt on Messerschmitt's part to improve their relations. He admitted that the designer was entitled to credit for his Me 109 fighter,

and he hoped that with the Me 309, which was due to commence production late in 1943, he would again produce a great aircraft.[2] But from
the Messerschmitt drawing-offices had flowed many ideas which had
not matched the Me 109's prewar success. Among some costly white
elephants were the Me 321 and 323: the former was a transport glider,
'Gigant', and the latter its powered equivalent. Of the Me 321, designed
to carry twenty tons of cargo including a medium-sized tank, Milch reported to Göring late in March 1942 that it was a swindle: '36 people
have already lost their lives test-flying it. Messerschmitt even went so
far as to shoot a film for the Führer's birthday with mock-ups.'[3] He
was equally opposed to Messerschmitt's other big aircraft project: to
meet a 1940 demand for a bomber able to fly to America and back, the
professor had designed the Me 264—a multi-engined giant on which a
big team was working at Augsburg.[4] Milch wanted all these projects
stopped and the really big aircraft design work left to Junkers or
Dornier.*

These problems were only minor compared with the disaster which
confronted the Luftwaffe over the Me 210—twin-engined fighter, high-
speed bomber and ground-attack plane. Messerschmitt subsequently accepted full responsibility for it, and again the company was nearly
forced into bankruptcy by Milch. Göring later proposed an eventual
epitaph for himself: 'He would have lived longer but for the Me 210.'
The aircraft had originally been designed by the company's leading designer, Waldemar Voigt, but the professor had adapted Voigt's blueprints to lessen the aircraft's weight and wind resistance. Although this
produced a radically different aircraft, the ministry (in Udet's time) had
ordered one thousand straight away, without waiting for the prototype
to fly. Test models went into a flat spin, side-slipped or suffered undercarriage collapses on landing (the professor had substituted a weaker
undercarriage than Voigt's to save weight).

Since November 1941 the Me 210's failure had brought increasing
technical and financial embarrassment to the company. Every day trainloads of costly components and sections for the aircraft were brought to
Augsburg and Regensburg; yet no finished aircraft were being completed or accepted by the ministry. Eventually four thousand workers
were laid off, and still the Me 210 production line was at a standstill.
Only one squadron, the second of ZG 1, had been equipped, but it had
suffered such calamities that they had abandoned the aircraft for an-

---

* Illuminating documents on the incoherence of German aircraft production,
design and planning will be found in the dossier assembled by Martin Bormann
for the purpose of discrediting Göring in the summer of 1944: file 315 of the
Schumacher collection, Bundesarchiv, Koblenz.

other. In February 1942 the imbalance between the purchase costs of raw materials, half-finished sections and components and advance payments from the ministry was twenty-five million marks, and Messerschmitt's monthly overheads were running at sixteen million marks.[5]

While ruin faced the company, the Luftwaffe still awaited the aircraft. Eventually the professor admitted to Göring that the aircraft was not fit for squadron service, after seventeen lives had been lost in one week alone.[6] Göring threatened to cancel the aircraft altogether. At the company's factories 370 half-finished Me 210s were lying around, visible to all the workers and staff, and materials were coming in for eight hundred more.[7] During an angry discussion between Milch, Vorwald and Messerschmitt at the ministry Milch gave the professor one last chance: the Me 210 was to revert to Voigt's original design. Ten samples were to be produced immediately, the first six being delivered by 1 April. Messerschmitt volunteered to begin mass production of this new version from 1 May—again a wholly unrealistic promise, since he must have known that the ten aircraft could not possibly have been built and tested by then. In fact the tests were not completed until September.

Back in Augsburg Messerschmitt broadcast appeals over the factory loudspeakers to his workers, and denied the rumours circulating among them.[8] He expressly denied that he had fallen out of favour with Göring. But at a staff conference in mid-April Milch mentioned the possibility of unseating Messerschmitt before his 'genius's skull' could do them still further damage. He sent his chief engineer, Lucht, to inspect the factories. Lucht returned with a gripping description of the catastrophic situation he had found: 'I found Messerschmitt a broken man. He was physically at a very low ebb and crazy with emotion. He was crying like a baby.' Lucht recommended that Messerschmitt should be removed from control.[9]

Milch agreed. He secured Göring's approval for the Me 210 to be struck from the aircraft programme. Only the new sample should be completed for trial purposes. When Messerschmitt's stunned chairman pointed out that this meant that the aircraft was finished, Milch agreed. On 25 April all work on the Me 210 stopped; throughout the industry the suppliers were ordered to cease manufacturing the components. 'Thus,' Milch summarized on the twenty-seventh, 'the aircraft can be considered a dead duck.'[10] He ordered the company to continue purchasing the completed equipment, materials, half-cut sections and components for the Me 210 from their suppliers, as it was not the latters' fault; many trainloads of the goods, totalling in all some sixty-eight million marks' worth, reached Augsburg and were stored in hangars on a nearby airfield.

All told Milch's decision cost the Messerschmitt company some thirty-eight million marks. The professor's alterations to Voigt's designs had cost the Luftwaffe over a thousand aircraft at a time when they could not be spared. But when the first reconverted Me 210s were completed in September 1942 and tested with DB 603 engines, they were found to be magnificent in every way; Milch ordered them to be redesignated the Me 410, and in this manner every trace of the unhappy predecessor was obliterated.[11]

On the same evening as Me 210 production ceased the RAF carried out the first of four violent attacks on Rostock and the nearby Heinkel aircraft factory at Marienehe. Nearly two-thirds of the town's built-up area was gutted by the fire-bombs and Heinkel's production there ceased for the time being. Had the RAF used more fire-bombs in attacking the factory the delay would have been even more extensive. Milch observed that purely explosive loads were useless for attacking industrial targets: 'A real effect is achieved only by the proper mixture, dropped over a long period. During the British attack on Rostock a few hundred cows, pigs and sheep lost their lives thanks to the stupidity of the public, as they took absolutely no action to put the fires out. But if the British had really set about attacking Heinkel's the right way, we would have been without any production at Marienehe for the next ten months.'[12]

These early raids were the storm signals for the future: a new officer, Air Chief Marshal Sir Arthur Harris, commanded the RAF bomber force and the bomb-loads were aimed predominantly against the towns rather than against the factories. In the wreckage of a Wellington bomber examined on the morning after the Lübeck attack Milch's enemy equipment expert, Engineer-Colonel Dietrich Schwenke, had found a new electronic device for accurate blind navigation (code-named 'Gee').[13] Angered by Lübeck, in mid-April Hitler commanded the Luftwaffe to carry out 'terror attacks on towns other than London'.[14]

Milch differed radically from Hitler in his proposals for combating the troublesome British bombing attacks by night. Hitler still believed in a strong defence by flak and searchlights. The state secretary, although a former artillery officer himself, was not enamoured of anti-aircraft artillery: he once calculated that besides the huge and costly ground organization it had taken on average 2,313 rounds of heavy flak and 4,258 rounds of light flak to bring down each aircraft they had claimed up to the end of November 1940.[15] Such a barrage undeniably had a deterrent effect on the bombers, but the cost, particularly in copper, was too high. At a conference with Hitler in January 1942

Milch proposed that more of these raw materials should be devoted to fighter and less to flak production.[16] He argued that they already had enormous stocks of flak shells in hand, and despite opposition from Keitel and Jeschonnek he stopped production of their aluminium time-fuses for three months. When Keitel curtly wrote to him protesting that the Luftwaffe was not supplying army factories with enough copper for the Führer's flak programme to be carried out, and that Hitler had therefore decreed 'that the raw materials are to be made available', Milch replied to Keitel with heavy sarcasm: 'The entire Luftwaffe copper quota would suffice to cover 74 per cent of the flak programme—provided, of course, that all aircraft production ceases.'[17] Privately he described Keitel's letter as a 'self-protection' letter: 'If anything goes wrong, Keitel himself is covered. If you see such a letter in future, and I have written "Self Protection" on it, that means it's somebody without the guts to take responsibility.'[18]

In his first few weeks of power Milch swept half of Udet's four thousand-strong staff out of the ministry and into industry, and replaced the old but fashionable system of liaison officers by twice-weekly mammoth conferences, great parliamentary assemblies attended by upwards of eighty officers, engineers and industrialists. Nobody was kept uninformed any more about planning and requirements. Reichstag shorthand-typists were called in to keep verbatim shorthand records of these discussions. They show that Milch ruled by the lash of his tongue, developing an invective that at times was not bettered by Goebbels himself. Over every industrialist hung the possible fate of a Koppenberg or Messerschmitt; learning that a leading airscrew factory had fallen twenty per cent below target, Milch swept out the managers and put in a *Kommissar*.[19] Learning that the Ju 88 had undergone fifty thousand design changes, even while under production, up to the previous summer, he now categorically prohibited virtually all last-minute design changes to any production aircraft.[20] Learning that twelve-cylinder Daimler-Benz cars were still being ordered 'for this highly placed personality or that', he persuaded Göring to forbid such non-military production at all: 'Any person working on any peacetime project from now on is liable to the death penalty,' he announced in mid-April.[21]

At the same time he introduced positive measures to increase production: he aimed at greater part-standardization of aircraft components, as in America, and together with the Industrial Council introduced mass-production techniques which had not even been thought of in western countries. Multiple drilling rigs were designed for a new engine-factory at Allach that could perform three dozen drilling operations in one eight-minute stroke instead of the thirty hours the old system had required.[22] He tried to shorten the 'pipeline' in the engine industry and established the air force's own machine-tool factory. Compared with twenty-eight thousand aero-engines turned out in 1941, Milch's factories were to manufacture fifty thousand in 1942.[23] Above all, he injected new optimism into his entire ministry: 'I often aimed high,' he admits, 'but I fired them with confidence in our certainty of ultimate victory, and with pride in our work.'

A few weeks after taking office as Munitions Minister in February Speer recognized that he still lacked influence on air armament. (He had even taken Milch with him for his first conferences as minister with the Führer.) Speer decided to create a small body comprised in effect of Milch and himself, so that Milch could not evade joint responsibility for the rest of the arms production spectrum.[24] Early in March Speer mentioned to the OKW's General Thomas the need for a 'small body of men gathered round the Reichsmarschall to direct central planning policy'.[25] At the end of the month he took the idea to Göring, and from the meeting there emerged a decision to establish a 'Supreme Court' to control raw materials, beyond which neither the industries nor the Services could appeal.[26]

This new authority, Central Planning, was to consist of three men—Milch, Speer and State Secretary Körner from Göring's Four-Year Plan Office. Their task was to find out where the slack in the German war economy was; Milch referred to the body, not inappropriately, as a 'lemon squeezer'. Initially Göring gave them control over all raw materials except coal, fuel and synthetic rubber. But they had no control over the procurement of labour, for which Hitler appointed a separate overlord in the shape of Gauleiter Sauckel, and this was to prove a major hindrance in organizing armament in depth.[27] The inclusion of Körner was symptomatic of Göring's fear that this body would otherwise usurp his powers; Speer was opposed to Körner, but Milch commented privately that it was better to have a Göring 'stool-pigeon' they recognized than to be spied on in some other, unknown way.[28] The decree signed by Göring stated that all three members were equal in status, but it was in the nature of things that Speer assumed control of Central Planning as time passed.[29]

The field marshal next saw Göring at the Rechlin research establishment on 11 May. He was exceedingly surprised by the Reichsmarschall's presence—his first visit since the famous 'magic display' in July 1939. 'I never really intended to set foot inside Rechlin again,' Göring told the Rechlin team, 'in view of the way you engineers lied so damnably to the

Führer and myself during the display in the summer of 1939.'[30] Again he was shown the powerful effect of the 30-millimetre MK 101 cannon. A few days before one fitted experimentally in a fighter had blown up a Wellington bomber with one round. This time he saw it mounted in a Henschel 129 'tank-killer' aircraft, its shells easily piercing eighty milli-metres of armour-plate. He recognized in this aircraft the ideal means of combating enemy tanks which had broken through the lines.[31] The MK 101 was the same weapon as had been displayed to Hitler in 1939; the later versions with belted ammunition feed, known as the MK 103 and MK 108, had actually lain fallow since then, until Milch had taken over, issuing immediate production contracts. But it would be 1943 be-fore they entered squadron service. Göring's anger was therefore under-standable: 'I keep searching like somebody demented for the devil who fouled up my Office of Air Armament like this.' And again and again he reached the same conclusion: 'Udet must take the blame—and in parts it is enormous—because he was downright incompetent; but I must share in that blame myself, because I burdened the man with more than he could carry. . . .'[32]

Of all the heavy aircraft inspected by Göring, Milch and Jeschonnek at Rechlin only the He 177 could carry out strategic bombing of Russian targets; but it had still not been resolved whether it should be able to dive-bomb, or attack on the level only; indeed it had still not been finally decided whether it was better with two or four propellers.[33]

The Germans saw no means of bombing the United States by direct flights, but they had studied partial solutions of the problem, such as mid-air refuelling or establishing mid-Atlantic staging posts. In mid-1941 preparations for mid-air refuelling of bombers had been put in hand: the bomber aircraft would take on seven tons of fuel from a sec-ond aircraft after flying 2,600 miles.[34] When Milch asked for his opin-ion General Jeschonnek said curtly, 'Quite pointless.' Milch asked to be kept informed should the Air Staff change its view: 'Until then I would request the idea of mid-air refuelling to be put to one side.' He added, 'There is also some idea of landing in Greenland and topping up with fuel from a U-boat there. I don't know how this is visualized pre-cisely, but I think it would be far better to fly over, drop the bombs, ditch the aircraft and ask, "Which internment camp have you picked for me!"'

A few days after his visit to Rechlin Göring, as head of the Four Year Plan, finally persuaded the Führer to adopt radical measures to cure the chaotic transport system inside Germany and behind the eastern front.[35] The man who had achieved what Stalin's armies and the RAF bombers had so far failed to do was the sixty-five-year-old Transport Ministry official heading the Reich Railways, State Secretary Kleinmann. For some time Hitler had protected this man and his even older minister, Dr Dorpmüller, and Dorpmüller had rejected Speer's suggestion late in March that Kleinmann should be replaced by a younger man.[36] Shortly afterwards Milch had been at the Führer's headquarters when Dorpmüller hinted to him that Hitler wanted Milch to put transport in order; when Milch saw the Führer immediately afterwards Hitler confirmed this briefly, explaining, 'You are a transport expert, after all.'[37] For some weeks Milch heard no more of this.

By late April a complete seize-up seemed inevitable. The OKW had ordered tens of thousands of coal trucks to be converted to flat tops for transporting guns and vehicles to the front, since none of the proper flat tops had been returned. Hundreds of locomotives had been knocked out by the winter through lack of provision for the extreme cold; once unloaded, nobody had bothered to send the wagons back, so now there were over 150,000 choking the lines behind the eastern front, and fresh, full-laden trains could not get through.[38] The great distances which now had to be covered had doubled the average running time of a wagon to seven days. In Germany, denuded of rolling stock, the crippling coal shortage was threatening to bring the munitions plants to a standstill: at least seventy thousand coal wagons a day were needed to sustain capacity. Within a few weeks major factories would be standing idle.[39] The only solution which General Gercke, the OKW's transport chief, could offer (as Hitler later told Milch) was to tip wagons and contents off the lines to clear a way, and return the locomotives in convoy to Germany.[40] This would hardly help Germany or the fighting front.

In this situation, Hitler recalled the two men who had already shown their ability: Albert Speer, who had developed and produced a heavy anti-tank gun in a matter of weeks where the Army Ordnance Office had asked for months; and Erhard Milch, who had saved the situation in southern Norway in 1940, and had rescued the Luftwaffe from the abyss more recently. 'Here were the men for whom, as for me, there was no such word as "impossible".' He sent for them both, together with a young Reich Railways district official Speer had mentioned to him, and harangued them on the need to overcome the transport catastrophe.[41]

He proposed means of solving the railway crisis: turn-round times must be shortened, unloading accelerated by the use of prisoners of war, and all unnecessary journeys avoided. (Milch later discovered that while the Reich Railways were crippled by shortage of rolling-stock, four express trains still nonsensically operated every day between Brussels and Paris.) Hitler expostulated, 'In wartime we don't need to transport beer from Munich to Berlin and from Berlin to Munich.' He ordered that rolling stock was to be withdrawn ruthlessly from the occupied countries: 'Here Germany's interests are paramount.' He wanted to see primitive locomotives and equipment built and extensive repairs to existing stock. To achieve all this, he announced, he was dismissing Kleinmann as state secretary and replacing him by Dr Ganzenmüller, Speer's choice. Meanwhile, Speer and Milch were to be given dictatorial powers over the entire transport system of the Reich.

For Hitler, only one thing mattered: 'We must not lose this war just because of a transport problem; therefore the problem must be solved.' Milch and Speer solved it essentially within three weeks. While Speer attacked the problem of mass producing locomotives and rolling-stock, Milch turned his attention to the railway and inland waterway systems. If Milch, two days later, was to describe his powers in these terms: 'I have been authorized to string up any railway official from any tree, right up to the highest directors (−and I mean it!)', then this was his usual hyperbole; but only just.[42] It was an opportunity to break every single railway regulation—the small print on posters in every ticket hall. He recognized his familiar enemy, red tape and the centuries-old 'megalomania' of the legal mind, and attacked it with relish.

There were the 'safe load' regulations—the compositions, heights, weights and maximum speeds of loads in railway wagons. 'The gentlemen in charge,' said Milch, 'are naturally fully conversant with these safety regulations, and know no way round them.'[43] Armed with Hitler's authority, he ordered the wagons to be overloaded by as much as twenty per cent with forbidden goods packed at random together, lengthened the trains and despatched them to the eastern front at speeds ten or twenty per cent above the permitted maximum. He ordered the canals and ports of the occupied countries to be searched for barges and tugs to take the load off the railway system—and stumbled on 2,300 assorted barges which had been assembled and converted by the navy for the invasion of England in 1940. About five hundred, with a capacity of two hundred thousand tons, were still serviceable; Milch ordered them to be towed back to Germany and the necessary tugs to be confiscated in the occupied territories.

When his staff expressed scruples about the morality of this, he retorted, 'All of us are bound to one common aim—winning this war. If the Dutch fall by the wayside one way or another, because we have to survive—that does not concern me. I could not care less if every Dutchman froze, drowned or starved to death, so long as Germany's future is assured. You may think this unadulterated selfishness, to think only about one's own country. But it is our task and our duty.'[44] He ordered seventy thousand wagons to be allocated to coal transport daily, before any more wagons were given to the military. He discovered that the OKW had been hoarding thousands of wagons for emergency troop movements to meet an Allied invasion: 'In a year's time that might well happen,' he conceded. 'But it might never happen. In the meantime the coal necessary to keep Siemens or AEG from grinding to a standstill is not being shifted.'[45] 'Stupidest of all are the Wehrmacht,' he complained on 12 June (and how revealing was this complaint, coming from the Lufthansa director turned field marshal!). 'They have no idea whatsoever about how to do things economically.' If the coal was shifted production—and that meant arms production—must increase.[46]

A major dictum revoked by Milch was the heresy that this was to be only a short war. 'We have to accept that this is a Thirty Years' War,' he warned his own staff. 'Not that this means it will last thirty years; but we must act as though it *could*. I forbid under penalty of extreme punishment any such expression as that things still under research or development will be too late to be of purpose in this war.'[47]

Germany's progress in some fields of research had been confirmed at Rechlin. There were two turbo-jet aircraft under development—the Arado 234 armed reconnaissance aircraft and jet bomber to be powered by four BMW 003 jet engines; the prototypes were to fly in the coming spring. And there was the Me 262 jet fighter, still awaiting its first jet-propelled flight.[48] Milch's attention was also caught by the Argus Tube: months before he had been puzzled to see a Heinkel 111 standing at Rechlin with a strange bulbous tube slung beneath one wing. The Germans were hesitant even to use it, lest the enemy copy it, because its principle was so simple and cheap: once in flight the Argus Tube drew in air through a number of flaps at the front, mixed it with paraffin vapour and ignited it; the hot air exploded out of the rear, since the compression closed the flaps in the front. If the tube was the right length, an organ-like resonance was set up, and considerable thrust was developed. 'Have you any use for it?' Milch had asked Udet at the time. Udet had shaken his head.[49] The original use, as a source of brief extra power for Ju 88 bombers, had been disqualified by the tube's own wind-resistance.

Milch had kept thinking about the Argus Tube. Soon he had linked three things in his mind: explosive warhead, automatic pilot and Argus Tube. In May he urged his scientists that the Argus Tube was 'of importance for the future', indeed, as important as the jet engine. 'What I keep thinking is this: somewhere, we set up a conveyer belt production of these Argus Tubes. But first we must find a use for them. . . .'[50] In fact he had already visualized a small, cheap, expendable pilotless aircraft packed with high explosives, flying faster than the fastest enemy fighter plane. A flying-bomb, in fact.

Three days later Admiral Lahs, Chairman of the Reich Society of Aircraft Manufacturers, brought an aircraft designer to see him—Robert Lusser.[51] Lusser's qualifications could not have been better: he had been thrown out by Heinkel, and by Professor Messerschmitt before that. Milch sketched out his idea and a few days later the designer returned to his office with a case full of drawings and calculations. On that day the flying bomb (later known as 'V-1') was born. By early June 1942 the project had been code-named 'Cherry Stone'.[52] In its proposed final form it was a small, straight-winged aircraft, with the Argus Tube attached to the top of its tailplane. It would carry nearly a ton of high explosive, fly at a top speed of 440 miles per hour at low altitude, making it virtually impossible for any modern fighter to catch, and hit any large target of about five by three miles at a range of 160 miles; it would descend on its target at a speed of 650 miles per hour. If it were launched from France, therefore, London would be well within range.

Against it there was virtually no defence, for it would take a brave fighter pilot to come within range of a ton of high explosive and try to blow it up. The weapon's wings contained a special knife-edge for cutting through the tethers of barrage balloons. The whole fuselage would be constructed of thin steel plate.[53] The beauty of the project was that it used no aluminium, and it was fuelled with cheap paraffin. Each such weapon would probably cost only 550 man-hours to manufacture, plus the cost of the explosive and autopilot. Provided that it could be catapulted to an initial take-off speed of over 200 miles per hour, its wings could be made short and stubby. The necessary catapult was already being developed by experts in rocket propellants; it would be ready in the autumn and then the ministry could have the first handmade 'Cherry Stones' completed and ready for testing. Milch selected Peenemünde, on the Baltic coast, as the best location for its trials.[54]

Thus was one opportunity realized, by the Luftwaffe, at the same time as another was lost: on 4 June 1942 Milch, Speer and many leading scientists and industrialists were invited to hear Professor Werner Heisenberg, the famous nuclear physicist, lecture on atomic fission in Berlin.[55] Heisenberg headed an atomic research laboratory at the Kaiser-Wilhelm Institute of Physics in the capital, and was already experimenting with atomic piles. 'He described the excellent start that they had made,' Milch recalled in his memoirs, 'but complained that nobody took them seriously and supported them.'[56] Heisenberg actually mentioned the feasibility of making an atomic bomb. Milch stood up and asked him approximately how large such a bomb would have to be to destroy a whole city, and the professor replied: 'About as big as a pineapple.'

At this, Speer also became interested and asked what Heisenberg needed for his research. In his mind he had a figure of about a hundred million marks as being an appropriate sum.[57] Either Heisenberg or his deputy, Professor von Weizsäcker, replied that they had been asking for some time for an allowance of ten thousand marks for building purposes.[58] Speer and Milch exchanged ironic looks. The Munitions Minister granted this request immediately. On 7 August 1945, Field Marshal Milch read the news of Hiroshima, and recalled bitterly that afternoon with Speer and the German atomic scientists in Berlin: 'If Germany had discovered this,' he wrote that day, 'instead of spending the money on the war (the USA put the cost at $2,000m so far), then we could have achieved without bloodshed all that we needed, and all we were entitled to.' $2,000m was about the amount of money that the Luftwaffe had spent on armaments in three months of war.

# THE DEAD RACEHORSE

## (*June–October 1942*)

After six months in office Milch had clear plans for the future. His experts had told him what the RAF was planning, and from General Bötticher, the former military attaché in Washington, he had heard a detailed briefing on the American air force's plans to assist.[1] Milch asked that the industry should develop fighter aircraft with greater fire-power and aim for supersonic speeds, with jet engines eventually; at night their exhausts should be invisible, and there should be an effective system of ground control worked out for all the fighters. He asked for a purpose-built night fighter aircraft (the Heinkel 219 seemed most suitable), so that the output of medium bombers did not have to be raided for this purpose.

He also asked for a high-speed bomber with a one-ton payload, 650 miles of penetration and a top speed of 440 miles per hour and later of the speed of sound. Like the new generation of fighters, the bombers must have greatly increased ceilings of operation, using superchargers and additives like nitrous-oxide ('GM-1') or alcohol–water injection; by 1943 he wanted the bombers to have a ceiling of 45,000 feet, and even more by 1944 or 1945. The bombers were to be fitted with exhaust flame-dampers, radar devices to warn of enemy fighter attack, and to adopt jet propulsion as soon as possible. Long-range bombers like the Hs 177 and the generation after that were to be equipped with guided missiles like He 293 and remote-controlled bombs like Fritz-X for attacking enemy shipping in mid-Atlantic.[2]

These were the tasks to which Milch was to apply himself for the next two years. But the Luftwaffe had already lost the initiative. At the end of May 1942 over a thousand British bombers attacked the city of Cologne in a raid lasting about one and a half hours; 469 people were reported killed, over five thousand injured and forty-five thousand homeless.[3]

After the failure of the Battle of Britain this was the second relapse

Göring's reputation suffered. Soon he would be looking back with nostalgia to 1940 and the Luftwaffe's carefully prepared attacks on Britain. 'The British have learned it all from us,' he sighed. 'That's the most depressing thing about it. Except for this electronic warfare side, they have learned it all from us—the whys and wherefores of concentrated attacks—they have copied the lot.' He added wistfully, 'How beautifully they were botching it to start with . . . !'[4]

Milch also came in for criticism. The Cologne Gauleiter reported to Hitler that the flak had had to cease fire because of lack of ammunition. Hitler attributed this to Milch's relentless campaign against flak; Milch ordered an investigation and established from the local flak battery commander that they had more than adequate ammunition, but stored too far away.[5]

By mid-June Milch's planning staff had produced modest figures for their possible aircraft production over the next few years, rising from 1,500 a month in 1942 to 2,860 in 1945, including 840 bombers, 1,240 single-engined and 200 twin-engined fighters.[6] Milch wanted more. From an agent highly placed in the British Air Ministry they were receiving regular and (they believed) reliable figures on British production. At the end of June he warned Göring: 'Comparison of German aircraft production with the figures available to us from Britain shows that the British are making both more bombers and more fighters than we are.'[7] This the Reichsmarschall refused to believe.

Nor was this all, for the British had begun operating at least one aircraft superior to anything known to the Germans—the Mosquito. Colonel Galland, chief of the day-fighter squadrons, told Milch that his fighters were completely outclassed by it. At the end of May the first such aircraft had been shot down and investigated; it was evidently a high-speed, high-altitude bomber, made largely of wood. The prisoners captured from the first Mosquito crash stated that its top speed was 450 miles per hour, and it could well reach altitudes of 38,000 feet—a very serious threat indeed.[8] A high-powered Intelligence investigation of the Mosquito began. A second crashed and completely burnt out, but it was clear that it had carried four one-thousand-pound bombs, and had been crewed by high-ranking officers.* Milch predicted, 'I am bound to suspect that one day the British are going to start coming with these aircraft *en masse*.' A few weeks later it was reported that the black-

---

* The first had been crewed by a squadron leader and wing commander and the second by a wing commander and group captain. 'For the RAF this is quite exceptional,' Milch was told. 'Perhaps they consider this aircraft particularly safe.'

painted Mosquitoes were also being used as night-fighters, armed with four cannon and four machine-guns: 'This aircraft is going to be the deadliest for us,' said Milch.[9]

The wooden Mosquito was not his only headache. Three British four-engined bomber types had made their appearance—the Lancaster, Halifax and Stirling. A Stirling was captured almost intact when it made a forced landing in Holland. The Germans repaired the minor damage with parts from other Stirlings, levelled out a thousand-yard runway, primed a special crew with instructions from captured take-off papers and flew the bomber with German markings to Rechlin.[10]

The American four-engined bombers were now also appearing in the European theatre. In July the B-24 Liberator appeared in North Africa.[11] When Schwenke briefed Jeschonnek on the coming armada of American bombers, and on the numbers of B-17 Flying Fortresses being ferried across the Atlantic, Jeschonnek was positively delighted, and boasted: 'We will fetch these four-engined bombers down just as quickly as the twin-engined ones; and the loss of a four-engined bomber means a much higher loss to the enemy.'[12]

Milch's own planning foresaw the use of the Me 109, powered by the 1,475-horsepower DB 605, as the standard daylight fighter until the Me 309 eventually replaced it; as for the FW 190 fighter, its BMW 801D double-row radial engine had earlier been unreliable and until July 1942 Milch had not dared hope for too much from the aircraft. The engine was now satisfactory, and in July Galland made a very favourable report on the FW 190 to Milch.[13] By this time the faults in the troublesome DB 605 engine had been overcome: the overheating of the valves was cured by exchanging them for components with greater chrome and nickel content, and a minor adjustment to the ignition timing had been proposed. By early summer the crisis with both engines was past. The DB 605 was running smoothly and the Me 109G was to prove one of the best high-altitude fighters in the world.[14]

As Hitler gathered the Axis forces for the summer offensive in Russia, the lunge towards the Caucasus and its oilfields, Milch set out his own philosophy: in his view it made more sense to have a thousand aircraft, with something like four thousand muzzles between them, than just a handful; not that the extra aircraft would cause any extra ammunition to be fired, but by proper use of a vast number of aircraft in one operation one could frequently spare the need for twenty or thirty others. 'We saw the proof of this in France. If we had not used the means at our disposal correctly, we would have found ourselves in a war which would have swallowed up colossal amounts of ammunition. The thousand guns too few we had in 1914 would have sufficed to settle the war in our favour by that Christmas.' He added: 'If we could say today that after six months' winter production effort we had six thousand fighters and six thousand bombers, instead of just the 1,800, with ammunition, crews and fuel, then the war would be over very quickly.'[15] By May 1942 the position was that the Luftwaffe had about 15,000 aircraft, of which 6,600 were scattered along the various fronts, 4,300 were in the training schools, 447 in reserve, about 3,000 under repair and 685 'on the way'. ('Those are the aircraft that have just been lost,' said Milch. 'They are not on the way, they are just missing—mislaid *en route*.')[16]

Yet there were insuperable obstacles in the path of increasing bomber production—problems of selection, rather than of engine-design. Bomber 'B' would not appear for some time; the He 111 was obsolescent, and only the latest Ju 88—which Göring agreed to rename the Ju 188 ('so that the enemy gets the impression it's something new,' admitted Milch)[17]—seemed worth concentrating on. Milch was aware that they were approaching the most important season: 'What we manage to turn out now will still be in time for the great offensive; what we turn out in four months' time will come too late for this year's decisive battles.'[18] His experts told him that if they cancelled Bomber 'B', but still kept the Heinkel 177, they could eventually produce 840 Junkers 188s a month instead of the 750 currently projected.[19] To Milch the Ju 188 was incomparably a more worthwhile aircraft than Bomber 'B', when considerations of cost, bomb-load and range were borne in mind; Göring shared this view, but both of them came up against the stubborn requirement of the Air Staff for the Ju 288, Bomber 'B'. 'It is adequate neither in range, nor in speed, nor in bomb-load, and suffers from a number of congenital diseases, particularly in that it is powered by two *coupled* engines, of whose reliability and operation we are still anything but convinced,' Milch grumbled, at the end of June. 'If we add to all this the fact that its dive capability is nullified by the big airscrews, then I am at a loss to explain why it is required.'[20] For many months yet, however, Milch was forced to sustain the costly Bomber 'B', an aircraft which was never to fly.

There was still no prospect of attacking the United States in *direct* flight, but early in August Milch's bomber expert von Lossberg outlined to him a proposal for bombing Washington or New York: a Blohm and Voss 222 aircraft would fly across the Atlantic and land near a U-boat stationed about eight hundred miles off New York to refuel and make up its bomb load to eight tons; it would repeat the operation one night later before flying back to Europe.[21] The navy and the aircraft manufacturer both supported the plan, but not Jeschonnek, who turned it down as impracticable. Milch believed the Chief of Air Staff was interested only in the Russian campaign.

Von Lossberg assured him he would be prepared to make the flight any time himself. He proposed predominantly incendiary bomb-loads—in each attack they could rain about four thousand fire-bombs on New York. 'The 2.2-kilo magnesium bomb has an explosive segment which detonates after four to ten minutes. . . . If they could be laid in a swathe across New York, and the bombs kept exploding round the ears of the fire-fighters like hand-grenades, it would have a terrific effect.' He proposed they attack first of all the city's Jewish quarter or dockyard area; but the project, after being briefly resuscitated in the summer of 1944, was never put into effect.

Plans were drawn up by the Air Ministry for a factory designed for conveyer-belt production of a thousand bombers a month; it would employ fifty-five thousand workers.[22] Milch told his staff, 'I want the foundations laid this autumn, so that it can commence production at the end of next year. . . . Half a year from today the war will certainly look quite different from now, so that it is by far the best if we make our demands immediately.'[23] By this he meant that the war would have switched its main emphasis to Britain and her allies in the west again. Early in August 1942, as German troops launched the first stage of their thrust towards Stalingrad, Milch confidently predicted, 'The major fighting in the east will be over by next year; a colonial type of warfare will of course continue.'[24]

This optimism did not last. Milch soon learned that the Russian air force would still have to be contended with. Soviet industry was believed to be producing about five hundred aircraft and fifteen hundred aero-engines a month. As the Wehrmacht rolled deeper into Russia all summer, they found that the Russian aircraft industry had vanished: the whole industrial Donets region had been evacuated; aircraft engine plants had been uprooted from round Moscow, too, and were probably already producing again. Milch was full of admiration for this lightning Soviet industrial evacuation: 'The Russians are doing things we would have said were impossible.'[25]

All his endeavours to increase German aircraft production ran up against his inability to procure and assign fresh manpower, now that Sauckel had been put in charge of labour procurement by Hitler. Milch had significantly less control over manpower allocation than Speer, who controlled the Armaments Inspectorates which recruited local German labour. The problem became more urgent in the summer, when Hitler abandoned his undertaking to restore top priority to Luftwaffe production in 1943, and advised his Munitions Minister that army production 'must be expedited with the same priority as the Luftwaffe's even after the successful conclusion of the operations in the east'.[26] At this time ninety per cent of the aircraft industry was not even able to work a second shift because of the labour shortage.[27] In the autumn of 1941 it had employed 1,850,000 workers, but the heavy military call-up of the following months had reduced it considerably.[28]

The shortage was aggravated by the problem of workers who malingered, changed jobs or just hid to avoid regular shift work. It was no small problem: from January to June 1942 the air industry had been allocated 403,000 workers; but the fluctuation caused by the shirkers was so great that the actual net increase was only 60,000.[29] Milch recommended that these people be turned over to Himmler's well-known facilities: 'He knows how to deal with them even though they haven't broken any laws.' Meanwhile, while Speer built up the effective labour force by closing down less essential consumer industries, Sauckel brought in the foreign labour—those from western Europe coming initially on a contract basis, and those from the east as slaves.[30]

Milch never neglected the needs of the German public (which, he once insisted, must be considered first even if the rest of Europe had to starve). He considered that the entire economy was being maladministered in the continuing tussle between the Services, the Four-Year Plan and the war industries. He had discovered one instance of this military selfishness himself: when the navy had protested that it must have greater steel allocations, and the civilian economy less, Milch had without warning sent inspectors round some of the navy's biggest shipyards: at the end of August 1942 they reported to him that there were huge quantities of steel lying round the yards at Wilhelmshaven, Kiel and Hamburg; the workers had said that the steel had lain there for years.[31]

In September he reported the work of Central Planning to Hitler.[32] He protested at the huge sums being spent on armaments, and estimated that forty per cent of the money was being squandered. 'If one cannot buy a glass or saucepan it does not matter to these people,' he complained, referring to the High Command.

It's all right by them that thousands of families today have to cook in tin cans. But they themselves must have everything: *ten million safety razors are manufactured annually for the Wehrmacht, and twenty to thirty million toothbrushes!* There are only seven million soldiers altogether! Twenty to thirty million combs, the same number of hairbrushes, and so on. But can any member of the public buy combs or hairbrushes today? The war cannot be won by the Wehrmacht alone, but only by the whole German nation.[33]

Even as a Luftwaffe field marshal, Milch did not hesitate to take the public's cause to the seat of the war economy—the Central Planning commission. Much has been written of Albert Speer's opposition to Hitler's 'scorched earth' orders in 1945; but that was opportunism, in apprehension of certain defeat and not improbably with an eye to the Allied trials to come. Milch's effort for the German people began much earlier, when victory still seemed possible. The controversy in question was Central Planning's distribution of nitrogen and electric power. In short, Milch argued that Speer's refusal to support the nitrogen needs of agriculture would scorch the earth more effectively, though less spectacularly, than any Führer directive.

It was a double dilemma: the first was that Speer's explosives factories competed with fertilizer production for the available nitrogen supplies; the second was that Speer's armaments factories competed with nitrogen production for the available electric power. In Central Planning Milch resolutely but unsuccessfully championed the demands of agriculture and the German people.[34] Speer sided equally relentlessly with the demands of war: the huge losses of the previous winter had to be replaced. When the Minister of Agriculture protested at this attitude, and particularly at Speer's decision to switch off the nitrogen plants during the coming winter and cover the 140,000-tons nitrogen loss entirely from fertilizer production—'the loss of 140,000 tons will result in a collapse of our food supplies!'—Speer replied sardonically, 'You are free to tell this to the Führer; but alone.'[35]

Milch argued that Germany should now meet all agriculture's demands, since she had built up considerable stocks of explosives: 'The ground is becoming increasingly exhausted.' Speer refused to share this view, believing that in the present situation with the German army beginning its decisive battle for Stalingrad, 'each ton of explosives is more vital than a ton of cereal'.[36]

In other respects Milch had cause to worry about Speer's Ministry. Despite clear standing orders from Göring to the contrary, Speer's local armaments inspectors had begun seizing labour from aircraft industry factories in their territory, for army production. In one 120 workers had been drafted from the Fieseler aircraft factory in Kassel into the army programme. 'Out of the question,' said Milch when told of this; learning that the culprit had earlier been in the Army Ordnance Office, Milch grumbled, 'The Führer said a few days ago that these gentlemen should have read a bit more Karl May, and a bit less military manual; then they would be fit for something in this war.' General von Gablenz suspected it was Albert Speer himself who encouraged these raiding parties: Speer had long held the view 'that the Luftwaffe comes *after* the Army.' Milch shut his ears to such talk: 'It wasn't Speer,' he said loyally. 'It was one of his agencies.'[37]

At the end of August 1942 General von Gablenz was killed in an air crash during a thunderstorm in Turingia. Although Milch continued to inquire hopefully about the cause—after Todt's death Hitler had ordered the Luftwaffe to develop a crash-proof magnetic wire-recorder for the cockpit of such aircraft—it was never established with certainty.[38] The pain caused by the loss of yet another close friend from such a familiar cause really troubled Milch. He unbent enough to write one word in his diary: 'Shocking'. That evening he met Albert Speer at Horcher's; Speer, fourteen years his junior, put his arm round the field marshal's shoulders and commiserated, 'This afternoon you lost a life-long friendship. Can I offer you a new one?' The dour field marshal, who had never offered the familiar *Du* to anyone in his life, accepted.

The remarkable Speer–Milch alliance, which was to last over a quarter-century through many vicissitudes, dated from that evening. Indeed, they became inseparable. It would be hard to imagine a less likely combination: Milch was short, stocky, choleric and balding: Speer was a tall ascetic figure, ill at ease in uniform. His conversation was polished and intellectual, albeit weakened under the impact of Milch's lieutenant's jargon. The field marshal was rough, robust and ruthless, and privately scoffed at the juristic precision with which his friend consolidated his empire: 'His ministry was well known to me for its penchant for *decrees,*' he was to testify. 'There were too many experts there and each one wanted to issue a decree.'[39] Milch's ministry worked by mass conference behind guarded doors, at which he could harangue his generals and engineers from ten in the morning until four or five in the afternoon. Speer copied his shorthand-record idea, but mocked the conference principle. When Milch later persuaded him to hold joint conferences to hear the Luftwaffe's most urgent requirements, Speer's court historian described: 'To lend the necessary emphasis to these requirements, the Luftwaffe assembled each time in almost company strength, so that the large conference room of the Air Ministry was only just big enough.' 'The quantity of Luftwaffe participants,' the chronicler added sarcastically, 'appeared necessary in view of the somnolence of the individual members.'[40]

Yet Milch's methods worked. By the autumn of 1942 the air industry was already producing fifty per cent more aircraft, but he could do little to amend the existing aircraft projects. A new aircraft took four years from drawing-board to squadron, so Milch was still stuck with those begun in 1938.

Among these was the Air Staff's greatest hope, and Milch's despair, the 30-ton Heinkel 177 heavy bomber and long-range reconnaissance aircraft. Jeschonnek wanted at least one squadron to carry out long-range bombing operations in Russia, but in May he had advisedly told the Reichsmarschall: 'For such operations the reliability of the engines is of paramount importance.'[41] Milch wanted the bombers for carrying out mass attacks on Allied convoys in the Atlantic, and Admiral Dönitz wanted the reconnaissance version to enable his U-boats to engage the transatlantic convoys too. All the technical opinion was unanimous that it had magnificent handling characteristics;[42] but by September 1942 only 102 had been produced, of which the Quartermaster-General had accepted only 33 for squadron service; and of these, only two were still operational. The Daimler-Benz coupled engines were still plagued with faults, and major design errors in the airframe were just coming to light.

'If one sees how the first He 177 flew on 20 November 1939, and that the aircraft are still not in service, one can only weep,' said Milch at the end of August 1942.[43] Göring echoed him: 'It really is the saddest chapter. I do not have one single long-range bomber. . . . I look at these four-engined aircraft of the British and Americans with really enormous envy; they are far ahead of us here.'[44] The principal delay to the He 177 had been caused by the basic requirement that it should be able to dive-bomb. It was tempting to blame Udet for this (he had explained to Professor Heinkel in 1938 that there was no future for the aircraft otherwise).[45] Milch refused to blame a dead man now: 'I have never done so, on principle,' he was to say. 'I have been taught to take responsibility for my subordinates; it is all too easy to say once somebody is dead, "It was an error of leadership". We must not assume so here.'[46] Even so, he deeply regretted the delay; how many He 177s they would have had by the end of 1942 otherwise! 'What still has some small effect in 1943 would have had a major effect in 1942, and a decisive effect in 1941.'[47]

One basic error Udet had committed was to trust Heinkel too implicitly. At the beginning of 1942 Lieutenant-Colonel Petersen had visited the factory to investigate the delay. The works staff complained that the professor devoted all his attention to the profitable He 111 series, 'and devotes no capacity to the He 177'. As the original serial production order had been cut back to five He 177s a month pending the solution of all the problems, this was only human.[48] In February 1942 the first engine-fire had occurred, and since then the aircraft had been dogged by outbreaks of fresh faults about every three months.[49] By the summer it was obvious that the wing structure had been wrongly designed, for it could not withstand the stresses of diving; Heinkel himself woke up to this only after the first wing fractured in August. Meanwhile, Petersen had ordered over 1,300 minor modifications as a result of the flight trials; these modifications were carried out with 'catastrophic lethargy' by the factory: 'We have proof,' Milch was later told, 'that from the time of the conferences concerned Heinkel took three months before he even began to attend to minor modifications to the prototypes.'

Milch knew that only a major change could save the aircraft; by this he meant dropping the dive requirement, and making the bomber a pure four-engined aircraft, instead of using two coupled engines.[50] But his development staff pointed out that this would mean a completely new aircraft, and that would take four years to realize.[51] So the coupled-engine version was retained, while engineers struggled to prevent the engines—first the DB 606, later the DB 610—from catching fire in the air.

Göring had always believed that the aircraft was a pure four-engined design. When he saw the strange new beast that had developed by the time he visited Rechlin in May 1942, his anger knew no bounds: 'I have never been so furious as when I saw this engine. Surely it must be as clear as daylight! How is such an engine to be serviced on the airfields? I believe I am right in saying you cannot even take out all the sparking plugs without pulling the whole engine apart!'[52] The shock took him months to get over; much later he still reproached his state secretary, 'It is absolute stupidity. I told Udet right from the start I wanted this beast four-engined as well. At some time or other this crate must have been in a four-engined form. . . . Nobody mentioned this hocus-pocus with two welded-together engines to me at all. A charming surprise that was for me.'[53]

Throughout the summer the He 177 crashes continued. In mid-June, as Milch and Speer visited Peenemünde research establishment to watch an (unsuccessful) launching of von Braun's A4 rocket missile, they saw a brand-new He 177 taking off with four tons of bombs on a test flight; after it had flown out of sight, it banked steeply to the right and side-slipped into the ground from five hundred feet up, killing everybody aboard. 'The investigation has shown that a coupling sleeve broke on the propeller shaft,' Petersen reported to Milch, and he added that a week before the very same sleeve had snapped on another aircraft before it could take off. Not only had this incident been kept secret by Heinkel and Daimler-Benz, but six identical cases had been uncovered during the factory's test programme.[54]

In the meantime, production suffered. Only two He 177s were operational. 'It's no use,' said Milch in mid-August. 'The question is, can we leave Heinkel—who bears most blame for this with his Oranienburg factory—in charge?' He sighed and added, 'On the other hand, he has done much good for us.'[55] Professor Heinkel claimed he needed more designers, but to Milch this was an all too familiar ploy. 'The cause is not the manpower situation,' he said on the twenty-sixth, 'but the complete failure of the Heinkel company, a failure for years in this field. There's just no excuse for it.'[56]

Three weeks later Göring made a speech to the aircraft industrialists which left a very bitter taste in their mouths.[57] Messerschmitt and Heinkel were the principal objects of Göring's scorn; he reserved his most biting comments for the Heinkel 177 bomber and for its coupled engines. 'The things they told me!' Göring mocked. 'I asked them, "Why not go over to a pure four-engined type?" and they told me, "No—four-engined types are *passé* now; it is far better to have only two airscrews." So I said, "Well, well! The enemy is proving quite a nuisance to me with his four-engined types, they are a deadly nuisance. . . ." Not so, is the reply: "We are doing things differently. We are putting two together, or two in tandem."'

When Milch pointed to General Jeschonnek's requirement—that the bomber should dive—as the root of all the evil, Göring apologized that in that case the firm was exonerated; but he added, 'It is straightforward idiocy to ask of a four-engined bomber that it should dive. Had I been told of this for one moment, I should have exclaimed at once: what kind of nonsense is that! But now we are stuck with it.' He asked Professor Heinkel, 'Are you going to manage, or is it quite hopeless?' Heinkel assured him that the engine-fires were as good as cured and explained: 'The airframe has to be strengthened for the dive-bombing. . . .' 'It does not *have* to dive,' thundered Göring. Heinkel, as astounded as Milch by this swift decision, replied, 'Then it can go straight to the squadrons.' Three more times Göring repeated that the bomber was not required to dive; he wanted it only for carrying torpedoes and the guided missiles like Hs 293 and Fritz-X to shipping targets far out in the Atlantic, and for occasional raids at high-level on targets like Sverdlovsk. Milch gratefully repeated this decision to his staff: 'The Reichsmarschall has ordained that dive-bombing by the He 177 is no longer a requirement. He has quite properly described this requirement as crazy, and prohibited it.'[58]

In the meantime, despite Professor Heinkel's assurances, design faults were still encountered. In investigating yet another accident, Milch's engineers discovered still more weak spots in the main wings, which tended to buckle under stress. 'That's no minor fault,' erupted Milch when he was told. 'That's a major foul-up!'[59] Early in October Major Scheele, commanding one of the prospective He 177 units (the first squadron of KG 50), refused to take responsibility for sending the aircraft out on operations. When a ministry engineer cited none the less expert opinions that the He 177 was otherwise the best aircraft in the world, Milch could only snarl: 'What use is the best aircraft in the world if it can't stop falling apart? What use is the finest racehorse if it displays the best speed over 200 yards and drops dead after 300!' In one graphic phrase he characterized the medical history of this bomber: 'First of all we tried a minor ear operation. Then we cured its teeth. And now we find it's got a chronic heart ailment and is probably being kept alive only by artificial means.'

Very soon after Göring's tirade about Allied superiority Milch was brought firm evidence of just this. The B17 Flying Fortress had now reached them; it was clearly designed for daylight operations.[60] By early October the remains had been reassembled at Rechlin. There were altogether eleven heavy machine-gun positions in the bomber, loaded with a hitherto unknown incendiary ammunition. Colonel Galland was full of praise for this dangerous aircraft: 'It unites every possible advantage in one bomber: firstly heavy armour; secondly enormous altitude; thirdly colossal defensive armament; and fourthly great speed.' Others echoed this praise. In formation the B17 was virtually impregnable—they had managed to collect this sample only when it drifted out of formation.[61]

At the same time a second daylight threat was developing: an exhaust turbine had been clearly identified on photographs of a B24 Liberator bomber; this would greatly increase its altitude. 'These are worries I just cannot get over,' Milch said late in October. 'We have got to accept that one day the enemy bombers attacking Germany will be flying at altitudes of 28,000 or 30,000 feet.'[62] From another Boeing crash they had recovered almost intact the famous Norden bombsight (of which a German agent in America had procured the blueprints before the war); this left no doubt as to the Americans' potential bombing accuracy. From the American bomber production figures and from the reconnaissance photographs of extensive new bomber airfield construction in eastern England, it was clear that 1943 would see the onset of a crushing bombing offensive from both the RAF and their American allies.

The field marshal took Göring a dossier on this coming Armageddon, on 11 October. Jeschonnek refused to modify his careless attitude towards the American bombers, and Göring also refused to take Milch seriously. A few days later Milch related with some concern to his own staff, 'The Reichsmarschall told me that there is no cause for anxiety about the American aircraft and that, four-engined though they may be, we can contemplate the future with equanimity. I told him that I do not agree. . . .'[63]

# NONE SO BLIND

## (*October–December 1942*)

As a patriot, Milch adopted a firm line on treason. The word covered many sins, from the action of the since-discredited Engineer-General Reidenbach back in 1941 in ordering nearly a million of a certain component not used anywhere in the Luftwaffe, to the active dispensation of secrets to the enemy.[1] Milch's attitude towards traitors, even when accidental, was brief and final. When a Panzer division's operations officer crash-landed behind Russian lines in a Storch (the enemy murdered him and captured his papers, revealing the offensive beginning nine days later) Milch showed no pity: 'He would have been sentenced to death anyway.'[2]

Not without reason he suspected treachery all round him. He warned his own staff, 'There are recalcitrants everywhere, and traitors. Nobody knows where the next one sits, ready to betray you!' It speaks volumes for his judgement of character that he privately suspected the loyalty of the *Abwehr* (military counter-espionage) organization directed by Canaris. He thought little of Canaris. The Admiral had once visited him clutching a lump of pressed coal. 'What's that, Canaris,' he had joked, 'are you going to set fire to me?' 'It's a bomb!' replied Canaris earnestly. 'We are going to sabotage the ships of the enemy!'[3] The field marshal placed his faith in the Gestapo. 'The traitors are lucky that I am not head of the Gestapo,' he once said. 'Then there would be far more death-sentences.'[4]

Treachery was even closer than he suspected. In the autumn he was informed that the Gestapo had uncovered a large communist spy ring, the 'Red Orchestra', with its seat in the Air Ministry and Milch's own Office of Air Armament.[5] About seventy people were rounded up and indicted. The agents had established numbers of wireless transmitters and had passed to the Soviet Union information on planned paratroop operations, the latest positions of Hitler's and Göring's headquarters, details on the withdrawal of flak defences and much else. One merchant had simply walked from room to room of the ministry collecting production and casualty figures; fortunately, he had confused production targets with actual achievements. 'That's probably just as well,' Milch commented. 'Otherwise I would have been ashamed of such low figures —the enemy would have laughed at us!'[6]

Kingpin of the 'Red Orchestra' was Lieutenant Schulze-Boysen of the Air Staff's Intelligence branch, whose wife was grand-daughter of the Prince of Eulenburg. Colonel Stumpff, the prewar chief of personnel, had turned him down for a commission because of suspected communist sympathies, but the Prince himself had intervened with Göring, and Göring had overruled Stumpff.[7] Learning the full details of the spying, Milch was shocked at the numbers of the nobility involved. 'The harmless Central European might say, "There goes the daughter of So-and-So—the family has given generations of fine officers to the State. Impossible to think wrong of her!"' He shook his head. 'Not so, unfortunately; not so. The father may well be a fine, outstanding gentleman; and the son can be a swine.' With grim satisfaction he added, 'Of course, they are all for the high jump. The lot of them.'

He announced new precautions for the ministry. In future everybody must submit to spot-checks and X-rays as they left the building. He betrayed his deep suspicions of the *Abwehr* too: 'The X-rays will be worthwhile only if they are made by the Gestapo. I forbid any kind of X-raying by the *Abwehr*, as otherwise we have no guarantee that it will be a "successful" X-ray.' Seeing the curious faces round the table he continued, 'The whys and wherefores I cannot say. But I have my reasons.'[8]

Göring did nothing to halt the drain on the aircraft factories' skilled labour. In October 1942 the OKW ordained a further major call-up for the army. 'The Führer says, quite rightly, "I want more soldiers",' complained Milch, 'and then everybody about him bows in unison and murmurs *Jawohl* and they simply grab more workers from our factories. I would like to know how many of the army's millions are really in the front-line areas! I doubt if there are more than 20 per cent of the infantry at the front; the other 80 per cent are somewhere in the rear.'[9]

To fill the gaps in the factories, air industry workers were switched by Speer to army armaments production before Milch could protest, and foreign labour was brought in. Gauleiter Sauckel was given sweeping powers by Hitler to procure more labour from France, and these produced absurd anomalies: as the biggest airscrew manufacturers were preparing to send German workers to a factory in France, Sauckel was busy pressganging French workers *from* it. Other German workers sent

to Paris factories were recruited by the OKW as soon as they arrived
there. Of two hundred men working on FW 190 engines in Paris,
Sauckel seized fifty overnight to deport to Germany.[10]

None of Milch's counter-measures helped. In desperation individual
factories turned to Himmler's concentration camps for manpower.[11]
The Heinkel company obtained six thousand prisoners from Oranienburg concentration camp to work on the He 177, and these were followed by thousands more for other Heinkel factories.[12] Messerschmitt's
opened direct negotiations with Dachau concentration camp for three
thousand prisoners for the Augsburg works.[13] Nobody else would
appreciate the air industry's predicament. Speer recognized the malady,
but could diagnose no cure. 'In every offensive, we lack just 10 per
cent . . .', he warned. 'If we cannot manage that 10 per cent more this
winter, by next summer our position will have deteriorated so much
that we will be reduced to a war of attrition.' At the end of October
1942 Speer mentioned to Milch, 'I spoke with Goebbels recently. He
is of the opinion that the public is actually waiting to be inspired to
this last great effort. The public often has a much better sense of realism
than the self-opinionated middle classes. The public has recognized
that this final effort is not being made.'[14]

Two months previously the German armies had reached the River Volga
and the outskirts of Stalingrad, and a long, exhausting struggle for this
focal point had begun. As the Russians massed for an autumn offensive
Hitler appealed to Milch to mount a superhuman effort against the
Soviet targets, bringing in the newest aircraft, even if they were still
imperfect. Jeschonnek wrote to Milch, 'In the last few days the Führer
has several times referred to the He 177 aircraft and said that he would
attach particular importance to sorties by this aircraft in the eastern
theatre, however primitively carried out.'[15]

The air force was heavily committed to supplying both the Afrika
Korps under Rommel and elements of the army groups on the eastern
front. When the Russian offensive broke as anticipated across the River
Don on 19 November 1942, the latter commitment was suddenly extended: within four days the German Sixth Army under Colonel-
General Paulus was encircled at Stalingrad; Hitler ordered the Fourth
Panzer Army to the relief, but if the Sixth Army was to hold out, its
three hundred thousand men would have to be supplied by air.[16]
Colonel-General von Richthofen, commanding the Fourth Air Force
which would have to operate this airlift, noted that Paulus believed such
an operation feasible, but he told his superiors he could not share this
view.[17] Had either Göring or Jeschonnek firmly challenged the pro-

posal, Hitler would certainly have abandoned it and ordered Paulus to fight his way out of the encircling ring; but the proposal passed unchallenged at this stage.

Initially the Sixth Army asked for 300 tons of fuel and 30 tons of ammunition a day; later they would need 150 tons of foodstuffs a day as well. This would require up to 800 Ju 52 transport aircraft, taking the very low serviceability on the eastern front into account. In the entire Luftwaffe there were only some 750 Ju 52s, several hundred of which were supplying Rommel's forces in Africa. Milch had warned all summer that the Air Staff requirement of only 60 new transport aircraft a month was totally inadequate. Now the gap would have to be bridged by temporarily converting He 111 bombers for transport purposes.[18] When Hitler telephoned Göring on 23 November to question him about an airlift, the latter, unprepared for such a question, agreed it sounded possible.[19] That afternoon he told his staff officers that he had given the Führer his word that the Sixth Army could be supplied by air. Every transport aircraft available was to be mobilized for this purpose —he himself was providing his own courier flight. There was no discussion.[20] The huge operation began next day.

In the hours that followed, Hitler ordered Paulus to stand fast until relief arrived; meanwhile air supplies were being mobilized. If Göring made any conditions (about the stabilization of the front line, about prolonged fine weather or the limit of the airlift's duration) these were not adequately heeded in the optimistic climate his undertaking had induced. He repeated on the twenty-fifth that the Luftwaffe could deliver an average of five hundred tons of supplies a day, assembling every possible aircraft, including Lufthansa's precious four-engined Ju 90s for this purpose.[21] Hitler waved aside the new-found pessimism of Jeschonnek, and the outright opposition of the Luftwaffe representative Colonel Christian next morning, assuring them 'it was all a matter of time', and that 'a particularly gifted organizer would manage things, equipped if need be with ruthless powers, and despite whatever obstacles the generals opposing the airlift (von Manstein and von Richthofen) might put in his way.' Göring left for Paris.[22]

'Wars can only be won by air power,' Milch hammered in to his staff as the new year, 1943, came. 'You will lose every war, in fact, if you do not have air superiority—not in all God's skies, but where you need it, in the *Schwerpunkt*. For ground forces without air superiority or air supremacy it is impossible to attain victory.' How well the setbacks Rommel had suffered since the British capture of Tobruk illustrated this: 'He had to retreat, and for no other reason than that it was not possible, for logistics reasons, to establish German air superiority over the British.'[23]

The aircraft industry was now producing fifty per cent more aircraft than in 1941, and the increase had only just begun; but it was still not enough. From his experts Milch had assembled the comparable figures for Britain, Canada and the United States both for 1942 and for the next two years: where Germany had averaged 367 fighters a month in 1942, these countries had averaged 1,959; where Germany had averaged 349 bombers, the enemy had averaged 1,378, of which many were four-engined.[24] 'God knows what the enemy is planning with this enormous number of bombers,' pondered Milch.

He took these ominous figures with him when he went to see Göring on 4 January, confronting the Reichsmarschall across the vast desk in his study with this proof of the enemy's capabilities. Göring, however, believed in the Führer and the Führer had once said: 'The simplest logic, my dear Göring! The Americans cannot have anything up their sleeves. They know how to make refrigerators and razor blades, and that's all.'[25] Göring turned the pages back and forth, then angrily challenged, 'Have *you* joined the defeatists now, Milch? Do you believe these fantastic figures?' Milch replied that he had every confidence in them. 'I don't want to be bothered with such rubbish,' bawled Göring. 'We can't work miracles; so nor can they.'[26] His attitude recalls the humorous lines of Christian Morgenstern about an equally blind optimist:

> . . . And thus in his considered view
> What did not suit could not be true.

Milch reported this encounter to his department heads next morning. 'The Reichsmarschall says—and he does not fully agree with me on the figures as he thinks they will manufacture fewer—"Even if they do reach these figures, it won't help them in Africa if they cannot keep the aircraft supplied, and that means shipping space." '[27] Göring, like Milch, saw the Luftwaffe's principal strategic objective now as attacking the enemy's shipping: 'That is his aorta, and if we sever it he must bleed to death. And then let's see if his God and his praying can help him! If he is to maintain an army from America or Britain, he must supply it, too.' But for this the He 177 bomber was indispensable. Both ends of a rapidly closing vicious circle were now becoming apparent.

Milch's own ideal was a totally different aircraft. For months he had been looking for a design for a high-speed, twin-engined bomber or heavy fighter aircraft capable of speeds up to five hundred miles per hour.[28] In December Junkers's Professor Hertel had shown him one promising design, which put both engines in one fuselage, powering two airscrews on the same axis—the shaft of one passing through the centre of the shaft of the other. Milch foresaw technical problems with this design.[29]

In the first week of January 1943, however, Professor Claude Dornier visited him with sketches of a strange aircraft, the Do 335; like Hertel, he put both engines in the fuselage, but instead of driving two airscrews at the front Dornier's design foresaw one in front and another at the tail of the fuselage. Milch's chief of technical development had turned the idea down; but Dornier predicted that his aircraft would fly at over 470 miles per hour and Milch knew him as a designer who kept his promises. Something clicked inside him: after a lifetime in aviation he sensed that this was a project which must work. He gave Dornier an immediate order for twenty Do 335s; from it developed one of the fastest propeller-driven aircraft in the world.[30]

Field Marshal Kesselring later wrote that had Milch replaced Göring at this time, the end of 1942, the Luftwaffe could still have been saved.[31] There is no doubt that Milch was nearing the summit of his achievements. Yet another honour was bestowed on him: the Chairman of Lufthansa, Emil-Georg von Stauss, had died shortly before Christmas and in mid-January Milch was elected to succeed him.[32] Thus the beginning of 1943 saw him charged with these high offices: State Secretary, Inspector-General and Deputy Commander-in-Chief of the Luftwaffe, Director of Air Armament and Chairman of Lufthansa.

He was about to be charged with a very different commission, one which was to tax his courage and ability to their utmost.

# PART IV

# SPECIAL MISSION:
# STALINGRAD

*After Stalingrad, Speer said: 'The trouble is that what with the Atlantic Wall, the eastern fortifications and so on all construction in the Reich is virtually stifled. Today, eastern fortifications are more important than building projects in the Reich, because with them I can spare labour, fuel. . . .'*

*'The only raw material which cannot be restored in the foreseeable future,' observed Milch, 'is human blood'.*[1]

# 'PANAMA!'

## (*January–February 1943*)

Twice already Hitler had acclaimed Field Marshal Milch as a man for whom the word 'impossible' did not exist. In mid-January 1943 he put this to the test. Milch was ordered to save the Sixth Army, which the Führer's stubbornness, Paulus's docility and Göring's vanity had trapped in Stalingrad, encircled by Soviet armies, while the eastern front receded ever farther from the beleaguered city.[2]

If one man had the drive, the tongue and the personal ruthlessness to save the situation, then he was Milch. His efforts were to raise his personal status to such a level that he could afterwards deliver Hitler the frankest lecture that he can ever have heard from a subordinate.

Von Richthofen's *Luftflotte* had organized a force of Ju 52 transport aircraft on the airfield at Tatsinskaya, each capable of carrying about two tons of supplies over the 160 miles to Stalingrad. A further force of He 111 bombers, which could carry about one and a half tons of supplies in 'supply bombs', was centred on the equally makeshift Morozovsk airfield, about 130 miles from Stalingrad. Göring's promise entailed landing three hundred aircraft at Stalingrad every day, an average of one every two and a half minutes; much therefore depended on the ability of the Sixth Army to unload the aircraft and distribute the supplies in time. By early December 1942 ten squadrons of Ju 52s (including eventually six hundred Ju 52s withdrawn from the air training schools) and various units of Ju 86s, FW 200s, Ju 90s and other aircraft had been assigned to the airlift; some Ju 290 prototypes had also arrived—big four-engined transporters capable of carrying ten tons of supplies into the fortress and returning with seventy wounded soldiers. The aircraft losses had been frightening, and it was great testimony to Luftwaffe morale that the airlift had been sustained at all; for once an aircraft was written-off in Stalingrad, its crew knew that they would never get out.

During December General Hoth's Fourth Panzer Army had begun its relief drive towards the city, but in the middle of the month a sector of the front held by the Italian Eighth Army collapsed; Hoth's advance was halted, and on Christmas Eve Russian tanks overran Tatsinskaya airfield as the last of the 124 transport aircraft there escaped. Two more airfields were lost early in January as Field Marshal von Manstein withdrew the front still farther; the transport squadrons had to fall back on to airstrips like Novocherkassk, 220 miles from Stalingrad. Much of the cargo had to make way for extra fuel and the number of sorties they could fly each day was reduced. In Stalingrad, meanwhile, Paulus's troops had begun to starve. Their commanders were already talking about their 'betrayal' by the Luftwaffe. There were few homes in Germany unaffected by the drama.

Milch's Stalingrad mission began late on 14 January 1943, when Bodenschatz telephoned from Hitler's headquarters, ordering him to report there immediately: Hitler wanted him to take over the airlift to the Sixth Army; by way of warning Bodenschatz added that until now Göring had been claiming that Milch could not be spared. Now the Führer had lost patience and overruled him.[3]

The field marshal took hurried leave of his staff, detailed his personal physician and Colonel Petersen to accompany him, and set out; as Albert Speer drove him to the Dornier parked on Gatow airfield he begged Milch to search for his younger brother, Corporal Ernst Speer, believed to be in a field hospital somewhere within 'fortress Stalingrad'.[4]

At Hitler's war conference that evening Milch recognized the catastrophic situation at Stalingrad for the first time. The fortress's last good airfield at Pitomnik had just fallen into enemy hands. Hitler stressed to him the strategic importance of the mission: about three hundred tons were to be flown in daily if the city was to be held; this would bind numerous large Russian formations which would otherwise be elsewhere employed. He issued special powers to Milch, giving him authority to issue orders and instructions to every military command.[5] There is evidence that Hitler believed Stalingrad could hold out for another six to eight weeks.* As Milch left, Hitler's Luftwaffe adjutant, Major von Below, appealed to him to search for his brother-in-law, one of Paulus's trapped army.

---

* Thus Speer, chairing Central Planning on 26 January, excused Milch's absence 'as he has been given a particularly important mission by the Führer on the eastern front, which will occupy him for the next six to eight weeks.'[6]

Over thirteen hundred miles separated Hitler's headquarters from the Black Sea town of Taganrog where von Richthofen and von Manstein had established their respective headquarters. Milch and his staff covered the distance in five hours. As their two aircraft landed it was snowing heavily and there was an icy gale blowing; the same forbidding weather conditions were to prevail for several weeks. At this stage he may not have been alarmed by the cold. Ever since October 1942 he had believed the Luftwaffe need not fear this second winter on the eastern front.[7] Since that spring a special commission had toured the squadrons, gathering experience for the coming winter. Milch had personally supervised the preparations: he had ordered three thousand prefabricated wooden huts for the airfields, most of which had been shipped to the front by late summer so that they would arrive before the snowfall.[8] Tens of thousands of chemically heated bags, muffs, electric blast heaters and special ground-crew overalls had been despatched; fitters had installed cabin heaters in the airborne and ground ambulances ('I do not want our injured to be transported back in open trucks for five days in thirty degrees of frost as they were last winter').[9]

Yet there was a factor he had overlooked—the human factor. He could not control the will-power of the Luftwaffe troops to struggle on; nor could he instil proper leadership and humanity into their commanders. Indeed the news that Milch, the organizer, was on his way evoked consternation at Taganrog. General Fiebig, commanding the Eighth Air Corps, commented in his diary: 'There is not much else to organize, for we can only drop supplies from the air from now on—a matter of pure chance.'[10] And when his superior, von Richthofen, angrily protested to headquarters, Jeschonnek assured him that Milch was just the Führer's last attempt to save the Sixth Army. The *Luftflotte* commander caustically observed in his diary: 'Nothing would delight me more than that Milch should chance upon the Philosopher's Stone which our supreme authorities evidently believe is lying round here somewhere. Certainly *we* have not found it.'[11]

By the evening of 16 January Milch had arrived in von Richthofen's warm and well-equipped command train. 'He is completely misinformed about the technical and tactical situation,' von Richthofen gloomily noted, 'and hence he is still quite optimistic.'[12] Milch immediately summoned the *Luftflotte* staff to report on available aircraft and units. For the first time he learned that far fewer transport aircraft were serviceable than was assumed at Hitler's headquarters; a truly staggering percentage, particularly of the Junkers transports, was immobilized by the cold. Aircraft availability at that moment was as follows: 140 Ju 52s of which only fifteen were operational; 140 He 111s of which only forty-one were operational; twenty FW 200s of which only one was operational. Only seven Ju 52s and eleven He 111s were actually scheduled to fly to Stalingrad that evening.[13]

About 5,300 tons of supplies had been lifted into the fortress, an average of about one hundred tons a day. Richthofen privately advised Milch that he had warned all along that the airlift was 'impossible', and now that Pitomnik, the fortress's last good airfield, had been over-run it was madness to continue.[14] The loading airfield at Sal'sk was 220 miles from Stalingrad, and if Novocherkassk were lost the fortress would be beyond Heinkel range. The Ju 52s were already operating at extreme range: their fuel tanks were unprotected and the air corridor was thick with Russian fighters and flak; the remnants of the fighter squadron based at Pitomnik had escaped just in time, but they could no longer reach Stalingrad without drop tanks and these were not available. It would be inhuman to speculate further on the reasons why so many Ju 52 crews—many of them drafted overnight from the accustomed luxury of ministers' personal crews—found it difficult to get their aircraft into the air. Milch recognized that the Luftwaffe was not above blame.

The Sixth Army inside Stalingrad had made virtually no provision for unloading the aircraft. It had thoughtlessly set up headquarters near a second airfield at Gumrak, and it had discouraged earlier attempts to ready the field for use in the airlift, not wanting to attract Russian bombing raids; now the loss of Pitomnik left them no choice, but the field had not been equipped for night landings and it had been prepared so haphazardly even for daylight landings that most of the aircrews were refusing to land, and were just throwing the cargoes out. Without petrol the army could not gather in the heavy containers; so they lay embedded in the snowdrifts, and the troops in Stalingrad continued in their deprivations. The loss of air superiority had turned a crucial situation into a desperate one.

During the evening increasingly hysterical appeals for help poured in on Milch from the Sixth Army: 'The fate of the army depends on tonight's airlift and on those of the 17th and night of 17/18th alone. . . .'[15] 'By 2300 hours only sixteen supply containers seen dropped. On what are troops supposed to live and fight tomorrow?' 'Fighting more and more pointless, as supply gap can no longer be bridged.' 'Numerous German soldiers lying starved to death in streets. . . .' 'Please act against vile allegations of aircrews. Gumrak landing ground is fully serviceable.' To rebuild the crews' morale first of all, Milch proposed to tour every squadron himself next morning; then he would fly in to Stalingrad to see for himself.

In a fierce blizzard, and thirty degrees of frost, Milch next morning drove off towards the airfield. As they bumped over a railway crossing, Milch—sitting in front next to the driver—saw a shadow move outside his window, opaque with frost. He sensed danger and shouted to the driver. The driver braked, the front wheels jammed inside the railway track and a heavy Russian-built locomotive crashed into the car at forty miles per hour, hurling it across the embankment into a railway hut, which collapsed in ruins. Two soldiers in the hut were killed outright.[16]

Milch was crushed—unconscious—in the tangled wreckage. He was driven in an ambulance to a field hospital and von Richthofen was informed. He was found to have a severe head injury from which he had lost a lot of blood, concussion and several broken ribs. The flight to the squadrons and Stalingrad was off; but nobody could restrain him from resuming the Führer's special mission. Within three hours he was carried back into the *Luftflotte*'s command train: 'Heedless of the shock and of the high temperature he is running, he has returned to Fourth Air Force headquarters and is in command as before,' recorded von Richthofen in his diary.[17]

Milch, his back and ribs encased in plaster, was propped up before a telephone. For the next two weeks his tongue would be his only weapon. The telephone line to Berlin was as clear as a local call. Soon he was discussing with Colonel Vorwald, his representative in Berlin, immediate steps like the provision of two long-range fighter squadrons and the gearing of industry to mass production of ready-filled air-drop containers.

From General Fiebig Milch recognized that there was clearly something wrong at the Stalingrad end of the operation. Fiebig said that several Heinkel 111s had actually landed at Gumrak airfield during the day: they had found no ground organization, and nobody in the Sixth Army took any interest in their cargoes at all. 'They handed over the foodstuffs they were carrying to troops passing by, and flew some injured back. The troops made a disorderly impression—our aircrews had to defend themselves with their small-arms against soldiers crowding in on them,' said Fiebig. They had reported seeing no Russian tanks outside the fortress, nor any major fighting. Milch ordered reliable air force officers to fly to Gumrak next morning to inspect the organization in person and reconnoitre possible air-dropping zones and a glider landing site nearer to the city itself, since fifty giant gliders were now available.[18]

Colonel-General Paulus continued to broadcast appeals for help. On the evening of 17 January he wirelessed Hitler, '*Mein Führer!* Your orders for the supply of the army are not being obeyed. Gumrak airfield has been serviceable since early 16 January. Numerous obstacles being raised by air force outside fortress. Airfield declared perfectly safe for night landings. Ground organization standing by. Immediate intervention urged, extreme danger.' This was followed by telephone calls to Milch from Hitler's headquarters, asking why he planned no missions that night. Milch again insisted that Gumrak had no night-landing organization. The upshot of these conflicting reports was that Hitler ordered a senior officer of the Sixth Army to be flown out to report to him next morning.[19]

Milch suspected that in fact the transport aircraft crews' morale had suffered, and that Paulus was not unjustified in his complaints. Later that evening Paulus again insisted that Gumrak was operational, but during the night no fewer than twenty-seven Heinkels flew at minimum altitude up and down the airfield, without sighting any flarepath; so again they could only drop out their loads in mid-air. Daylight missions were highly dangerous because of the Russian fighter patrols, but on Milch's insistence three more Heinkels took off at dawn, each carrying an officer with orders to contact Paulus in the fortress; with them they took a set of flarepath equipment so that Gumrak could operate by night.

On Milch's instructions, too, Colonel Petersen had toured the first airfields and his initial report on the Ju 52 squadrons at Zverevo was horrifying: there was a fifty-mile-per-hour gale blowing, and the aircraft were enveloped in huge snowdrifts, their engines frozen solid. There was no shelter, not even a trench, for the hundreds of airmen—just a vast, inhospitable, blizzard-swept field. The Air Transport Commander had been unable to make any provision for the men in the six weeks they had been there. After only a few minutes' work, the fitters' hands froze to their tools. Of the 106 Ju 52s standing round the field, forty-two were slightly damaged and awaiting repair; and of the rest only eight had taken off that morning, of which five had turned back short of Stalingrad. The figures spoke for themselves.

Milch summoned the Air Transport Commander to his command train and asked if he had any requirements. The commander said he had none—it was useless to import more technical staff as there was not enough accommodation or equipment as things were. The field marshal was irritated by this attitude. 'These men had no chance whatsoever of warming themselves up; the only thing accomplished for them was parking a stone-cold omnibus there. Just imagine what it means,' Milch described to his ministry staff a few days later, 'working in 25 degrees of frost with a fifty-mile-per-hour blizzard howling round your ears day and night without respite, and not being able to get away from it all at 6 o'clock each evening like in the ministry!'[20] He was unconvinced by the commander's excuses. When the latter explained he had written off for everything but nothing had arrived Milch challenged: 'Do you think that lets you off?' He asked why they had not built the simplest kind of huts, taking the materials from local villages. The commander replied they could not fetch materials without transport; Milch asked about the army trucks standing near the field. The commander protested, 'We cannot touch those. That would be larceny!' 'The only larceny done around here,' thundered Milch, 'is that somebody has made off with your brains.'[21] He ordered sixteen prefabricated huts to be rushed immediately to Zverevo airfield.*

'The Junkers squadrons had not the foggiest idea how to improvise,' he related not long after. 'I had to club some sense into them. At first they had nothing. But all at once they had a wooden hut with a small stove in it so they could keep warm. Then gradually they began to look at the correct cold-start procedure for the engines. I threatened anybody who neglected it with execution.'[22]

Over a hundred Ju 52 transport aircraft on hand, and only three flying! From that moment Milch recognized that the air force had let down the Sixth Army. The Fourth Air Force had totally failed to accommodate the armada of transport aircraft, and to take the necessary scale of organization into account. On Milch's recommendation, von Richthofen dismissed his chief of staff Colonel von Rohden on the spot. Otherwise, he kept his recognition of the culprits to himself.[23]

This was the familiar Erhard Milch, tackling a seemingly hopeless situation, surrounded by frightened and defeated men. Sitting painfully behind his desk in the command train, he summoned the squadron commanders one by one for the rough edge of his tongue. 'In any other circumstances,' he later said, 'I would have stayed in hospital. But there is a time in a man's life when he must put his own person second.'[24] The flak general, Pickert, who had flown out to Stalingrad a week before,

---

* The Commander, supported by the Stalingrad air veterans' association, has recently denied that there was any dispute with Milch. But the records of the Luftwaffe—and particularly the war diary of Milch's staff, the field marshal's contemporary notes and the verbatim Air Armament conference reports—produce a very different picture.

reported that at that time Paulus had expected to hold out only six more days.[25] Milch sent him to Hitler. 'I share your fears,' he told von Manstein privately shortly after. 'But we must assume that Stalingrad can be held, and do all we can to that end. Clearly there can be no question of our acting as though Stalingrad were already lost.'[26]

During the coming night, 18/19 January, six Heinkels and one FW 200 actually landed at Gumrak and disgorged their supplies; another forty-one Heinkels, one FW 200 and three Ju 52s made air-drops over the airfield. The containers fell into deep snowdrifts and few could be recovered. A Heinkel brought out a score of injured men, and early next morning the Panzer general, Hube, was flown out of the fortress on Hitler's orders, and added to Milch's staff.[27] Hube had lost one hand in the First World War and was an obvious leader of men. He complained that many of the earlier transports that had landed at Pitomnik had been only half full, and even now others were carrying quite useless stores. As for Gumrak, Hube questioned why so many aircraft had failed to risk the landing; he had himself seen the signal cartridges being fired as the transports circled overhead. Milch did not admit to Hube the conclusions he had drawn about the crews' morale.[28]

Alerted by Hube's complaint, Milch ordered some of the containers to be opened on the airfields. Many of the sacks were found to contain only fish-meal. Milch sent the sacks back and asked the army to have the victualling officer hanged. 'If we had not had the contents of these sacks sampled on the airfields, our aircraft would actually have flown fish-meal into Stalingrad!'[29]

With the arrival of Milch's special mission a new spirit prevailed. The rate of supply increased, new aircraft joined the squadrons and a new heroism was instilled into the exhausted crews. Two squadrons of fighter aircraft were on their way from Germany. Gumrak airfield now had an improvised flarepath of ten tank-lamps and a powerful radio beacon was in operation. Milch's experts toured the loading airfields, supervised cold-start procedures and established workshop and supply facilities. In the twenty-four hours before dawn on 20 January, the Sixth Army saw thirty He 111s actually land at Gumrak with petrol, ammunition, foodstuffs and medical supplies; and 130 injured men were flown out. Only one Ju 52 landed, a failure which angered Milch. 'I will have any commander acting against my orders shot,' he warned the Air Transport Commander.[30]

Colonel Petersen sent to Rechlin for cold-start squads to work on the sixty-five Junkers transporters abandoned to the Russian winter at Zverevo. They found that no attempt whatever had been made by the

Junkers crews to operate the trustworthy cold-start procedure. 'The Ju 52 squadrons did not even know of it,' Milch later related, 'because they had arrived from Africa.'[31] Special cold-start fuel was also available not far away; but the squadrons had no transport, and dared not appropriate the army's unused vehicles. Meantime, Milch had investigated what had happened to the accommodation and equipment the Air Transport Commander had written off for through service channels: 'They are probably still waiting for it,' he mocked three weeks later. 'I found out that the trains did actually set out, in part; but they were shunted off somewhere else, because more important stuff had to be transported. So they lay around . . . and who knows where they are today?'[32]

During the afternoon a Heinkel squadron commander reported to Milch; he had flown the round trip to Gumrak, but had had to wait five hours there before his aircraft was unloaded. His report left no doubt about the mood within the fortress. Paulus had reproached him, 'Today is the fourth day my men have had nothing to eat. Our heavy guns have had to be abandoned, because we have no petrol. Our last horses have been eaten. Can you imagine soldiers falling upon the carcass of a horse, smashing its head open and eating its brains raw. . . . ? What should I, the Commander-in-Chief of an army, say to a man who begs of me— "Herr Colonel-General! A crust of bread?"' Paulus's chief of staff had butted in, '—And now you dare to try to whitewash the Luftwaffe, which has committed the worst treachery in the history of the German people! *Somebody* must have suggested the airlift to the Führer! That a whole army, this magnificent Sixth Army, has to go to the dogs like this!' Paulus commented, 'We speak to you as though from another world already, for we are dead men. Nothing remains but what history may write of us.' Retaining an icy composure to the end, Paulus instructed the Luftwaffe major to tell Milch that only one thing was of use—that the transport aircraft must be ordered to *land* at Gumrak whether they liked it or not.[33]

During the night hours 113 transport planes took off, and 67 completed supply runs of which 21 Heinkels and 4 Ju 52s landed at Gumrak. The rest of the supplies were pushed out into the dark sky, in the hope that some would be found.

At Stalingrad teams of starving troops laboured to prepare a second landing-ground, eight hundred yards long and sixty wide. It was subjected to continuous Russian air attack. News reached Milch that a squadron of the latest Me 109G fighters was destined for Stalingrad, plus eighty mechanics for the Ju 52 ground crews.[34] Trainloads of transport gliders were on their way—Go 242s, Me 321s and even seventy-two DFS 230s. The extra aircraft pre-heating equipment had been despatched, and German industry had begun the production of air-drop containers. When von Manstein telephoned to ask when the fighters and bombers would arrive, Milch could reply, 'Very soon! The fighters have already reached Cracow.'[35]

He detailed a ground-control officer to fly with three others into Gumrak next day. Fiebig noted pessimistically, 'They want to be fetched out if the worst comes to the worst. I do not think it can be done. They are done for.'[36] At noon a Sixth Army staff officer reported to Milch that there were still about 160,000 German troops in the city, slowly freezing or starving to death. Nothing less than two hundred tons a day could keep this army alive: 'How long the fortress can hold out is not for me to say; things might be over very rapidly.'[37] Milch sent him to report in person to Hitler.

Early next day the ground-control officer returned prematurely. Paulus had ordered him out, saying he had been promised a Luftwaffe *general:* 'Whatever the assistance you are offering, it comes too late. We are all lost!' When the major had referred to other, more optimistic developments, Paulus had cut him short: 'Dead men are not interested in war history.' General Jänecke, commander of the Fourth Panzer Corps, who had been sent for by Hitler, accompanied him. While the Luftwaffe major reported that aircraft could land safely at the new Stalingrad landing-ground—but not take off—Jänecke said he gave the fortress three more days.

Time was now running out fast. Gumrak airfield was overrun by Russian troops. Eighty-one aircraft flew missions to the new landing ground and twenty-six attempted landings, but most were wrecked as they ran into bomb-craters concealed by the snowdrifts. The rest discharged their cargoes in mid-air. The Russians had launched a heavy assault on the western outskirts of Stalingrad and the new airstrip was overrun as well: ten more Heinkels managed to land and unload part of their fuel before the enemy arrived. From now on the airlift could be maintained by air-drops alone; no more injured could be evacuated. Some twenty-nine thousand injured troops had been successfully flown out. In grim anticipation of this final act, every soldier had been given the chance to write one last letter home; when the last Heinkel took off on 23 January it carried nineteen injured soldiers, and seven bags of mail.[38]

Altogether 116 aircraft completed missions on that day, proof of the work put in by Petersen and the ministry engineers; but all of them had to release their cargoes in mid-air. At ten o'clock that evening Milch learned that the fortress had been cut in two, with a northern pocket about ten miles wide and eight deep, and a southern one in the city's suburbs.[39] It would take two more days for the first fighter aircraft to arrive from Germany.[40] Göring continued to send lengthy telegrams to Milch and Hitler himself telephoned early on the twenty-fourth to inquire about the situation, clutching at any straws of hope Milch's staff could offer. 'He wanted a miracle to happen, and believed there would be one,' Milch later wrote. 'I myself saw no such chance.'[41] As dawn broke on the twenty-fourth, the weather worsened. Wireless contact was lost for several hours. A few planes flew low over the fog-shrouded ruins and dropped sacks of foodstuffs on brightly coloured parachutes, but few were found. Later that day Paulus's headquarters signalled, 'Ghastly conditions prevailing in the city. At least twenty thousand untended injured and stragglers are sheltering in the ruins of houses and cellars. Scenes of catastrophe on very largest scale. . . . Front line being held by small squads commanded by generals and high-morale officers, who are organizing the last battleworthy men together under fire.'[42]

That afternoon, Milch telephoned Speer from Mariupol. The Munitions Minister reported that the Führer recognized that the airlift had been speeded up, and was ruefully reproaching himself again for not having sent for Milch earlier.[43] The field marshal admitted that he had no news of Speer's brother in the fortress; Speer was not surprised. The family had now received a long-delayed postcard from Ernst, saying he had decided to die in the front line rather than in hospital. They never saw him again.

Although suffering agonies from blood poisoning and the inflamed injuries resulting from his crash a week before, Field Marshal Milch did what he could over the next few days to alleviate the long drawn-out death throes of the Sixth Army. Forty-five tons of supplies were parachuted into the two shrinking pockets during the night, but of the sixty-two Ju 52s operational at Zverevo again only eleven had actually flown. The Air Transport Commander blamed the cold engines; Milch admonished him, 'Any pilot aborting without good reason will be stood before a court martial.'*[44] On the following night, 26–7 January, no fewer than 124 transport aircraft completed missions over Stalingrad:

* Milch's Stalingrad diary quotes one Rechlin expert's statement in his command train on 27 January: 'This morning most of *KG 55*'s aircraft started without the use of the heating truck and despite a temperature of minus 15 degrees, *simply by applying the correct cold-start procedure.*'[45]

50 He 111s flew 104 sorties between them.* A hundred tons of food
—bread, ham and chocolate—and ammunition were released over the
dropping zones, now marked by criss-crossed lorry headlamps. The
Me 109G squadron had now reached Lemberg, six hundred miles away,
and the Me 110 long-range fighters were even nearer.

Milch sent urgent word to Berlin that he wanted engineers and oil-
cooler experts to work on the He 177s; he wanted specialists for ground
equipment, engineers familiar with parachute and air-drop techniques,
experts for aircraft repairs, armament and equipment.[46] By now one
trainload of filled air-drop containers and another of foodstuffs was
arriving every day at the loading airfields. Every three days a trainload
of transport gliders arrived as well. At Zverevo there were already
1,800 tons of foodstuffs and ammunition awaiting lifting into Stalingrad;
but the airlift itself was still the impassable bottleneck.

On the following night eighty-seven transports flew missions to the
dropping zone, now in Red Square itself, but little of the supplies
reached the German troops. The Luftwaffe signals officer within the
fortress now had all the radio beacons in operation; he must have
known the fate awaiting all of them. Milch emulated his courage and
asked Hitler's permission for General Hube and himself to fly one
Heinkel mission to Stalingrad in person. Permission was refused.[47]

Early next morning, 28 January, Milch was unexpectedly visited by
Hitler's chief adjutant, General Schmundt.[48] The field marshal frankly
told Schmundt, 'I believe it desirable for the Führer to detach himself
more from the individual problems of army command, and appoint a
leading personality Theatre Commander for the eastern front, like those
already existing in the west and south, to command all three Services.'
He warned that Germany's increased production effort could not match
those of the enemy until 1944, so the coming year must be one of defensive strategy.[49] The armies on the eastern front should dig in to
strongly fortified positions. Schmundt invited Milch to state this case to
the Führer, and Milch agreed provided that he could talk to Hitler
alone.

The defence of the two remaining strongholds was now seriously
hampered by the presence of some thirty thousand injured troops lying
untended among the ruins. Paulus's foodstocks were so low that he

* Major Beumelburg wrote in his June 1943 study: 'On the night of 26–7 January two crews flew two sorties each from Zverevo airfield, three crews flew two
sorties each from Stalino, six crews from Novocherkassk flew three sorties each
and seventeen crews flew two, and from Constantinovka four crews flew two
sorties each.' The courage needed to fly three sorties in one night to Stalingrad
can readily be appreciated.

ordered no food to be given to the injured or sick, so that those who were still fit enough to fight could do so. The heavy parachute containers were falling too far from Red Square, and settling down into the tall shells of ruined buildings where the troops could not retrieve them. Still the airlift continued. By dawn on 29 January another 109 aircraft had carried out supply drops, each releasing about one ton of food and ammunition. The whole airlift had now cost the Luftwaffe 330 aircraft and 791 airmen dead or missing; the latter losses were nothing compared with the Sixth Army's, of course.

The first twelve fighter aircraft had now arrived from the Reich. Milch ordered that on the morrow, the tenth anniversary of the Nazi seizure of power, there must be German fighter aircraft over Stalingrad.[50] 'The reputation of the Luftwaffe, and in particular of the fighter arm, in the eyes of the German army is at stake.'[51] Von Manstein's army group alone failed to rise to the occasion. It announced the next day's army password as one word, 'Panama!' To men of Milch's generation this was an elegant insult, derived from the fraud surrounding the building of the first Panama Canal. Milch ordered the password to be changed to, 'Long live the Führer!'[52]

Now Paulus changed his tone as well. He wirelessed Hitler, 'On the anniversary of your assumption of power, the Sixth Army sends greetings to the Führer. Still flutters the swastika over Stalingrad. May our struggle stand as an example to generations as yet unborn, never to surrender, however desperate the odds. Then Germany will be victorious.'[53]

Under Milch's control the airlift was now reaching its second climax. Overnight, 124 aircraft flew over the dropping zones, and this time almost all the supplies were retrieved. As dawn of the thirtieth broke Milch's fighters stood over Stalingrad. But already the Luftwaffe units there were wirelessing him their last farewells from within the fortress. A new discipline replaced the disorder and recrimination which had characterized the weeks before. Colonel Rosenfeld, commanding 10th Flak Regiment, signalled: 'In the basement ruins of Red Square, Stalingrad, surrounded by the thunder of enemy gunfire, we have read our Führer's proclamation. It has given us courage and resolution for these last hours of the battle for the ruins of the Red citadel on the Volga. Above us flies the swastika banner. The orders of our Supreme Command are being obeyed to the end. We turn our thoughts loyally to the Fatherland. Long live the Führer!'[54]

The southern pocket was almost finished. Returning aircrews told Milch that fires were raging round Red Square, and that the secret police building housing Paulus's headquarters was on fire.[55] That evening, sitting in von Richthofen's train, Milch listened to the broadcast of Göring's commemoration speech from the Air Ministry: 'Oh yes,' proclaimed Göring, 'there were those weaklings who came and warned that the Soviet Union had three, four or five times as many tanks, and ten times as many planes as we. Isn't that always the way that cowards act!'[56] Milch knew whom Göring's jibe was aimed at.

By next morning another 120 supply missions had been flown.[57] At 10 am it was clear that the southern pocket had been destroyed. The Luftwaffe signals troops there had wirelessed that Russian troops were smashing the door down, so they 'signed off'—a discipline which brought tears to the eyes of the field marshal who had created the Luftwaffe.[58] Hitler signalled the Ninth Army Corps, holding the tractor factory, 'I expect the northern pocket of Stalingrad to be held to the last man. Every day, every hour which is thereby gained is of decisive value for the rest of the front.'[59] The Corps predicted they would hold out for two more days.

His body aching and swollen, Milch was lifted into his Dornier to tour the loading airfields and harangue the crews himself.[60] The transport squadrons dropped ninety-eight tons into the northern pocket during the night, a momentous effort considering the distances now involved. But on the morning of 2 February the last German resistance in Stalingrad was overcome: 'Ninth Army Corps's six divisions have done their duty in heaviest fighting to the last man. Long live the Führer! Long live Germany!'[61] Milch telephoned this text to the Führer's headquarters at 11 am. It might have been a Soviet trick, so he still ordered aircraft out over the city in case there were signs of German fighting men; but they returned with their loads still on board. Columns of Russian troops had been seen marching into the lifeless factory. Signal cartridges had been fired aimlessly into the sky. Milch ended the airlift forthwith, and telephoned this decision to Hitler an hour before midnight struck.

We can imagine with what memories he took leave of von Richthofen next day. The nightmare impressions of apathy and lack of leadership, the bitter realization that so much more could have been achieved, the distracted midnight conversations with Hitler and the Reichsmarschall —three hundred thousand faces crowding in on him as his Dornier took off from Mariupol airfield, churning up a whirlwind of snow particles in its wake, bearing General Hube and himself to Hitler's headquarters.

To the field marshal's surprise the Führer sent privately for Hube first, and suspiciously inquired whether Milch had done everything in his power; to which Hube replied, 'All that and more!' Hube observed that if the Führer had sent Milch fourteen days before, Stalingrad would not have fallen. 'That,' regretted Hitler, 'is a judgement on me.'[62]

After Hube Hitler received Milch until 1.30 am, but it was painful to see Hitler's nerves at such low ebb. Milch made no bones about his views: had he been Paulus, he said, he would have disobeyed orders and commanded his army to break out of Stalingrad.[63] Hitler coldly replied that he would then have been obliged to lay Milch's head at his feet, and the field marshal, his neck bulging ominously red and his injured back hurting like the devil, burst out, *'Mein Führer*—it would have been worth it! One field marshal sacrificed, to save three hundred thousand men!' Hitler was not pleased by this remark, and Milch realized he could talk no more with him that night.

# TOTAL WAR

## (*February–March 1943*)

For twenty days Milch was unable to report to Reichsmarschall Göring. Göring's disgrace was complete, but one factor saved him after Stalingrad in Hitler's eyes: 'He is my own designated successor,' the Führer said, 'and that is why I cannot hold him publicly responsible for Stalingrad.'[1] The defeat had not been a glorious episode for the Luftwaffe. Professor Richard Suchenwirth, the first postwar biographer of Germany's air commanders, has observed: 'Of all the leading personalities in the air force in the whole unhappy period from November until February, we can see only the one man, von Richthofen, as a man of vision and resolution; and, in the final phase, exerting himself to the very utmost, the man on the spot whom the Luftwaffe generals so willingly dismissed as "a civilian"–the state secretary, Field Marshal Milch.'[2]

In seventy-two days and nights the Luftwaffe had successfully flown in 8,350 tons of supplies to the fortress, an average of 116 tons a day; the cost had been 488 aircraft destroyed, missing or written off, and about 1,000 airmen. It had cost the equivalent of five wings (*Geschwader*) or an entire air corps.[3] The training schools had been stripped of aircraft and instructors, and Lufthansa had also lost some of its finest pilots.[4] But what were these losses compared to those of the Sixth Army? Only 108,000 troops had survived to enter Soviet captivity; of these only 6,000 survived to return to Germany.[5] But we now know that the Stalingrad fighting tied down no fewer than seven Russian armies for the two months that it endured.

A long time afterwards Milch learned part of the background of Göring's undertaking to Hitler. Colonel Eschenauer, the Air Staff's supply officer, told him he had pointed out that 300 tons a day was impossible; he had found some difficulty at first in making Jeschonnek realize that the so-called '250-kilo' supply bombs would not hold anything like 250 kilograms of food, but far less (it just had the same shape as a 250-kilo bomb).[6] To Jeschonnek's credit, he immediately brought this to Gö-ring's attention, and asked him to warn Hitler that their calculations had been based on a wrong assumption. The Reichsmarschall forbade him to tell Hitler, and the outcome was inevitable.[7]

While Milch had been away much had happened that was to affect the air war. In broad daylight and unescorted American bombers had car-ried out their first attack on Germany on 27 January and three days later RAF Mosquitoes bombed Berlin in daylight too; that same night the British raided Hamburg in force, using the 9-centimetre H2S radar system for the first time—a system which more than any other contrib-uted to the German cities' ruin.[8] It was all happening just as he had prophesied.

Somehow the German army's losses in the east had to be replaced, for Hitler was already planning a spring counter-offensive. Speer an-nounced to Central Planning that Hitler had commanded a major tank production effort, rising to fifteen hundred tanks a month by the au-tumn.[9] Speer undertook that neither the Luftwaffe nor the submarine construction programmes would be inconvenienced in any way, but when Milch, on his return, appealed to him to accord aircraft produc-tion the same industrial priority this was delayed for three months, by which time the supply firms were so crowded with 'Panzer' and 'U-boat' contracts that the belated Luftwaffe contracts had little chance.[10]

For the first time Milch was meeting an influence as radical as him-self. Speer he could handle as a friend, but the minister's chief assistant, Karl-Otto Saur, was beyond control; Saur, a stocky, bustling engineer, was an acknowledged expert on armament and industrial problems. Aided by police he raided the Luftwaffe's most important factories and picked the best engineers for himself. Throughout February 1943 the complaints rained in on Milch, as overnight the irreplaceable welders and engineers vanished from the production lines at Junkers and Daimler-Benz.[11] When Milch drew attention to this Göring agreed that Hitler ought to make up his mind what he wanted: 'Even Speer is pow-erless when the Führer hammers him for tanks. That's why the Führer must decide in his own mind whether he will grant aircraft the same priority as tanks or not.'[12]

But the Führer's aircraft requirements varied constantly, as the tide of battle changed. In the aftermath of Stalingrad Hitler had impulsively demanded of Milch, 'I want transporters, transporters and more trans-porters!'[13] He suggested quite a primitive aircraft, capable of landing with up to four tons of cargo on rough, unprepared ground. But soon the evacuation of the Caucasus was in full swing, headed for the

Crimea, and now he asked for Ju 52 seaplanes too.[14] He also desperately wanted the He 177 bomber: the aircraft had flown nineteen supply missions to Stalingrad in all, and as usual had excelled as a fast, heavy aircraft; but five had been destroyed by engine fires in mid-air—a casualty rate of twenty-six per cent. 'The Führer spoke to me about it,' lamented Milch on his return from headquarters. 'I stood in front of the Führer like a very small boy who has not done his sums properly. I tried to go over the causes and explanations with him, but it is tough to explain the reasons to anybody who has not been immersed in it all, and it's even tougher if you cannot simply tell him, "That's the way I inherited it, it's not my baby. It's my predecessor that's to blame." That would be the coward's way out.'[15]

The spectacle of Stalingrad and the eastern front oppressed Milch, and he resolved to speak his mind to the Führer on the next occasion. When Speer launched into a monologue on the scarcity of materials and fuel, during a Central Planning session, Milch cut him short with the grim reminder, 'The only raw material which cannot be restored in the foreseeable future is human blood.'[16] He viewed the war very differently now. He discussed with Speer and Goebbels a proposal for a War Cabinet to relieve Hitler of the burden of political leadership while he directed the fighting.[17] He found Goebbels's attitude towards total war and the leadership closely allied to his own. On 16 February he told his departmental heads that Goebbels had recently pointed out to him that 'it is the first duty of the leaders of a State to keep their heads, and to pronounce upon the over-all situation calmly and reasonably, and without carping and grousing. Our nation must be properly led by us and it must *feel* that it is being led. Nobody must get the impression that we do not accept the efforts this nation is offering to us.'[18] This was the very eve of Total War.

On the evening of the eighteenth Milch witnessed the new age ushered in by Goebbels at a major *Sportpalast* speech, broadcast throughout Europe. Afterwards Goebbels invited Milch and a handful of his like-minded colleagues to his apartment; he found Göring's state secretary 'a fanatical champion of total war', and suspected he might well prove a valuable prop for the cause: 'Thus we shall also succeed in bringing the Reichsmarschall round to our side.'[19] But Göring's general lethargy defeated the plan for a War Cabinet. Speer put the proposal to him in their name, and was himself optimistic; Milch recorded the results more negatively, and Göring does not appear to have broached the possibility to Hitler at all.

\*        \*        \*

The Luftwaffe's dilemma after Stalingrad was formidable. It was plagued with a strange assortment of prewar aircraft designs long since overtaken by the changing patterns of air strategy; really effective weapons like the 30-millimetre cannon would still not enter production until mid-1943, and then only in minute series;[20] Milch's predecessor had fought tooth and nail against such devastating weapons as the 1-kilo anti-personnel bomb the Führer had himself suggested;[21] and several of the air force's leading generals, like the incompetent and corrupt General Loerzer, had reached their present positions only through influence in high places.[22]

The increasing shortage of trained aircrew, particularly for the bomber arm, was aggravated by the lack of aircraft and aviation fuel for the training schools, and by the huge numbers of front-line aircraft now being produced by the industry.[23] Once, Jeschonnek had assured Göring that if the front-line squadrons were to be given the petrol currently being allocated to the training squadrons, the war would be over before the latter crews were needed. Milch alone took the long-term view, and pressed for extra capacity for fuel production: without extra fuel they could not train aircrew to the proper standard, could not run in new aero-engines, could not transport stores or fight in the air.[24] If the Allies ever decided to concentrate their attack on Germany's synthetic oil refineries, there would be Armageddon: 'The synthetic oil plants are the worst possible place they could hit us,' he warned Central Planning during the spring of 1943. 'With them stands or falls our very ability to fight this war. After all, if the synthetic fuel plants are effectively attacked, not only our aircraft but the tanks and submarines will also come to a standstill.'[25]

Göring refused to be alarmed: 'I prefer,' he explained to Milch, 'to have a heap of aircraft lying idle, unable to fly because of a temporary fuel shortage, than to have no aircraft at all. . . .' By 1945 Göring's preference had been met, with a vengeance.[26]

On 22 February 1943 Milch saw Göring and the Air Staff for the first time since Stalingrad, to put to them the planning for the coming year.[27] Göring wearily complained that all the old familiar aircraft types were reappearing: 'The whole thing suffers from the complete absence of planning that reigned previously, from the tyranny of the old Office of Air Armament, and their reluctance to report defects in time to the Commander-in-Chief.'[28]

When the conversation turned to the lack of heavy bombers, Milch recalled to him with some bitterness the events of 1937: 'In 1933 or 1934 a four-engined aircraft was built by both Junkers and Dornier.

These planes were rejected later, and scrapped. At that time people believed the medium bomber was the true aircraft, and killed off the four-engined one. At the same time,' he emphasized, 'the British and Americans went over to four-engined designs.'[29]

At this conference Milch noticed that Göring's power of speech frequently failed him; his eyes seemed glazed, and he confused the aircraft types: 'What use are the finest remote-controlled bombs and all those contraptions if we can't get right out and attack the ships far beyond the range of fighter aircraft?' Göring asked him. 'And the Russian spaces present certain clear tasks to us as well. I must insist that we tackle the four-engined problem, by the quickest possible means—by a crash-programme or whatever you call it. Whether we build on the Focke-Wulf, or take the He 177 as the appropriate aircraft, or an enlarged Ju 288 . . . I don't know how.' Then in confusion he asked, 'How many engines does this Junkers 290 have?'[30]

On 1 March over 250 four-engined RAF bombers attacked Berlin, releasing six hundred tons of bombs; the extensive damage included five hundred big fires raging out of control, twenty thousand homes damaged, thirty-five thousand people homeless and seven hundred civilians killed. As Dr Goebbels hurried back to tour his stricken *Gau*, Göring left by special train in the opposite direction for a brief vacation in Rome. From his hunting lodge, Milch saw the fires against the skyline and hastened to the ministry: a heavy bomb had hit one wing, his own office had been demolished and fire brigades were in action everywhere.

But the news Milch gave his colleagues next morning was that the fight was still on. For the first time they had produced over two thousand aircraft a month in February, including 725 single- and 133 twin-engined fighters and over 650 bombers.[31] 'That is just the beginning, the increase must continue,' he said. 'There can be no going back. By the end of this year we must reach three thousand aircraft and eight thousand engines a month.' Next day an RAF photographic reconnaissance Mosquito circled high over Berlin in broad daylight. Neither the German fighters nor the flak could reach it.[32]

To assuage German public opinion Hitler ordered reprisal attacks on London, a target he had recently been sparing.[33] Of a hundred tons of bombs carried by his aircraft to London on 3 March, however, only twelve fell within the capital's boundaries.[34] Göring was still in Rome. At a midday conference the Führer derided the Third Air Force's inability to find London, a target thirty miles across and only ninety miles from the French coast. On the same night the first really heavy RAF attack had fallen on Hamburg. 'When is the Reichsmarschall going to come?' Hitler repeatedly asked. 'This way we'll never make the British give in!'[35] He summoned Milch to his headquarters and repeated to him his demand for the urgent manufacture of a high-speed, high-altitude bomber.[36]

That evening, 5 March 1943, Milch dined alone with Hitler until the early hours of the morning.[37] His basic arguments were two—that for 1943 Germany must restrict herself to the defensive, conserving strength for a resumption of the offensive if need be in 1944;[38] and that Germany's leadership meantime must be overhauled.[39] Göring, whom he suspected of succumbing again to narcotic influences after a ten-year interruption, should resign the Luftwaffe command and be appointed Theatre Commander of the eastern front instead: 'But once he is there you must draw a line on the map, which he may not cross to the west without your express permission. Otherwise he'll be off shopping in Paris again.' He suggested that Hitler also appoint a proper chief of staff for himself, like von Manstein.[40]

For the planned spring offensive in the east, Milch continued, the German forces were at present too weak and their transport was inadequate over such great distances. Inspired by his recent observations ('there were sixty-five thousand army troops at Tagarog, while one lieutenant and six men had to hold each kilometre of the front!'[41]) he challenged the Führer to investigate how many soldiers were actually fighting in the east, of the ten million troops on army strength. He refused to believe that more than a few hundred thousand were actually fighting; the other millions were tucked away in the Wehrmacht's vast bureaucracy and rear areas.*

For the Luftwaffe, Milch suggested that they aim for a production of five thousand fighters a month. He warned that the Allied bomber production figures were no mirage. 'When these bombers come, Germany and her whole armament industry will be destroyed and it will all be over.' Equally he warned against underestimating the Russians: the individual Soviet soldier was inferior to the German, but his leadership in this war could not be faulted. Hitler interrupted to say, 'I will certainly treat Stalin well when he is my prisoner!'

Milch concluded with a strong hint that Hitler should make peace now. 'Mein Führer, Stalingrad has been the gravest crisis for the nation and armed forces so far. You must do something decisive to bring Germany out of this war. It is still not too late, and there are

---

* A year later Milch triumphantly related in Central Planning: 'In November [1943] the Führer ordered a survey and found out that there are only 265,000 men permanently fighting on the eastern front.'[42]

certainly many who think as I do. You must act now—act without ceremony, and above all act now.'

It was 3.15 am when they separated. The field marshal had talked himself into a cold sweat. Hitler had listened to his arguments without anger, but Milch recognized that he had not convinced him.[43] He met Göring for the first time after this talk ten days later. After luncheon the Reichsmarschall took him for a drive in the grounds of Karinhall. Milch very properly reported in full his advice to Hitler that Göring should relinquish the Luftwaffe's command. The latter allowed this to pass without comment.[44] Milch suspected that his mind was far away, in consequence of more narcotics, but a year later Göring was to repeat to him word for word everything he had said.

# PART V

# THE YEAR OF THE CLENCHED TEETH

*'Things don't look rosy for our big cities'*
—Field Marshal Milch, March 1943

# TERROR RAIDS

## (*March–May 1943*)

On the night of Milch's talk with Hitler the RAF destroyed the big Ruhr city of Essen and devastated its Krupp steelworks and armaments complex in the process. Captured British crews admitted that the aiming points in these raids were now invariably the residential areas. The object was to burn and kill, to bring political pressure to bear on Berlin.* The destruction of military targets like dockyards and air bases was left almost exclusively to the still rare incursions of the American daylight bomber formations.

Almost every night during the coming months one German, French, Czech or other target was singled out for destruction in a methodical attack, heralded by skyborne showers of coloured pyrotechnic flares released by 'Pathfinder' aircraft; the latter were guided by 'H2S' or 'Oboe' radar systems. 'H2S' portrayed a city's outline on the aircraft's radar screen while 'Oboe' was a precise method employing radio beams and ground controllers in England, enabling single aircraft to release marker flares or bombs with an accuracy of a few hundred yards on targets as distant as the Ruhr.

To combat the growing Allied bombing offensive, the Germans had General Kammhuber's fighter aircraft defence system, and flak. The defences were highly dependent on ground and airborne radar systems. Kammhuber had established a line of night-fighter 'boxes', each with a 'Freya' early warning radar, a 'Würzburg' precision radar and a ground-controlled fighter-aircraft; but it was a costly and elaborate system and it was rigid and vulnerable to Allied interference.

There was another, indirect and hence less certain, means of defence —for the Luftwaffe to strike back at Britain's civil population; but Göring was in Rome and his absence only angered Hitler more.¹ On

---

* As the official historians succinctly wrote (*The Strategic Air Offensive against Germany*, vol. II, p. 22), the object of the general-area attacks was 'to render the German industrial population homeless, spiritless and, as far as possible, dead'.

8 March 1943 nearly eight hundred tons of bombs were aimed by the RAF at Nuremberg, one of the holiest of Nazi shrines. On the ninth the RAF attacked Munich in force, and on the eleventh they attacked Stuttgart. Hitler ordered Göring to return to Germany and commanded an 'intensification of the air war against Britain', for which he handed absolute responsibility to the twenty-nine-year-old Lieutenant-Colonel Dietrich Peltz as 'Attack Commander, Britain'.[2] This further commitment, and its further failure, were to bring Göring still greater reproach from Hitler. Göring waited, 'Look around Stalingrad—that's where my bombers are, strewn wrecked across the countryside.'[3]

For a while Milch was also deflected from his belief in the need to concentrate on the Reich's defence. Perhaps it was the head injury at Stalingrad that caused his now more frequent outbursts; his staff noticed that he was more irritable than before.[4] 'We must attack Britain,' he told them, 'otherwise Britain will smash us to smithereens. Our entire armaments effort—air, army and navy—is dependent on whether we can clear our own skies by carrying out the appropriate attacks on the British home base—either on their airfields or on their industry or on their civilians and cities.' 'It's not a matter of precise aim, but of terror raids pure and simple! Look what *they* accomplish with their terror raids even without aiming. They didn't aim at this Ministry or at anything else, they just plodded bravely overhead.'[5]

Göring did not like being admonished by Hitler; nor did he like having been summoned back from Rome. In a towering rage he summoned his generals and industrialists for a five-hour tirade of insults and recriminations.[6] 'I can only express to you my strongest disappointment about the complete failure in virtually every field of aviation technology today—and my disappointment, too, that I have been deceived in the past on a scale to which I have hitherto been accustomed only in variety acts by magicians and conjurers,' Göring complained. 'There are some things which were reported to me as absolutely ready before this war, which are not even ready today!' Twice he emphasized that when he spoke of 'the enemy' now, he meant the western Allies, for he considered the German forces still the equals of the Russians.[7] Germany's present aircraft were useless except for the Russian front, he added: 'In 1940 I could at least fly as far as Glasgow with most of my aircraft; but not now—not any longer.'[8]

Much of Göring's speech was devoted to the abortive aircraft projects inspired by Messerschmitt—like the Me 264 and Me 309—and Heinkel. 'I was promised a heavy bomber,' Göring recalled with sarcasm, 'the Heinkel 177. Then, when one calamity after another happened to it, they told me: "Well, if the plane did not have to dive, it would be the finest plane in the world, it could be sent to the squadrons at once—at once!" I immediately announced, "It does not *have* to dive!" How could anybody think of such a mode of attack? But where it has been tried out on [level] operations,'—meaning Stalingrad—'it has resulted in catastrophic losses, none of them caused by the enemy.' Thus they still had no means of long-range reconnaissance for the submarine wolf-packs, and attacks on enemy shipping with special missiles like Fritz-X and Hs 293 were impossible.[9] Later he challenged the professor, 'Now, Herr Heinkel. . . . What do you say today. Will it work, or won't it!'

'It will work in summer, Herr Reichsmarschall. . . .'

'. . . And how many out of ten aircraft will catch fire,' jeered the Reichsmarschall. 'Half of them!' 'How much fun was made of the enemy's backwardness,' Göring goaded his audience, 'about the enemy's "plodding four-engined crates" and so on. . . .' 'Make no mistake, gentlemen, the British are going to go from strength to strength with their much-mocked "four-engined crates", or whatever other fine adjectives you dream up for them. He is going to take on city after city. It makes no difference to him: he flies with the same sure navigation to Munich or Berlin, he can fly as far as Warsaw or Vienna.'[10]

Then there was the British Mosquito high-speed bomber: 'It makes me furious, when I see the Mosquito,' he admitted. 'I turn green and yellow with envy. The British, who can afford aluminium better than we can, knock together a beautiful wooden aircraft, and give it a speed which they have now increased yet again. What do you make of that! That is an aircraft that every piano factory over there is building.' He recalled with bitterness his experts' advice years before that such a wooden aircraft was impossible. Udet had warned him the whole world would laugh them to scorn. Who, asked Göring, was laughing now? Why did not the air industry simply copy the captured Stirling bomber, Göring asked: 'Then at least I would have an aircraft with which I could do something.' And why not copy the Mosquito?

Professor Messerschmitt was stung into retorting that it was much simpler to convert an existing aircraft to wooden construction, than to design a completely new aircraft.* Göring interrupted him, 'I am just telling you, you should take the Mosquito!' The professor had not meant that, and obstinately continued, '. . . but it could be any other aircraft.' Again Göring roared at him, 'Why not take the best one!' Messerschmitt wearily explained, 'I think it is more complicated than

---

* Milch complained at one meeting that Professor Messerschmitt showed no inclination to visit the displays of captured Allied aircraft.

that. Wooden construction is by no means simpler.' 'It could hardly be more complicated than your crates!' retorted Göring.

Milch shared this irritation at Professor Messerschmitt's attitude. Discussing the unsuitability of the Me 309 prototype for night-fighting, Messerschmitt actually claimed, 'I ordered it to be dropped because there is not enough capacity for tool-making for its mass production. . . .' 'Messerschmitt!' Milch exploded. 'The 309 was cancelled because it was totally unsatisfactory in rate of climb and ceiling, because it did not match the enemy at all.' The Reichsmarschall agreed, and with heavy sarcasm reiterated the Luftwaffe's basic requirements for a fighter: 'The most modest is that the aircraft must take off and land at night without the pilot risking every bone in his body.'*

The second great area of Hermann Göring's discontent was radar. By this time the Luftwaffe had long lost the initiative in what is now referred to as electronic warfare; and worse was to come. 'I have long been aware of the fact,' Göring rasped, 'that there is nothing the British do not have. Whatever the equipment *we* have, the enemy can jam it without so much as a by-your-leave. We accept all this as though it were God's Will, and when I get worked up about it, the story is, "We haven't got enough workers." . . . Gentlemen, it's not manpower you've got too little of, it's brainpower in your brain-boxes, to make the inventions we need!'[11] The Reichsmarschall—who occasionally confessed he was incapable of switching on his own radio—did not mince his language about German radar: 'I have frequently taken a look inside such sets,' he explained disarmingly. 'It does not look all that imposing —just some wires, some more wires and a few other bits and pieces; and the whole apparatus is remarkably primitive even then. . . .'[12]

It is true that German radar, operating on half-metre wavelengths, was more susceptible to noise jamming than the 9-centimetre wavelengths favoured by the British. A creeping campaign of jamming had begun, first from transmitters based in southern England, and then in specially fitted four-engined aircraft over Germany and the occupied countries. But British scientists had also developed the simplest jamming method of all—the release of myriads of metal foil strips into the air, exactly half the German wavelength in size. So simple and effective was this device, code-named 'Window', that RAF defence commanders had successfully delayed its introduction by the bombers, in case the

* As they left the room for luncheon, according to Messerschmitt's note on the conference, Milch crossed the room to him and stated that at times he had been so angry with the professor that he had had to restrain himself from 'rushing over and tearing out the last hairs from his head.'

Germans should discover the technique as well.[13] (From Milch's documents we find that the Germans had already had precisely the same idea, and were prevented from using it for precisely the same reasons by General Martini, the shy, academic Chief of Air Signals.)

In April 1942 Milch had offered researchers a prize for the invention of a means of avoiding radar detection.[14] It constantly occurred to him that it ought to be possible to get protection 'by some kind of wire' or other.[15] A few weeks later his chief engineer confirmed, 'If you scatter out wires the radar picture is so distorted that it is impossible to make accurate calculations. You don't even need a jamming transmitter for this—just a few leaves of aluminium or something.'[16] In August Colonel Schwenke had reported primitive British attempts to dupe their 'Freya' early warning radar by floating metal foils towards Germany suspended on balloons. 'They would have a degree of success, if these were used in much larger scale under certain weather conditions,' he advised.[17]

Armed with hindsight, we can see that an urgent investigation of counter-measures should have followed this report. But even more explicit information did not have this result. Early in September 1942 it was alleged to Milch that the British night bombers were 'ejecting clouds of fine aluminium dust' to confuse the night-fighters' airborne radar, 'Lichtenstein'.[18] His experts now advised him that there was a possibility that the enemy would start a jamming campaign against the main German radar systems, and their defences would then be overwhelmed: 'It is a big headache for Martini.'[19]

Milch had instinctively demanded, 'We must use the same means over there, and deceive the enemy,' but Schwenke pointed out that it would lead to a real jamming offensive on both sides, which would affect Germany as well. Milch retorted, 'Let's not start turning soft. You might as well say, "Then I won't make bigger weapons than he's got!"'

By the end of November 1942 the picture of what the British could do if they ever developed this simple means of jamming was complete. An engineer told Milch, 'If they shower clouds of these strips out over a big city, they will remain suspended for about twenty or thirty minutes in the air, and render our "Würzburg" radar temporarily blind. . . . General Martini says this is so secret, that he thinks we must test only over the sea, so that these things are destroyed by the waves after we have released them; because at present we have no antidote.'[20]

When, in January 1943, Milch pressed for an extensive jamming campaign against British radar, he was told that Martini was emphatically opposed to any jamming: 'He asks that all such experiments to jam the enemy's radar should be dropped for the time being, because there is a simple means whereby the enemy can jam our entire radar system, against which we have no antidote.'[21] For the next six months no research was carried out. Only when the British first used 'Window' in mass attacks on Hamburg in July and the German radar system was overwhelmed, as predicted, did the Luftwaffe begin research on counter-measures.

Göring and Milch both accepted that the German electronics industry had fallen far behind that of the enemy. A basic reason was that while Britain and America had actively encouraged amateur radio enthusiasts, in Germany the amateurs had been systematically persecuted by the Reich authorities;* another was that each Service had developed and manufactured its own equipment (and continued to do so until early 1944).[23] Hearing for example in September 1942 that the navy had developed a simple warning device for submarines to warn them when an enemy radar set was locating them, Milch demanded a similar set for German aircraft ('So that the pilot knows immediately, "Aha—some-body's onto me!"—just as a girl suddenly senses a man's looking at her').[24]

The British H2S radar particularly fascinated them. It had been sal-vaged from an aircraft near Rotterdam in February, with two prisoners. Both stubbornly refused to answer questions and maintained they knew nothing about the equipment; this behaviour alone proved to the Germans the equipment must be something special.[25] It weighed about three hundred pounds, filled half a dozen cabinets and was clearly being mass produced. 'It was installed in a place in the fuselage where we have also found a hollow space provided in the Stirling at Rechlin,' Milch was told. 'In the Lancaster bomber there is already a remote-controlled platform installed ready for it.' One thing was certain: H2S could not easily be jammed. When Milch commented to Göring that the cabinets were so voluminous that no German aircraft was big enough to carry them, Göring caustically observed, 'That's because they have built those "old four-engined crates" for themselves—aircraft so big you could lay out a dance floor in them!'[26]

As usual, the British had designed something the Germans could not even imitate. When the unfortunate Martini explained that radar prob-lems could frequently be solved in two or three different ways—'and

---

* In March 1943 Göring stated, 'The main blame belongs to Ohnesorge [Min-ister of Posts]—he never wanted to relax his grip on anything. We smashed up the amateur radio "ham" clubs and wiped them out, and we made no effort to help these thousands of small inventors. And now we need them.'[22]

there may even be a fourth or fifth way which we haven't yet discerned'—Göring retorted: 'You can be dead certain that if you have not found out about it, the enemy has!' 'I have never seen such nonsense in my life,' he raged. 'I refuse to be led a song and dance like this. The enemy can actually see through the clouds whether he is over a city or not. We cannot jam him. And then you tell me we also have something, but in the same breath you add, "But it can all be jammed by the enemy!" Are you trying to make a fool of me? What am I supposed to tell the Führer! He would think me a complete nincompoop if I repeated to him what you tell me. I ask you again, do we have any such radar set?' 'Not yet,' stammered Martini. 'Aha! Not yet! But the British do. Can we jam them?' 'We hope to be able to in a year's time. . . .' 'That does not interest me two hoots! Can we jam them now, at this moment?' 'No.' 'Good. That is a clear answer. And can the enemy jam the equipment we use for navigation, or can he not?' '*Jawohl.*'[27]

Six weeks later Göring transferred electronic research and development from Martini to Milch.[28]

Göring's discomfiture would be almost comic, were it not for the growing scale of the Allied attacks. During March 1943 the RAF had delivered powerful attacks on many German cities by night, releasing nearly a thousand tons over Duisburg, and 1,450 tons in two attacks on Berlin; on 3 April nearly a thousand tons were dropped on Essen, causing extensive damage to the Krupp factories. The American heavy bomber formations battered targets by day in the Nazi-occupied countries on Germany's periphery. On 4 April they killed 228 Parisians in an attack on the Renault motor factory and 221 Italians in an attack on Naples; on the fifth they killed 2,130 civilians, including 300 children, in Antwerp (Belgium had suffered some six thousand military casualties in the Nazi invasion three years before). All this time Göring contemplated developments with increasing lethargy.[29]

Milch warned Goebbels at this time that for the rest of 1943 the outlook for the Reich's great cities was melancholy, and added that Göring's completely false direction of the air war must terminate in disaster.[30] He used this dangerous language on the telephone in the certain knowledge that Göring's telephone tappers would report it to him. Goebbels invited him to tour the Ruhr's devastated towns a few days later. In the Propaganda Minister's sleeping car, Milch displayed his usual bluntness. 'Field Marshal Milch spoke in the most biting and contemptuous manner of the Reichsmarschall,' recorded Goebbels. 'He accuses him of allowing the Luftwaffe's technical development to go to the dogs. He had fallen asleep on the laurels he had won in 1939 and

1940. . . . The consequence is our almost complete defencelessness in the face of this British airborne terror.'[31]

The damage in Essen was very severe. Together they climbed a tall tower at Krupp's and surveyed the gutted shells of the factory buildings. They spoke to a meeting of the anxious Gauleiters and mayors of the biggest west German cities, and Milch defended the Luftwaffe's record as well as he could. Privately, he was able to discuss the future more frankly with Goebbels than with the others. 'It will not be possible to reply on a large scale to the British attacks until November,' Goebbels summarized. 'And it will not be until next spring—in other words a whole year—before we can really repay them in the same coin. . . . Until then, the British, if they know their business, will be able to blast and burn a major part of the Reich. Milch views the war in the air as very grave.'

In an editorial in *Das Reich* Goebbels had himself spoken of 'adequate means' which would soon be employed against Britain. He had been referring only to organizational changes but the public unanimously believed Germany had developed some deadly new secret weapon.[32] In fact no retaliation would be possible until the autumn, as Milch had warned. Even 'Cherry Stone', the flying bomb, could not be ready until then.

Its tests had gone perfectly. One fine April day, on the northern tip of Peenemünde West's airfield, where the Baltic lapped the deserted beaches of a one-time holiday haven, Milch watched his engineers prepare a strange steel-shelled aircraft with no cockpit on the landward end of a high ramp pointing out to sea. Several prototype flying bombs had been launched from aircraft during November, and wind-tunnel tests were also now complete.[33] Catapult launchings had begun on Christmas Eve, and the pilotless aircraft was functioning perfectly. Milch watched as the weapon's Argus Tube was ignited, the catapult was triggered, and the aircraft was hurled into the sky. At about three thousand feet it levelled out and streaked away towards the distant horizon, followed by a fast spotter aircraft. Milch was pleased as he flew back to Berlin.[34]

Albert Speer had never been a soldier, and he lacked the experience that four years on both fronts had instilled into the field marshal. When the army reported its ammunition, clothing, food or explosives 'consumption' the Führer and Speer automatically believed them. Milch, guardian of the public interest, did not. 'If anything is cut back on,' he told Central Planning, 'it naturally hits the weakest first, and that's the German domestic economy.'[35] He argued for a more critical scrutiny of the Wehrmacht's claims. 'What do they really mean by "consumption"?' he asked. 'Consumption is certainly not what they have actually fired. I am convinced they do not count up the ammunition that has actually passed through the gun barrels. They list as "ammunition fired" the quantity they draw from the ammunition dumps.' The point was that they made no mention of the quantities they simply abandoned during retreats.[36] Milch proposed that they show Hitler the quantities of artillery ammunition actually fired during the First World War, compared with the huge stocks still left at the time of the Armistice. 'The raw materials squandered here are urgently needed for agriculture,'[37] he pointed out. The two government nutrition experts he had summoned to the Central Planning meeting fully supported his argument. 'We must still have food to eat in 1947. If we shut our eyes to this, then we are deceiving ourselves.' He reminded his colleagues that it was the starvation of 1918 that had caused the final collapse then, and he repeated his insistence that the nitrogen demands on German agriculture be met.[38]

As on earlier occasions, Speer disagreed with Milch. 'If you challenge the Führer about ammunition,' he warned, 'you are banging your head against a brick wall.'[39]

The British bombing offensive was becoming increasingly accurate. Late in April 1943 the Germans found why—they recovered intact the new British Mark XIV bombsight, superior even to the American Norden bombsight already in their hands.[40] The British device was fully automatic and coupled to a small computer which allowed for the aircraft's most violent evasive actions. Furthermore, from reports of conferences between the British Minister of Aircraft Production (Sir Stafford Cripps) and the Air Council, supplied by an agent in Whitehall, the Germans also knew that the British had produced 1,920 front-line aircraft during April, with ever-increasing emphasis on the 'four-engined crates' to which Göring had referred.[41]

By May 1943 there had been several violent attacks on the Ruhr. 1,500 tons of bombs were dropped each night on cities like Duisburg and Dortmund. A handful of RAF Lancaster bombers, each carrying one special rotating bomb, smashed the dams controlling the water supplies of the Ruhr; a week later a squadron of Mosquitoes carried out a low-level daylight attack on the Zeiss optical factory at Jena, and not one was shot down. Göring remonstrated with his generals, 'My own men say, "We are not quite sure whether we will be able to find London in bad weather." But the gentlemen on the other side come over and find a dam lying swathed in mist at night, and whack right into it!'[42] And on another occasion, 'I have to admit, my respect for those gentlemen grows with every hour. I don't mind having to put up with the occasional tip-and-run attack on the coast, but Jena lies right in the heart of Germany! One has to admit, what dash and courage on the one hand, and what *contempt* for our own fighter defences on the other!'[43]

On 8 May Hitler told Milch, 'There's something wrong with the Luftwaffe, and it's either with its tactics or its technology.'[44] Milch suggested it was the current tactics that were wrong, and patiently explained his steps to bring aircraft production up to three thousand a month by the end of the year. He himself had no control over how they were tactically employed. Hitler demanded that each of the new fighter aircraft must be capable of carrying a bomb.[45] After seeing Hitler on the same day, Goebbels summarized:

The technical failure of the Luftwaffe results mainly from useless aircraft designs. It is here that Udet bears the fullest measure of the blame. Well may he have tried to expiate this by his suicide, but this has not helped our situation very much. Speer is very disturbed by all this, but believes that Milch will probably succeed in leading us out of the woods. The public shows its common sense when they rumour that it is Göring himself who is to blame. Göring has put his old First World War comrades too much to the fore, and these are obviously not equal to the burdens of leadership that war places on them.[46]

Hitler shared Speer's view of Milch. When General Galland visited the Führer on 25 May, the latter confided in him that the Luftwaffe without the field marshal 'just did not bear thinking about'.[47]

# 'AS THOUGH AN ANGEL'S PUSHING'

## (*May–July 1943*)

The Messerschmitt 262 jet aircraft first flew in July 1942; it did not enter squadron service with the Luftwaffe until the autumn of 1944, too late to have a decisive effect on the outcome of the war. In retrospect we can see where the mistakes between those dates were made: Air Ministry priority was granted too late, and as soon as it was granted Professor Messerschmitt lost interest in the aircraft and turned his attention to still newer projects; and at a late stage in the fighter version's production programme Hitler insisted that a bomber version be manufactured first, a decision for which Messerschmitt himself was principally to blame, as we shall see.

The aircraft had barely been mentioned in production studies before February 1943, and then, as Milch told the Reichsmarschall in that month, only so that it would not be overlooked completely.[1] Göring, who had been shown the research long before the war, unhappily reflected in March: 'When I asked at that time when we should be seeing them, I was told, "In one and a half to two years' time." And now that I get the facts from the horse's mouth I hear that it is still two years—at least that's the way it looks!'[2]

The professor, of course, has never accepted responsibility. Looking back after Germany's defeat he inevitably recognized the delays to his most prestigious aircraft as a major factor, but he confidently blamed Milch, by then incarcerated by the Americans and unable to reply.[3] More recently he has declared: 'Milch regarded the whole thing as a frivolity and prohibited us to work further on it.'[4] Messerschmitt has also alleged that he himself winced at Hitler's 'intrinsically absurd' idea for a bomber version of the Me 262. After the war the British captured the Air Ministry records, however, and seized the personal papers of Professor Messerschmitt; they are still held in London and present a historically unalterable picture of the tortuous path followed by the controversial project.

The novelty was the Junkers turbo-jet engine, and not the Messerschmitt airframe.[5] For years the main difficulty had been the design of the axial compressor. In July 1939 the Air Ministry had issued a contract for the development of a jet engine with 1,300 pounds thrust to Professor Otto Mader, head of the Junkers engine research laboratory.[6] The over-all design work was carried out by the designer of the successful Jumo 210 piston-engine, and the jet engine Jumo 004 had its first hot run at the time the Battle of Britain was at its height. For eighteen more months the engine underwent improvement, modification and tests, and in June 1942 the first pair were delivered to the Messerschmitt company.

The Air Ministry had issued a contract for the design of a corresponding airframe four years before, and the result, the Me 262, was ready when the engines arrived. The engines were installed and the aircraft's first pure jet flight took place on 18 July.[7]

It was a tragedy for the project that its development should have lain in the hands of a personality, Messerschmitt, in whom Milch had little faith. 'I know only too well how Messerschmitt likes to talk big,' he would remark.[8] After Udet's suicide Milch had seen the industry's immediate duty as being to provide enough of the existing aircraft types to prevent the Luftwaffe's total collapse. Throughout 1942 he had lived in a climate of disaster. He was entitled to fear that the Jumo 004 jet engines might develop the same maladies in mass production as had plagued the power plants of the He 177 and the Ju 288 bombers, and in this he was to prove right. Moreover, in January 1943 there was still no Air Staff requirement for a jet fighter.[9] Nevertheless, before departing for the Stalingrad mission Milch had asked General Vorwald 'as a last request' to put pressure on Messerschmitt to complete the Me 262, and the result was that a few days later the ministry accorded priority to the completion of a small number of prototypes.

By the spring of 1943 the Messerschmitt company was tooling up for production of the piston-engined Me 209, a successor to the Me 109G, to be powered by the new Daimler-Benz 603 engine. As recently as the end of March Milch's view had been that the company should concentrate on this and the Me 410, desperately needed for the war against Britain, and on nothing else;[10] the jet fighter prototypes should be completed by some other firm. Messerschmitt was wounded by Milch's lack of faith in him, but did little to promote the Me 262 despite the ministry's January priority order. He removed designers working on it to work on the Me 410 instead, and in April he wrote to the ministry that the jet fighter had been shelved *sine die* for this reason.[11] He had however drawn up a 'crash programme' under which (given top priority) forty jet aircraft could be manufactured by the end of 1944. This was hardly likely to attract Milch's enthusiasm.[12]

The final cloud in the midst of this climate of mutual mistrust between Messerschmitt and Milch came in May: Milch was told confidentially that the piston-engined Me 209, due to enter squadron service early in 1945, would probably be *inferior* in rate of climb and manoeuvrability to the Me 109G and the FW 190D which were already in service. Thus the question of the next generation of fighter aircraft was suddenly wide open again. In April one of Galland's pilots had test-flown the jet fighter and reported that it was so good it could be sent to the squadrons as it was. Milch now turned his attention to the possibility of converting directly, without an interim fighter, to the Me 262 —a possibility fraught with risks.[13] Torn between his confidence in the Junkers power plant and his mistrust of Messerschmitt, he asked Galland, whose judgement he trusted implicitly, to test the Me 262 himself.[14]

On 22 May Galland flew the aircraft for the first time, and telephoned Milch in excitement that it flew 'as though an angel's pushing'.[15] He wrote an exemplary one-page report, which was to shake the whole aircraft programme: 'The aircraft could be our biggest chance, it could guarantee us an unimaginable lead over the enemy if he adheres to the piston engine.'[16]

Galland's proposal was that the inadequate Me 209 fighter should be scrapped forthwith, and the design and production capacity transferred immediately to the Me 262. 'I think the decision is correct,' one of Milch's departmental heads said. 'But what a decision!' Milch agreed: 'A clear course of action!'[17] Top priority was now granted to the Me 262 jet fighter at last, subject to Göring's consent. The company was invited to manufacture the first hundred before the year was over.[18] Milch ('I may hesitate about unimportant matters, but on important ones there's nobody who decides faster!') informed the Reichsmarschall by telephone of the proposal to cancel the Me 209, and Göring approved without hesitation.[19]

They were none too soon with the decision. Three days later Colonel Schwenke announced that a reliable British prisoner had reported seeing a British jet aircraft flying 'very fast' at Farnborough, Britain's Peenemünde.[20]

\*     \*     \*

On 26 May Milch flew to Peenemünde, where the army's 14-ton A4 rocket was to be matched against the Luftwaffe's flying-bomb. Both could carry a 1-ton warhead to London, but Wernher von Braun's rocket would cost about a hundred times as much as each of Milch's

Galland and Mölders, the German fighter aces          [*Sketch by Ernst Udet*]

flying bombs. The rocket's history went back seven years, so the army was understandably loath to cancel it; and as it was an army project even a level-headed weapons man like Speer felt it his duty to support this anachronism in an age of Total War. Had it been designed with the specific object of destroying the basis for Milch's increased aircraft production, it could not have selected scarcer commodities. By the first months of 1944 it was to employ two hundred thousand skilled workers, consume a thousand tons of aluminium a month and tens of thousands of tons of liquid oxygen, pure alcohol and hydrogen peroxide; it would swamp the electronics and precision mechanisms industry with contracts and use up every available machine tool.

The Fi 103 flying-bomb had been designed to avoid these bottlenecks. Made of thin sheet steel and fuelled with paraffin, it promised to tie down a significant proportion of Britain's air defences when it was employed, while the A4 rocket (the later 'V2'), being invulnerable to attack, would not.

Precisely at noon the army launched its A4 rocket: it vanished into low clouds and radar tracking stations followed it up sixty-four miles into the stratosphere; it impacted 175 miles away, only three miles from its target centre—a very flattering performance for the otherwise inaccurate missile.[21] At the Luftwaffe airfield meanwhile, Luftwaffe engineers had prepared a flying bomb on its catapult; Milch watched aghast as it plunged into the sea after flying barely a mile. A second flying bomb repeated this unspectacular trajectory. When von Braun's technicians launched a second A4 rocket, it leapt towards the high ceiling of thin cirrus clouds atop a lengthening pillar of dazzling white flame; then something went wrong, it began to topple and within seconds it had crashed into the airfield within sight of everybody. The smile returned to Milch's face. The decision was taken to allow both missile projects to proceed side by side, but Speer allowed the A4 rocket to be placed into the highest priority rating, DE.

Milch forbade further demonstrations: 'However high and mighty the personage who visits Peenemünde, the bomb is not to be demonstrated.'[22] He knew it would work when the time came. He planned mass production to start with a hundred in August, rising to five hundred a month in September and five thousand a month from April 1944.[23] Three thousand tons of steel would be needed over the next three months for the bombs and their catapults. Milch suspected that Speer would object that the weapon could not be ready if it did not always function properly; but his staff urged him to proceed none the less, although they admitted that Speer was boasting that the rocketeers would get their campaign started first. Soon Speer's lieutenant Saur was demanding the release of skilled workers for A4 electronic components production.[24] The struggle between the rocket and the flying-bomb, and the desperate needs of home defence, was just beginning.

In the last week of May the British continued to ravage the Ruhr's larger cities, with two thousand tons of bombs dropped in single attacks on Dortmund and Düsseldorf on the twenty-third and twenty-fifth; on the twenty-seventh an 'Oboe' attack on the Ruhr town of Wuppertal killed 2,450 civilians and made 118,000 people homeless within barely fifteen minutes. Milch repeated his warnings of the need to do more for the home front.

The German people [he said] have become accustomed to the fact, as far as one can become accustomed to such a thing, that each night one town or other is heavily bombarded. But it will not understand it, if one fine day perhaps a squadron of Flying Fortresses appears in broad daylight over Berlin and drops its bombs with parade-ground precision without the least action being taken to prevent it. The attack on Jena has struck deeply at public morale and at its faith in the Luftwaffe, although the damage itself was not all that severe. It is not a pretty situation, and we cannot have many more of them. . . . What has happened in Dortmund, in Bochum and in Wuppertal is far worse than anything that has happened at the front. Because, when things get as bad as that, the soldier just gives up the fight; but the civilian population has to stick it out.[25]

The devastation continued. On 11 June Bomber Command released two thousand tons of bombs on Düsseldorf, killing vast numbers and rendering a hundred thousand homeless. On the next night 1,500 tons were dropped on Bochum, and after that the target was Oberhausen, a steel town. A German bomber commander, Major Hajo Herrmann, gave Milch an eye-witness account of the Düsseldorf attack: 'The tactics are remarkably primitive: the first aircraft arrives and releases his cascades of markers over the target and on the target itself; then he puts out a red fireball about 15,000 feet up. Every minute a green flare is emitted from this fireball; when this goes out, another one is emitted, so that even the stupidest pilot can see the signal from as far away as the Thames Estuary.' The city itself was enveloped in a cumulus of smoke, rising to ten or twelve thousand feet like a huge thunder-cloud through which the radar-controlled flak batteries had continued to fire at the aircraft. 'From a distance it looked as though the whole city was one huge sea of fire.'[26]

Milch spent some days in the west inspecting the radar and fighter defence systems. He reported to Göring that the defences were still numerically too weak, and he asked that the daylight fighter squadrons should be quadrupled 'until the Americans lose all pleasure in their handiwork'.[27] At wing level he had found the leadership excellent, but he suggested a radical change in the command structure in the west—the whole air force there should be put under one commander, with a Flak Command and three others identical in purpose to the RAF's Fighter, Bomber and Coastal Commands subordinate to him; he much admired the British system, and had made a similar suggestion to Hitler during their talk in March.

He called a Berlin conference to discuss a revision of their fighter defence tactics.[28] It was evident that more flexible tactics than those so painstakingly developed in the Kammhuber Line were necessary if the mass incursions by the RAF night bombers were to be halted. In 1940 he had in vain called for the use of single-seater fighters at night; this proposal had been ignored until recently, when Major Herrmann had commenced unofficial night-fighting experiments with borrowed single-seater (i.e. day-fighter) aircraft over Berlin. They were unofficial experiments, because Kammhuber had again rejected the idea as recently as February 1943.[29]

The need for an improved defence was ever more pressing. In the third week of June the RAF dropped two thousand tons of bombs on Krefeld, 1,640 tons on Mülheim and Oberhausen, 1,660 tons on Wuppertal and 1,300 tons on Gelsenkirchen. In the town of Wuppertal the civilian deathroll was brought up to eight thousand in the two attacks. On the twenty-second Hitler assured Goebbels he had ordered a major expansion of the Ruhr's defences and promised that by autumn reprisal attacks by rocket and bomber would have begun against the British Isles. Goebbels recorded afterwards, 'Air force generals make rotten technicians. If the Luftwaffe's expansion had been entrusted at the right time to Milch—or better still, to Speer—then we should most certainly be far better off than we are at present.'[30]

Five days later Hitler summoned the seven top aircraft designers to the Obersalzberg and interrogated each in turn.[31] Heinkel—now displaced in his own factory by a government 'Kommissar'[32]—excused his He 177's tardiness by the 'hitherto unshakable requirement that it should dive-bomb' (although Göring had emphatically removed this requirement ten months before). Messerschmitt's contribution to Hitler's state of mind was even more remarkable. For an hour he heaped criticism on Milch, and actually warned Hitler and Speer—who chanced to come in—against the folly of mass producing the Me 262 jet fighter, since its fuel consumption was, he alleged, higher than that of piston-engined fighters like the Me 209 which Milch in his sublime ignorance had now cancelled.* Thus at the very time that Milch was campaigning for priority for the jet fighter, its own designer was sowing the seeds of doubt in Hitler's mind.[34]

Milch was an advocate of *Schwerpunkt* fighting.[35] He believed that the Luftwaffe should be applied in strength to only one front at a time, and by that he meant the defence of the home base. And within that front the maximum possible number of aircraft should be brought to bear on the enemy. This was where the Kammhuber Line failed: the enemy bombers invaded each night in a mass bomber stream, but only a handful of the night fighters could be brought into action. All the others had to remain inactive in their 'boxes'.[36]

Herrmann's solution was the establishment of a *Schwerpunkt* by hurl-

---

* He did not mention that the jet engine used low-grade fuels, which needed one less stage of hydrogenation and were thus far more plentiful than aviation spirit.[33]

ing masses of fighters at masses of attacking aircraft, and this meant striking where the bombers foregathered, right over the target area itself —exploiting the illumination caused by the fires, searchlights, bomb flashes, parachute flares and target-indicator pyrotechnics.[37] Each night in the Ruhr attacks the radar-controlled searchlights held up to 140 aircraft for several minutes in their beams; these would be easy prey for single-seater fighters, if the flak would stop firing. Herrmann suggested crewing a hundred or more normal single-seater fighters with freelance bomber pilots and sending them to hunt down the enemy bombers right over the target cities as though it were broad daylight.

Milch suggested to Göring that this freelance system (later known as 'Wild Boar') be put to the test as soon as possible: 'If the weather is right we can expect considerable results.'[38] Herrmann moved his experimental flight from Berlin to the Ruhr, began selecting crews, and waited for the next RAF attack.

When Milch's planning staff now asked, 'Does *Herr Feldmarschall* approve that we now concentrate on single- and twin-engined fighter production, at the expense of bombers?' he replied, 'Indeed I do.'[39] He wrote to Göring repeating a two-month-old suggestion that one month's entire fighter production (about a thousand aircraft) be allocated immediately to the Reich's defence.[40] But Göring would not receive him, so Milch invited the Führer's adjutant von Below to ministry conferences, and to meet the foremost Luftwaffe officers and ministry experts privately at his hunting lodge.[41] This must have had some effect, for early in July 1943 the Führer approved that the western fighter defences should be intensified.[42]

The state secretary had not seen Göring for six weeks. While Milch toiled in Berlin's stifling heat, Göring holidayed on the Obersalzberg, forcing Milch to put all his communications on paper throughout June: he appealed for protection from draft for the skilled workers now engaged on the Me 262 jet fighter, on its jet engines, on night-fighters and on the *TSA* precision bombsight recently developed by Zeiss;[43] he suggested that they plan now for massive defences for the flying-bomb catapult sites in France, since 'after this weapon offensive begins, our fighters and flak will find magnificent opportunities of annihilating the enemy air force which will be forced to attack them.'[44] And of course he sent Göring a lengthy report on his tour of the western air defence system.

He finally saw the familiar pearl-grey uniform and flashing rings on 2 July at Göring's hunting lodge, Rominten, in East Prussia; the Reichsmarschall had summoned all the *Luftflotte* commanders to discuss the new eastern offensive, 'Zitadelle', due to begin in three days' time.[45] Here the estrangement between Göring and his state secretary was made more public than ever before. When Göring referred on the following day to the 'cowardice' of their flying personnel, Milch was the only officer present to speak out against him.[46] He had assessed aircrew morale very highly in his inspection report in June, and he referred to the proposals he had made for improving the command structure. In front of all the other field marshals and generals, Göring angrily rounded on Milch: 'You don't imagine that I actually read the rags you send me!' Milch stonily commented that in that case it was superfluous for him to make further inspection trips as Inspector General; Göring retorted that as far as he was concerned, he need not.[47] Milch returned angrily to Berlin.

That night, six hundred RAF heavy bombers attacked Cologne, on the fringe of the Ruhr. This time, Major Herrmann had twelve single-engined fighter aircraft ready—five FW 190s and seven Me 109s—to test his proposals over the city, which was soon brilliantly lit up by fires and flares. He reported to Milch three days later: 'I opened fire on one bomber, which began to burn at once but carried on flying for about four minutes although it was on fire. So I let him have it again from one side, right in the cockpit, and then it went down like a stone—the crew must have been hit.' Within the space of a minute, he had seen ten or fifteen aircraft, clearly identifiable from their exhaust flames and sitting targets for a fast single-seater. If in doubt, one only had to wait around near the target-indicator flares. He estimated that given enough aircraft he could shoot down up to eighty enemy bombers a night. He already had 120 crews picked out for 'Wild Boar', but they still had only fifteen aircraft scraped together from different establishments.[48]

'Didn't the flak down below know you were there?' asked Milch. 'They had no idea!' said Herrmann. 'I suppose they were amazed when the bombers started dropping like flies?' 'They were astounded to find ten or eleven down, when they had shot down only two the day before,' laughed Herrmann. General Vorwald and Field Marshal Milch both exclaimed in relief, 'It seems we have broken the spell.'

A few days later, the German agent in the British Air Ministry provided further transcripts of Whitehall conferences, which showed that the RAF's recent losses of heavy bombers were even more severe than the Germans knew. Schwenke suggested to Milch that if they could increase British casualties by about a fifth, the enemy would have to give serious consideration to means of avoiding further losses.[49] This was a problem to which RAF Bomber Command had already faced up; the solution was reached on 15 July, with a decision that as from 23 July the embargo on the use of the secret metal-foil strips to jam Kamm-huber's radar system would be lifted.[50]

Five days after operation 'Zitadelle' began, the Allies landed in Sicily supported by three thousand aircraft; on 12 July the Russians opened a counter-offensive; Hitler ordered Zitadelle to be halted, and air rein-forcements rushed to Italy.

In vain Milch argued at Hitler's headquarters that the defence of the home base was a prerequisite for any operations by the Germans in Sicily or anywhere else.[51] 'If something happens to us here,' he pointed out, 'whatever happens elsewhere is of no interest.' Returning to Berlin he told his departmental heads, 'I have just been up there trying to sort them out a bit about the future. I can only keep saying, for us 1943 is a year to sit tight and clench our teeth.'[52] Discussing the allocation of twin-engined fighter aircraft in mid-July, he again emphasized: 'Let us first of all set our houses in Germany, Italy and Japan in order.' When an Air Staff general protested, 'Herr Feldmarschall, it's like this: there's heavy fighting down in Sicily, and they . . .' Milch interrupted him: 'I know, they are screaming blue murder! But the more the people scream, the calmer we must keep.' For him the coming battlefield was not in Sicily or at Kursk, but in the Reich itself. 'There is only one worry,' he said, 'and that is that in some way the enemy again catches us on the hop with some radar trickery or other, and we have to start trotting after him again.'

# A WREATH UPON OUR COFFIN

## (*July–September 1943*)

In the last few weeks before the Hamburg catastrophe in the summer of 1943, Field Marshal Milch exhorted the leading German politicians and officers to support his campaign for concentration on the defence of the Reich.[1] Hitler did not believe that the low casualties the night-fighters were currently inflicting on the enemy would alone prevent the air attacks: 'You can only smash terror with counter-terror,' he told Göring and Milch. 'You have to counter-attack. Anything else is useless.' When they touched on the possibility of night intruder aircraft attacking British airfields, Hitler observed that if the Luftwaffe could not find London by night, it was hardly likely to find an individual bomber airfield.

'It's a scandal!' Hitler told his own staff two days later. 'And I said precisely that to the Reichsmarschall. I did not mince my words. And then I have to listen to some nincompoop telling me, "Yes, *mein Führer,* if they come to Dortmund from Britain with their present radio beam system they can lay their bombs down on factory buildings 500 yards wide by 250 yards long." But we can't find London, thirty miles across and only a hundred miles from our shores!'[2]

On 24 July catastrophe fell upon Hamburg. Seven hundred heavy bombers attacked the port and city, first releasing cascades of millions of strips of metal foil about twelve inches long into the sky—the simple means of jamming the gunlaying and fighter control 'Würzburg' radar sets which Martini had feared all along.[3] While the searchlights wandered aimlessly over Hamburg's sky, and the blinded night-fighter aircraft fumbled in the darkness, fifteen hundred civilians were killed and much of the city devastated. Only twelve bombers were shot down. The Luftwaffe's ignominy was complete, for no counter-measure had been developed against the dreaded metal-foil strips.

Next day over a hundred American bombers again attacked Hamburg to hamper the fire-fighting, and that evening six hundred British bombers attacked Essen. 'Gentlemen!' observed Milch on the twenty-seventh, 'we are no longer on the offensive. For the last one and a half or two years we have been on the defensive. This fact is now apparently recognized even at the highest levels of the Luftwaffe command.' He continued, 'For the last three months I have been asking for one month's fighter production to be assigned to home defence. This would have made attacks like those yesterday on Hamburg and Hanover quite impossible. . . . I keep getting the feeling that anything may still happen!'[4]

That evening Hamburg suffered renewed violence. Again enveloped in metal foil, the bombers released 2,300 tons of high explosives and fire bombs over the city, tinder-dry after weeks of drought. Tremendous fires broke out. The water mains had been smashed in the earlier attacks, and soon the fires were out of control, sweeping across the city with horrifying speed; tens of thousands of the inhabitants were sucked into the inferno by the artificial hurricanes raging through the streets, incinerated alive in the giant concrete air-raid shelters or poisoned by the carbon-monoxide, a feature of these 'fire-storm' attacks. Fifty thousand people died. Now at last Göring ordered the *Schwerpunkt* to be switched to the defence of the Reich.[5] Milch was ordered to report to him and Hitler on the twenty-ninth.

Milch asked Colonel Victor von Lossberg, a bomber expert, to pilot him. During the night, an idea occurred to von Lossberg for a fighter defence system to defeat—indeed to exploit—the British metal-foil jamming, a night-fighter system which promised to bring a greater weight of aircraft to bear on the enemy than Kammhuber's rigid system: squadrons of twin-engined fighters should assemble over Holland, awaiting the enemy bomber stream; each unit would follow a shadower, itself transmitting a radio beacon, guided by a ground controller into the very vanguard of the approaching bomber stream (by means of the Y radio-beam guidance system); once guided into the stream, the fighters would hunt freelance, using the latest radar sets. Von Lossberg also recommended reinforcing Herrmann's increasingly successful 'Wild Boar' operations over the target area. In this way the British aircraft would be engaged not only by the Kammhuber Line, but along the whole route from the coast to the target and over the target itself.[6]

'By these means,' suggested Lossberg, 'between two and three hundred night-fighters inclusive of the Herrmann Wing could be brought to bear, in other words at least a threefold increase on the present rate.'[7] The British bombers could soon be suffering enormous losses every night. Göring ordered a full-scale investigation of the proposals. Meantime Hamburg had again been heavily attacked; over two thousand tons of bombs were released on the residential areas. But thanks to Herrmann's new 'Wild Boar' tactics, the British losses were mounting too. Twenty-eight bombers had been shot down, despite the radar-jamming effort.[8]

It is evident that Milch believed that Germany's home front now faced a threat no less than confronted the Sixth Army at Stalingrad: 'It is one minute to twelve. It is a matter of trying to turn back the clock of Germany's destiny, no less.' He tackled this crisis with the same energy and decisiveness as had characterized his special mission at Taganrog. Despite the Führer's emphatic objections he ordered that their new *Schwerpunkt* was to be the production of fighter aircraft; to square his own conscience, he listed the flying-bomb as well. In a brief preliminary discussion on 30 July he laid the foundations of a 'Reich Defence Programme', retargeting fighter production alone at *three thousand a month* instead of two thousand, by the summer of 1944.[9]

When the investigation of von Lossberg's proposal began, as commanded by Göring, Milch warned: 'What has happened in Hamburg has never happened before, not even during our attacks on Britain. The casualties in Hamburg—dead alone—are put at fifty thousand as of today, most of them caused by the immense conflagrations. . . . These attacks on Hamburg strike deep at our nation's morale.' Weighing his words carefully he continued, 'If we do not succeed in smashing these terror attacks by day and by night very soon, then we must expect a very difficult situation to arise for Germany.' Kammhuber attempted to block the new proposals, but was overruled.[10] That afternoon the first Lichtenstein SN-2 radar sets were installed in the Ju 188s which were to serve as the 'shadowers'.

To Germany's leaders, Hamburg seemed momentarily to spell the beginning of the end. Speer candidly prophesied in Central Planning: 'If the air raids continue on this scale, three months will see us relieved of many a problem exercising us today. Things will slide downhill smoothly, irrevocably and comparatively fast! The pressing question is simply this: can we manufacture more single-engined and more twin-engined fighters? And if so, what can we shut down to that end? Otherwise we might as well hold the last meeting of Central Planning!'[11] At Milch's hunting lodge Speer expressed himself even more pessimistically two evenings later.[12] To the Führer, on 1 August, Speer predicted that if things continued in this way within eight weeks he could no longer guarantee a production effort; and if the same catastrophe were to befall just six more cities, the war would be over.[13]

Even Milch's iron shell of optimism was corroded by this mood of defeatism. When the ministers and gauleiters assembled on Hitler's instructions in Berlin on 2 August for Dr Goebbels to 'inject some cement into them', Milch repeatedly interrupted a discussion on the war in the air with the almost treasonable outcry, *We have lost the war! Finally lost the war!'* Goebbels had to appeal to his honour as an officer before he would quieten down, and the minister complained to his staff afterwards, 'I would just like to see one of my state secretaries dare behave like that—however right he was!'[14]

During the night the British attacked Hamburg yet again. 'My own view is this,' Milch lectured to the silent officers who gathered in his ministry. 'It's much blacker than Speer paints it. If we get just five or six more attacks like these on Hamburg, the German people will just lay down their tools, however great their willpower. I keep saying, the steps that are being taken now are being taken too late. There can be no more talk of night-fighting in the east, or of putting an umbrella over our troops in Sicily or anything like that. The soldier on the battlefield will just have to dig a hole, crawl into it and wait until the attack is over. What the home front is suffering now cannot be suffered very much longer.' That day he cabled Göring in these terms: 'It is not the front which is under attack and struggling for survival, but the home base, which is fighting a desperate fight.' When General Meister, deputy Chief of Air Staff, declined his suggestion that two idle long-range fighter squadrons should be taken out of the eastern front and sent back to the Reich, Milch reproached him, 'I keep getting this feeling that we are all sitting out on a limb. At this limb, the British keep sawing away! Here at home I can hear the rasp of the saw. You out there, Meister, are farther away, and are deaf to it. . . .'[15]

By now he was manufacturing over a thousand new fighter aircraft every month, but still they were being dissipated in every theatre. From a military point of view this was not acceptable: in the air the battle should have been fought from the rear forwards, just as on the ground. The enemy bombers should have been swept away from the centre of Germany, and finally far beyond the English Channel if that were pos-sible.[16] But this could be done only by summoning up every ounce of fighter strength. This was going to be the 'year of clenched teeth', Milch had often warned. When Colonel Peltz volunteered the better part of his bomber strength for the defence of the Reich, Milch praised his vision: 'Attacking Britain with twenty or thirty aircraft only makes us look ridiculous. We don't impress the British like that, we just show them what we are capable of under circumstances like these. But if we do nothing, then they will say, "They must be up to something." '[17]

In many senses Milch *was* up to something. The Fi 103 flying-bomb was scheduled for operation by the autumn; the first hundred jet fighters were planned for the spring of 1944, and the Ar 234 jet bombers were to reach squadron service later in the year. Of the secret flying-bomb catapult sites being constructed along the Channel coast, Milch predicted: 'This is where we will bury the British air force. If they bring over their bombers and we can collect our fighters just as they attack, then we shall no longer need fighter defences in the rear; we can throw them right forward to the coast.'[18] He prophesied that the Americans would also soon have to devote their effort to daylight attacks on the catapult sites in France (since the RAF night-bombers were not suited for such work). 'In a short time we can tear them limb from limb. After one or two battles like that they will be so washed up that they will need two weeks before they can attack again. And the aircraft and airmen we knock out over there cannot visit us in Germany any more.'[19]

Yet the flying-bomb was still encountering difficulties. The whole project needed nearly three thousand more workers, and nobody was parting with them, least of all the army, which had the A4 rocket project to look after. Speer had used the aftermath of Hamburg to chisel out of Hitler a formidable decree assigning top priority to the rocket's mass-production.[20] The test launchings of the flying-bomb at Peenemünde had unexpectedly produced a disappointing number of failures. One ranging shot had however covered 140 miles, and the bombs were otherwise travelling at cruising altitudes of four thousand feet and speeds up to four hundred miles per hour.[21] By August only about sixty per cent of the test launchings were successful, but Milch observed, 'I will be satisfied if the Fi 103 works at all. . . . A weapon against which the public sees there is no real defence has such catastrophic morale effects that by itself—regardless of what the weapon is —it must have immense consequences.'[22] He expected that Londoners could withstand the damage for two or three days under heavy bombardment, or 'if they are real roughnecks' for four days; but after that it would all be over, and the fires would rage unchecked. Given a production of 3,500 flying-bombs a month they could theoretically launch one every twelve minutes. 'They will never endure it. It will be the end of any real life in the city.'*

Early in August 1943 an unexpected blow hit the Me 262 jet-fighter project. The Führer suddenly ordered that the Me 209 piston-engined fighter was *not* to be cancelled, although both Milch and Galland believed its performance to be inadequate.

Three months had passed since Milch's decision to cancel the Me 209 in favour of immediate jet-fighter production. Since then somebody had alerted Hitler to the supposed risks of concentrating on jet fighters. 'The Führer sees it as taking too great a risk,' Milch explained to his disappointed departmental heads. He himself regretted this: 'But I have my orders. I am a soldier, and must obey them. We must observe the element of prudence demanded by the Führer.'[24] The Messerschmitt company had undertaken some months earlier to complete the pilot series of a hundred by May 1944, manufacturing sixty per month thereafter.[25] This new decision would inevitably set back their plans for mass production: 'Obviously Messerschmitt cannot now convert a hundred per cent to the 262, as he would otherwise have been able.' The next generation of fighter aircraft after the Me 109 and the FW 190 would apparently have to be the Me 209 or Kurt Tank's Ta 153 after all, of which the former was inevitably chosen, even though it had still not flown, since the company had more factories at its disposal and claimed (falsely) that the tooling-up for the aircraft was eighty-five per cent complete.[26] Milch was angry that he could no longer promote the jet fighter's production as he had wanted in May: 'But this is an intervention from on high, so the problem will have to be solved some other way.'[27] He was convinced Messerschmitt had himself brought about the Führer's change of mind.[28]

Milch's Reich Defence Programme called for the production of four thousand fighter aircraft per month by September 1945; on General Galland's advice he set Me 262 jet-fighter production at a quarter of that total. But for the August 1943 decision it could have been far more.

Meanwhile, Berlin awaited disaster. Everybody knew it was coming. In the first week after Hamburg Dr Goebbels had ordered all non-essential civilians to leave; a million people were evacuated in anticipation of the raids to come.

---

* Colonel von Lossberg proposed that they use mainly incendiaries in the flying-bomb warheads. 'One need only look at London as an example. For half a year we bombed London, and still London is not in ruins. For three days they bombed Hamburg—and Hamburg is *kaputt!*'[23]

At Hitler's headquarters the position of General Jeschonnek, Chief of Air Staff, became intolerable. He had never busied himself much with defence problems; and he had watched in concern as Göring, shunned by Hitler, set up his own little 'Air Staff' with Diesing and two or three other colonels, to bypass Jeschonnek.[29] Göring began meantime to search for a replacement; von Richthofen was among the possible candidates.[30] After the American daylight attack on Wiener Neustadt's aircraft factories on 13 August the Führer berated him for over an hour in private. Jeschonnek afterwards complained to Meister, 'Why does the Führer say all this to me, and not to the Reichsmarschall?' The answer was of course that Göring was Hitler's chosen successor. Four days later unescorted American bomber formations penetrated deep into Germany and struck at the ball-bearing factories at Schweinfurt and the Messerschmitt complex at Regensburg, killing four hundred Messerschmitt workers.[31] The Luftwaffe destroyed sixty American bombers that day, but again Hitler sent for Jeschonnek and upbraided him unmercifully.[32] That night the RAF attacked Peenemünde, the rocket research station, in great force, killing 750 scientists and workers there. The defence effort was a fiasco: two hundred of Herrmann's and von Lossberg's fighters assembled over Berlin by mistake, where the flak opened fire on them, because of orders Jeschonnek had issued.[33] He took the only way out, and his body was found in the morning with a bullet in the head. He left a note: 'It is impossible to work with Göring any longer. Long live the Führer!'

The new Chief of Air Staff was Colonel-General Günter Korten, commander of the First Air Force, who had been Milch's staff officer until October 1936. Milch thought very highly of him: 'While the newcomer Korten soon learned how to gain Hitler's confidence, his relations with Göring became very strained,' he wrote. 'Korten, in his diplomatic way, prevented things from coming to a head for a long time. At the end of June 1944, however, he confided to me, as his former chief, that by August 1944 at the latest he wanted to resign the post as with the best will in the world he could not get on with Göring.'[34] Before that month came, however, Korten had also met a violent end.

The writing was plainly on the wall. As the hot summer streets in Berlin lay empty and deserted, and those who remained reacted nervously to every siren's sound, Messerschmitt wrote to the industrialists that 'they could tick off on their fingers' the months Germany's armaments industry could expect to survive.[35] With Jeschonnek dead, Milch persuaded Göring to transfer a number of fighter squadrons to Germany from other fronts: 'In my view this has been done so late as to be almost lunatic,' he commented, 'but at least it has been done.'[36] He was already searching for dispersal sites for the vital aircraft factories. There was talk of giant bomb-proof factories, but the Luftwaffe's share of construction projects had shrunk in 1943 to half that of the previous four years (the Luftwaffe was now ranked only sixth, coming after the Reich Railways).[37]

During the summer Milch managed to find over thirty million square feet of floor space for evacuation of the factories, but the actual transport was hindered by his shortage of transport and fuel; on the railways Speer had secured top priority for the needs of the 'Adolf Hitler Panzer Programme', and by autumn the Luftwaffe's railway wagon allocation had been halved.[38] Göring attacked Milch over every damaged factory as though he were personally to blame, but when Milch asked for temporary use of the Luftwaffe's sixty thousand lorries, the Reichsmarschall refused point-blank. With masters like these the Luftwaffe seemed doomed to defeat.[39]

During August 1943 Major Herrmann's 'Wild Boar' unit had been increased by over 150 aircraft; those crews who still had no planes 'borrowed' the equipment of day-fighter squadrons. The major arranged for high-flying bombers to light up the whole target area with parachute flares, to aid his freelance pilots in their search for enemy bombers; the flak would put up a barrage of starshells, and the searchlight batteries were to illuminate the base of any cloud layers present. Milch hoped the RAF would meet its Waterloo over Berlin: 'One thing is clear: the enemy is only a hero when there is no defence! If he runs up against determined opposition or meets with a disaster, then for ninety per cent of them that's an end to the heroics. And then they will have to think very hard about whether to carry on.'[40]

Three nights later the RAF launched its assault on Berlin.[41] Within an hour they had lost fifty-six bombers, mainly to Herrmann's nightfighters; many more were damaged beyond repair. Milch triumphantly reminded his men that by March 1944 they would be producing two thousand fighter aircraft a month: 'I give my word that then these night attacks will cease altogether.'[42] Nothing could prevent the Allies from manufacturing bombers by the thousand; but if the Allied aircrews lost their nerve, this alone would defeat the attacks. Again and again the same bleak realization dogged the field marshal: 'If we had had enough day and night fighters before, all this would never have happened. Then we would not now be having to disperse our factories. Then no enemy bombers would be coming over.'

It was an enigma to him that he stood alone in his fight for the defence

*Above* Frau Clara Milch, the field-marshal's mother, and the man to whom she bore her children. The Church would not have allowed them to marry.

*Left* Erhard Milch before 1914.

German civil aviation after the First World War suffered numerous indignities at the hands of the British and French control commissions. Stockpiled engines and fuselages were searched out and put to the sledgehammer, like these at Lübeck airfield in 1919.

At thirty-three Milch (*right*) was one of the three directors of the new German national airline Lufthansa. Two years later – despite conflict with his fellow directors Wronsky and Merkel, *left* and *centre* – he rescued the airline from financial ruin.

Mishaps were frequent. The first Lufthansa flight from Vienna to Berlin brought Milch down in the treetops of Saxony.

In 1932 Milch, still a civilian airline manager, chartered Lufthansa aircraft to Adolf Hitler for his election tours of Germany. A mutual respect sprang up between them.

In 1935 the Luftwaffe was officially born. Milch, by now a full Luftwaffe general, inspects the Luftwaffe guard of honour drawn up outside the Air Ministry building. His rapid promotion earned the envy of career officers.

In 1933 Milch and the Luftwaffe's first chief of staff Wever had issued contracts for the design of bombers capable of flying right round the British Isles. But four years later Göring ordered the resulting four-engined Dornier 19 (*above*) and Junkers 89 (*below*) prototypes to be scrapped.

This was the heyday of British appeasement. In October 1937 General Milch took a party of Luftwaffe generals (including Ernst Udet, *left*) round R.A.F. airfields and headquarters in Britain.

In 1940 he directed the campaign against the R.A.F. in Norway: a wooden airfield (*below*) was constructed near Trondheim for the Nazis by volunteer Norwegian labour.

Milch (seen above with Göring and his chief of Intelligence, Colonel 'Beppo' Schmid) took notes on everything. The diary – apparently from 1936, but in fact filled by Milch at the height of the Battle of Britain – records a conference at 3 p.m. on 14 September 1940 with 'der Führer'.

MAY, 1936.

MAY, 1936.

Rogation Sunday. **Sunday 17**

Monday **18**

Milch's friendships were rare and explosive. Speer (*above*, with Professor Porsche of the Volkswagen works) served twenty years in Spandau, outwitted him and outlived him.

Udet, the Bohemian caricaturist and former stunt flier (*below*, at Karinhall) alternately idolized and mistrusted Milch. Udet succumbed to narcotics and envy, and took his own life in 1941.

Before the war the Air Staff issued a requirement for a replacement for the Junkers 88. 'Bomber B' was to be a heavy bomber with five-ton bombload, dive capability and great speed. By 1941 the two contenders were the Junkers 288 (*below*) and the Focke-Wulf 191 (*above*).

In 1939 Göring was still powerful. On the eve of war he proudly showed Hitler and his staff round a boastful display of futuristic Luftwaffe equipment at Rechlin airfield (*right*). But as Göring's indolence and unpopularity increased, Milch stood in for him at the important Nazi ceremonies with Hitler, Keitel and Himmler. Eventually Göring rid himself of this dangerous 'crown prince' in 1944.

The Heinkel 177 was the Luftwaffe's 'dead racehorse', as Milch put it, Udet's posthumous bequest to the bomber squadrons. A long-range bomber and reconnaissance aircraft, it was fitted with two weird Daimler-Benz 610 coupled-engines so that it could skit like a dive-bomber. In September 1942 Göring complained, 'Never was I more furious than when I saw this engine. . . . How is such an engine supposed to be serviced in the squadrons? I don't think you can even get out the spark plugs without dismantling the entire engine!' Thousands were ordered, hundreds were impatiently awaited by the Luftwaffe, Hitler and the submarine crews, but only a handful ever flew.

Earlier, Göring, Milch and the Chief of Air Staff Hans Jeschonnek (*centre*) appeared the best of friends in public. But after the R.A.F. firestorm raids began with a grisly series of attacks on the city of Hamburg in July 1943, Jeschonnek put a bullet in his head at Luftwaffe headquarters.

The results of the R.A.F. attack on Hamburg in July 1943. This was what caused Milch to demand priority for Reich defence.

Professor Messerschmitt believed the Messerschmitt 262 jet could be altered to carry bombs – of up to 1,000 kilogrammes if necessary – within fourteen days. Milch protested to Hitler, 'Mein Führer, the smallest infant can see that it's a fighter, not a bomber aircraft!' After nine months the Me 262 began operations with two 250 kilo bombs (*below*) in the autumn of 1944.

The Arado 234 was designed as a jet bomber and armed reconnaissance plane from the outset.

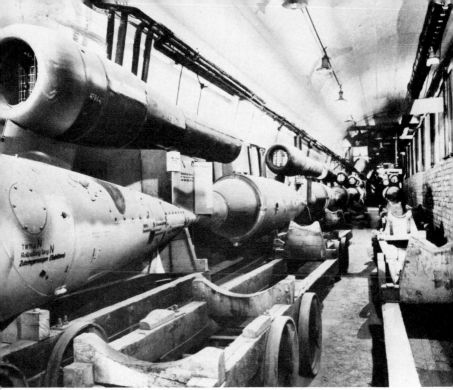

When Milch abdicated in June 1944, Germany's secret weapons research was just bearing fruit: *above*, the V1 flying-bomb in its underground mass-production line in the Harz mountains; *left*, the record-breaking Dornier 335 fighter-bomber with twin engines powering a propeller at each end; and *below*, the Junkers 287 supersonic jet bomber, with its unconventional forward-swept wings.

On trial for his life by an American post-war tribunal at Nuremberg (*left to right above* Judges Speight, Phillips, Musmanno and Toms), Field Marshal Milch was defended by Dr Friedrich Bergold and (*right*) his lawyer brother Dr Werner Milch. He was acquitted on one count, and sentenced to life imprisonment on the other two.

of the Reich. He found it shameful that the other two Services did not volunteer vital assistance—raw materials and manpower—for his defence programme. 'Not one swine helps us,' he reflected on 31 August 1943. 'We have to help ourselves. Each of them expresses deepest sympathy, and promises to lay a wreath upon our coffin. . . .'[43] That night six hundred bombers again assaulted Berlin. The conditions were good for the night fighters, and they were marshalled into the bomber stream from airfields as far afield as northern Denmark and central France—a classic example of *Schwerpunkt* formation. Between them they destroyed most of the forty-seven bombers shot down that night. Milch had ordered every means possible to increase the glare on the clouds by searchlights, fires and even by burning pots of magnesium in the outskirts, and he had ordered special aircraft to stand by to lay thin trails of mist if the clouds had been inadequate.[44] As he told Speer next day, 'The enemy bombers crawl across them like flies on a tablecloth.'

Three nights later the RAF attacked the capital again, operating only the powerful Lancaster squadrons now; twenty-two were shot down, and the series came to an abrupt end. Of the total of 1,719 sorties despatched against Berlin on the three nights, only twenty-seven had dropped their bombs within three miles of the aiming point. By night at least, within one month of Hamburg, the tide was turning firmly in favour of the Luftwaffe's new night defences. On 2 September Field Marshal Milch reported to Göring at his East Prussian hunting lodge, and found that all the Reichsmarschall's old hostility towards him had disappeared.[45]

# DEFENCE OF THE REICH

## *(September–October 1943)*

Until August 1943 the aircraft production programmes established by Milch were adhered to; but with the commencement of the Combined Bomber Offensive the first major setbacks were experienced. The bombing of the five biggest aircraft factories and the two biggest repair plants reduced the August output by 150 fighters.[1] Not only were the big factories severely harmed, but the smaller foundries, press-shops and components manufacturers were affected by the area attacks: the shortage of airscrews after Hamburg was such that of forty-two Ju 188s due for delivery in one month, only four could be completed.[2]

Speer's staff persistently claimed that Milch's new Reich Defence Programme ('224') was unattainable and that even '223', which had been issued in April, had stretched the limits imposed on aircraft production anyway by the bottleneck in engine crankshaft supplies.[3] When Milch appealed to Speer to set fighter production at least on a par with other top-priority programmes for supplies, this request was rejected.[4] A number of components, workers and machine-tools were promised but none arrived. Speer's representatives denied that these items were really needed.[5] It seemed to the Air Ministry that the Munitions Ministry* was adopting blocking tactics to secure eventual control of aircraft production for itself, as it had of the naval construction programme a few weeks before.†

Professor Messerschmitt also wished to see the industry wrested from Milch's grasp. To Speer and Saur he criticized the one-shift operation of the air industry (inevitable because of the manpower shortage); he urged the ruthless closing down of the bomber factories in favour of fighters; and he advocated production of one million Fi 103 flying-bombs

---

* In September 1943 it became the Ministry of Armaments.

† When Speer took over aircraft production in June 1944, his ministry approved programmes in excess of '223' and almost as high as '224', both of which it had declared 'impracticable' when Milch was still in control.[6]

a year.[7] On 7 September he again secured Hitler's ear for his proposals: he alerted Hitler to Milch's 'incompetence' and spoke of the wonders of the Me 209 fighter aircraft and of the flying-bomb project.[8] Then he talked about the Me 262 jet fighter: he considered that this aircraft met the requirements recently raised for a fast bomber for attacking Britain: 'Its technical lead is so great that this aircraft cannot come into service fast enough, as otherwise we must expect the enemy to start coming over with similar aircraft before us, or at the same time.' Unhappily, he did not have adequate capacity for mass production of the Me 262, he said; he proposed that the rival projects—Milch's favourite Dornier 335 and the Ar 234 armed reconnaissance aircraft and jet bomber—should be cancelled.[9] Hitler had never seen a jet aircraft, but the possibility of using the Me 262 as a jet bomber must have lodged in his mind, because he asked about it when he saw Göring a month later; and by the time he saw Milch a month after that, the idea had become a requirement. We need look no further for the origins of Hitler's 'absurd notion' of using the Me 262 as a jet bomber.[10]

Italy's separate Armistice with the Allies at least brought some relief to the German war economy. Germany had had to supply her ally with 2 million tons of oil fuel in 1941 and 1.2 million tons in 1942.[11] But the Italian defection also brought major strategic problems: by 27 September British forces had seized Foggia and the fifteen airfields surrounding the town; American bomber and fighter squadrons moved in. Milch was advised that they had no choice but to evacuate what they could of the Italian factories: 'One thing is clear. The way their base at Foggia lies, the British and Americans have limitless opportunities. They can flatten the whole of Upper Italy.'[12] To Milch, who shared Hitler's dislike of the Italians, this prospect was not without its attractions. 'On the other hand,' he mused, 'we ought to leave the factories a certain element of activity, to keep them valid as bomber targets, and not us!'[13]

Reluctantly, he now had to give up all hope of manufacturing Professor Gabrielli's exceptionally fast piston-engined fighter, the Fiat G55, in Italy.[14] While hundreds of thousands of disarmed Italian soldiers went into captivity, German troops took over. The evidence of Italy's bad faith that they found staggered even Milch. The Italians had concealed vast stockpiles of raw materials for themselves, while pleading with Germany for more: 'They had bigger stocks of copper than we have!' fumed Göring. 'The most amazing is the fuel oil: in two tunnels we have found enough fuel oil to have kept their entire navy operational for a year! The swine put it away, barrel by barrel, and then came to me for more: "We would dearly love to fly, but we need the fuel!" I gave them another thousand tons—and now we find they had sixty-five thousand tons tucked away.'[15]

On 1 October the American air force began bombing missions against the Reich from the newly occupied base at Foggia. The first target was the Messerschmitt factory at Wiener-Neustadt. 'The south and southeast are now in the firing line as well,' Milch admitted. 'Our "safe" has been blasted open. I have worked out for myself that the distance from Foggia to Vienna is shorter than from London to Berlin.'[16]

The heavily armoured American squadrons were daunting opponents for the German fighters, most of them still armed only with relatively small-calibre machine-guns. During the summer the enemy began appearing with P-47 ('Thunderbolt') escort fighters as far east as Aachen, and this complicated the fighter defence task still further. Milch's scientists devised many ways of combating the threat. Because of Air Ministry hostility towards rocket development, there were still no adequate ground-to-air or air-to-air missiles, but much effort had been expended on more complex methods like proximity fuses for bombs and shells operating by remote radio control or on acoustic or magnetic principles; the most awe-inspiring was a rocket-propelled 500-pound or half-ton bomb, which a twin-engined Me 410 could lob into the bomber formations from a range of about a thousand yards.[17]

In September a glider pilot who had survived the hazardous operations against the Belgian forts and Crete wrote suggesting a suicide squadron for attacking vital enemy targets; he and his comrades considered they were living on borrowed time anyway, and would like a chance to sacrifice themselves for their Fatherland. Milch asked General Korten to discuss the idea with Göring. Petersen suggested packing ageing Ju 88s with explosives and heading them for the bomber formations; the pilot could jump out at the last moment, if he could. Milch thought the prospects over: 'I do not know if *I* would have the courage for this myself.' He had always insisted the pilot must have a chance, however slim, of surviving. An engineer pointed out that it only needed an attractive girl to cross the man's path during his suicide-squadron training and the effort would be wasted. Milch related to the engineer one such episode of his own experience: 'There was this man who was about to throw his life away, for nothing. So he was told, wait a while; we have a little job you can do, where you can still throw away your life, but for the good of your country. You will be trained for it, and in the meantime you will be given everything you want—good accommodation, fine food and perhaps even the young maiden you'—indicating the engineer —'mentioned. It all took some time, and when finally the day came the man said, "Nothing doing! I've changed my mind. Life is too beautiful to throw away." '[18]

Göring asked Korten to open a list of airmen willing to undertake such missions.

Meanwhile the RAF was still dormant after the retreat from Berlin.[19] The mood was very different from a month before, when Britain's (and some of Germany's) leaders were predicting Germany's imminent collapse. The autumn of 1943 saw the German fighter arm increasing daily in its strength.[20]

This was Milch's achievement alone. In the three months since 1 July German fighter strength in the west had increased from 1,288 to 1,646, an increase which confounded the predictions of the British Air Staff. The latter had allowed for Germany emerging from the pre-invasion campaign against aircraft factories and the fighter defences with perhaps 650 fighters in the west; but they now estimated that the Germans would have over 1,700 fighters on the western front on the eve of the Allied invasion in 1944.[21] By early November 1943, when these Allied estimates were made, the prospects of defeating the Luftwaffe before an invasion had evidently vanished, and Sir Arthur Harris, chief of Bomber Command, was tempting the Prime Minister with the same alluring prospect as had been held before Hitler in different circumstances in 1940: 'We can wreck Berlin from end to end if the USAAF will come in on it,' Harris promised. 'It will cost between 400 and 450 aircraft. It will cost Germany the war.'[22] Churchill authorized the attempt.

The Germans expected it. To defeat the H2S radar sets carried by the bombers, they spent the remaining months of the summer dotting the lakes around Berlin with metal rafts as radar camouflage; they designed special jamming transmitters ('Roderich') and a simple receiver ('Naxos Z') to enable the night-fighters to home on to H2S transmissions; and the ground-spotting organization was alerted to track the H2S emissions of careless bomber crews heading into Germany.[23] Major Herrmann's organization was expanded into three wings, the night-fighters were equipped as far as possible with an improved radar, less affected by the metal-foil jamming, and with infra-red detectors (Spanner); the ground organization was improved, General Kammhuber was replaced by Lieutenant-General Schmid as commander of the night-fighter squadrons, and scores of airfields, including those of aircraft factories, were prepared to receive exhausted fighters landing after the night's battles. On some nights the ground controller would have over 250 fighter aircraft following his commentary on the movements of the marauding enemy bomber stream.[24]

The British deduced what was happening and adopted counter-measures. They split the bomber stream and attacked several cities simultaneously, leaving the German controller guessing until the last moment, and then jamming his wireless communications. Using heavy aircraft laden with nothing but transmitters, they would interpolate fake instructions to the fighter pilots, ordering them to the wrong end of Germany or, more subtly, predicting worsening weather or ground fog.[25] Major Herrmann reacted by loading a special Ju 88 with fake Pathfinder flares and releasing them over open country at the precise moment of the British 'Master Bomber's' broadcast. It was a growing nightmare, but Milch kept his nerve, confident that the Luftwaffe was winning the air war by night; as, for the next six months, it was.

The new German tactics took some weeks to organize. In the early RAF attacks on Bochum and Kassel some German night-fighters were hit by their own flak.[26] In early October the RAF surprised the de-fences at Kassel by first feinting towards Hanover and Magdeburg, causing an angry outburst from Milch about the inability of the ground-spotting organization to report that the bomber stream had switched its course. 'What upsets me is that it is still not possible for us to take proper command by night, although we have been employing hundreds of thousands of people for this.' He predicted, 'You will live to see the day when they don't just attack cities lying on the Rhine, but perhaps Munich and Berlin simultaneously. Let's see how your command system tackles that!'[27]

The RAF had also begun operating long-range night-fighters over Germany equipped with very efficient radar sets. Milch had often recom-mended that similar German intruder operations should be carried out over RAF bomber airfields, and on the night of 2 October there were twenty-two German night-fighters mingling with the British bombers as they returned to their brightly illuminated airfields after attacking Munich.[28] Hitler disapproved of these intruder operations, which were disconcerting for the enemy but not spectacular. He told Göring that it was infinitely preferable for the Luftwaffe to sustain an attack on British cities than to interfere with the landing manoeuvres of enemy bombers; and when it was suggested that the intruders created great confusion among the RAF bombers Hitler acidly pointed out, 'They may be confused, but they keep coming!'[29]

To add to the injury, the American bomber squadrons now resumed their daylight assault on Germany's aircraft industry. During the attack on Emden on 2 October H2S-type radar sets were detected aboard the bombers for the first time; evidently they had adopted elements of British blind bombing technique.[30] Milch made no secret of his respect for American accuracy: 'When the Americans lay down their carpet of bombs somewhere, then anything beneath is pretty well matchwood.'[31]

The industrial quarter of Frankfurt was the 'matchwood' on 4 October. As the first news of the attack reached Hitler, his staff assured him, 'We knew this attack was on, from an agent. So the defence commander was forewarned.'[32] Forewarned was not forearmed, however. Galland's fighter squadrons failed almost completely to deter the heavily armoured bomber formations. Isolated packets of fighter aircraft came sporadically to within a thousand yards of the bombers, but then peeled away after a few ineffectual machine-gun bursts. (The eighteen-bomber formations could between them concentrate the fire-power of two hundred heavy machine-guns on attacking fighters.)

After Hitler's evening war conference Göring reported to Milch, 'The Führer is insisting, and he says he has to insist on this as spokesman of the German people, that whatever the cost these mass attacks by day have got to be stopped.' He added: 'After this daylight raid on Frankfurt I heard people say, "We all saw the enemy aircraft over Frankfurt, but not one German fighter was to be seen, far or wide."' Milch tried to defend Galland's squadrons, but Göring interrupted him: 'A large number of the fighter pilots are pussy-foots!' Milch persisted that Göring's harsh criticism upset the pilots sorely. 'They don't need to get upset,' snorted Göring. 'They only need to close in to four hundred instead of a thousand yards; they only need to shoot down eighty instead of twenty bombers, just once. Then their blues will be gone, and I'll doff my cap right respectfully to them. . . .'[33]

It annoyed him that the pilots were regarded as national heroes; he believed they bore a large measure of the blame. 'The German public doesn't care two hoots about the fighter casualties,' he reminded Galland. 'Try going to Frankfurt and asking what impression your fighter losses that day left on them. They'll tell you: "You can't be serious! Look at our *thousands* of dead!"'[34] He admitted the daylight battles were more costly because of the Thunderbolt escort; but no position was wholly impossible. 'The most famous and important battles have been decided by attacks launched from the most hopeless positions,' he reminded his generals. 'In one legendary battle Alexander carried his troops to victory through crumbling river beds, slippery mudbanks and across heights dominated by the enemy; it was *because* the position was so bad that the enemy never believed his attack could succeed.' It was not an encouraging argument.

Two days after Frankfurt Göring undertook his first air journey for some years, as he returned from speaking to an assembly of gauleiters in Posen. As his aircraft droned in stately luxury across Central Europe towards southern Germany, his imagination came into play. For four hours he imagined himself trapped in an American bomber's gun turret, as hundreds of Luftwaffe fighters attacked from every quarter without respite; after an hour his guns were useless, their last ammunition gone. By the time Göring landed near the Obersalzberg he believed he knew just how an American airman would feel, *if* the fighter onslaught could be maintained for hours on end: 'There's no squadron that could stand it, even if they were lions at heart!'[35]

Next day he inquired of Galland how long his fighters could keep firing. Galland replied, 'Seven minutes!' Göring calculated out loud that a fighter pilot could therefore land to rearm and refuel several times in one battle: 'So if you really roll up your shirtsleeves, you can each engage the enemy three times or so during a four-hour battle?' Galland agreed. Göring continued, 'I herewith order: three times!' Thus Hermann Göring must go down in history as the architect of a victory which Galland's fighters shortly secured, when the American squadrons returned to Schweinfurt on 14 October—a day the Americans now remember as Black Thursday.

# LIFE-OR-DEATH QUESTIONS

## (*October 1943*)

It was convenient to blame Udet for the technical backwardness of the Luftwaffe in the autumn of 1943. In one outburst on 9 October Göring said of him, 'If I could only find some explanation of what Udet really thought he was up to! He led our aviation into absolute chaos. If he were still alive today I would say to him, "You are the destroyer of the German air force!" '[1] Behind Milch's back Göring readily added him to his list of culprits, and even tried to blame him for not having copied the Mosquito ('I told him I would quite shamelessly copy anything the enemy had built that was any good, without any hesitation. Let Churchill say what he liked!').[2] Referring to the bomber production in Milch's new Reich Defence Programme, Göring complained: 'It drops lower and lower! During this October we get 410 bombers a month; and by next October it will be 266! What on earth is the field marshal thinking of?'*

Nobody defended the absent field marshal. 'I want to see an end to this perpetual business of fraud,' Göring seethed. 'It's even worse than in Udet's time.' And moments later he erupted again when Colonel Diesing, his technical officer, claimed that daylight bombing of Britain was difficult because German aircraft had no rear gun turrets.† 'I am bound to ask,' retorted Göring, 'what these people have in their brain-boxes. They knew about the enemy's rear turrets, but the thought of building our own never occurred to them. We really ought to send for Reidenbach this very evening and stand him in front of a firing squad.' Something inside him snapped. Within seconds Göring had indeed ordered the arrest of Udet's chief lieutenants Reidenbach, Ploch and Tschersich by the Gestapo. 'With every day that passes I recognize their crimes more clearly. There will be a summary court martial, not a

---

* In fact Milch's programme showed an *increase* of 169 bombers a month by October 1944.[3]

† The Heinkel 177 bomber had always had a rear gun turret. Colonel Diesing was to succeed Milch as 'Chief of Technical Air Armament' in June 1944.

lengthy trial. If their failure is proven, they will be shot.' Göring added: 'The field marshal talks in every conference of "having people shot"! But when I say it, I mean it, and it will be ruthlessly carried out. I don't just mouth threats—I mean them!'[4]

Milch's Reich Defence Programme was therefore unacceptable. Göring ordered Milch to reinforce the bomber arm quickly for a resumption of the campaign against Britain.[5] Over-all bomber production, including the new Junkers types, was to be increased from the present 410 per month to 600 and then 900 as soon as possible. The field marshal believed this change of emphasis was all wrong: 'It is precisely in these coming months that we must avoid weakening the Reich Defence Programme,' he warned Göring on the fourteenth. 'Otherwise the enemy will smash all our bomber production anyway, and that's an end to your Junkers 188 and 388 production.'[6] He believed they would find themselves falling back onto their original target figures eventually, and suggested instead that they develop ways of packing more explosives into the Me 410 bomb-bay—for example by producing bombs cast of special explosives, dispensing with a bomb-casing altogether. 'It is to be a pure terror-bomb!' Milch explained.[7]

The second week of October 1943 brought crisis to the American squadrons stationed in England. On the eighth, attacking Bremen and Vegesack, they lost thirty bombers, with major damage to over a score more; on the ninth they attacked Marienburg and Anklam in East Prussia, where ninety per cent of the Focke-Wulf factories were devastated. Göring exclaimed, 'We cannot continue like this!' He asked Speer to start work on six bomb-proof concrete factories for fighter production.[8] For the first time that day Galland's squadrons had operated multiple sorties: every aircraft had been brought in, including some from France, and some had flown two or three sorties against the Americans. Twenty-eight of the 378 bombers had been destroyed, but it was still not good enough for Hitler or Göring. Galland, who illicitly joined in the battle himself, could see why: a few weak single- and twin-engined fighter units appeared, opening fire at too great a range, making generally irresolute attacks and then breaking away too early. He now agreed with Göring's low opinion of fighter morale.[9]

On the tenth the Americans bombed the centre of Münster, in revenge for the casualties they had suffered. The Germans destroyed thirty of the 236 bombers, a much higher percentage. In three days, therefore, eighty-eight American bombers and nearly nine hundred men had been lost. This was vivid justification of Milch's emphasis on fighter defence. 'The Americans certainly know their business in these daylight attacks,' he conceded to Göring. 'At Marienburg not one bomb hit the town—every one landed on the target area.'[10] While he congratulated the Luftwaffe on its three great victories, he warned: 'There is no place in Germany proof against air attack.'[11]

Göring would dearly have loved to bomb America, and on 14 October he again examined with Messerschmitt the Me 264 project—a bomber capable, the professor said, of carrying several tons of bombs to the mid-West of America. 'If only we could do that!' sighed Göring. 'If only we could chuck a few bombs at them, so that they had to have a blackout over there. . . .'[12]

This day, 14 October, was Black Thursday. Earlier, three thousand American airmen had been briefed for a renewed assault on Schweinfurt. Morale in the bomber squadrons was already at crisis point. The medical diary of one unit which had suffered heavily in the earlier attack noted, 'The mental attitude and morale of the crews is the lowest that has yet been observed.' When the briefing for the attack began, 'The mention of the word "Schweinfurt" shocked the crews completely.' No estimate was announced of the number of German fighters based along the route. The medical officer checked and found this omission was intentional: 'The entire German fighter force of 1,100 fighter aircraft was based within eighty-five miles of the course. The implications were obvious. As I went round to the crews checking equipment, sandwiches, coffee, etc., the crews were scared and it was obvious that many doubted that they would return.'[13]

As the three hundred American bombers crossed the German frontier and the Thunderbolts withdrew, the first German fighter squadrons closed in. An awesome air battle ensued. The German tactics were so expertly coordinated that the Americans suspected that the mission had been betrayed by an agent in Britain. Many fighters had now been equipped with improvised 21-centimetre rocket launchers: 'If a squadron or even only a flight of aircraft closes in in tight formation and all their rocket launchers open fire,' Milch had been promised a month before, 'then something's got to catch it!'[14] As wave after wave of single-engined and twin-engined fighters attacked with rockets, 20-millimetre cannon and even bombs, the powerful formations of Flying Fortresses fell apart, crippled bombers slewed out of station and were mercilessly destroyed. It was the bloodiest battle in the American air force's history, with the entire German fighter force, day and night, hurled against the attackers. Galland later said his men had flown eight hundred sorties.[15]

The short-range fighters landed, refuelled and rejoined the battle, giving the enemy no respite as Göring had insisted. At 2.40 pm the remnants of the American First Air Division started its bomb run on Schweinfurt. Ten minutes later Göring was told of the beginning of the attack. He took the news calmly: the Americans had been defeated once before at Schweinfurt, and they had been prevented from inflicting severe damage because the local flak commander had switched on fog generators in good time.[16] Then he was stabbed by the sudden thought: 'Would the man have switched them on this time?' He relaxed, confident that the generators had been switched on. But they had not, and this time the damage was severe.* By 2.57 pm the last American plane had unloaded its bombs. The ball-bearing factories had been heavily damaged.

As the bombers turned for home, 160 fighter aircraft attacked simultaneously from every angle, delivering the most concentrated onslaught yet. The running fight was kept up all the way to the Channel coast and beyond. By early evening the battle was over: south-western Germany was strewn with the wrecks of sixty Flying Fortresses; seventeen more had been irreparably damaged, and many of the others carried dead crew members as they struggled back to England. Göring telephoned Hitler to report his airmen's finest hour.[18] But Hitler was dining with Speer; Speer telephoned—with some difficulty—the works foreman of one of the ball-bearing factories, and was able to report to Hitler, not without some relish one suspects, that the factories had in fact suffered grievous damage.[19]

The hindrance to arms production turned out to be less than Speer feared. He and Milch had already spent several weeks devising means of economizing on ball- and roller-bearings; they had discovered that the army alone had hoarded enough ball-bearings to make good the entire losses of the previous attack on Schweinfurt, and Milch suspected that the Luftwaffe must somewhere have the same kind of hoard.[20] Speer later wrote that not one tank, aircraft or other product less was manufactured because of the shortage of ball-bearings.[21]

Schweinfurt was not immediately recognized for the tactical victory that it was; fearing further attacks on this scale, Hitler ordered that the de-

---

* The Reichsmarschall later told Milch why the flak commander had not switched on the fog generators in time: 'The idiot decided to test the atmospheric humidity first! I can only say, every time I hear of enemy bombers approaching I tremble at the thought of the follies that can happen—at the damage that these God-forsaken idiots can do.' With wry humour he added, 'I am going to round up the most monumental idiots I can find, by circularizing every branch, and add them to my staff, so that by consultation with them I can get some expert idea of what this or that idiot in the field might get up to.'[17]

fence of the Reich was to take precedence over all other needs.[22] Speer noted the Führer's demands for more flak, more fighters and more 200-centimetre searchlight production. Hitler also demanded that fighter aircraft should be equipped with the latest armament, particularly the very heavy 50-millimetre KWK—an anti-tank gun normally mounted on armoured cars, with a 21-shot magazine.[23] Galland was bitterly opposed to this, and it soon became a *cause célèbre* similar to the 30-millimetre cannon and the use of the Me 262 as a bomber.[24] On the day before Schweinfurt, Speer and Milch had still been arguing over the increased fighter production programme, but now Milch's planners confidently began studying a new programme, '225', whereby, while increasing bomber production, they could also bring fighter production up to five thousand a month.[25] This study was short-lived as Speer's ministry rejected it as totally impracticable, and Milch advised his planners, 'The [supply] difficulties for programme "224" are already great enough, according to the minister.'[26]

By night the Luftwaffe still had to contend with the RAF's increasingly sophisticated electronic warfare and deception tactics. In the latter part of October they dropped 1,700 tons of bombs on Hanover and 1,100 tons on Leipzig. The basic problem of beating the metal-foil jamming had still not been solved. Göring conceded his admiration for the British electronic devices: 'In the field of radar they must have the world's greatest genius,' he said. 'They have the geniuses and we have the nincompoops. . . . The British would never have dared use the metal foil here if they had not worked out a hundred per cent what the antidote is.' He added, 'I hate the rogues like the plague, but in one respect I am obliged to doff my cap to them. After this war's over I'm going to buy myself a British radio set, as a token of my regard for their high-frequency work. Then at last I'll have the luxury of owning something that has always worked.'[27]

Paradoxically, Göring's popularity with the public was still undeniable. In the last week of October he toured the fighter organization in the west, and wherever his Mercedes halted in the Ruhr and Rhineland cities he was mobbed and cheered by the populace. For the generals who accompanied him it was mystifying. In a private speech to them at fighter defence headquarters in Holland, Göring emotionally exclaimed: 'I am human too, and I would have understood if these people who stand among ruins—nothing but rubble to left and right!—and who have put up with over a hundred air raids, had taken the chance of a passing visit by one of the dignitaries who is actually responsible for this mess and had . . . well, not exactly chucked rotten eggs at me, but at least put on a sour face or hollered "You fat slob!" at me.' He smiled wanly: 'Nor would I have intervened if they had!'[28]

This public acclaim strengthened Göring in his contempt for his officers. By the morning of 23 October, as hundreds of fighter pilots gathered in one of the hangars at Arnhem to hear him speak, huge fires were sweeping Kassel, devastated by 1,800 tons of RAF bombs during the night. Nearly six thousand civilians had died between dusk and dawn. Göring put it to the pilots that they were 'pussy-foots, and some of you somewhat more'. He angrily reminded them how, when he had withdrawn fighter squadrons to the defence of the Reich, they had assured him, 'Just let those four-engined rattletraps try coming! What a party that will be—what a thrashing! Well, the party's over and still they keep coming. Look at it this way: the German public has suffered indescribably from the enemy bombing terror, by day and night. At night-time the public can just about understand the problems of making contact with the bombers; but what it will never understand is what problem there is by day, particularly in clear weather. I am not going to single out one squadron, or one flight, as particularly bad. But of one thing you must rest assured: I will not have cowards in my force—I intend to winkle every one of them out!'[29]

Milch did not believe it right to blame the fighter pilots. Schweinfurt and several of the RAF night battles had shown what these officers were capable of given proper equipment and adequate leadership. It was in the Luftwaffe's higher command that he saw the responsibility for the long-term planning errors which had reduced the Luftwaffe to its present defensive stance. He showed the new programme study for '225', the five thousand fighter per month programme, to Göring next day and urged him to secure support from Hitler; above all the industry must be protected from the drastic recruitment planned by Hitler for the next three months—no fewer than 60,000 to be culled from the 435,000 'reserved' German workers alleged by Speer to be employed in the air industry.[30] Milch was convinced Speer's staff had faked this figure—he believed that the correct figure was nearer 250,000.[31] But in the struggle for labour the Luftwaffe consistently lost, as Speer could use his local armaments inspectorates to transfer workers from a purely air force factory to one manufacturing army equipment.[32]

Göring next saw Hitler on 27 October, but totally failed to persuade him to halt the recruiting. Hitler would not believe the air industry had fewer than five million workers (the real figure was 1,920,000).[33] The other service C-in-Cs present evidently related moving stories of their own plights. The rest of the discussion dissolved into an exchange of humorous anecdotes about manpower wastage in the Services. Milch learned this from Göring next day, and wrote in his diary: 'Big conference at Karinhall. Terrible row. [Göring has] bad conscience as he got nowhere with the Führer.'* On the twenty-ninth he informed his ministry heads, 'A clear decision has now been reached. The recruitment goes on.'[35] Sauckel had promised to procure three million Italian prisoners for German industry, but these proved unreliable: they volunteered for military service, were therefore transported back to Italy, where they melted away into the mountains. The workers who remained were given kid-glove treatment until Milch found out. He told Göring, 'I have ordered that they are to be beaten if they do not work.'[36]

Of one thing Hitler had persuaded Göring in particular: that whether or not the German lines in Russia were pushed back a few hundred miles was immaterial compared with whether by the spring of 1944 Germany would be sufficiently invulnerable in the west to prevent the establishment of an Allied second front. 'This is where the air force is of decisive importance,' Hitler had emphasized.[37] If once an enemy army set foot on French soil, it would spell the end for Germany. This was an infinitely greater danger than any attack on their cities.

In vain Field Marshal Milch reminded Göring that it was not the cities as such but the armaments industries they had to defend—the very basis of their military strength: 'I am thinking, in this context, of the *real* life-or-death question, apart from the eastern front—namely whether next spring the home front will be adequately protected when the American long-range escort fighter appears!'

Göring impatiently replied, 'Even if every German city is razed to the ground, the German people will still survive! . . . I am not against the defence of the Reich—it was I who buttressed the Luftwaffe on the home front, it was I who recalled the front-line squadrons to the Reich against the bitterest opposition.' He repeated that there were two real dangers for Germany: the first was when one fine day they heard, 'The Russians (Army Group So-and-so) have entered Silesia, with another army group in East Prussia; one of them is massing on the river Vistula, the other is coming up the river Oder.' And, 'Then there is danger Number Two. And that is Britain.' This was why he felt justified in regarding bombers as an essential arm of the Reich's defence. 'I have to start attacking them over there,' exclaimed Göring. 'For one whole year the British public suffered air warfare just like us now. But for two years

---

* The record of the conference shows Göring berating Milch: 'All of a sudden I can't trust anybody. I have had my fingers burnt too often! You must not try to intoxicate me with figures the way you tried before.'[34]

now they have had no air raids.' He continued, 'The moment the British try and invade France to establish a second front, I will not leave a single fighter aircraft to the defence of the Reich; that same day every single aircraft which is airworthy will be sent forward, and the Reich itself will not have an aircraft to its name—come hell or high water.'

'If the British once get a foothold on our coast,' he summarized, 'that would be fatal. For them to bomb German cities for two or three days would be unpleasant—but not fatal.'[38]

# 'WHO NEEDS MESSERSCHMITT?'

## (*October–December 1943*)

Nobody now doubted that the Messerschmitt 262 jet aircraft was vital
for reasserting Germany's air superiority, but there soon arose controversy on how it should be employed. The fighter squadrons' commander
Galland repeatedly asserted, 'It will give us such a lead that even a few
would make an enormous difference to us.'[1] But Hitler, who had still
not seen it, envisaged it as a fighter-bomber, and he hoped it would
play a decisive role in defeating the Allied invasion in the coming spring.

In October 1943 he defined to Göring the critical phase of the coming
invasion as the first hours of confusion on the landing beaches, when
the area would be choked with tanks, guns and troops: in those hours
the fast Me 262s should make their sensational first appearance—as
high-speed bombers.[2] They need not carry much—'Even if they carry
only a couple of 150-pounders I should be pleased enough', Hitler
explained—and they would not need to aim precisely; they would merely
streak along the landing beaches at low level, hurling bombs into the
midst of the disembarking troops and equipment. Even a few hours'
delay forced upon the enemy could be vital, for it would give Hitler
time to move up his reserves. Göring agreed, but thought to himself,
'*I don't know if we'll have the Me 262 by then!*' Accordingly, he said
out loud that they would also try to do this with their existing fighter-
bombers.[3] He undertook to discuss the bomber version with Milch
and Messerschmitt.

The first one hundred of the pilot series were currently due for completion by May 1944, and mass production would begin at Regensburg
and Augsburg in November 1944. But Professor Messerschmitt maintained his demands for more skilled labour, more draughtsmen and
more jigmakers and by mid-October 1943 Göring very properly enter-
tained doubts about whether the jet aircraft would ever enter squadron
service: 'I would not like the Me 262 to enter service half a year too
late,' he told Milch.[4] It was a prophetic utterance.

The Air Ministry had done its best to satisfy Messerschmitt's demands, even to the extent of winding up rival companies and giving him their labour force.[5] Messerschmitt still asked for more. At Neuburg airfield he tackled Göring in person and demanded four thousand new workers: 'I ought to warn you that the Me 262 is going to be three months late as it is; and if you don't give me the workers, half a year!'[6] When Göring repeated this to Hitler, the latter 'almost had a fit', as he told Milch. Hitler decreed that the workers would again have to be found from some other aircraft company.

Milch disapproved very strongly of the professor's tactics: 'He did not report anything to *us* about any delay,' he complained to Göring. He suggested that the delays were actually caused by the company's having concentrated too much effort on the piston-engined Me 209. When Göring tamely defended the professor, Milch angrily interrupted him, 'Herr Reichsmarschall, who needs him? We have far better designers than Messerschmitt in the fields in which he works.'[7]

It must be said that at this stage nobody criticized the Führer's inclination to regard the Me 262 as a potential fighter-bomber—Messerschmitt least of all, when Milch and Göring travelled down to see him a few days later.[8] Before they toured the sprawling factory buildings and hangars the Reichsmarschall mentioned Hitler's requirement. Messerschmitt exclaimed, 'Herr Reichsmarschall, from the very outset we have provided for the fitting of two bomb pylons so that it can drop bombs—either one 500-kilo or two 250s!' And he volunteered, 'But it could also carry a 1,000-kilo bomb, or two 500s.' Asked by Göring how long this modification would take, the professor responded: 'That is relatively easily done—say, fourteen days.'*[9]

Before they left Göring and Milch were shown the newly completed sixth prototype in flight—the first to have a retractable nose-wheel—and a Me 163 rocket-propelled interceptor, a suitable chariot for a suicide squadron if ever there was one.

Two days later they visited the Junkers works, where the jet engines were under manufacture.[10] This important production line was soon to be evacuated to an army barracks at Zittau, and mass production was to begin in January. Göring urged them to find underground tunnel space if possible, and to provide realistic fire-fighting equipment meantime for the surface factories: 'Experience shows that however great the devastation of a factory by high-explosive bombs, the damage can always be repaired, even if the entire crop falls on every single machine tool; but where once the fires have ravaged, nothing can ever be made

* A shorthand record was taken of their discussion, on Göring's insistence.

good.'* Before they left Dessau they were also shown the prototypes of the latest Junkers bomber designs—the Ju 388 (essentially a Ju 188 powered by two BMW 801 double-row radial engines)[12] and a heavy jet bomber, the Ju 287, powered by six Jumo 004 engines; with its forward-swept wings, this bomber was designed to approach the speed of sound. Its prototype made its first test-flight eight months later.

Finally, Göring and Milch toured the Arado works, now in the midst of evacuation to Landshut.[13] The new site would start jet bomber production in September 1944, with twenty-six thousand workers. The first hundred Ar 234s would be manufactured by the end of 1944. Five had already been assembled, with a top speed of five hundred miles per hour and a range of a thousand miles; but the project had been set back some weeks by the crash of the first Ar 234 some weeks before, killing their best test pilot; and the present dispersal would cost them another two months.[14] Milch insisted that the original production programme should be not only maintained but increased, and the company duly undertook to manufacture two hundred by the end of 1944 and a thousand by mid-1945, given the necessary materials and manpower.[15]

We can well visualize with what optimism Göring concluded his tour of the jet-engine and aircraft factories. Yet a few days of well-aimed saturation bombing could destroy all this. He anxiously initiated a major campaign to 'get my entire outfit underground', as he put it. While Air Ministry officials scoured the countryside for suitable empty caves and tunnels, Göring addressed the gauleiters on 8 November, appealing to them to co-operate and outlining his plans for the future: 'Britain has already suffered air warfare once, in the most violent manner,' he recalled. 'Like a true Germanic country, she clenched her teeth and took it on the chin.' But for many months she had been left alone, while for the German public raids had become a common occurrence. All the greater would be the anguish for the British when his reprisal raids began, before the end of 1943. London would not be the only target: 'It is always better to wipe out a town of a hundred thousand citizens completely, than to make a dent in a giant city!' He spoke of the six tons of bombs the He 177 could carry, and of the 'Trialen' explosive in them, twice as powerful as the British explosives.[16]

The cloud on his horizon was the Me 262. By late autumn it had fallen several months behind schedule just as he had feared. In January

---

* Speer said much the same a few days later: 'If today we only had to deal with blast effects, things would not be half so bad.' And Dr Werner, speaking of the Schweinfurt raid, added: 'Where there's fire, it's all over: the spindles burn out and you might just as well throw the machines on the junk heap.'[11]

1944 Messerschmitt was to write a lengthy memorandum denying responsibility for this and blaming the Air Ministry;[17] this was less than fair. Since as recently as June 1943 he had campaigned against replacing the Me 209 with the Me 262; the 209 was, he then claimed, ninety-five per cent ready for production.[18] Despite Milch's embargo, he continued to invest skilled labour and draughtsmen in the 'dead' 209 at the expense of the jet aircraft against the outspoken objections of his own colleagues.*[19] Milch recalled how many aircraft had gone sour in the past—the Me 110, the Me 210, the Me 264 and the Me 309; and even the Me 410 had not owed much to Messerschmitt. But then again, where would the Luftwaffe have been in 1939 without the Me 109 fighter? 'It is unfortunately very hard to tell in advance with him whether he has another hit or another miss,' he sighed.[21] The upshot had been that late in September Milch cautiously asked his staff 'while avoiding any misunderstanding, to look at the question whether we really need the 209 in view of its performance and delivery dates'.[22]

The expert opinion, especially of Galland, was unanimous: they did not need the Me 209. It had still not even flown by the end of October, although it was due to enter mass production in June 1944. Now Messerschmitt was demanding a thousand more draughtsmen, and even then could not guarantee to deliver the fighter before early 1946.[23] Göring's technical officer stated, 'The only person who will fight against cancellation of the 209 is Messerschmitt. But all his colleagues realize they are only obstructing themselves with it, and that they will never get a breathing space for sensible projects if they go on like that.'[24] It was calamitous that the Me 209, sheltered by the injured pride of one brilliant aircraft designer with the ear of Hitler, should have blocked the path of the jet fighter for so long. In mid-November the professor tactlessly complained to the Führer's special representative about the 'superfluous' aircraft under development, which were wasting manpower; this was the last straw for Milch: 'If Messerschmitt complains he has too many different types,' he snarled, 'I can only say, we have tried to take one after the other away from him.' He ordered all work on the Me 209 piston-engined fighter to cease, and secured Göring's approval for this a few days later.[25]

Albert Speer refused to accept responsibility for the new aircraft programme planned by Milch, designated '225'. At that time, the prevailing

---

* Deputy Chairman Fritz Seiler chided Messerschmitt in a letter in July 1943: 'Milch . . . was also able to refer to the fact that you, the entire board and I were emphatic during one of the big conferences on the 262 that the 262 can only enter service rapidly if we *concentrate* on that aircraft.'[20]

programme was '223', with a target of 3,700 single- and 1,194 twin-engined fighters a month in 1945, plus 720 bombers; the post-Hamburg Reich Defence Programme, '224', issued in the second week of October, had raised these targets to 4,160 single- and 1,256 twin-engined fighters, plus 820 bombers by 1945.[26] Göring had ordered him to place greater emphasis still on bombers, and the resulting 'revenge' programme, '225' aimed at 4,585 single- and 1,264 twin-engined fighters and 930 bombers (Göring had called for 900) by 1945. Fighter production would be marginally lower during 1944, but not because of the increase in bombers—(Milch said, 'Whatever I am ordered, I would not dream of cutting back on fighters')—so much as because of a shortage of suitable engines.

Speer would not even consider the new programme: 'It's pointless,' he objected. 'These are Utopian figures!' He added, 'I refuse to discuss anything over and above programme "224". If the Luftwaffe wants to go ahead and adopt programme "225", nobody will stop it; but I must state officially here and now that the necessary supplies will not be forthcoming.'[27]

Milch patiently asked his office to prepare a new study,[28] the first of many, in an attempt to reconcile the two positions. His friendship with Speer was saved in this month of strain by an unexpected drought: by mid-November it was recognized that the drought would be so severe that during 1944 there would be less aluminium available than ever before. This new limiting factor was disclosed by Speer to Milch in mid-November and Milch had no option but to accept it.[29]

The drought was the worst for ninety years in Germany. The loss of hydro-electric power would cause considerable production losses of nitrogen, high-grade steels, synthetic fuels and aluminium; moreover, the Danube was so low that oil barges from Rumania could carry only 300 instead of 700 tons each; in November the amount transported would be 80,000 tons compared with 144,000 tons in October, and there were 323,000 tons waiting in Rumania to be shipped to Germany.[30] Of Reich aluminium production estimated at 40,000 tons a month for the next few months, the Luftwaffe would now be allocated 22,000 tons a month. This appeared to rule out programme '225' altogether.[31]

On the night of 18 November Sir Arthur Harris, C-in-C of Bomber Command, began his attempt to 'wreck Berlin from end to end'. He followed this raid with an even heavier attack on the night of the twenty-second. Munitions and Air Ministries both suffered; soon Speer's building was blazing fiercely, and the neighbouring Army Armaments Office also caught fire. The night's casualties were 3,500 dead and 400,000 homeless. On the following night the British bombers again attacked Berlin in force.[32]

At the same time, the recruiting of fresh soldiers from Milch's factories was increased. Milch watched these developments with consternation. At the end of October he had again reminded Göring that the army had eight million men in uniform: 'But how many of those are really at the front, as combat troops? Certainly far fewer than twenty-five or thirty per cent.'[33] On 8 November Hitler finally agreed that there was an imbalance between front-line and rear areas, and he ordered the High Command to investigate; he invited Admiral Dönitz and the Reichsmarschall to headquarters on the twenty-fourth to discuss ways of increasing the combat strength.[34] Göring asked Milch to brief him.[35] Milch again claimed that of 8.3 million soldiers, less than two millions were actually at the front: 'On the eastern front,' he claimed, 'there are only 260,000 soldiers.' Given the chance he believed he could round up two million soldiers and add them to the front line, without any need to raid the armaments factories at home.[36]

In the event, precisely the opposite happened. So weak was Göring's position—particularly now that Berlin was suffering again—that he not only failed to repeat Milch's statistics to Hitler, but declared he was convinced a large number of front-line soldiers could be obtained from the Luftwaffe's rear areas.[37] This was the Luftwaffe's fate: its commander-in-chief was reluctant to state its requirements to the Führer with the necessary forcefulness; while Milch, who shared none of Göring's inhibitions, was steadfastly prevented by Göring from confronting Hitler directly.

Milch—like Speer—had always cultivated good relations with Heinrich Himmler, chief of the SS; they had always exchanged birthday greetings and once Milch had said, 'I prefer working with him than with other military authorities.'[38] It was probably just the admiration of one organization man for another; both had created from nothing a politically conscious fighting élite.[39]

When the agitation among the legions of foreign workers in his factories threatened production, Milch was able to refer to his association with Himmler:

I spoke to Himmler recently about this, and told him his main task must be to see to the protection of German industry if unrest breaks out among this foreign scum. If, for instance, there is a mutiny at X, an officer with a couple of men, or a lieutenant with thirty troops, must appear in the factory and let fly with their machine-guns into the mob. The object is to lay out as many people as possible, if mutinies break out. This is the order I have issued, even if the people are our own foreign workers. . . . Then every tenth man is to be picked out, and every tenth man will be shot in front of the rest.

He generally favoured giving Heinrich Himmler close control over their vital armaments factories, as was the SS chief's desire. 'Why should we stand in his way?' Milch asked his staff. 'Speer is letting him in too.'[40] (Needless to say, none of Milch's draconic proposals was ever carried out.)

On 20 November, after they had both attended the Führer's speech to four thousand officer cadets at the Century Hall in Breslau, Milch invited Himmler to his nearby estate, 'Althofdürr'. Like Hitler, the SS chief possessed the most punctilious manners and charm, and he conversed at length with Milch's mother, who had lived here since the destruction of their fine home in Königsallee in a recent Berlin air raid. Milch poured out his heart to Himmler about the difficulties with Göring, and the urgency of support for the Reich's defence.[41] Himmler promised support.

For purposes which we can readily surmise, Göring had ordered Milch to prepare at short notice a display of the most modern aircraft and weapons for Hitler at Insterburg airfield. The display was to include both jet aircraft projects, the flying bomb and the two guided anti-shipping missiles Hs 293 and Fritz-X, and film of the new panoramic radar sets and the 'Korfu' receiver stations tracking the RAF bombers by their radar emissions during a night attack on Berlin a few days before.[42] Hitler agreed to come with his staff on 26 November; Himmler also attended.

Göring deliberately snubbed Milch at the display and introduced his own technical officers to Hitler as those to whom credit was due.[43] Milch was speechless with anger. More was to come: the Reichsmarschall took the printed programme out of Milch's hands and began introducing each aircraft to Hitler, working his finger down the list. He was unaware that one of the fighter prototypes had had a mishap at Rechlin and there was thus one aircraft missing; the remaining aircraft had each been moved along one place in the line. Milch saw what was going to happen and took his revenge: he stepped tactfully back into the second row. Where the missing fighter should have been, there was now a medium bomber. Göring announced it to Hitler as the single-seater; for several more exhibits this farce continued until the Führer decided that enough was enough, and pointed out Göring's error.

The next mishap occurred as they inspected the Me 262 jet fighter. The Führer repeated his inquiry: could it carry bombs? Before the others could stop him, Messerschmitt stepped forward and said that it could carry one 1,000-kilo or two 500-kilo bombs without trouble. Hitler thanked him: 'This at last is the aircraft I have been demanding for years! Here it is—but nobody recognized it!' Colonel Petersen later commented, 'Thus the bacillus was planted.' Even now nobody protested, least of all Göring, who had only a few months before scorned Milch's interim efforts to fill the high-speed bomber gap: 'With the high-speed bomber you gentlemen took the easy way out. You slung a bomb under the fastest fighter, and there's your high-speed bomber! But a fighter is no bomber.'[44] Long of tongue, and short of memory, the Reichsmarschall now approved a modification of the jet fighter project which, in time, was to set it back by many months.

Partly for security reasons (the need to avoid compromising the jet engine in a crash over enemy territory) and partly because of his desire to promote the fighter version, Milch had always urged caution on jet bomber development. In May Major Herrmann had asked for the Me 262 as a bomber, too, but Milch had answered evasively: 'First we will build it as a fighter, and then look for something answering your purpose.'[45] Colonel Peltz had echoed Herrmann: 'The jet bomber would be so superior, if it came today, that the enemy would never bring it down.' In July he asked for a hundred of the Ar 234 jet bombers as soon as possible and regretted that the reconnaissance version was planned for release first, as one crash in Britain would compromise its secrets.[46] Milch knew that a host of technical problems— special bombsights, strengthened landing gear and improved visibility —would have to be solved first and might take years of work. When Colonel Diesing advised him that even Hitler now envisaged jet engines more as a power plant for bombers Milch sharply disagreed.[47] However, a few days later Göring also described the jet bomber as 'a point of extreme urgency' for their research and development; he was thinking of both a small bomber and one with a two-ton bomb-load, and he told Milch: 'A positive effort is to be made on the development of a jet bomber.'[48] At the time of Insterburg one thing was certain: the Me 262 was not capable of carrying any bombs, however small.

Another fiasco occurred at Insterburg when Hitler stepped in front of the static flying-bomb exhibit. He asked the group leader of the Luftwaffe research unit at Peenemünde when the weapon would be ready; this man, thinking only of the development progress, replied, 'The end of March 1944.' (Even then some weeks would be necessary before the weapon could go into operation). But March was bad enough, and General Bodenschatz hissed to Petersen, 'Who was the pessimist who arranged this display?'[49]

After it was over, Göring suggested they watch each aircraft fly past from the roof of the control tower. Hitler agreed, but invited only Milch and his adjutant to accompany him, as he wanted an 'expert commentary' on each plane. Göring stayed below. The Me 262, which swept past several times, made the greatest impression on him. Then he returned to headquarters, having demonstratively congratulated Milch on the exhibits. Milch hurried to his aircraft and took off for Berlin. As they curved back over the airfield, he saw that the Reichsmarschall had returned from the station; he ordered his pilot to fly towards Göring's group at zero feet, and secured some satisfaction from their response.

The flying-bomb project had indeed fallen about two months behind schedule. In October Hitler had asked when the three secret 'reprisal weapons'—the A4 rocket, the flying-bomb and a huge underground gun battery with multiple barrels four hundred feet long aimed at London—would open fire.[50] The army were saying their A4 rocket would be ready by the end of the year; the Luftwaffe were striving to achieve the same date with their flying-bomb, but General Jodl disputed this: 'You will trail a long way behind.' 'That may well be so,' Milch admitted; the rocket project had been under way for thirteen years already, compared with the flying-bomb's fifteen months.

Milch's fears were not without substance. By mid-December the ninety-six catapult launching sites for the weapon had been completed in France, along the whole coastline facing England; and in March the first two of the planned bombproof bunkers for launching the flying-bomb would also be complete; throughout the country caves and tunnels were being extended and reinforced to house the dumps for rockets and flying-bombs.[51] But the mass production of the bomb was now running about two months behind schedule, the weapon having encountered a series of difficulties during trials. The compass and dive-mechanism were faulty, the auto-pilot was imperfect and some of the bombs broke up in mid-air because of faulty spot-welding. In September ninety bombs should have been test-launched, but only fourteen had been tried out, with only thirty-five more in October. The RAF attack on Peenemünde had set them back about three weeks, and the mass attack on Kassel on 22 October had forced the evacuation of the Fieseler works manufacturing the pilot series to another site, where there was no compressed air, no electricity, and no telephones or transport. The full-scale mass-production was scheduled to begin at the Volkswagen works at the end of October; but to reach the target of five thousand a month the works needed 250 more workers and seven hundred more machine tools.[52]

When November came it was estimated that up to 150 more flying-bombs still had to be tested, but that this could be completed by early February 1944.[53] Long before then, however, further faults disrupted the flying-bomb programme. Meantime Himmler, impressed by what he had seen, afforded the flying-bomb project one whole tunnel in 'Central Works', a vast underground complex being adapted by the SS and tens of thousands of concentration camp prisoners near Nordhausen; here the weapon would eventually have a bombproof production line independent of Volkswagen.

On the day after Insterburg Göring promised Hitler that the Luftwaffe would execute a heavy bombing attack on London, in revenge for the continued raids on Berlin.[54] To his generals he disclosed that the Führer had made it a point of honour to carry out this operation within two weeks, but he would consider waiting a further ten days should the full moon promise better results.[55] He ordered Peltz to scrape together as many Ju 188s, Ju 88s, Me 410s and He 177s as possible over the next few days; Peltz told him, 'Anything that can carry bombs is good enough for me.'

Ideally, the He 177 could carry two 2,500-kilo bombs, of which one hundred had already been stockpiled with a so-called 'England mixture' of Trialen and Hexogen explosives. Göring planned to marshal at least 300 for the first strike, denuding the Italian front if necessary to provide them; these would be followed by 100 aircraft in a second wave and 150 more the next night. The attack, delayed by many circumstances, took place eventually on 22 January, by which time Peltz had assembled 524 bombers (including some He 177s) and fighter-bombers, of which 462 were serviceable. They attacked London in two waves six hours apart, but had some difficulty in finding the capital, for only thirty tons of bombs fell within its boundaries.[56] The wretched He 177 suffered particularly heavy losses. 'They can't even get *that* far,' lamented Hitler afterwards. 'This rattletrap is obviously the worst junk ever to have been manufactured. It is the flying *Panther*—a reference to one of Germany's less fortunate tank designs—'and the *Panther* is the crawling Heinkel!'[57]

The RAF's assault on Berlin was by this time drawing to its climax. Tens of thousands of tons of high explosives and fire bombs were falling on the capital every week, spreading rumours, fear and panic throughout Germany. The RAF's Bomber Command was shrugging off the normally crippling losses inflicted by the night-fighters as though of no consequence. Yet the German air industry was by no means declining: it had manufactured 15,700 aircraft in 1942, and 25,871 in 1943, with a further 18,600 reissued after repairs; the 1944 target was 51,800 aircraft.[58] Milch regretted time and again that this upsurge had not come a year earlier. Even now, there were still those who sought to cut back aircraft production to allow more steel for truck production, more aluminium for A4 rockets, or more manpower for the thousands of frivolous occupations still tolerated in this desperate war situation: at Baden-Baden the casino was still open and fully staffed, while the Me 262 jet-fighter programme was fighting for any kind of labour. The Speer Ministry could not be induced to take any interest in either the Me 262 or the flying-bomb. It was said that Speer's deputy, Saur, would cooperate only if he were given complete control over the projects: 'If he is permitted to manufacture the Fi 103 and the Me 262, he will support them to the hilt; but so long as we are responsible and he is only the supplier, he won't help.'[59]

Milch was forced to admire the excellence of the RAF's night navigation, compared with the Luftwaffe's. The enemy could unerringly find his way to Berlin across hundreds of miles of darkened Europe. 'In Britain seamanship was always their strong point,' he reflected. 'It's a question of getting fixes and dead-reckoning the whole time. It's in their blood. Our aviation emanates, as you know, from the army side. . . . The army has no need to navigate. They read the signposts at the crossroads, and that tells them where to go.'[60] The British moreover could jam every electronic aid used by the Germans, while the Germans did not even know the British wavelengths, as the Air Staff still refused to make aircraft available for radio-reconnaissance missions over the British Isles.[61] Neither the 'Berlin' radar set nor the one hundred 'Panorama' ground radar sets needed for the future fighter-control organization could be ready until late 1944. Meanwhile *'Wasserfall'*, the Luftwaffe's radio-controlled, liquid-fuelled surface-to-air missile, was being blocked by the highly similar A4 rocket.[62] Milch was advised that the A4 was swallowing up so much of the Speer Ministry's capacities that they were having to 'mark time' on every other similar project: 'The importance of [anti-aircraft] rocket research does not seem to have sunk in to them.'[63]

Yet the picture was not entirely black for the Luftwaffe. The Air Ministry had found a partial solution to the Mosquito problem, by fitting Ju 88R night-fighters with the secret 'GM 1' kit, a system for injecting nitrous-oxide gas into the engine, giving it superior high-altitude performance.[64] The RAF bombers were now suffering severe losses at the hands of the night-fighters, and on 20 December massive

RAF attacks began on the 'secret weapon' sites in France, just as Milch had expected. The Do 335 tandem-engined prototype had made its first flights, reaching four hundred miles an hour at ground level, and nearer five hundred at its proper altitude; Milch saw it as the piston-engined high-speed bomber and day-fighter of the future.[65] Only the Speer Ministry's stubbornness stood in his way still, and his bitterness increased with every air raid and with every joint meeting. When Saur announced in January 1944 that the Armaments Ministry was going to accord equal top priority to still further army equipment (an assault-gun programme) Milch angrily rebuked him: 'What's the use! If we cannot make aircraft, it is useless to manufacture such equipment. . . . If we had been a year earlier with our present programme, everything that has happened in Germany in 1943 would never have happened.'[66]

# PART VI

# 'CRASHED IN FLAMES'

*'Air force armament has just not been given the proper treatment and support—that's why things look so black today. If we carry on like this we shall be forced to our knees before the coming year is out. I am convinced of it. Why beat about the bush?'*
—Milch, early in January 1944

# FIGHTER STAFF

## (*January–April 1944*)

On 4 January 1944 Field Marshal Milch attended Hitler's war conference for the first time in many months.[1] He had been summoned to headquarters with Speer and Sauckel to debate with the military the necessary means of raising more than four million new workers for the coming year.[2]

This was the first problem of 1944. The second was the threatening Allied invasion. That evening, Milch and Speer dined alone with Hitler until the early hours of the morning, and listened to the Führer's plans for defeating the Allies. Hitler reminded them of the importance he attached to the new submarine (the Type XXI) and to the jet aircraft, the Me 262 and the Ar 234. Milch in turn reported to his ministry, 'The Führer says, "If I can get these in time I can thwart the invasion." This is the thought which inwardly pre-occupies him the most. He has told this to the Reichsmarschall too.'[3] Within two days the British government had officially released details of its own jet aircraft development, and Milch was urgently recalled by Hitler to discuss this new threat, and the need for the Luftwaffe to develop counter-measures.[4]

The Me 262 as a fighter-bomber figured prominently in Hitler's anti-invasion planning. Milch did not explicitly discourage this opinion. Early in November he had cabled Göring that it had been foreseen all along that the Me 262 should be capable of bombing.[5] On 3 December he reminded his engineers that at Insterburg Hitler had particularly emphasized this, and had also expressed an urgent interest in seeing the Me 410 fighter armed with the unorthodox 50-millimetre cannon;[6] two days later Hitler had again stressed the strategic importance of having jet fighter-bombers 'in action in large numbers by the spring'.[7] Although Milch knew that only the tenth prototype, V-10, was being equipped experimentally with two bomb pylons for 250-kilo bombs, and that this was not due for completion until early May 1944 itself, neither he nor Göring dispelled the impression Hitler had evidently gained. Indeed late in December after a visit from Göring Hitler e plained to his commanders,

Every month that passes makes it more and more probable that we w get at least one squadron of jet aircraft: the most important thing is th they [the enemy] get some bombs on top of them just as they try to invad That will force them to take cover. And even if there is only one such a craft in the air they will still have to take cover, and in this way they w waste hour after hour! But after half a day our reserves will already l on their way. So if we can pin them down on the beaches for just s or eight hours, you can see what that will mean for us . . .[8]

But Milch took no discernible action to promote the Me 262 as fighter-bomber, as he was anxious not to delay its début as a fighter.

He regarded the flying-bomb Fi 103 as one of the most important pro ects of the coming year. But severe manufacturing problems had beset He had authorized mass production before the trials were concluded the same gamble as had been taken by Udet with the Ju 88 and the N 210—and the gamble had not come off.[9] Cheap production metho had resulted in a run of failures; at the end of November 1943 th Volkswagen mass production series was halted for the time being, an the two thousand bombs already partly finished were scrapped as the structures were too weak. Eventually the ministry resolved that th works should proceed with the manufacture of one hundred entire new flying-bombs with the most up-to-date modifications incorporated; final decision would be reached on the basis of their performance, b they would not be delivered until mid-February.

In the meantime Flak Regiment 155(W) had been activated to ma the catapult sites and supply lines, and its five thousand officers an men were transferred to France during December.[10] The C-in-C the flak artillery was quick to publicize this newly acquired weapo although he was regrettably unaware of the technical delays. As a resu of his report the Führer decided that the flying-bomb campaign again London should begin on 15 February.[11] Early in January 1944 th Führer's headquarters was told that the Volkswagen works would man facture 1,400 flying-bombs in January, 2,000 in February and increas to 8,000 a month by September—figures devoid of any accuracy. Milc knew that nothing like 1,400 bombs would be manufactured durin January, and on his return to Berlin on the fifth he announced: 'I forbi anybody else to make reports to the High Command. . . . I am strong opposed to those gentlemen meddling in our affairs.'[12] When Fiel

Marshal Keitel cabled him expressing disappointment, Milch unblushingly told his staff: 'I have now received an idiotic telegram from Keitel and I have sent back an equally idiotic reply. I have asked him, "Why do you question the people who are not responsible for this?"'

The final decision on whether to cancel the flying-bomb was postponed until 24 January. When, meanwhile, Speer's own Me 262 troubleshooter, Dr Krome, asked whether the various secret weapon projects could possibly release skilled workers for the jet fighter, Milch soberly replied: 'I cannot speak for the A4.' Krome pointedly asked, 'Which do we need more—A4 or Me 262?' Milch rasped, 'We need the Me 262 more than anything else—more than submarines and more than tanks, because without this aircraft all armament production will become impossible. . . .'[13] 'That is what I said four weeks ago,' replied Krome, 'but nobody drew the necessary conclusions.' 'Nor will they draw them in Germany!' exclaimed Milch. Turning to Saur, he appealed: 'Cannot the submarine and tank people realize that in four or six months' time Germany will not be able to manufacture one more tank or submarine? Saur, cannot you realize that something must be done?' Saur made a non-committal reply.[14]

The auguries for the coming year were clear and well-defined for those who wished to read them. On 11 January the Americans resumed their strategic attack on the fighter defence structure: all three bombardment divisions, 663 bombers, set out to attack Milch's aircraft factories at Halberstadt, Brunswick, Magdeburg and Oschersleben. Two divisions had to be recalled because of bad weather; the German fighters exploited the gaps left in the ragged escort with deadly effect, destroying fifty-nine bombers and five of the escort fighters, for the loss of forty defenders.

When Göring's advisers proposed transferring BMW's Allach factory underground, Milch agreed but added: 'One day like 11 January, with real combat between our fighters and an attacking enemy, is worth far more than any cave. I don't mean to belittle our cave campaign, but it is far more important for the enemy to get a good thrashing, so that he doesn't come back; and the requirement for that is that we manage to turn out enough fighters this month. It's the famous "One Year too Late" again.'[15] Hitler asked Göring how much progress had been made with fitting the Me 410s with the 50-millimetre cannon displayed to him at Insterburg. Göring cabled Milch, 'Again and again the Führer inquires how many aircraft are already in service with this. Unhappily I have had to advise the Führer that virtually no such aircraft is yet in service, and that only two or three such aircraft have been so equipped.

The Führer accordingly beholds in such displays the same kind of symp
toms as once upon a time at Rechlin'[16]—meaning the notorious displa
of July 1939. To those who knew Göring, this was certainly menacin
language, and Milch put great pressure on the Rheinmetall compan
to equip the first thirty Me 410s with the formidable—and in due cours
brilliantly successful—weapon by the end of the month.[17]

By night, the RAF bombers continued to pound Berlin, but the prom
ised victory was not yet in sight. On 20 January the RAF droppe
2,400 tons on Berlin—a noteworthy achievement when compared wit
the difficulty the Luftwaffe experienced a year before in transporting
hundred tons of supplies two hundred miles to Stalingrad. Togethe
Milch and Saur toured the air industry's most vital factories in a specia
train, checking the production arrangements for the Do 335, the M
262 and the Ar 234.[18] As they returned to Berlin the sirens wer
sounding for a British attack on Magdeburg. During their last thre
attacks on Germany the British had lost 130 heavy bombers, but stil
they kept coming.

The only relief for the German cities in this ordeal was the increasin
diversion of Allied bombing effort to the strange secret weapon site
under construction in France. By the end of January the ninety-si
catapult sites for the flying-bomb, with their conspicuous ski-shape
buildings, were being heavily attacked; twenty thousand of the thirty-fiv
thousand French workers had been scared away, and a quarter of th
sites damaged; but the Allies had expended tens of thousands of ton
of bombs, and had lost aircraft and crews as well. All this time, wit
ten thousand workers, Milch was constructing fifty prefabricated cata
pult sites a month some distance *behind* the ring of 'ski sites' currentl
under attack, and these had not yet been detected by the Allies. It wa
from these that he now intended to open the attack; he had no intentio
of using the other sites if he could help it. Whether or not the flying
bomb campaign ever opened, he saw that his strategy of luring th
enemy bombers into 'fighter and flak traps'[19] far from German territor
was having good effect. 'The attacks on these sites are worth thei
weight in gold to us,' he triumphed. 'Otherwise we would have caugh
the bombs elsewhere!'[20]

It dismayed him that ambitious generals had reported too optimisti
cally to Hitler about the weapon's readiness: 'All the Führer's order
have been based on the assumption that we open fire on 15 February,
he complained. 'The Führer says, "You humbugged me once before a
Rechlin, and now it has happened all over again." '[21] By mid-February
this ordeal of waiting was over: he could tell Göring that the first fiv

f the new Volkswagen series of one hundred had been tested, and all ad functioned perfectly, travelling 140 to 175 miles with only about ne degree deviation.[22] On the fourteenth Milch was advised that lmost all the rest had worked equally well. He ordered mass production o be restarted immediately, and telephoned the Führer's headquarters. The long-range bombardment of London could begin in about two nonths' time.[23]

A month had passed since Speer had entered the SS clinic at Hohen-ychen with knee trouble; Milch watched with concern as the original nalady was complicated by lung troubles. With the minister's deputy, Saur, Milch could not reach any kind of understanding: Saur was ruth-ess, energetic and blindly partisan to the needs of the army. 'I knew ull well,' Milch was to state in his resignation speech in June, 'that it was he who had caused us the greatest damage in chasing his own arms roduction.'[24] Milch could see only one solution. In his snow-covered unting lodge in the forest outside Berlin he would lie awake all night, istening to the rumble of the bombers over the capital, and pondering n the future. It was futile to expect Speer's staff to collaborate with im, still less in their minister's absence. Only his total abdication of oower to Speer would release to the air industry the manpower, ma-erials, transport and construction capacity, and the extra foodstuffs and clothing allowances which Speer had monopolized. 'If somebody works on tanks in a factory,' he observed, 'he is showered with food parcels. If the same man works twice as hard on aircraft production, he gets nothing.'[25]

During his visits to Speer Milch proposed his own abdication for the good of the air industry, if this was the only way. Speer approved the suggestion.

Milch did not have long to wait for the right occasion. On 20 February 1944 the American bombers' 'Big Week' began; in effect, their directive was to destroy in ten days an industry to which Milch had devoted the ast eighteen years; this was to be the eclipse of the Luftwaffe—it was to open the doors to the Allied invasion in the spring.[26] It was an unex-oected feature of the industrial reorganization carried out in 1941 that t was unusually vulnerable to daylight attack, since Milch had re-grouped the individual 'production rings' into tight geographical units. Now this was exploited to the full: 'Big Week' opened with a thousand Flying Fortresses and Liberators, heavily escorted all the way by British and American long-range fighters, striking at a dozen air industry targets, and particularly at the Me 109 factories situated round Leipzig, where thirty-two per cent of all Me 109 production was concentrated. The factories had survived the RAF attack during the previous night, but nothing could have withstood the American saturation bombing next day.

By the time the campaign was halted by bad weather five days later 10,000 tons of bombs had been dropped by the Americans on target accounting for 90 per cent of Milch's air industry; and these had been followed by 9,200 tons of bombs released at night on ball-bearing centres like Stuttgart, Steyr and Schweinfurt, and on Augsburg; between them the two air forces lost nearly three hundred bombers, but the results were a catastrophe for Germany. In the industrial targets seventy five per cent of the buildings had been destroyed; Milch had lost 350 complete Me 109 fighters at the Leipzig factories, another 150 at the various Messerschmitt factories and 200 more at Wiener-Neustadt. He had lost his entire production of twin-engined fighters, the only aircraft capable of carrying the advanced 'SN 2' radar, and at Junkers the current production of 365 Ju 88s per month had been halved.[27] On 24 February, with the German air force now fighting desperate battles by day and by night, Göring departed on three weeks' leave to his castle at Veldenstein.[28]

Milch and Saur had already arranged a tour of the industry to discuss means of dispersing it in face of air attack. The tour could not have begun at a more opportune time.[29] A lesser man might have admitted defeat, seeing the buckled machinery, the blazing buildings and the hundreds of half-finished aircraft wrecked on the production lines. But the sheer scale of the damage that met Milch's eyes acted as a challenge. His first shrewd decision was that these main factories should *not* be completely evacuated. At Oschersleben and Brunswick he ordered half the factory to be left where it was, explaining, 'The enemy shall continue to attack them. I want them to believe that the factories are still there!'[30] As dawn rose on the twenty-third their train was standing on a siding near the stricken Me 109 factories at Leipzig. Here 450 workers had been killed in their slit trenches, and the survivors had fled from the area and refused to return.[31] Milch recognized that it was madness to expect the workers to shelter in the heart of the factory area during American saturation attacks, and ordered that in future as soon as the air-raid warning sounded the entire factory staff was to form up in column of threes and 'march singing' out of the works to a distance a thousand yards away: 'They can dig their slit trenches there and watch their factory, and then if necessary return for rescue, salvage and fire-fighting operations.'[32] Despite angry intervention by the local gauleiter, he also ordered that the foreign workers and prisoners killed in the attacks were to be accorded the same heroes' funeral as the Germans.[33] When the final American attack fell upon Regensburg on the twenty-fifth, the Messerschmitt factory was totally destroyed, but there were only five casualties, as the labour force had been evacuated three thousand yards away in good time.[34]

It was as their train had been approaching Leipzig that the idea of a 'Fighter Staff' was officially born.[35] This body should control the urgent dispersal and reconstruction of fighter aircraft production. It would consist of the principal officers of Milch's and Speer's ministries, and be vested with special powers by Hitler himself. The factories themselves had no spare labour, no construction workers and scarcely any transport. 'The local State authorities and Wehrmacht bodies confront these problems, as I have seen with my own eyes,' said Milch, 'with an impotence and helplessness that is frankly staggering.' And back in Berlin next morning he harangued their joint staffs: 'The fight is not a hopeless one—it can be won!' 'The object is to give the enemy such a fright that they can no longer bear the casualty rate. Every time they try brute force—because their political leadership is much more callous than the airman who actually has to fly the mission—they have got to be trounced.' Otherwise, he predicted, the same armada which was at present methodically ruining Berlin would in future be able to wipe out towns like Brunswick or Hildesheim, five or six at a time. 'What is the use of building a wall in Norway, if meanwhile the home base is destroyed? What is the use of emplacing one gun more or less in the Atlantic Wall, if we can state with certainty that the day will come, not long after the Luftwaffe has been defeated, when the guns will not arrive—because there will be no more trains running, no railway lines left crossing the Rhine, Weser, Elbe or Oder. Just try and visualize that, if you can!' These were prophetic words, deserving of a better audience. 'If you agree with me, then I will sacrifice all I have to carry out this programme as the Führer and Fatherland would wish. I can see no other way for Germany than this.' A memorandum advocating an inter-ministry 'Fighter Staff' was now drawn up and signed.

Within six hours the whole organization had been agreed upon.[36] When Milch showed Speer the document, he adroitly left the impression that all this had been Speer's own idea. Milch suggested Saur should head the Fighter Staff, as it was he who had sabotaged aircraft production all along. Now he should bear partial responsibility for it.[37] Göring, still ensconced at Veldenstein, and Hitler both warmly approved the Staff's formation.[38] Hitler commanded that as its first task it should construct two huge bomb-proof factories to house their most modern aircraft projects like the Me 262 (which the total destruction of Augsburg had fortuitously left virtually unscathed).[39] The factories should enclose a floor space of between seven and nine million square feet. Milch reported on the results of 'Big Week', and on their possible future production figures, but he leavened this picture with one promise which he now knew he could keep: they could open fire with flying-bombs on London at any time the Führer so commanded. 'Only the Führer can make this decision,' he explained a few days later. 'I suggested to him that we ought to open fire on his birthday [20 April] and then not as an annihilating attack, but as the most evil torture you can imagine: just picture for yourselves a large high-explosive bomb falling on Berlin every half-hour, and nobody knowing where the next will fall! Twenty days of that will have them all folding at the knees!'[40]

He returned to Berlin on the day after his talk with Hitler. At midday American bomber squadrons flew in splendid formation high over the capital and released 1,600 tons of bombs; they lost 68 bombers and 11 escort fighters to the defences, but the blow to German morale was undeniable.[41] On the eighth, seeing that the weather was again brilliant, Milch hurried to the First Fighter Division's operations room with Galland, arriving in time to see the next American attack begin, the glittering squadrons of heavy bombers flying in perfect formation overhead— 'An awesome spectacle with their condensation trails,' as Milch jotted in his diary. A hundred fighters tried to intercept the enemy, but failed to reach them in time.[42] Milch left that afternoon for the Fighter Staff's first tour of the stricken air industry.

During the next three months the Fighter Staff achieved a near-miracle. It presided over the Phoenix-like resurrection of the fighter aircraft industry from the ashes of its factories, and achieved greater production than ever before. Milch and Saur toured the factories, harangued the weary workers and took emergency action backed by the full resources of the Armaments and Air Ministries. Incompetent managers were dismissed or arrested, the rubble was cleared, temporary buildings erected and a *seventy-two-hour* working week was proclaimed throughout the industry.[43] Now the Speer Ministry provided the additional food rations to make the extra work-burden possible, and extra clothing allowances as an incentive for hard workers. The hardships were extreme: 'We must not forget,' Milch commented at the end of the first month of this gruelling winter test of will-power, 'that most of our workers are accustomed to working in heated buildings, and are now out in the open air, exposed to all the elements.'[44]

After the aircraft factories they toured the steel works, exhorting Krupp workers to hold out despite the mighty Allied bombing campaign. At that moment the American bombers were attacking Berlin again, and that night the RAF unloaded over *three thousand* tons of bombs on Frankfurt. Small wonder that when Milch mustered the quartermasters and chief engineers of the Luftwaffe a few days later to urge them to scour their stores for spare parts now vitally needed for the production lines, he lost his temper when the treatment of foreign workers was touched upon and bellowed, 'There is no such thing as international law!'—an utterance with which the judiciary to whom it was exhibited three years later profoundly disagreed.[45]

The Volkswagen works, he now learned, would complete 1,700 flying-bombs in April and 2,500 more in May. 'My own view is,' he said, 'that we might begin at the end of April, if we do not wish to do so on too heavy a scale.' The flak commander did not disagree, but proposed that they wait until a 'really sadistic' bombardment lasting many months could be sustained against London; it was unrealistic to attempt this with only three thousand bombs in hand—three thousand could all be launched within twenty-four hours, he thought. Milch replied with a warning: the catapult sites in France might suddenly find themselves in the middle of a battle zone once the Allied invasion began. 'That's why we can't waste one day, not even a minute. In my view the thing must be put into action fast. June is too late. I personally would open fire on 20 April, loose off fifteen hundred during April and the rest in May.' He gloated, 'Every half-hour or so, a flying-bomb! That will suffice to disrupt the life of this city over a very long period.'[46]

Then, a week later, the Luftwaffe inflicted a very severe defeat on the RAF's night-bombers. On 30 March over seven hundred bombers set out to destroy Nuremberg. It was a clear, frosty night, and their condensation trails showed conspicuously the course that they were following. Many of the night-fighters had by now been equipped with SN 2' radar, or with 'Naxos Z' for homing on to the bombers' radar emissions. Conditions were perfect for the von Lossberg and Herrmann pursuit techniques, and that night ninety-five bombers were brought down over Germany and twelve more crashed in England. RAF Bomber Command felt this an appropriate moment to halt the night offensive almost completely. The Battle of Berlin, which Sir Arthur Harris had predicted would end the war, had ended in a severe reverse for the bombers, as had Göring's similar assault on London in 1940. To Milch this was the long-awaited turning-point, and he too recalled the parallel with the Battle of Britain, and the Luftwaffe's attempt to destroy the RAF. Britain had survived that crisis; Germany could survive this.[47]

# BREAKING-POINT

## (April 1944–May 1945)

The Fighter Staff's principal functions had been to restore component production in the shattered factories and to safeguard them by dispersing them into tunnels, caves and vast bomb-proof factories, or by decentralizing them so as to multiply and reduce in size the targets for daylight attack. This was a race against time, since the Allies often attacked the secret dispersal sites as soon as they were occupied. Between 9 and 13 April 1944 the Americans carried out systematic attacks on scores of such new locations, particularly on the ball-bearing factories. 'There is no means in the world,' observed Saur, 'to keep secrets with six million foreign workers in Germany.'[1]

Yet the production miracle continued. In April Germany produced over two thousand fighters (2,021) for the first time, and in May 2,212. By September 1944 the climax would be reached with 3,375 fighters manufactured in one month. Obviously this would have been impossible had the ground not been prepared many months before by Milch and his staff; but it was Saur who effectively exploited these hidden reserves, and made the production possible in face of all-out air attack.[2]

Albert Speer was joint chairman of the Fighter Staff with Milch, but only in name; by late May he had not attended a single session.[3] When, after the war, Speer allowed his interrogators to see in him the architect of this production recovery after 'Big Week', Milch commented in his diaries: 'Young Speer does not seem to have been so much in the picture after all. That I was the one who first thought of a Fighter Staff, that he went on leave during March, April and May so that the whole burden fell on me, these things are not mentioned. Nor that its setting up was not primarily because of the air raids, but because of Herr Saur's dwindling of air force production.'[4] Speer had in fact left Germany for the Tyrol, and had settled on a mountainside high above Merano; he referred to his absence as a convalescence, but to the hard-working Milch it was an unnecessarily extended leave. To Göring it was an unexpected opportunity to floor a rival and recoup his lost position in Hitler's favour.

Once, the Führer had incautiously hinted that Speer was a suitable candidate from the younger generation to succeed him, and this obvious high regard had earned Speer the abiding enmity of both Bormann and Göring.[5] Göring exploited Speer's absence to introduce to the Führer the quiet-spoken head of the Todt organization, Xaver Dorsch, as being greatly superior to Speer as a construction overlord. Göring's most powerful ammunition was his allegation that Speer had patently neglected the Führer's six-month-old order, issued in October, for the construction of colossal bomb-proof factories;[6] at that time Speer had shown Hitler Dorsch's proposals for artificial caves constructed by laying a mighty slab of concrete on the ground, and excavating the gravel beneath it; Dorsch had also designed a bomb-proof aircraft factory to be built this way.[7] The obstacle was that Speer's organization alone was responsible for construction within the Reich; Dorsch could build only in the occupied territories.

Speer opposed such large projects for quite definite reasons: they would be too costly, too late and in themselves they would set back production by four or five months.[8] But he had agreed none the less in October to build at least two such factories.[9] Seven months later, no such factory had even been begun. When the Air Ministry investigated projects of its own for protecting its vital factories, particularly the BMW aero-engine factory at Allach, the Speer Ministry had refused to assist in any way;[10] and when the Luftwaffe then found a suitable autobahn tunnel in which to install part of the Me 262 jet-fighter production, Speer tried to requisition it for ball-bearing production instead, causing Göring angrily to remind him, 'You will recall that the Führer has ordered you to build two big bomb-proof fighter factories.'[11]

Milch also felt that the German economy could not support such huge construction projects. On 6 April he and Saur persuaded Hitler to agree to only one such factory, since the rest of the floor space could be found in an extension of Himmler's underground 'Central Works' tunnel complex at Nordhausen, where the A4 rocket was already being manufactured.[12] This extension would be allocated to the assembly of a thousand Messerschmitt jet fighters a month and the manufacture of the Junkers jet engine and all its components.[13] Milch afterwards told Göring that the Fighter Staff's intention was for Junkers, and not Messerschmitt, to control the Me 262 production line; when the whole complex was finished it would also house an assembly line for a further two thousand piston-engined fighters and their engines.[14] By late April however, no decision had been reached on either the site or the shape of the above-ground bomb-proof factory. This was the position when Hitler intervened.

Hitherto, Hitler had shown little interest in the defence of the Reich's cities. When foreign visitors pressed him for his views on the harrowing scenes they had witnessed, Hitler replied coldly that experience showed that a man who had lost everything made a truly 'fanatical warrior'; and he would remind his questioners of how many times in the last centuries entire German cities had been gutted by fire, only to arise anew.[15] But he did recognize the need to defend his armaments factories. Alarmed at last by the growing weight and accuracy of the Allied offensive, he impatiently rejected a navy suggestion that manpower be temporarily diverted from the air industry for repairs to a factory involved in submarine construction; 'I also need assault guns and tanks desperately; but nevertheless, I have to have an umbrella of fighter aircraft over the Reich. That is the alpha and omega of it.'[16] When he criticized the inexplicable delay in the construction of the bomb-proof factories he had ordered in October, Dorsch advised him that his Todt organization could build only in the occupied territories; so the factories were Speer's province. Hitler replied that he would brook no further delays—he had had enough of this bureaucracy. He ordered him to take over the work immediately.[17] It was a slap in the face for Speer, and Göring welcomed it.[18]

Dorsch had his six-month-old blueprints flown down from Berlin for Hitler to see. Hitler now asked for ten mushroom-like bomb-proof hangars to be built on selected airfields as well.[19] The Reichsmarschall, impressed by the engineer's unassuming manner, impulsively promised to place the entire Luftwaffe construction department at his disposal. Hitler again stressed to Göring the need for the bomb-proof factories, and explained, 'I could never put everything underground—that would take years. My highest priority is to put up a fighter umbrella over everything I cannot accommodate underground, and that means an actual front line of two thousand fighters to defend the Reich.'[20] This was the gospel that Milch had been preaching to deaf ears since the beginning of the Allied air offensive. Hitler ordered Göring to summon all the Fighter Staff and Todt organization officials, but not Speer, to a conference immediately.[21]

Milch was among those ordered to the Obersalzberg; he had not seen Göring for six weeks. A remarkable confrontation between them preceded the main conference.[22] Göring picked over all the old familiar bones of contention between them, and added Milch's behaviour at

Insterburg; he even repeated word for word what the field marshal had told him of his post-Stalingrad audience with Hitler—how Milch had recommended the replacement of Göring as commander-in-chief—and quoted to the field marshal a number of insults he had uttered against him in telephone conversations. Milch recognized that his telephone had been tapped. He gleaned a possible clue to Göring's rancour when he talked with the Chief of Air Staff that evening: Korten said that General Zeitzler was asking for Milch to command an airlift for the beleaguered troops at Sebastopol—the same kind of mission as he had had at Stalingrad. How many festering recollections this must suddenly have stirred up in Göring's bruised memory!

The main conference began early on 19 April. Göring announced that the Führer had decided that Dorsch should construct the bomb-proof factories and hangars, since Speer was unreliable. At least one of the factories was to accommodate a monthly production of five hundred fighters, 'and the Führer particularly wants it for the jet fighter Me 262'.[23] Milch and Saur reminded him that the jet fighter was to be assembled in the 'Central Works' complex; Göring said that in that case the Tank 152 (a beautiful fighter to be powered by either the DB 603 or the Jumo 213 engine, with exceptional high-altitude performance) could go into the bomb-proof factory. Previously Hitler had objected to three-shift working in factories since this would triple the production loss if such factories were destroyed; but with the bomb-proof factories he had no such objections—he wanted to see the maximum possible concentration of manpower and machinery in the space. Göring again lamented that he had asked for all this once eight months before: 'All this could have been ready long ago.'

Before they left, Göring briefly mentioned the danger that the Allies would attack the synthetic fuel refineries: 'I have heard that the enemy is not attacking them as they want to keep them for themselves after the war. They believe it will be enough to destroy our aircraft.'[24] That same day, on the far side of the North Sea, the American Eighth Air Force commander, General Spaatz, was given permission to divert the bombing offensive to these refineries; but it was to be mid-May before this offensive, which had been Milch's constant dread these last twelve months, became a reality.[25]

At the Obersalzberg the Chief of Air Staff General Korten left Milch in no doubt of his inability to work much longer with Göring, and he quoted a telling aside by the latter to the effect that Speer too was 'already finished'. Speer also considered his usefulness at an end. Hearing of Göring's latest dealings, he wrote to Hitler from Merano warning of the folly of starting still further giant construction works, and regretting the dubious role he considered the 'illoyal' Dorsch to have played; he threatened to resign if his views were not accepted.[26] Hitler was evidently minded to let him go, and Saur certainly did not defend his absent minister.

After inspecting a big display of the new German armour at Klessheim Castle with Hitler on the twentieth, Milch asked if he might speak to him alone on Speer's behalf. He argued that Hitler would be losing his best lieutenant in Speer, and one whom he could not well replace, through the intrigues of far lesser men.[27] Together they stood staring through a window at the tanks and guns displayed on the terraces below; Hitler began drumming his fingers absently on the glass. Milch asked Hitler for some word of comfort for Speer, to restore their former basis of mutual confidence. At first Hitler would not answer. Milch repeated the request. '*Jawohl, gut!*' answered Hitler curtly. 'Tell Speer from me that I am very fond of him. Is that enough?'[28] Milch drove at once to Merano, and performed his last great service for the war effort, restoring Speer to his previous favoured position with Hitler.

The Armaments Minister returned to Berlin early in May. Gradually control of the air industry was moving into his hands. Milch did not consider he had failed in any way—far from it. The RAF now hardly ventured into German skies by night, while by day the American bombers were wastefully committed to attacking the flying-bomb sites in France; both air forces had also begun attacking the French transport system, prior to the launching of the invasion. When shown a map of the railway sites selected for attack, Milch commented: 'They are attacking all the approach roads for this entire area. Here is the area they are trying to cut off—from here to there. . . . You can see from the density of the bombing that here is his *Schwerpunkt*.' He pointed at Normandy. He suggested sending the map to the High Command immediately.[29]

Within a few months, he hoped, they would be producing hundreds of Me 262 jet fighters to confront the American bomber formations. A new Fighter Staff production programme, '226', was being drawn up—far in excess of programmes the Speer Ministry had previously dismissed as unrealistic.[30] But the studies for the new programme aroused the open hostility of the Air Staff, on account of its meagre bomber production figures. In February, March and April the industry had manufactured 567, 605 and 680 bombers respectively. Study '1026', on which the new programme was based, foresaw a production of about 550 bombers a month, which would sustain forty squadrons (*Gruppen*), so the other eleven squadrons would have to be dissolved; but a further study, '1027', anticipated production of only 284 bombers a month to allow for expanded fighter production, and this would suffice for only twenty-six bomber squadrons from 1 October 1944. General Korten saw this as the death of the bomber arm.[31] Milch's argument that with the opening of the flying-bomb campaign against Britain a number of manned bomber squadrons would become superfluous anyway, was not accepted.

General Karl Koller, Korten's able deputy, prepared a lengthy memorandum highlighting the jeopardy their bomber arm was in, and suggested that all aircraft production should be concentrated within Speer's Ministry, while Milch's remaining departments for development and research were regrouped under the Air Staff;[32] and two weeks later he supported his suggestions with an explicit study on the bomber force needed to maintain the German position in Europe.*[33] These memoranda were submitted to Hitler.

No arms production could survive without air power to protect it, however; and no aircraft could fly without fuel or pilots. On 12 May the Americans initiated their attack on German oil production: the synthetic oil refineries at Leuna and Pölitz were extensively damaged. At an emergency conference called by Hitler between Speer, Milch and Keitel on one side and the synthetic oil industry's experts on the other, the experts described in stark detail the position confronting Germany if the crippling American offensive continued.[34] Yet Hitler still hankered after a powerful bomber arm, and on the same day, 23 May, we find him discussing with Göring a vast future Luftwaffe with a front line of fourteen thousand aircraft supported by a monthly production of five or six thousand planes; he agreed with Göring that in the final analysis it was always the Luftwaffe which had turned the scales in his campaigns, and he dismissed the Fighter Staff's meagre planned bomber production as 'quite out of the question'.[35] His earlier exhortations on the need for a 'fighter umbrella' over the Reich were forgotten.

Thus opinion again strongly diverged. Milch recognized only one hope of defeating the crippling American daylight attacks, whether they be against oil, industry or transport—the Me 262 jet fighter. For this reason he had silently ignored the autumn 1943 ordinances to develop it primarily as a fighter-bomber, and had concentrated on the pure fighter version only. By May 1944 about twenty of the pilot series were nearing completion, and ten prototypes had already taken to the air, but three

* Milch did not receive it until the end of the month, when he filled its margins with caustic comments indicating where the *Air Staff* had committed its errors in the past.

had crashed—two because their undercarriage had collapsed, and a third had spun into the ground on 19 May after its pilot had radioed that he 'did not feel well'.[36]

These technical setbacks paled into insignificance compared with the disruption that a radical policy change concerning this aircraft now inflicted. On 23 May Göring summoned a conference on the Obersalzberg to discuss the Fighter Staff's programme '226'; Milch, Speer and Saur were among the participants.[37] He advised them of the Führer's resumed interest in a strong bomber force, and reviewed the history of their production effort so far. In searching for the errors, intentional or otherwise, they had made since 1938, he concluded that 'they had gone completely wrong as far as bombers are concerned'. Thanks to Udet, they had concentrated earlier on the single-engined dive-bomber. (Mellowed by time, Göring now conceded: 'It will always be recognized as his greatest contribution that he created the weapon with which we achieved such magnificent victories.') This had encouraged them to proceed to twin-engined, and finally four-engined dive-bombers like the Junkers 88 and the Heinkel 177, while the Allies had methodically perfected the purely conventional heavy bombers like the Lancaster and Flying Fortress. The time had come to halt this process.

Göring recognized the need to promote the fighter arm initially to allow for any kind of armaments production under its umbrella. Echoing General Korten, he pointed out, 'But the thing is, that at present this is to be done at the expense of the bomber arm; and if this goes on the bomber arm will be finished, numerically if no other way!' He now aimed to restore the bomber force to a front line of at least 2,600 aircraft, based on a monthly output of eight or nine hundred bombers.[38] His recent conversations with Hitler had enlightened him as never before, he added: only the Heinkel with four separate engines (termed the He 277) had any future as a heavy bomber. Therefore the Führer had asked for this production to be brought forward, and planned at two hundred a month.[39] For the fighting in the west they would need the high-speed bombers like the Junkers 388 and the Do 335, and 'as interim fighter-bombers' the Ar 234 and the Me 262. As for the future, Professor Hertel's swept-wing Ju 287 jet bomber would restore German air superiority; this 530-miles-per-hour bomber would be produced at a rate of one hundred a month from December 1945.[40] The first three prototypes would be ready late in 1944.[41]

Milch objected to the description of the Me 262 as a fighter-bomber: like the Ar 234 it could carry only five hundred kilos of bombs (about a thousand pounds) and it had not been designed for the purpose. He could not conceal from his listeners that 1944, like the year before, was to be a 'year of clenched teeth'. The time for optimism seemed to recede further and further into the future. As the conference broke up, Göring announced that Hitler wished to examine the details of the programme that afternoon.

Milch certainly did not suspect that the storm was now almost upon him. With Colonel Petersen, director of the research establishments, he now joined Göring and Speer in a large unheated room at Hitler's Berghof, with a large picture window overlooking the Alps.[42] Hitler listened absently to the details of the Fighter Staff programme, apparently gazing out over the mountains, until the planning for the Me 262 jet fighter was mentioned. Here he interrupted, 'I thought the 262 was coming as a high-speed bomber? How many of the 262s already manufactured can carry bombs?' Milch told him: 'None, *mein Führer*. The Me 262 is being manufactured exclusively as a fighter aircraft.'[43] There was an awkward silence. Milch explained that the aircraft could not carry bombs without extensive design changes, and even then no more than five hundred kilos.*

Hitler lost his composure. He now realized that with the Allied invasion in France due any week, the wonder aircraft on which he had rested a large part of his hopes of defeating it could not possibly come in time. He excitedly interrupted Milch, 'Never mind! I only wanted one 250-kilo bomb!' He demanded precise statistics on the loads carried by the fighter version—its armour plate, guns and ammunition. 'Who pays the slightest attention to the orders I give?' he exclaimed. 'I gave an unqualified order, and left nobody in any doubt that the aircraft was to be equipped as a fighter-*bomber*.'[44]

Saur produced the load statistics and Hitler totted them up out loud. The total was far more than five hundred kilos. 'You don't need any guns,' he pointed out. 'The plane is so fast it doesn't need any armour plate either. You can take it all out.' Turning to Petersen he asked if this was not so; Petersen, overawed, nodded and replied: 'It can be done without any difficulty!' (Göring rebuked him next day: '*Jawohl*, Petersen—you can look it up for yourself in the transcript!') Milch, dismayed at this turn of events, urged Hitler to hear the others, but nobody else spoke out. General Korten stayed silent, and Galland was so badly savaged by the Führer after barely a dozen words that he lapsed into silence too. In desperation the field marshal appealed to Hitler to think again, but he was subjected to a torrent of abuse; and before he

---

* No note survives of Hitler's conference, but the language used there was quoted during the 'post-mortem' discussions on it with Göring over the next two days, and these were recorded in shorthand transcripts.

could control himself he shouted back, *'Mein Führer,* the smallest infant can see that this is a fighter, not a bomber aircraft!'[45]

Hitler turned away from him, and refused to address himself to Milch for the rest of the discussion. The man sitting on Petersen's left whispered one word to describe what they had seen: *'Aufschlagbrand!—* crashed in flames!' Milch's days of office were evidently numbered, and the number did not exceed two figures.

Speer told Göring afterwards that the Luftwaffe had not made clear enough to the Führer the problems still besetting the Me 262.[46] But the basic objection to a bomber version was that the jet fighter carried its six hundred kilos of armour plate and armament *forward* of the centre of gravity; these could not be taken out without redistributing the aircraft's loading, which might even mean altering the position of the wings. The first hundred Me 262s and the parts already manufactured for the rest were nearly all for the pure fighter version. There could be no basic design change for the next five months. Told of this on the morning after the Führer conference, Göring raged, 'You gentlemen appear to be stone deaf—the lot of you! I have referred again and again to the Führer's order, he doesn't care two hoots about getting the Me 262 as a fighter, but wants it only as a fighter-bomber.' He himself had insisted on this long before Insterburg in November.[47]

'The Führer must have the strangest impression of you. From every side, including Messerschmitt, he was left in doubt about this, right from the start. And then, in my presence [at Insterburg] Messerschmitt told the Führer that his company had provided right from the start for it to be manufactured as a fighter-bomber. And now suddenly it is impossible!'[48] When Colonel Petersen enlarged on the structural and engine problems the jet aircraft had run into, Göring unhappily replied: 'I would have been grateful had you uttered ten per cent of these remarks yesterday! The Führer says, "As far as I am concerned you can cremate the fighters!" He needs an aircraft which can force its way through by virtue of its sheer speed, despite the enormous mass of fighters guarding the invasion forces. What no civilian dares to do—simply ignoring superior orders—you gentlemen venture time after time after time.'[49]

Milch could see everything he had built up being destroyed. True, Göring had now spoken in terms of a standing force of three thousand fighters for the Reich defence, encouraged by Saur's estimate that he would produce a thousand fighters in the next week alone. (Milch sarcastically entered in his diary, 'Göring discovers the defence of the Reich!')[50] But where would the crews now come from? With the modification of the Me 262 to fighter-bomber, Milch considered the war finally lost. He felt bitter at the lack of support during the Führer's conference. Even Galland had acquiesced in the dreadful decision although he knew that the Me 262 was their only hope of finally exorcizing the Mosquito menace (Galland once said 'For the Mosquito there is no escape once a 262 has sighted it').[51]

Milch privately appealed to Göring to make one last attempt to change Hitler's mind; then he returned to Berlin, resolved to swim against the tide no longer.

Speer now prepared to take over Milch's aircraft production. On Friday 26 May 1944 he attended his first Fighter Staff meeting, at the Air Ministry. It was the familiar Emperor Speer: he expressed himself well pleased with Saur's achievements in his absence. His staff chronicler recorded: 'The individual members of the Fighter Staff were introduced to him and he was apprised of their efforts so far and the current status of the various campaigns. Through the minister's illness, the Fighter Staff, which he established, has become too entrenched in the Air Ministry. The minister gathers the reins into his own hands. Milch greeted him in tones of the warm comradeship which has united both men to the benefit of all armaments production.'[52]

Milch recognized that the end of his long road was in sight. Over the next few days Göring called further conferences, and Milch was not invited. On 27 May Göring did indeed advise Hitler that Colonel Petersen now withdrew his assurance that the Me 262 was suited to carry bombs. ('I told the Führer you did not mean it,' Göring afterwards told the colonel. 'But it's no good! It's written down in the transcript!')[53] Hitler repeated that none of his orders had been carried out. He himself was satisfied that a jet bomber could be built, capable of attacking area targets from an altitude of a few thousand feet; as targets he had been thinking of any troop embarkation movements on the other side of the English Channel, or the disembarking mass of tanks and troops swarming round the landing beaches.

In fact, Hitler had strong doubts whether the Me 262 fighter version would really be of any use against the Allied fighters, which alone were the guarantee of enemy air supremacy; he believed the jets would find it tactically difficult to engage the far slower but more agile piston-engined Mustangs and Thunderbolts; the enemy would only have to curve and the jet would overshoot him. (This fear was to prove well-founded, and in combat the Me 262 fighter's chief success was to force the American long-range escort fighters to jettison their fuel tanks and which obliged them to turn back early; actual combat victories by the jet fighters were disappointingly few.[54]) Göring pledged that every man working on the aircraft would now honourably try to achieve what Hitler ordered. On 27 May he telegraphed Milch emphatically: 'The Führer has ordered that the Me 262 aircraft is to enter service exclusively as a high-speed bomber. The aircraft is not to be regarded as a fighter until further notice.'[55]

At a conference summoned by Göring two days later, 'to clarify things once and for all', Professor Messerschmitt and even Petersen blamed the absent Milch for the 'misunderstandings' which had arisen. Göring announced that he was transferring the project from Galland's office to that of the General of Bombers 'to avoid further errors'.[56] When Petersen admitted that the jet engine had a tendency to 'flame out' above twenty-eight thousand feet if throttled back to reduce speed, Göring triumphed, 'Then I can only say, the Führer was right again, with his brilliant and instinctive touch!'[57] And when Professor Messerschmitt began to explain how, after releasing its bomb, the Me 262 was just like a fighter again, Göring anxiously interrupted, 'Not like "*a fighter*" again, but "*super fast*" again. Stop calling it a "*fighter*"!'[58] That evening Colonel Petersen brought Milch the news that Göring was going to transfer air armament in its entirety to Saur.

To have resisted the Armaments Ministry's overtures would have harmed the Reich. Milch did not resist. He stayed at his lakeside hunting lodge for many weeks, returning to Berlin only to sign important papers. He travelled for one day with the Fighter Staff to Hungary for the signing of the State agreement on joint aircraft production, but otherwise he slipped out of active life.[59]

When Göring complained half-heartedly to Hitler that the present huge upswing in aircraft production proved how greatly the Speer Ministry had obstructed them in the past, Speer replied that the increase had been attained solely by exploiting the Luftwaffe's own reserves.*[60]

The Reichsmarschall's reputation was approaching its lowest ebb. A week earlier German oil production had again been heavily attacked. When on 6 June the Allied invasion of France began, the Luftwaffe was able to fly only 319 sorties against the 14,700 flown by the British and American air forces that day. On the seventh the Führer ordered Saur to hasten production of the Do 335 high-speed bomber and the Me 262 bomber version.[61] (In Central Planning that afternoon, Milch

---

* But Speer appeared to contradict this in his speech at the Flick Building on 9 June 1944: '. . . Since February we have on the quiet brought in capacities from the armament and Panzer industries into the aircraft industry. This is the reason, in my opinion, for the speedy success of the Fighter Staff.'

burst out, 'We are not on the offensive, but on the defensive! This is going to have to be recognized!')[62] So low had Göring's star sunk that during a war conference Hitler caustically asked him whether, in view of the lack of air victories during the Allied invasion operations, it was true that the Luftwaffe had taken out a 'knock-for-knock' insurance policy with the enemy?[63]

A greater fiasco was to follow. On the night of 12 June the flying-bomb attack was opened against London, two days prematurely. The struggling catapult crews managed to launch only ten bombs, of which four immediately crashed; of the remaining six, two were never seen again, one destroyed a railway bridge in London and the other three impacted elsewhere. It was an inauspicious start to a campaign in which Milch had vested such high hopes.[64] The flying-bomb regiment explained that as the High Command had advanced the planned zero-hour by two days, the methodical timetable for the final installation of the heavy prefabricated catapult rigs had been thrown out of joint.[65] Göring anxiously reminded Hitler that Milch was the author of this unspectacular weapon.

Two days later the offensive was resumed. In the first night 244 flying-bombs were launched, and German reconnaissance aircraft reported that fires were sweeping the British capital.[66] Göring retracted his earlier statement on the authorship of the flying-bomb idea, but on 17 June Hitler telephoned Milch from France and congratulated him on the weapon: 'It has exceeded our wildest expectations!'[67] By next day five hundred had been launched, and by the twenty-second one thousand; during the next three months this weapon (which had cost £12 million) inflicted over £47 millions' worth of damage—in terms of cost effectiveness a clear vindication of all Milch's strategy since mid-1942.[68]

Three days after Hitler's telephone call, Göring told Milch that all military arms production was to be consolidated under Speer, which would mean Milch's resignation as Director of Air Armament; this was confirmed by Hitler soon after. In Hitler's presence, Göring added that Milch was also to resign as state secretary, but in order to keep their dispute private he would prefer Milch to remain as Inspector General.[69]

Speer invited him to accept the post of 'deputy minister' in the Armaments Ministry; Milch saw this as a token of his friend's clouded conscience. 'Speer,' he noted, 'has persuaded the Führer to make the change. Göring did not dare to refuse and Speer has a guilty conscience towards me. He asks if I am happy with the arrangement. My reply is that he ought to be able to judge that for himself.'[70] The full extent of the change cannot at first have been appreciated by Milch. He wrote in his diary, 'I transfer with air armament production to Speer and remain Inspector General of Luftwaffe.'* It soon became clear however that *Saur* was to manage the industry. At some indeterminate date Milch sadly modified the diary entry to read, 'I go! Air armament transferred to Speer, I remain Inspector General of the Luftwaffe.'

Speer circularized the government authorities about Milch's new appointment as deputy Armament Minister, but he also made it brutally clear that his own departmental heads' right to see him and act in his name was not affected in any way by this.[72] When Hitler addressed an Arms Convention at Linz on 26 June he praised Speer and Saur for the miracle they had achieved, 'together with their colleague, Field Marshal Milch'.[73] But within a month he had forgotten whatever role Milch had ever played, and explaining to Mussolini why he had taken all arms production out of the hands of 'the military', he said: 'Thus fighter aircraft production, which under military direction reached only 1,100 a month, was increased to 2,600 after just four months and then to 3,000, and is going to reach 5,000.'[74] That he himself had fought tooth and nail against increasing fighter production, and that any increase was impossible unless it had been planned and provided for at least nine months earlier (when 'the military' was still in control) was overlooked.

On the last day of June 1944 Milch confidentially explained, in a bitter farewell speech to his staff, why air armament had had to be abdicated to Speer's Ministry. He conceded that the changes would lead to rumours and unrest, and that it was a remarkable decision to take in the fifth year of a war: 'But the decision has been recognized as the proper one, by everybody, including our superiors.' He emphasized that the reorganization was not a consequence of any failure by the Luftwaffe or the Office of Air Armament; it had become inevitable as a result of the air raids—it had been inevitable as the only means of overcoming the obstructionism of the Speer Ministry: 'We did not have the construction capacity, we did not have the truck transport,' he reminded them. 'Every request we expressed in these connections was turned down with a smirk by the offices concerned. . . . Nor did we have any means of giving our workers the extra rations necessary for them to work a 72-hour week. So far as material allocations and parts supplies were concerned, we were treated like lepers.'

He recognized, he said, that ignorant outsiders would now claim: 'They fell down on their job. They failed!' He also recognized that his

---

* The British official historians of the strategic bombing offensive commented: 'Milch had not expected to be replaced by Saur, but to continue to manage the industry inside the Speer organization.'[71]

programme of industrial rationalization was still incomplete. 'I do not believe I have been an easy-going leader—I have had to use some rough language and some harsh methods. Nor am I sorry for having done so, however wrong I may occasionally have been.' He still believed in ultimate victory. But had Germany done what he had demanded for two years as Director of Air Armament, things would have been different today. He ordered the transcript of the speech to be destroyed except for one copy placed on his confidential file.[75] At a State funeral next day he saw Hitler briefly for the last time.

The doctrine Milch had always preached—the doctrine of massive reinforcement of the Reich's fighter defences—continued to attract support even after his abdication. This was small wonder, for on 20 June fifteen hundred American bombers, escorted by a thousand fighters, had again attacked the vital oil refineries; on the following day the same armada had attacked Berlin itself, releasing two thousand tons of bombs, and on the twenty-second the great Russian summer offensive had begun, supported by four thousand aeroplanes. On 25 June we find Hitler stressing the importance of checking the Allied air superiority, and asking how many extra fighters could be built if the planned two hundred Heinkel 177s per month were cancelled.[76] Saur put the increase at a thousand a month. The next day the Führer emphasized: 'In our position all that matters is the manufacture of fighters and still more fighters! With high-speed bombers as well. . . . We shall just have to put up with the long-term loss of a strategic air force that that will entail.'[77] Surely this was the familiar heresy which had resulted in Milch's abdication? But Hitler repeated it on the twenty-seventh and again on the twenty-ninth, after which Göring issued to his staff the extraordinary command that 'all production of bombers, torpedo bombers and the like, and all training for such aircraft, is to cease forthwith'.[78] He stonily overruled General Koller's protests, proclaiming: 'It is the Führer's will that only fighter aircraft are to be manufactured from henceforth.' Now that Milch had gone, extreme chaos was overtaking the air industry's long-term planning.

On 20 July 1944 cruel destiny robbed the Luftwaffe of its Chief of Staff, General Korten, standing a few paces from Hitler as an assassin's bomb exploded. Milch heard of the murder attempt and providently wrote in his diary: 'Midday: attempted assassination of the Führer. Thank God, miscarried.' He cabled Hitler, 'Mein Führer! I beg to express my heartfelt joy that a merciful Providence has shielded you from this base murder attempt and preserved you for the German people and its

Wehrmacht. May God continue to protect you and grant you the total victory you deserve.' He signed himself, 'Your loyal Erhard Milch, Field Marshal.'[79] Perhaps these sentiments were sheer opportunism. But he maintained his contempt for the murderers of one of his best friends even when a more temperate attitude might have benefited him. When a Nuremberg interrogator put it to him that the assassination of a tyrant was in obedience to God's Will, Milch replied, 'There was no plaque on the Reich Chancery saying, "I am a tyrant".' And when a prosecutor confused the date of his dismissal, Milch pounded the witness-box and shouted, 'Will you please note it was 20 *June,* not 20 July! I attach great importance to not being associated with those vermin!'[80]

After the murder attempt Göring developed a throat infection and withdrew from headquarters for over a month. Hitler proposed the very experienced General von Greim as Korten's successor, but on 24 July Göring selected a more harmless alternative, Lieutenant-General Werner Kreipe. He later told Kreipe of the qualms he had had: 'I hesitated at first to appoint you my chief of staff, since you—like your two predecessors—were Milch's staff officer.' And he referred to Milch in terms of extreme coarseness.[81] Korten's own deputy, General Koller (a former NCO who had actually been Kreipe's *superior* in the Third Air Force), was passed over.[82] Koller attributed this slight to Göring's technical officer Diesing: 'After all, as the new Chief of Technical Air Armament Diesing will be subordinate to the Chief of Air Staff. He must have leant over backwards to thwart my promotion. He knows full well I emphatically advised Korten against having him as Chief of Technical Air Armament. . . . I consider him the most two-faced and deceitful officer in the entire air force. Korten was of the same view, as were Milch, Speer and many others.'[83]

When the order for the transfer of the Office of Air Armament to Diesing as of 1 August was complete, Colonel Aldinger, the ministry's organization officer, had the thankless task of showing it to Milch. 'I know why you are here,' said Milch, 'and I know you are not to blame for this scrap of paper.' Aldinger knew few men who would have displayed such self-restraint and sovereign good temper at such a moment.[84]

In Göring's absence, Hitler occupied every war conference with recriminations against the Luftwaffe. In vain Koller pointed to the planning errors from 1939 to 1942 as the cause; the Führer extended the failure to more recent years.[85] When Kreipe reported to Hitler for the first time on 11 August Hitler lectured him at length on the failure of Göring's technical advisers, by whom he meant Udet, Jeschonnek and now

Milch, and on the manner they had deceived him with 'over-hasty promises'; it was Kreipe's job to ensure that in future 'clarity and honesty' reigned within the Luftwaffe.[86]

Over the next few weeks the scales fell from Kreipe's eyes. Hitler relentlessly demanded the transfer of the fighter squadrons from the Reich to France. Milch privately reminded Kreipe of the urgency of devoting fighters to the defence of the remaining synthetic fuel refineries (each should have its own fighter squadron, given the sole duty of defending that refinery).[87] In time Kreipe learned the history of the Führer's order forbidding the use of the Me 262 as a fighter: 'Galland tells me of the Insterburg display which led to Milch's downfall,' he noted. 'This has set back the Me 262 by nine months.'[88] When Kreipe broached the subject of this order, Hitler interrupted him. 'In a growing temper he made short work of me,' Kreipe noted that day. 'Now I was stabbing him in the back as well! Irresponsible elements in the Luftwaffe like Milch and Galland had talked me into it!'[89] For some days Hitler weighed the possibility of abolishing the Luftwaffe altogether except for a jet aircraft force, relying otherwise solely on a tripled flak defence.[90] Eventually Göring forbade Kreipe to communicate with Milch in any way.

During these months Milch faded out of the war picture. With Speer he discussed an idea for operating manned V-1 flying-bombs against vital enemy targets; several hundred were actually manufactured, and about a hundred pilots for them trained, but they were never launched.[91] Milch took his leave of the flying-bomb designers and engineers, and then of the ministry's staff. 'I was a broken man, as the further course of German history could no longer be in doubt.'[92] He continued to attend Speer's staff conferences and accompany the minister on his journeys. In mid-August they watched the launching of one of the new Type XXI U-boats, and went on a submarine journey in the new Walther-Type submarine U793. It was the last time Milch saw Danzig, with its memories of the pioneering days of aviation.[93]

Late in September they toured paratroop and army units in the west. One afternoon, as they were all dozing—exhausted by early starts and long drives—in a field in Holland, they were awakened by the thunder of aero-engines, to see the American Eighth Air Force passing high overhead into Germany. Milch guessed they had seen a thousand bombers, glittering in the summer sunlight. One of Speer's officials counted 987, undisturbed by flak or fighters.[94]

Thanks to the continued activities of General Galland, the Me 262 did in fact first go into service as a fighter aircraft. On 3 October 1944 an experimental squadron was established with forty Me 262s under Major Walter Nowotny. The Inspector of Day-Fighters personally supervised the first few days' operations, and selected the squadron the best pilots from the piston-engined squadrons for them. The unit none the less had an inglorious existence. On the very first day four Me 262s took off from Achmer; two were destroyed within minutes by enemy fighters as they took off, and a third as it came in to land. Two more took off from Hesepe airfield and one was destroyed by fighters on landing. Between them they claimed three or four enemy bombers.[95]

Numerous reports reached the Messerschmitt company of the pilots' 'inadequate leadership, poor training and frivolous attitude'; there had been no advance study of the proper fighter tactics, and although the unit was once grounded for ten days by bad weather Nowotny took no action to train the pilots. So severe was the shortage of fuel caused by the American destruction of the refineries that jet aircraft awaiting final flight tests at Obertraubling airfield had to be moved to dispersal areas by horses and oxen.[96] By 24 October Nowotny's unit had managed to fly only three missions; in November Nowotny himself was killed, and the unit was disbanded, having destroyed about twenty-six enemy aircraft.

By late October about 265 Me 262 aircraft had been manufactured, of which 30 had been destroyed in attacks on the Messerschmitt works; production in November was expected to be 130, and in December 200. The first bomber unit to operate the Me 262 was KG 51, and by the autumn eight more former bomber units were being converted to the aircraft. Further Me 262 fighter squadrons were also established, including aircraft fitted with racks of a dozen R4M air-to-air rockets under each wing; but the aircraft had come too late, and there had been inadequate attention to the proper tactics and targets for such advanced aircraft, so the real threat never materialized in the way the Allies had feared.


On the way back from the battlefields of Arnhem on 1 October 1944—he and Speer had stayed to watch a before-dawn German counter-attack—Field Marshal Milch's driver skidded at high speed, the car hit a tree and swerved into a ditch. Milch broke the steering column over his long-suffering back, and recovered consciousness only in hospital.[97] With crushed ribs and increasing lung complications, he lay immobilized at his hunting lodge until early 1945, as the war approached its end. On one October day the RAF released nine thousand tons of bombs on one German town, the final proof of complete air superiority.

Uninvited, Milch appeared at Karinhall for the last time on Göring's birthday in January 1945. The Reichsmarschall was astounded and openly unpleasant.[98] Three days later Milch received a week-old letter from Göring dismissing him from his last office, that of Inspector General. The office now remained empty to the end.[99]

Milch still remained in contact with affairs. Early in January one of Hitler's intimates told him that Stalin had offered a negotiated peace, but that Hitler had refused to listen. Two weeks later the Soviet invasion of Silesia began.[100] Milch was advised to evacuate his family from the Althofdürr estate.[101] Hitler evidently missed Milch's loyalty, because once he commented that it would probably have been far better if he had handed the Luftwaffe long before to the field marshal: 'Then perhaps Udet might still be alive now.'[102] And when Speer suggested a Transport Staff under Milch to repair the internal transport system, on 1 March the Führer expressed his agreement to the plan, only to change his mind within two weeks as other elements round him persuaded him of Milch's unsuitability.[103]

In the privacy of Milch's home Speer informed him of Hitler's decrees for the destruction of Germany's industries before they fell into enemy hands, and of his fight against these orders.[104] Here too Speer drafted a wireless speech appealing to the German people to obstruct them. There was the usual birthday greeting from Hitler at the end of March ('The Führer sends greetings, but not Göring and his vermin!' Milch entered in his diary). When the Führer's air adjutant visited Milch two days later, he offered to return to the capital and fight in the ranks; perhaps he longed for a howitzer battery like the one he had commanded in 1914. Now Germany was being cut in two by the Allied armies, and Speer formally commissioned Milch to act for him in the northern half. Coming from Hitler's bunker on 21 April, he reported that the Führer had made a very fine impression on him, but not 'that dodger Göring'.[105] According to Milch's diary, he confidentially mentioned a few days later his plans for escaping to Greenland in an aircraft, or alternatively living in a small canoe on Germany's canals and waterways; two months after the war's end he would return 'to take over Germany's leadership'.[106] This was their last meeting for many months.

The headquarters of the High Command were evacuated to a hut in the forest not far from Milch's hunting lodge. Here Jodl told him Göring had cabled from Berchtesgaden announcing that he was taking over; the Führer had disagreed and ordered the Reichsmarschall's arrest. (Speer chuckled on the telephone to Milch, 'Göring has committed a tiny *Dummheit!*')[107] Two days later, at 2.30 am on the twenty-sixth, Milch left his hunting lodge for the last time, heading for northern Germany by car. He met both German and Russian tanks along the road, but he drove without headlights and was not stopped.

Hitler's suicide left Milch less perplexed than his appointment of Admiral Dönitz instead of Göring or Speer to succeed him. Milch refused to be traded from one slavemaster to the next 'as in the most reactionary Middle Ages', and declined Speer's invitation to join the admiral at Flensburg. Instead he waited for events to overtake him in Sierhagen Castle near Neustadt on the Baltic coast.

# PART VII

# JUDGEMENT AT NUREMBERG

*'Was ist gut? fragt Ihr. Tapfer sein ist gut.'*
—Nietzsche: *Also sprach Zarathustra* (Tenth Speech)

# IN ALLIED HANDS

## (*May 1945–November 1946*)

At the castle Milch put on his full-dress uniform with interim baton and braid and the rows of medals he had won in two world wars, and awaited capture. At midday on 4 May two British gunners appeared at his lunch-table. They disarmed him and drove him off to a nearby village where a Royal Artillery unit had set up headquarters; he was handed a cigarette and driven off by a major towards Neustadt. The gunners returned meanwhile to Sierhagen and looted his valuables; in their mess that evening they displayed two of Milch's gold watches, his gold field marshal's baton and an inscribed gold cigarette case given to him by Göring in happier days in 1936.[1]

British troops had witnessed some grim scenes of Nazi brutality in northern Germany, but few grimmer than here at Neustadt. It had been entered by Royal Marine commandos the day before. Three German transport ships had been sunk offshore by Allied fighter-bombers and hundreds of the drowned passengers and refugees were drifting in the bay as the commandos arrived.[2] The British had taken over the former submarine school at Neustadt, now being used as a transit depot for prisoners. The town's market place was crowded with tanks and ar-moured cars as the Mercedes carrying Milch into captivity arrived. He was handed over to a squad of commandos and put under guard in a restaurant being used as their headquarters. Moments later a com-mando strode in. He stopped in front of Milch, rounded on the field marshal and shouted that all the generals were criminals—they were guilty of the concentration-camp atrocities. Milch pointed out that he was in the German air force but the commando was not satisfied by this explanation. He suddenly tore the field marshal's baton from his hands and began raining blows on the back of Milch's skull until the heavy wooden baton snapped. Milch staggered and fell to the ground, shouting, 'I am an officer—a field marshal!'[3]

Milch was then marched into the local submarine school and forced to contemplate the infernal scene the commandos had found there. The officers shouted to the surviving prisoners, 'This is your field marshal—you owe it all to him!' Milch had become hardened to horrifying sights after air raids on Berlin and other cities but even he was sickened. In his diary, he wrote: 'It was an abominable spectacle—dead, diseased camp inmates, dressed in naval uniforms, lying about in the open air and in the exercise sheds.' Later that day he was turned over to a Scottish regiment at Lübeck, where he was given a proper meal and even some cigars before he was transferred to a prisoner-of-war cage at Lüneburg to await shipment to Britain.

Here his relatives were allowed to visit him. On his mother's farewell visit she mentioned the rumours that he had been mishandled by the commandos—his head still bore the untreated scars—and as he gave her his hand to say goodbye he felt something cold and hard pressed into it. His mother said quietly, 'If they ill-treat you again, or torture you, use this.' It was a small screw-capped phial of cyanide. This seemed the supreme act any mother could perform for her own son.

On 18 May 1945 Milch was flown to England, his mother's cyanide capsule still concealed about him. As his plane crossed southern England and landed at Croydon he was surprised at the general lack of bomb damage. An Air Ministry officer drove him through London and out towards Oxford; after twenty miles the car halted outside a white house in wooded parkland, the first of several interrogation centres. Here he was to live for some days while his interrogators courteously attempted to persuade him to accept Germany's sole guilt for the war and to give evidence incriminating his brother officers.

The most important such centre was that at Latimer, a 'Combined Services Detailed Interrogation Centre' (CSDIC) to which Milch was transferred at the end of May.* He found General Koller, General Schmid (the former chief of Air Intelligence) and many other former colleagues there. The prisoners were told that they were there to write expert studies on their experiences, but it was the microphones hidden in the communal and private rooms—and even among the trees along the woodland paths—that made the top secret CSDIC reports so rewarding. Milch suspected this and wrote in his diary on the first day there: 'They opened a door into a small room, and I found myself confronted by the astonished gaze of General Galland. . . . We had much to tell

---

* The commandant of the CSDIC at Wilton Park, L. St Clare Grondona, has described his own experiences in an article in the Royal United Services Institution *Journal* (December 1970), but he was not permitted to disclose the use of hidden microphones.

each other, and this was no doubt the ulterior motive for one could take it that there was a highly sensitive listening device in there.'

Milch was to spend a record four months at this centre, interrogated almost every day by British and American officers known only by their pseudonyms. The American Major Emery (or 'Evans', as he introduced himself to Göring who was being held on the Continent) was an air force officer, whose real name was Ernst Englander. The interrogations were of a military nature, unassociated with the war crimes trials proceeding elsewhere. Milch's assertion* that the American daylight attacks on transport and oil plants had defeated Germany was an evident embarrassment to the British interrogators. 'I think they are annoyed at me for speaking this obvious truth,' recorded Milch. 'Again and again I have been interrogated on this point. I can only repeat, the British inflicted grievous and bloody injuries on us—but the Americans shot us in the heart.'[4]

Englander found the best approach was by 'getting reasonably chummy with the prisoners', as he wrote a few months later.[5] He had already interrogated Göring at some length at Augsburg and confided to Milch, 'Göring is such a liar that he cannot tell when he's lying himself now.'[6] From the field marshal's reactions and the transcripts of his private conversation in the interrogation centre it was obvious that there had been no love lost between him and the Reichsmarschall. A year later Englander was to write, 'Göring and Milch hated each other, and we have it in their own words—there can't be any question about that.'

He furnished Milch with increasingly unpleasant details about the Reichsmarschall: the man was once more a drug addict and had the gall to refer contemptuously to Milch as 'that fat little man'. But somehow Milch was sure that in general Göring would have to speak well of him and his other colleagues, if only to ensure that he was covered by them in turn.[7] 'Göring is going to cost Germany dear even now,' Milch suspected in private. 'How the Germans clung to him until almost the last moment—how they trusted him!' But during these weeks Göring for his part resolved to make his final public appearance a last great act on Germany's behalf. He was not afraid of death. 'My philosophy is that if the time has come, the time has come,' he told his defence counsel. 'Accept responsibility and go down with guns firing and colours flying! It's the defence of Germany that is at stake in this trial—not just the handful of us defendants who are for the high jump anyway.'[8] Many months before, in November 1944, Göring had already proclaimed to

* For example, in his (recorded) conversation with Englander on 3 June 1945, in CSDIC (UK) report SRGG 1313 (C).

his generals: 'To stay alive at any price has always been the philosophy of the coward.'*

From a cell in an English prison camp the scene was not the same. Milch sat in his cell and watched as Germany began to pay for the war: divided, dishonoured and starving, the ordinary people were bearing the brunt of the defeat. General Stumpff arrived, bringing ugly news of the pillaging and looting in the Russian zone. There were also rumours that the Americans had reopened the former SS concentration camps like that at Dachau.

After the Potsdam conference the future looked even bleaker for the Nazi prisoners. On 10 August Milch read in *The Times* of the Four-Power pronouncement that the first major trial of war criminals was to take place at Nuremberg, with Göring among the first defendants. But on the same day an American officer whom he tentatively approached to assist him in his defence should he also be brought to trial reassured him that the prisoners brought to Britain were not considered to come into the category of war criminals. None the less word soon reached him that he might be shipped to Nuremberg as a witness. He wrote in his diary, 'The Lord preserve me from such a fate!'

The more he heard about his former boss Hermann Göring, the more he inwardly raged against him. He obtained evidence of the corruption which seemed to have flowered within the Luftwaffe. He met one Heinkel director in captivity who had himself signed a cheque for forty thousand reichsmarks for a senior test pilot to persuade him to report favourably on the ill-conceived Heinkel 177 prototypes.[10] Göring seemed to have been financially involved in many aircraft companies. 'Late in the afternoon Fritz Siebel joined us. He didn't want to talk about Göring. When I asked about the latter's rake-off from his aircraft factory, he suddenly went red!'[11] And again,

General Kreipe came back on to the theme of the aluminium plants in Norway, which I had opposed both verbally and in writing. Today I am beginning to suspect that Göring was getting his cut from these as well, like Koppenberg and friends. After all, one and a half billion marks were invested for a return of nil point nil. We never got as much aluminium out of Norway during the war as the existing factories had produced there in peacetime. . . . The crook's proper place is before a German court martial![12]

* Personal papers of General Koller. The quotation is from Göring's lengthy speech to the Air Staff when Kreipe was replaced by Koller. Göring continued, 'Besides, the life in this world is by no means so sublime that I am not willing to pass on with great wonderment and curiosity to find out what it is like in the next.'[9]

Towards the end of August 1945 Milch was flown back to southern Germany in a Flying Fortress. Quite informally, he had thus been transferred from British to American custody, a technicality which was to cause some anxious moments for the Allies when sentence came to be passed on him. He was imprisoned in the Air Interrogation Centre at Kaufbeuren, a former lunatic asylum where Nazi doctors had been engaged in liquidating the mentally handicapped patients for some years. Milch had no idea what was wanted of him until late in September, when the uncertainty began to clear. On the twenty-third Englander visited him, explaining that he was about to call on Albert Speer, who was a witness in the coming trial, and would Milch like to go to Nuremberg as a witness as well? The field marshal emphatically declined.[13] Englander's invitation was evidently purely a formality for on 12 October Milch was called for anyway by car and driven off to Nuremberg. At two o'clock that afternoon he was in the prison yard of the forbidding Palace of Justice, within the walls of Hitler's erstwhile capital of the Nazi movement, and meeting the prison commandant for the first time.

The Nuremberg Trials have already exercised enough minds to make any discourse upon them here superfluous. Ironically, Milch had been brought to Nuremberg as a witness for the prosecution: news of his unconcealed hatred for Göring was no doubt the reason for his presence here; but in the prison's confines he suffered such indignities at the hands of the Americans, and heard such remarkable reports through the prison grapevine of the transformation his former commander-in-chief had undergone, that he resolved to *defend* the Reichsmarschall to the best of his ability. Besides, he met the ailing and elderly Field Marshal von Blomberg again and he was also speaking more favourably of Göring now; together with General Guderian (Hitler's former army chief of staff), Milch and Blomberg formed one of the factions in the witnesses' wing of the prison. A rival faction formed round the General Staff: Halder ('who refused my proffered hand'), von Falkenhorst ('servile as ever') and the younger von Brauchitsch belonged to it, as did General Warlimont, Jodl's deputy.[14]

Eleven days after the gates of Nuremberg Prison closed behind him, Milch was summoned before Major John J. Monigan, Jr, for his first interrogation.[15] It began harmlessly, touching on Milch's official relations with Speer (who was in fact indicted among the defendants) and on the history of Central Planning. But after about an hour Monigan changed the subject. 'Leaving Central Planning for the moment—part of your duty in the Air Ministry was the development of new equipment, was it not?' Milch agreed that since 1941 this was so—'technical developments like aeroplanes and so forth'. Monigan pressed him, 'What was the situation regarding the use of the pressure-chamber in the development of aviation?' The field marshal gave a neutral answer, but the major persisted, 'Were you familiar with the experiments which were carried out with pressure-chambers?' Monigan now asked how Heinrich Himmler and the SS had become involved in the experiments and whether the Luftwaffe's Surgeon-General Dr Hippke was involved. And had not Himmler approached Hippke about airmen who had parachuted into the sea, to ask if the Air Ministry would assist in low-temperature experiments on human beings?

Milch replied that Hippke had refused the SS overtures, because such experiments were superfluous. 'After all,' he added, 'we had enough experience—we had saved several hundred airmen who had been swimming in the Channel at very low temperatures. And we had several doctors who tried out these experiments on themselves until they lost consciousness, and so all the questions connected with this matter were perfectly clear to us.' Monigan asked about a former Luftwaffe doctor who had been transferred to the SS: 'The name was Rascher.'* Milch did not know him. The Americans then asked if he had seen a film of experiments on human beings and Milch replied, 'I say again, on oath, that I never saw a film or anything that had any connection with people who were undergoing water-cooling.'

When he returned to his cell he could see ahead more clearly than for a long time. In his diary he mused, 'I only knew that Hippke complained to me that the SS was now trying to work its way into this as well, and that he had rejected a proposal for a combined research project.' Next day he was confronted with a letter signed by him in 1942 actually referring to Dr. Rascher.[16] It read, 'Dear Herr Himmler, Many thanks for your letter of 25 August. I have read with great interest the report of Dr Rascher and Dr Romberg.† I have been informed of the

---

* Dr Sigmund Rascher and his wife had conducted these experiments on concentration-camp prisoners at Dachau; both were shot by the SS in April 1945 for fraud. The background and medical value of the experiments are investigated in the report prepared by Major Leo Alexander, MC, US army: 'The Treatment of Shock from Prolonged Exposure to Cold, Especially in Water' (CIOS Black List Item 24, Medical).

† Dr Hans Romberg was put on trial in the doctors' trial, which ran parallel to the Milch trial, for the low-pressure experiments on human beings; but he was acquitted (as was Milch on this count). As for not having recalled the name 'Rascher', Milch's personal assistant was to testify that the field marshal once signed eight hundred letters in three days and his adjutant testified that the daily postbag of Air Armament alone was about three thousand letters.[17]

current experiments. In the near future I shall ask the two gentlemen to talk to my people and show them a film.'[18] Having read this, Milch suggested that it was just a diplomatic reply to a letter from Himmler which he himself had no recollection of receiving. But there was another document confronting him on the interrogation table, a letter from him to Himmler's former chief of staff, SS General Karl Wolff. This stated that Hippke considered that the continuation of a different set of experiments on the effects of high altitude (or low pressure) being conducted at Dachau had no point, but that the ministry *was* interested in other experiments relating to the problems of air-sea rescue, and in particular the effects of low temperature on human bodies; the Luftwaffe's Dr Rascher would be seconded to the SS until further notice for this purpose. The letter concluded, 'The low-pressure chamber is not required for these low-temperature experiments, but it is urgently needed elsewhere and thus cannot be left at Dachau any longer. I wish to express the thanks of the commander-in-chief to the SS for their great assistance and remain, with best wishes to an old comrade-in-arms, always yours, E. Milch.'[19]

At first Milch believed that the Dachau experiments referred to were the standard physiological experiments on Luftwaffe volunteers. But it was evident from further documents in this Nuremberg dossier that the SS experiments conducted by Rascher using borrowed equipment from an aeronautical research institute had overstepped this harmless concept. The wretched concentration-camp prisoners had been partially immersed in ice-cold water and their bodily functions had been measured until they died (or could be resuscitated, which was not often). These savage and barbarous Nazi experiments had been filmed and the film had been shown to an (evidently hostile) audience of aeromedical experts at the Reich Air Ministry on 11 September 1942.[20] To the Dachau scientists' annoyance the state secretary, Erhard Milch, had still not seen the film when it was removed from the ministry building three days later.[21]

If the intention was to intimidate him the two-hour interrogation was not without success, for his diary reflected a more pensive mood that evening; but his outward reaction was to offer an even more determined resistance to the subsequent American pressure on him to testify against Göring and Speer in the coming trial. On 27 October 1945 he was again taken into the interrogation room; this time they tried unsuccessfully to convince him that Göring had prepared the German air force for a war of aggression.[22] The mental pressure on him was stepped up: perhaps it was his rank that was the source of his fortitude? The Americans raided his personal effects and stripped all badges of rank from his uniform. Milch still proved unco-operative. The witnesses were now being treated only marginally better than the defendants on whom the indictments had recently been served. The cells were unheated and open to the winds, and for days at a time they were allowed no outside exercise at all. 'Just twelve minutes outside today!' complained Milch on the last day of October.[23] But even so he was being treated better than the tens of thousands of slave labourers who had worked (and often perished) in the aircraft factories, and this was to become a point of contention when Milch's own trial began.

To Milch it seemed that the Allies were trying to exploit the rivalries and jealousies of the German leaders to divide the enemy camp before the trial began. Göring was the principal target of this campaign. Milch wrote, '[Field Marshal] von Brauchitsch has been told of insulting remarks Göring has uttered about the army and navy. What does this idiot think he is up to? Can he still not see that after Hitler he bears the greatest blame in the eyes of the German people? This antique-dealer and yellow-belly!'[24] Yet he also knew that Göring was loyally keeping the secret of Milch's parentage, and perhaps it was this that warmed him towards his former boss. Göring correctly informed the Americans that he had requested State-Secretary Stuckart of the Ministry of the Interior to alter Milch's birth certificate in accordance with certain facts that had been established,* and his other state-secretary, Paul Körner, confirmed this. That there was far more than this to the truth was a secret manfully kept by all who knew it and the Americans never found it out.

For the Germans and for the forces of occupation alike a hard winter was beginning. On 20 November 1945 the main Nuremberg trial began. Meantime, lack of food and exercise was beginning to tell on the prisoners; Milch had attacks of giddiness and was losing weight fast. The sentries made it increasingly difficult for the prisoners to sleep: all night long there were commotions, spotlights were suddenly beamed into their faces and lighted cigarette butts were tossed on to the sleeping men. Field Marshal von Blomberg fell ill with cancer and died on the Americans' hands; like Field Marshal Busch, who had died at another CSDIC in England and was buried on a false death certificate on waste ground in Aldershot, Blomberg was buried without formality in an unmarked grave; and he was just one of the witnesses. Milch wrote, 'I do not believe we can expect any different fate from his.'[25]

* See pp. 332 ff.

This was how the Americans achieved what may seem to the reader to have been the impossible, in transforming Milch into an active defence witness for his old enemy. Göring's defence counsel ascertained that Milch was prepared to be called on his behalf. On the way back from a discussion with Speer's counsel Milch saw Göring briefly for the first time in fourteen months—the Reichsmarschall looked much fitter and slimmer—and they hailed each other in passing.[26] Göring was going to need all the help that he could get; in February 1946 he asked for General Koller as a witness, but the Americans replied that Koller could not be traced (although Englander himself had interrogated him at a CSDIC in Britain).[27]

When Milch stepped into the witness-box at Nuremberg a few days later the transformation was complete. Göring muttered nervously to his defence counsel that he must expect to be thoroughly blackened by the field marshal as their relations had been very strained. But Milch did his best and refused to be cowed by the questioning. His two days in the witness-box left both British and German newspapers perplexed but curious. Walter Suskind, reporting the trial for the authoritative *Süddeutsche Zeitung,* wrote of him as 'a powerful, stocky man not unlike John Bull in appearance, clever and emphatic and not without a sense of humour'. Suskind relished the precise and unrehearsed nature of Milch's answers:

Instructions for the German soldier on the laws of war are printed at the back of their paybook,' he says. Then he checks himself, says, '—I have my paybook here', and fetches it out to read out some of the items. The effect is very strong—the simple gesture speaks volumes for his ability to improvise and for his judgement, and when the day's session is adjourned soon after, we cannot help looking forward with excitement to the cross-examination still awaiting this witness from prosecuting counsel.[28]

And *The Times* commented, 'No witness could have spoken with a greater air of confident sincerity than Field Marshal Milch.'[29]

Erhard Milch was himself in no doubt that he had won the first round. 'I was called as a witness at 3.30 pm,' he wrote afterwards.

. . . A description of my journeys abroad was cut short by the President, Lawrence. When I was asked about Göring's attitude towards prisoners of war Jackson [the American chief prosecutor] interrupted, 'We have shown enough patience, but this is going too far. I object!' The court sustained his objection and poor Stahmer, somewhat confused, asked me one more short question and sat down. When Laternser [Jodl's defence counsel] asked for the reasons for the air force's lack of striking power in 1939, the President again intervened and cut me short. At about 4.30 the court adjourned until Monday at 10 am. The defendants were mostly pretty low in spirits. For instance, I saw Jodl being led away and there were tears in his eyes.

The courtroom's magnetic recorders engraved for posterity the misguided attempts of the American prosecutors to brand Milch as a turncoat Jew—an exchange of some poignancy, it will be seen, when the truth of Milch's parentage is learned.*

JACKSON: . . . Didn't you know that the decrees which excluded Jews and half-Jews from positions were issued by Göring?

MILCH: No, I did not. As far as I know the decrees were issued by the Ministry of the Interior, the department concerned with that.

JACKSON: Uh, as a matter of fact did you not have to take certain proceedings to avoid the effects of those decrees yourself?

Milch paused for many seconds before replying.

MILCH: No. I know what you are referring to. That was a matter that was cleared up long before.

JACKSON: How long before that was it cleared?

MILCH: As far as I know, in '33.

JACKSON: 1933—right after the Nazis came to power!

MILCH: That's right.

JACKSON: And that time Göring had you—so we'll have no misunderstanding about this—Göring had you made what's called a full Aryan? Is that right?

MILCH: I don't believe so—not that I was 'made one' by him. I *was* one already.

JACKSON: Well, he had it established, let us say.

MILCH: He was of great assistance in clarifying what was very obscure to me.

JACKSON: That is, your mother's husband was a Jew. Is that correct?

MILCH: That is not what I said.

JACKSON: You had to demonstrate lack of ancestry through any Jewish source. Is that correct?

MILCH: *Jawohl*—same as anybody else.

JACKSON: . . . and in your case it involved the . . . your father, your *alleged* father. Is that correct?

MILCH: *Jawohl*.[30]

With the conclusion of his evidence in defence of Göring on the second day, 11 March 1946, Milch withdrew from the witness-box. The

* One of the American team had passed a note to Jackson saying that 'Milch was made a full Aryan on the request of Göring, in spite of his Jewish father'.

correspondent of *The Times* complained, 'Milch was enabled by the tactics of the prosecuting counsel to draw most of their fire upon himself. For nearly five hours he was engaged in a battle of wits in which the prosecution was apparently at such pains to discredit his evidence that it often seemed that Milch, rather than Göring, was the accused man.'[31] Milch answered challenge with counter-challenge. Asked for his attitude towards air raids on civilian populations Milch replied (so far as he could recall when writing his diary that evening), 'I can think of nothing crueller and more objectionable than such air raids; and anybody who still has any doubts has only to take a look at Hamburg, Berlin, Leipzig, the Ruhr cities and particularly Dresden to see what I mean.'[32] When the British prosecutor, the particularly able and well-spoken G. D. Roberts, suggested that the 1941 air raid on Belgrade was pure murder (as undoubtedly it was) Milch replied that the unpunished murder of Germans was currently a commonplace. Asked by Jackson whether he was an American prisoner, Milch replied that he was a British prisoner who had subsequently been declared an 'internee' by the Americans in violation of international law.[33] Challenged on weak spots in his memory, he explained that it was impossible to remember everything, 'particularly as my memory has suffered from the severe manhandling I received after my capture, when I was beaten about the head'.[34]

When Roberts inquired of him, in his cool and level tones, 'You are of course aware that Norway's neutrality was violated?' Milch, mindful of the *Altmark* incident, replied *Jawohl!* To our knowledge, and in our view, it was violated twice!'[35] When he finally stepped down, Milch had declined to answer only one question—whether he considered Göring lazy or not. In general the defence counsel spoke of him as the first witness to have worthily defended the German cause.[36] *The Times* commented, 'Unless means is found of keeping witnesses to the point, the Nuremberg defence will become an opportunity for Nazi polemics and false trails. The defence moreover is by no means incapable of using the trial as an attempt to divide the Allies, which is still the clearest trend that emerges in Germany today.' Milch proudly wrote in his diary: 'I must have knocked their plans into a cocked hat!'[37]

On 3 April he was removed from the witnesses' wing at Nuremberg and transferred to Dachau concentration camp, where he was committed to the notorious 'bunker'.

In the days when Dachau had been run by the SS the bunker had been one of its main features. It was a low building housing a number of low-ceilinged concrete punishment cells about eight feet square, designed to accommodate one prisoner; each had an open lavatory in one corner and a ventilation slot high up in one wall. Milch was marched into a dark and tiny cell, in which—as his eyes adjusted themselves to the gloom—he could make out the forms of *five* other inhabitants. He recognized the voices of Field Marshals Kesselring and von Brauchitsch among them. Most of the space was taken up by four bunks; the two remaining prisoners had to sleep on the floor.

For many weeks he was confined to the bunker, with only liquid nourishment and less than five minutes' fresh air every second or third day. ('The United Nations War Crimes Commission states that twenty-two German generals are now held in the former concentration camp at Dachau,' reported *The Times* on 8 May. 'Among them are Field Marshals Walter von Brauchitsch, Albert Kesselring and Erhard Milch as well as Generals Alexander von Falkenhausen and Nicolaus von Falkenhorst. They are housed and fed as prisoners of war.') Eventually the International Red Cross and an American army chaplain heard rumours about the bunker and demanded to see the captives; but Milch and the others had been moved to a hospital outside the Dachau camp perimeter before the Red Cross delegate, Bickel, arrived.[38]

Meanwhile Ernst Englander—by now a lieutenant-colonel—was so astounded that Milch, whom he believed he knew so well, had turned up as a 'star witness' for Göring's defence that he wrote from America to Mr Justice Jackson to ask whether the unchallengeable evidence (obtained, of course, by concealed microphones at the CSDIC camp in England) had been available to him: 'I feel sure that with the evidence taken down in Milch's own words one could break him down in court to such an extent that he would have to reverse himself and admit perjury,' he assured Jackson. 'I should like to see those boys hang and sweat rather than to make themselves out as heroes and martyrs.'[39] The chief American interrogator sent a woman to question Milch in Dachau, but the field marshal could only (truthfully) assure her that as far as he knew no shorthand record had been taken of his informal talks with Englander. Since Englander had not mentioned the microphones to Jackson in his letter his suggestions were rejected as unhelpful.[40]

For several months Milch had no official indication as to whether a war crimes trial awaited him or not. During July, however, he heard the first rumours that the new trials were about to begin and he thought it advisable to look for a lawyer. He wrote to Dr Dix, who had successfully defended Hjalmar Schacht, and asked him if he would stand by. Dix declined to represent him until the financial question was settled and the field marshal was still not legally represented when late in August 1946 he was suddenly returned from Dachau to Nuremberg Prison, ostensibly for the purpose of further interrogation.[41]

Soon afterwards he was taken with other prisoners to a room where they were showing a film of the Jewish death camp horrors. 'Horrifying scenes, complete with a commentary by a German doctor!' he wrote in his diary. 'Hitler, Himmler and consorts must have gone quite mad. Even though we suspected none of this, the burden of guilt stands heavily upon us all. The more senior we are, the heavier the burden. I cannot comprehend how human beings can become such animals—and how different was the impression we all had of Hitler in those first years after 1933! But why are our victors doing precisely the same things now?'[42]

He resigned himself, in his tortured state of mind, to certain 'liquidation' by the Americans, and began to write his life story, a painful labour in an unheated cell from which every item of furniture had been removed, along with his spectacles, and with no usable light once dusk fell.[43] All night long on 14 October he lay awake listening to the noise of the carpenters hammering in the prison gymnasium—constructing the gallows for the eleven major war criminals who were to be hanged two days later.[44] As he had always expected, Göring was sentenced to be among them; and so were Sauckel, Keitel, Jodl and Ribbentrop. Albert Speer had attracted a lesser sentence and was to serve twenty years in Spandau Prison instead. ('You'll have to get at least fifteen years,' he called out half jokingly as he was led away past Milch). When Frau Göring called to take leave of her husband the Reichsmarschall asked her to convey to Milch his gratitude for his courageous defence in the witness-box. So after ten years of long and harmful feuding Hermann Göring and Erhard Milch parted in a spirit of atonement. Göring wrote one last long letter to Winston Churchill (which has never been published) and swallowed poison, thus escaping execution. Of the other condemned prisoners who were hanged in the gymnasium a few hours later Milch learned: 'They all died bravely. One Yank said they must have had ice in their veins.'[45]

Some days passed after the executions. One night a week later, as an icy draught was blowing across from the barred, glassless window to the ever open Judas hole in his cell door, the sleeping field marshal had his final confrontation with Adolf Hitler, who was still alive somewhere and came to him in a dream. Milch's telephone had rung and when he had answered a voice had said that it was the Führer's secretary speaking and would *Herr Feldmarschall* like a few words with the Führer? If so he was to tap twice on the telephone (Milch's muddled brain understood that this was to prevent the line from being bugged). He had tapped twice and the familiar guttural Austrian accents had come on to the line, as hard as ever for Milch, a north German, to understand. The sequel was as inane as most dream conversations are. Milch just asked, 'How are you getting on?' Hitler said, 'Is that all you have to say to me?' At a loss for further conversation Milch retorted, 'I was faithful to you for longer than you have been faithful to the German people and to me!' At this Hitler had evidently hung up, but this weird conversation was still drifting across Milch's memory when he woke next day, and he recorded it in his diary.[46]

The interrogations on the Dachau medical experiments continued. Towards the end of one of them, the interrogator complained that he had been able to work any admission of responsibility he wanted from a subaltern, but that the higher up he went the less this was possible. Each general just passed the buck on to another. As the interrogator stood up to go, Milch stopped him: 'May I say the following! I am not interested in my fate—I should like to make that quite clear. If somebody says to me, "You were a field marshal, you were in a high position, we are going to hang you", then all I can say is, "Go right ahead! I am not concerned about my own life. But I will not accept responsibility for cruel acts of which I know nothing whatsoever, and which are totally foreign to my nature." '[47] There must have been a further brief conversation after the shorthand-typist had been dismissed; at least Milch recorded in his diary that when he said he had a good idea why dirt was being dug up against him the interrogator replied that this was his impression too: 'They want to pin the dirt on some people while they will let others off scot free.'[48]

# ON TRIAL FOR HIS LIFE

## (*November 1946–April 1947*)

Despite the numerous earlier assurances of Allied officers that there was no likelihood of Erhard Milch's being put on trial as a war criminal, on 14 November 1946 the American court marshal, Colonel Charles Mays, served a formal indictment on him at Nuremberg Prison.[1] He was charged with war crimes and crimes against humanity; the first and third counts detailed in the six-page indictment referred to the enslavement, deportation and maltreatment of millions of people—civilian forced labourers and prisoners of war; the second count accused him of participation in criminal medical experiments on human beings, and in murders, brutalities, cruelties, tortures, atrocities and other inhumane acts. The 'high-altitude' and 'freezing' experiments at Dachau formed the main basis for the second count.

Perhaps it is necessary to explain how the Americans came to put enemy prisoners of war on trial, and why they decided to afford Field Marshal Milch a trial by himself—unique among the American trials at Nuremberg. To put into effect the terms of the Moscow Declaration of October 1943 and the subsequent London Agreement of 8 August 1945 and its appended charter, and to provide a uniform basis for the prosecution of suspected war criminals, the Four-Power Control Council for Germany had enacted Control Council Law No. 10 on 20 December 1945. This provided for each of the occupying powers to arrest and try suspects within its own zone of occupation; the military governor in that zone was to decide the form of tribunal and its rules of procedure.[2] The new law emulated the statute of Nuremberg under which Göring and his co-defendants had been tried (but it did specifically exclude a number of defences that would otherwise have been available under international law).

On 18 October 1946 the American zone governor, General Joseph T. McNarney, promulgated 'Ordinance No. 7', establishing military tribunals within his zone to try the suspected war criminals; and on the twenty-fourth he appointed Brigadier General Telford Taylor, one of the most respected members of Jackson's earlier team, as Chief of Counsel for War Crimes. Taylor was confronted with something of a problem, for the new trials had begun somewhat precipitately: he had had all summer to prepare the trial of twenty-three leading Nazi doctors which was just beginning, but a second panel of judges was already arriving at Nuremberg and no case was ready for them. A full-scale generals' trial —in which many of Milch's former colleagues were to be defendants— was planned but these indictments were still incomplete. Taylor decided, rather than have the new judges sitting round with nothing to do, to 'pitch Milch in all alone'; the field marshal was a big enough personality to warrant a trial all to himself and the indictment against him was virtually complete. In one sense the decision worked in Milch's favour: in large group trials there was always the danger that the appalling guilt of some defendants would 'slop over' on to the innocent, as Telford Taylor now points out; but in another sense the decision may have worked to his disadvantage, for these early trials were conducted in an atmosphere very different from that prevailing later, after the descent of the Iron Curtain and the birth of the Cold War. Harsh sentences against the Germans were still a commonplace.[8]

The indictment signed by Telford Taylor was served on the field marshal in his cell. He had expected this development ever since leaving Dachau and he handed the bearer of the document, Colonel Mays, a letter in which he formally notified him that he was a prisoner of the British and could not therefore recognize the jurisdiction of an American tribunal.[*4] The threatened trial may be argued with justification as constituting a breach of the provisions of the July 1929 Geneva Convention on the treatment of prisoners of war, which had been ratified by the United States, Britain, Germany and thirty-two other nations (and could not be abrogated[†] by any of them unilaterally): for example, Article 60 provided that before the opening of a trial against a prisoner

* The carbon copy of the letter is in Milch's files, but the original apparently did not travel far enough, as Alvin J. Rockwell of OMGUS's Legal Division was to write in a memorandum on Milch's subsequent petition to the US Supreme Court: '. . . nor does it appear that during any stage of the proceedings petitioner objected to the jurisdiction of Military Tribunal II' (Official Court File, Case 2, Nuremberg state archives).

† It would be improper not to refer here to Brigadier Telford Taylor's comment to the author that the signatories of the August 1945 London Charter (see p. 313) included 'with very few exceptions' all the twenty-nine Geneva signatories, and that he did not therefore consider it stretching the facts to regard the charter as a superseding treaty. In the author's view, however, the fact that 'the few exceptions' included all the vanquished countries and that the signatories were the victors or the neutrals made it a unilateral abrogation.

of war the detaining Power was to advise the protecting Power (in this case, Switzerland); it was perhaps academic under the circumstances, but no such notice had been sent. Moreover, and more important, Article 63 provided that the court must be the same, and follow the same procedure, as in the case of an officer of the armed forces of the detaining Power. Legally Milch could be tried only before a British court martial comprised of officers of field marshal's rank. This does not gainsay the possibility that a military court martial might have passed an even harsher sentence than was to fall to him: it was a British court martial that sentenced Kesselring to death in Italy, and it was an American court martial that passed the same sentence on Yamashita. (Kesselring's sentence was subsequently commuted.)

A state of war still formally existed between the United States and Germany and the unconditional surrender of Germany's authority in no way altered the provisions of Geneva. The British Queen's Counsel who defended von Manstein has written, 'The status of the prisoner of war is the right of the prisoner and it does not depend on the discretion of the captor. So long as a state of war continues, the captor cannot alter the status of a prisoner of war.'[5] These were very real obstacles, and the Allies adopted various devices to overcome them; the Control Council issued 'Proclamation No. 2' seeking to nullify the provisions of Geneva: 'The Allied representatives will give directions concerning the . . . revival or application of any treaty, convention . . . to which Germany is or has been a party.'[6] Since no action had been taken by the Allies to revive Germany's participation in the Geneva Convention, this removed the Allies' legal obligation to comply, it was argued.*[7]

Milch's legal status as a *British* prisoner of war still further complicated the issue (since the convention strictly prohibited one country from transferring its prisoners of war to another's custody). On 10 and 11 September 1946 and again early in October Brigadier-General Telford Taylor conferred with the British authorities on Milch's formal transfer from their jurisdiction—in itself, an act prohibited under the convention. The British officers, Brigadier Lord Russell, Group Captain Somerhough and Mr McAskie (the British Legal Director in Berlin) agreed orally to his release to the American zone commander.[8] Milch continued to insist that he was still a British prisoner; this was ignored until he appealed to the US Supreme Court, when it was explained by the occupation authorities that 'due to a series of lost letters and delays

---

* On which argument, however, OMGUS's Legal Division itself privately commented: 'It should be noted that this argument is contrary to the view as to the *continuing* effect of the Geneva Convention in Cable W-88419, dated 26 December 1946.' Thus tortuous the legal mind!

in mail delivery' the written confirmation of the transfer was not received until 22 April 1947, some days after the conclusion of the trial. Further evidence that the Americans took Milch's prisoner-of-war status very seriously was that two days after the trial began an American prisoner-of-war discharge team arrived at Nuremberg to 'release' him from that status; Milch refused to acknowledge his release and endorsed the document to that effect. He had been appointed a field marshal by Hitler; traditionally a field marshal remains active until the end of his days and no US army corporal could deprive him of the rank that the Nazi leader had bestowed on him in July 1940.

With the indictment now served on him, Milch asked to be represented by an American lawyer, but this was refused him.* A list of local German lawyers was shown to him and he selected Dr Friedrich Bergold. He never regretted this choice, for although an anti-Nazi Bergold was a loyal and fearless advocate at Nuremberg. He had earlier been picked to defend the loathsome Martin Bormann *in absentia* and in doing so he had learned much about Allied procedures: the British Lord Justice Lawrence (the late Lord Oaksey) had interrupted his final defence speech and after a brief adjournment directed him to omit a number of pages in which it was objected that trial *in absentia* was contradictory to the customs of every other European country.[9] Lawrence assured him that the missing pages would still appear in the printed record, but neither they nor the discussion between Bergold and himself are to be found in those volumes.

A death sentence on Milch would (rightly) be a certainty if the prosecution could establish that he had participated in the criminal experiments at Dachau. Prima facie the documentary evidence on this count against Milch was damning and was more than sufficient basis for the indictment. The prosecution team began to process other prisoners, whose outlook was somewhat bleaker than his (and most of whom were subsequently hanged for direct participation in the experiments). During November and December a number of these prisoners signed statements incriminating the field marshal. It was the kind of evidence that no properly constituted British court would have admitted, but for Nuremberg the normal rules had been expressly waived. Thus the SS colonel Wolfram Sievers, head of the infamous *'Ahnenerbe'* (Racial Purity Institute) alleged: 'Dr Rascher was a Luftwaffe medical officer until the end of 1943. His superior was the Surgeon-General Dr

---

* Manstein was defended by a British counsel; and in the 'Wilhelmstrasse' trial that followed Milch's in Nuremberg the diplomat von Weizsäcker was allowed an American attorney, Warren Magee. Both their clients were convicted.

Hippke. To my knowledge Dr Hippke was directly subordinate to Field Marshal Milch as Inspector General of the Air Force. Milch must have been informed of Rascher's experiments.'[10] (Sievers was later executed.) Similar statements were procured from Dr Siegfried Ruff of the medical section of the German Aeronautical Research Institute (*DVL*) and from one Walter Neff, who testified for the Americans that Milch's name was 'frequently referred to' at Dachau, where he worked, and that Dr Rascher had said that he had personally contacted Milch: 'The low-pressure chamber was brought to Dachau and taken away again as a result of orders for which Milch was responsible.'[11] Clearly, if this could be proved Milch could not escape responsibility for the experiments.

This file of evidence was complete by 23 December 1946. Milch confidently expected that both Dr Hippke, who had actually drafted the incriminating letter* to General Karl Wolff, and Wolff himself could clear him if they gave evidence. Bergold asked the Americans to trace them for him; his colleague Dr Fritz Sauter, a defence counsel in the doctors' trial, also applied for Dr Hippke to be produced as a defence witness. Bergold's application was dated 21 December. A few days later, however, word reached him that neither Hippke nor Wolff could be found.

From every quarter news was now reaching Nuremberg of other trials. General von Mackensen and Field Marshal Kesselring had been sentenced to death by a British court martial, but not yet executed.[12] Milch wrote grimly in his diary, 'I have resolved what to do if the time comes. . . .'[13] For the last twenty months he had been carrying the concealed aluminium capsule of cyanide that his mother had given him. He had been X-rayed twice since Göring's suicide, but each time he had managed to conceal it in the palm of his hand while dressing and undressing.

On 14 December 1946 the American deputy military governor established Military Tribunal II, which was to try Milch at the Palace of Justice in Nuremberg. Under the glare of film arc-lamps Field Marshal Milch was led into the court room for the first time six days later, to be formally arraigned by the People of the United States of America. He entered a plea of 'not guilty' on all three counts of the indictment.

The three American judges who were to try the case against him were Robert Morell Toms (as presiding judge), Fitzroy Donald Phillips and Michael A. Musmanno;[14] Judge John Joshua Speight was available as

* See pp. 304–5.

an 'alternate'. All were state, not federal judges, but of the four the one who was to play the most fateful part in the final sentencing was Musmanno. Musmanno had his good as well as his bad points: he was patriotic, energetic and versatile, and his genuine concern for the betterment of social conditions accounted for much of his political support in Pennsylvania. One of the eight sons of a poor Italian immigrant and fifty years old, he had risen through the courts of Pittsburgh to affluence and renown; he had defended the anarchists Sacco and Vanzetti in the twenties. As a commander in the US naval reserve he had acted as General Mark Clark's naval aide in Italy. On passing through Nuremberg he formed more than cordial relations with two of Hitler's former female staff who had been summoned there for personal interrogation. (He was writing a mawkish book on Hitler's last days entitled *Ten Days to Die*.) Another of Hitler's secretaries who met him described his passion for uniforms: he had multiple photographs taken with his arm round her outside the blitzed ruins of her home in Munich, changing into a different uniform for each shot. When Brigadier-General Telford Taylor heard of Musmanno's selection he cabled to the War Department a tactful suggestion that his rank was inappropriate for the trial of a field marshal (in truth he objected to the judge's emotional tendencies); the Pentagon responded by promoting Musmanno to captain, a rank he displayed in official photographs by drawing back enough of his gown to reveal the rings on his sleeve.[15] The other judges, and particularly Phillips, were sincere and professional arbiters of the law.

The key role was to be played by the prosecutor, Clark Denney, a tall, handsome, hawk-eyed attorney, prematurely balding. He was of a complex character. To assist him he could call on a large staff of researchers, translators and secretaries and the full resources of Telford Taylor's office.

Milch's defence counsel, Bergold, had also obtained an assistant—the field marshal's brother, Dr Werner Milch, who was a trained lawyer himself. On Christmas Eve the latter was asked to trace Dr Hippke at all costs.* The Allied authorities had now been broadcasting appeals

---

* The court file shows that Bergold formally applied for Hippke as a witness on 21 December 1946 and furnished the doctor's address to the prosecution in so doing. Under the Nuremberg rules defence counsel had to explain precisely what they expected each witness to establish (a procedure very useful to the prosecution, of course, as Mr Justice Jackson himself observed to fellow Allied prosecutors). From Bergold's application the prosecution learned that Hippke would be able to testify . . . that witness [Hippke] talked only once with Milch about the Dachau experiments on the occasion of the answer to Himmler, that Milch and witness agreed upon the fact to decline any participation, however to disguise this refusal carefully, that Hippke made the draft of the letter to Himmler, that the Luftwaffe carried out their experiments with their own physicians even in

for Hippke to come forward for some months without success and they finally informed Bergold that the doctor was presumed to have fled beyond the pale, to eastern Germany.[16] Werner Milch went to the surgeon-general's last known address at 23 Klopstock Strasse in Hamburg; here the missing doctor's wife told him that her husband had left one morning for work as usual some days before but had vanished without trace. The occupation authorities knew nothing about him. But among the neighbours one woman remembered seeing a man being arrested that morning by British soldiers, and the description fitted Hippke. Milch's brother inquired at each of Hamburg's prisons and finally learned that Hippke was in Fühlsbüttel Prison.[17]

'Nothing enrages so much as injustice,' the philosopher Kant once observed. 'All other evils endured are as nothing by comparison.' But the fact that the outcome of a trial is different from what one might have expected, knowing all the facts (the ten-year sentence on Dönitz is a case in point), does not alone mean that an injustice has been done. It is in the fairness with which a trial is conducted that we can identify justice, not only in the result.

'Mr Denney,' invited Judge Toms when the trial began on 2 January 1947, 'you may proceed with your opening address.'[18]

'Your Honours,' proclaimed Denney, 'the defendant Erhard Milch was a field marshal in the German air force, state secretary in the Air Ministry, Director of Air Armament, sole representative of the armed forces in the Central Planning commission, chief of the Fighter Staff and a member of the Nazi party.'[19] After relating Milch's early career, Denney continued:

The defendant never went far from the aims and ideals of German militarism. He was one of that silent army of men who nurtured their memories, kept hoping and hating; but unlike the others, this man did not lie idle. He did not wait passively until Germany rose again, but devoted himself actively to that end. In 1921, one year after his discharge from the army, we find him already heading the air service of the new branch of commercial aviation.

Just how intimate Milch had been with Hitler was shown by his presence at the notorious conference of 23 May 1939, attended by only a

---

peace time, that Milch never cared about medical questions and did not understand them, that he never read Rascher's reports, that moreover Hippke and Milch only knew that in Dachau criminals who had been sentenced to death by regular courts presented themselves as volunteers in order to obtain a leniency of the punishment [official American translation].

handful of others: 'The prosecution will prove that Milch was a main instigator of the enslavement of the civil populations of the occupied countries; we shall show that he took part in the murder and maltreatment of prisoners of war. . . .'

To the judges, the words may have seemed initially stronger than the substance. After Denney had spent some hours reading into the record a mass of documents relating to Sauckel and labour procurement, Judge Speight asked him, 'Are you going to be able to establish some kind of connection between these documents which you are reading into the record and the defendant?' By way of answer Denney read out on 6 and 8 January interrogations of Sauckel and Göring apparently made shortly before they were sentenced to death; the statements attributed to them were damaging and inaccurate, and enough records survive in Washington to indicate—at least in Göring's case—that he was under a wholly false impression at the time he was questioned; but he and Sauckel had both been dead for over a year, so Bergold's difficulties as defence counsel can well be imagined.[20] He protested that the International Military Tribunal (IMT) that had tried Göring et al had ruled more than once that such testimony should be accepted only if defence counsel had the opportunity of testing the witnesses concerned under cross-examination.[21] This would place Denney in a predicament no less awkward than Bergold's, for much of his case rested on such statements, from people whose lips had been sealed for ever. After a brief adjournment he reminded the court of Article 19 of the IMT's statute: 'The Court is not bound by normal rules of evidence.' And he pointed out next day that when Ordinance No. 7 governing these subsequent proceedings was issued it expressly stated that such interrogations were admissible. 'Obviously,' commented Denney, 'the people who drew up this ordinance realized that certain of the defendants in the first trial would not remain alive much longer.'[22] The presiding judge had no option but to disallow Bergold's objection.

This was not the only problem confronting the defence. 'Your Honours,' Dr Bergold was again obliged to complain on 15 January,

. . . I have to ask for an adjournment for the following reasons. The case of the defendant Milch is particularly difficult from the point of view of time. I have of course already been working for the defendant Milch since November, but as I have already had to explain to the Court on an earlier occasion, by the time the trial began I had still not received the documents. I still do not have the transcripts of the Central Planning meetings.* I am allowed to read these conference minutes only in the prosecution's

* The court file shows that Bergold applied for these on 3 November 1946.

information room, I am not allowed to remove them from the room, and I cannot give them to my secretary to copy, but must sit and read them there and then. The office shuts at 6 pm. I am here at court nearly every day, so when the court adjourns each evening I have only one hour to read them. I still have none of the transcripts of the Fighter Staff's meetings. I have been unable to speak to any of the witnesses we have applied for. . . .

Your Honours, I beg you to accept that I am doing all in my power, and that I would willingly work from morn till night; but I still do not have the documents. I have heard by chance that the prosecution has already been working on this case for several months, while I have seen the documents only since the hearing of this case has begun.[23]

Musmanno objected to the adjournment requested but his fellow-judges outvoted him.

In the meantime—a bewildering feature to any observer familiar only with the workings of British justice—a forceful press campaign had begun in Germany against Milch.[24] ('The Luftwaffe general Milch has pleaded Not Guilty, but what other plea has yet been entered by any of the Nuremberg defendants?') The campaign was directed by a German claiming to be a former concentration-camp prisoner, Gaston M. Oulman. For example, a month after the trial began Oulman wrote, under the heading 'The Aryanized Field Marshal', the following commentary in the German national newspapers:

In the trial which began earlier this month against the former Field Marshal Erhard Milch, the defendant appears to be not entirely unmoved, unperturbed or insensitive to the hard accusations of the prosecution, who challenge that his private and public life has been that of a traitor. The twisted features of the small, stocky man flush purple with anger, as he nervously leafs through his papers, seemingly following the prosecution's statements. The seriousness of the crimes of which Milch is accused, and his personal character, have been well brought out by Clark Denney, in a manner calculated to bring a flush of shame to even the most hardened person's cheeks.

Milch, wrote Oulman, was 'one of the least likeable people one could think of'. He was accused of 'sending his men ruthlessly and uselessly to their deaths'. And the columnist went even further:

All this fits in with the picture yielded by letters reaching the American prosecutor Mr Robert M. W. Kempner, in which distant relatives or friends of Milch attest that he—whose part-Jewish parentage is beyond doubt—steeled himself against their entreaties and shipped them to certain death in concentration camps. One relative of Milch lived in 1943 in the Netherlands: a man called Maurice Robert Milch asked the field marshal to help him emigrate. Milch's adjutant replied that the writer and his family would be sent forthwith to a concentration camp if they dared write one more personal letter to him. That was in January 1943. In the spring, Maurice Robert Milch and his whole family were deported to Sobibor in Poland. None of them has ever returned. . . .[25]

Had this infamous allegation been true, it takes little imagination to visualize with what alacrity it would have been investigated by the conscientious Denney's staff. As it was, it was not even mentioned in the case against the field marshal. Nor had any such 'relative' been heard of by his family.

The campaign against Milch as a Nuremberg defendant was not without its repercussions, however. Thus Dr Erich Hippke, who arrived from Hamburg and was summoned first to Denney's office for an interview on 16 January, explained to Bergold that he was fearful for his own future if he testified for Milch.[26] Another key witness, a senior foreign ministry official who was being held in solitary confinement at Nuremberg and was wanted by Bergold to establish 'that Soviet Russia [before the war] denounced all treaties of the Czar Government, among them the Geneva Convention and the Hague Law on Land Warfare,* was afflicted by a 'sudden loss of memory' and Bergold was obliged to do without him.[27] Friends of long standing cabled Milch that they could not come. Another witness was called before the US Counter Intelligence Corps (CIC) and advised to absent himself. General Wolff could still not be found. When Bergold asked leave to call the former French ministers Delbos and Cot to testify on his prewar endeavours for a Franco–German *entente,* and the former Belgian premier Van Zeeland and ambassador in Berlin van Denterghem, the court denied the applications.

Albert Speer, at least, had nothing to lose by defending Milch.[28] Dr Bergold learned on 3 February that the Allied Control Council had agreed to his evidence being taken in private commission in the presence of one judge, Musmanno. Learning that he would be called, Speer (who was under severe psychological and physical strain after the conclusion of his own trial) wrote in his diary, 'Thought a lot about this.'[29] But here too subtle forces came into play, for Speer had evidently

---

* From the court file. Since Milch was accused of illegally employing Soviet prisoners on arms production (forbidden by the Geneva Convention) this was a very pertinent inquiry.

drawn over-optimistic conclusions from the frequent visits certain high-ranking Americans had paid on him and his hopes still centred on the dream that one day he might be suddenly returned to a senior governmental post in Germany—a hope that sustained him for the next twenty years in Spandau. He was taken in handcuffs to be questioned by Musmanno on 4 February. As he and Bergold were waiting for the hearing to begin Musmanno entered and shook hands with him. This harmless act had an unpredicted effect on Speer. 'Did you see that!' he whispered to the defence counsel. 'He shook hands with me!'[30]

He was feeling very ill and the strain of the months of imprisonment had clearly told on him. In his own diary Speer recorded, 'No press or newsreel men present [in the courtroom]. Very pleased, as this allows a clearer testimony. . . . I sapped a lot of energy, as I was exhausted. Prosecution declined to cross-examine me. [Milch's] counsel satisfied. Hope I did my duty towards Milch—by helping take some of the load off his shoulders.'

Bergold was anything but satisfied, however. The testimony of the former armaments minister was hardly what he had expected. Twice Speer had tripped him up on details and he had even insisted that Central Planning *did* concern itself with labour procurement, an allegation that Bergold had been at pains to disprove. Seeing his client soon afterwards Dr Bergold lamented: 'Herr Milch, I thought you said Speer was your friend!'[31]

Meantime—and this may have been a natural consequence of the general disorganization reigning within the ruined and defeated Germany—Bergold was having difficulties in securing his other witnesses. In court next day he rose and said, 'I would like to put to you a further worry of mine, your Honours. There is a large number of witnesses approved by this court, including several in the hands of the American occupying forces, who have not yet been brought to Nuremberg. I have made frequent representations about this already.' His carefully organized timetable for hearing each defence witness was in danger of collapse and the prosecution authorities were certainly not making life easier: Dr Hippke, whom he had traced with such difficulty, had now been arrested by the Nuremberg authorities and was being held incommunicado. 'There is an order by the prosecution posted downstairs in the interrogation room,' Bergold protested on 6 February, 'that for eight days no defence counsel is to be allowed to speak with Hippke. That in my view is something not allowed even under American law.' Bergold declared that he was sure that Mr Denney had nothing to do with this, but he continued: 'My difficulty is as follows. I have to begin tomorrow to deal with that count of the indictment concerning the Dachau experiments. My key witness is Dr Hippke, whom I had wanted to call to the witness-stand tomorrow morning. Your Honours will understand that I must speak to him today—in fact I had really wanted to see him yesterday.'

Denney denied all knowledge of the incident and Bergold willingly accepted his assurances. From the court file we know that Bergold had applied for Hippke on 21 December, specifying Hippke's hitherto unknown Hamburg address. Denney now stated that the prosecution had been searching for Hippke for several months. 'We were not able to find him. He was in the British zone and was arrested in about December—I think it was about the twenty-first.'[32] But he disposed of any suspicions that might otherwise have lingered in the court's mind: 'I can assure the court that I did not take [Bergold's] application into my hands, read it and then order somebody: "Arrest that man!"' The court ordered that nothing should be put in the way of Dr Bergold's interviewing the surgeon-general that evening and putting him into the witness-box next day.*

Dr Erich Hippke entered the witness-box on 7 February.

With his first answers the 'Dachau experiments' case against Milch collapsed. He testified that while he *had* been directly subordinate to Milch up to 1940 or 1941, he had thereafter been transferred to the Head of Air Defence (General Rudel, who was succeeded by General Foerster).[33] He explained that he himself had drafted the letter to General Wolff and that Milch had tried his utmost to keep the SS from meddling in the air force's medical affairs. The Dachau experiments of the SS were believed to be of no importance to the Luftwaffe and the Air Ministry had certainly never been informed of any fatalities they had caused. In cross-examining him Denney unfortunately lost his temper and confused the experiments on concentration-camp prisoners with the Luftwaffe experiments on volunteers. When Hippke pointed out quite simply, 'They are two quite different categories', Denney shrilled at him, 'We don't want any speeches from you!'[34] Dr Bergold objected to this type of browbeating ('We are not in America, and these are German witnesses!'). Denney apologized and candidly attributed his outburst to high blood pressure.†

---

* Brigadier-General Telford Taylor has stated to the author that he recalls enough to state with confidence that there was no basis for the suggestion that the prosecution was holding back on either Hippke or Wolff, and it must be said that apart from the incidents set out in the text no obstacles were put in Bergold's way.

† From the shorthand record of the trial.

The trial was not without its more comical aspects either. When Milch's seventy-one-year-old personal assistant, Karl-Eitel Richter, arrived to give evidence he was at first mistaken for a prosecution witness, driven off by limousine to a luxurious apartment and prepared an ample dinner; as soon as the error was detected he was whisked off to an unheated cell in the prison building and the food remained uneaten.[35] A week later General Wolff was also in the witness-box: Bergold had found him incarcerated in a Nuremberg lunatic asylum. Wolff was a strange character indeed: despite eight months' solitary confinement he—as Himmler's adjutant until 1943—had *volunteered* to answer for the SS alongside General Ernst Kaltenbrunner before the IMT; when this offer was turned down he had volunteered his services as a defence witness, only to find himself removed, as he said in evidence, to a lunatic asylum, where the military had locked him in one room with sixteen insane, paralytic, tubercular and incurably deranged patients.

After speaking his testimony for Milch, Wolff seized his chance and asked the judges if they could believe he was 'insane'. The guards attempted to remove him from the courtroom, but the presiding judge replied, 'My colleagues and I are ready to affirm that your bearing in the witness-box, the rapidity with which you responded, your excellent understanding and your ability to answer questions have convinced us personally that you are an intelligent and mentally perfectly normal human being.'[36] Wolff could not be returned to the asylum after that.

The prosecution had not neglected its own case meantime. From the shorthand records of the meetings of the Fighter Staff and Central Planning and—as surprise exhibits towards the end of the trial—Milch's own Air Armament conferences, the prosecution extracted every incriminating passage that it could, be it a furious outburst after Hamburg, or the mention by SS General Kammler that thirty forced labourers had been hanged by the SS to set an example. (The defence of *tu quoque* was explicitly denied to defendants under the Nuremberg statute, but Bergold did not fail to remind the court that General Eisenhower's Ordinance No. 1 had similarly provided for any German workers in occupied areas who refused to work to be shot.) Whether Milch had actually issued criminal orders, or had any powers to issue the orders attributed to him; whether Central Planning had any function other than allocating raw materials; whether these documents had been signed by, addressed to or even seen by Milch—all these were points the court did not contemplate. Bergold found it particularly trying that he was not allowed to examine the *unextracted* part of the conference transcripts for any material that might have been helpful to the defence.

Yet he fought with great tenacity. To establish the legality of Milch's actions in relation to the 'slave labour' programme he reminded the court on 5 March 1947 that Proclamation No. 2 of the Allied Control Council had empowered the Allies to deport German labour for reparations.[37] As far as Russian prisoners were concerned, the Soviet government had defined on 1 July 1941 that there were no restrictions on the type of work that could be demanded of German prisoners.[38] Perhaps it was a measure of his success that an American campaign of persecution began against Milch's defence counsel and his staff. On 6 March Bergold's Nuremberg home and its contents were confiscated by the American military authorities and placed at the court's disposal. Bergold protested to Judge Toms in his private room, 'Here I am *collaborating* with the Americans, and that is the gratitude I get!' Toms was so angry that he contacted the occupation authorities at once, and when they refused to rescind the order the judge declared (in Bergold's presence), 'Then I shall discontinue the trial and return forthwith to the United States. I shall there tell the press that defence counsel has been treated in this shameless way. I dislike this trial anyway!' Bergold's home was returned to him.[39]

Throughout this spring the field marshal's endurance was also severely tested; his diary records how his liquid nourishment was almost totally removed and his cell windows were smashed; there was no heating and again there was no light in the evenings, until he tried to sleep, and then a spotlight was turned on. The table and chair had vanished long ago and these were followed by his mattress and blanket. (It was the American army that was responsible for this, not the judicial authorities.) Whereas in December he had been allowed out in the fresh air seven times (three hours all told), in January he had only two hours and in the whole of February, at the height of his trial, only one hour fifty minutes.[40] Despite this lack of exercise, Milch showed surprising resilience in the witness-box. For four days he battled with grim humour against what he (mistakenly) saw as 'the forces of the Old Testament'* arrayed against him. Bergold had adjured him to keep his temper and he succeeded well until he was examined by Judge Phillips about the Polish workers' conditions in Germany. His temper snapped: 'I would like to ask your Honours to accept that we in Germany were not all public torturers. I would say that the greater part of the German people were well-intentioned and treated other people properly.' Then his neck

* Milch's diary.

went red, his eyes bulged and he shouted at the president, 'Or you may think—and you are perfectly entitled to—that *all* Germans are criminals. And then you must say you are justified in simply hanging the lot. In which case you had better make a start with me!'[41] Bergold sank his head into his hands.

There were altogether thirty-one witnesses for the defence. The Americans had broadcast repeated appeals for direct evidence of Milch's activities over the wireless system, but not one witness had come forward. By the time the trial began, they had found only three men willing to testify against the field marshal—two French labourers and a German who professed to be a qualified aircraft engineer, one Josef Krysiak. Taken together, their evidence gave a vivid impression of the cruel conditions encountered in various armaments factories.

The emotional effect of Krysiak's evidence moved even Milch to write sympathetically about him that evening as a 'German engineer from Messerschmitt's thrown into Mauthausen concentration camp in 1940—poor devil'.[42] The testimony was devastating.

KRYSIAK: I swear by Almighty God to speak the truth, the whole truth and nothing but the truth.

DENNEY: What is your profession?

KRYSIAK: A qualified aircraft engineer.

DENNEY: And when did you terminate your studies?

KRYSIAK: In 1936, in Berlin-Charlottenburg.

DENNEY: And were you professionally employed thereafter?

KRYSIAK: Yes, at Fokker's in Amsterdam and at Messerschmitt's in Augsburg.

DENNEY: Would you tell us what happened in 1940?

KRYSIAK: On 9 December 1940 I was arrested for sedition against the armed forces and for defeatist remarks . . . and I was sent for political re-education to the concentration camp at Mauthausen near Linz on the Danube.*[43]

Gradually the whole tragic story was elicited from him—how he had had to work for twelve hours a day in a Messerschmitt plant three hours' drive from the camp, with starvation rations and frequent thrashings. In the camp four men had had to sleep to each bed. 'Most of those at Mauthausen and Gusen II died. As a rule nobody was released and the gaps caused by these convict deaths were filled by new transports.'

* The reason for quoting Krysiak's remarkable evidence will become plain on p. 338.

Judge Musmanno himself leaned forward to ask: 'What was your health like before your experiences in concentration camp?'

> KRYSIAK: I can only say that I am now ill in my lungs and am under-going medical treatment. That's what the five years cost me.
> MUSMANNO: What was your health like before?
> KRYSIAK: I was a sportsman and long-distance runner, so my health must have been good then—my lungs were perfect.

Krysiak was the last witness to be heard before the final speeches.

One more surprising feature became known to the defence in this case on 25 March, the day of the closing speeches. The court asked for Bergold's defence speech to be heard *first*. It lasted until that afternoon. Bergold regretted that he would have no chance to reply to the prosecution's final speech, the practice he had been accustomed to. Of Denney's final speech, which lasted a further two hours, Milch predictably observed that it 'maintained all the old lies intact. Illogical, confused, but diabolical.'[44]

Today [began Denney] we close the case against a Major War Criminal, a leader of the slave programme, of an enormity unparalleled in history and a principal instigator of crimes of murder in a horrible masquerade of scientific progress that leaves both the world of medical science[45] and laymen aghast. The evidence discussed before this tribunal has shown that Erhard Milch is particularly incriminated as a leader of the forced labour programme which brought workers to Germany and distributed them to the various sectors of the German war economy and systematically exterminated them as soon as their value for science was at an end.[46]

The prosecution formally demanded the death sentence on all counts.

When Milch himself spoke for the last time, he did so for only three minutes. He made no mention of the charges laid against him but talked instead about his life's work for Germany since becoming a solider in 1910. He recalled how he had built up German civil aviation and promoted increased international understanding. In war he had done his duty in his country's defence. 'My personal fate is of no consequence in this connection,' Milch concluded. 'I have only one wish—that the German people may soon be released from its endless suffering, and enter as an equal partner into the community of nations.'[47]

Word of the conclusion of the trial had been noised about the prison and the American soldiers guarding him were impressed. By evening a can of toddy, chocolates and cocoa and malt, scores of cigarettes, cigars and pipes of tobacco, pencils and beer had found their way to his cell.[48] One American told him that he was now rated with Speer and Wolff among the most popular inmates of that grim hostelry. Another said to him in very broken German, 'I won't use truncheon or shoot if you run away.' Milch declined to make the effort and sadly reflected that with men like that one could soon settle one's differences, 'but the Denneys. . . .'

Four days after the court adjourned the Chinese-American soldier assigned to guard him, Private Lee, confided that he had just come off guard duty in the judges' room: 'You get two years and two months!' This would be a notable sentence, for it would effectively result in Milch's immediate release, as he had served that time already. Bergold heard a similar rumour from one of Denney's own team—that a sentence of about two years' imprisonment was to be handed down to Milch.

Originally the verdict had been expected within about a week. Soon it was announced, however, that judgement had been postponed.[49] On Easter Monday, 7 April, a lieutenant warned Milch that the verdict was expected next day. That night they took away his belt so that he could not hang himself.[50] He ended his diary and dedicated it to his closest friends and relatives, but eight more days passed before judgement was pronounced.

At 2 pm on the sixteenth the tribunal met to announce its verdict.[51] Judge Musmanno announced at once that he was submitting a separate opinion. The tribunal then proceeded to consider the three counts of the indictment. On the second of the three counts, concerning the criminal medical experiments at Dachau, Judge Phillips announced their verdict that it was obvious that Milch had never been an accessory, and he was acquitted completely on this count. Then Musmanno read the tribunal's finding on the first count, the charge that Milch was responsible for the deportation of foreign labour to Germany, resulting in its 'enslavement, torture and murder'*. He was found guilty. So far as the third count of the indictment was concerned, the court found no evidence that Milch was guilty of crimes against humanity, but found him responsible for the torture and deportation of 'large numbers of Hun-

---

* Brigadier-General Telford Taylor who was in court took exception to Musmanno's theatrical and flamboyant reading of the judgement and afterwards interviewed the judge about it. Musmanno acknowledged his error on this occasion and promised to keep better control of himself in future. On that basis he remained in Nuremberg and sat as presiding judge in a later case.[52]

garian Jews' and other citizens of Hungary and Romania (a difficult verdict to understand, since these deportations were decided on long after Milch had relinquished office in June 1944, and since no instance of deportation of Romanian labour had actually been discovered). On this last count he was therefore also found guilty.

Sentence was passed next day, 17 April 1947. 'High Court of Military Tribunal No. II. Court is now in Session! God bless the United States of America and this High Court.' Dr Werner Milch, seated with Dr Bergold, could hear low voices murmuring over the odds that sentence would be death by hanging. The court marshal banged his gavel: 'Those present in Court Room A are requested to be silent.' Milch was ordered to rise to his feet.[53]

Until this moment he had been handcuffed to a burly US sergeant next to him. Private Lee, who had snapped the handcuffs on to him in his cell, had begun weeping with emotion for some reason, and even the Prison Office sergeant had apologized. In a subdued voice the court president read out the sentence:

This tribunal takes no pleasure in performing the duty which confronts it, but the deliberate enslavement of millions must not go unexpiated. The barbarous acts which have been revealed here originated in the lust and ambition of comparatively few men, but all Germans are paying and will pay for the degradation of their souls and the debasement of the German honour caused by following the false prophets who led them to disaster. It would be a travesty of justice to permit those false leaders, including this defendant, to escape responsibility for the deception and betrayal of their people.

It would be an even greater injustice to view with complacence the mass graves of millions of men, women and children whose only crime was that they stood in Hitler's way. Retribution for such crimes against humanity must be swift and certain. Future would-be dictators and their subservient satellites must know what follows their defilement of international law and of every type of decency and fair dealing with their fellow men. Civilization will be satisfied with nothing less.

Raising his voice, he pronounced, 'It is the sentence of this tribunal that the defendant, Erhard Milch, be confined to the Rebdorf prison for the remainder of his natural life.' Milch scrutinized them dispassionately. The president ordered, 'The Court Marshal will remove the defendant from the courtroom.'[54]

The handcuffs were replaced. As Milch was marched across the prison yard he caught sight of General Vorwald looking out of a cell window high up in the wall ahead. Milch raised his arm, defiantly jerking the army sergeant's arm aloft as well, as he saluted him.[55] Some of the defendants in another case, against the industrialist Friedrich Flick, called out to ask the sentence. Milch shouted back, 'Let off with a reprimand!' Then he was put into Cell Eleven, where the rest of his life was to begin.

# EPILOGUE: A DISCLOSURE

## (*April 1947–January 1972*)

So, for Erhard Milch, two years after most people, the war was over at least. He had survived again. There was now hardly any risk to which he had not been exposed—he had crashed four aircraft, two cars and one railway locomotive. In the Second World War alone he had made over five hundred flights, forty of them operational in the battles for Norway and France. Now he had escaped a death sentence too.

After it was all over the judges expressed sincere regrets to Milch's counsel for the contemptible publications propagated by Gaston Oulman (before the year was out Oulman had himself been arrested and imprisoned for repeated forgery of documents: he had never been in a concentration camp—he had forged the certificates to that effect himself).[1]

The rumours of Milch's Jewish parentage had started in the autumn of 1933.[2] They were nourished by Milch's own reticence on the subject they were believed even by his closest friends like Udet and they left behind a legend which will live on long after the field marshal's death The whole truth was not disclosed even to him until the autumn of 1933, after Göring had first mentioned the rumours to him. In Nazi Germany for a state secretary to have partly Jewish blood could have only one consequence. Milch could only reply that he had never heard talk of a Jewish strain in his family before: Anton Milch, who had married Klara Vetter at the end of the 1880s, had been, as we have seen, a naval apothecary; and if in turn Anton's father had admittedly been called Benno, that was a normal Catholic name at the time.[3] But the evidence against Milch could not be overlooked; he backed up his allegation with a dossier including photographs of a tombstone in a Jewish graveyard in Breslau, bearing the one word 'Milch'.[4]

An investigation was immediately carried out. The unwholesome truth the authorities shortly uncovered was the cruellest blow that any man could have expected: in one sense there was relief, for Milch's father was unquestionably Aryan; but that was not all, for he was not Anton Milch, and he was not a man whom the Church would ever have accepted as Klara Vetter's husband. So awful were the implications that Erhard Milch knew that this one fact about his parentage could never be revealed. He concealed it from the author, and when the truth nevertheless emerged from the family papers he asked that the confidence should be respected about his father's identity. All his life Milch had longed for a father. Anton Milch he had scarcely known. Now the tragedy was complete, for at nearly forty years of age he had identified his real father, a man he had known and admired like no other as a boy, but a man already dead for a quarter of a century.

Soon Milch had in his hands a document which dispelled any last doubts that might have lingered in his mind, a letter his mother had written six months before (in March 1933) to her son-in-law, whose career had also been threatened by the rumours.[5] Four pages long, the letter responded to his appeal that she should set out in writing the truth about her marriage: briefly summarized, it was that her parents had decided that she should marry an apparently orphaned naval apothecary, Anton Milch; she however was consumed with illicit love for another man, who wanted to marry her—a union which would have been disallowed by the Church but not illegal in those days. Her mother and father had insisted that the wedding to Anton, humble and unloved, should go ahead. Her unhappiness had changed to horror when she learned by chance that Anton's mother was in fact still alive, but incurably insane in an asylum; Klara vowed that she would never bear his children. In distraction, Anton had pleaded with her and out of pity she consented to the marriage on condition that all their children should be by her heart's true desire, the man whom Göring's investigation had identified. Thus the unique combination had come about, to the contentment of all parties.

On 7 October 1933 the then state secretary drove up to Kiel for one last meeting with Anton Milch, still alive but with not many months to live. A more poignant occasion can scarcely be imagined. Anton dictated to him a two-page statement, admitting everything Erhard had now found out.[6] He signed the document at its foot. He had no children of his own and before he died he disinherited the four who had been born to him by his wife. Thus the matter was finally settled. Apart from Göring, who never revealed the truth—which no man knowing it could ever forget—only a few people were informed. The letter of Milch's mother and Anton's confession were produced to Hitler, and on 1 November Milch recorded in his diary, 'Afternoon: Göring has spoken with Hitler, von Blomberg and Hess about my parentage.' A few hours later he added the telling phrase, 'Everything in order.'[7]

Yet the long-drawn-out agony of indignity was to continue much longer, inflicted first by his fellow-Germans and then by his captors at Nuremberg, to whom his 'Jewish' background and his subsequent 'clean billing' by Göring were anathema. His mother was still alive: Milch could only bite his lip and contain the truth within himself. We have seen how the American prosecutor Jackson bluntly challenged Milch upon this point; and Dr Robert Kempner, his assistant, continued to work this haemophiliac wound in the interrogations over the years that followed. From Milch's diary we can sense his agony of mind: 'Kempner grills me about father (AM) and mother. . . . I turned it all over in my mind, then answered in line with my original official papers. Should I have disclosed the truth, shameful as it is, about C—to him? But now Kempner will exploit all this,' he wrote in frustration, 'It makes me sick!'[8]

From the autumn of 1933 onwards there had been one thing of which he was now certain: he could expect to advance no further if he admitted the truth about his parentage. It would have been unthinkable under the rigid Prussian code of ethics for a minister or a commander-in-chief to have a concealed history like his.[9]

As Milch's life sentence now began, members of Denney's own prosecution team privately urged Dr Bergold to lodge an appeal with the US Supreme Court, a course which no other German lawyer had yet considered. On 2 May Bergold did indeed petition the military governor either to quash the sentence as illegal under the Geneva Convention or to reduce it as certain findings had not been supported by the evidence.[10] At the same time Bergold petitioned the US Supreme Court, challenging the legality of Military Tribunal II, and applying for a writ of habeas corpus.[11] As to the first petition, the US deputy military governor, Major-General Frank A. Keating, upheld the tribunal's findings.[12] As to the second, Keating forwarded it to Washington with a recommendation that the application should be rejected.

The device used by Dr Bergold in applying for a writ of habeas corpus had been overlooked by the planners of the Nuremberg statute, and the petition could not be prevented from going all the way to Washington. In the American capital it nearly succeeded: it reached the very doors of the Supreme Court, but by four votes to four the court ruled that it was unable to hear it (Justice Jackson very properly abstained from voting).[13] Subsequently Bergold appealed to the Swiss government as

the protecting Power about what he alleged were the American violations of the Geneva Convention in putting Milch on trial. In reply the
Swiss government disclosed that the United States had withdrawn their
recognition of Switzerland as the protecting Power in early 1945
(Britain and Canada had not). This did not, in their view, lessen the
force of the Hague Treaty of 1907 or the Geneva Convention concerned, but there was nothing they were prepared to do about it.[14]

All this time people like Professor Messerschmitt and Dr Heinkel,
who were—as the documents indicate—*personally* responsible for the employment of concentration-camp prisoners in their factories, were free,
as was indeed Karl-Otto Saur, Milch's joint chief in the Fighter Staff.

For the first three months of his sentence the field marshal was imprisoned with the seven major war criminals who had survived the first trial.
He passed the time in long private talks with Speer, Hess and the others,
who were not to leave Spandau for many years to come. Milch was
an accurate observer and a conscientious recorder of detail and the
diaries he kept thus have a certain interest.

Rudolf Hess appeared to be the only one left with any faith in National Socialism. All the others had recanted to a greater or lesser degree. He was evidently writing a book: a typewriter clattered constantly
in his cell, and from time to time he would emerge to grill Milch and
Speer on the details of the important weapons-project failures, like the
four-engined Ju 89 stopped by Göring in 1937; he evidently considered
these responsible for the German defeat.

I told him that all these were just minutiae, and not the decisive factors.
We were defeated because Hitler went to war after only four or five years'
rearmament, with no rising class of military leaders. I said the same was
true of the civil sector: the conflict between the State and Party, and the
disorganization that this caused. And on top of that virtually useless people
acting as administrators—gauleiters, district leaders and the like.[15]

It was one of a number of somewhat brittle conversations conducted
in an atmosphere of forced politeness; Speer often found some excuse
to leave the discussions early on. He told Milch privately that he thought
that Hess was trying to prove that Hitler and National Socialism had
been let down by the incompetence of the lesser leaders. Milch could
see that not only was Hess's faith in Hitler unshattered, he had a growing belief in his own National Socialist mission.[16] In June 1947 the
erstwhile deputy Führer stunned him with a remark that he was 'trying
to find a better name for the Ministry of Propaganda'.[17] 'He is a strange

man,' concluded Milch, 'partly intelligent, partly very mixed-up, but such a fanatic and ascetic that it is not possible to regard him as completely sane.' And after he saw him for the last time, 'He has donned the mantle of a martyr and sees every occurrence only as an act of spite against his person.'[18]

The field marshal's relations with Grand-Admiral Raeder, now seventy-two years old, were at first strained. Both had attended Hitler's secret speech of 23 May 1939, but when Milch had asked him in February 1947 to testify to its true nature, which was very different from what Hitler's adjutant had recorded, the admiral sent word back to Bergold that 'if I have come a cropper and been convicted I see no reason why the others should not suffer too'.[19] Later he had said of Milch, 'I can't abide the fellow!' But now that the ordeal of both was over, a belated friendship sprang up between Milch and the reserved and charmless admiral. Raeder now confirmed what Milch had remembered of Hitler's 1939 speech to them and pointed out that had the Führer at that time started his firm intention of declaring war, the navy would have entered the hostilities far better prepared than it did.[20]

It was Albert Speer who still fascinated Milch: he regarded him with a mixture of envy, loyalty, amusement, cynicism and admiration. 'Speer thinks nothing of soldiers. After all, he himself never served. Strongly egocentric—particularly interested to know what the Yanks and Germans think of him. Still has the same old ambitions—very outspoken against Göring, Keitel and Saur. His memory only good in parts.'[21] By his own account the minister had lived through many dramatic events, sometimes as observer, sometimes as conspirator. Of the last days in Berlin Speer described how Hitler had planned his suicide:

> Hitler really wanted to stay alive and remain in Berlin until he had organized the resistance. This latter intention he, Speer, foils by persuading Colonel-General Heinrici and his chief of staff [Colonel] Kinzel to abandon Berlin. Only in this way can Speer prevent the large-scale demolition of Berlin's bridges and industry as ordered by Hitler in the event of a battle. The OKW detects this sabotage attempt, and Hitler sends Keitel and Jodl out of Berlin. They dismiss Heinrici, but cannot undo what has been done. Only at Nuremberg do Keitel and Jodl learn that Speer was the *spiritus rector*.

To this Milch added, 'Well, well!'[22]

The field marshal also maintained a healthy scepticism about Speer's claim to have planned to assassinate Hitler, and he questioned him privately about this on at least three occasions. Speer's account grew more detailed with each telling.

About the middle of February 1945, he [Speer] plans to infiltrate a new poison gas, capable of penetrating any filter, into Hitler's bunker at the Reich Chancery, by means of the ventilation shaft. In the evenings there are usually only Hitler, Bormann and Goebbels down there in the bunker. Speer intends to procure the gas from Stahl, of the Main Munitions Committee. The idea fails for three reasons: the chemicals have to be activated by an explosion, impossible in the air intake duct; secondly, on Hitler's orders the intake duct has suddenly been bricked up to a height of ten feet, and thirdly the garden round the shaft is patrolled by several sentries. He does not want to run any personal risk. Thus he toys with the idea in his mind until the end of March—now for, and now against. Then he goes to the Ruhr on about 23 or 24 March 1945, where he talks, unrecognized, to an elderly miner who displays a childlike faith in the Führer. Whereupon, says Speer, he gives up his assassination idea!

He was asked about it during the trials by Lawrence and Jackson. The 'plot' has been of the utmost value to him. Jackson has let him know that he is the only defendant he respects.*[23]

Milch purposely avoided discussing with Speer his repeated claims to have increased aircraft output after the field marshal's resignation. ('What's the point of bickering—it's all over and done with!')[24]

After the lorries finally rolled out of Nuremberg Prison, carrying Speer and his fellow prisoners away to Spandau in Berlin, Milch put down on paper his private assessment of his former colleague:

Of the younger ones, his is the most marked personality—highly intelligent, artistic in temperament and ambitious to the point of power-hunger; knows what he wants and what his worth is. Temperamental, well suited for higher office with the reservation that he frequently displays poor judgement of character. Very accommodating, but at times also abrupt. Always unpredictable. Sometimes belligerent, sometimes peaceable. Usually opposed to the general trend and whatever one would normally expect. Personally courageous, and intercedes for others without thought of his own safety. Desires publicity, as he suffers from a certain vanity. . . . Germany could make better use of him elsewhere, even today.[25]

Finally there was Walther Funk, the flabby, homosexual former Economics Minister. Like Hess he was a sick man and every personal attack

* Jackson's respect for Speer also speaks loudly from his private papers: given a choice as to which defendant he would have acquitted, he wrote in a memoir he would have acquitted Speer.

wounded him deeply. When the German press announced that '45,000 bottles of wine and several hundredweight of flour' had been found hidden in his home—a total invention, of the kind which found ready credence in postwar Germany—he flew into an impotent rage which repelled Milch.[26] Funk's sensitive nerves had worse to suffer next day: SS General Pohl, on trial for his life, confessed that he had sworn his affidavit against Funk (which had figured prominently in the evidence before the IMT) only after considerable maltreatment.*

A few weeks later, early in September 1947, it was Milch's nerves that suffered. It was unexpectedly discovered during the Pohl trial that Josef Krysiak, the sole German witness produced by the American prosecution in the case against Milch, was a perjurer of astounding audacity and a convict with a criminal record.[27] He had never been inside a concentration camp in his life, let alone worked for Messerschmitt's or in the aircraft industry. Yet this was clearly the witness who had made most impression on Judge Musmanno; altogether fifty-six lines of his written opinion were devoted to the harrowing, but entirely fictitious, evidence of this thirty-six-year-old German:

In contrast to the idyllic picture of harmony in an explosives factory or of 'Strength through Joy' at Nuremberg, one recalls the picture of the final witness in this trial to one's memory: he too was a German. He too worked in a war factory. In December 1940 he commented in a conversation with friends that Germany could not win the war if America entered the European conflict. The Gestapo learned of this remark and he was put into a concentration camp. . . . The collapse of this man's health is perhaps only a fraction of the real damage he has suffered. In the witness box he gave the impression of a man broken by the hell of these five years. His voice trembled, his shoulders dropped, his looks were far away. He was alive, and there was something in him that had already died. Perhaps he was musing on the real tragedy—that all these horrors had been inflicted upon him by his fellow-countrymen, not because he had turned against his own country, but because he had spoken the truth, which—had it been heeded—could have prevented not only his misfortune but also the ruination of millions of his brothers. . . .

The Americans tried to introduce Krysiak again as their witness during the Pohl case. Dr Georg Fröschmann, a colleague of Dr Bergold, established from the civil police records that Krysiak had a long criminal record, starting at the age of nineteen, with twelve convictions for re-

* Full details are in the shorthand record of Case IV, USA v. Oswald Pohl et al.

peated fraud, begging, illegal frontier-crossing, illegally wearing a uniform to perpetrate marriage frauds on rich widows, embezzlement and forgery; in October 1941 the regular criminal courts had sentenced him to death as a habitual criminal, though the sentence was later commuted to ten years' penal servitude.[28] In his evidence in the Milch case he had perjured himself from one end to the other. Yet despite his background the Americans had made this creature an official 'property trustee' after the Milch case, working in their Property Control Division. Here he reverted to form, for within eighteen months he was back in prison on two counts of embezzlement, the fraudulent use of an academic degree and forgery.[29] Bergold and Fröschmann both appealed to the tribunals to convict Krysiak for perjury, but in August 1948 Judge Toms finally ruled that perjury was not an offence under international law, so they had no jurisdiction.

Milch remained in Landsberg Prison, watching the constant flow of prisoners, some less fortunate than he, with the red jackets that marked them out as 'candidates' for the hangmen. His bitterness turned to stoicism. He learned carpentry and glazing (he jokingly told a visitor that Landsberg was the only jail that could boast about its priceless 'Milchglas').* Early in 1951 the Allies reduced his life sentence to fifteen years and he was released on parole after serving two-thirds of this sentence, in mid-1955.[30] Much in the world outside had changed, but much was the same as ever. A new Lufthansa airline had been founded and a new German air force under General Josef Kammhuber was in its infancy. Once again Milch was the outsider, but this time there could be no return: he had been stripped of all his possessions and was forbidden under the terms of his parole to meet his wartime colleagues and friends. The memory of Milch faded from the public mind.

Industry—the Fiat aviation division and the Thyssen steel combine—did not forget him and employed him almost to the end as an adviser. He lived with relations in Düsseldorf until illness carried him to hospital at the end of 1971. On 30 December his field marshal's baton, which had been taken from him in 1945 and been purchased after many wanderings by a Scottish family in memory of three sons they had lost in the RAF in the war, was returned by their generosity to Germany, and formally handed back to Milch in a small ceremony by a Bundeswehr general at his bedside. When he died not long after, the newspapers published the announcement with the words he had requested: 'Erhard Milch, Field Marshal: born 30 March 1892, died 25 January 1972, signs over and out.' It was characteristic of him to use the same phrase

---

* An expensive opalescent glass.

that the Luftwaffe unit, trapped inside Stalingrad, had signalled to him as the enemy broke down the door twenty-nine years before.

The tragedy of the German air force was wrought by the three men who had ruled its fortunes—Göring who had fathered it, Milch who had created it and Hitler who used it. Its ultimate defeat cannot be attributed to any insuperable disadvantage in materials or resources. (Even the oil shortage which reduced the hours of flying training and finally grounded the operational squadrons themselves would not have become crucial had the energetic defensive measures of 1944 been adopted two years before, as Milch had recommended.) The principal cause of its defeat was its unreadiness and the high-level conflicts over how it should be committed to battle: the blade that destroyed the Polish and French air forces was still too brittle to survive the exhausting conflict that lay ahead, and was shattered in its turn.

Of its two principal officers, Göring was characterized by a pathological vanity and hunger for power, while his deputy Milch was motivated by a more congenial alchemy of personal ambition and deep-rooted nationalism. Between them reigned an endless, alternating cycle of *Hassliebe*—Milch refusing to recognize his minister's qualities, Göring reluctant to trust his state secretary further than he could throw him. Of the two, Göring may in some respects be considered the more attractive personality: he possessed undoubted personal authority, indeed he was a lion among lambs. Before the war his reputation among foreign diplomats was enviable and his attributes were sufficient to cloud his faults. He knew how to inspire great deeds in his men: the dogged bravery of the Luftwaffe crews in the Battle of Britain, as indeed at Stalingrad, testify to that. He was a hard worker, though only in spasms, and was defeated by the sheer multiplicity of his offices. He would work for a long stretch in the capital, then tire suddenly and depart for Italy, France or the Netherlands, however real the crisis he left behind. Small wonder that he mistrusted the more consistently able officers of the Luftwaffe command—men like Milch, Koller and von Greim—and contrived to keep them far from Hitler's headquarters.

In his personal life, Göring was contentedly married, a mark of personal stability which cannot be overlooked; but unlike Milch, Göring was not a man of vision, as is shown by his ready abandonment in peacetime of Milch's ten-year plan for the creation of a well-exercised and -staffed strategic air force in favour of rapid armament in breadth, and by his reluctance to invest in the defence of the Reich in wartime. In this Göring ignored a basic tenet of strategy—that the home base from which all operations are launched must be defended first and foremost.

By 1942 at the latest, the provision of adequate air defences for the Reich should have found first priority. The truth was that the Reichsmarschall lacked the courage to represent this to Hitler; he was possessed of great moral and physical courage at other times, but was awestruck in Hitler's presence. This weakness was a major factor in the over-extension and defeat of the Luftwaffe. Another contributory element was Göring's uncertain judgement of character—how else could he have appointed officers like Udet, Loerzer, Kreipe and a host of others to the positions that they held?

It must be added here that Milch's judgement was not flawless either. His unconcealed prejudices against able officers like Kesselring (and even Jeschonnek) and his ready acceptance of indolent and harmful commanders like Sperrle testify to this. Nevertheless, Göring's initial choice of Milch—insensitive, ruthless but outstandingly capable as an organizer—was one that he cannot have regretted. In other circumstances history would probably have ranked Milch with Lord Brabazon, Juan Trippe and other great airline pioneers as the promoter of flying without fear; even now history should still compare him with Mr Robert S. McNamara, as the civilian manager of a large commercial undertaking suddenly plunged into a world of military strategy and high politics.

For the first years after 1933 it is difficult to fault Milch's administration, although it was increasingly circumscribed by the jealous actions of his master. No regime could have picked a better architect for its air power. When he began there was virtually nothing; out of these small beginnings he created by 1940 the biggest air force in the world. Even in war his achievement was undeniable: faced with the diminishing resources of a blockaded nation at war, and by annihilating air attacks, he more than trebled aircraft production between 1941 and 1944.

Yet as much as the Luftwaffe was Milch's creation, the field marshal was himself a product of the Nazi era: he adapted his language and adopted its methods. His enemies began to outnumber his friends. In later years he ruled the ministry by bluster and fear, by threats of courts martial and firing squad. Though the threats were never carried out, the court martials ordered were profuse and when Speer took over in 1944 he had to declare a general amnesty and stop all the proceedings Milch had initiated. Milch argued to the end that to combat the mass destruction and terrorizing of the Reich, ruthless measures alone would suffice; without them, it was impossible to stamp out despondency and defeatism. At the same time Milch showed great positive virtues: among them were his outstanding loyalty towards his friends (evidenced above all by his refusal to undermine Speer's early position) and his buoyant optimism in spite of the most catastrophic situations.

From the time of Udet's death in November 1941 Milch alone championed the need to defend German air-space above all else. This was a realization that dawned on Hitler and Göring only later, in 1944. By then Milch had given up the unequal struggle, and had engineered his way out of the war using the Fighter Staff as his bridge.

History will hold against him many matters, which are not all identical with those counts on which he was formally found guilty. He must have recognized that the Hitler of 1943 was different from the Messiah he had seen ten years before, a dictator irrevocably committed to the domination of territories to which Germany had not even the pretence of a legal claim; yet from this man Hitler flowed his own rank and his authority. When he 'thanked God' for the Führer's escape from the assassin's bomb in July 1944 he really meant it. For Milch too there was no going back, and he shut his eyes to what was happening about him. He had exulted in the splendours of the Nazi rise; he had marched next to Hitler in Munich, he had taken the salute in Vienna, he had banqueted in Berlin; that he suffered also in the decline and fall cannot entirely have surprised him.

# BIBLIOGRAPHY

## 1. PRIMARY SOURCES

The material used in this biography has primarily been quarried from the unpublished private and official records kept by Erhard Milch. Since the material will prove a blessing to future historians, this author has taken the trouble, while preparing the book, of assembling the documents in sequence and microfilming them, as a collection complementary to the microfilms of Milch Documents recently produced by the Imperial War Museum's Foreign Documents Centre in London; a set of this author's microfilms has been donated to the Centre, and to the Militärgeschichtliches Forschungsamt in Freiburg, West Germany, with the consent of the field marshal. These personal papers are cited in the notes as 'MPP'.

Milch's personal papers include about 5,000 pages of diaries and notebooks, which vary considerably in content from 1910 to 1950: from the First World War until 1923 the diaries are wordy and intact; as his offices expanded, Milch compiled two diaries—a vest-pocket version which has survived complete, and a more bulky book of which latter all but a few were looted by Allied troops in 1945 and must be presumed lost. The most important texts of the diaries have been transcribed by this author and can be found on his microfilm DJ-59, together with selected items of his correspondence. The diaries themselves are microfilmed throughout on microfilms DJ-54, 55, 56, 57, 58a and 58b. The personal papers also included a number of studies, including a manuscript autobiography, which are listed in Section 2 below.

The 60,000 pages of captured Milch Documents (cited as 'MD') previously held by the Air Historical Branch, Ministry of Defence, London, were temporarily transferred to the Imperial War Museum, London, and they were microfilmed throughout by the museum before the original files were restituted to the Bundesarchiv, Germany.

Considerable use was made of this collection, for which this author is indebted to Dr Leo Kahn and his assistant Miss Angela Raspin of the Foreign Documents Centre at the museum; among the fifty thousand pages of the documents are the stenographic minutes of the *Generalluft zeugmeister* conferences (Office of Air Armament), bound in volumes numbered 13 to 41; of the Night-Fighter development conferences (vol. 43); of flak conferences (vol. 42); of Central Planning conferences (vols. 46–49); Fighter Staff conferences (vols. 1–8) and Armaments Staff conferences (vol. 9). Indispensable to historians are the records of conferences presided over by Göring, frequently taken down verbatim (vols. 62–65), cited in the following notes as GL-, Night-Fighter, Flak-, Central-Planning, Fighter-Staff or Göring conf respectively. Where possible precise volume and page numbers are given (MD: 62, p. 5242). Many of the captured Foreign Documents ('FD') cited have also been microfilmed by the museum. This author has prepared a 200-page index as a somewhat primitive tool with which to garden in this formidable acreage of conference reports; the remaining volumes of the Milch Documents, which contain Milch's and Udet's correspondence and memoranda, are adequately catalogued in the Air Ministry's report ADI(K) No. 414a/1945: 'Files belonging to General-Feldmarschall Milch'. It remains a source of regret that in accordance with official policy the Ministry of Defence was unable to grant access to the post-war British interrogations of Milch as a prisoner, of which ADI(K) No. 333/1945, a complete survey of the production situation, would seem one of the most important; the Cabinet Office was similarly unable to open reports by the CSDIC, numbered SRGG 125(C), 1313(C), 1323(C), and 1324(C) on Milch's conversations in custody, but these were partly obtained from non-British sources. As usual, the United States archival authorities proved exceptionally cooperative, with the signal exception of the USAF Historical Division at Maxwell Air Force Base, Alabama; through the courtesy of the National Archives in Washington the author obtained important additional material in the form of OSS reports, USFET and State Department interrogation reports and the complete files of pre-trial interrogation records on Milch, Göring, and numerous other defendants and witnesses at Nuremberg.

The Milch diary is cited in the notes simply as 'Diary'; diaries of others are identified thus: 'Jodl Diary'. A name followed by a month ('Prof Telford Taylor, Oct 1969') indicates a source interviewed by the author. The German transcript of the American war crimes trial of Milch is cited as Milch Case Hearings or MCH. The various Nuremberg trial documents are identified by number (ND:343-PS).

## 2. PUBLISHED AND UNPUBLISHED WORKS

AIR MINISTRY: The Rise and Fall of the German Air Force (*London, 1949*). This official monograph, based on interrogations and captured documents, was kept restricted for far too long, and is now available in a pirated American edition.

—— Intelligence report: The History of German Night-Fighting (ADI[K] Report No. 416/1945, of 8 December 1945).

—— Intelligence report: The career of Generalfeldmarschall Milch (ADI[K] Report No. 360/1945).

—— Intelligence report: Personalities in the German Aircraft Industry (ADI[K] Report No. 304A/1945).

—— Intelligence report: Files belonging to Generalfeldmarschall Milch (ADI[K] Report No. 414A/1945). A 40pp catalogue of the volumes recently held in the Imperial War Museum, London.

ALBRECHT, ADMIRAL CONRAD: diary, part published in *Vierteljahreshefte für Zeitgeschichte (VfZ)* 1968, p. 148 et seq.

BAUMBACH, WERNER: Broken Swastika (*London, 1960*). An early attempt at exploiting the Luftwaffe records, marred by persistent errors of fact and dates.

BAUR, HANS: Ich flog Mächtige der Erde (*Kempten, 1960*). A disappointing biography, in view of the high vantage-point occupied by its author as Hitler's pilot and confidant.

BEKKER, CAJUS: Angriffshöhe 4000 (*Oldenburg, 1964*). This contains useful appendices, especially No. 12, a 1954 statement by Kesselring on the heavy-bomber controversy.

BEWLAY, CHARLES: Hermann Göring (*Göttingen, 1956*). This biography is stated by Göring's intimates (Bodenschatz *et al.*) to be the one work to do the Reichsmarschall justice.

BLUNCK, RICHARD: Hugo Junkers, der Mensch und das Werk (*Berlin, 1942*).

BOELCKE, WILLI A.: Deutschlands Rüstung im Zweiten Weltkrieg (*Frankfurt am Main, 1969*). This prints the principal entries in the minutes of the conferences between Hitler and Speer or Saur, 1942–5, with a useful commentary.

BROSS, WERNER: Gespräche mit Hermann Göring (*Flensburg, 1950*). Notes taken by one of Göring's defence counsel during their private consultations; authentic and revealing.

BRUSTAT-NAVAL, CAPT. FRITZ: Unternehmung Rettung–Letztes Schiff nach Westen (*Kohlers Verlagsgesellschaft, 1970*). The tragic events off Neustadt in May 1945.

COLLIER, BASIL: The Defence of the United Kingdom (*HMSO, London, 1957*): the official history, accurate in detail but lacking in magnanimity towards a defeated enemy.

CAIDIN, MARTIN: Black Thursday (*New York, 1960*). The American attacks on Schweinfurt—the style does not commend itself, but the author secures some useful material from official sources.

Documents on British Foreign Policy, Third Series (*HMSO, London, 1950 et seq.*).

Documents on German Foreign Policy 1918–1945, Series D (*HMSO, London, 1950–64*).

DEICHMANN, GENERAL PAUL: unpublished study, Why did Germany have no four-engined bomber in the Second World War? (Archives of Militärgeschichtliches Forschungsamt, Freiburg, *MGFA*).

EBERHARD, WOLF: unpublished diaries and notebooks from his service as adjutant of Keitel (Chief of the *OKW*), 1936–1939; in the sole possession of this author.

ENGEL, LIEUT.-GENERAL GERHARD: unpublished notes, 1938–1943, to be published by the Institut für Zeitgeschichte, (*IfZ*) Munich. The diaries, of somewhat problematic source value, were maintained by Engel as Hitler's Army adjutant.

EYERMANN, KARL-HEINZ: Der grosse Bluff (*East Berlin, 1963*). Based on documents in East German archives, not generally available from western sources, the book contains useful material if the obvious political line is overlooked.

FIEBIG, GENERAL MARTIN: unpublished diaries, 1942–1943. Fiebig commanded the Eighth Air Corps under von Richthofen at Stalingrad.

FISCHER, LIEUT.-COL. JOHANNES: historical paper on The Decision to Supply Stalingrad by Air, published in *Militärwissenschaftliche Mitteilungen*, No. 2, 1969; by far the most authoritative study, even if the final conclusions do rest heavily on the slightly questionable Engel diary of November 1942.

FÜHRER'S DIPLOMATIC CONVERSATIONS, 1939–1944: recorded by Dr Paul Schmidt, Walther Hewet *et al.*, in the German Foreign Office political archives.

—— Headquarters: war diary of, August 1939–July 1942, unpublished.

—— Secretary (Martin Bormann): diary notes, January 1934–June 1943, unpublished.

—— Speeches: certain selected speeches, published as Es spricht der Führer, by Hildegard von Kotze (*Gütersloh, 1966*).

—— Table Talk, published by Henry Picker as Hitlers Tischgespräche (*Stuttgart, 1963*).

—— War Conferences, published by Helmut Heiber as Hitlers Lagebesprechungen (*Stuttgart, 1962*).

FOREIGN DOCUMENTS, FD. 3049/49: files of Karl-Otto Saur, including original Führer-Decrees and interrogations of Saur.

—— FD. 2690/45: Speer's files.

—— FD. 4355/45: several folders of Prof. Messerschmitt's personal papers, memoranda, letters, records of works conferences and his meetings with Hitler.

—— FD. 4439/45: a German Air Ministry report on the reasons for increased aircraft production March to June 1944, establishing that Speer had previously put obstacles in Milch's way.

—— FD. 4829/45: Udet's file on production and supply figures for the aircraft industry, 1933 onwards.

—— FD. 4921/45: results of air attacks on Messerschmitt's.

—— FD. 4924/45: some official papers of Fritz Seiler, a former Messerschmitt chairman.

—— FD. 4940/45: a similar file on aircraft production figures.

—— FD. 5444/45: a file of General Georg Thomas' memoranda.

—— FD. 5454a/45: a further file from Thomas' branch.

—— FD. 5515/45: a file of Heinrich Koppenberg, relating to Junkers 88 and aluminium production efforts.

GALLAND, ADOLF: The First and the Last (*London, 1953*): like Baumbach's book this frequently cited work is marred by crude errors of date and detail, often erring by many months.

GOEBBELS, JOSEF: diaries, 1941–1943. The author has relied on the original typescripts, which are very much more voluminous than the selection published by Louis P. Lochner (*London, 1948*); but Lochner performed his editing task on the sections available to him at the time (many unpublished sections including the years 1928 to 1941 have since come to light) with remarkable objectivity and perspective.

GREINER, HELMUT: Die Oberste Wehrmachtführung 1939–1943 (*Wiesbaden, 1951*).

—— The campaigns against the Western Powers and in the North (US foreign military studies, manuscript C-065d).

GRITZBACH, ERICH: Hermann Göring, Werk und Mensch (*Munich, 1940*): a colourful biography based on sources no longer available, but spoilt by hero-worship and plain untruths.

HALDER, GENERAL FRANZ: diaries, published as Kriegstagebuch, by Hans-Adolf Jacobsen (*Stuttgart, 1962*).

VON HAMMERSTEIN, BARON CHRISTIAN: Mein Leben, privately printed memoirs of the chief of the German Air Ministry legal branch (*IfZ*).

HEINKEL, DR ERNST: Stürmisches Leben (*Stuttgart, 1953*), edited by Jürgen Thorwald; the memoirs are somewhat more moderate towards Milch than the serialization which appeared in *Quick* during 1953.

VON HASSELL, ULRICH: diaries, published as Vom anderen Deutschland (*Frankfurt am Main, 1964*). Hassell was unusually well-informed for a man technically in retirement, although his sources were very occasionally more fanciful than factual.

HÜBNER, GENERAL GERBERT: study, The Engineer problem in the Luftwaffe 1933–1945 (in *MGFA* archives).

— — Study, The actual Sequence of Requirements, Planning and Aircraft Selection for the Luftwaffe (*ibid.*).

HOMZE, EDWARD L.: Foreign Labour in Nazi Germany (*Princeton University, 1967*). A well-documented account of the strained Speer–Sauckel–Milch relationship.

JANSEN, GREGOR: Das Ministerium Speer (*Berlin, 1968*).

JODL, GENERAL ALFRED: diaries, 1937–1945. Fragmentary diaries and notebooks survived the war, published apparently at random in the Nuremberg volumes, while other important sections (like those in 1781-PS) were ignored, and the section covering 1943–1945 was not even registered as a Nuremberg document, resulting in the almost total ignorance of historians today of their existence. The best transcript is that embodied by General Warlimont in his commentary on them, in US foreign military studies, Manuscript P-215, but even that omits some sections.

KESSELRING, FIELD MARSHAL ALBERT: Soldat bis zum letzten Tag (*Bonn, 1953*). A meticulous autobiography, clearly pulling its punches in its loyal references to Milch.

KLEIN, BURTON H.: Germany's Economic Preparations for War (*Harvard Univ. Press, Cambridge, Mass., 1959*).

KOEPPEN, DR WERNER: unpublished series of lengthy memoranda on Hitler's conferences and table-talk from September to November 1941. The bulk of these—not unlike the Picker and Heim notes on Hitler's table talk—were destroyed at Rosenberg's headquarters, but these surviving 28 reports have so far eluded the scrutiny of historians.

KOLLER, GENERAL KARL: unpublished papers of, 1941–1945. A collection of diaries, daily reports and memoranda of Koller as deputy CAS and then CAS; of particular interest the transcript of Göring's speech of 25 November 1944 therein. In this author's possession.

— — His official reports and studies can also be found on National Archives microfilm T-321, roll 10, for the period 1943–1944.

KOPPENBERG, DR HEINRICH: The Development of [Junkers works] Dessau during 1934; an unpublished report of January 1935.

KREIPE, GENERAL WERNER: unpublished diaries, 1944. Revealing entries by the Chief of Air Staff highlighting Göring's declining influence at the Führer's headquarters, and the personalities in the Luftwaffe.

LICHTE, DR AUGUST: The political persecution of Prof. Hugo Junkers by the Nazi Regime; an unpublished study by the official historian of the postwar Junkers company.

— — and Fritz Böttger: The Development of aircraft Jet Engines by Junkers Research; paper dated 1 August 1963.

LIEBMANN, LIEUTENANT-GENERAL CURT: unpublished memoranda on Hitler's and Blomberg's principal speeches and conferences from 1933 on; IfZ file ED. 1.

— — Account of events of 1938 and 1939, written down in November 1939 (ibid.).

LINGE, HEINZ: diaries kept by him, unpublished, from March 1943 to February 1945, recording minute details of Hitler's daily appointments.

MEINCK, GERHARD: Hitler und die deutsche Aufrüstung 1933–1937 (Wiesbaden, 1959). A reliable dissertation on the period, based on primary sources.

MILCH, FIELD MARSHAL ERHARD: unpublished study, Aerial Reconnaissance, 21 February 1920.

— — Study, Struggle for Air Supremacy, 24 February 1920.

— — Lecture, Technical Developments in Aviation (Essen, 24 May 1928).

— — Article, Technical Problems of Lufthansa; published in Nachrichtenblatt des Reichsverbandes der Deutschen Luftfahrtindustrie, Berlin, 23 April 1928.

— — Study, Thoughts on Air Warfare, January 1937.

— — Study, The Development of the German Air Force, June 1945.

— — Study, The Principal Reasons for the Defeat of the Luftwaffe.

— — Hitler and his Subordinates, written at Kaufbeuren internment camp, September 1945.

— — Memoirs, unpublished, 1946–1947, manuscript written in captivity in Nuremberg prison. Principally a description of his prewar years and the expansion of Lufthansa. A transcript has been deposited by this author with both the MGFA and the IfZ.

— — A confidential study on the life of Göring, 17 May 1947; located in file of Pre-Trial Interrogations of Milch, National Archives, RG-238.

VON MANSTEIN, FIELD MARSHAL ERICH: Verlorene Siege (Bonn, 1955).

MILWARD, ALAN: The German Economy at War (*London, 1965*). A monograph on the German armaments miracle, in which Fritz Todt is given his just credit; based almost wholly on primary sources.

MÜLLER, MAX: The Todt Case, an Attempt to Solve the Mystery; an unpublished study made available to me by Herr Albert Speer.

NATIONAL ARCHIVES, WASHINGTON: Preliminary Inventory of Textual Records of the US Military Tribunals, Nuremberg (*Washington, 1966*).

— — Report and Documents of the Simpson Commission of Inquiry; NARS record group RG-335. A disturbing account of American military interrogation and trial procedures in the Dachau and Malmedy trials, investigated by an American commission.

NAVAL CONFERENCES, FÜHRER'S: this author used the original German documents of these 1939–1945 conferences, rather than the very abridged English translation available in *Brassey's Naval Annual 1948;* historians should be warned that many of the minutes are wrongly dated, and that Raeder's minutes are by no means complete records of the matters discussed.

NAVAL STAFF WAR DIARY: recourse was had to the original bound volumes in the US Navy Department historical division, which frequently disclose matters of Luftwaffe interest.

NUREMBERG: Trial of the Major War Criminals before the International Military Tribunal (*Nuremberg, 1947–48*). Especially vol. IX, containing Milch's testimony; this was compared by the author with the earlier mimeographed text, and with the wire-recording stored at the National Archives, Washington, when alarming discrepancies between the sound recording and the published version were found. This author's text is based on the sound recordings.

— — documents, collection Rep. 501, item *LX*, in Bavarian Archives, Nuremberg: writs, petitions, OMGUS Legal Division Documents and other papers on the Milch Case (Case II).

— — Official Transcript of the US Military Tribunal II in the Case of the United States of America *versus* Erhard Milch, defendant, at Nuremberg, Germany, from 2 January to 17 April 1947; this full (2,544 pp) transcript, available in both the German and English versions, is preferable to the selective extracts published in the one Green Volume on Case II. The transcript is available at the Wiener Library, London; the *IfZ*, Munich; the Bavarian archives, Nuremberg; and National Archives, Washington.

VON OVEN, WILFRED: diaries, published as Mit Goebbels bis zum Ende (*Buenos Aires, 1949–50*).

PAGET, REGINALD T., QC: Manstein, his Campaigns and Trial (*London, 1951*).

PENDELE, COLONEL MAX: fragmentary extracts from the diaries kept by P., Udet's adjutant until the end; unpublished.

PICKERT, GENERAL WOLFGANG: unpublished diaries, 1942–1943. Pickert commanded the 9th Flak Division at Stalingrad.

PRICE, ALFRED: Instruments of Darkness (*London, 1967*). A reliable account of electronic warfare between the Air Forces, based on restricted British sources.

RIECKHOFF, GENERAL H. J.: Trumpf oder Bluff? (*Geneva, 1945*). The first post-war history of the Luftwaffe, by one of its generals.

VON RICHTHOFEN, FIELD MARSHAL WOLFRAM: unpublished diaries, 1940–1944. These were generously made available by the family.

ROEDER, MANFRED: unpublished summary of the legal investigation into Udet's suicide, by the Judge Advocate concerned; written in Nuremberg, 27 June 1947.

ROOT, WAVERLEY: The Secret History of the War (*New York, 1945*).

ROSENBERG, ALFRED: diaries, published as Das politische Tagebuch Alfred Rosenbergs, by Hans-Günther Seraphim (*Gottingen, 1956*). The edition is unfortunately fragmentary, as the original diaries were acquired by one of the American prosecution team at Nuremberg and have not been seen since.

SPEIDEL, HELM: paper on the Reichswehr and the Red Army, published in *VfZ*, 1953, pp. 18 *et seq*.

SEILER, FRITZ: unpublished memoirs, made available to this author by courtesy of Seiler.

—— Typescript study, The Udet Case; based on Messerschmitt company records.

—— Postwar memorandum, How to Explain that my Career was ruined by the Work-Prohibition imposed from 1946–1949; an unpromisingly titled study which in fact gives much insight into the Messerschmitt Company affairs.

SPEER, ALBERT: unpublished official chronicles of office, 1941–1944. The 1943 volume is FD. 3037/49; copies of the other volumes were kindly provided by Herr Speer, but there are indications that these are not *complete* copies of the originals, which were retained by Speer's clerk Wolters.

—— Erinnerungen (*Berlin, 1969*). A volume of memoirs which will confirm Milch's assessment of his former Armaments Minister—more a *pièce justificative* than a straightforward history, but full of revelation none the less.

SUCHENWIRTH, PROF. RICHARD: Milch, an Essay; dated 29 June 1955, this unpublished manuscript was one of a series of biographies commissioned by the US Forces in Europe on leading Luftwaffe personalities. The Milch study is less accurate than those on Göring, Jeschonnek and Udet, which were also available to this author.

THOMAS, GENERAL GEORG: basis for a history of the German defence and armaments economy (completed 1944), Nuremberg Document 2353-PS; published with useful appendices in full by the Bundesarchiv, Koblenz, as Monograph No. 14: Geschichte der deutschen Wehr und Rüstungswirtschaft (*Boppard am Rhein, 1966*).

THORWALD, JÜRGEN: Ernst Udet, Mein Fliegerleben (*Berlin, 1954*).

U.S. STRATEGIC BOMBING SURVEY: Aircraft Division Industry Report (No. 4).

—— The Defeat of the German Air Force (No. 59).

—— V-Weapons (Crossbow) Campaign (No. 60).

—— British Experience during German Air Raids (a British source document, filed as 64.b.q. (15)).

VÖLKER, KARL-HEINZ: Die Entwicklung der militärischen Luftfahrt in Deutschland 1920–1933 (*Stuttgart, 1962*). Völker is the official historian of the Luftwaffe. Of particular interest in this volume the memorandum by Jeschonnek on p. 273, in which he advocates killing off civil aviation as 'useless for military purposes'.

—— Die deutsche Luftwaffe 1933–1939, Aufbau, Führung, Rüstung (*Stuttgart, 1967*).

—— Dokumente und Dokumentarfotos zur Geschichte der deutschen Luftwaffe (*Stuttgart, 1968*).

WAGNER, GENERAL EDUARD: diaries and letters, published as Der Generalquartiermeister, by his widow Elisabeth Wagner (*Munich, 1963*). It is to be hoped that the remaining Wagner diaries, at present in private hands, will also soon become available to historians of the period.

VON WALDAU, GENERAL HOFFMANN: unpublished diaries, 1939–1943; these diaries of Jeschonnek's deputy, with appendices, were kindly made available by von Waldau's widow.

WEBSTER, SIR CHARLES, and DR NOBLES FRANKLAND: The Strategic Air Offensive against Germany (*HMSO, London, 1961*). Official history, courageous and just, though less adequate in its description of Bomber Command's adversaries in occupied Europe.

WEHRMACHT, OBERKOMMANDO DER: war diaries, 1940–1945. Published as Kriegstagebuch des Oberkommandos der Wehrmacht (*Frankfurt am Main, 1961–1965*).

VON WEICHS, FIELD MARSHAL MAXIMILIAN: unpublished memoirs of, in Bundesarchiv-Militärarchiv collection N-19.

VON WINTERFELD, HANS-KARL: unpublished memoirs of this Lufthansa official and adjutant of Milch.

—— unpublished report on 1943 reception of the German air attachés by Milch *et al.,* 24 August 1945.

WÜNSCHE, MAX: unpublished diary, June to November 1938; minute account of Hitler's movements and minor decisions, kept by his aide.

YOUNG, DESMOND: Rommel (*London, 1950*).

# NOTES AND SOURCES

1 Diary, 10 Mar 1938. Memoirs, and Pre-Trial Interrogation, 17 Oct 1946. An earlier hint of coming events can be found in Milch's diary, 15 Feb 1938: 'Evening with the Führer. Dinner. [He discussed] the assimilation [*Angleichung*] of Austria.'

  The source cited in the Part heading is the British Air Ministry's restricted monograph, *The Rise and Fall of the German Air Force* (1948), a 422 pp volume deserving of a far wider public.

2 MCH, 12 Mar 1947, p. 1810. Cf Werner Bross: *Gespräche mit Hermann Göring*, pp. 116f. Milch, IMT vol. IX, p. 84. Also, K. H. Völker: *Die deutsche Luftwaffe 1933–1939* (Stuttgart, 1867; cited hereafter as Völker: *Luftwaffe*) Milch's diary, 12 Mar 1938, and letter Milch to author, 1 Sep 1968. And Documents on British Foreign Policy, Series 3, vol. I (cited hereafter as DBFP) p. 27: Palairet to Halifax, 12 Mar 1938.

3 Diary, 15 Mar 1938. Memoirs, and Milch, Feb 1967. The programme for the parade is in MPP. The German general in the fly-past was Wolff, Sperrle's chief of staff in the Third Air Group, Munich (who from 12 to 31 Mar 1938 acted as C in C of the Luftwaffe in Austria.

4 Milch, Nov 1968. A copy of his birth certificate, dated 31 Mar 1892, issued on 14 Dec 1937 with a further (significant) endorsement by the Minister of the Interior (sgd. pp. Stuckart) on 18 Feb 1938, is in Milch's personal papers (cited: MPP).

5 MCH, 11 Mar 1947, p. 1755.

6 *Berliner Lokal-Anzeiger*, 26 Jun 1906.

7 Milch's officer's record (*Personalnachweis*) in MPP. Also MCH, 11 Mar 1947, pp. 1954f. For a minor act of bravery on his part—rescuing a drowning boy—see the citations in *Berliner General-Anzeiger*, 28 Aug 1908, and *Amstblatt der Königlichen Regierung im Stralsund*, 10 Dec 1908 (MPP).

8 Milch, Nov 1968.

9 Letters from Fritz Herrmann, 22 Aug 1968, and Richard Falke, 29 Aug 1968, to the author. The former was seven years Milch's senior and served in the same regiment, the latter was a fellow officer at Anklam.

10 Werner Beumelburg; Ein Leben im Dienst der Luftfahrt, *Deutsche Soldatenzeitung*, 30 Mar 1953.

11 Diaries. Milch also wrote a notebook of essays during the early months of the First World War. This chapter is also based on the 334-page typescript of the hand-written memoirs written by Erhard Milch in Nuremberg prison (MPP). The diaries are on the author's microfilm DJ-54.

12 This was a remarkable coincidence, for in the battle of Langemarck in autumn 1914 in Flanders, the young German regiments also attacked singing the German national hymn.

13 Diary, 14 Feb 1915.

14 Memoirs; and diary, 12 Jul 1917: 'British prisoner of war (shot down near Anermoy) joins us in the mess. Douglas Weld, from Canada. A small party is held.'

15 Capt. Helmuth Wilberg, who played a significant role in the Reichswehr phase of the Luftwaffe's history, was *Kofl 4* (commanding air units, Fourth Army) at this time.

16 Memoirs.

17 Diary, 1 Oct 1918; and memoirs.

18 Diary, 11 Nov 1918; and memoirs.

19 Diary, 14 Nov 1918; and memoirs.

20 Milch in MCH, 11 Mar 1947, pp. 1756ff.

21 Letter Major E. von Stülpnagel (70 Inf Brig) to Capt Milch, Stolp, 3 Jul 1919 (MPP).

22 Memoirs.

23 Doc. 6, in Karl-Heinz Völker: *Dokumente und Dokumentarfotos zur Geschichte der deutschen Luftwaffe* (Deutsche Verlagsanstalt, 1968) cited hereafter as Völker: *Dokumente*. This is a list of the police air squadrons, dated 31 Mar 1920. The invitation to Milch came from Major Streccius, *Fliegerführer* of the Army Command North.

24 Käthe Patschke, born 28 Aug 1889, was the daughter of the landowner Paul Patschke of Schöneck.

25 Diary, 1 Nov 1919.

26 Milch: Report on the incident at the Flour Mill, on 13 Aug 1920 (MPP); see also *Ostpreussische Zeitung*, Königsberg 13 Aug 1920: 'Blood on the conscience of rioting strikers. One dead, many injured.' (MPP)

27 Milch's officer's record (see note 7). On the dissolution of German flying units, see Völker: *Dokumente*, Doc. 1, dated 9 Apr 1920; Doc. 2, dated 6 May 1920; and Doc. 4, dated 13 Jan 1921.

28 Letter from German Airlines to Milch, 22 Nov 1920. (MPP)

29 Letter from Herr Porr to Capt Milch, 22 Nov 1920. (MPP)

30 Memoirs, and letter Milch to author, 3 Aug 1969; Milch's diary had not spoken kindly of Sachsenberg before (17 and 19 Dec 1919).

31 The card shows flight time from Berlin to Königsberg via Schneidemühl and Danzig as 5½ hours; it is undated but probably before May 1921.

32 Diary, 23 Apr 1921.

33 Diary, 4 Jun 1921; and memoirs.
Diary, 26 Jul 1921 et seq; and memoirs, and letter Milch to Sachsenberg, 27 July 1921 (MPP).

34 Diary, 29 Jul 1921; and memoirs.

35 Characteristic of airline operating problems then are the letters Milch to Lloyd Eastern Airways, Devau, 31 Jul 1921; Harry Winter to Milch,

Danzig Air Mail, 2 Aug 1921 (MPP); Milch to Sachsenberg, 11 Aug 1921, and Hermann Müller to Milch, Riga, 25 Sep 1921 (MPP).

36 Milch, Dec 1968; and circular re Processing of War Experiences in Aviation, Berlin, 5 Jan 1920 (signed Kraehe, and counter-signed Wilberg) in MPP; and Völker: *Luftwaffe* p. 61. Milch's two studies are 'Aerial Reconnaissance', 21 Feb 1920: and 'Struggle for Air Supremacy', 24 Feb 1920 (MPP); Milch's papers also contain a lengthy study he wrote in 1917 on the future development of air power in war—a study which has proved very accurate in time.

37 Milch: comments on *Frankfurter Illustrierte* articles, 2 May 1952 (MPP): 'The Reich Defence Ministry put the money at his [Junkers's] disposal. I myself had to collect the first instalment from the Reichsbank.'

38 Affidavit Dr Ernst Brandenburg, 29 Oct 1949: he described the Fili affair as 'one of the most hateful and grievous experiences in my life'; also report of State Prosecutor Lämmler, Dessau, to the Reich Air Ministry, 5 Feb 1934 (Berlin Document Centre, file: Junkers–Milch) and Junkers company, Main Office: Description of the Relations between the Reich Defence Ministry (Army Command) and Professor Junkers from Autumn 1921 to Autumn 1926 (dated 8 Dec 1926, in the Junkers archives). This latter report was circulated *inter alia* to Reichstaff deputies Quaatz, Kulenkampff and Wieland, and this constituted the treason of which Junkers was later accused.

39 Milch: Half-annual report on the operations of Danzig Air Mail from 5 May to 30 Sep 1922. (MPP) and Memoirs.

40 Memoirs, and letter Milch to Junkers company, Aviation Department, 4 Aug 1922 (MPP).

41 Memoirs; and *Frankfurter Illustrierte*, 27 Apr 1952.

42 Ibid, 15 June 1924.

43 Diary, 16 July 1924; and Milch in MCH, 11 Mar 1947, p. 1761.

44 Diary, 21–28 Jul 1924.

45 Letter Brandenburg to Prussian Ministry of Trade, 23 Nov 1924; quoted in Karl-Heinz Eyermann: *Der grosse Bluff* (based on documents in East German archives); cf Willy Polte: *Uns aber gehörte der Himmel*, (Bonn, 1956), p. 145.

46 Memoirs.

47 Von Gablenz: note on telephone conversation between Koch and Dr Kaufmann, 13 Nov 1925 (MPP). Milch, letter of Aug 1969.

48 Memorandum, Dessau, 15 Nov 1925, in which the whole episode is recounted by von Gablenz stage by stage (MPP). Cf Diary, 14 Nov 1925: 'In Berlin with Koch and Fisch: would I like to become manager (instead of Sago [Sachsenberg])?—Yes, provided Prof [Junkers] also asks me to.'

49 Memorandum of 24 Nov 1925 (MPP).

50 Milch: Memorandum of 24 Dec 1925.

51 Brandenburg: affidavit, 29 Oct 1949: 'From that moment on this company [Lufthansa] was like a red rag to a bull for Junkers. As Milch had

previously been employed by Junkers Airways Company, he was regarded by the professor and by many of his partly innocent but misinformed colleagues as a deserter.'

52 Milch, letter of Aug 1969.

53 Memoirs; and memorandum of 24 Dec 1925 (MPP).

54 Memoirs.

55 *Frankfurter Illustrierte,* 27 Apr 1952; the pioneers were led by Dr Robert Knauss and Lt Cdr (ret.) Georg von Winterfeld.

56 The licence was awarded on 27 Jan 1927.

57 Cf article 'Air Traveled Germany' by W. Jefferson Davis in *Saturday Evening Post,* 19 Nov 1927.

58 Milch in MCH, 11 Mar 1947, p. 1762; and memoirs.

59 Diary, 21 Mar 1927; and memoirs.

60 Milch, lecture: Technical Developments in Aviation, delivered at Essen, 24 May 1928 (MPP).

61 On the successful east–west transatlantic crossing by Lufthansa's Captain Köhl (an attempt which Milch flatly opposed) see Milch's memorandum on confs with Herr Köhl early and mid-Mar 1928, dated Berlin 12 Apr 1928; and on 22 Jun 1928, dated 23 Jun 1928 (MPP). And diary, 12 Apr 1928, 13 Apr 1928.

62 Memoirs.

63 MCH, 11 Mar 1947, pp. 1762ff.
Milch, letter of Aug 1969; and draft OSS biography of Hermann Göring, 18 Jun 1945 (NARS).
Milch: A confidential study on the life of Göring, 17 May 1947 (NARS: RG-238; in file: Pre-Trial Interrogations of Milch).
Diary, 4 Dec 1928. Milch evidently did not consider Göring of sufficient importance to commemorate his earlier meetings with him in his diary. Hermann Göring was born at Rosenheim, 40 miles east of Munich, on 12 Jan 1893.

64 Letter Milch to Deutsche Bank, 30 May 1928 (quoted by Eyermann, op. cit., p. 320).

65 Letter, Deutsche Bank to Lufthansa, 6 Jun 1929 (ibid, pp. 356f). Under German criminal law (paras. 331 et seq. of Reich Penal Code) bribery of Reichstag deputies did not constitute a crime. To the author Milch disclaimed any part in the decision to make payments to Göring.

66 Memoirs.

67 Memoirs; see also Milch at GL conf, 12 Feb 1943 (MD:35, p. 3222): '. . . This was what Junkers devised, and this was how he tried to kill off Lufthansa.'

68 Ibid. Dr Stüssel and Dr Schatzki were the engineers who made the F 24, Ko, as the single-engined version was called, possible.

69 Diary, 14 and 15 Sep 1928.

70 Cf. Milch's comments 2 May 1952 (note 37): 'I played no part whatsoever in Merkel's dismissal.' But see his memorandum of 23 Jun 1928 on the Köhl affair.

71 Diary, 15 and 26 April, 11 and 15 May, 29 Nov 1928.

72 This notebook is tucked into the beginning of the *following* year's diary, 1929, the year in which Merkel went.

73 There are references to Milch lunching with Göring at the Kaiserhof in diaries, 28 Jan, 12 Feb, 6 Mar, 8 Apr and 9 Apr 1929, etc.

74 Diary, 9, 11 Apr; 10, 26, 27 May 1929.

75 Gritzbach: *Hermann Göring, Werk und Mensch* (1940), pp. 121f.

76 Diary, 18 Jun 1929: 'Audit committee: "The bombshell bursts". Heck, to tell him my views,' 28 Jun 1929: 'Afternoon, audit committee: Grulich, von Schröder, Schmidt dismissed.' Cf also diary, 29 Jun, 1 and 2 July 1929.

77 MCH, 13 Mar 1947, p. 1895.

78 Memoirs. Milch comments, 2 May 1952 (note 37); and Diary, 4 Jul 1929.

79 Memoirs.

80 Letter Milch to Fritz Horn, Shanghai, 1 Nov 1929 (MPP). Horn had been a fitter in Milch's squadron in the First World War.

81 *Bremen* first launched her aircraft 250 miles from New York on 22 July 1929; *Europa* 500 miles from Europe in 1931.

82 Cf Eyermann, p. 115.

83 Letter Milch to Horn, 1 Nov 1929.

84 Memoirs. The Deutsche Bank (Dr Kurt Weigelt) headed a consortium of five major banks granting Lufthansa three-monthly credits of six million Reichsmarks.

85 Milch: lecture (see note 60); cf his article, 'Technical problems of Lufthansa', in *Nachrichtenblatt des Reichsverbandes der Deutschen Luftfahrtindustrie* Berlin, 23 Apr 1928.

86 Lufthansa business report, 27 Sep 1929; quoted in Eyermann, op. cit., pp. 106f. Cf Gritzbach, op. cit., pp. 123f: 'The nucleus of German aviation was always Lufthansa. There was a number of minor companies apart from her, mostly of a local character. The parsimonious spirit of the time never understood that quite apart from their real civil aviation job, these companies had vital duties to fulfil, in keeping Germany abreast of the technical progress made by the world's aviation.'

87 Letter Werner Milch to Milch, 15 Nov 1923 (MPP).

88 Memoirs.

89 MCH, 11 Mar 1947; Memoirs.

90 Berlin Document Centre: Parteikorrespondenz, Erhard Milch.

91 Diary, 13 Oct 1930, lists the following people at Göring's apartment: Hitler, Goebbels, August Wilhelm of Prussia and his son, the Duke of Prussia, Prince zu Wied and his wife, Niemann and his wife, the photographer Hoffmann and his daughter who was acting as Hitler's secretary, Rudolf Hess and his wife, Paul Körner, Esser, Schulze-Naumburg and his wife and daughter, Frick and Epp.

92 Milch also recollects Frau Karin Göring and the adjutant Wilhelm Brückner as being present; cf Memoirs.

93 Memoirs; and Milch, Oct 1967. Cf diary, 7 Mar, 27 Apr 1931.

94 Cf Eyermann, op. cit., pp. 146f. Milch again related this story at GL conf, 12 Dec 1942 (MD: 34, p. 2654), adding that it was documented in the files of Lufthansa.

95 Polte, op. cit., p. 206; the first 32 Ju 52s were named after German air pioneers who had lost their lives.

96 Diary, 15 Jun 1932. Memoirs; and Polte, op. cit., pp. 209f.

97 Diary, 28 Jul 1932. *Junkers Nachrichten,* May 1936.

98 *Junkers Nachrichten,* Mar 1962.

99 Meinck: *Hitler und die deutsche Aufrüstung,* p. 16.

100 Diary, 16 Sep 1931; and Memoirs, and MCH, 12 Mar 1947, p. 1803.

101 Memoirs; and diary, 4 Apr 1932.

102 Diary, 28 Apr 1932: Milch records those present as Göring, Hitler, Kube, Ludwig Grand Duke of Hesse with his Greek wife, Prince zu Wied and his wife and daughter, Prince zu Waldeck, Putzi Hanfstängl, Rudolf Hess, Bruno Loerzer, Frau Käthe Milch and Levetzow. Cf also Milch's other meetings with Hitler, on 31 Aug at Göring's, and on 8 Sep with several others present at the Kaiserhof. It is known that during the Jul 1932 elections Hitler took the opportunity of a visit to Dessau to tour the Junkers works, and made generous promises about his rearmament plans after the Nazis seized power (Dr Adolf Dethmann, quoted by Dr Ing August Lichte, in his study: The political persecution of Prof Hugo Junkers by the Nazi Regime).

103 Letter of Milch to author, 22 June 1969; and MCH 11 Mar 1947, pp. 1770ff: '. . . Hitler said he would make available quite different means for aviation, when he took over the government. He even named a figure to me, which seemed quite fantastic at the time, but was in fact only one-fifth of the Luftwaffe's running costs in one month's war, for one year.'

104 Letter Milch to author, 22 Jun 1969; but see also his memoirs and his MCH testimony, where he makes no mention of Hitler's discourse on *military* air power. Hitler had occupied himself with Germany's weak air position since 1928 at least (cf Hitler's *Second Book* Institut für Zeitgeschichte, 1961), pp. 148, 173. The high opinion Hitler had of Milch is confirmed by the wish he expressed to Göring in 1932 to have Milch as a personal Chief of Staff; Göring dissuaded him from this.

105 Diary, 5 Aug 1932: 'P.m.: Göring telephones about an Air Ministry.' Memoirs and MCH, 11 Mar 1947, p. 1774.

106 Diary, 31 Aug 1932: Milch lists those present as Göring, Hitler, Goebbels, Strasser, Röhm, Frick, Prince of Hesse, Prince zu Wied, Brückner, Körner, and Hess; and diary, 8 Sep 1942: Heck, Hitler, Göring, Goebbels, August-Wilhelm, Kube, Körner, Brückner, Kerrl.

107 Diary, 6 Nov 1932; Milch also voted for the Nazis in Jan 1933 (cf MCH 11 Mar 1947 p. 1771; and Military Government of Germany, Questionnaire completed by Milch Oct 1945, in NARS: RG-238).

108 Diary, 28 Nov 1932. Cf Ibid, 10 Dec 1932.

109 Hans-Karl von Winterfeld: memoirs (unpublished MS); one of the officers of the postwar Lufthansa, he was present at this discussion.

CHAPTER 2

1 Diary, 28 Jan 1933; and Memoirs, and Milch at IMT, vol. IX, pp. 93f, and MCH, 11 Mar 1947, pp. 1775ff.

2 Diary, 12 May 1948: '. . . In reality he [Brandenburg] was sorely wounded in his pride and vanity, as he had wanted to head Germany's aviation. If only he knew that I actually proposed him rather than me to Göring, though in vain, but that Göring scornfully turned him down, which was not my fault. Anyway, he would hardly have been suited to the job as he was too sensitive in temperament, and too full of theory.' Milch also relates why Hitler chose Dr Fritz Todt, rather than Brandenburg, to build the autobahns.

3 Diary, 29 Jan 1933.

4 Ibid, 30 Jan 1933.

5 MCH, 11 Mar 1947, p. 1777; cf diary, 24 May 1945: 'So Göring was still addicted to this vice, although he gave me his word at the beginning of 1933, when I mentioned the rumours to him and added I must have a clear answer, as I refused to have any truck with morphine addicts.' Cf diary, 3 Jun 1945, on Milch's interrogation by Major Ernst Englander.

6 Diary, 31 Jan 1933; and MCH, 11 Mar 1947, p. 1776.

7 Völker: *Dokumente,* Doc. 40, p. 131, dated 2 Feb 1933. Milch was formally appointed state secretary by Hindenburg on 22 Feb 1933. He joined the NSDAP after Hitler's landslide election victory in Mar 1933, being allocated an artificially early number (123,685) but his membership lapsed when he was re-commissioned in Oct 1933. In the Mar 1933 election he also voted for the NSDAP (Questionnaire, 20 Oct 1945).

8 Völker: *Luftwaffe,* passim; and Helm Speidel: Reichswehr und Rote Armee (in *Vierteljahreshefte für Zeitgeschichte,* 1 1953, p. 18).

9 Hitler: speech on 3 Feb 1933 to Army and Navy commanders; in Inst. f. Zeitgeschichte file Liebmann Papers, ED 1, pp. 191ff. Milch was not present. Blomberg has stressed the defensive nature of the rearmament, and pointed to the violations of German sovereignty during the disarmed period: 'There was the separation of the Rhineland, the occupation of the Ruhr region, and the fights in Upper Silesia to alter the plebiscite results; even little Lithuania had been able to take Memel from us!' (SAIC/FIR/46, dated 13 Sep 1945). Cf Diary, 24 Feb 1933.

10 Diary, 9 Feb 1933: '10.50 am. Reported to Hindenburg as deputy Reich Commissar for Aviation. Afternoon and evening individual talks with Reichswehr. 5–7.15 pm. Ministerial Council [grants] 40 millions for aviation. I am sworn in.' On 7 Nov 1933 (diary) Milch was guaranteed RM 1,100m. for the 1934/35 budget by Schacht and Wilhelm Keppler.

11 Memoirs; and diary, 11 Mar 1933.

12 Göring's main office was at first the Prussian Ministry of the Interior and subsequently in the building next to his official residence, Leipziger Platz 7a.

13 Völker: *Luftwaffe*, pp. 44, 61, 66. The former *DLV* (German Flying Sport Association) had been founded in 1920 and had over 50,000 members. The *DLV*'s chief of staff Major (GS) Nordt soon asked to be relieved because of friction with Bruno Loerzer.

14 According to Col Gen Stumpff, head of the Personnel Dept at the time, the Reich Air Ministry took on 182 army and 42 navy officers for the secret Luftwaffe in 1933, all with some flying experience (letter to Milch, 27 Apr 1964); the figures in the text are from Völker: *Luftwaffe*, p. 16. Milch's comments on Blomberg: MCH, 12 Mar 1947, p. 1807; and Memoirs.

15 Memoirs; and diary, 11 Apr 1933, and Milch, Oct 1967. Göring saw Mussolini at 4 pm., 11 Apr 1933 (cf Documents on British Foreign Policy, Series 3, vol. V, pp. 144ff) (cited hereafter as DBFP). Gritzbach's account of their flight home (op. cit. p. 23) is largely fictitious.

16 Diary, 25 Apr 1933; 'Saw Göring about the agreement reached with Reich Defence Ministry. We get the lot.'

17 Diary, 13 May 1933: 'Major technical etc conf on thousand-aircraft programme.' Cf Völker: *Luftwaffe*, p. 27, and Gritzbach, op. cit., p. 130.

18 Capt (ret) Dr Robert Knauss: The German Air Force (memo dated May 1933) quoted in Völker: *Luftwaffe*, pp. 29f, 34. Milch states that the phrase 'Risk Air Force' was his; he had in mind the 'Risk Navy' of the First World War (Milch, Dec. 1969).

19 Order of Reich Defence Minister creating Air Ministry, 10 May 1933 (Völker: *Dokumente*, Nr. 41, p. 131); cf Völker: *Luftwaffe*, pp. 12, 224ff. This simple division of the ministry into two large departments, military and civil aviation, stayed effective until 31 Aug 1933.

20 Milch, Dec 1969. The air adviser to the Army Command had been Captain Helmuth Wilberg, followed by Hugo Sperrle and Hellmuth Felmy; the air advisers to the German Admiralty had been Adm. (ret) Lahs, and Rear-Adm. Ralph Wenninger. Wilberg was retired as army commandant of Breslau Fortress shortly before 1933, but reactivated on Milch's recommendation; he died in an air crash in Nov 1941.

21 Diary, 17 May 1933: '3 pm. Reichstag. Hitler's big speech on Geneva—magnificent. Hitler greets me.'

22 Völker: *Luftwaffe*, p. 26, citing memo by *Ministerialdirektor* Fisch to Milch on phone conv of 20 May with Major Reinicke (civil aviation department) in Geneva; this Reinicke, brother of the later General in the *OKW*, died in an air crash. Cf diary, 25 May 1933; 'Two and a half hours with Hitler and Göring on air expansion and Geneva.'

23 Liebmann: remarks of the Reich Defence Minister on 1 Jun 1933 at Bad Wildungen. (See note 9.)

24 Telegram Rumbold to Simon, 24 Jun 1933 (DBFP(3), Vol. V, p. 375). The air attaché considered the incident a clumsy attempt to justify the

construction of fighter aircraft. He doubted whether there had been any such leaflets dropped. But see diary, 22/23 Jun 1933: 'Socialist leaflets showered over Berlin'; and 24 Jun 1933: 'Noon: press conf re leaflet.' See also Herring's note on his conv with Capt (ret) Bolle, 10 Jun 1933 (DBFP(3) Vol. V, p. 378). Milch complained about Herring's tendentious reporting (Newton to Vansittart, 14 Aug 1933) and secured Herring's recall to London. Cf DBFP(3) Vol. V, pp. 496, 499ff.

Herring's note on his conv with Milch, 26 Jun 1933 (ibid, pp. 383ff). Hansard: *Parliamentary Debates,* vol. 279, col. 1469.

Telegram Vansittart to Newton, 27 Jul 1933; and 3 Aug 1933 (DBFP(3) Vol. V, pp. 450ff, 468f).

Herring: note on conv with State Secretary von Bülow, 29 Jun 1933 (ibid, pp. 456ff, 462f).

25 Diary, 24 Jun 1933.

26 Pre-Trial Interrogation of Göring, Nuremberg, 17 Oct 1945.

27 It is difficult to state with certainty when this was. It may have been on 8 Jun 1933; diary: 'Morning, reception of British by Hitler; afternoon Cabinet meeting, as Göring's deputy.' Milch, Nov 1967, Nov 1968. (See also note 28.)

28 Cf diary, 9 Jun 1933: 'Midday to see Schacht, with Göring, v. Blomberg, re: finance. My new job.' Cf pre-trial interrogation of Göring, 17 Oct 1945: 'In 1933 Schacht, in cooperation with the Ministry of Finance, assumed the obligation to raise funds for the rearmament, which was kept secret up to 1935. Göring confirms the fact that any money used for armament purposes which was not covered in the Budget had to be raised by secret means unknown to foreign nations. At the conference where the secret means of raising funds were discussed, Hitler, Göring, Blomberg, Schwerin von Krosigk, Schacht, Reichenau and the Supreme Commanders of all three branches of the Wehrmacht were present; all the state secretaries concerned and the Secretary of the Reich Chancery were also present at this conference . . . Schacht made proposals about the ways and means to raise secret funds for the rearmament programme, especially about the famous Mefo bills.'

29 Dr Hjalmar Schacht: *1933—wie eine Demokratie stirbt* (1968).

30 Milch, conf with Col von Reichenau of Reich Defence Ministry, on the activation of air force units, 19 Jun 1933 (Völker: *Dokumente,* Nr. 79, pp. 193f).

31 Order on camouflage of Luftwaffe (sgd. pp. Milch) 25 July 1933 (Völker: *Dokumente,* Nr. 71, p. 183).

32 Diary, 21 Jul 1933: 'To see Dorpmüller about the freight routes!' Cf Völker: *Luftwaffe,* p. 16.

33 From the unpublished memoirs of Hans-Karl v. Winterfeld, head of the 'Traffic Inspectorate' (which in fact was commanded by Knauss with Major Fütterer as its second in command).

34 Milch, Dec 1969.

35 Letter Göring to Junkers company, Jan 1933 (Junkers archives).

36 The security risks were identified to Junkers as Dr Adolf Dethmann, Fiala v. Fernbrugg and Drömmer; all were arrested at the end of Mar 1933 and forbidden to work in Junkers again (report of Lämmler, Dessau, 28 Apr 1934).

37 Prof. Junkers' Diary, 12 Mar 1933 (Junkers archives). Cf. Memo on Prof. Junkers' conf with Milch and *Ministerialrat* Panzeram, Berlin, 6 Apr 1933; and Junkers' diary, 7 Apr 1933. On 27 Apr 1933 Prof Junkers wrote to Hitler requesting an interview; his notes show he intended to propose the development of a mass-production fighter aircraft as a defence system. The agreed interview was cancelled at short notice, however.

38 Diary, 1 Jul 1933.

39 Instructions on setting up air training schools (sgd. Milch) 14 Aug 1933 (Völker: *Dokumente,* Nr. 81, pp. 195ff).

40 British Air Ministry: *The Rise and Fall of the German Air Force,* pp. 7f. Of the 4,021 aircraft included in the programme, which was superseded by another in Jan 1935, 1,714 were land-based operational types, 1,760 were trainers, 89 were communications and 309 miscellaneous (experimental series etc). They were distributed as follows: Lufthansa 115, units 1,085, training 2,168, research 138, airfields 156, flak schools 5, target-towing 48, clubs 33, Reichsbank 12, Hitler 10, miscellaneous 80, wastage 171. Cf diary, 13 Sep 1933: 'Berlin. Noon to Hitler to discuss aircraft for Party (twelve) and publishing-house (six)'.

41 ND: 1708, 1715, and 1724-NI.

42 Pre-Trial Interrogation, 6 Nov 1946; in 1933 Junkers manufactured 41 aircraft and thereafter the following numbers: 1934, 238; 1935, 433; 1937, 529; 1939, 922; 1942, 1,782; 1944, 3,106, or altogether 12,530 from 1933 to 1945; the licencee factories manufactured 17,522 Junkers aircraft from 1933 to 1945.

43 Junkers diary, 24 Aug 1933. *Junkers Nachrichten,* Mar 1962.

44 Diary, 24 Aug 1933.

45 Manpower of air industry, statistics, Berlin, 14 Aug 1939 (Udet file: FD. 4940 45). The annual labour statistics for the air industry, divided as to airframes, motors, signals and national equipment, bombs and ammunition (not including Army Ordnance Dept contracts) show 230,000 workers in 1937, 269,000 in 1938, 325,000 in 1939, and an anticipated total of 340,000 in 1940, 400,000 in 1941 and 500,000 in 1942.

46 Milch, May 1968; and Memoirs. Wever's appointment as chief of staff (*de facto*) took effect from 1 Sep 1933; Milch stated to the author that besides Wever the then Col Stumpff also had his personal file endorsed, 'Suitable for a later C-in-C of the Army.'

47 Diary, 25 Aug 1933.

48 Milch, May 1968: Milch stressed that there was never any talk of a 'Urals bomber', a word subsequently attributed to Wever. Cf Völker: *Luftwaffe,* p. 30, where the recollections of the then head of the Technical Department, Col Wimmer, are cited. Cf Milch at GL conf, 27 Apr 1943 (MD: 20, p. 5212): 'In 1933 we set wheels in motion in this field, but

we stopped the development work again in 1937. That was the Ju 89 and the Do 19. I never understood why.'

49 Hindenburg was told that since the flak commander was expected to take orders from Göring, the latter must have a military rank. Diary, 19 Oct 1933; MCH, 11 Mar 1947, pp. 1779f.

50 Völker: *Die Entwicklung der militärischen Luftfahrt in Deutschland, 1920–1933*, pp. 212ff.

51 Telegram Phipps to Simon, 24 Oct 1933 (DBFP(3) Vol. V, pp. 717ff.

52 Diary, 16, 17 Oct 1933: 'Big conference on increasing production programme.'

53 Diary, 12 Oct 1933.

54 Diary, 14 Nov 1933.

55 Diary, 20 Oct 1933; also 23, 24 Oct 1933. And Blomberg: Directive for the event of Sanctions, 25 Oct 1933 (IMT, vol. XXXIV, pp. 487ff.) Meinck, op. cit., pp. 50f; and diary, 1 Nov 1933: 'Discussion [with Göring]: he was dissatisfied, because Blomberg had signed the *A* [mobilization] order.' Diary, 22 Oct 1933: 'read Douhet'.

56 Dr Heinrich Koppenberg: introduction to Report, The Development of Dessau during 1934; early Jan 1935 (Junkers archives). Koppenberg was born on 15 Mar 1890.

57 Draft (by Milch) of letter Röhm to Prof Junkers, with covering letter Milch to Röhm, 6 Dec 1933 (Berlin Doc Centre: file 'Milch-Junkers'). Kesselring: affidavit, 4 Sep 1948.

58 Report by Lämmler, Dessau, 28 Apr 1934. Also letter Dr Wiegand to Milch, 17 Sep 1934 (Junkers archives); Wiegand was a close friend of the professor. Also Reich Air Ministry memo on Junkers Case, 8 Aug 1934 (in BDC file, see note 57).

59 Basically, the allegations resulted from the Fili episode (see Chapter 1, note 38). After the Locarno treaty, the Fili factory became a political embarrassment to the German government, who stopped all subsidies; Prof Junkers claimed he had made nothing but loss from Fili, and after a lengthy battle, partly fought in public in the Reichstag, received a further 17 million Reichsmarks. This brought the Fili affair to the public attention (cf *Manchester Guardian*, Dec 1926). The Central Criminal Office at Dessau seized Junkers' company accounts and claimed proof that of the original 9.7m Reichsmarks subsidy given for Fili, Junkers had diverted nearly 5m for other purposes outside Russia. Milch told the author he believed the allegations were true, but that Prof Junkers himself was not to blame.

60 Cf diary, 18 Oct 1933: 'Noon, with Körner to see Röhm. Junkers has relinquished 51 per cent of Junkers Aircraft Company.'

61 It is not known whether Milch was as concerned in this affair as the Administration Dept officials Kesselring, Höfeld and v. Hellingrath. Cf diary, 16 Nov 1933: 'Big Junkers conf, with Keppler and Koppenberg.'

62 Cf Junkers diary, 21 Nov 1933.

63 Prof Junkers: note on conv with Dr Eschstruth, 16 Feb 1934. August
Lichte, op. cit., p. 63. And appendix to report to Rudolf Hess, 15 Aug
1934 (ibid. p. 78).
Letter to Air Ministry (Admin. Dept) to Wiegand (sgd. Milch, counter-
signed Kesselring) 28 Aug 1934; diary, 28 Aug 1934: 'Speeches about
Junkers, Gürtner.' Milch wrote to Prof Sauerbruch on 29 Aug 1934 to
assure him that no arrest of the sick Prof Junkers was planned. One of
Junkers' lawyers, Dr Semmler, published a very erroneous article blaming
Milch for the professor's death, in *Basler Nachrichten*, 27 Jan 1948.

64 Early in May 1935 Milch opened negotiations with a consortium of
Flick, Thyssen, IG Farben and Stahlverein to purchase 75% of Junkers'
shares. (ND: 10114-NI: note on Milch-Koppenberg conf, 2 May 1935.)

65 Letter Koppenberg to Milch 5 Jan 1935.

66 Plan for expansion of Junkers concern, Dessau, 6 Jul 1934. Appendices
to Koppenberg report (see note 56).

67 Liebmann: C-in-C conf, 2 Feb 1934 (see note 9). Cf Meinck, op. cit.,
pp. 81, 126. Diary, 2 Feb 1934.

68 Tschersich: memo on monthly output planned by 1 Oct 1938, dated 6
Jan 1934 (FD. 4829/45).

69 Telegram Newton to Simon, 31 Aug 1933 (DBFP(C) Vol. V, p. 564.)

70 Milch notes, 1934.

71 *Geheimrat* Bosch's principal aides were Prof. Krauch who was expert
on synthetic fuel manufacture, and Dr Ambros, the expert on synthetic
rubber. Cf Milch notes, 31 Jan 1934: 'Conf [with Gen.] von Bockelberg
[Head of Army Ordnance] and Udet. Production 1.) at Leuna; 2.) in
the Ruhr; 3.) elsewhere inside Germany. Dr Ruperti, Benzole; Dr Rott,
Ruhr Coal; Dr Krauch IG [Farben], Dr Fischer of IG. A small plant,
150,000–200,000 tons annually, total production in Germany 800,000
tons. 3.5 m tons needed. IG: 350,000 tons from lignite. Production cost
35m marks for 100,000 tons, 65m for 200,000 tons. I [insist on] 1.)
stockpiling as interim measure, 2.) stockpiles of lubricants, 3.) anti-knock
qualities.' Cf also Milch notes, late Apr 1934: 'Convert four nitrogen factories in Reich to petrol production forthwith.' And notes, autumn 1934:
'Von Blomberg says: synthetic fuel cannot be used for aircraft.?? [ask]
Krauch.'

72 Diary, 7 Nov 1933. Milch now comments that all these figures in his
diaries were momentarily the genuine ones.

73 *Reichsgesetzblatt*, 26 Mar 1934. The published budget had increased from
78.3m marks in 1933/34, to 210m in 1934/35. Diary, 22 Mar 1934:
'Afternoon: Cabinet meeting. Budget etc. Hitler discusses Air Force etc
with me alone.' And ibid, 23 Mar 1934: 'Afternoon, Cabinet. (Reich)
Finance [Minister] on budget objections.' Cf DBFP(C) Vol. VI, pp. 595ff.

74 Telegram Phipps to Simon, 9 Apr 1934; Simon to Phipps, 10 Apr 1934;
and letter von Neurath to Phipps, 11 Apr 1934 (DBFP(C) vol. VI,
pp. 613ff, 621f).

75 Milch, Oct 1967. An identical admission is quoted in Hewel diary, 2 Jun 1941.

76 There is a list of 63 such camouflaged names in Völker: *Dokumente, Dok.* 73, dated 12 Apr 1934.

77 Von Winterfeld: memoirs.

78 Diary, 24 Mar, 28 Mar, 1 and 5 Apr 1934. Memoirs.

79 MCH 11 Mar 1947, p. 1772; and Milch, Dec 1968.

80 MCH, 12 Mar 1947, p. 1803; cf diary, 28 Feb 1933 and 17 Mar 1934.

81 Milch had attended Ernst's marriage: diary, 17 Sep 1933.

82 Cf diary, 4 Jun 1933: 'Midday: Röhm, about Duel.' He had previously seen Hitler on 6 May 1934.

83 Milch: Hitler and his Subordinates. For other details on Theo Croneiss' career, see Prof Willy Messerschmitt's obituary speech on him, Nov 1942 (Messerschmitt file: FD, 4355/45, vol. I) The records of the Führer's *Adjutantur* (Bundesarchiv files NS-10) show that Croneiss was also active later as Martin Bormann's technical adviser.

84 Diary, 29 Jun 1934, records only: '9.45–10.45 a.m., solo flights in Kadett. Noon with Teucci [Ital. Attaché] Then Head of Army Command, von Fritsch.'

85 Diary, 30 Jun 1934; notes, 30 Jun 1934.

86 Bross: *Gespräche mit Hermann Göring*, p. 19.

87 Milch: Hitler and his Subordinates.

88 Milch, Dec 1968.

89 But cf OSS, Research and Analysis Branch, secret report 3152: Hermann Göring as a War Criminal, Washington, 25 Jun 1945. Göring had in fact first set eyes on his men in uniform ten days before. Cf Milch.
Diary, 20 Jun 1934: 'Schorf Heath. Burial of Karin Göring. The Führer. Air Force [*Fliegertruppe*] presents arms for first time.'

90 Diary, 1 Jul 1934, 2, 3 Jul 1934. Milch: Hitler and his Subordinates. Göring later insisted that the *putsch* was real enough. 'I myself was present as SA-General Ernst's headquarters was cleared out. As I looked by chance out of the window, I saw to my amazement that my troops were staggering out under crates of machine-guns and ammunition . . .' (Bross, op. cit., p. 18). But see Milch diary, 13 Feb 1948, 25 Feb 1948 (his discussions with SA General Jüttner).

91 Seiler and Kokothaki, Nov 1969: Seiler was a close friend of Croneiss and saw the ceremonial dagger he had received from Röhm; after the purge Rudolf Hess took Croneiss under his wing, as aviation expert on his Liaison Staff. Prof Willy Messerschmitt proposed that Croneiss should be asked to leave the company, as a political embarrassment, but Seiler bitterly opposed this mark of illoyalty.

92 *The Rise and Fall of the German Air Force*, pp. 7ff.

93 Milch: The Development of the German Air Force, Jun 1945. Diary, 31 Jul 1934.

94 Pre-Trial Interrogation, 25 Oct 1946.

95 Diary, 22, 23, 31 Aug 1934; and notes, 1945, thereon. Ibid, 9, 10 Sep 1934. Ibid, 11 Sep 1934, and 1945 notes thereon. Diary, 21 Sep 1934.

96 W. S. Churchill: *The Second World War*, vol. I, pp. 106ff. Pre-Trial Interrogation, 6 Nov 1945; Basil Collier: *The Defence of the United Kingdom*, pp. 27ff. Also records of the Technical Dept., quoted in *Rise and Fall* (note 92) pp. 11f. Cf Völker: *Luftwaffe*, pp. 56f.

97 Diary, 9 Oct 1934: 'C-in-C's to see Blomberg.' Cf Liebmann: conf Minister von Blomberg on 9 Oct 1934 (see note 9) pp. 228ff.

98 Memoirs. Cf Milch, notes ca Aug 1934: 'Von Blomberg: 1.) [. . .] 2.) if we reach agreement with Britain, what to demand? They won't put up with Equality.' And notes, early Feb 1935; 'Navy 35 per cent of Britain (Russia?); Army 100 per cent of French; air 100 per cent of British, assuming British as strong as French. We place our hopes on Britain, against Russia.'

99 Diary, 12 Jan 1935; 'Big conf of C-in-C's in Reich Defence Ministry'. Notes, 12 Jan 1935. Cf Liebmann: conf on statements by Minister [Blomberg] and Chief of Army Command [Fritsch] on 12 Jan 1935 (see note 9) pp. 233ff. Milch's notes contain the following a few days later: Funds (now calculated by calendar years). 1935–8, 223m, of which 5,500m in [Mefo] bills. Of which Army [receives] 4,000m, Navy 760m, Air 3,300m (2,900m). Supply build-up [*Bevorratung*] of these could be sacrificed, saving additional 570m. Altogether including SA etc, 9,600m. Schacht prepared to provide 6,000m. [Funds required by] SA, SS etc—266m. There is also a note on a conversation with Schacht late in Jan 1935: 'Should we publish the budget? A danger for our image!'

100 Milch; and Völker: *Luftwaffe*, p. 78.

101 Memoirs; and Kesselring, op. cit., p. 34.

102 Reich Air Minister: order for setting up of reserve airfields and expanding ground organization (sgf. pp. Milch) 8 Oct 1935 (Völker: *Dokumente*, Nr. 103).

103 Diary, 5 Feb 1935: 'Speech to Gauleiters. Koch (of East Prussia) hostile to me, but Streicher, Goebbels, Hess on my side.' Cf Rosenberg diary, 24 Feb 1935.

104 Koppenberg's report, 3 Jan 1935.

105 Ordinance on Luftwaffe's Officer Corps (sgd Milch), 18 Feb 1935 (Völker: *Dokumente*, Nr. 138).

106 Milch, Nov 1967.

107 Führer decree on Reich Luftwaffe, 26 Feb 1935 (Völker: *Dokumente*, Nr. 44).

108 Reich Defence Minister: directive for uncamouflaging the Luftwaffe, 26 Feb 1935 (Völker: *Dokumente*, Nr. 75).

109 Reich Air Minister: instructions for uncamouflaging the Luftwaffe (sgd. pp. Wever) 27 Feb 1935 (Völker: *Dokumente*, Nr. 76, cf Nr. 78).

110 Völker: *Luftwaffe, passim*. Diary, 7 Oct 1935.

111 Diary, 24 Oct 1935: '2 pm to see von Blomberg. Asked for 616m Reichsmarks more.'

112 *The Rise and Fall of the German Air Force*, p. 12.

113 Heinkel: op. cit., pp. 329, 339.

114 Reich Air Minister: directives for operations in first phase of a war (sgd. Wever), 18 Nov 1935 (Völker: *Dokumente*, pp. 445ff.)

115 Diary, 16 Nov 1935; cf. Völker, *Dokumente*, pp. 445ff.

116 IMT Vol. XXXIV, pp. 644ff: Blomberg's order of 2 Mar 1936 described the remilitarization of the Rhineland as 'a peaceful operation to transfer troop units into locations prepared for them.' Cf Völker: *Luftwaffe*, pp. 147f.

117 Diary, 6, 7 Mar 1936.

118 IMT Vol. IX, p. 83; Milch. Oct 1967.

119 Air Force Manual: 'Air Warfare' (*LDV 16*) May 1936, and regularly brought up to date thereafter. Cf Völker: *Luftwaffe*, pp. 198ff.

120 Dipl. Ing Alpers, who took on the Special Aircraft unit in the Technical Department under von Richthofen early in 1934, describes Wimmer as 'open, correct, exemplary but unimaginative.' Von Richthofen found Udet an uncongenial new Chief, and arranged to be replaced by Lt Col Jungk. (Alpers, Dec 1969.)

121 Milch, Oct 1967, Nov 1967, May 1968; and letter Milch to Prof Suchenwirth 3 Jan 1957.

122 Letter Milch to Suchenwirth 10 Jan 1957.

123 Milch, Dec 1969. Diary, 26 Jul 1936. Völker: *Luftwaffe*, pp. 148ff. There are references to Special Staff 'W' until late 1938 in the Milch documents, reporting experiences with new weapons (letter Bodenschatz to Udet, 9 Dec 1937, MD: 65, p. 7482) and forwarding requests for more war materials (letter Göring's office to Milch and Stumpff, 21 Oct 1938, ibid, p. 7439).

124 *Rise and Fall of the German Air Force*, p. 13; cf Völker: *Luftwaffe*, p. 149.

125 Diary, 3 Aug 1936; and 8, 9, 14 Aug, 23, 24 Sep 1936.

126 Diary, 29, 30 Oct, 2, 4, 5, 6, 7 Nov 1936.

127 Diary, 6 Nov 1936.

128 Ibid, 14 Nov 1936.

129 Bodenschatz: memo on Göring conf, 2 Dec 1936 (in fact the date was probably 3 Dec 1936: cf Diary) (ND: US exhibit 580).

130 Milch, May 1968; cf Milch: The Development of the German Air Force.

131 Udet: memo on his conf alone with Göring, 16 Nov 1936 (MD: 65, pp. 7532f).
Milch, Nov 1967.
Diary 8 Sep, 24 Dec 1936.
Milch for his part had solicitously attended to Göring and his wife: cf diary 24 Mar, 10 Apr, 11 Apr 1936.
Notes, 24 Dec 1935.

132 Diary, 26 Nov 1936, and 1945 comment thereon. Cf *Inter Avia*, Aug 1946, p. 12.

Reich Air Minister: order altering establishment of fighter units (sgd. Wever) dated 15 Apr 1936 (Völker: *Dokumente*, Nr. 88).

Udet: memo on conf with Göring, 11 Jan 1937 (on increased production programme) MD: 65, p. 7529. Among others the new programme called for the total output by 1 Apr 1938 of 850 He 111s (previously 831), of 184 Me 110s (104), of 444 Do 17F (270), of 570 Do 17E (518), of 345 Ju 87s (264). Cf Diary, 11 Jan 1937.

133 Collier, op. cit., p. 46.

134 Milch, Oct 1967.

135 Memoirs; and IMT, vol. IX, p. 56.

136 Diary, 21, 22 Jan 1937, and esp. 19 Jan 1937: 'Big discussion with Courtney: [exchange of] statistics.' Also: memo on conf with Air Vice-Marshal Courtney on 19 Jan 1937 (MD: 56, pp. 3003ff).

German Embassy, London: note on conf in British Air Ministry, 28 Jan (MD: 56, pp. 3006f.) Wg Cdr C. E. H. Medhurst was head of the Directorate of Operations and Intelligence.

Letter Wenninger to Milch, 28 Jan 1937 (MD: 56, pp. 3010f).

Webster and Frankland, op. cit., vol. I, p. 73.

137 Diary, 28 Jan 1937; Milch, Oct 1967.

138 Milch: Thoughts on Air Warfare, ca. Jan 1937 (MPP), with cover letter Bodenschatz to Milch, 1 Feb 1937. Milch's statistics appear to have been obtained from a report by the head of the operations branch of the Air Staff, Major (GS) Paul Deichmann: Basic Facts for Strategic Air Warfare, dated 29 Oct 1936 (Völker: *Dokumente*, Nr. 198). Cf Diary, 24 Oct 1936.

139 Diary, 3 Feb 1937; (cf diary 4 Jun 1936: '*Personal* feud with Raeder set aside.')

140 Rear-Adm. von Puttkamer, Mar 1970.

141 Diary, 30 Jan 1937. This was the occasion on which the Minister of Posts, Eltz v. Rübenach, refused to accept the badge and resigned. Cf Pre-Trial Interrogation, 16 Sep 1947; Milch, Nov 1967.

Letter Eltz v. Rübenach to Führer, 1 Feb 1937 (ND: 1534-PS) and *Völkischer Beobachter*, 31 Jan 1937 (ND: 2964-PS).

142 Cf Diary, 5 Feb 1937: 'Afternoon: lecture by Heydrich'; and 2 Jun 1937: 'Party leaders in Air Ministry: lecture by Himmler on homosexuals and Abortion. Very good.—Afternoon, Führer speaks to Party, two and a half hours on foreign policy.'

143 Diary, 9, 15 Feb 1937, 16, 17 Feb 1937.

144 Ibid, 2 Mar 1937.

145 Diary 2–17 Mar 1937 shows Milch in Italy. Diary 18, 23 Mar 1937 shows Milch's attempts to see Göring. Cf diary 25 Mar, 3 and 19 Apr 1937; and Milch: Development of German Air Force.

146 It is difficult to be precise about the date of the decision. Latterly 29 Apr 1937 has been accepted, because of Milch's testimony to IMT: but

his diary that day reads only 'Ju 86 [and Jumo 205] diesel engine cancelled.' Neither his diary, nor, more significantly, his Jan 1937 study (see note 138) mentions the role of heavy bombers, or the decision to stop them. (On the Ju 86 decision, see Udet's memo on his conf with Milch, 5 May 1937, MD: 65, pp. 7512ff). Many legends have grown up round the far-reaching decision on the Ju 89 and Do 19, and General Paul Deichmann even blamed Milch in an MGFA study, postwar: 'Why did Germany have no four-engined bomber in the Second World War?' Deichmann relates an audience he secured with Göring to protest against the decision (he was then a major). Milch's diary shows no such conference. See also General Kesselring's statement, 17 Mar 1954, printed as App. 12 to Cajus Bekker: *Angriffshöhe,* p. 463; and Völker: *Luftwaffe,* pp. 132ff, 208f. Völker suggests that the four-engined bombers were dropped because of the lack of a suitable engine, but this is disputed now by the Junkers aero-engine experts.

147 Milch, 16 May 1968. See especially a letter from Adm. Lahs, Pres. of Reich Assn of Aircraft Manufacturers, to Milch, 1 Nov 1942 (MD: 53, pp. 780f): Udet's military advisers had turned the four-engined bombers down in favour of twin-engined medium bombers. 'The task of anti-shipping warfare across vast ocean distances had apparently not been recognised.' Junkers and Dornier had both produced prototype heavy bombers by 1936: 'Had they been systematically developed still further they would by now, 6 years later, have been superior to *all the American and British heavy bombers.'*

148 IMT vol. IX, p. 72; and memoirs. Memo on Göring conf, 24 Feb 1937 (with Körner, Udet, Ploch) (MD: 65, p. 7526). Milch was in hospital at the time.

149 Cf diary, 24 Mar 1946: 'Göring has testified, "There has been much talk of two- and four-engined bombers." Nobody could pass judgement on that except himself. He would have built a four-engined one if he had had a serviceable type and enough aluminium . . .' Note that a programme schedule dated 26 Jun 1936 (file FD. 4829/45) lists the Do 19 and Ju 89, *and* a Ju 90 airliner.

150 Diary, 8 May 1937. Milch: Development of the German Air Force, and cf Völker: *Luftwaffe,* pp. 78f.

151 Diary, 30, 31 May 1937. Göring: order on reorganization and line of command in Reich Air Ministry, 2 Jun 1937 (Völker: *Dokumente,* Nr. 48). Völker states that this reorganization of the command structure of the Luftwaffe was drafted by the Air Staff. Cf diary, 1 Jun 1937: 'Major row with Göring.' And 3 Jun 1937, ibid.

152 Diary, 8 Jul 1937: 'To see Göring with Stumpff and von Richthofen, re: Spain.' Ibid, 10 Jul 1937: 'New ordinances by Göring, against me!' Cf MCH, 12 Mar 1947, p. 1799; and diary, 13 Jul 1937: 'Udet and Greim to see Göring.'

153 Milch: The Development of the German Air Force (MPP).

CHAPTER 3

1 Reich War Minister: Directive for unified preparation of a possible war, dated 26 Jun 1936; ibid, dated 24 Jun 1937. (IMT, vol. XXXIV, pp. 733ff.)

2 Col. Max Pendele: Udet timetable, 25–27 Jun 1937. Udet: notes for conf with Minister on 13 Jul 1937 (MD: 65, p. 7501).

3 Diary, 7, 8 Jun 1937; cf letter Wenninger to Milch, 28 Oct 1937 (MD: 56, p. 3026). Memoirs.

4 Memoirs; and Völker: *Luftwaffe*, p. 157. Diary, 23–27 Jul 1937; and Polte: op. cit.

5 Memoirs; and diary, 23 Aug 1937.
Diary, 1 Sep 1937.
Pre-Trial Interrogation, 18 Oct 1946.

6 Udet: note on Göring conf, 24 Feb 1937 (MD: 65, pp. 7526f).
Diary, 11 Sep 1937.
Col Georg Thomas of the Military Economics Branch complained of the Air Ministry's 'dynamism', and wrote in 1944: 'The desire to go its own way was one of the determining features of the Luftwaffe, and the need for a centralised direction of the war economy, as Field-Marshal Milch was to represent by his transfer to the Reich Armaments Ministry in 1944, was unfortunately not realised at that time [1934]. On the contrary, the very thought was most emphatically opposed by the Luftwaffe.' Thomas: Basis for a history of the German Defence and Armaments Economy (ND: 2353-PS).

7 Memo on teleph. conv Lt Col Hünemann (for Thomas) to Maj Schmid, 3 Jun 1937 (MD: 53, p. 867); letter Volkmann to Reich War Minister, 31 Aug 1937, re Effects of Iron and Steel Shortage on Luftwaffe's Rearmament (MD: 53, pp. 850ff). Udet had been assured monthly quotas totalling 99,800 tons from May to Sep 1937, of which only 35,000 tons would in fact be delivered by the end of Sep 1937.

8 Cf letter Milch to Göring, draft, 30 Oct 1937, enclosing table of iron and steel requirements of Luftwaffe, 'as basis for the conference provisionally planned for Monday 1 Nov with the Führer.' (MD: 53, pp. 849ff). This document puts the Hossbach protocol of the Führer conf on 5 Nov 1937 in its proper perspective.

9 Memoirs; and Völker: *Luftwaffe*, p. 158.

10 Later Milch recalled how difficult it had been to persuade von Richthofen (one of Wimmer's subordinates) to accept the 'Storch' project. GL conf, 19 Jun 1942 (MD: 15, p. 1114): 'Nothing was harder than to push that through. It actually took several years for the gentlemen in the Department to understand that such a plane was necessary.'

11 Amb. Vicco von Bülow-Schwante: affidavit, 11 Aug 1948 (head of Protocol in the German For. Office, 1935–38): 'Milch enjoyed great respect among the diplomatic corps, as he was accustomed to speaking his mind about everything.'

12 Diary, 11 Aug 1937; and memoirs.
Diary, 4 Oct 1937.
Ibid, 5 Oct 1937.
MCH, 12 Mar 1947, p. 1794.

13 Diary, 10 Oct 1937; cf Pre-Trial Interrogation, 17 Oct 1946.

14 Letter Wenninger to Milch, 28 Oct 1937 (MD: 56, pp. 3026f).
The shadow factories visited were the Austin works at Birmingham, and the Standard and Humber works at Rugby: 'All the factories are working at 70 per cent strength these last four to six weeks, will achieve top output in four to six more weeks.'
Diary, 17–25 Oct 1937; appendix to letter Wenninger to Milch (note 340).

15 Peter Townsend: *Duel of Eagles* (London, 1970), p. 134; and Speer in MCH, 4 Feb 1947.

16 Diary, 19 Aug 1945. Milch also copied into his diary, without comment, the following extract from Churchill: *My Early Life*, p. 370 (first published in 1939): 'To cope with all this [Boer War guerilla activity against the British in South Africa] the British military authorities found it necessary to clear whole districts of their inhabitants and gather the population into concentration camps. As the railways were continually cut (!) it was difficult to supply these camps with all the necessaries of life. Disease broke out and several thousands of women and children died.' (Milch inserted the exclamation mark.)

17 The meeting and conversation with Mr Churchill are related in identical terms in CSDIC (UK) Report SRGG 1313 (C), 3 Jun 1945; and Memoirs.

18 Memoirs; diary, 1 Nov 1937; and Milch: Hitler and his Subordinates.

19 Pre-Trial Interrogations of Milch, 17 and 18 Oct 1946. Diary, 2 Nov 1937. Cf MCH 12 Mar 1947, pp. 1746f; and Milch, Oct 1967.

20 Diary, 2 Nov 1937.

21 Memoirs; cf Meinck, op. cit., p. 226: 'Such treaties can assume an aggressive character only too easily, as the early history of the Great War showed.'

22 Meinck, op. cit., p. 149; and Liebmann: note on von Fritsch's conf with von Blomberg, 24 Apr 1935. Milch diary, 11 Apr 1935 and 18 Apr 1935: 'Göring, on seriousness of situation in long term. Until 9 pm drawing up plans in the Ministry.'

23 Diary, 2 May 1935: '[To see] von Blomberg: three C-in-C's, Czechoslovakia plan.' Also letter of Reich Defence Minister, 2 May 1935 (IMT vol. XXXIV, pp. 485f). At Nuremberg it was wrongly assumed that the codeword *Schulung* referred to the remilitarization of the Rhineland.

24 Diary, 15 and 16 May 1935.

25 Diary, 20 Jan 1938: 'Conf on battle directive *Green* [Czechoslovakia]'.

26 Ibid, 21 May 1938.

27 Ibid, 22, 28, 29 May 1938. Cf E. M. Robertson: *Hitler's Pre-War Policy*, p. 125.

28  Diary, 30, 31 May, 1 Jun 1938; cf Völker: *Dokumente*, Nr. 69: Order setting up Air Defence Zone West (sgd pp. Milch); cf Völker: *Luftwaffe*, p. 111.

29  Diary, 7–11 Jun 1938.
    Milch notes, 20 Jun 1938; cf diary, 23 Jun 1938: 'Morning [conf on] Plendl's system, *Green* [Czechoslovakia].'

30  *The Rise and Fall of the German Air Force*, p. 19. And Udet: notes for conf with Milch, 21 Jun 1938 (MD: 65, p. 7457).

31  Diary, 8 July 1938; and Göring speech to gentlemen of the air industry, Karinhall, 8 Jul 1938 (ND: R-140).

32  Völker: *Luftwaffe*, pp. 154f. The C-in-C of First Air Group was General Kesselring.

33  Milch, Mar 1967, May 1968. Diary, 15 Aug 1938, and notes of same date. For full report on Führer's speech, see Eberhard diary, 15 Aug 1938; and cf Liebmann: personal experiences 1938–1939 (Inst. f. Zeitgeschichte, file ED/1, pp. 417f).

34  German Air Staff: 'Extended Case *Green*', dated Berlin 25 Aug 1938 (ND: 375-PS).

35  Letter Wenninger to Göring, 23 May 1938 (MD: 56, pp. 3024f, 3018f). The quoted passage was underlined by Milch, and he placed '!!?' in the margin next to it.

36  Liebmann (see note 33) wrote that Hitler's adjutant Capt Engel asked early in Sep 1938 whether he had had a row with a senior Luftwaffe officer recently; Liebmann recalled the row with Milch, 'Engel then told me he had by chance overheard a conversation between Milch and Göring, in which my name had been mentioned as one of the Army's "troublemaker" generals.' Liebmann was replaced in Nov 1938 in his command

37  Diary, 20 Aug 1938.
    Heinkel, op. cit., p. 402; Alpers, Dec 1969.

38  Letter von Winterfeld to author, 23 Sep 1969.

39  Manvell and Frankel: Göring, p. 141.

40  Völker: *Luftwaffe*.

41  See note 35.

42  Diary, 23 Aug 1938.
    See note 397; and preamble to Second Air Group study on 'Planning Case *Green*', 22 Sep 1938; cf Suchenwirth: Jeschonnek, p. 38f, and Völker: *Luftwaffe*, p. 159. Also Diary, 25 Aug 1938: 'War Game *Green*.' On the inadequate range of Luftwaffe aircraft, see diary, 28 Feb 1938: 'Göring: range of He 111'; and letter Göring to Udet, via Milch, 20 Sep 1938 (MD: 65, p. 7440).

43  Notes, ca 17 Sep 1938: 'Felmy, special unit for war with England.'
    Second Air Group study on Planning Case *Green*, 22 Sep 1938.

44  Diary, 21, 22 Sep 1938.

45  Capt (GS) Pohle: 'Lecture during Air Staff journey, Jun 1939' cited by Völker: *Luftwaffe*, pp. 191ff.

46 Lichte; also Junkers company chart: Chronology of Ju 88, dated 13 Nov 1940.

47 Völker: *Luftwaffe*, p. 191.

48 Lahs at Göring conf, 8 Jul 1938, p. 37 (see note 31). For early licence production plans for Ju 88 see Udet's papers (MD: 65, p. 7425), a document dated 30 May 1938.

49 Milch at GL conf, 20 Aug 1942 (MD: 15, p. 1986f).

50 The conf was most probably on 27 Sep 1938; Milch *recalls* the conf as being at Karinhall, attended by Udet, Lucht, Koppenberg, Stumpff, Lahs, Jeschonnek and others. (Cf MD: 57, p. 3227).

51 Göring at conf, 18 Mar 1943, stenogram (MD: 62, p. 5474).

52 Göring's commission to Koppenberg, signed and forwarded by Göring to Koppenberg on 30 Sep 1938 (MD: 57, pp. 3230ff).

53 Milch, Mar 1967; cf diary, 24 Jun 1946, and affidavit, Dachau, 24 Jun 1946; Bross has the same story, op. cit., p. 70.

54 Memoirs; cf Wünsche diary, 30 Oct 1938.

55 Thomas: conf with Göring on 14 Oct 1938 (ND: 1301-PS); cf Pre-Trial Interrogation, 30 Oct 1946. Milch was not present.

56 Diary and notes, 15 Oct 1938; notes, 24 Oct 1938.
Diary and notes, 26 Oct 1938; cf Udet's notes for this Göring conf (MD: 65, p. 7436).

57 Memo by fuel supply office, 5 Dec 1938; quoted in Völker: *Luftwaffe*, p. 138.

58 Suchenwirth suggests it was about 8 Jan 1939; this author suspects it was earlier.
Cf diary, 13 Dec 1938: 'Iron conf with Göring and Wehrmacht chiefs. Will not release raw materials, but adhere to the Big Programme.'

59 Diary, 28, 29 Nov, 1 Dec 1938; cf Suchenwirth: Jeschonnek, p. 46.
Udet: notes for Göring conf, 13 Dec 1938 (MD: 65, pp. 7409ff).

60 Göring order dated 23 Jan 1939 (MD: 65, pp. 7403f); and Memoirs.
Cf diary, 16 Jan 1939.

61 Baron v. Hammerstein quoted by Suchenwirth: Udet, p. 28.

62 Memoirs. As an example of Jeschonnek's 'narrow-mindedness', Milch has drawn attention to the then Capt Jeschonnek's Aug 1932 memorandum (Völker: *Die Entwicklung der militärischen Luftfahrt in Deutschland, 1920–1933* [1962] p. 273) in which he advocates the killing off of 'civil aviation, which is useless for military purposes'. In so far as it was to to be allowed to survive, it must be ruthlessly subjected to the needs of the Reich Defence Ministry.

63 Milch, Oct 1967; cf also Suchenwirth: Jeschonnek, pp. 120, 164. The conflict between Milch and Jeschonnek continued with occasional pauses until the latter's suicide in Aug 1943. Cf diary of von Richthofen, 12 Feb 1943, and 15 Mar 1943 ('conf with Jeschonnek. Jeschonnek has made peace with Milch.') Cf also Milch's diary, 24 Feb 1943: 'Bury the hatchet with Jeschonnek, at my suggestion.'

64 Diary, 12 Mar 1939. Letter Maj Gen Schlichting to author, Oct 1969: Stumpff ordered him to memorize the message.

65 Göring was opposed to the occupation of Czechoslovakia and wrote trying to dissuade Hitler from it (USFET-MISC Interrogation of Göring, OI-RIR/7, dated 24 Oct 1945). That he was previously unaware of any such plans can be seen from his conf with Udet, 28 Nov 1938, where he advocated expenditure of several million Reichsmarks in foreign currency on machine tools and iron in Prague. Also, 'Field-Marshal [Göring] recommends purchase of shares in Czech factories'. (MD: 65, pp. 7429f). Cf Wagner: *Der Generalquartiermeister*, p. 79.

66 Diary, 13 Mar 1939.

67 Milch remained Insp. Gen until Jan 1945. Göring's order dated 30 Jan 1939, (Völker: *Dokumente*, Nr. 53); and service instructions dated 6 Feb 1939 (ibid, Nr. 54).

68 Letter Maj Gen Schlichting to author, Oct 1969.

69 Udet: report on journey of *Generalluftzeugmeister* to Prague, and other documents went to Göring in San Remo on 27 Mar 1939 (MD: 65, p. 7395). See also the report on Göring's conf with Mussolini, 15 Apr 1939 (ND: 1874-PS).

70 Diary, 22 Mar 1939, 23 Mar 1939.

71 Diary, 25 Mar 1939.
Führer's brief to C-in-C, Army, 25 Mar 1939 (ND: 100-R); Directive for unified preparation for war of Wehrmacht, 1939/40, dated 3 Apr 1939 (ND: 120-C).

72 US State Dept interrogation of Göring, 6–7 Nov 1945.

73 Diary, 27 Apr 1939: 'Big speech by Jeschonnek on *White*.'

74 Conf of Gen Felmy with Jeschonnek, 2 May 1939 (in MGFA, cited by Suchenwirth: Jeschonnek, p. 39).
Diary, 13 May 1939; cf Völker: *Dokumente*, Nr. 199: final conf of war exercise of Second Air Group on question of air warfare against Britain and at sea (13 May 1939).

75 German Air Staff: report, 22 May 1939; quoted in Suchenwirth; Jeschonnek, p. 39.

76 Cf Milch, IMT, vol. IX, p. 57: 'I was suddenly sent for, since the Reichsmarschall was not present.' When the prosecution ignored this, Milch insisted, on 11 Mar 1946, 'May I state that my recollection is that Field Marshal Göring was not present. My recollection is that I was sent for to stand in for him, at the last moment.' (ibid, p. 134). Cf Pre-Trial Interrogation, 17 Oct 1946, 18 Oct 1946: Göring had by then been dead for several days, so it cannot be held that Milch was trying to defend him. And in particular Milch's Diary, 23 May 1939: '. . . Air Defence college Wannsee opened by Göring. Funeral Count Schulenburg, Potsdam, Lustgarten, 4–8.30 pm. Führer, Commanders-in-Chief, grand plans. I as Göring's deputy, called in at last moment by Bodenschatz.'

77 Report on conf in Führer's study, 23 May 1939 (ND: 79-L). For an analysis of the anachronisms in the '1939' document, see Dr Friedrich

Bergold's defence closing speech, MCH, 25 Mar 1947. Göring, shown the document at Nuremberg under Pre-Trial Interrogation, at first denied knowledge of the conf, but was then persuaded that he must have been there as his name was on the list. Bodenschatz (interrogated 6 Nov 1945) said: 'I must honestly say that I cannot remember this thing in this form . . . I do not want to say I was not present there, but I cannot recall this form of the conference as it has been drawn up here by Schmundt.' Halder (29 Oct 1945) also stated: The [Schmundt report] does not reproduce the trend of the thoughts expressed there.' Warlimont also denied that he was present.

78 MCH, 12 Mar 1947, p. 1816.
Diary 30 May 1947; cf also diaries, 7 Nov 1945, 17, 19 Jan, 19 Feb, 12 Mar, 18 Nov 1947; and 21 Mar, 1 Apr 1948. The conf was discussed in MCH pp. 1814ff, 2283ff, and 2367ff.

79 Letter Bodenschatz to Udet, 21 Jun 1939 (MD: 65, p. 7371).

80 Report on 2nd session of Reich Defence Council, 23 Jun 1939 (ND: 3787-PS) cf IMT, vol. XVII, p. 438.

81 Letter Udet to Milch, 20 Jun 1939, re raw material quantities for July 1939 (MD: 65, p. 7341); Milch sent this to Göring on 23 Jun 1939. Also letter Keitel to Göring, 15 Jun 1939, re determination of metal and rubber quotas for the coming months (MD: 65, p. 7343); note on conf, 27 Jun 1939 (ibid, p. 7354); and Tschersich: points touched upon by Göring during his conf with Udet on 20 Jul 1939 (ibid, pp. 7318ff).

82 On the strength of Raeder's assurance, Adm Dönitz, the submarine commander, went on leave (CCPWE, interrogation of Dönitz, 4 Aug 1945).

83 Diary, 26 May 1939; cf Ciano diary, 3 Feb 1939: 'He [Duce] said once more that he regards war as inevitable.' On the Italian–German air force exchange of aircraft and information, see Milch: note on conf with Udet, 29 Jun 1939, with an Italian delegation (MD: 65, pp. 7368f). On 23 Jun Göring ordered that no flak batteries were to be handed to Italy and on 14 Jul he amplified this, 'but the Italians are to be advised that there may be partial delivery in 1940 according to how the raw materials situation is.' (Letter Udet to Göring, 11 Jul 1939; Bodenschatz to Milch, 14 Jul 1939; MD: 65, pp. 7327ff).

84 Diary, 8 Jun 1939; an extract from a letter from Hess to Göring subsequent to this visit is in MD: 65, pp. 7348f.

85 Tschersich: report on supplies position, Jul 1939, dated 15 Aug 1939 (FD. 4940/45). This states that the Luftwaffe consumed 52,000 cubic metres of aviation spirit in Jul 1939: 'The stocks have thereby been reduced from about 712,600 to 691,300 cubic meters (adequate for 3.9 war months); but of this quantity only about 420,000 can be regarded as fit for use, as no more can be ethylised in consequence of the release by us of 512 cubic metres of ethyl fluid.' See also Dr Karl Gundelach's study in *Wehrwissenschaftliche Rundschau*, 1963, p. 687. On the general issue of the unreadiness of the Luftwaffe, cf Völker: *Luftwaffe*, pp. 194, 203, 205, 210, 214.

86 *Chef OKW* (Keitel) had reported to the C-in-C's on 7 Dec 1938 that Hitler had ordered the Services to concentrate on producing weapons rather than ammunition.

87 Report by Milch to Göring, 18 Apr 1939 (MD: 51, pp. 5667f).

88 Diary, 26 Jun, 3 Jul 1939. Heinkel: op. cit., pp. 490ff.

Article: The Secret Fight that Doomed the Luftwaffe, *Saturday Evening Post*, 8 Apr 1950: 'Messerschmitt laughingly disclosed to an American reporter after the war, "The plane that Wendel flew was no Me 109 (horsepower 1065) but a stripped down special Me 209 (horsepower 2300) a plane no ordinary pilot could ever handle." '

That the cold-start procedure was displayed to Hitler on this occasion was recalled in a document of 11 Apr 1942 (MD: 56, p. 2678) when the reasons for the German *Army's* ignorance of the procedure were discussed (the Battle of Moscow).

89 Suchenwirth: Udet, p. 44. But Suchenwirth: Jeschonnek, p. 42f, cites Lt Gen Josef Schmid's postwar recollections of a statement by Hitler on this occasion: 'I must forge the Great Reich with weapons. We will have a war, I don't know when. Under all circumstances this war must end in victory for us. Whether it lasts one, two, or ten years is all the same to me—it must be won.' Diary, 8 May 1947; von Below also regarded Hitler's policies as bluff (diary, 21 Mar 1948).

90 Göring speech to air industry, 13 Sep 1942 (MD: 62, pp. 5277ff.).

91 Eng. Gen. Gerbert Hübner: The engineer problem in the Luftwaffe 1933–1945, p. 21 (MGFA).

92 Kreipe diary, 11 Aug 1944.

93 Alpers, Dec. 1969. Hitler's closing speech at Rechlin was recalled by Göring, in his conf on 14 Oct 1943 (MD: 63, pp. 6185f), see also memo Techn. Dept to Milch, 21 Oct 1943, explaining why the 30mm cannon had been delayed (MD: 51, p. 329). The MK 101 was an early and very heavy weapon (178 kilos) developed by Rheinmetall Borsig since 1935 from the tank weapon MKS–18–1000, of 20mm calibre. It would only fire from a drum magazine, a maximum of 30 rounds. It was to be replaced by the MK 103 (weighing 143 kilos) and later by the MK 108 (weighing 62 kilos), both belt fed, and the latter with very rapid fire, important for fighter aircraft. Later on Milch fitted fighters with 75mm and even with 88mm guns, in experimental versions. (Letter Maximilian Bohlan to author, 31 Jan 1970.) Göring's emphasis on these is in MD: 63, pp. 6185f. The next conf was on 12 Jul 1939 (Milch was not present). Cf letter Bodenschatz to Udet, 14 Jul 1939 (MD: 65, p. 7326) and letter Schmid to Udet (MD: 65, p. 7325).

94 Tschersich: points touched upon by Göring during his conf with Udet on 20 Jul 1939 (ibid, p. 7318).

95 Heinkel, op. cit., p. 413.

96 Lichte and Böttger: The development of aircraft jet engines by Junkers research, study dated Aug 1963; letter from Erich Warsitz, 26 Jan 1970;

letter from Milch to author, 19 Mar 1970. The Jumo 004A engine had its maiden run in Oct 1940; the operational version, the Jumo 004B, first ran in summer 1943.

97 Diary, 21 Jul 1939; Pre-Trial Interrogation, 27 Oct 1945; and *Development of the German Air Force*.

98 Ciano diary, 15 Apr 1939.

Göring conf, 18 Mar 1943, stenogram (MD: 62, p. 5474).

99 Udet: notes for Göring conf on 21, 22 Aug 1939 (MD: 65, pp. 7309ff). Heinkel: op. cit., p. 434.

100 Letter Jeschonnek to Udet and others, 9 Aug 1939 (in file FD. 4940/45). By Oct 1939 Udet's staff were already issuing an aircraft production programme with completely different figures.

101 Letter Bodenschatz to Milch, 9 Aug 1939 (MD: 65, p. 7313).

Udet: note for conf of 14 Aug 1939 (FD. 4940/45).

Cf Diary, 15 Aug 1939.

Führer order for expansion of Ju 88 and Flak Programmes dated 21 Aug 1939 (FD. 4940/45), and other documents in the same file.

102 Halder diary, 14 Aug 1939; cf Keitel, Memoirs, pp. 208f. Milch diary, 15 and 16 Aug 1939; cf Pre-Trial Interrogation, 17 and 27 Oct 1945.

103 Memoirs; cf MCH 12 Mar 1947, p. 1833.

104 Milch, May 1968; cf diary, 4 Mar 1915.

105 Diary, 22 Aug 1939: '12 noon: all C-in-C's and army commanders with Führer: the situation and his intentions, directives. 5.40–7.47 pm. [flew] Ainring to Berlin.' Milch disputes Hans-Bernd Gisevius' version *Bis zum Bitteren Ende*, vol. II, p. 103, according to which caviar was served during the luncheon. He accepts the text prepared presumably by Adm. Canaris: Führer's speech to C-in-C's, 22 Aug 1939 (ND: 798-PS) as being correct. Cf Albrecht diary, 22 Aug 1939, printed in *Vierteljahreshefte für Zeitgeschichte*, 2/1968, pp. 148f.

106 Diary, 25 and 26 Aug 1939: 'Overnight in Air Ministry. Then to Karinhall, and thence to Reich Chancery. Lunch with Führer. Then to Air Ministry and Wild Park. At 3.30 a.m. Göring comes, and we await him at his train. He says Italian King blocked Mussolini!' Also Milch, Mar 1967, Oct 1967, May 1968; and *The Development of the German Air Force*.

107 Diary, 27, 28 Aug 1939; Milch's draft inspection report to Jeschonnek and others, 29 Aug 1939 (MD: 51, p. 485).

108 Diary, 31 Aug 1939.

CHAPTER 4

1 Völker: *Luftwaffe*, pp. 182f.

2 Milch: Reasons for the Defeat of the Luftwaffe.

3 Report of Air Staff, 6th Div., 2 Sep 1939 (cited in Völker: *Luftwaffe*, p. 189).

4 Kesselring, op. cit., p. 59.

5 Gen Wilhelm Speidel: The Polish Campaign, vol. I, appendices 1–10.

6 Milch puts the bombs consumed at about 60 per cent of the total stocks. Cf Göring, quoted in *Inter Avia*, Jul 1946, p. 17.

7 Notes, diary, 1940: 'Casualties east, casualties west.'

8 Halder diary, 27 Sep 1939; cf Helmut Greiner: The Campaigns against the Western Powers and in the North (MS: C-065d). Diary, 28 Sep 1939.

9 Ibid, 12 Oct 1939.

10 Cf diary, 31 July 1937; and 16 Jan 1940: '. . . Conf with Udet on bombs. For concrete [bombs] I propose Degelow.'

11 GL conf, 10 Nov 1942 (MD: 17, p. 3193). See also Milch at GL conf, 29 Jul 1942 (MD: 34, pp. 1672ff): von Richthofen had seen the bomb early in 1940 and been impressed by its fragmentation effect. By Jul 1942 there were 1½ million 50-kilo concrete bombs in stock.

12 Heinkel, op. cit., p. 440; diary, 1 Nov 1940.

13 A relation of the better-known Colonel (GS) Diesing on Göring's staff. Cf Göring interrogation SAIC/13, 19 May 1945: '. . . Hitler asked Göring to inform him as soon as a period of fine weather days was in sight, so that the Luftwaffe could be committed for at least five days in a row . . . Göring claims that at that time he was very much opposed to the invasion in France, and suggested repeatedly that it be postponed until Spring. He was in constant fear all through the winter that a period of fine weather might precipitate the offensive against France . . .'

14 Milch, May 1968; and diary, 7 Nov 1939; weather confs were also called on 8, 10 and 20 Nov 1939.

15 Jodl diary.

16 Milch, May 1968; ND: TC-58a; Jodl diary, 11 Jan 1940; and diary, 12 Jan 1940: '. . . Evening, to see Göring: "Belgian papers have been burnt." '

17 Bross, op. cit., p. 130.
GL conf, 15 Aug 1942 (MD: 15, p. 1926): 'The Reichsmarschall also says that the affair in 1940 was a frightful blow to his prestige with the Führer.'

18 Kesselring, op. cit., p. 66. Hitler also ordered that experiments be carried out on self-destructor devices, for couriers' briefcases in the event of their capture.

19 Milch, Nov 1968.

20 Göring, 19 May 1945. (See Note 13).

21 Milch, May 1968. German Air Intelligence put the combined British and French front-line air strength at 1,782 bombers and 1,823 fighters on 1 Jan 1940 of which perhaps 60 per cent were serviceable. Comparable figures for 20 Jan showed the German air force to have 4,724 war planes, of which 72 per cent were serviceable. The number increased by about 800 by the end of March. Milch knew that both Britain and France were purchasing aircraft from USA—he knew the precise figures—and it was a matter of time before the enemy was numerically equal. Hitler repeatedly stressed that time was working only for the enemy.

22 Cf Göring conf, 29 Jan 1940, recorded in Milch's notes: present were Göring, Milch, Jeschonnek, Bodenschatz, Sperrle, Koller, Kesselring, Speidel, von Waldau, von Seidel, Martini and Schmid. Also Göring conf, 3 Feb 1940, with the same participants plus von Greim, Plocher, Grauert, Loerzer, Korten, Meister, Keller, von Richthofen, Seidemann, Genth, Geisler, and Harlinghausen.

23 Four Year Plan: memorandum on conf on acceleration of arms production, 9 Feb 1940 (MD: 65, pp. 7281ff); cf Milch's notes, 9 Feb 1940: those present were Göring, Milch, Udet, Neumann, Todt, Krauch, Gritzbach, Funk, Becker, Witzell, Keitel, v. Hannecken, Hernekamp, Thomas, Kleinmann, Landfried, Zimmermann; and diary, 9 Feb 1940.

24 Letter Udet to Four Year Plan office, 21 Feb 1940 (MD: 65, p. 7280).

25 Heinkel, op. cit., p. 442.

26 Diary, 1 Mar 1940, 2 Mar 1940; and Milch, Nov 1967, May and Nov 1968.

27 Diary, 26 Dec 1947. Milch adds: 'What on earth was the *General Luftzeugmeister* thinking of?'

28 Göring conf, in Milch's notes, 13 Mar 1940. Cf diary, 13 Mar 1940: 'First [Göring] conf with Udet.'

29 Diary, 17 Feb 1940: 'British *Schweinerei* against the *Altmark*.' In this incident the German tanker *Altmark*, carrying 299 British captives taken by the raider *Graf Spee*, was boarded in neutral waters by a party from a British destroyer, and nine of the unarmed German seamen were killed. Cf US Army Pamphlet No. 20–271: *The German Northern Theater of Operations 1940–1945*. Diary, 11 and 13 Jan 1940; Milch, May 1968.

30 Diary, 14 Jan 1940: 'Morning, first "Oyster" conf—and last.' Cf Jodl diary, 21 Jan 1940: '6 pm: C-in-C Army and chief of staff. Operation "Oyster". C-in-C Air Force.'

31 Jodl diary, 23 Jan 1940: 'Study N[orth] withdrawn on Führer's orders and will not be processed by Services. Activation of special unit in C-in-C Luftwaffe's staff is to be stopped. Processing only by *OKW*.'

32 Eyermann, op. cit., pp. 160, 310–311.

33 Diary, 11 and 12 Apr 1940; and Göring conf, noted in Milch's notes, 12 Apr 1940.

34 Diary, 13 Apr 1940.

35 Notes, 14 Apr 1940: conf in Reich Chancery with Hitler, Göring, Raeder, Milch, Jeschonnek, Keitel and Bodenschatz.

36 Diary, 17 Apr 1940.

37 *Royal Air Force, 1939–1945*, vol. I, p. 86.

38 Diary, 26 Apr 1940: 'Row with Harlinghausen!' And 27 Apr 1940: 'Morning, Falkenhorst here: very downcast. "Impossible to make progress without strong air activity!" Agreed. Midday: we capture Kuam and Bagn: Group XXI holds up its head again . . .'

39 Führer–Speer–Milch conf, 24 May 1942 (MPP); also published by Boelcke, *Deutschlands Rüstung im Zweiten Weltkrieg*, pp. 127ff.

CHAPTER 5

1 Diary, 23 May 1940; Milch was apparently at Göring's headquarters all day.
2 *Inter Avia*, Jul 1946, p. 17.
3 Engel notes, 23 May 1940.
4 Milch, May 1968; cf Gen Josef Schmid: Background of the Luftwaffe's operations at Dunkirk; cited by Suchenwirth: Göring, p. 99, and Jeschonnek, p. 61.
   Engel, notes, op. cit.; Kesselring and v. Richthofen also objected to the decision. Cf Richard Collier: *Sands of Dunkirk*, pp. 24ff.
5 Engel notes, 23 May 1940.
6 Memoirs; cf also description by Gen v. Waldau, diary, May 1940.
7 Diary, 5 Jun 1940; CSDIC (UK) report SRGG1313 (C), dated 3 Jun 1945.
8 Bross, op. cit., p. 47; Milch does not consider this an adequate excuse.
9 Diary, 19 Jul 1940.
10 Memoirs; Milch, and Nov 1967, May 1968.

CHAPTER 6

1 Jodl: The Continuation of War against Britain, 30 Jun 1940 (ND: 1776-PS).
2 Ibid.
3 RAF fighter production since Jun 1940 was 490 monthly; while Me 109 production was 164 in June, 220 in July, 173 in August, 218 in September 1940.
4 German Air Staff order, 30 Jun 1940.
5 *The Rise and Fall of the German Air Force*, p. 75.
6 Notes, 21 Jul 1940: a long record of a conf attended by Göring, Milch, Sperrle, Kesselring, Speidel, Stumpff, Jeschonnek, v. Waldau, v. Seidel, Udet, Grauert, Loerzer, Kühl, Weiss, Martini, Bodenschatz, Gritzbach, v. Richthofen, Schmid, Keller, v. Greim, Coeler, Dessloch, Kastner, Putzier, Witzig. Cf also Luftwaffe ops staff staff memo on the conf, 21 Jul 1940. Milch had first demanded radio to enable ground controllers to communicate with fighter pilots, and escort fighters with bombers, in 1934. Cf GL conf, 10 Sep 1943 (MD: 38, p. 4566): 'I never found out why our bombers were unable to communicate with their escort fighters in the attacks on Britain.'
7 Conf of three C-in-C's with Führer, 21 Jul 1940 (in German Naval Staff War Diary, 21 Jul 1940); Göring was represented by Jeschonnek.
8 See note 6.
9 Führer naval conf, 31 Jul 1940; cf Naval Staff war diary, 31 Jul 1940, and OKW war diary, 1 Aug 1940.
10 Führer directive No. 17, 1 Aug 1940.
11 Luftwaffe ops staff, directive, 2 Aug 1940.

12 Diary, 6 Aug 1940. Most problematic was the realization that the bomber formations could not defend themselves adequately. Robert Lusser, Messerschmitt's chief designer, had warned since 1936, from his knowledge of the Me 110's armament, that German bombers with their drum-loaded MG 15 machine-guns were far too weakly armed. In Jan 1939 he proved to the Reich Air Ministry that a standard fighter (Me 109) was not seven times, but *five hundred* times, superior to the standard bomber (He 111) in any air combat. No action was taken on Lusser's report. (Cf Report Lusser to Milch, 15 Jan 1942, MD: 53, p. 817).

13 OKW war diary 12 Aug 1940.

14 The figures are of serviceable aircraft. Basil Collier, op. cit., Appendix XI.

15 Diary, 13 Aug 1940. In fact not all Second Air Force's units received the recall message (*KG 2* for example), and thus made their attack without fighter escort. Cf Richard Collier: *Eagle Day,* pp. 55ff.

16 Diary, 15 Aug 1940; and notes, 15 Aug 1940.

17 OKW war diary, 16 Aug 1940. On the 18th, dive bombers had attacked Portsmouth and mislaid their fighter escort—'a small mishap'—and German losses that day were 147, compared with 49 enemy aircraft.

18 Diary, 19 Aug 1940; and notes, 19 Jan 1940; see also the part report on the conf, MD: 65, pp. 7251ff, circulated in no fewer than 920 copies. Cf Basil Collier, op. cit., p. 203.

19 Cf notes, 27 Aug 1940: 'Sperrle believes that enemy can be softened up by night attacks. Jeschonnek thinks differently.'

20 Baron von Hammerstein, to Suchenwirth, in: Jeschonnek, p. 72. He also related this in his privately printed memoirs, *Mein Leben,* pp. 131f.

21 Milch: inspection report, 20–25 Aug 1940 (MD: 51, pp. 538ff).

22 Notes, 20–25 Aug 1940.

23 Notes, 30, 31 Aug 1940; and inspection report, 27 Aug–4 Sep 1940 (MD: 51, pp. 530ff).

24 Notes and diary, 4 Sep 1940: 'Führer approves larger quota for 1000 kilo bombs.'

25 OKW war diary, 4 Sep 1940. In fact the RAF had 650 fighters serviceable.

26 Ibid, 30 Aug 1940. Cf notes, 4 Sep 1940: 'Point 1: when London?' and OKW war diary, 4 Sep 1940: 'London still not released for attack by Führer.'

27 OKW war diary, 6–9 Sep 1940.

28 OKW war diary, 10 Sep 1940.
   *Time,* 26 Aug 1940, pp. 21–4.

29 Diary, 13 and 14 Sep 1940; the latter conf was attended by Hitler, Milch, Keitel, Jodl, Bodenschatz, v. Brauchitsch, Halder, Jeschonnek, Raeder, v. Puttkamer, Schmundt and a major.

30 Notes, 14 Sep 1940; cf Halder diary, 14 Sep 1940; and OKW war diary, 14 Sep 1940: The Führer had ordered, 'Terror raids against purely residential areas must be reserved for use as an ultimate means of pressure.'

Cf also German Naval Staff war diary, 14 and 15 Sep 1940. Keitel's version is in ND: 803-PS.

31 Diary, 16 Sep 1940; and notes, 16 Sep 1940. Those present were Göring, Sperrle, Kesselring, Milch, Greim, Pflugbeil, Martini, Bodenschatz, v. Döring, Loerzer, Jeschonnek, Zech, Kastner and others.

32 Between 24 Aug and 6 Sep 1940 the RAF had lost 103 pilots killed and 128 seriously injured, and 466 fighters were destroyed or seriously damaged. In general, see Warlimont's report, in OKW war diary, 23 Sep 1940.

33 Naval Staff war diary, 17 Sep 1940.

34 Letter Erich Warsitz to author, 29 Jan 1970.

35 Major Storp later became Technical Officer on Göring's staff: as a lieutenant he had served under Jeschonnek in the Greifswald unit.

36 Göring conf, 7 Oct 1943, stenogram (MD: 62, p. 5713).

37 Notes, 2 Sep 1940. Cf Milch at GL conf, 20 Aug 1942 (MD: 15, pp. 1986f): 'I had to consider the matter very thoroughly once about two years ago. Major problems had arisen in the operations of the Ju 88 as it then was. This resulted in an inward rejection of the Ju 88 by the mass of the squadrons. I am not talking of those people who believed I was personally opposed to the Ju 88. I was as neutral towards the Ju 88 as towards the He 111 or Do 217, etc. I have no interest in standing out for or against a firm or office. In my reports I purely forwarded the squadrons' opinions, without suggesting they were proper ones. But I had to report what the subjective views of the squadrons were, and I tried to narrow the causes down for the technical authorities; but the technical authorities begrudged me that, and said, "This is an attack on us—it looks as though we have failed." '

38 Milch: inspection report dated 15 Oct 1940 (MD: 51, pp. 522ff). Cf notes, 12–15 Oct 1940. See also Werner Baumbach's version in *Broken Swastika*, where he suggests Milch recalled the third squadron of *KG 30* from the front 'as a punishment for mutiny and defeatism.' And cf notes, 13 Oct 1940.

39 Koppenberg: note on Göring conf, 12 Nov 1940 (in file: Correspondence with Dr Koppenberg, FD 5515/45).

40 Diary, 13 Oct 1940; cf ibid, 5, 16, 17, 18, 27 Sep, 1 Oct 1940.

41 Heinkel, op. cit., p. 422.

42 Diary, 20 Oct 1940.

43 Ibid, 23, 25, 28 Oct 1940; cf Heinkel, op. cit., p. 444, and letter Prof Kalk to author, 11 Dec 1968.

44 Diary, 28 Oct, 12, 14 Nov, 10 Dec 1940.

45 Letter von Winterfeld to author, 22 Dec 1969; Lieut. Simniok was the signals officer.

46 Diary, 3 Oct 1940; and notes, 3 Oct 1940.

47 Pre-Trial Interrogation 6 Nov 1946; the Inspectorate was returned to Milch on 13 Oct 1940.

48 Diary and notes, 12 Oct 1940.

49 Notes, 30 Oct 1940. Cf Koppenberg's note on Göring conf, 8 Nov 1940 (see note 39): 'The *General Luftzeugmeister* [Udet] is considering similar measures to increase the industry in Germany by 400,000 workers, and start up the French industry again with 200,000 workers, in other words an increase in manpower by 600,000 to 1,200,000 altogether.'

50 Diary, 15 Oct 1940; and notes; 15 Oct 1940. Cf letter Milch to Göring, 15 Oct 1940 (MD: 56, pp. 2790ff).

51 Memoirs.

52 Diary and notes, 31 Oct 1940.

53 Engel notes, 4 Nov 1940.

54 Milch: inspection report 27 Aug–4 Sep 1940 (MD: 51, p. 534).

55 Diary, 14 Nov 1940.

56 Waldau diary, 16 Nov 1940.

57 Diary, 25 Nov 1940: '4.30–4.50 pm with Führer: situation and measures to be taken, Mediterranean. Telephone Göring at Rominten: I am to return to West, Jeschonnek to go to him.' And notes, 25 Nov 1940.

58 Diary, 3 Dec 1940. Notes, 3 Dec 1940. Waldau diary, 3 Dec 1940: 'In the evening, went to Insterburg, thence to Rominten. Wet autumn day. A very warm and personal discussion with Reichsmarschall (mostly in his hunting landau, which was taking us to the feeding place of the world record deer "Matador"). Night, returned to Berlin.'

59 Diary, 4 Dec 1940; and notes, 4 Dec 1940. Cf letter Hitler to Duce, 4 Dec 1940 (personal papers of Mussolini, NARS film T-586, roll 405).

60 Notes, Nov 1940: the 1,845 Germans had been killed in a period of severe petrol rationing of motor vehicles; over the same six months in 1938, there were 4,280 people killed in traffic accidents.

61 Diary, 11, 12 Dec 1940.

62 Cf war diary of Führer's HQ, Appendix; and Bormann diary, 24, 25 Dec 1940. Milch Diary, 25 Dec 1940: 'Minister Hess visits us, early. Then to Führer, for conf (his train near *Asia*). East first! Adm. Darlan visits Führer.' Hitler had signed the OKW directive No. 21 (Case *Barbarossa*) on 18 Dec 1940: 'The German Wehrmacht must be prepared to knock out the Soviet Union in a rapid campaign, even before the war with Britain is over.'

CHAPTER 7

1 Cf diary, 17 Dec 1939: 'Morning at Karinhall with Udet, conf on deliveries to Russia.' Notes, 30 Mar 1940: a conf on supplies to Russia (in some detail); also Alpers, Dec 1969.

2 Bross: op. cit., pp. 76ff.
   Göring's last public speech in Berlin, 30 Jan 1943 (reported in *Völkischer Beobachter*, 2 Feb 1943).

3 US State Dept interrogation of Göring, 6–7 Nov 1945; and USFET report OI–RIR/7 on Göring, 24 Oct 1945.
   *Inter Avia*, Jul 1946, p. 17. *The Rise and Fall of the German Air Force*, p. 162, states that the engineers' reports 'were not believed by Oberst [Col]

Schmid who suspected Udet's engineers of being the victims of Russian bluff.' One of them was *Oberstingenieur* Dietrich Schwenke: cf GL conf, 9 Dec 1942 (MD: 17, pp. 3614ff, 3716f) for his experiences there; on Russian production in general see GL confs 21 Jul 1942 (MD: 15, p. 1551ff); 17 Nov 1942 (MD: 17, pp. 3246ff); and 23 Mar 1943 (MD: 19, p. 4763).

4 Bross, op. cit., p. 26: 'I [Göring] tried in vain to dissuade him; for three hours I harangued him. Of course this won't have the slightest effect on this trial.' Cf also Göring interrogation SAIC/13, 19 May 1945; and OI-RIR/7, 24 Oct 1945; and Pre-Trial Interrogation of Göring, 11 Oct 1945; and US State Dept interrogation, 6–7 Nov 1945.

5 Diary, 13 Jan 1941; cf Waldau diary, 6 Jan 1941: 'Jeschonnek recalled to Berlin and Obersalzberg after being back here barely half a day!' And 13 Jan 1941: 'Jeschonnek returns with basic directives, then goes back to Berlin.' Cf Pre-Trial Interrogation, 18 Oct 1946; and MCH 12 Mar 1947, p. 1839. And letter Col Edgar Petersen to author, 3 and 18 Dec 1969: from Dec 1940 to Mar 1941 Petersen was the expert on navigation and blind flying on Jeschonnek's staff at Le Déluge; he is certain that the date was 13 Jan 1941.

6 Diary, 1 Feb 1941.

7 Kesselring, op. cit., p. 111.

8 Pre-Trial Interrogation, Oct 1946; cf IMT vol. IX, pp. 57ff; and MCH 12 Mar 1947, pp. 1839f. 'From the Memoirs of Field Marshal Milch' reproduces the dialogue from memory; cf Memoirs.

9 Milch, May 1968; cf Bross, op. cit., p. 46, where Göring takes the credit. MCH, 12 Mar 1947, p. 1841; and Memoirs.

10 Cf Goebbels diary, 15 May 1942: 'Naumann tells me about yet another instance of the War Office's neglect. They ordered rubber boots for the mud period in the East, which will not be ready until July, probably. The Army always complains about the better clothing of the Luftwaffe and SS. This can only be attributed to the fact that people there worked more promptly and responsibly than in the Army. The Army is governed by a scarcely tolerable bureaucracy.' Milch himself recalled this period at GL conf, 9 Dec 1942 (MD: 17, p. 3669): '. . . Everybody knew at the time that the Eastern affair was coming. It was long before June [1941]: I was asked in the Supply Department whether we were to prepare for the winter or not. That was months beforehand. Thereupon I gave the order: "Prepare everything for the winter. The war in the East is going to last for years!" At that time the official view was different. I know the East, its expanses; I have been there often enough myself . . . Do you believe the winter measures could have been carried out if we waited until the order was finally given? Then it would have been far too late.'

11 Göring conf, 8 Jan 1942 (MD: 62, pp. 5161ff): Von Seidel: 'Since 22 Jun 1941 winter orders and directives have been continually issued. Every-

thing possible has been done. There are still stocks in hand for further units going out there.' Suchenwirth: Milch, p. 20, gives credit to both von Seidel and Milch, but the latter correctly points out that von Seidel's orders were issued, if at all, in Aug 1941; this is supported by Vorwald (Jun 1968), at the time head of the Equipment Branch of the Air Staff. In about Sep 1941 (when GAF headquarters was already at Goldap, East Prussia) Jeschonnek told him, 'Telephone Seidel that everything must be stocked up for the Luftwaffe—cold-start equipment, clothing, etc.' (Jeschonnek himself was not on speaking terms with Seidel.)

12 Memoirs; cf MCH 12 Mar 1947, p. 1884ff, and IMT, vol. IX, p. 60. Cf also von Brauchitsch in MCH, 20 Feb 1947, p. 1281: 'I do recall one remark, in April or May 1941, that Field Marshall Milch went to the C-in-C of the Luftwaffe in a conference to advise him that it would not be possible to wage a war against Russia, and asked him to make the appropriate representations to the Führer.'

13 Waldau diary, 28 Mar 1941: he ordered KG 51, KG 2, *Stuka 77* and *JG 54* immediately to the new front.

14 Diary, 30 Mar 1941; this version is based on Waldau's note.

15 Halder diary, 30 Mar 1941.

16 The Fourth Air Force's commander, Col Gen Alexander Löhr, and General Fiebig, were executed by the Yugoslavs after the war for the attack on Belgrade.

17 Waldau diary, 6 Apr 1941; Milch diary, 7 Apr 1941.

18 Rieckhoff: *Trumpf oder Bluff*, p. 135.

19 Robert Lusser: memorandum to Milch on development and research planning in German air armament (MD: 53, pp. 804ff) dated 15 Jan 1942; Lusser was with Messerschmitt company until Jun 1939 when he transferred to Heinkel's as chief designer.

20 Rakan Kokothaki: on the reasons and sequence of cancellation of Me 210 production (Mar 1970). Cf letter Udet (sgd Reidenbach) to Prof Messerschmitt, 17 May 1941 (FD. 4355/45, Vol. 5).

21 Baron von Hammerstein, op. cit., p. 132; cf Udet's notes for conf with Göring 7/8 Feb 1941, point 6.
von Hammerstein, op. cit., p. 132.

22 Heinkel op. cit., p. 446.

23 Göring to Milch, conf, 7 Oct 1943, stenogram (MD: 62, pp. 5697f).

24 Milch Nov 1968; diary, 31 Oct 1940; and Manfred Roeder: Investigation after suicide of Col Gen. Udet (dated Nuremberg 27 Jun 1947).

25 von Brauchitsch in MCH, 20 Feb 1947, pp. 1283f.

26 von Hammerstein, op. cit., p. 133; cf Baumbach: op. cit., p. 104.

27 Diary, 16 May 1941.

28 Milch in MCH, 12 Mar 1947, p. 1844; cf von Brauchitsch, MCH, 20 Feb 1947, p. 1283.

29 Diary, 22 May 1941; *The Rise and Fall of the German Air Force*, pp. 165, 76. Pendele: chronology, 23 May 1941.

30 Heinkel: op. cit., pp. 450f.

31 Diary, 29 May 1941. 'Midday: with Udet at Horcher's'. It cannot be denied that Milch was jealous of Udet's ready accessibility to Göring, for MPP contains a scrap of paper on which Milch listed the numbers of Udet's confs with Göring each year, as compared with his own.

32 Pendele: chronology; Milch diary, 11 Jun 1941.

33 Milch, GL conf, 22 Jun 1943 (MD: 21, p. 5772). Göring to Milch at conf, 7 Oct 1943 (MD: 62, pp. 5697f).

34 Diary, 12 Jun 1941; MCH, 12 Mar 1947, p. 1844.

35 Diary, 14 Jun 1941.

36 Waldau diary, 14 Jun 1941; Halder diary, 14 Jun 1941.

See also Warlimont: *Im Hauptquartier der deutschen Wehrmacht.* Cf Pre-Trial Interrogation, 18 Oct 1946, and Milch at IMT vol. IX, p. 65: 'We sat round a large table and each of the Army Group and Army commanders outlined their tasks and planned operations on a map, while Hitler signified his approval or made minor corrections.' And diary, 15 Jun 1941: 'Major conf of Luftwaffe at Karinhall: *Luftflotten,* Air Corps, Air Zones.'

37 OKW directive, 18 Dec 1940.

38 Diary, 22 June 1941.

39 The Soviet publication, *History of the Great Patriotic War of the Soviet Union,* suggests that by noon of the first day, 22 Jun 1941, twelve hundred Soviet aircraft had been destroyed, including 800 on the ground.

40 Diary, 22–26 Jun 1941. Göring claimed the Russians lost 2,700 aircraft in the first three days, mostly on the ground (*Inter Avia,* Jul 1946, p. 18).

CHAPTER 8

1 A. Milward: *The German Economy at War,* p. 43.

2 Diary, 20 Jun 1941: '. . . Göring [gives me] Special commission to quadruple the Luftwaffe. . . .'

3 Thorwald: *Ernst Udet; Mein Fliegerleben* (Berlin, 1954), p. 178.

4 Milch at MCH, 13 Mar 1947, p. 1910. Cf Milch at GL conf, 22 Jun 1943 (MD: 21, p. 5772): 'I am thinking of the times of the late Dr Todt. There was perpetual argument about whether Udet had been given the workers or not. He proved that Udet had received 60,000, each month and Udet said he had not received one.'

5 MCH, 13 Mar 1947, p. 1911. The date in Jun 1941 is uncertain.

6 Ibid; and diary, 21 Jun 1941.

7 Göring: special authority to Milch, Jun 1941. (MD: 57, pp. 3206ff). The only copy is in the Milch Documents, among the papers left by Udet: it was evidently typed in Göring's office, and initialled by Pendele for Udet on 25 Jun 1941 (p. 3208); the copy shown to Udet was not signed by Göring, and it was undated.
Ibid, p. 3209.

8 MCH, 13 Mar 1947, p. 1911.

9 *Chronik* of Inspector-General of Construction in Reich Capital (cited hereafter as Speer, *Chronik*) 23 Jun 1941. Cf Speer: *Erinnerungen,* p. 197. Cf Thomas' note (see note 11): '. . . with the provision that the factories are to be torn down after the war, to avoid any incentive to invest huge sums in them.'

10 Memoirs; and notes for conf with Field Marshal Milch, undated (MD: 65, pp. 7118ff).

11 Diary, 26 Jun 1941; Milch and Dr Todt had known each other since 1915, at Verdun, where both were stationed on the same airfield. And cf Thomas: note on conf in State-Secretary Milch's office, 26 June 1941 (publ. in OKW war diary, vol. I, pp. 1016ff).

12 Milch: speech to Industrial Council, 18 Sep 1941, stenogram (MD: 53, pp. 1162ff).

13 GL conf 3 Aug 1943 (MD: 23, p. 6597).

14 In Nov Koppenberg was given special powers by Göring to double Norwegian aluminium output to 120,000 tons a year by mid-1942, with the Air Ministry as sole beneficiary. He established Hansa Leichtmetall AG for this purpose. By Jul 1941 he was talking of expanding Norway's aluminium smelting capacity to 250,000 tons a year (letter Koppenberg to Krauch, 11 July 1941, in FD. 5515/45); the added capacity would come from Herven II, Eitrheim, Aura and Ulvik. By mid 1941 his main problem was securing raw materials—alumina and bauxite; he looked to France (letters to Udet, 31 Mar, 4 Apr 1941, ibid), Greece and Yugoslavia (letter to Udet, 23 Apr 1941, ibid); on 23 Jun 1941 he was already considering Russian sources (letter of 2 Jul 1941 to Udet, where reference is made to a conf of 23 Jun). (Koppenberg was most interested in the alumina works at Kandalashka, but he advised that the biggest aluminium smelting plants, with a capacity of 27,000 tons a year, were on the Dnieper, with associated aluminium, electrode and cryolith factories.) Koppenberg was frequently thwarted by Dr Westrick's rival United Aluminium Works, a Reich company, which attempted to secure a monopoly of Yugoslav bauxite; cf note on conf, 17 Jul 1941, where Krauch proposed dividing Soviet Union into a northern area for Koppenberg's Hansa, and a southern one for Westrick (FD. 5515/45). Cf Milch diary, 23 Jun 1941.

15 Conf of 26 June 1941. Similar information on enemy air forces including the American, compared with Germany, was given to the OKM by the Air Staff liaison officer and by Schwenke during Aug 1941. Cf Naval Staff war diary, 5 and 13 Aug 1941.

16 Milch: speech, 18 Sep 1941 (see note 12). Göring shared Milch's admiration for Knudsen: 'What Mr Knudsen, the organizer and leading figure of the US armaments industry, is capable of we are all capable of.' (See chapter 6, note 39 for source). Knudsen had visited Milch in Germany.

17 Memoirs.

18 Milch in MCH, 12 Mar 1947, p. 1845.

19 Note on Programme for Jumo 222: conf in Reich Air Ministry, 30 Aug 1941 (Junkers archives).

20 Vorwald in MCH, 10 Mar 1947, p. 1672.

21 Memoirs. And Thomas: note on staff conf under Field Marshal Keitel, 14–16 Aug 1941 (publ. in OKW war diary, vol. I, p. 1046). Milch, Nov 1967.

22 Diary 8–11 Jul 1941, and 1945 note thereon: 'Udet's deception of Göring.' Cf Udet's notes in MD: 65, p. 7133.
From a letter of State prosecuting authorities dated 8 Apr 1942 it appears that 'Moose' programme was dated 5 Jul 1941 (Udet's version) and 15 Jul 1941 (Milch's redraft)–MD: 56, p. 2556. Also Milch, Nov 1967.

23 Diary, 15, 16 Jul 1941: 'At headquarters, Rostken: report to Göring Luncheon, then Göring called to Führer. Went for a walk. Göring still with Führer. My attendance a waste of time.' We now know that Hitler was holding an important conf with Göring, Ribbentrop, Lammers and others on the exploitation of the Soviet Union after its defeat (ND: 1221-PS, 2360-PS; and Thomas: note on result of confs with Reichsmarschall and FM Keitel on 17 Jul 1941, NARS film T-77, roll 441).

24 Diary, 17 Jul 1941; and 1945 notes thereon. Cf Roeder in MCH, 3 Mar 1947, pp. 1395f.

25 Statistics in MD: 53, p. 742.

26 Diary, 7 Aug 1941; and Milch, May 1968.

27 Messerschmitt, interviewed on Second German Television, 17 Feb 1970.

28 Milch: speech, 18 Sep 1941 (see note 12).

29 See note 21, conf of 14–16 August 1941. Also diary, 16 Aug 1941. Thomas evidently discussed the conf in some detail with Amb. von Hassel, cf Hassel diary, p. 196f.

30 Heinkel, op. cit., p. 451. Diary, 12–17 Aug 1941.

31 Milch: speech, 18 Sep 1941 (see note 12).

32 Letter of Milch to Maj Gen Ploch, c/o Udet, 4 Sep 1941 (MD: 56, pp. 2682f). On 18 Sep 1941 (see note 12) Milch assessed the cost of the whole air industry expansion as about 1,200 million marks.

33 Note on Programme for Jumo 222, conf in Reich Air Ministry, 30 Aug 1942 (Junkers archives).

34 Milch believes this discussion was about 28–30 Aug 1941. (Milch, May and Nov 1968.)

35 Diary, 6 Sep 1941: '. . . At Rominten: big conf on factory construction programme. Göring: large number of aircraft, postpone Bomber "B", cancel Jumo 222 . . .'

36 Pendele: chronology, 25 Aug 1941. Roeder in MCH, 3 Mar 1947, p. 1395: 'It resulted in a lengthy discussion [between Udet and Göring] in the garden of Karinhall, which ended with Udet taking six weeks' leave.'

37 Diary, 1 Sep 1941.

38 Milch in MCH, 12 Mar 1947, p. 1846.

39 Diary, 9 Sep 1941; cf Milch's note on *Frankfurter Illustrierte* series, 2 May 1952 (MPP).
Suchenwirth: Udet, p. 75.
Milch, May 1968. Letter Göring to Koppenberg, relieving him of his commission, 20 Oct 1941 (MD: 57, p. 3205).

40 Diary, 9 Sep 1941; and Milch: speech, 18 Sep 1941 (see note 12). The original composition of the Industrial Council was Milch as Chairman; Director William Werner (Man. Dir of Auto Union) as deputy; Karl Frydag (of Henschel, later of Heinkel); Heyne (of AEG), with Albert Vögler (of United Steel), Westrick (of United Aluminium), Bruhn (of Auto Union) and Adml Lahs (Pres. of the Association of Aircraft Manufacturers).

41 Ibid., the figures Milch gave for future monthly output, with current output in brackets, were: He 111: 160 (100); He 177: 120 (0); Do 217: 100 (24); Me 210: 140 (90); Me 109: 200 (200); FW 190: 485 (170); Ju 87: 156 (55); and Ju 88: 300 (220).

42 These fears were confirmed in letter Roeder to Milch's lawyer, P. H. Gordan, 7 Dec 1953 (MPP).

43 Pendele: chronology, Sep 1941. Roeder in MCH, 3 Mar 1947, p. 1395.

44 Diary, 25 Sep 1941: '[Rominten]. Conference with Schmid, chief of Intelligence. Early morning hunt, for "Klumpenbalis", without success. Agreement reached with Udet. Morning and afternoon, big organization and personnel conf with Göring, re: Office of Air Armament. Agreement reached. All my proposals accepted.' Milch, May 1968, Nov 1967.

45 Suchenwirth (quoting Ploch) in Udet, p. 76.
Göring conf, 9 Oct 1943, stenogram (MD: 63, p. 6317). Göring had by then read extensively in the reports of the Udet Case.

46 Conf on Opel, 10 Oct 1941 (MD: 65, pp. 7107ff).

47 Diary, 20 Oct 1941.

48 Diary, 21 Oct 1941.

49 Seiler Papers: The Udet Case (a 13-page description of the events from 22 Oct to 17 Nov 1941).

50 Milch, May 1968. On Milch's plan to visit Paris with Udet, see also Pre-Trial Interrogation, 25 Oct 1946 and his note, dictated in Landsberg 27–28 Jul 1953 (MPP).

51 Diary, 15, 16, 17 Nov 1941: 'Left Schill for Berlin. There [received] news that Udet died approx 9.15 am!!! Evening with [Prof] Kalk at hunting lodge Bärenwiese. Telephone conversation with Göring.'

52 Frau Inge B[leyle] interviewed by *Münchner Illustrierte* 8/1953 (21 Feb 1953); Suchenwirth: Udet, p. 78.
Cf Pendele: chronology, 17 Nov 1941: '9 am: after a telephone conversation with Milch and then with Frau Bleyle, the end comes.' There is no mention of such a telephone call in Milch's diary, and he states that there was none (Udet would not have known his telephone number at Breslau, he states); the car journey to Berlin must have taken Milch 3½ hours, so Udet may have tried in vain to reach him.

53 Letter Gordan to Pendele, 23 Oct 1953; letter Roeder to Gordan, 7 Dec 1953; letter Lawyer Dr Justus Koch (Körner's lawyer) to Gordan, 25 Jan 1954 (MPP).

Körner, in interview with Thorwald, Jan 1953; letter Thorwald to Gordan, 16 Aug 1953 (MPP).

54 Roeder, op. cit.; Pre-Trial Interrogation of Milch, 25 Oct 1946; and diary, 21 May 1942, and 1945 notes thereon; and Memoirs.

55 Telegram Dr v. Ondarza (Göring's office) to Gen v. Witzendorff, 18 Nov 1941 (MD: 51, pp. 444f).

56 Göring was deeply distressed by the sudden loss of Udet and Mölders. When Ciano met him in Berlin three days after the funeral, tears came to Göring's eyes when he mentioned them (Ciano diary, 24 Nov 1941); after a period of vehement recrimination against Udet (Oct 1943) he softened again. Reviewing the reasons for Germany's loss of air superiority in his speech to Air Staff officers on 25 Nov 1944 (Koller Papers), Göring recalled: 'Things got completely out of hand for the controllers of our arms production. One of them, seeing the chaos coming, then took a step which obviously one cannot approve of, but one now understands better than ever.'

57 Führer war conf, 1 Feb 1943. Hitler continued to blame Udet to foreign statesmen, for example see Führer-Antonescu conf, 5 Aug 1944.

CHAPTER 9

1 Diary, 16 Jul 1946.

2 Intercepted despatch of French amb in Washington, in Naval Staff war diary, 7 Mar 1942.

3 Petersen: notes on the organization of Luftwaffe technology, 20 May 1944 (MD: 56, p. 2561).

4 Air Ministry, Techn. Dept: On the reasons for the Increased Aircraft Production Mar to Jun 1944 (undated, probably Aug 1944). FD. 4439/45. This document sets out to establish that the Fighter Staff achieved its great mid-1944 production figures only because of the provisions already made by Milch and by lifting the obstacles that the Speer Ministry had refused to lift when Milch was responsible. For comparative figures of airframe and aero-engine production 1941 and 1942, both in Germany and abroad, see Milch, GL conf, 5 Jan 1943 (MD: 18, pp. 3932ff).

5 Papers of Fritz Seiler, Munich; in particular his memorandum (postwar), 'How to explain that my career was ruined by the work-prohibition imposed from 1946–1949'. Seiler, born in 1895, was a financial expert specializing in doctoring sick companies; in Jul 1923, although only 29, he was appointed general manager of a respected Hamburg banking house, Carlo Z. Thomsen. He had saved the famous Dyckerhoff cement concern for that family in 1933, from the clutches of five major banks, and at the request of Manfred Stromeyer took over the financial affairs of the Raulino family (which owned Messerschmitt's company) which was

threatened by disaster as the result of an uncovered attempt at fraudulent transfer of capital abroad.

6 Pre-Trial Interrogation, 25 Oct 1946.
Diary, 6 Aug 1949.

7 Report Petersen to Milch, 13 Aug 1942 (in Milch file: He 177, FD. 5514/ 45) cf report Petersen to Milch, 7 Oct 1942, re He 177's structural strength (ibid.)

8 Göring: speech to air industry, 13 Sep 1942 (MD: 62, p. 5294).

9 Letter Lahs to Milch, 11 Jan 1942 (MD: 53, p. 783): the DB 603 and Jumo 213 engines were both between 1,800 and 2,000 horsepower.

10 Techn. Dept: comparison of DB 603 with Jumo 213, 3 Nov 1941 (MD: 53, pp. 835ff); and diary, 27 Nov 1941: 'Air Ministry. Staff conf with industry on Jumo 213.' On the long, sad history of the DB 603, see Eisenlohr's remarks, GL conf 1 Jun 1942, and Milch, GL conf 9 Jun 1942 (MD: 14, pp. 845f, and 958ff). Milch: 'Do you know when the DB 603 was first offered to us, with 1,400 to 1,500 horsepower?—On 4 Sep 1936!'

11 Cf Eisenlohr, GL conf, 5 May 1942 (MD: 13, pp. 327f).

12 Göring conf, 13 May 1942 (MD: 62, p. 5202); Milch, May 1968.

13 Göring conf, 6 Mar 1942 (MD: 62, p. 5174).

14 Von Hammerstein, op. cit., pp. 130ff. According to Roeder the warrant for the inquiry was issued on 17 Mar 1942. 'Scars': see Judge Advocate Dr. Kraell's circular dated 8 Apr 1942 (MD: 56, pp. 2556f).

15 Roeder says the closing conf with Göring was on 17 Oct 1942.
Göring also expressed his relief to Milch; Milch, May 1968. In Jan 1942 when Munich asked permission to name a street or square after Udet, Göring agreed (NARS film T-84, roll 8, frame 8229); but by Jul 1942 his attitude had hardened. He decided that the question of naming the plaza in front of Tempelhof airport after Udet 'should be postponed to the end of the war.' (ibid, frame 7691).

16 Göring conf, 7 Oct 1943, stenogram (MD: 62, pp. 5698f); cf Göring conf, 29 Jun 1942 on the need to convert to wooden construction as quickly as possible: 'I gave Udet this order two years ago.' (MD: 62, p. 5242).

17 Air Staff order: Division of Occupied Eastern Territories into Air Zones, sgd Jeschonnek, countersigned Hoffmann, dated 15 Oct 1941 (MD: 53, p. 1065).

18 OKW order: Armaments 1942, dated 14 Jan 1942. (MD: 51, pp. 435f).

19 Diary, 24–29 Jan 1942. Hitler's Table talk, 28 Jan 1942.

20 Breith, at GL conf, 20 Oct 1942 (MD: 16, p. 2849).

21 Seidel, Göring conf, 8 Jan 1942 (MD: 62, p. 5165).

22 Herrmann: report to Milch on Cold Start Procedure for Vehicles, 11 Jan 1942 (MD: 56, p. 2678); there were Army and SS liaison officers at the Rechlin display on 3 Jul 1939. See also Technical Instructions of *General Luftzeugmeister:* Cold Start Procedure by means of Diluting

Lubricant, 18 Oct 1942; and ibid: Measures against Cold Effects (MD: 65, pp. 7188ff, 7192f); cf also Herrmann at GL conf, 7 Aug 1942 (MD: 34, pp. 1721f): means of determining degree of dilution of a lubricant.

23 Milch at GL conf, 7 Apr 1942 (MD: 13, p. 59).

24 Hitler's evening table talk, 19 Feb 1942; Speer was also present.

25 Memoirs. On Ley's role, see Goebbels diary, unpubl., 14 Feb 1942.

26 Milch, May 1968; MCH, 12 Mar 1947, pp. 1856f.

27 Foul play was ruled out: Letter Ilsabill Todt to Milch, 6 Oct 1946; Milch replied that he did not believe it had been sabotage. Milch, May 1968. Cf Max Müller: The Todt Case, an attempt to solve the mystery. He cites the terminal report of Air Zone I, Königsberg, 8 Mar 1943 (Bundesarchiv: Zentralnachweisstelle).

28 Speer (op. cit., p. 211) says Hitler called for him at 1 pm and said, 'I appoint you Todt's successor in all his offices'. This seems improbable, as Speer, Chronik shows Speer still being appointed to the other offices on 9 and 12 Feb. Cf Milch diary, 2 Aug 1947: 'Speer told me at the time he really wanted to fly with Todt in the same aircraft to Berlin, but changed his mind at the last moment. He always did want to be in the thick of the danger!'

29 For the 'attempts', see Saur report, 9 Jul 1945 (FD. 3049/49, file 1); and Milch diary, 11 Feb 1942.

30 Ibid, 12 Feb 1942: 'First conf with Speer [then] big conf with Funk and others, "Command structure". To see Reichsmarschall with Speer. Todt funeral. . . .' Cf. Speer, op. cit., p. 215.
Cf Speer, Chronik, 12 Feb 1942.

31 Diary, 13 Feb 1942; Speer, op. cit., pp. 215f. Cf Col Neef's memo on Conf of Armaments Inspectors, 13 Feb 1942 (FD. 5444/45 page J. 007442ff): Milch had agreed with Speer, the Luftwaffe and the OKW to concentrate joint planning under Speer: 'This issue will be put to the Führer this afternoon in conference.' Milch was very frank about his own role in this; cf GL conf, 10 Aug 1942 (MD: 38, p. 4736): '. . . Real brains know how to get on together and work together. About a year ago [in Feb 1942] I was confronted by the same problem: the problem then was, "Who is to head German arms production, Minister Speer or I?" I said, "Speer is to head it, and I will support him 100 per cent." I can happily do without any medals or decorations.'

32 Memoirs. Cf Speer in MCH 4 Feb 1947, p. 1447: 'Funk proposed Milch as the senior for this post. But I felt it important that I should get it.' And see Goebbels diary, 10 and 14 Feb 1942, unpubl, relating to events of the 13th; and Speer, Chronik, 13 Feb 1942.

33 Diary, 22 May 1948.

34 Diary, 21 Jul 1946; and 22 May 1948.

35 Cf Saur notes, on 13 Feb 1942: '4 pm. Führer introduces Speer in presence of Funk, Dorpmüller, Ley, Hupfauer, Maienbach, Vögler, Zangen, Milch, Witzell, Schulze-Fielitz, Schäde, Fromm, Leeb, Keitel,

Thomas, Kessler, Landfried.' Cf Speer in MCH, 4 Feb 1947, p. 1447; and Saur report, 9 Jul 1945 (FD. 3049/49).

Saur, op. cit. Hitler made a similar statement to Rosenberg on 8 May 1942 (Rosenberg memo, ND: 1520-PS).

36 Milch wrote notes of the speech in his 1942 diary.

37 Letter Görnnert to Schrötter, 24 Feb 1942 (NARS film T-84, roll 8, frames 8146f).

38 Milch, Dec 1969.

Cf *Hitlers Lagebesprechungen*, p. 901.

39 Roeder. Cf diary, 6 Oct 1947.

40 Vorwald, MCH, 10 Mar 1947, p. 1674.

Milch, GL conf, 5 Jan 1943 (MD: 18, p. 3932).

*The Rise and Fall of the German Air Force*, p. 207. Cf also Göring conf 29 Jun 1942 (MD: 62, p. 5237): Milch then planned to turn out 1,600 aircraft a month at the end of 1942, 2,500 at the end of 1943, and 2,800 by the end of 1945.

41 Letter Milch and Jeschonnek to Göring, re choice of Bomber B, 27 Feb 1942 (MD: 62, pp. 5178f); diary, 26, 27 Feb, 6 Mar 1942.

42 GL conf 30 Jun 1942 (MD: 15, pp. 1350f).

43 GL conf, 17 Aug 1942 (MD: 15, p. 1844).

44 Burton H. Klein: *Germany's Economic Preparations for War* (Harvard, 1959) pp. 198f. This conf transcript is not in the MD files in London, cf Milch diary, 21 Mar 1942: 'Rominten. Minus 26 degrees C!! Major conf with Göring and Jeschonnek. Latter would not know what to do with more than 360 fighters [a month]. Midday with Speer, then bomber production programme etc. Evening by special train to Berlin.'

45 Milch, GL conf, 5 Jan 1943 (MD: 18, p. 3946).

46 Milch, GL conf, 29 Jun 1943 (MD: 21, pp. 5718f); Milch, Oct 1967.

47 Jeschonnek, Göring conf, 6 Mar 1942 (MD: 62, p. 5168); cf Koller diary, Mar 1942.

48 Göring conf, 21 Mar 1942 (MD: 62, pp. 5181ff).

49 Milch at GL conf, 7 Apr 1942 (MD: 13, p. 107).

50 Memo Görnnert to Schrötter, 27 Mar 1942 (NARS film T-84, roll 8, frame 8129).

51 Letter Hitler to Milch, 30 Mar 1942 (MPP).

Memoirs.

52 Vorwald, in MCH 11 Mar 1947, pp. 1709, 1743; both Milch's former employers, Lufthansa and Junkers, presented small paintings to him, and these he accepted.

## CHAPTER 10

1 Von Winterfeld: report on reception of the German air attachés by Milch, Steengracht and Goebbels [etc], 24 Aug 1945.

2 Milch, at conf on 23 Apr 1942 (MD: 53, p. 796); and see Petersen's biting criticisms at GL conf, 19 Jun 1942 (MD: 15, pp. 1125f).

3 Göring conf, 21 Mar 1942 (MD: 62, p. 5187). Milch was equally hostile towards the Me 323, the Me 321's powered equivalent: Göring conf, 8 Aug 1942 (MD: 62, p. 5258): the Me 323 used four (and later six) Gnome-Rhone 14–N engines.

4 Telegram Urban to Messerschmitt company, 30 Mar 1942 (FD. 4355/45, vol. 5); cf Milch at GL conf, 4 Sep 1942 (MD: 34, p. 2002): It had been 'absolutely wrong' to start the company building big aircraft.

5 Kokothaki.

6 Göring conf, 6 Mar 1942 (MD: 62, pp. 5167ff).

7 The production position varies from document to document: cf conf of 23 Apr 1942 (MD: 53, p. 795), GL conf 27 Apr 1942 (MD: 13, p. 282) and Göring conf, 13 May 1942 (MD: 62, p. 5203).

8 Messerschmitt: speech to his workers, 25 Mar 1942 (FD. 4355/45, vol. 1).

9 GL confs, 14 Apr 1942 (MD: 13, p. 129); 21 Apr 1942 (MD: 13, pp. 191f); and 23 Apr 1942 (MD: 53, pp. 791ff). Milch had a very high opinion of Seiler's capabilities (see GL conf, 17 Nov 1942, MD: 17, p. 3240).

10 Milch, GL conf, 27 Apr 1942 (MD: 13, p. 282). And Messerschmitt company meeting, 30 Apr 1942 (Seiler papers): the main decisions reached were that Messerschmitt should restrict himself to his job as chief designer; and that Croneiss should become Chairman, with Seiler as Managing Director.

11 Note on phone call from Lt Col Petersen, 3 Sep 1942: Me 210 had just flown with two DB 603s, reaching top speed of 525 km per hour at ground level. Milch orders it to be named Me 410. (FD. 4355/45, vol. 4).

12 Milch, GL conf, 5 May 1942 (MD: 13, pp. 380ff); cf Milch at GL conf 10 Sep 1943 (MD: 38, pp. 4505): '. . . I am the one who sent one appeal after another to the authorities about this in 1940 and 1941. It is nonsense, this high explosive load; a mass of fire bombs belongs in every load of high explosive.'

13 Schwenke, GL conf, 26 May 1942 (MD: 14, pp. 691f).

14 Air Staff: directive on air warfare against British Isles, 14 Apr 1942; cf Basil Collier, op. cit., Appendix XXXVI.

15 Milch, 1940 notes. Cf Milch, GL conf, 7 Aug 1942 (MD: 34, p. 1729): 'I can never forget how General [Otto] Rüdel believed we would be able to shoot aircraft down with 47 rounds apiece, no more, no less. Then he worked out, the enemy has 6,000 aircraft, multiply it by 45 (or for that matter a hundred), gives 600,000 rounds of 88 mm flak ammunition. According to that sum, I cannot need any more. Fortunately we did not all believe that before the war broke out.'

16 The Chief of Naval Construction, Adm. Witzell, reported this to Raeder, adding that they must be prepared for attempts to cut the naval quotas in favour of the Luftwaffe; he privately stated that the overall raw ma-

terial allocations to the navy 'were not all that bad', however (Naval Staff war diary, 3 Feb 1942).

17 Letter Keitel to Milch, 6 Mar 1942 (MD: 49a, p. 216). Jeschonnek also wrote to Milch insisting that the Führer's flak production programme be adhered to. On the copper shortage, see also Göring conf, 6 Mar 1942 (MD: 62, pp. 5167ff), and Milch, GL conf 7 Apr 1942 (MD: 13, p. 94).

18 Milch, GL conf 27 May 1942 (MD: 14, p. 798); letter Milch to Keitel, 11 Mar 1942 (MD: 49a, pp. 213f). Cf GL conf 7 Apr 1942 (MD: 13, p. 94): Milch: 'It is out of the question for us to hand over the copper to them for [searchlight] production.' And cf GL conf 14 Apr 1942 (MD: 13, p. 170).

19 Milch at conf, 23 Apr 1942 (MD: 53, p. 796).

20 GL conf, 7 Apr 1942 (MD: 13, p. 36); Milch: speech, 18 Sep 1941 (MD: 53, pp. 1166f).

21 Milch, GL conf, 14 Apr 1942 (MD: 13, p. 124).

22 Milch, May 1968.

23 GL conf, 5 Jan 1943 (MD: 18, p. 3941).

24 Speer in MCH, 4 Feb 1947, pp. 1447f; Milward, op. cit., p. 83.

25 Military Economics Branch: note on conf with Speer, 2 Mar 1942 (FD. 5454a/45); Milward, op. cit., p. 79.

26 Memoirs; and diary, 2 Apr 1942; cf Speer, *Chronik*, 2 Apr 1942. See Milch's Central Planning file (MD: 48, pp. 8196ff).

27 Speer in MCH 4 Feb 1947, p. 1452.

28 Cf Görnnert: note for Göring at Führer conf, 3 Apr 1942: (NARS film T-84 roll 8, frame 8040). And decree establishing a Central Planning commission, 22 Apr 1942 (MD: 53, p. 1035).

29 Speer: Führer conf, 4 Apr 1942; see also Speer in MCH, 4 Feb 1947, pp. 1447ff.
Milch gives a somewhat different version in Pre-Trial Interrogation, 18 Dec 1946; cf Milch at IMT, vol. IX, p. 75; MCH 4 Feb 1947, p. 1449; and Körner at MCH, 5 Feb 1947, p. 1668f; and Speer: *Erinnerungen*, p. 235.

30 Hübner.

31 Göring conf, 13 May 1942 (MD: 62, p. 5200). For details of the production and contract for the MK 101 and MK 103 see GL conf, 12 May 1942 (MD: p. 486f).

32 Göring conf, 7 Oct 1943, stenogram (MD: 62, pp. 5712f).

33 Göring conf, 29 Jun 1942 (MD: 62, p. 5235). Cf Jeschonnek's report to Göring, 13 May 1942 (MD: 62, p. 5204).

34 Friebel at GL conf, 13 May 1942 (MD: 14, pp. 527ff).

35 Görnnert: note for Göring conf with Führer shows that railway matters were to be discussed with Hitler on about 3 Apr and 22 May 1942 (NARS film T-84, roll 8, frames 8039, 8003f).

36 Military Economics Branch: conf with Reichsmarschall on 26 Jun 1941, para 2, 'The Führer does not wish to drop Kleinmann'. (FD. 5444/45.)

37 Milch, Dec 1969. This may have been on 20 Apr 1942, the occasion Milch last saw Hitler before 24 May.

38 Goebbels diary, 24 Apr 1942; cf ibid 16 Apr 1942 and 20 Sep 1943 ('the Führer has awarded Dorpmüller and Ganzenmüller the Knight's Cross of the War Service Medal—Dorpmüller for his failure, and Ganzenmüller for his exceptional achievements, which at times have been decisive for this war.')
Speer, *Chronik*, 21 May 1942; and *Erinnerungen*, p. 237.

39 Milch, GL conf, 19 Jun 1942 (MD: 15, p. 1121); cf Webster and Frankland, op. cit. vol. I, p. 481. For Reich railway statistics, see GL conf 26 May 1942 (MD: 14, p. 690).

40 So Hitler told Milch; Milch, Dec. 1969.

41 Conf in Führer's HQ, 24 May 1942 (MPP).

42 Milch, GL conf, 2 Jun 1942 (MD: 14, p. 811) and 26 May 1942 (ibid, p. 690); cf Speer, *Chronik*, 24 May 1942 and 11 Jun 1942.

43 GL conf, 20 Aug 1942 (MD: 15, p. 2013).

44 Conf on inland waterways and rail transport, 3 Jun 1942, stenogram (MD: 55, pp. 1832ff) and on 8 Jul 1942 (ibid, pp. 1892ff). And GL conf, 19 Jun 1942 (MD: 15, p. 1121).

45 GL conf, 2 Jun 1942 (MD: 14, p. 808).

46 GL conf 12 Jun 1942 (ibid, p. 1078f).

47 GL conf, 27 May 1942 (ibid, p. 794).

48 Friebel at GL conf, 12 May 1942 (MD: 14, pp. 556, 507f).

49 Milch, May 1968; memoirs, p. 302.

50 Milch, GL conf, 27 May 1942 (MD: 14, pp. 786ff).

51 Diary, 29 May 1942; but cf diary, 11 May 1947.

52 Milch at GL conf, 9 Jun 1942 (MD: 14, p. 978). Milch saw the flying-bomb Fi 103 as a means of economizing on manned bomber sorties, and above all of exacting reprisals without risk to one's own crews, should German cities be further bombarded (Cf Brée at GL conf, 16 Oct 1942, MD: 34, p. 2228).

53 This in itself was an innovation. Milch predicted (GL conf 26 Aug 1942, MD: 15, p. 2106): 'The future [aircraft] construction material will be steel. Aluminium is not the real material—it has only been the interim material. The ultimate material will be steel.' He added that it would have to be made especially for the purpose.

54 GL conf 19 Jun 1942 (MD: 15, pp. 1195ff).

55 Cf diary 5 Jun 1942 (entered under wrong date): 'Air Ministry. Afternoon: "Atom smashing", at Kaiser-Wilhelm Foundation . . .' Cf Otto Hahn diary, 4 Jun 1942, and Speer, *Chronik* 4 Jun 1942.

56 Memoirs.

57 Speer, May 1968. At the GL conf 4 Sep 1942 Milch stated that the cost of airframe and engine procurement for the Luftwaffe was now 6,000 million marks a year (MD: 34, p. 2045).

58 Cf diary, 7 Aug 1945 (when news of Hiroshima reached Milch). In his memoirs he puts the figure at 60,000 Reichsmarks.

CHAPTER 11

1 Gen von Bötticher in GL conf, 2 Jun 1942 (MD: 14, pp. 855ff).

2 These demands were summarized by the Techn. Dept. in their study: Guidelines for Aircraft Development, 20 Oct 1942 (MD: 65, pp. 7073ff).

3 Police-president report on attack on Cologne, 30–31 May 1942; cf final report on same attack dated 15 Jun 1942 (NARS film T-175, roll 65). Görnnert's files contain a letter apparently from Göring to Lt Göring, dated 3 Jun 1942: '. . . Finally, I expect the report from Gauleiter Grohé on the air raid on Cologne will interest you.' (NARS film T-84, roll 8, frame 7564).

4 Göring conf, 8 Oct 1943, stenogram (MD: 62, p. 5723).

5 Milch, Jan 1967, and May 1968.

6 Sellschopp at GL conf, 19 Jun 1942 (MD: 15, pp. 1101ff). This was the new study '1011'.

7 Göring conf, 29 Jun 1942 (MD: 62, p. 5241).

8 GL conf, 12 Jun 1942 (MD: 14, pp. 1092ff); cf Schwenke, GL conf, 7 Jul 1942 (MD: 15, pp. 1368ff).

9 GL conf, 20 Aug 1942 (MD: 15, p. 1966).

10 GL conf 7 Jul 1942 (MD: 15, p. 1368). And Schwenke, GL conf, 20 Aug 1942 (MD: 15, pp. 1964f) and GL conf, 1 Sep 1942 (MD: 16, p. 2185).

11 Schwenke, GL conf, 14 Jul 1942 (MD: 15, pp. 1421f).

12 Corr between Schmid and Schwenke cited by Suchenwirth in: Jeschonnek, p. 113. One RAF prisoner volunteered to return to Britain as a German spy: cf Schwenke, GL conf, 20 Oct 1942 (MD: 16, p. 2810).

13 Göring conf, 21 May 1942 (MD: 62, p. 5220); in Mar 1942 Milch had advised Göring on problems with the BMW 801 engine (Göring conf, 6 Mar 1942, MD: 62, p. 5173); cf also letter Lahs to Milch, 24 Jan 1942 (MD: 53, p. 800); and Göring conf, 11 Jul 1942 (MD: 62, p. 5245). On the DB 605 see GL conf 5 May 1942 (MD: 13, pp. 327ff and 331) and Petersen at GL conf, 24 Nov 1942 (MD: 17, pp. 3303f), and especially Milch at GL conf 27 Nov 1942 (MD: 34, pp. 2634f).

14 Dietrich at GL conf, 19 May 1942 (MD: 14, p. 610); and memoirs. Milch, GL conf, 26 May 1942 (MD: 14, p. 703).

15 GL conf, 12 Jun 1942 (ibid, p. 1032).

16 GL conf, 23 Jun 1942 (MD: 15, p. 1249).

17 GL conf, 26 May 1942 (MD: 14, p. 758); cf Göring conf, 21 May 1942 (MD: 62, p. 5222).

18 GL conf, 5 May 1942 (MD: 13, p. 346).

19 Sellschopp, GL conf, 19 Jun 1942 (MD: 15, pp. 1103, 1106); Milch, GL conf, 30 Jun 1942 (ibid, p. 1350f); Göring conf, 29 Jun 1942 (MD: 62, pp. 5221f).

20 GL conf, 30 Jun 1942 (MD: 15, p. 1352); cf GL conf, 17 Aug 1942 (MD: 34, pp. 1811f).

21 Von Lossberg, GL conf, 7 Aug 1942 (MD: 34, pp. 1811f).

22 Göring conf, 29 Jun 1942 (MD: 62, p. 5237).

23 Milch, GL conf, 7 Jul 1942 (MD: 15, p. 1381). Cf Milch at GL conf, 26 Aug 1942 (ibid, pp. 2147f): Herr Pöhlmann was appointed his Commissar to carry out the task; cf GL conf 16 Oct 1942 (MD: 34, pp. 2205ff).

24 Milch, GL conf, 7 Aug 1942 (MD: 34, pp. 1728f).

25 Milch and Schwenke ('the statistics [on Russian aircraft production] are available in detail') GL conf, 21 Jul 1942 (MD: 15, p. 1553). On 17 Nov 1942 Milch was told Russian production was: 150 bombers, 600 fighters and 350 low-level attack aircraft. This caused him to ask, 'How do the Russians manage such a production? They have lost their "Ruhr", and yet still they turn out fighters and more fighters—50 per cent more than we do!' (GL conf, MD: 17, p. 3247).

26 This new decision was reported by Milch to his staff on 17 Aug 1942 (MD: 15, p. 1785).

27 Milward, op. cit. Hertel assessed on 20 Oct 1942 that only 20 per cent of the factories were running a second shift on that date (GL conf, MD: 16, p. 2828).

28 Frydag and Speer, at Göring conf, 28 Oct 1943 (MD: 63, pp. 6018f); cf FD. 4439/45, pp. 12f and appendices 8 and 9.

29 GL conf, 18 Jun 1942 (MD: 15, p. 1932). Cf GL conf, 26 Aug 1942 (MD: 15, pp. 2096f). In general a well-documented account of the strained Speer–Sauckel–Milch relationship will be found in Edward L. Homze: *Foreign Labour in Nazi Germany* (Princeton Univ. Press, 1967).

30 Cf Bross, op. cit., pp. 28f. Göring pointed out that the Dutch government having fled had *de jure* passed government status to the occupiers; in Belgium the King had surrendered unconditionally, and the French and Danish manpower was supplied under an agreement with the constitutional governments.

31 Milch in Central Planning, 21 Aug 1942 (MD: 46, p. 8595). Cf GL conf, 9 Sep 1942 (MD: 16, pp. 2361f).

32 Diary, 7 Sep 1942; cf Speer: Führer conf, 7–9 Sep 1942 (Boelcke, op. cit., pp. 179ff).

33 Milch, Central Planning, 4 Sep 1942 (MD: 46, p. 8650).

34 Central Planning, 22 Jul 1942 (MD: 46, p. 8491).

35 Central Planning, 29 Oct 1942 (MD: 46, pp. 8892ff).

36 Speer, Central Planning, 18 Nov 1942 (MD: 46, pp. 9189ff).

37 GL conf, 20 Oct 1942 (MD: 16, p. 2860). Milch was with the Führer at midday and on the afternoon of 14 Oct 1942, with Speer. And GL conf, 17 Aug 1942 (MD: 15, p. 1785).
Vorwald, Jun 1968. It was von Gablenz's decision in 1938 against recommending Lufthansa to give the Siebel company a contract for light aircraft (the Si 104) which almost ruined the firm.
Diary, 21 Aug 1942.

38 The precursor of today's 'Black Box' system in modern airliners. Cf GL confs 14 Apr 1942 (MD: 13, pp. 130f); 21 Apr 1942 (ibid, p. 184);

27 May 1942 (MD: 14, p. 788); 2 Jun 1942 (ibid, p. 829); 26 Aug 1942 (MD: 15, p. 2127); 9 Oct 1942 (MD: 16, p. 2667); and 28 Aug 1942 (MD: 34, p. 1954). For a good survey of the two projects, *Unfall-wächter* (Accident Monitor) and *Telephon* see statements of Wendroth and Milch, GL conf, 16 Oct 1942 (MD: 34, p. 2300f).

39 Milch, MCH 13 Mar 1947, p. 1876.

40 Speer, *Chronik,* 25 Aug 1943.

41 Göring conf, 13 May 1942 (MD: 62, p. 5204).

42 Göring conf, 16 May 1942: KG 40's representatives stressed the excellent manoeuvrability of the aircraft, which the two crews had highly praised (MD: 62, p. 5214).

43 GL conf, 26 Aug 1942 (MD: 15, pp. 2145f).

44 Göring conf, 13 Sep 1942, stenogram (MD: 62, pp. 5277ff).

45 Heinkel, op. cit., p. 411.

46 GL conf, 12 Feb 1943 (MD: 35, p. 3233).

47 GL conf, 9 Oct 1942 (MD: 16, p. 2698).

48 Ibid, pp. 2689f.

49 Göring conf, 22 Feb 1943, stenogram (MD: 62, pp. 5356f); cf Friebel at GL conf, 4 Sep 1942 (MD: 34, pp. 2034ff); and Prof Seewald's report at GL conf, 30 Oct 1942 (ibid, pp. 2360f). In general see Petersen: chronology of accidents to He 177, dated 27 May 1943 (MD: 53, pp. 745ff).

50 Göring conf, 29 Jun 1942 (MD: 62, p. 5235): 'The Air Armament Office proposes the He 177 should better be built with four separate engines.' Cf Von Gablenz, GL conf, 18 Aug 1942 (MD: 15, p. 1909).

51 Milch, GL conf, 12 Feb 1943 (MD: 35, p. 3220).

52 Göring conf, 13 Sep 1942, stenogram (MD: 62, p. 5294).

53 Göring conf, 22 Feb 1943, stenogram (MD: 61, p. 5373).

54 Petersen at GL conf, 19 Jun 1942 (MD: 15, pp. 1167ff).

55 Milch, GL conf, 17 Aug 1942 (MD: 15, p. 1795).

56 Milch, GL conf, 26 Aug 1952 (MD: 16, p. 2100). On 7 Sep 1942, Eng. Gen. Lucht inspected the Heinkel works and established a 'neglectful and dawdling treatment of the question of the structural strength' (report to Milch, 9 Sep 1942; in Milch file, FD. 5514/45); he warned Prof Heinkel of the ominous parallel between the He 177 and the Me 210 affair (Heinkel: memo on Lucht's visit to Marienehe, 7 Sep 1942 [ibid]).

57 Messerschmitt: memo on Reichsmarschall's speech to an assembly of air industry representatives in Reich Air Ministry on 13 Sep 1942 (FD. 4355/45, vol. 4). See also Heinkel, op. cit., pp. 458f. And especially Göring conf, 13 Sep 1942, stenogram (MD: 62, pp. 5277ff). Cf diary, 12 Sep 1942; '. . . Midday at the Ministry. Preparations for Göring's speech.'

58 GL conf, 15 Sep 1942 (MD: 16, pp. 2398f).

59 GL conf, 9 Oct 1942 (MD: 15, p. 2687). Cf Milch, GL conf, 20 Oct 1942 (ibid, p. 2861).

60 Schwenke at GL conf, 15 Sep 1942 (ibid, p. 2429).

61 GL conf, 6 Oct 1942 (ibid, pp. 2628f).

62 GL conf, 27 Oct 1942 (ibid, pp. 2936f).

63 Diary, 11–14 Oct 1942; Milch, GL conf, 20 Oct 1942 (ibid, pp. 2762ff).

CHAPTER 12

1 GL conf 26 Aug 1942, 1 Sep 1942 (MD: 15, pp. 2108f, MD: 16, pp. 2173f): Reidenbach had ordered 900,000 nuts with 11mm metric thread.

2 GL conf, 21 Jul 1942 (MD: 15, pp. 1520f).

3 Milch, May 1968.

4 Milch, GL conf, 20 Aug 1942 (MD: 15, pp. 1974f).

5 USFET interrogation, Alexander Kraell, 6 Sep 1946.

6 Milch, GL conf, 20 Oct 1942 (MD: 16, pp. 2731ff): only his departmental heads appear to have been present.

7 Letter Milch to author, 19 Jul 1969.

8 GL conf, 20 Oct 1942 (MD: 16, pp. 2731f).

9 Milch, GL conf, 27 Oct 1942 (ibid, pp. 2923f). For a similar remark, see Milch, GL conf, 6 Oct 1942 (ibid, p. 2614).

10 GL conf, 6 Oct 1942 (ibid, p. 2595); and 27 Oct 1942 (MD: 16, pp. 2612, 2977).

11 Brückner, GL conf, 20 Oct 1942 (MD: 16, p. 2886). Milch, GL conf, 27 Oct (ibid, pp. 2898f and p. 2907). And Brückner, GL conf, 3 Nov 1942 (MD: 16, p. 3008).

12 Vorwald, MCH, 10 Mar 1947, p. 1667; and remarks of SS *Obersturmführer* Karl Sommer (of the SS dept: Manpower) to Milch, in latter's diary, 28 Oct 1947. The first approach came to the Oranienburg concentration camp from Heinkel's Director Hayn in person. Cf GL conf, 16 Oct 1942 (MD: 34, pp. 2247ff).

13 Letter Prof Messerschmitt to SS *Sturmbannführer* Weiss, Dachau, 20 Jul 1943 (FD. 4355/49, vol. 3).

14 Alpers at GL conf, 5 Feb 1943 (MD: 35, p. 3086); reported to Milch, GL conf, 9 Feb 1943 (MD: 18, pp. 4357f). The negotiating parties were Prof Messerschmitt and Director Hentzen, and Dr Schieber of the Munitions Ministry, and SS Lt Col Maurer of the SS Manpower Office. Of all these, Milch alone was imprisoned for the use of concentration camp prisoners in the air industry.

15 Letter Jeschonnek to Milch, 28 Oct 1942 (MD: 51, p. 479). And Letter Milch to Jeschonnek, 12 Nov 1942 (MD: 51, pp. 474f).

16 Bundesarchiv military archives: Fourth Air Force at Stalingrad, 20 Jul 1942–21 Mar 1943 (monograph). Cf Suchenwirth: Jeschonnek, pp. 100ff.

17 Von Richthofen diary, 21 Nov 1942.

18 Göring conf, 8 Aug 1942 (MD: 62, p. 5256); cf Milch, GL conf 19 Jun 1942 (MD: 15, pp. 1120ff). Cf Göring: speech, 13 Sep 1942 (MD: 62, p. 5304).

19 The best study of the decision to supply the Sixth Army in Stalingrad by air is Lt Col Johannes Fischer: On the decision to supply Stalingrad

by air, in *Militärgeschichtliche Mitteilungen,* 2/1969; and General Fiebig diary, 26 Nov 1942 (Fiebig's Eighth Air Corps was assigned solely to the airlift from 30 Nov 1942 onwards). Cf also von Richthofen diary 21 Nov 1942 and 10–12 Feb 1943. Göring, interrogated on 19 May 1945 (SAIC/13), suggested he implored Hitler to let Paulus break out. 'Hitler called Göring [by telephone] one day and asked him for a statement on the total number of transport planes available and their total loading capacity. Göring told him but added that the number of planes would be inadequate for the task ahead. Hitler then asked Göring whether it would be possible to carry in supplies by bomber, and Göring told him that it could be done, but that it was not advisable since many bombers were being used in the battle against Britain . . . Göring protested bitterly, stressing the impossibility of the job due to a number of factors, including the weather.' Much of this sounds like hindsight.

20 Letter Vorwald to Milch, 27 Jan 1970.

Engel 'notes', Nov 1942: this source must be viewed with some misgivings, in view of conclusions drawn by Lieutenant Colonel Manfred Kehrig's forthcoming official German government history of Stalingrad.

21 von Richthofen diary, 25 Nov 1942; cf Koller diary, 20–22 Nov 1942.

22 Engel, notes.

23 Milch, GL conf, 5 Jan 1943 (MD: 18, p. 3953).

24 The 1942 average German monthly production (with 1941 in brackets) was: fighters 366.5 (251.7); twin-engined fighters, 109 (64.2); bombers 349 (291); dive-bombers 75 (43.5); transporters 48 (42.8).–Ibid, p. 3932. Cf also Schwenke, report to Milch on estimated possible aircraft production in Britain and USA, 16 Dec 1942 (MD: 53, pp. 1281f).

25 *Inter Avia,* Jul 1946, p. 18.

26 Vorwald in MCH, 10 Mar 1947, pp. 1672f; and Vorwald, Jun 1968. Milch, IMT, vol. IX, p. 96.

27 Milch, GL conf, 5 Jan 1943 (MD: 18, p. 3950f).

28 See discussion in GL conf, 13 Nov 1942 (MD: 34, pp. 2458ff) on a high-speed bomber; on Milch's ideal, see esp ibid. pp. 2475ff.

29 Cf Friebel, GL conf, 12 Dec 1942 (MD: 34, p. 2652); Milch again discussed his requirement (p. 2655). The Hertel and Gropler proposals were discussed.

30 Diary, 8 Jan 1943; Milch, May 1968. Milch also describes Dornier's visit at GL conf 29 Oct 1943 (MD: 39, p. 5117). It was decided to make the Do 335 at Dornier's Wismar works (GL conf, 26 Jan 1943, MD: 18, p. 4207). See also Reidenbach, GL conf, 20–21 Jan 1944 (MD: 32, pp. 930f) on the history of the Do 335.

Milch, GL conf, 5 Jan 1943 (MD: 18, p. 3945); cf also GL conf, 7 Aug 1942 (MD: 34, p. 1783).

31 Kesselring, op. cit., p. 466.

32 Dr Kurt Weigelt: notes for a speech on the election of a new Chairman, 11 Jan 1943 (Deutsche Bank archives); and letter Weigelt to Knipfer, 16 Jan 1943 (ibid; quoted by Eyermann, op. cit., p. 69, p. 28).

CHAPTER 13

1 Central Planning, 12 Feb 1943 (MD: 47, p. 9408).

2 The diary of Milch's special staff has survived intact and is in the Bundes-archiv military archives under file III L78 1–5. Milch also remained in contact with Col Angermünd at the Ministry, who reported regularly at the GL conferences; a further source of importance is Gen Hube: Report of Proceedings on the Airlift to Fortress Stalingrad, 15 Mar 1943 (publ. in Jacobsen: *Der Zweite Weltkriek in Chronik und Dokumenten*, pp. 365ff). Reference has also been made to Maj Gen (ret.) Fritz Morzik's study: Airlift Operations of the German Air Force (NARS: MS No. AF–167) where the cruel conditions prevailing on the eastern front are vividly described. Also to Maj Werner Beumelburg: Stalingrad, a report based on documents and individual testimony, dated 8 Jun 1943 (MPP).

3 Diary, 14 Jan 1943; Memoirs; and Milch at MCH, 14 Mar 1947, pp. 1991ff.

4 Speer, Dec 1968; Milch: affidavit, 12 Jul 1947; Speer, op. cit., p. 264.

5 Special staff diary, 15 Jan 1943; OKW war diary, 15 Jan 1943; and Führer directive, 15 Jan 1943.

6 Speer, Central Planning, 26 Jan 1943 (MD: 47, p. 9236).

7 The final conf on the status of winter preventive measures was on 20 Oct 1942 (GL conf, MD: 16, pp. 2844ff).

8 The special commissar, Eng. Col Breith of the Eighth Air Corps, reported regularly at GL confs after 7 Apr 1942 on his recommendations for the coming winter (MD: 13, pp. 45ff); cf GL confs, 5 May (MD: 13, p. 375), 26 May (MD: 14, p. 751); 9 Jun (ibid, pp. 914f), 30 Jun (MD: 15, p. 1303), 21 Jul (ibid, pp. 1570ff), 20 Aug (ibid, p. 2013) and 9 Sep 1942 (MD: 16, p. 2364).

9 Milch, GL conf, 20 Aug 1942 (MD: 15, p. 2013): 'I do not want our injured to be transported back in open lorries five days long, with 30 degrees of frost, as they were last winter.'

10 Fiebig diary, 16 Jan 1943; Gen Wolfgang Pickert, commanding the Ninth Flak Division, expressed identical sentiments (Pickert diary, 16 Jan 1943).

11 Von Richthofen diary, 15 Jan 1943.

12 Ibid, 16 Jan 1943.

13 Eng. Gen. Weidinger, Chief Engineer of Fourth Air Force, conf with Milch, 18 Jan 1943 (Special staff diary); cf von Richthofen diary, 15 Jan 1943; and Beumelburg, op. cit., p. 55: 'That of the 483 aircraft avail-able [on 16 Jan] only 87 were momentarily serviceable.'

14 Memoirs.

15 Special staff diary, 16 Jan 1943.

16 Memoirs; letter from Prof Dr Heinz Kalk, Dec 1968; Petersen, Jun 1968; Milch, Oct 1967.

Diary, 17 Jan 1943.

17 Memoirs.

Von Richthofen diary, 17 Jan 1943.

18 Phone conv Milch–Fiebig, 17 Jan 1943 (Special staff diary).

19 Phone convs Milch–Jeschonnek and Milch–Lt Col Christian (Special staff diary, 17 Jan 1943).

20 Milch, GL conf, 9 Feb 1943 (MD: 18, pp. 4336f). Cf Col Morzik's conf with Milch, 18 Jan 1943 (Special staff diary).

21 GL conf, 9 Feb 1943 (MD: 18 pp. 4376f; cf p. 4338).

22 Ibid, p. 4337.

23 Cf phone convs Milch–Fiebig, and Göring–Milch, 18 Jan 1943 (Special staff diary).

24 Milch, Oct 1967.

25 Pickert diary, 18 Jan 1943, describes Milch as 'looking somewhat the worse for wear'.

26 Phone conv Milch–von Manstein, 18 Jan 1943 (Special staff diary).

27 Col (Ret.) Kühl, conf with Milch, 19 Jan 1943 (Special staff diary). Kühl was Air Transport Cdr, Novocherkassk.
Memoirs. Diary, 19 Jan 1943: '. . . Von Manstein, conference: recommend despatch of three front-line officers to the Führer!!'

28 Conf Milch–Hube, 19 Jan 1943. And see conf Milch–Lt Col von Beust, Col Kühl, 19 Jan 1943 (Special staff diary); Beust was Air Transport Cdr, Voroshilovgrad.

29 Milch, GL conf, 9 Feb 1943 (MD: 18, p. 4285; cf p. 4339).

30 Phone conv Milch–Morzik, 20 Jan 1943 (Special staff diary).

31 Milch, GL conf, 9 Feb 1943 (MD: 18, pp. 4336f).

32 Milch, GL conf, 16 Feb 1943 (MD: 18, pp. 4438f).

33 Fiebig diary, 20 Jan 1943; and Major Thiel: report to Milch, 21 Jan 1943, on serviceability of Gumrak landing ground, and on conv with Col Gen Paulus (Appendix to Fiebig diary, page K. 2294ff).

34 Phone conv Milch–Lt Col Christian, 21 Jan 1943 (Special staff diary).

35 Phone conv Milch–Manstein, 21 Jan 1943 (ibid).

36 Fiebig diary, 20 Jan 1943.

37 Conf Milch–Maj von Zitzewitz, Sixth Army staff, 21 Jan 1943 (Special staff diary).

38 Beumelburg, op. cit., p. 60.

39 Phone conv Army Group Don–Milch, 23 Jan 1943 (ibid).

40 Conf, 24 Jan 1942 (ibid).

41 Diary, 23 Jan 1943: 'Farewell conf with von Manstein, one hour. 12.30–12.55 p.m. flight Taganrog West to Mariupol South. The new airfield is lost! No communications. Swinish weather.—Until 2 or 3 am long telephone conversations with Führer's headquarters. Göring sends lengthy telegrams.'
Memoirs; and letters from Milch, 1 Sep 1968, and Kalk, 11 Dec 1968.

42 Sixth Army signal to Fourth Air Force and Eighth Air Corps, 24 Jan 1943 (Special staff diary).

43 Diary, 24 Jan 1943.
   Speer, Dec 1968; Speer, op. cit., p. 264.
44 Cf Von Richthofen diary, 28 Jan 1943.
45 Conf, 27 Jan 1943 (Special staff diary); cf GL conf, 9 Feb 1943 (MD: 18, p. 4338).
46 Col Angermünd at GL conf, 26 Jan 1943 (MD: 18, pp. 4153f); diary, 25 Jan 1943.
47 Phone conv, Milch–Christian, 28 Jan 1943 (Special staff diary).
48 Conf, Milch with Gen Schmundt, 28 Jan 1943 (Special staff diary).
49 This was a view Milch had also expressed to his department heads on 5 Jan 1943 (GL conf, MD: 18, p. 3936).
50 Conf, 29 Jan 1943 (Special staff diary). Cf Milch, GL conf, 17 Apr 1944 (MD: 29, p. 9565).
51 Phone conv, Milch–Maj Wilke, 29 Jan 1943.
52 Diary, 30 Jan 1943.
53 Col Gen Paulus, signal to Führer, 29 Jan 1943.
54 Flak Regt 104, signal to Eighth Air Corps, 30 Jan 1943.
55 Beumelburg, op. cit., p. 64.
56 Göring: speech, printed in *Völkischer Beobachter*, 2 Feb 1943; cf Memoirs, and Vorwald in MCH, 11 Mar 1947, p. 1707 (Vorwald testified that everybody at the Ministry knew that Milch was meant).
57 Beumelburg, op. cit., p. 64.
58 Memoirs; Fiebig diary, 31 Jan 1943, and Milch diary, 31 Jan 1943: 'End of Stalingrad South approaches. Our Luftwaffe officers "sign off"!! . . .' Cf Beumelburg, op. cit., p. 65: 'Air Signals unit 129 signalled, 'Rest of Stalingrad Unit is now signing off. All best wishes to the Fatherland.' (Signal timed 4.22 am, 31 Jan 1943.)
59 Hitler: signal to Ninth Army Corps, 5.25 pm, 1 Feb 1943.
60 Diary, 1 Feb 1943.
61 Signal, Ninth Army Corps to Army Group Don, 2 Feb 1943.
62 Memoirs. Cf Hube's report (See Note 2): 'Field-Marshal Milch and his staff could have had a decisive effect on the airlift to the Fortress Stalingrad, if he had been sent out earlier. His measures needed ten to fourteen days to take effect. So had he been in charge from the time the fortress was besieged [23 Nov 1942] the effect would have been felt by mid December at the latest and if kept up the airlift would have made it possible for the fortress to hold out for many months.'
63 There is little doubt that Milch did make this dangerous statement; he made an identical one to Goebbels (Goebbels diary, 9 Apr 1943); cf Milch diary, 28 Sep 1947.

CHAPTER 14
1 Erich von Manstein: *Verlorene Siege* (Bonn 1955), p. 395.
2 Suchenwirth: Jeschonnek, p. 109.
3 Beumelburg, op. cit., pp. 43, 49.

4 In comparison with sorties flown, loss rates were: Ju 52: 10 per cent; He 111: 5.5 per cent; Ju 86: 21 per cent; FW 200: 9.7 per cent; He 177: 26 per cent. The British Bomber Command operated on the assumption that no air force could maintain flying operations in the face of a sustained loss-rate exceeding 5 per cent, which again testifies to the courage of the Luftwaffe aircrews.

5 *FAZ*, 27 Jan 1968.

6 This is presumably the Eschenauer report mentioned (at third hand) to Suchenwirth (cf his: Jeschonnek, pp. 105f.) Milch had it from Eschenauer direct (diary, 21 May 1946). It was more likely that it was the 250-kilo supply bomb that was meant (cf GL conf, 9 Feb 1943, MD: 18, p. 4283: 'My own experience is that I was only too pleased not to have got the thousand-kilo ones . . . The 250-kilos were somewhat better.' The supply bombs were in use from 26 Nov 1942 at Stalingrad (cf Beumelburg, op. cit., p. 30).

7 Diary, 21 May 1946: 'Deceit plus incompetence equals one Reichsmarschall!! One guessed it already, but now one gets the proof for it, one can't help vomiting all over again.'

8 Cf Schwenke, GL conf, 12 Feb 1943 (MD: 35).

9 Speer, Central Planning, 26 Jan 1943 (MD: 47, p. 9236).

10 Milch, GL conf, 16 Feb 1943 (MD: 18, p. 4466). Cf FD. 4439/45, p. 8 and p. 22: decree of Munitions Ministry, 28 Jan 1943. Subsequently the Transport Codeword 'Panzer' played equal havoc with transport of Luftwaffe requirements.

11 Hertel, GL conf, 18 Feb 1943 (MD: 18, p. 4467.) And Milch, GL conf, 2 Mar 1943 (MD: 19, p. 4488).

12 Göring, conf 22 Feb 1943, stenogram (MD: 62, p. 5403).

13 Diary, 4 Feb 1943; cf Milch at GL confs, 9 Feb 1943 (MD: 18, pp. 4375f) and 12 Feb 1943 (MD: 35, pp. 3187f); also MCH 14 Mar 1947, p. 1992.

14 Diary, 17 Feb 1943: '. . . Evening at hunting lodge. Führer telephones about Ju 52, floatplane version.' MCH, 14 Mar 1947, p. 2008.

15 Milch, GL conf, 12 Feb 1943 (MD: 35, pp. 3226f).
Details of the He 177 losses were reported to the GL conf on 16 Jan (MD: 18, p. 4122) and 29 Jan 1943 (MD: 35, p. 2976); also conf in special staff diary, 31 Jan 1943 attended by a representative of first squadron of FKG. *50*, the squadron operating the aircraft. General Fiebig considered the He 177 useless as a transport plane: it could carry only eight '250'-kilo containers, a total of about 1,120 kilos of food, for which it used four tons of fuel! (Fiebig diary, 14 Jan 1943).

16 Central Planning, 12 Feb 1943 (MD: 47, p. 9408).

17 Diary, 12 Feb 1943; alternatively the conversation may have been that on 17 Feb 1943 recorded in Milch's diary and Speer, *Chronik*.

18 Diary, 15 Feb 1943; Goebbels diary, 16 Feb 1943; Milch at GL conf, 16 Feb 1943 (MD: 18, pp. 4481f, 4461.)

19 Memoirs; and diary, 18 Feb 1943.

Goebbels wrote, 'I discuss with Milch the question of the airlift to Stalingrad. The Luftwaffe did not fail here after all—the difficulties were just insuperable.'

20 Cf notes of Eng. Col. Hauser, GL conf, 10 Nov 1942 (MD: 17, pp. 3090ff): three prototypes of the MK 103 cannon had been made, and from Apr to Jul 1943 200 more would be manufactured. Production of 300 a month was guaranteed from early 1944, rising to 1,000 at the end of 1944. He also reported the difficult position with the MK 108: this was scheduled at 500 a month in factories at Poasen, Karlsruhe and Liege; but there was a serious shortage of the necessary machine tools.

21 The Führer had evidently asked for the SD 1 bomb early in 1942. It had been demonstrated by the Luftwaffe in mid-1942 at Peenemünde, when Col Gen von Richthofen had immediately demanded its mass production. Cf Milch, GL conf, 10 Nov 1942 (ibid, p. 3192): 'The position on the SD 1 is that firstly the Führer demanded it very urgently, and secondly we sent the pilot series of the first ten thousand straight to the squadrons—in other words we dropped the trial series not at Rechlin but actually in action; and the word got round about it, and suddenly everybody wanted it.' On 9 Feb 1943 (GL conf, MD: 18, p. 4319) Milch added: 'The pacemaker must be the one-kilo bomb . . . The SD 1 and its containers must be given special priority, equivalent at least to that of the Panzer programme. The Führer keeps telling me, "This is what I always wanted." ' And again three days later, Milch added: 'The Führer is a man who peers very deeply into the needs and necessities, and without being an engineer has a very sound common sense about technical things. Consider the notorious one-kilo bomb, which the last Director of Air Armament [Udet] and his entire staff turned down, until we put pressure behind it last year, so that today we can say: the most valuable bomb we have is the one-kilo bomb. It was the Führer who said it, not one of us . . .' (GL conf, 12 Feb 1943, MD: 35, p. 3191).

22 On Loerzer, cf Baumbach's letter to Jeschonnek, 12 Dec 1942, in *Broken Swastika*, pp. 137ff.

23 The shortage of fuel for training squadrons became acute in July 1942. Cf letter von Brauchitsch to Milch, 23 May 1942 (MD: 57, p. 3055); Göring conf, 29 Jun 1942 (MD: 62, pp. 5243f); Milch at GL conf, 7 Jul 1942 and 28 Jul 1942 (MD: 15, pp. 1398f, pp. 1636f). The fuel then available was enough to train only 40 per cent of the fighter and 20 per cent of the bomber crews required. This shortage began to have its effect on the squadrons early in 1943. Cf Milch, Oct 1967: 'I demanded 45,000 tons of fuel a month to be set aside for training; I was allowed 15,000 tons.'

24 Eisenlohr at GL conf, 1 Sep 1942 (MD: 16, p. 2193): new aero-engines needed five hours' running in; but they were now being accepted from factories after only 2½ hours' running in because of the fuel shortage.

25 Central Planning, 22 Apr 1943 (MD: 46, p. 9657). Cf letter Milch to Göring, 23 Jun 1943: 'In this connection I wish to mention that more than 50 per cent of all synthetic oil capacity is concentrated within the confines of the Ruhr.' (MD: 51, p. 426).

26 Göring conf, 22 Feb 1943 (MD: 62, pp. 5355); cf Göring conf: re Training, 24 Feb 1943, stenogram (MD: 62, pp. 5416ff; particularly Milch's opening speech, pp. 5417ff.

27 Diary, 22 Feb 1943: 'Air Ministry. Major programme conf with Göring. Study "1015" approved.' Göring conf, 22 Feb 1943, stenogram (MD: 62, pp. 5350ff).

28 Ibid, pp. 5368f.

29 Ibid, p. 5370.

30 Ibid, p. 5371.

31 Diary, 28 Feb 1943: '2,004 new aircraft manufactured in February!' Cf Milch, GL conf, 2 Mar 1943 (MD: 19, pp. 4489f).

32 Diary, 3 Mar 1943.

33 Cf Col Theo Rowehl's remarks at GL conf, 28 Aug 1942 (MD: 34, p. 1874): three Ju 86Rs had bombed small British towns from 40,000 feet up: 'London is prohibited as such.'

34 Basil Collier, op. cit., p. 314.

35 Führer: war conf, 5 Mar 1943.

36 Milch, MCH, 14 Mar 1947, p. 1992.

37 Diary, 5 Mar 1943: 'Reich Air Ministry. 11.05–1.45 pm: Gatow [airport] to Kalinowka, Speer there. Dinner with the Führer. [Conf on] high-altitude and high-speed bombers, etc. Overall situation. Discussed all questions with the Führer alone until 3.15 am.' Cf Vorwald in GL conf, 5 Mar 1943 (MD: 36, p. 3410).

38 This version is based principally on his recollection of the discussion (the original memo Milch wrote afterwards was lost). Milch: Hitler and his Subordinates, 1 Sep 1945; Milch afterwards told Goebbels (on 8 Apr 1943) that the bombing of England could not be resumed until Nov 1943 or the spring of 1944.

39 Cf Vorwald, MCH, 11 Mar 1947, p. 1734: Vorwald stated that upon his return Milch related how he had proposed the dismissal of von Ribbentrop and Keitel, and making peace with France. See also Gert Buchheit: Hitler der Feldheer, p. 331 (Grote, Baden. 1958).

40 Milch, May 1968. In his Nuremberg diary, 11 Aug and 23 Aug 1946, Milch wrote passages showing he had completely changed his attitude towards von Manstein, for personal reasons; and he recalled how he had recommended him to Hitler after Stalingrad.

41 Milch, Central Planning, 1 Mar 1944 (MD: 48, pp. 9987f).

42 Ibid, p. 9983: 'On 3 March last year [sic] I proposed to the Führer that the Army, Luftwaffe and Navy had enough manpower between them to mobilise the necessary extra combat troops . . .'.

43 This advice to Hitler seems credible, since we have seen on earlier pages how Milch was making the same provisions about visits to the Eastern Front and France by his own subordinates.

44 Vorwald, MCH, 10 Mar 1947, p. 1681.

CHAPTER 15

1 Goebbels diary, 7–8 Mar 1943.
2 Ibid, 12 and 15 Mar 1943. Milch.
   Diary, 13 Mar 1943: 'Demonstrations at Rechlin. [Führer has ordered] intensification of air war against Britain.'
   Telegram Göring to Milch and others, 17 Mar 1943 (MD: 65, p. 7071f); Basil Collier, op. cit., pp. 314f.
3 Bross, op. cit., p. 16.
4 Richter, MCH, 11 Feb 1947, p. 900.
5 Milch, GL conf, 9 Mar 1943 (MD: 19, pp. 4669f).
6 Messerschmitt: memo on industrial conf with Reichsmarschall at Karinhall (FD. 4355/45, vol. 2). And especially Göring conf, 18 Mar 1943, stenogram (MD: 62, pp. 5461ff). Those present included Göring, Milch, Martini, Dornier, Rottgardt, Plendl, Lüschen, Hertel, Heinkel, Messerschmitt, Franke, Kammhuber, Peltz and Nallinger. Cf diary, 18 Mar 1943: 'At Karinhall: the chiefs of development. Major onslaught!'
7 Cf ibid, p. 5463: 'I am not speaking of the eastern theatre, because we are absolutely equal to, and in part superior to the enemy; I am talking about the enemy in the west . . .'
8 Ibid, p. 5473.
9 Ibid, p. 5466. Cf p. 5503.
10 Ibid, pp. 5476f.
11 Ibid, p. 5471.
12 Ibid, p. 5482 and p. 5473. Cf Milch's report on Göring, 17 May 1947: 'Almost proudly he boasted to anybody he met that he was so untechnically minded that he did not know how to switch on his radio set; one of his servants had to do it for him.'
13 For the whole 'Window' story, see Alfred Price: Instruments of Darkness (London, 1967), passim.
14 Milch, GL conf, 24 Apr 1942 (MD: 13, p. 398).
15 Milch, GL conf, 5 May 1942 (MD: 13, p. 351).
16 Lucht, GL conf, 12 Jun 1942 (MD: 12, p. 1094).
17 GL conf, 20 Aug 1942 (MD: 15, p. 1868).
18 Milch, GL conf, 1 Sep 1942 (MD: 16, p. 2229).
19 GL conf, 27 Oct 1942 (MD: 16, pp. 2952f); cf Göring conf, 14 Oct 1942 (MD: 62, pp. 5324ff). For Milch's view on General Fellgiebel, military chief of signals, see GL conf, 20 Oct 1942 (MD: 16, p. 2825): '. . . If one of us is a stupid pig, then it certainly isn't me!' Once Göring asked of Martini, 'What can this man Fellgiebel do, if anything?' And Martini replied, 'He is an excellent horseman!' (Milch, Dec 1969).

20 Nebel, Vorwald and Milch at GL conf, 27 Nov 1942 (MD: 34, pp. 2575f).

21 GL conf, 5 Jan 1943 (MD: 18, p. 3990).

22 Cf Göring conf, 18 Mar 1943 (MD: 62, p. 5552).

23 Milch, GL conf, 20 Aug 1942 (MD: 15, pp. 1971ff).

24 Milch, GL conf, 9 Sep 1942 (MD: 16, p. 2337).

25 Schwenke, GL conf, 12 Feb 1943 (MD: 35, p. 3263). Göring conf, 18 Mar 1943, stenogram (MD: 62, pp. 5472).

26 Ibid, pp. 5498, 5545.

27 Ibid, pp. 5491f, 5546f.

28 Göring: order on responsibility for execution of radar and radio navigation programme, 2 May 1943 (MD: 52, pp. 677ff).

29 Goebbels diary, 6 Apr 1943. (Unpublished fragment: NARS Microfilm T-84, roll 272.)

30 Ibid, 7 Apr 1943.

31 Ibid, 9 Apr 1943 (publ.) and Milch diary, 8, 9 Apr 1943.

32 Goebbels diary, 2 Apr 1943 (unpubl).

33 GL conf, 27 Nov 1942 (MD: 34, p. 2607).

34 Diary, 16 Apr 1943.

35 Central Planning, 23 Apr 1943 (MD: 47, pp. 9608ff).

36 Ibid, p. 9729. In this connection Milch was referring to two million bombs abandoned by the Luftwaffe. Cf Milch, GL conf, 9 Mar 1943 (MD: 19, p. 4606): 'As the Führer tells me [on 5 Mar] two million of our two-kilo bombs were allowed by the Fourth Air Force to fall into enemy hands, instead of being dropped in action . . . The question arises how such a thing was possible.'

37 Ibid, p. 9729ff.

38 Ibid, pp. 9730f. Milch returned to this subject again in Central Planning on 4 May 1943 (MD: 47, p. 9796): 'It would be important to find out once and for all how much ammunition each of the Services has, and how much has been manufactured, so that we can work out if the figures are correct: where the quantities are, how much should be there, what the likely consumption will be and how much has been wasted in the various operations.'

39 Ibid, pp. 9737f.

40 Schwenke, GL conf, 20 Apr 1943 (MD: 20, pp. 5234f).

41 GL conf, 1 Jun 1943 (MD: 21, pp. 6062f).

42 Göring conf, 8 Oct 1943, stenogram (MD: 62, p. 5804).

43 Göring conf, 7 Oct 1943, stenogram (MD: 62, pp. 5632f).

44 Diary, 8 May 1943: 'At Reich Air Ministry. Noon to see the Führer, War conference. Then conf on small bomb containers, armament. Führer says, "Either Luftwaffe's technology or its tactics are out of order." I prove to him that the technology is all right.'

45 Milch, GL conf, 11 May 1943 (MD: 20, pp. 5278f).

46 Goebbels diary, 22 May 1943.

47 Diary, 27 May 1943.

CHAPTER 16

1 Study '1015', discussed by Milch with Göring in conf, 22 Feb 1943 (MD: 62, p. 5413).

2 Göring conf, 18 Mar 1943 (MD: 62, p. 5475).

3 Messerschmitt, in *Saturday Evening Post*, 8 Apr 1950. Messerschmitt's war papers are filed as FD. 4355/45 at the Foreign Documents Centre, Imperial War Museum, London, and are available on microfilm.

4 Messerschmitt, in Second German Television programme, 17 Feb 1970.

5 Cf Milch, GL conf, 31 Mar 1943 (MD: 19, p. 4832).

6 Lichte, Böttger: The development of the Jet Engine by Junkers, 1 Aug 1963.

7 Messerschmitt: Survey of development chronology of Me 262 (FD. 4355/45, vol. 2), dated 31 Mar 1944.

8 Milch, GL conf, 17 Apr 1943 (MD: 20, p. 5201).

9 Sellschopp, Vorwald at GL conf, 16 Jan 1943 (MD: 18, pp. 4112, 4114).

10 Milch, Göring conf, 18 Mar 1943 (MD: 62, p. 5521).

11 Vorwald, GL conf, 23 Mar 1943 (MD: 19, p. 4788); and Galland, GL conf, 13 Apr 1943 (MD: 19, pp. 5030f).

12 Antz, GL conf, 22 Mar 1943 (MD: 36, pp. 3729f).

13 GL conf, 14 May 1943 (MD: 36, pp. 4164ff). Cf Milch, GL conf, 31 Mar 1943 (MD: 19, pp. 4824, 4828).

14 Milch, GL conf, 20 Aug 1942 (MD: 15, p. 1998); Milch, GL conf, 4 Aug 1942 (MD: 15, p. 1738) 'One gets the impression that one is speaking to a man who knows more than an engineer about his own subject.'

15 Galland: *The First and the Last;* and in Second German Television programme, 17 Feb 1970.

16 Report, Galland to Milch, 25 May 1943 (MD: 56, p. 2620).

17 GL conf, 25 May 1943 (MD: 20, pp. 5468ff); cf GL conf, 18 May 1943 (MD: 20, pp. 5430f).

18 GL conf, 25 May 1943 (MD: 20, p. 5473).

19 Diary, 25 May 1943: 'Massage. GL conf with department heads. Lunch with Speer. Afternoon, telephone Göring: "Drop the Me 209, put Me 262 in its place. I propose an anti-invasion [Air] Corps . . ."' The latter Corps was to consist of airborne troops, special fighter and fast bomber units fitted with special weapons for combating an Allied invasion attempt wherever it might be made. (Memoirs.)

20 Schwenke.

21 A4 rocket-firing records in Peenemünde archives in Deutsches Museum, Munich; cf David Irving: *The Mare's Nest* (London 1964), pp. 58f. Diary, 26 May 1943.

22 Milch, GL conf, 4 Jun 1943.

23 The programme was: Aug 1943: 100; Sep 500; Oct 1,000; Nov 2,000; Dec 2,500; Jan 1944 3,000; Feb 3,500; Mar 4,000; Apr 5,000.

24 GL conf, 15 Jun 1943; Heyne, GL conf, 22 Jun 1943 (MD: 21, p. 5803) (von Below was also present); GL conf, 13 Jul 1943 (MD: 22).

25 Milch, GL conf, 4 Jun 1943.

26 Herrmann, GL conf, 15 Jun 1943.

27 Milch: report on inspection trip 7–12 Jun 1943, dated 29 Jun 1943 (MD: 51, pp. 512ff). On page 4 is a note that it was discussed on 3 Jul.

28 GL conf, 15 Jun 1943.

29 Milch, GL conf, 6 Jul 1943 (MD: 21); Herrmann, ibid, pp. 5566f. Cf diary, 15 Jun 1945, where an Allied officer 'reminds me of Kammhuber, who to the Luftwaffe's misfortune "governed" its organization for a long time.'

30 Goebbels diary, 23 Jun 1943, unpubl.

31 Heinkel, op. cit., pp. 459ff. (He incorrectly dates the meeting 23 May 1943). Messerschmitt dates it 27 Jun 1943, and this is confirmed by Bormann diary ('Führer confers with the most important designers'); cf Speer: Führer conf, 26 Jun 1943 (Boelcke, op. cit., p. 272). In general much of Heinkel's version seems unlikely: quite apart from making no mention that Göring had dropped the requirement for the He 177 to dive in Sep 1942, Hitler had long been fully aware of the He 177's technical background: cf Führer's war conf, 1 Feb 1943 (pp. 139ff).

32 Pasewaldt, Milch at GL conf, 2 Mar 1943 (MD: 19, p. 4545); Milch approved the replacement of Heinkel by Dr Harald Wolff as Commissar (GL conf, 9 Mar 1943: MD: 19, p. 4672). Cf Heinkel, op. cit., p. 547. Milch said at GL conf, 23 Mar 1943: 'Whenever he [Heinkel] gets some facts, he duplicates them and sends them to just about everybody except us; or Heinkel reports what a magnificent achievement it was to turn out a few He 111s, and sends a telegram to the Führer. Next time I'll put him inside! What he should report [to the Führer] is ". . . moreover, I report that for two long years I have been unable to complete the He 177, because I haven't cared a hoot about it."–Not that he will ever do that.' (MD: 19, p. 4715).

33 USSBS interrogation of Prof Messerschmitt, 11 May 1945.

34 Messerschmitt: comments on letter of Herr Kokothaki, 19 Jan 1944 (FD. 4355/45, vol. 6): '. . . The Führer and Reichsminister Speer both expressed reservations about converting the entire fighter programme to jet fighters, for fuel supply reasons.'

35 Milch to Maj Herrmann and others, GL conf, 6 Jul 1943 (MD: 21).

36 Col von Lossberg: Proposal for a new Night Fighting Tactic, 29 Jul 1943 (MD: 56, p. 2613ff).

37 Göring conf, 27 Jun 1943 (MD: 63, pp. 5842ff); Milch was not present. Cf Herrmann at GL conf, 6 Jul 1943.

38 Report Milch to Göring, 29 Jun 1943 (MD: 51, p. 514).

39 Alpers, GL conf, 29 Jun 1943 (MD: 21).

40 Report Milch to Göring, 29 June 1943 (MD: 51, p. 513).

41 Diary, 30 June 1943; and MCH, 14 Mar 1947, p. 2008.

42 Milch, GL conf, 6 Jul 1943. He added, 'The Führer has approved a considerable reinforcement of the home defences, particularly in the west.'

43 Letter, Milch to Göring, 19 Jun 1943 (MD: 51, pp. 423f); cf Milch, GL conf, 22 June 1943 (MD: 21, p. 5809).

44 Letter Milch to Göring, 30 Jun 1943 (MD: 51, p. 425).

45 Diary, 2 Jul 1943: '. . . [Flight] Insterburg to Goldap (by Storch) for conf of Luftflotte commanders at Rominten on "Zitadelle".'

46 Ibid, 3 Jul 1943: 'Continuation of Rominten conf. I oppose Göring on "cowardice" of air crews.' Cf von Richthofen diary, who describes other conf events, 3 Jul 1943; and Milch, May 1968. Von Brauchitsch, MCH, 20 Feb 1947, pp. 1278f, relates the episode to 'a conference in East Prussia, where [Milch] tabled proposals for modifications in the manner of Luftwaffe operations . . .' (And see note 27.)

47 Memoirs. Cf Milch, MCH, 14 Mar 1947, p. 2008; Maj Englander, quoting Milch in Inter Avia, Aug 1946, p. 12, used almost identical wording. Cf von Richthofen diary, 3 Jul 1943; he describes how after lunch Göring discussed with him, during a long forest walk, the possibility of replacing Kesselring as C-in-C, South, with an Army officer, and of making Kesselring Inspector-General (Milch's office!).

48 Herrmann, GL conf, 6 Jul 1943 (MD: 21, pp. 5566ff).

49 Schwenke, GL conf, 9 Jul 1943.

50 Price, op. cit., p. 149.

51 Diary, 13 Jul 1943: '. . . Göring conf, with Jeschonnek; Göring conf, 13 Jul 1943 (MD: 63, pp. 5847ff); cf memo on visit of Italian ambassador Alfieri to Milch on 16 Jul 1943 (MD: 53, pp. 1116f).

52 Milch, GL conf, 16 Jul 1943.

CHAPTER 17

1 Diary, 15–20 Jul 1943; MCH, 13 Mar 1947, p. 2009.

2 Cf Führer, at war conf, 25 Jul 1943: 'That was precisely the tenor of the remarks made at that discussion a few days ago, when I asserted, "Terror . . . [etc]" ' See Milch diary, 23 Jul 1943: '. . . by Dornier from Oranienburg to Rastenburg. Technical conf with Göring. Afternoon: with the Führer . . .'

3 In a cable to Milch, the Chief of Air Signals Martini mentioned on 4 Aug 1943 the GL's radar research unit at Werneuchen commanded by Major August Hentz, 'which six months ago, on the basis of its experiments, recognized the great danger of enemy jamming.' (MD: 56, p. 2589). Martini tried to place sole blame for the embargo on research into counter-measures on Göring after the war (cf The Rise and Fall of the German Air Force, p. 277); the flavour of the Milch Documents suggests that Martini was at least equally responsible.

4 Milch, GL conf, 27 Jul 1943.

5 Richter: memo on telephone message, 11.30 am, 28 Jul 1943 (MD: 51, p. 421); cf von Brauchitsch, MCH, 20 Feb 1947, p. 1279. And Milch, GL conf, 30 Jul 1943: 'The day before yesterday the Führer agreed that

the absolute *Schwerpunkt* of the industry is to be the defence of the home territory: "All else must take less priority." '

6 Von Lossberg, letter to the author, Aug 1969.

7 Diary, 29 Jul 1943.
Ibid; and 1945 commentary thereon.

8 Of the 28, Herrmann's Wild Boar fighters were credited with 18 (GL conf, 30 Jul 1943).

9 Diary, 30 Jul 1943; Milch, GL conf, 30 Jul 1943; and letter Milch to Göring, 30 Jul 1943 (MD: 56, pp. 2592ff).

10 Göring: order for expansion of night fighter force, to Milch, 1 Aug 1943 (MD: 56, pp. 2599ff); cf telegram Milch to Göring, 3 Aug 1943 (MD: 56, p. 2590).

11 Speer, Central Planning, 29 Jul 1943 (MD: 48, pp. 10443f, 10445); Milch, who was not present, lined both passages in the margin.

12 Diary, 31 Jul 1943.

13 Speer, GL–Speer conf, 3 Aug 1943 (MD: 23); in his memoirs, Speer dates his warning to Hitler 'three days after' 29 Jul 1943; there is otherwise no record of a Speer–Führer conf on 1 Aug 1943.

14 Wilfred von Oven: *Mit Goebbels bis zum Ende*, vol. II, pp. 77ff: diary of 4 Aug 1943; there is no corresponding entry in Milch's diary (and Milch indignantly denies having made the remark as quoted) but the Speer *Chronik* records: 'On 2 Aug Dr Goebbels spoke in the presence of Minister Speer to the ministers and state secretaries, in his Ministry.'

15 Milch, GL–Speer conf, 3 Aug 1943 (MD: 23, pp. 6607f).

16 Memoirs.

17 GL–Speer conf, 3 Aug 1943.

18 Milch, GL conf, 10 Sep 1943 (MD: 38, pp. 4523f).

19 Ibid, 4525.

20 Führer decree: production of A4 rockets (FD. 3049/49); and Speer; Führer conf, 25 Jul 1943. After the war, Speer suggested that he had always been opposed to the costly A4 project. Cf Milch diary, 21 Jun 1946: '[Read] Speer interrogation, very interesting. He says the V2 [i.e. the A4 rocket] was madness, and ordered from above against his will!!'; see also Speer, op. cit., p. 374: 'It was again Hitler who made the moves which aided the enemy air offensive in 1944'; one such move was the 'absurd idea' of reprisal attacks on Britain.

21 Krüger, GL conf, 29 Jul 1943.

22 GL conf, 24 Aug 1943 (MD: 24, pp. 7056ff).

23 Milch, GL conf, 10 Sep 1943 (MD: 30, pp. 4507f, 4522).

24 Milch, GL conf, 17 Aug 1943 (MD: 24, pp. 7234ff). On the pre-history of how Messerschmitt secured Hitler's decision, see Seiler, GL conf, 4 Jun 1943; letter Prof Messerschmitt to Seiler, 2 Jun 1943 (FD. 4355/45, vol. 6); GL conf, 27 Jul 1943; GL conf 3 Aug 1943 (MD: 23, p. 6555): 'The [Me 209s] design work is 95 per cent complete.'
3 Aug 1943 (MD: 23, p. 6554); and Galland, GL conf, 10 Aug 1943 (MD: 38, pp. 4722f).

25 Cf GL conf, 22 Jun 1943 (MD: 21, pp. 5804f). The plan was sent in on 17 Jun and approved on 22 Jul 1943 (Bley at GL conf, 29 Jun 1943, MD: 21, p. 5702). Each Me 262 would cost on average 24,000 manhours for the first 100, reducing to 3,500 in mass production, compared with 4,200 manhours for the Me 109. Telegram Messerschmitt AG to Colonel Petersen, 20 Jul 1943 (MD: 65, p. 7051).

26 GL conf, 10 Aug 1943 (MD: 38, pp. 4726, 4687ff, 4694, 4699).

27 Milch at GL conf, 10 Aug 1943 (ibid, p. 4726).

28 Milch at GL conf, 20 Aug 1943 (MD: 24, p. 7134); cf GL conf, 17 Aug 1943 (MD: 24, pp. 7233f, 7238). Milch had meanwhile discovered that Messerschmitt's tooling up for the Me 209 production was only 60 per cent complete (p. 7234f).

29 Suchenwirth: Jeschonnek, pp. 132ff.

30 Von Richthofen diary, 27 Jul 1943, et seq.

31 Results of Air Attack on Messerschmitt AG (FD. 4921/45).

32 US State Dept. Interrogation of General Warlimont, 26 Sep 1945. This may have been at 1.25 pm, 17 Aug 1943 (cf Linge diary).

33 Milch, von Lossberg at GL conf, 20 Aug 1943 (MD: 24 pp. 7068ff); and Night Fighter conf, 31 Aug 1943 (MD: 30, pp. 283f).

34 Milch: Hitler and his Subordinates.

35 Letter Messerschmitt to Frydag, 23 Aug 1943 (FD. 4355/45, vol. 3).

36 GL–Speer conf, 25 Aug 1943 (MD: 30, p. 411).

37 Memoirs, p. 320; FD. 4439/45, p. 16; cf diary, 7 Aug 1943.

38 FD. 4439/45, p. 22.

39 Memoirs, p. 320.

40 GL conf, 20 Aug 1943 (MD: 24, p. 7077).

41 During the attack on Berlin about 400 were killed, 300 missing, and 65,000 left homeless—Milch at Night Fighter conf, 31 Aug 1943 (MD: 30, p. 283f).

42 Night Fighter conf, 31 Aug 1943 (MD: 30, p. 285).

43 Night Fighter conf, 31 Aug 1943 (MD: 30, p. 227).

44 GL–Speer conf, 1 Sept 1943 (MD: 30, p. 3771); cf Night Fighter conf, 31 Aug 1943 (MD: 30, p. 206).

45 Diary, 2 Sep 1943. Rumour of Herrmann's successes soon spread: see Note of discussion Ribbentrop–Antonescu, 3 Sep 1943. 'A new tactic has been worked out whereby using the existing aircraft types about 20 to 25 per cent of the attacking aircraft can be shot down.'

CHAPTER 18

1 GL–Speer conf, 25 Aug 1943 (MD: 30, pp. 411ff).

2 Cf Milch at Göring conf, 7 Oct 1943 (MD: 62, p. 5704).

3 FD. 4439/45: 'As machine tools reserved for aircraft production had to be released at short notice en masse on account of the shortage of crankshafts for tanks, a considerable shortage of crankshafts for our own purposes arose.' Cf GL–Speer conf, 25 Aug 1943 (MD: 30, pp. 390ff).

4 GL–Speer conf, 25 Aug 1943. Cf FD. 4439/45. The accuracy of Milch's planning war contested: Speer *Chronik*, 1 Sep 1943; and GL-Speer conf, 1 Sep 1943 (MD: 30, p. 328ff).

5 FD. 4439/45. Cf Speer *Chronik*, 15 Sep 1943.

6 FD. 4439/45.

7 USSBS interrogation of Prof Messerschmitt, No. 6, May 1945. Letters Messerschmitt to Frydag and Lusser, 23 Aug 1943 (FD. 4355/45, vol. 3). Messerschmitt had independently had the same idea for the 'uninterrupted bombardment' of London with flying bombs powered by the 'amazingly cheap' Argus Tube. (Letter, Messerschmitt to Croneiss, 15 Sep 1942; ibid, vol. 4).

8 USSBS interrogation of Messerschmitt. Linge diary, 7 Sep 1943, '4.20–5.25 p.m.: Prof Messerschmitt and Colonel von Below [with Führer].' Hitler admitted that if the same happened to Berlin as had happened in Hamburg, he might have to liquidate the war.

9 Messerschmitt's notes on his conference with Hitler, 7 Sep 1943 (FD. 4355/45 vol. 1.) It should be noted that he had also ascribed bomber characteristics to the Me 262 in his correspondence with Frydag, 23 Aug 1943 (FD. 4355/45, vol. 3).

10 Speer, p. 372, refers to a telegram from Hitler to Milch early in Sept 1943, ordering him to stop mass production preparations for the Me 262. This is not evident from the archives.

11 Fischer and Thomas, in Central Planning, 29 Oct 1942 (MD: 46, p. 8934). Becht also said, 'On the outbreak of war the Italians had about a million tons of heating oil in store; they have reduced this volume so much that they do not even have enough now for their ships.' (p. 8936).

12 GL conf, 5 Oct 1943 (MD: 25, p. 7454).

13 Ibid, p. 7456.

14 Cf Göring conf, 22 Feb 1943: Göring: 'If the Italian aircraft is any good, we must not be ashamed, but mass produce it. Let's have no embarrassment about it!' Milch: 'We would win a year like that.' Galland: '. . . and it would do our own designers a power of good!' (MD: 62, pp. 5397f). Milch and Kesselring had seen the Fiat fighter in Italy early in December 1942. Cf Milch at GL conf, 9 Dec 1942: 'Field-Marshal Kesselring tells me the Italian fighter is first-class, absolutely the equal of ours.' On the Fiat G-55 fighter, see also Milch at GL conf, 5 Oct 1943 (MD: 25, p. 7439). Cf also note of discussion between Führer and Mussolini, 19 Jul 1943. The Führer said, 'According to the Luftwaffe, Italy turns out magnificent airframes.'

15 Göring conf, stenogram, 14 Oct 1943 (MD: 63, p. 6228). Cf. note on discussion between Hitler and Antonescu, 26 Feb 1944: Rumania had supplied Italy with oil, which Italy had 'secretly tucked away'. On these secret stocks in Italy, see also GL-Speer conf, 27 Oct 1943 (MD: 31, p. 754).

16 GL conf, 5 Oct 1943 (MD: 25, p. 7486).

17 Cf GL conf, 9 Dec 1942 (MD: 17, p. 3681); 22 Dec 1942 (ibid, p. 3824); and Göring conf, 8 Oct 1943 (MD: 62, pp. 5753f).

18 GL conf, 14 Sep 1943 (MD: 25, pp. 7634ff).

19 Diary, 20 Sep 1943; cf Goebbels diary, 21 Sep 1943, and GL confs 14 and 21 Sep 1943 (MD: 25, pp. 7648f and p. 7519); 12 Oct 1943 (MD: 38, p. 4285).

20 Webster and Frankland, op. cit., vol. II, p. 45.

21 Ibid, p. 46.

22 Sir Arthur Harris to Mr Winston Churchill, 3 November 1943, ibid, p. 48.

23 Camouflaging lakes and important factories against H2S radar was discussed at GL conf, 24 Aug 1943 (MD: 24, pp. 6996ff), 19 Oct 1943 (MD: 26, p. 8345), 3 Dec 1943 (MD: 39, p. 4848f), and GL-Speer conf, 16 Dec 1943 (MD: 32, pp. 1251ff.) On active devices against H2S, see Night Fighter conf, 31 Aug 1943 (MD: 30, p. 277).

24 See also ADI(K) Report No. 416/1945: The History of German Night Fighting, 8 Dec 1945, paras, 52ff.

25 In general on German radio counter-measures: the jamming of 'Gee': GL conf, 4 Aug 1942 (MD: 15, p. 1748); and 15 Sep 1942 (MD: 16, p. 2426); the coming role of RCM: GL conf, 20 Aug 1942 (MD: 15, pp. 1975ff); jamming enemy radar, GL conf, 6 Apr 1943 (MD: 19, pp. 4938ff); deceiving British jammers, Night Fighter conf, 13 Dec 1943 (MD: 43, pp. 6659ff). Measures against 'Window' jamming: GL conf, 10 Aug 1943 (MD: 38, pp. 4746f), Night Fighter conf, 31 Aug 1943 (MD: 30, pp. 172f), 5 Nov 1943 (MD: 43, pp. 6707ff) and GL conf, 14 Dec 1943 (MD: 27, p. 8645). Tracking H2S transmissions by 'Korfu', GL conf, 24 Aug 1943 (MD: 24, p. 7009f), homing on H2S by 'Naxos Z', or jamming with 'Roderich', Night Fighter conf, 31 Aug 1943 (MD: 30, pp. 277f), GL conf, 16 Nov 1943 (MD: 26, p. 8001) and 14 Dec 1943 (MD: 27, p. 8648).

26 Von Lossberg at GL conf, 5 Oct 1943 (MD: 25, p. 7506).

27 Röderer, ibid. For a lengthy statement by Schwenke on Allied electronic warfare, see GL conf, 30 Nov 1943.

28 In several conferences Milch talked of the need for intruder operations against RAF airfields.

29 Christian at Führer's war conf, 4 Oct 1943. Hitler: 'I spoke yesterday with the Reichsmarschall . . . [etc.]'. Cf Linge Diary, 3 Oct 1943, 12.30 pm: 'War conference (with Reichsmarschall).'

30 Schwenke at GL conf, 26 Oct 1943 (MD: 26, p. 8191). Cf The Army Air Forces in World War II, vol. II, pp. 692ff. The first H2S attack was on 27 Sep 1943 against Emden, but two of the four H2S sets broke down before the target was reached.

31 GL conf, 26 Oct 1943 (ibid, p. 8183).

32 Christian at Führer's war conf, 4 Oct 1943.

33 Göring conf, 7 Oct 1943, stenogram (MD: 62, p. 5658). Cf Linge Diary, 4 Oct 1943: '9.30 pm conference (conversation with Reichsmarschall)'. And 5 Oct 1943: '3.05–4.30 pm: Reichsmarschall, General Korten, Colonel Peltz, Colonel Christian, Lt. Col. v. Below [with Führer]; 4.30–5 pm:

Reichsmarschall, Major Waizenegger [with Führer].' Cf. Milch at GL conf, 5 Oct 1943 (MD: 25, pp. 7504ff): 'Tell this to him [Diesing] immediately, because there is a conference today between the Führer and Reichsmarschall.' Göring did not see the Führer again until 27 Oct 1943.

34 Göring conf, 7 Oct 1943 (MD: 62, p. 5665): 'I am quite properly held to be principally responsible.'

35 Ibid, p. 5626f.

CHAPTER 19

1 Göring conf, 9 Oct 1943 (MD: 63, p. 6309).

2 Göring conf, 8 Oct 1943 (MD: 62 pp. 5748f.) Milch was not present.

3 Provided the Ju 290, the He 111 *Kampftransporter* and the new high-speed bombers were included—Memorandum by Vorwald for Milch, 27 Dec 1943 (MD: 63, pp. 6277f.)

4 Göring conf, 9 Oct 1943 (MD: 63, pp. 6308f.).

5 Telegram Göring to Milch, 11 Oct 1943 (MD: 53, pp. 732f.).

6 Milch at Göring conf, 14 Oct 1943 (MD: 63, p. 6191). According to Göring on 2 Nov, during the Marienburg attack a large number of BMW 801 engines had been destroyed, as they had all been stored in one building (MD: 63, p. 5967).

7 GL conf, 12 Oct 1943 (MD: 38, pp. 4315 and 4382).

8 Göring conf, 9 Oct 1943 (MD: 63, pp. 6311f.).

9 Galland: *Die Ersten und die Letzten.*

10 See note 6.

11 GL conf, 12 Oct 1943 (MD: 38, pp. 4285f.). The Germans claimed to have destroyed 62 US bombers in the Anklam attack.

12 Göring conf, 14 Oct 1943 (MD: 63, pp. 6147ff).

13 Martin Caidin: *Black Thursday* (New York, 1960).

14 Pasewaldt at GL conf, 14 Sep 1943 (MD: 25, p. 7640).

15 GL–Speer conf, 27 Oct 1943 (MD: 31, p. 751).

16 Göring conf, 14 Oct 1943 (MD: 63, p. 6134).

17 Göring speech at Arnhem, 23 Oct 1943 (MD: vol. 63, pp. 6133f). Colonel von Below has said that this was typical of the Führer's views as well.

18 Linge diary, 14 Oct 1943, records inter alia: '9 pm: dinner with Minister Speer, Herr Dorsch, Herr Saur (telephone conversation with Reichsmarschall).'

19 Speer, p. 298.

20 More damaging for the Luftwaffe was the shortage of airscrews for many types after Schweinfurt; the aircraft had to be stockpiled without them (Milch at Göring conf, 2 Nov 1943, MD: 63, p. 5969).

21 Speer, p. 299. Milch at Göring conf, 14 Oct 1943 (MD: 63, p. 6228); cf GL conf, 12 Oct 1943 (MD: 38, pp. 4291f). Milch and Speer had arranged on 11 Oct to reduce ball-bearings for motor transport in favour of the air industry; the latter would also do without so many ball bearings, 'as we too have been making pigs of ourselves with ball bearings.'

22 Diary, 15 Oct 1943. Cf Milch at GL conf, 15 Oct 1943 (MD: 39, p. 5243): 'I have heard this morning that the Führer, in Speer's presence, yesterday . . . [etc].'

23 Cf Speer's record of the conference with Hitler.

24 At Insterburg on 26 Nov 1943, Hitler was to pronounce that he considered the combination of Me 410 with the 50-millimetre KWK cannon 'the backbone of the Reich's defence.' (Telegram Göring to Milch, 12 Jan 1944, MD: 51, pp. 414f). Galland had always opposed the weapon as too slow-firing—only one round every 1.8 seconds (GL conf, 26 Oct 1943, MD: 26, p. 8245). Cf Galland: *Die Ersten und die Letzten.*

25 Speer *Chronik*, 13 Oct 1943. FD. 4439/45. The related Programme Study, '1018', was concluded on 23 Oct 1943.

26 Milch at GL conf, 29 Oct 1943 (MD: 39, pp. 5119f). Speer repeated the refusal at his conference with Göring on 28 Oct, so Milch was not in the position to issue the programme.

27 Göring conf, 8 Oct 1943 (MD: 62, pp. 5750ff).

28 Göring conf, in officers' mess at Arnhem, 23 Oct 1943, stenogram (MD: 63, pp. 6119f).

29 Göring: speech to aircrews of Third Fighter Division, day-fighters, in hangar at Arnhem-Deelen airfield, 23 Oct 1943, stenogram (MD: 63, pp. 6091ff).

30 Diary, 24 Oct 1943; Memoirs, p. 321f.
Speer: Führer conf, 14–15 Oct 1943, point 20.
Speer at Göring conf, 28 Oct 1943 (MD: 63, pp. 6062ff).

31 Milch at Göring conf, 2 Nov 1943 (MD: 63, p. 6007). Cf Milch at GL conf, 12 Nov 1943 (MD: 39, p. 4964): 'The whole figures are false! Speer is talking of 435,000 men. According to *our* calculations it cannot be more than 259,000 of the 1.9 million men.'

32 Milch at GL conf, 29 Oct 1943 (MD: 39, pp. 5108f).
Vorwald in MCH 10 Mar 1947, p. 1656. Compared with air armament's 1,920,000 workers in Sep 1943, army armament had originally employed 1,600,000 and had now risen to 1,900,000, while Speer assessed air armament's labour force as 1,852,000 of which 817,000 were German men (44 per cent) and the rest women (25 per cent), or foreigners (23.5 per cent male, 7 per cent female).—Figures in MD: 63, p. 6024.

33 Linge diary, 27 Oct 1943.
Göring conf, 28 Oct 1943 (MD: 63, pp. 6018ff). Cf Vorwald in MCH 10 Mar 1947, p. 1659: 'During our activities from 1941 to 1944 our labour force did not expand, but barely remained constant as we covered the gaps caused by disease, absenteeism and death with workers from *GBA* [Sauckel].'

34 Göring conf, 28 Oct 1943 (MD: 63, pp. 6019ff.) By 21 Sep 1943 there were 190,000 Italian prisoners of war in Germany, according to Speer (GL–Speer conf, 22 Sep 1943, MD: 30, p. 45).

35 Milch at GL conf, 29 Oct 1943 (MD: 39, pp. 5108f).

36 Ibid, p. 6021ff. Cf Milch at Göring conf, 4 Nov 1943 (MD: 63, pp. 5938f).

37 Göring conf, 28 Oct 1943 (MD: 63, p. 6080).

38 Ibid, pp. 6084f. Cf Göring conf, 9 Oct 1943 (MD: 63, pp. 6294f).

CHAPTER 20

1 Galland at GL conf, 26 Oct 1943 (MD: 26, p. 8261f).

2 Göring, ibid, p. 6080f. Von Below has commented on Göring's 'amazingly accurate reproduction' of Hitler's language. Cf also Göring conf, 2 Nov 1943 (MD: 63, pp. 5961ff).

3 Göring admitted thinking this. Conf, 28 Oct 1943 (MD: 63, p. 6080).

4 Göring conf, 14 Oct 1943 (MD: 63, pp. 6261f).

5 Milch at Göring conf, 28 Oct 1943 (ibid, p. 6058).

6 Ibid, p. 6021.

7 GL conf, 29 Oct 1943 (MD: 39, p. 5117ff). Milch: '[Kurt] Tank understands three times more about fighter aircraft than Messerschmitt, because he climbs in himself. Messerschmitt never has sat in one of his aircraft.'

8 Cf Milch at GL conf, 29 Oct 1943 (MD: 39, p. 5174).

9 Göring conf, 2 Nov 1943, at Messerschmitt works at Regensburg, stenogram (MD: 63, p. 5963).

10 Göring conf, 4 Nov 1943, at Junkers works, Dessau, stenogram (MD: 63, p. 5923; ND:NOKW-180).

11 Speer at GL–Speer conf, 10 Nov 1943 (MD: 31, p. 697).

12 The Junkers 388 was in an assembly building, with one of the two BMW 801 engines already installed. Göring asked later for it to be shown to Hitler at Insterburg: 'No need for it to fly, just for the Führer to see it.' (Göring conf, 23 Nov 1943, stenogram, MD: 64, p. 6666).

13 Göring conf, 5 Nov 1943, at Arado works, stenogram, (MD: 63, pp. 5706ff).

14 On 2 Oct 1943 Flight Captain Selle had carried out test dives to test the Ar 234's dive performance. At 9000 metres altitude the left-hand jet engine flamed out. He dived to 4,500 metres hoping to cut the engine back in. Selle was heard to radio, 'All my instruments are dead', and then 'The ailerons and wing flaps are vibrating.' At 1,500 metres a flame was seen licking out of the left engine. The pilot jettisoned the cockpit cover, but could not get out in time. (Vorwald at GL conf, 5 Oct 1943, MD: 26, pp. 7433ff).

15 Letter Arado company to Milch, re Ar 234 production situation, Potsdam, 19 Nov 1943 (MD: 53, pp. 727ff). Lt Col v. Below had inspected the factory on 18 Nov for the Führer to ascertain whether the Ar 234 could be regarded purely as a bomber, while the Me 262 was regarded as a fighter.

16 Göring: speech to the Gauleiters, stenogram, 8 Nov 1943 (MD: 63, pp. 5859ff). Goebbels diary, 9 Nov 1943.

Cf Göring conf, 14 Oct 1943: 'Just watch our first attack on London with 150 aircraft—only with 150—and then read the British Press! And then down with the *Trialen* [aluminized explosive] and new fire bombs . . . The British have only one pleasure in war, and that is when they are the only ones doing the hitting. Just watch what happens when we are knocking them around again, *and* their bombers start saying, "We are suffering terrible losses." I can see the squaring of accounts coming.'

17 Memorandum on letter from Herr Kokothaki, 19 Jan 1944, by Messerschmitt (FD. 4355/45, vol. 6).

18 Letter Prof Messerschmitt to Fritz Seiler, 4 Jun 1943 (ibid).

19 Memorandum, 31 Mar 1944 (FD. 4355/45, vol. 2). The original document also gives the half-monthly figures.

20 Letter Seiler to Messerschmitt, 22 Sep 1943 (FD. 4355/45, vol. 6).

21 GL conf, 29 Oct 1943 (MD: 39, p. 5162).

22 GL conf, 26 Sep 1943 (MD: 38, p. 4489): 'We are severally come to the opinion that we are holding up too much other work with it, and that we do not really need it.'

23 GL conf, 15 Oct 1943 (MD: 39, p. 5207). Vorwald: 'That's what Messerschmitt had to admit yesterday, although he carped no end beforehand, when the Reichsmarschall reproached him about these figures.'

24 GL conf, 29 Oct 1943 (MD: 39, p. 5161f). Messerschmitt's visits to the Führer were frequently debated. Cf Milch at GL conf, 12 Nov 1943 (MD: 39, p. 4926): '. . . And then he scurries off with it to the Reichsmarschall or to the Führer, and lies until he is in the clear again.'

25 GL conf, 16 Nov 1943 (MD: 26, p. 8046); letter Seiler to Messerschmitt, 22 Sept 1943, FD. 4355/45, vol. 6.

26 See Milch at GL–Speer conf, 27 Oct 1943 (MD: 31, pp. 733ff) and 17 Nov 1943 (MD: 31, pp. 609ff) on the history of these programmes. '223' had been issued in Apr 1943.

27 GL conf, 27 Oct 1943 (MD: 31, p. 742). Speer: 'Even agreeing to Programme "224" was something approaching lunacy in my view.'

28 The first such study, '1019', suggested 3,000 single- and 1,090 twin-engined fighters a month, by 1945, with 610 bombers. This was not shown to Göring (GL–Speer conf, 17 Nov 1943, MD: 31, pp. 593, 603).

29 Sellschopp at GL–Speer conf, 17 Nov 1943 (MD: 31, p. 593); and see the biting sarcasm about Milch's conference in Speer *Chronik*, 17 Nov 1943.

30 Central Planning, 22 Nov 1943 (MD: 48, pp. 10257ff). Although energy capacity had increased by over 700,000 kw (6 per cent) and load had increased by only 3 per cent, there was now an energy gap of 930,-000 kw compared with 1942; part of this, 400,000 kw, had been caused by enemy action. In addition several power stations now lay idle for want of repairs, as they had no manpower. Agriculture would suffer as usual. Von Trotha said, 'The 35 per cent reduction in carbide and calcium nitrate means that fertilizers will not be manufactured at all.' (MD: 48, p. 10265).

31 Göring conf, 23 Nov 1943 (MD: 64, pp. 6632ff).

32 Speer *Chronik,* 23 Nov 1943. Cf Frydag at Göring conf, 23 Nov 1943. For description of these early raids' results, see Milch at GL conf, 30 Nov 1943 (MD: 26).

33 Göring conf, 28 Oct 1943 (MD: 63, pp. 6036f).

34 OKW War diary, vol. III: 27 Nov 1943 (p. 1214f). And letter Korten to Milch, 17 Nov 1943 (MD: 53, pp. 1026ff): Korten points out that 'reducing the force by 25 per cent would mean around 430,000 men from the military strength, or virtually the dissolution of the Luftwaffe.' An investigating commission was to investigate both the Luftwaffe and its industry.

35 Cf point 23 of telegram, Göring to Milch, 21 Nov 1943 (MD: 51, p. 418): 'For Führer conference: Statistics and proposals for saving in manpower in the Army, Luftwaffe and Navy in rear areas, particularly in headquarters, military stores, supply authorities, etc, with a view to considerably reinforcing the combat troops as proposed by Field-Marshal Milch and Reichsminister Speer in the conference with Herr Reichsmarschall.'

36 Göring conf, 23 Nov 1943 (MD: 63, pp. 6691f): Göring stated that the entire Luftwaffe front line from Kirkenes to the Crimea was 247,000 men.

37 Dönitz: Führer conf, 25–26 [sic] Nov 1943. The dates must be wrong as both the Göring conf quoted and the Linge diary make it clear the date was 24 Nov 1943. Cf also diary of Chief of Army Personnel, Schmundt, 27 Nov 1943.

38 Diary, 7 Oct 1940: 'Congratulated Himmler [on his birthday] by telegram.' Also Milch at GL conf, 19 Oct 1943 (MD: 26, p. 8391).

39 For a description of how Milch delayed the deportation of Jews from Holland, see affidavit Dr Herbert Rohrer, 13 Sep 1954 (MPP) and of lawyer, Gerhard Wilcke, 18 Apr 1950. Rohrer was Trustee of the Phillips concern from 1943 to 1944.

40 Milch at GL conf, 19 Oct 1943 (MD: 26, p. 8391).

41 Diary, 20 Nov 1943; Himmler diary, 20 Nov 1943: '8 p.m.: with Field-Marshal Milch.' Cf Milch in MCH, 14 Mar 1947, p. 2010; and 20 Mar 1947, p. 2244.

42 Telegram Göring to Milch, 21 Nov 1943 (MD: 51, p. 419). Göring ordered that apart from his own entourage, Milch, Speer, Korten, Vorwald, Galland, Peltz, Petersen, Knemeyer, [Lieut Col] Werner, Heyne and Frydag were to take part, together with Messerschmitt, Hentzen, Tank, Hertel, Tiedemann, Cambeis, Franz, Dornier, Franke, Blume, Nallinger, Lusser, Wagner and Günther from the air industry.

43 Diary, 26 Nov 1943: '. . . Insterburg. Equipment inspected by Führer. Göring pushes me aside.'
Petersen, Jun 1968; Vorwald, Jun 1968. Interview of Prof Messerschmitt on Second German Television, 17 Feb 1970.

44 Göring conf, 18 Mar 1943 (MD: 62, p. 5475).

45 Herrmann at GL conf, 25 May 1943 (MD: 20, pp. 5486f).

46 GL conf, 28 May 1943, and 9 Jul 1943. Re the Ar 234 reconnaissance plane, see also Colonel Theo Rowehl at GL conf, 19 Jul 1943 (MD: 22).

47 GL conf, 20 Aug 1943 (MD: 24, p. 7134).

48 Göring conf, 2–3 Sep 1943 (MD: 62, pp. 5595ff).

49 Kröger at GL conf, 1 Feb 1944.

50 Vorwald at GL conf, 3 Nov 1943 (MD: 39, pp. 5061ff).

51 Bilfinger at GL–Speer conf, 10 Nov 1943 (MD: 31 pp. 680ff).

52 Cf also Heyne, Vorwald and Offenhammer at GL conf, 19 Oct 1943 (MD: 26, pp. 8354ff).

53 See note 50.

54 OKW War diary, vol. III, p. 1313: 27 Nov 1943.

55 Göring conf, 28 Nov 1943, stenogram (MD: 64, pp. 6593ff). Cf Goebbels Diary, 7 Dec 1943.

56 Basil Collier, op. cit., p. 327.

57 Führer war conf, 28 Jan 1944.

58 Cf Milch at GL–Speer conf, 19 Jan 1944: (MD: 32, pp. 1114ff): 'At present the Americans alone are producing 8,800 aircraft a month, the British 2,600 and the Russians 2,300 to 2,400, of which 1,200 are four-engined bombers. This year will also see the new American B-29 and B-32, and these aircraft can attack at altitudes of 11 to 12 thousand metres.'

59 GL conf, 30 Nov 1943 (MD: 26, pp. 7918ff).

60 Milch at GL conf, 14 Dec 1943 (MD: 27, pp. 8674f).

61 GL conf, 14 Dec 1943 (MD: 27, p. 8672).

62 GL–Speer conf, 16 Dec 1943 (MD: 32, pp. 1309ff).

63 Memorandum by Eberhard, 10 Jan 1944: he urged that intensive attempts should be made to brief Speer on the importance of ground-to-air missile development (MD: 53, p. 873f).

64 Von Lossberg at GL conf, 14 Dec 1943 (MD: 27, p. 8663).

65 Letter Milch to von Below, 11 Nov 1943 (MD: 51, p. 511). On the Do 335 see also GL conf and Night Fighter conf, 13 Dec 1943 (MD: 43, pp. 6606ff).

66 Milch at GL–Speer conf, 19 Jan 1944 (MD: 32, pp. 1114f).

CHAPTER 21

1 There is no space to detail in the text all the subjects discussed at Hitler's headquarters from 2 to 4 January 1944. One of them was the unsatisfactory organization of electronics research: as a result of the criticism by Speer and Dönitz of electronics research under Staatsrat Plendl, Hitler approved its removal from Göring's control to Speer's on 2 Jan 1944. Cf Führer naval conf, 19–20 Dec 1943; Göring conf, 3 Jan 1944 (MD: 64, pp. 6568ff); and Führer naval conf, 3 Jan 1944, and Speer–Führer conf, 3 Jan 1944. Speer's *Chronik* and Himmler's diary, 3 Jan 1944, show Milch, Funk, Speer and Lammers dining with the Reichsführer SS before the important manpower conf with Hitler next day.

2 To examine the crucial manpower crisis in this book would have filled many pages and impeded the narrative. The Milch documents are a fund of information on this sorely neglected aspect of war policy and further researchers should not ignore them.

The Jan 1944 conf arose from Sauckel's belief that French workers were more productive in factories in Germany than in the 'protected' factories Speer was establishing in France. Speer objected that most of the deported Frenchmen escaped long before reaching the Reich. (Central Planning, 21 Dec 1943, MD: 48, p. 10165). The dispute was settled by Hitler on 4 Jan 1944, at a conf attended by Keitel, Speer, Backe, Himmler, Sauckel, Milch and Hitler himself; on this there is a number of reliable sources, so Speer's recollected version in his memoirs is best read last. Lammers: memorandum of 4 Jan 1944 (ND: 1292-PS) and circular, 8 Jan 1944 (on NARS film T-84, roll 175, frames 4886ff); Sauckel and Milch discussed the conf at length during Central Planning conf on 1 Mar 1944 (MD: 48, esp. pp. 9953ff, 9987f, 9994, 10003f and 10012f). See also Milch's diary, 4 Jan 1944: 'War conf with Führer. Midday, lunch with Führer. Afternoon, manpower conf (Führer). Evening, dinner with Führer and Speer. Tea-house with [Führer], Bodenschatz, Speer and Schmundt.' Speer's version, op. cit., pp. 333ff, differs from the wartime records: e.g. Speer himself, not Bormann, arranged the conf (Central Planning, 21 Dec 1943, MD: 48, pp. 10126 and 10165). And Sauckel was emphatic he could *not* guarantee the 4,050,000 new workers needed in 1944 (Central Planning, 1 Mar 1944, MD: 48, pp. 9953ff).

On the nagging, but unresolved question of increasing the use of female labour in the Reich, which Hitler would not tolerate (explaining that there could be no comparison between 'our long-legged, slender women' and the 'stocky-legged, primitive and healthy Russian women' (Sauckel, Central Planning, 1 Mar 1944, MD: 48, pp. 9958, 0076f, 9980) see also Speer's testimony, MCH, 4 Feb 1947, pp. 1459ff who suggests it was *Sauckel* who always opposed the employment of women. This is not borne out by the sources. At GL conf on 27 Nov 1942 Milch interestingly stated that if the same percentage of the German public would work, including women, as worked in Britain then 'at least ten million more would be in our labour force' (MD: 34, p. 2563). There were fewer women working in the Junkers factory now than pre-war, and Milch argued that the 'huge dependent-relatives allowance' paid to soldiers' families was a disincentive to their finding employment. (GL–Speer conf, 16 Dec 1943, MD: 32, pp. 1306ff; at GL conf, 14 Dec 1943, MD: 27, and in Central Planning, 16 Feb 1944 (MD: 48, pp. 10040f).

3 Diary, 5 Jan 1944. Cf Speer *Chronik*, 5 Jan 1944. Speer's protocols are missing for many of his conferences at this time. See also Milch at GL conf, 5 Jan 1944 (MD: 32, p. 1203).

4 Diary, 8 Jan 1944. The Air Ministry release announcing the British jet aircraft research was timed 11.50 p.m., 7 Jan 1944. Cf Speer, p. 372.

5 GL conf, 3 Nov 1943 (MD: 39, p. 5080); cf GL conf, 29 Oct 1943 (MD: 39, p. 5174): 'The Reichsmarschall said yesterday, the 262 is to carry bombs without fail!'

6 GL conf, 3 Dec 1943 (MD: 39, p. 4870).

7 Telegram Göring to Milch, 6 Dec 1943 (MD: 53, p. 730f.); cf GL conf, 7 Dec 1943 (MD: 27, p. 8748).

8 Führer war conference, 20 Dec 1943. Cf Linge diary, (for Hitler) 18 Dec 1943: '12.30 pm: conference (with Reichsmarschall); 2.25 lunch (with Reichsmarschall); 4.30 pm [to 5.45 pm] Major Buchs (with Reichsmarschall).' Cf Göring conf, 3 Jan 1944 (MD: 64, pp. 6576f).

9 GL conf, 25 Jan 1944 (MD: 27, pp. 8411ff, 8437ff). Cf GL conf, 3 Dec 1943 (MD: 39, pp. 4857ff).

10 War Diary of Flak Regiment 155(W).

11 Jodl diary, 15 Dec 1943.

12 GL–Speer conf, 5 Jan 1944 (MD: 32, p. 1214). Cf Milch at GL conf, 1 Feb 1944: 'Of course our Chief of Air Staff must be told everything.' Cf GL conf, 18 Jan 1944 (MD: 27, p. 8611f).

13 GL–Speer conf, 19 Jan 1944 (MD: 32, p. 1152).

14 Cf diary, 19 Jan 1944: 'GL–Speer conference. Lively. In the evening depart in new special train with Air Armaments Office and Speer's men.'

15 GL conf, 18 Jan 1944 (MD: 27, p. 8554).

16 Telegram Göring to Milch, 12 Jan 1944 (MD: 51, pp. 409ff). Milch replied on 14 Jan.

17 GL–Speer conf, 25 Jan 1944 (MD: 27, pp. 8399ff, 8421ff).

18 This was the first so-called 'Operation Hamburg'; the conferences with Dornier, Messerschmitt, Blume etc were all recorded (MD: 32, pp. 929ff).

19 On 3 Nov 1943 Milch recalled the demands he had made in June: 'I said at the time we must transfer appropriate forces of flak and fighters to the district to defend all the launching sites.' It was his strategic objective to establish 'flak and fighter traps' for enemy bombers, far from German soil. (GL conf, MD: 39, pp. 5024ff).

20 GL conf, 25 Jan 1944 (MD: 27, p. 8470).

21 GL conf, 1 Feb 1944; cf GL–Speer conf, 2 Feb 1944 (MD: 33).

22 Göring conf, stenogram, 8 Feb 1944 (MD: 64, p. 6561).

23 Diary, 14 Feb 1944. Cf GL conf, 25 Jan 1944 (MD: 27, pp. 8410ff, 8437ff).

24 Farewell speech to GL conf, 30 Jun 1944 (MD: 56, pp. 2701–14).

25 This was the most common criticism. Milch in Central Planning, 16 Feb 1944 (MD: 48, p. 10072f).

26 *The United States Army Air Forces in World War II*, vol. III, pp. 30ff.

27 GL–Speer conf, 23 Feb 1944.

28 Diary, 24 Feb 1944: 'Göring departs for three weeks' leave.'

29 Diary, 20 Feb 1944.

30 GL–Speer conf, 22 Feb 1944.

31 Cf Milch's remarks at GL–Speer conf, 23 Feb 1944; and at GL conf, 25 Feb 1944 (MD: 41, p. 5826); and in Central Planning, 1 Mar 1944

(MD: 48, p. 9982). Describing his visit to the Böhler factory at Kapfenberg, he said: 'Things are so bad that in one factory which had been disastrously bombed three times I myself had to step in and lay down regulations on how the factory was to be evacuated. It is stupid to keep the workers in a factory under saturation bombing attack, as the orders previously said, if there are not enough shelters of the right type available.'

32 Central Planning, 1 Mar 1944 (MD: 48, p. 9982). For Milch's praise of US tactics on 20 Feb 1944, see GL–Speer conf, 23 Feb 1944.

33 Fritz Seiler, Rakan Kokothaki, Nov 1969.

34 Results of air attack on Messerschmitt's (FD. 4921/45).

35 GL–Speer conf ('Operation Hamburg') 23 Feb 1944, 11.45 pm. On the early history of the Fighter Staff, see Milch's Pre-Trial Interrogation, 14 Oct 1946: 'The man who put us at a disadvantage was this Herr Saur . . . For months on end we held weekly conferences with Speer to by-pass all these injustices. Much was promised, but the promises were not kept . . . The result was that we could not turn out enough fighters.' Cf also Pre-Trial Interrogation, 6 Nov 1946: 'I was extensively throttled —I'm trying to use moderate language—by the Speer Ministry to its own ends. I got nothing—neither the workers nor enough materials . . .' (NARS: RG-248).

36 Diary, 23 Feb 1944; Speer *Chronik,* 23 Feb 1944; and Speer, Dec 1968.

37 For further details of the Fighter Staff's foundation history, see Milch's opening speech at GL conf, 31 Mar 1944 (ND:NOKW-417) and MCH, pp. 2181ff; and Speer's testimony, MCH, 4 Feb 1947, pp. 1464ff; and Vorwald's testimony, MCH, 10 Mar 1947, pp. 1685ff.

38 Saur: Points from a conference with Göring, 4 Mar 1944 (MD: 64, pp. 6510ff). And Saur: Points from a conference with the Führer on 5 Mar 1944 (MD: 64, pp. 6505ff). Diary, 5 Mar 1944, and Memoirs, p. 324.

39 Petersen at GL conf, 29 Feb 1944.

40 GL conf, 24 Mar 1944 (MD: 28, p. 8838f).

41 Diary, 6 Mar 1944.

42 Diary, 8 Mar 1944. On this occasion one hundred fighters were scrambled, but they failed to reach the bomber formation on time; had they done so, Galland told Milch later, they would have shot down eighty or a hundred bombers.

43 Vorwald testified (MCH, 10 Mar 1947, p. 1670) that Milch had previously opposed the 72-hour week as similar attempts had led to a decline in output.

44 GL conf, 31 Mar 1944 (MD: 29, p. 9579ff).

45 Diary, 25 Mar 1944. Cf Vorwald's testimony in MCH, 11 Mar 1947, pp. 1645 and 1729f, and 21 Mar 1947, p. 2348. Also testimony of Pendele, MCH, 18 Feb 1947, pp. 1201ff.

46 GL conf, 24 Mar 1944 (MD: 33, p. 8837f).

47 GL conf, 31 Mar 1944 (MD: 29, p. 9579ff).

CHAPTER 22

1 Cf Saur in Göring conf, stenogram, 19 Apr 1944 (MD: 64, pp. 6478f).

2 These figures are from USSBS report, Effects of Strategic Bombing, Table 102, p. 277: Reclassification of German figures (Aircraft Division, USSBS). The Speer Ministry's figures are somewhat higher, 1830 in March, 2034 in April, 2377 in May 1944. ('Output survey, Weapons and Equipment', 18 Oct 1944). Air Force acceptance figures are lower: cf Milward, op. cit., p. 148.

3 Speer himself made no bones about having attended none of the Fighter Staff's sessions: MCH 4 Feb 1947, p. 1470.

4 Cf The Observer, 5 Aug 1945. Milch commented on this in Diary, 6 Aug 1945. Milch's attendance in Fighter Staff sessions fell from 15 in March to 8 in April, 5 in May and only two in June 1944.

5 Milch: Hitler and his Subordinates. Cf Speer, p. 289.

6 Göring conference, stenogram, 4 Nov 1943 (MD: 63, pp. 5935f).

7 Dorsch in MCH, 24 Feb 1947, p. 1369. Göring conf, stenogram, 1 May 1944: bombproof fighter factories and hangars (MD: 64, pp. 6400ff).

8 Speer in MCH, 4 Feb 1947, pp. 1467ff.

9 GL–Speer conf, 13 Oct 1943 (MD: 31, p. 844).

10 Göring conf, stenogram, 28 Oct 1943 (MD: 63, p. 6040). GL–Speer conf, 10 Nov 1943 (MD: 31, pp. 680ff); cf FD. 4439/45, p. 16.

11 Göring conf, stenogram, 8 Feb 1944: Leonberg autobahn tunnel as factory site (MD: 64, p. 6520ff).

12 Diary, 6 Apr 1944. Cf Speer in MCH, 4 Feb 1947, p. 1487. Saur: Points from conference with the Führer, 6–7 Apr 1944; and cf Milch, IMT vol. IX, p. 74.

13 GL conf, 7 Apr 1944; and Saur at Göring conf, stenogram, 19 Apr 1944 (MD: 64, p. 6480).

14 Göring conf, stenogram, 19 Apr 1944 (MD: 64, p. 6479).

15 Note on Führer's discussion with Bulgarian representatives, 18 Oct 1943.

16 Cf Führer naval conf, 12–13 Apr 1944, and Speer in MCH, 4 Feb 1947, p. 1480; at this time the Führer recognized that fighters must be given priority over bombers in production. The Führer's words were repeated by Göring at his conference with Dorsch, Milch and Saur on 19 Apr 1944, stenogram (MD: 64, p. 6481): 'This was the opinion expressed by the Führer when the Grand-Admiral [Dönitz] tried to make small inroads into the fighter programme, by asking for equal priority for certain naval items . . .'

17 Ibid, pp. 6458, 6460.

18 Ibid, p. 6459.

19 Dorsch in MCH, 24 Feb 1947, pp. 1369f; also Dorsch: Protocol of Führer conference of 14 Apr, including conference with Reichsmarschall, dated 17 Apr 1944 (Boelcke, p. 349ff; cf Speer, p. 348).

20 Göring conf, stenogram, 19 Apr 1944: 'The Führer sent for me the day

before yesterday and we both walked up and down for some time, discussing it all over again . . .' (MD: 64, p. 6480f).

21 Göring's opening remarks were: 'The Führer commanded me to hold today's conference, and he also prescribed exactly who was to take part; he did so because he desires this matter to be tackled with vigour.' (Ibid, p. 6458).

22 Diary, 18 Apr 1944.
Memoirs, pp. 324f.
Milch in MCH, 17 Mar 1947, pp. 2079f. Interview, May 1968.

23 Göring conf, stenogram, 19 Apr 1944. Subject: concrete construction projects. Those present were Göring, Milch, Bodenschatz, Korten, Diesing, v. Brauchitsch, Saur, Dorsch and Knipping (MD: 64, pp. 6457ff). Cf Speer, p. 348, and Milch diary, 19 Apr 1944: 'Major conference with Göring, Dorsch and Saur. Intrigues [against] Speer.'

24 Ibid, p. 6499.

25 *The United States Army Air Forces in World War II*, vol. III, pp. 175ff.

26 Speer: Memorandum for the Führer, A Survey on Construction Work in the Reich, and Proposed Reorganization of the Todt organization, dated 19 Apr 1944 (FD. 2690/45). Cf Speer, op. cit., pp. 348ff.

27 Milch: 'Hitler and his Subordinates'. Diary, 20 Apr 1944; cf *Völkischer Beobachter*, 25 and 26 Apr 1944.
Diary, 5 Aug 1947; and interviews, Milch May 1968, Vorwald Jun 1968.

28 1945 commentary on diary, 20 Apr 1944. Cf Speer *Chronik*, 20–21 Apr 1944.

29 Milch in Central Planning, 18 May 1944 (MD: 55, p. 2276). Ganzenmüller reported that 40 to 42 trains were being shot up daily on average (ibid, p. 2269f).

30 Office of Air Armament: On the reasons for increased deliveries under the Luftwaffe programme, from Mar to Jun 1944, dated approx. Aug 1944 (FD. 4439/45) p. 4.

31 Korten was following a very independent line already. 'Korten is very optimistic,' wrote Field Marshal von Richthofen in his diary on 22 May 1944. 'I.e. in this connection he exactly follows the views of the Führer's headquarters. He has far-reaching plans for the reorganization of Luftwaffe command. Conflicts with Milch and his organization, but of a concrete nature and fully justified. Plans to expand the Luftwaffe; what Korten wants is quite sensible—But he is no fighter, so we must wait and see whether he manages to avoid all the pitfalls.'

32 Koller, letter to Chief of Air Staff, Korten, 5 May 1944, and appendices, re: Structure of Production Programme, Study of Aircraft Supply Position for Bomber Units (in OKW War Diary, appendices vol. C: NARS film T-321, roll 10).

33 Chief, Luftwaffe operations staff: Study on Necessary Minimum Strength of German Air Force to Maintain Position in Central Europe, dated 19 May 1944. (From the papers of General Karl Koller, loaned to this author by the Führungsakademie der Bundeswehr). A copy is in the Milch

Documents (MD: 53, pp. 706ff). Milch received it on 30 May, and pencilled bitter comments in its margin.

34 Diary, 22 May 1944; cf Speer, p. 357f (he wrongly puts the date as 23 May).

35 Göring, quoted this at his conf the next day, 23 May 1944 (MD: 64, p. 6846).

36 Saur, at Göring conf, 25 May 1944 (MD: 64, p. 6726); Milch at Göring conf, 24 May 1944 (MD: 64, pp. 6906, 6911); and Messerschmitt at Göring conf, 25 May 1944 (MD: 64, pp. 6727f).

37 Göring conf, stenogram, 23 May 1944. Subject: Programme and Planning conference. Those present were: Göring, Speer, Milch, v. Richthofen, Korten, Koller, Vorwald, Galland, Eschenauer, Diesing, Marienfeld, Petersen, v. Below, Knemeyer, Krause, Zurmühlen, Schieber, Dorsch, Saur, Werner, Frydag, Heyne, Schaaf, v. Brauchitsch, Schubert (MD: 64, pp. 6826ff). Cf Vorwald's testimony in MCH, 10 Mar 1947, p. 1696.

38 Göring conf, 23 May 1944, p. 6833. German bomber production in 1944 was: May, 648; June, 703; July, 767; August, 548; September, 428; October, 326; November, 412; December, 262.

39 Ibid, p. 6835. At the GL conf on 25 Feb 1944, Colonel Petersen had reported flying the four-engined version of the He 177, and said its qualities were 'amazingly good' (MD: 41, p. 5833).

40 Ibid, p. 6836.

41 The following Ju 287 jet bomber production was planned: one each in Aug, Oct and Dec 1944; two in Jan and Feb 1945, three in March, six in Apr, 13 in May, 21 in Jun, 26 in July, 30 in Aug, 35 in Sept, 55 in November and a hundred a month thereafter. (Ibid, pp. 6785f).

Göring had a very high opinion of von Richthofen, rating him, with Kesselring, as the best operational commander in the Luftwaffe (USSBS Interrogation, No. 56, 29 Jun 1945).

42 Diary, 23 May 1944: 'Technical conference with Göring, Speer. Afternoon to see Führer, Me 262! Fighter-bomber!—Evening, Korten.' Baumbach and various other writers have put this important conference in April 1944 or even in 1943. From the diary and from references in the subsequent Göring conferences (24 and 25 May) it was unquestionably on 23 May 1944. Cf Saur's postwar notes on Speer's Führer-conference protocols (FD. 3049/49, file 1, p. 0364): '23 May 1944: the additional protocol on the conference with Göring, Milch, Speer, Saur and Petersen on the 262 is missing.' Cf Von Richthofen Diary, 23 May 1944.

Colonel Petersen, Jun 1968; and letter to author, 2 Jan 1970.

43 Galland: *Die Ersten und die Letzten,* p. 355.

44 Göring conf, 24 May 1944 (MD: 64, p. 6905). Von Richthofen, who was evidently present during the Führer conference, noted only: 'Afterwards Milch and the Reichsmarschall came [to see the Führer] to discuss technical air matters. I sat in on this. Immediately afterwards, the things I reported to the Führer were ordered from the Reichsmarschall.' That evening, von Richthofen asked for a private talk with Saur: 'Milch accom-

panies him, as he thinks there is going to be talk against him and his system. Bad sign for Milch. Saur makes a splendid impression and (in Milch's presence) criticizes what has been done hitherto only in moderation. One can view Saur's future actions with equanimity.'

45 Milch, May 1968. The words are repeated almost verbatim by General Rieckhoff: *Trumpf oder Bluff*, p. 136ff (Milch was not the source).

46 Göring conf, stenogram, 24 May 1944 (MD: 64, p. 6901).

47 Ibid, p. 6901.

48 Cf also Göring at his conf, 25 May, stenogram (MD: 64, pp. 6718f).

49 Göring conf, stenogram, 24 May 1944. Subject: Shape of Programme and Planning. Those present were as in Note 37, except for von Richthofen. (MD: 64, pp. 6907, 6972f).

After the war, Göring put the blame on Hitler. He blamed the Me 262 'fighter-bomber' decision on 'Hitler's madness. When the first Me 262 was ready, I had it displayed to him, full of hope that at last I had my hands on something which would throw the Allies out of Germany's skies and put some spirit back into the Luftwaffe. But to my, and everybody's horror the Führer announced, "The aircraft does not interest me in the least as a fighter". He insisted on having it operated as a fast bomber and ordered that nobody was to speak of the Me 262 as a fighter. It was to be called "Blitz bomber", and I had to issue an order to that effect.' —*Inter Avia*. Jul 1946, p. 14. This is repeated in Ninth Air Force interrogation of Göring, 1 Jun 1945, paras 116ff. But in his interrogation by USSBS on 29 Jun 1945 he stated, 'The Führer had originally directed that it be produced as a fighter, but in May 1944 he ordered that it be converted into a fighter-bomber. This conversion is one of the main reasons for the delay in getting this plane into action in any quantity.'

50 Diary, 24 May 1944.

51 Göring conf, 29 May 1944, stenogram (MD: 64, p. 6333).

52 Speer *Chronik*, 26 May 1944. Milch in MCH, 17 Mar 1947, p. 2053.

53 Göring conf, 29 May 1944, stenogram (MD: 64, pp. 6323ff). Subject: Me 262. Those present were Göring, Korten, Bodenschatz, Galland, Marienfeld, Thierfelder, Behrens, Messerschmitt, v. Brauchitsch, Schubert and Petersen.

54 Hitler's doubts about the Me 262's usefulness as a fighter have often been criticized, but there is operational evidence in support of them. Prof Kurt Tank commented on the superior Allied fighter tactics against the Me 262 (in report by Dipl. Ing. Wolfgang Hupe: Note on a Visit to Prof. Dipl. Ing. Tank, Lindau, 2 Feb 1945: NARS film T-178, roll 4, frames 9201f); and Messerschmitt's own Dipl. Ing. Ludwig Bölkow reported that jet fighters were particularly vulnerable during landing and taking off because of their slow speeds, and that enemy piston-engined fighters could easily dodge the fire of a jet fighter by tricks like side-slipping, throttling-back, and lowering their flaps: 'This was clear from the outset to all the experts.' Bölkow blamed the Air Staff for failing to adapt their tactics accordingly. On the other hand, the bomber version

Me 262 had flown up to eight sorties a day in KG 51 without breakdowns. (Report by Bölkow with appendices, Oberammergau, 25 Oct 1944: Seiler Papers, FD. 4924/45).

55 Telegram Göring to Milch and others, 27 May 1944 (MD: 53, p. 730f); Milch received it 30 May.

56 See Note 53. MD: 64, p. 6326.

57 Ibid, p. 6332.

58 Ibid, p. 6336.

59 Diary, 2 Jun 1944; and Vorwald in MCH, 10 Mar 1947, p. 1702. The ratio of aircraft production was to be three for Germany for every one for Hungary.

60 Speer–Führer conf, 3–5 Jun 1944 (Boelcke, p. 375). Göring continued to maintain this argument after the war: cf USSBS interrogation No. 56, 29 Jun 1945. See also FD. 4439/45 and Milch's remarks in his farewell speech to the Office of Air Armament.

61 Saur: Führer conf, 7 Jun 1944 (Boelcke, pp. 380f); and Saur at Fighter Staff conf, 8 Jun 1944 (MD: 7, pp. 3218ff). Göring was not present at the Führer conf on 7 Jun.

62 Milch in Central Planning, 7 Jun 1944 (MD: 7, p. 2138): he was complaining about the additional bombers added to the Fighter Staff production programme by Göring on the Obersalzberg.

63 *Inter Avia*, Aug 1946, p. 12.

64 Diary, 13 Jun 1944: ' "Cherry-stone" [flying bomb] flops, as zero hour advanced two days.'

65 War Diary, Flak Regt. 155 (W), 13 Jun 1944.

66 Diary, 15 Jun 1944.

67 Diary, 17 Jun 1944: 'Telephone call from Führer at 1735 hrs from his journey in west: "Thanks for 'Cherry-stone', has exceeded our wildest expectations. According to Below it was I [Milch] who personally had the idea." '

68 David Irving: *The Mare's Nest* (London, 1964), pp. 302f.

69 Diary, 19–20 Jun 1944.
Milch in MCH, 18 Mar 1947, p. 2082. Cf his Pre-Trial Interrogation, 30 Aug 1946: '. . . because on 20 June I was discharged from my offices.'

70 1945 commentary on Diary, 20 Jun 1944.

71 Webster and Frankland: *The Strategic Air Offensive against Germany*, vol. II, p. 280. Cf USSBS Aircraft Division Industry Report No. 4, p. 35.

72 Speer circular to highest Reich authorities, Berchtesgaden, 21 Jun 1944 (MPP, and MD: 56, p. 2699). Cf Speer: speech at armaments convention in Linz, 24 June 1944: 'I have appointed Field-Marshal Milch my deputy. I make it quite clear that the department heads will continue to remain responsible only to me for their programme . . .' (Bundesarchiv file R3/ 1550, pp. 149f). Cf Speer in MCH, 4 Feb 1947, p. 1491; the fact that he had stated that the department heads were to deal with him as before meant that in reality Milch was *not* his deputy. Cf Speer *Chronik*, 24 Jun 1944.

73 *Es spricht der Führer*, p. 359. Diary, 26 Jun 1944: 'Armaments convention, Linz. Air raid alert. By car through St Florian to Berchtesgaden. Führer's speech to armaments chiefs. Conference with Führer on (a) tanks; (b) the Heinkel 177. Then special conference between Führer, Speer and me. Evening, departed for Berlin.'

74 Note of Führer–Mussolini conf, 20 Jul 1944. Hitler: 'With the aid of these fighters the protection of the battlefields and the production centres would be guaranteed first; and only then could Germany go in for counterattacks.' He spoke of the new 'jet fighters', of which production was to reach 1,200 a month, and which he intended to operate against the beachhead in Normandy: 'The effect would certainly be decisive.'

75 Milch's farewell speech to Air Armament Office, 30 Jun 1944. The pages of the GL conf concerned were placed in his private file (MD: 56, pp. 2701ff), away from the rest of the conf record (MD: 29, pp. 9162ff). Cf diary, 30 Jun 1944; and Milch in MCH, p. 2018.

76 Koller: notes on Führer's war conf, 25 Jun 1944. Cf Saur diary, 25 Jun 1944 (postwar).

77 Koller: daily record, 26 Jun 1944.

78 Koller: notes on Führer's war conf, 27 Jun 1944; and daily record, 29 Jun 1944. Koller objected to Göring that the directive would mean an early end not only to bombing operations, but also to sea-mining operations. The new aircraft programme ('Göring programme') was finalized with Hitler on 7 Jul 1944 (cf Speer: Führer conf, 6–8 Jul 1944; Boelcke, p. 396). Diary of Milch, 7 Jul 1944: 'Führer holds [aircraft] programme conference, attended by Göring, Saur, Diesing. Nobody told me—thank God!' Cf also Speer *Chronik,* Jul 1944.

79 Diary, 20 Jul 1944. Telegram Milch to Führer, 21 Jul 1944 (MD: 53, p. 1091).

80 Interrogation by Kempner, 1 Oct 1947.
Diary, 8 Oct 1947. For Milch's attitude to the murder plot, see also diary, 6 Apr, 16 Sep 1948, and 5 Feb and 2 Mar 1950.

81 Milch: 'Hitler and his Subordinates'.
Lieutenant-General Werner Kreipe, diary, 24 Jul 1944 (Foreign Military Studies, MS: P-069); ibid, 19 Aug 1944; and letter from Hans-Karl von Winterfeld, 13 Sept 1969.

82 Koller diary, 24 Jul 1944: 'Was General Korten, who repeatedly emphasized in his speeches that he and I were the closest personal friends, really so faithless? Or is there a lack of moral courage somewhere else, is somebody taking cover behind the dead general?'

83 Koller diary, 26 Jul 1944: '. . . The Jeschonnek and Milch episodes are common knowledge. Brauchitsch and Diesing once told me they were sick of the game and wouldn't ever intrigue again, but "cats can't stop mousing"!'

84 Letter from Major-General Hermann Aldinger to author, 9 Nov 1969.

85 Koller diary, 8 Aug 1944.

86 Kreipe diary, 11 Aug 1944.

87 Letter Milch to Kreipe, 8 Aug 1944 (MD: 53, p. 1084).

88 Kreipe diary, 12 Aug 1944.

89 Ibid, 30 Aug 1944.

90 Ibid, 3 Sep 1944.

91 Diary, 29, 30 Jul; 1 Aug 1944. Milch's documents originally contained a memorandum on a conference on this topic with SS-General Skorzeny on 31 July 1944 (cf MD: 53, p. 691) but it is now missing. The history is set out in a letter from Dipl. Ing. Otto Skorzeny to the author, 11 Jun 1970.

92 Diary, 19 Jul, 9 Aug 1944. Memoirs.

93 Diary, 15 Aug 1944.

94 Ibid, 28 Sep 1944.

95 Report of Dipl. Ing. Ludwig Bölkow, 25 Oct 1944 (Seiler Papers: FD. 4924/45).

96 Report to Minister [Speer?] 'Production and Operations of Fighter Aircraft of the Messerschmitt Group', dated 30 Oct 1944 (ibid.)

97 Speer *Chronik*. Milch diary, 1 Oct 1944.

98 Diary, 12 Jan 1945.

99 Diary, 15 Jan 1945. Interview, Oct 1967. Pre-Trial Interrogation, 14 Oct 1946.

100 Milch interrogation, CSDIC (UK) Report SRGG 1255 (C), 23 May 1945; top secret.

101 Diary, 19, 20, 21 Jan 1945.

102 Sepp Dietrich related this to Milch at Nuremberg. Diary, 1 Dec 1947, 21 Mar 1948.

103 Diary, 1 Mar 1945. Pre-Trial Interrogation, 30 Aug 1946. And diary, 13 Mar 1945, and Speer in MCH, 4 Feb 1947, p. 1490: 'Hitler then sent for me and told me that on no account was Milch to be allowed to take up any such activity. I replied that I should like to know why. Hitler did not give any reasons, but he said he had material from Kaltenbrunner and that this would be more than enough to justify preventing Milch from returning to active life.'

104 Diary, 3 Apr. 1945: 'Transport Staff conference. Speer relates his struggle with the Führer over demolitions.'

105 Diary, 21 Apr 1945.

106 Diary, 22 May 1948. Speer, Dec 1968, states that when the Dönitz government was formed, and not the Himmler one he had feared, he dropped the idea as pointless.

107 Diary, 24 Apr 1945.

CHAPTER 23

1 Diary. Milch also wrote a number of sworn statements on the circumstances of his capture of which my account is necessarily non-specific.

2 Cf Captain Fritz Brustat-Naval: *Unternehmung Rettung—Letztes Schiff nach Westen* (Köhlers Verlagsgesellschaft, 1971); and even more recently the excellent East German account by Rudi Goguel: *Cap Arcona* (Röder-

berg Verlag, Frankfurt/Main, 1972). Allied records indicate that the British aircraft responsible came from the Second Tactical Air Force. *Cap Arcona*, a luxury liner, was 27,560 tons.

For an alternative view of what happened, see the official captions on the British war photographs BU 5424 to 5430 in the Imperial War Museum, London: 'Some 80 Polish women and children and a few men were being removed for some reason or other by the Germans by barge [sic]. Our aircraft unfortunately strafed the barge, putting it out of commission, but the German SS troops opened up machine-guns on the shipment, killing every occupant.' See also the memoirs of Brig. Derek Mills-Roberts (Wm. Kimber, London) and Michael Horbach: *Out of the Night*, p. 249. In fact 7,300 prisoners and seamen were drowned.

3 Milch affidavit, 8 Mar 1948; and his statement at Nuremberg, IMT vol. IX, p. 125. See also the letter of Milch's counsel, Dr Fritz Bergold, to Princess Josia zu Waldeck, 8 Mar 1948; and Diary. Milch's secretary, Frau Elisabeth Hesselbarth, was one of those who themselves saw Milch's head injuries next day (interview, Dec 1969).

4 Diary.

5 Letter Lt. Col. Ernst Englander to Judge Robert H. Jackson, 18 May 1946 (NARS: Jackson Papers, Box. 179).

6 Diary, 30 May 1945.

7 Diary, 5 Jun 1945.

8 Werner Bross: *Gespräche mit Hermann Göring*, pp. 85f (entry of 20 Feb 1946).

9 Reichsmarschall's speech to the Air Staff officers, 25 Nov 1944 (Koller Papers): 'The German must display his greatest strength as being able to contemplate the most awful difficulties, and above all the prospect of Eternity itself, with a certain equanimity and calmness . . . For me Life is only one of many phases, a phase in which I am to deport myself on this globe as well as possible, but nothing else . . . To Hell with the lot of them, before I would allow myself to be pulled into the mire, or forced to drink the vinegar sponge!'

10 A handwritten note amongst Milch's prison papers.

11 Diary, 29 Jul 1945. Speer confirms that Göring was financially involved in the Siebel company (interview, Dec 1968).

12 Diary, 20 Aug 1945. On Koppenberg's alleged financial involvements with Göring, see Pre-Trial Interrogation of Milch, 6 Nov 1946.

13 Diary, 22 Sep 1945.

14 Ibid, 15, 19 Oct 1945.

15 Ibid, 23 Oct 1945. Pre-Trial Interrogation, 23 Oct 1945.

16 Diary, 24 Oct 1945.

17 Richter (MCH, 11 Feb 1947, p. 897); and Pendele (ibid, 18 Feb 1947, p. 1206f).

18 Letter Milch to Himmler, 31 Aug 1942 (ND: 343-PS); letter Himmler to Milch, 27 Aug 1942 (ND: 1607-PS).

19 Letter Milch to SS-Ogruf. Wolff, 20 May 1942 (ND: 343-PS).

20 Dr Romberg: 'Short report on the briefing arranged for 11 Sep [1942] in Herr State Secretary Milch's presence.'

21 Ibid; and diary, which shows that on 11 Sep 1942 Milch was at Rechlin and Neuruppin with Speer all day.

22 Pre-Trial Interrogation, 27 Oct 1945.

23 Diary, 31 Oct 1945.

24 Diary 16, 19 Feb 1946; 14–15 Mar 1946; cf Seventh Army Interrogation of von Blomberg, 13 Sep 1945: 'Blomberg despises his fellow officers of the German General Staff. He is grieved by the knowledge that none of his former subordinates was sufficiently courageous and independent to keep in touch with him after his separation from the Wehrmacht.' (SAIC/FIR/46).

25 Ibid, 6 Mar 1946.

26 Cf. Bross: *Gespräche mit Hermann Göring* (25 May 1946).

27 Statement of Dr Kurt Kaufmann, Kaltenbrunner's defence counsel, who also stood in for Dr Stahmer, 19 Jan 1947 (MPP); cf. Dr Werner Milch, 'Letter to a friend in America', a detailed report on the background to the trial, given wide circulation (amongst others to Senator Taft) in the US and Canada early in 1948. (Cited as: Werner Milch, op. cit.)

28 *Süddeutsche Zeitung*, 12 Mar 1946.

29 *The Times*, London, 9 Mar 1946: '. . . And the most remarkable statement he made was that it was not until 12 October 1939, with the Polish campaign almost concluded, that Hitler gave his assent to a full-scale programme of bomb production.'

30 Printed record of International Military Tribunal, Nuremberg (a body which was neither international, military, nor tribunal) 8 Mar 1946, vol. IX, p. 63 (cited as IMT, vol. IX). The German text has been used, and corrected where necessary against the sound recordings held in Washington.

31 *The Times*, 12 Mar 1946.

32 Cf. IMT, vol. IX, p. 138. This was omitted from page 5661, line 32, of the *mimeographed* transcript; the passage concerned is on Disc 1440B (NARS). The further part quoted by Milch does not figure on the discs, although there is no evidence that the original wire-recording of the US Signals Corps was not 'edited' before the discs were made. Dr Bergold also recalled Milch's having made the missing statements.

33 IMT, vol. IX, p. 88 (disc 1430B).

34 IMT, vol. IX, p. 125 (disc 1437B).

35 This was missing from the mimeographed transcript (p. 5660, line 20) but restored in the printed transcript, IMT, vol. IX, p. 137 (disc 1440B).

36 Diary, 11 Mar 1946.

37 Diary, 21 Mar 1946. And see *Süddeutsche Zeitung*, 15 Mar 1946.

38 Cf. also Diary, 18 Apr 1946: 'In the evening wireless announces that twenty officers are in Dachau and are being treated in accordance with Geneva Convention. So something of our maltreatment must have been rumoured abroad.'

39 On the Dachau bunker, see also Kesselring, op. cit., p. 429.
40 Letter Thomas J. Dodd to Jackson, 10 Jun 1946; cf Milch diary, 4 June
   1946. And OUSCC Buckslip, Lt Col. J. Amen to T. J. Dodd, 7 Jun 1946.
41 Letter Milch to Dr Dix, 22 Jul 1946. Diary, 21 Aug 1946.
42 Diary, 6 Sep 1946.
43 Cf Pre-Trial Interrogation, 18 Oct 1946: 'Might I ask for a table. It
   is extremely tiring to write on a bed.' And ibid, 6 Nov 1946.
44 Ibid, 14 Oct 1946.
45 Ibid, 17 Oct 1946.
46 Ibid, 24 Oct 1946.
47 Pre-Trial Interrogation, 8 Nov 1946.
48 Diary, 8 Nov 1946.

CHAPTER 24

1 Bill of Indictment, signed Brig. Gen. Telford Taylor, Nuremberg, 13 Nov
   1946 (in Nuremberg Staatsarchiv); Diary, 14 Nov 1946.
2 Control Council Law No 10, especially Article III, section 2. See also
   the introduction to NARS publication, 'Preliminary Inventory of Textual
   Records of the US Military Tribunals, Nuremberg, 1966'.
3 Professor Telford Taylor, Oct 1969.
4 Diary, 14 Nov 1946; Erhard Milch: petition for Writ of *habeas corpus,*
   31 May 1947.
5 R. T. Paget, QC: *Manstein, his Campaigns and Trial,* p. 80.
6 Control Council Proclamation No 2, section 6.
7 The legal division of OMGUS itself commented in a memorandum on
   Milch's petition (Berlin, 12 June 1947, cited hereafter as OMGUS
   memorandum).
8 OMGUS memorandum.
9 Dr Fritz Bergold, Dec 1968 and Jan 1969. Letter from Bergold to author,
   7 Nov 1968.
10 Affidavit SS-Standartenführer Wolfram Sievers, 19 Nov 1946 (ND:
   NOKW-264).
11 Affidavit Dr Siegfried Ruff (ND: NOKW-140). Interrogation of Walter
   Neff, 23 Dec 1946.
12 Diary, 2 Dec 1946.
13 Ibid, 9 Dec 1946.
14 On the status of the American Military Tribunal Judges, see Paget, op.
   cit., p. 115.
15 Prof. Telford Taylor, Oct 1969; Interview, Frau Traudl Junge; this is
   confirmed by the British court interpreter Harold Kurtz (Sep 1970).
16 Letter Dr Werner Milch to author, 8 Nov 1968.
17 Diary, 31 Dec 1946.
18 Official transcript of the US Military Tribunal II in the Case of the
   United States of America versus Erhard Milch, defendant, at Nuremberg,
   Germany (cited above and hereafter as Milch Case Hearings or MCH)

2 Jan 1947, pp. 9ff. (The transcript is available at the Wiener Library, London: the Nuremberg Staatsarchiv; and NARS).

19 Ibid, pp. 9ff.

20 Interrogations of Fritz Sauckel, 22 Sep 1946 (ND: 3721-PS) and of Hermann Göring, 6 Sep 1946 (ND: NOKW-311). This was after the final speeches and before sentence was pronounced in the IMT.

21 MCH, 6 Jan 1947, pp. 130f, 272, 273, 443.

22 MCH, p. 154f, and p. 188.

23 MCH, pp. 477f.

24 Dr Werner Milch, op. cit.; R. T. Paget, QC, writes similar criticism of the British Press's behaviour during the Manstein Trial: 'As a military tribunal was not a real court they were not restrained by any fear of contempt of court.' (p. 82).

25 Dr Gaston M. Oulman: 'Der "arisierte" Feldmarschall', in *Münchner Mittag*, 24 Jan 1947. And Bergold's letter of protest to the Secretary-General of Military Tribunal II, Nuremberg, 8 Apr 1947 (Nuremberg Staatsarchiv: Rep 501, LXC Nr. 9 u. 9a).

26 Diary, 15, 16 and 31 Jan 1947.

27 Bergold, Dec 1968.

28 Milch had applied for Speer as a witness on about 6 Jan 1947 (Speer diary).

29 Speer diary, 3 Feb 1947.

30 Bergold, Dec 1968. Speer diary, 4 Feb 1947. Cf MCH 4 Feb 1947, pp. 1444ff.

31 Letter Frau Käthe Herbst (Bergold's secretary) to author, 17 Dec 1968.

32 MCH, 6 Feb 1947, pp. 727ff.

33 MCH, 7 Feb 1947, p. 771.

34 MCH, 11 Feb 1947, p. 862. *Hamburger Freie Presse*, 12 Feb 1947.

35 MCH, 11 Feb 1947, p. 899.

36 MCH, 18 Feb 1947, p. 1271.

37 Among the Jackson Papers (NARS) is a Top Secret British memorandum of 27 May 1945 in which the British government approves of the deportation and forced labour of German workers and prisoners of war.

38 MCH, 5 Mar 1947, pp. 1542ff. On German knowledge of Soviet plans to use German forced labour postwar, see also the Goebbels diaries, 12 and 21 Nov 1943.

39 Bergold, Jan 1969. Diary, 6 Mar 1947.

40 Diary, 31 Dec 1946, 31 Jan, 28 Feb 1947.

41 MCH, 14 Mar 1947, p. 1980. Cf diary.

42 Diary, 21 Mar 1947.

43 Testimony of Krysiak, MCH, 21 Mar 1947, pp. 2379ff.

44 Diary, 25 Mar 1947. Cf Dr Werner Milch, op. cit.

45 It is not uninteresting to find among official American files the following note, dated 22 Jun 1945: 'The Aero-Medical Section of the United States Strategic Air Forces wish to interrogate the following German scientist

—Stabsarzt Rascher. With the SS. Did experiments in cold-water decompression and explosive decompression at Dachau.' (NARS: special film).

46 Closing speech by Denney, MCH, 25 Mar 1947, pp. 2452ff.

47 Closing speech by Milch, MCH, 25 Mar 1947. (MPP).

48 Diary, 25 Mar 1947.

49 Ibid, 3 Apr 1947.

50 Ibid, 7 Apr 1947.

51 MCH, 16 Apr 1947, pp. 251ff.

52 Prof. Telford Taylor, Oct 1969.

53 MCH, 17 Apr 1947, p. 2543; Dr Werner Milch, op. cit.

54 Diary, 17 Apr 1947. The British interpreter Harold Kurtz said (Sep 1970) that as sentence was passed Milch defiantly thrust his jaw out, and marched out with his head up as though he had won a victory.

55 Vorwald, Jun 1968.

EPILOGUE

1 Diary, 22 Apr 1947; and Werner Milch, op. cit. On Milch's sentence it should be stated that according to Telford Taylor, Judge Phillips believed Milch's sentence could have been 'increased' if he had been charged with preparing a war of aggression as well. See also Diary, 25 Apr, 29 May 1947.

2 In general on the issue of Milch's parentage: Milch, Nov 1967; letter to author, 7 Aug 1968; interview Nov 1968. Körner, Göring's other state secretary, had evidently discussed the allegation privately with Milch a week before the motor journey which took place on 18 Aug 1933. Diary, 11 Aug 1933: 'Körner re parentage . . . Evening, with Körner to see [SS Chief of Police] Daluege at Döberitz.'

3 In his officer's record (*Personalnachweis*) Milch's religion is entered as 'evangelical'. In his answers to the American Questionnaire (see Ch. I, note 107) Milch also wrote 'evangelical' in answer to the questions: 'What religion? Which church do you belong to? Which religion did you enter in the National Census of 1939?' The records of the Reich Office of *Sippenforschung* (Family Research) held at the Deutsches Zentralarchiv, Potsdam, have no file on Milch.

4 Seiler wrote in his unpublished memoirs: 'At the time, I did not know he [Milch] could not stand Croneiss.' Croneiss showed the 'Milch' dossier to some of his fellow directors at the Bavarian Aircraft Works; interviews of Seiler (successor of Croneiss and deputy chairman after 1940), Nov 1969; and Rakan Kokothaki, commercial manager, Nov 1969.

5 Letter, Klara Milch (née Vetter) to Fritz Herrmann, 16 Mar 1933 (MPP).

6 Statement dictated by Anton Milch, Kiel, 7 Oct 1933 (MPP). Diary, 7 Oct 1933.

7 Diary, 1 Nov 1933. That Milch accepted that the tragic fact discovered by the authorities and related by his mother was true, is indisputable: he marked the date his true father had died in his pocket diary, and every

year after that he marked the man's birthday along with those of his wife, mother, and colleagues in his diaries, and he continued to do so long after the war had ended. Although the name of Anton Milch is given as his father in his officer's record (*Personalnachweis*) the date of his death is given as 23 June 1906, the date the other man died. Cf Diary, 10, 11 Oct 1933: 'Körner, re Croneiss . . . Evening: I confess to Göring about [---]'—the real father's name. 14 Oct 1933: '. . . Göring sees Croneiss, throws him out. Rage at all these trouble-makers.'

8 Diary, 31 Aug 1948.

9 Milch said in Feb 1969, 'That was always my big handicap.'

10 OMGUS memorandum, 12 Jun 1947.

11 Petition of Erhard Milch to the Supreme Court of the United States. Nuremberg, 31 May 1947 (MPP).

12 Cf *Stars and Stripes* (European edition), 8 Jun 1947.

13 Bergold, Dec 1968.

14 Letter Swiss Consul-General, Munich, to Bergold, 14 Nov 47 (in diary).

15 Diary, 8 May 1947.

16 Ibid, 10 May 1947.

17 Ibid, 8 Jun 1947.

18 Ibid, 10 May and 18 Jul 1947.

19 Ibid, 19 Feb 1947.

20 Ibid, 18 Jul, 30 May, cf 8 May and 20 Jun 1947.

21 Ibid, 26 Apr 1947.

22 Ibid, 9 May 1947.

23 Ibid, 14 May, cf. 9 May 1947. After Speer had gone, one of his senior officers, Dr Schieber of the Armaments Supply Office, told Milch that he was sorely disappointed in his chief: 'The assassination thing has badly damaged his public image—in fact it was all quite different, he planned it against Bormann and Himmler (the rivals!)' (Diary, 28 Aug 1947). In connection with Speer's plan cf also diary, 6 Mar, 21 June 1946; 9 and 14 May, 28 Aug 1947, and 22 May 1948.

24 Diary, 20 June 1947.

25 Ibid, 18 Jul 1947.

26 Ibid, 9–10 Jun 1947.

27 Ibid, 20 Aug, 4 Sep 1947.

28 Certified copy: previous convictions of Josef Krysiak, born 8 May 1911 in Dortmund. Cf statement by Dr Fröschmann in the Pohl Case, Mil. Tribunal II (Case IV) at Nuremberg, 4 Sep 1947, pp. 7310ff.

29 In February 1952 Krysiak resumed his career of fraud, (cf. letter 'Hanse' Grosshandel GmbH, Hamburg to Bergold, 21 Mar 1952. Bergold files: Krysiak).

30 Letter, John H. McCloy (US High Commissioner for Germany), 31 Jan 1951. Memorandum No 9, War Crimes Prison No. 1, 7 Feb 1951 (MPP).

# INDEX